THE WICKED + THE DIVINE

BOOK ONE

GILLEN

McKELVIE

WILSON

COWLES

KIERON GILLEN
WRITER

JAMIE McKELVIE
ARTIST

MATTHEW WILSON
COLOURIST

CLAYTON COWLES
LETTERER

HANNAH DONOVAN
DESIGNER

SERGIO SERRANO
DESIGNER

CHRISSY WILLIAMS
EDITOR

DEE CUNNIFFE
FLATTER

NATHAN FAIRBAIRN
GUEST COLOURIST #4, PP 1–2

ALISON SAMPSON
#7 MAP DESIGN, PP 6–7

TOM MULLER
#7 FLYER DESIGN, PG 25

IMAGE COMICS, INC.
Robert Kirkman, CHIEF OPERATING OFFICER
Erik Larsen, CHIEF FINANCIAL OFFICER
Todd McFarlane, PRESIDENT
Marc Silvestri, CHIEF EXECUTIVE OFFICER
Jim Valentino, VICE-PRESIDENT
Eric Stephenson, PUBLISHER
Corey Murphy, DIRECTOR OF SALES
Jeff Boison, DIRECTOR OF PUBLISHING
PLANNING & BOOK TRADE SALES
Jeremy Sullivan, DIRECTOR OF DIGITAL SALES
Kat Salazar, DIRECTOR OF PR & MARKETING
Emily Miller, DIRECTOR OF OPERATIONS
Branwyn Bigglestone, SENIOR ACCOUNTS MANAGER
Sarah Mello, ACCOUNTS MANAGER

Drew Gill, ART DIRECTOR
Jonathan Chan, PRODUCTION MANAGER
Meredith Wallace, PRINT MANAGER
Briah Skelly, PUBLICITY ASSISTANT
Sasha Head, SALES & MARKETING PRODUCTION DESIGNER
Randy Okamura, DIGITAL PRODUCTION DESIGNER
David Brothers, BRANDING MANAGER
Ally Power, CONTENT MANAGER
Addison Duke, PRODUCTION ARTIST
Vincent Kukua, PRODUCTION ARTIST
Tricia Ramos, PRODUCTION ARTIST
Jeff Stang, DIRECT MARKET SALES REPRESENTATIVE
Emilio Bautista, DIGITAL SALES ASSOCIATE
Leanna Caunter, ACCOUNTING ASSISTANT
Chloe Ramos-Peterson, ADMINISTRATIVE ASSISTANT
www.imagecomics.com

GILLEN McKELVIE WILSON COWLES

THE

WICKED

+

ƎNIΛIᗡ

ƎHⱢ

THE WICKED + THE DIVINE: BOOK ONE
DATE: April 2016
First Printing
ISBN: 978-1-63215-728-7
Forbidden Planet ISBN: 978-1-63215-811-6
Books a Million ISBN: 978-1-63215-813-0
Kinokuniya ISBN: 978-1-63215-812-3
Published by Image Comics Inc.
Office of publication: 2001 Center St, Sixth Fl, Berkeley, CA 94704.

For information regarding the CPSIA on this printed material call: 203-595-3636
and provide reference # RICH – 668247. Representation: Law Offices of Harris M.
Miller II, P.C. (rights.inquiries@gmail.com).

This book was designed by Sergio Serrano, based on a design by Hannah
Donovan and Jamie McKelvie, and set into type by Sergio Serrano in Edmonton,
Canada. The text face is Gotham, designed and issued by Hoefler & Co. in 2000.
The paper is Escanaba 60 matte.

"Ah, Faustus,

Now hast thou but one bare hour to live,

And then thou must be damn'd perpetually!

Stand still, you ever-moving spheres of Heaven,

That time may cease, and midnight never come"

Christopher Marlowe
Doctor Faustus

"BOOM, BOOM, BOOM, BOOM"

Vengaboys
'Boom, Boom, Boom, Boom!!', *The Party Album!*

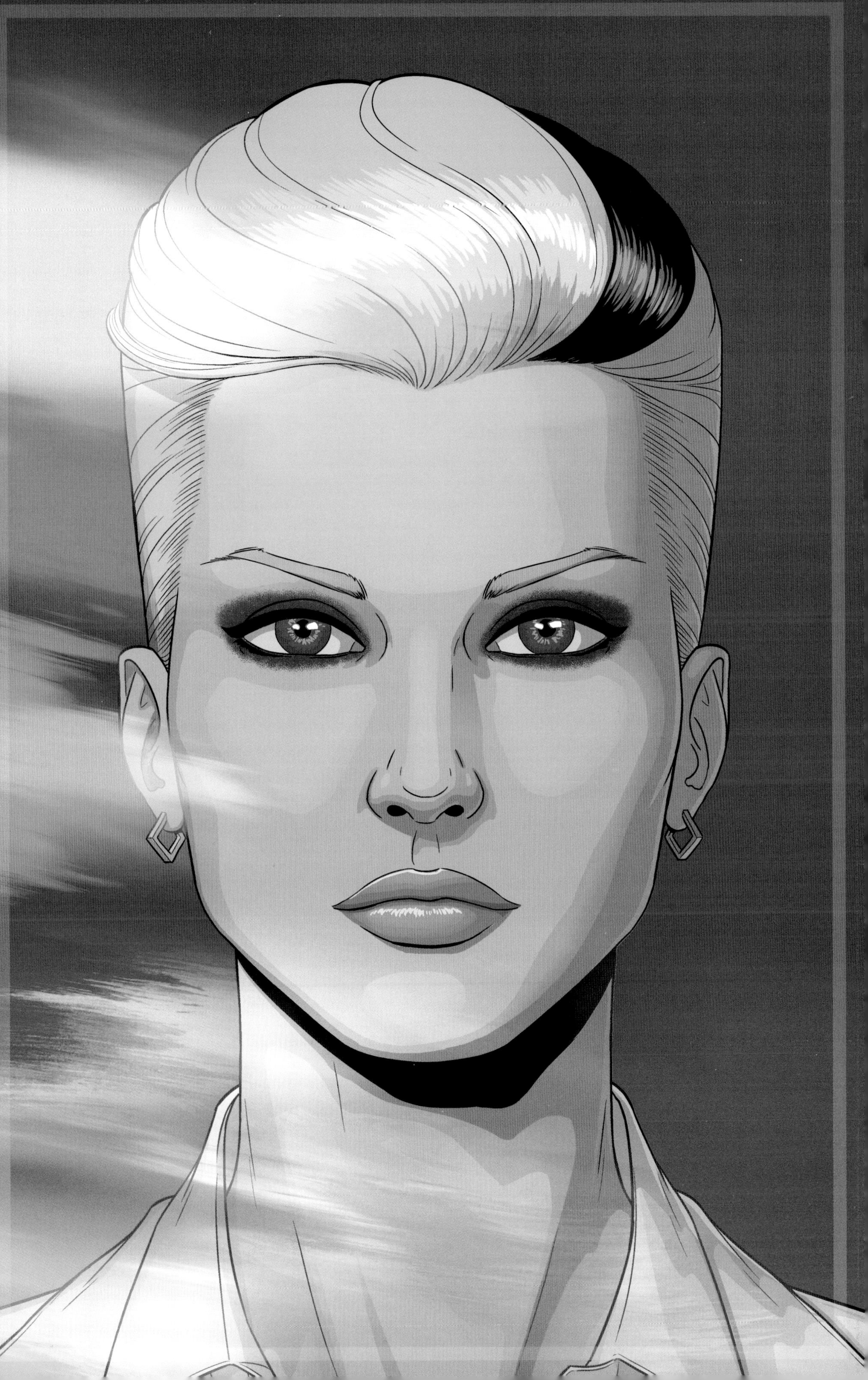

ONCE AGAIN

31 DECEMBER 1923

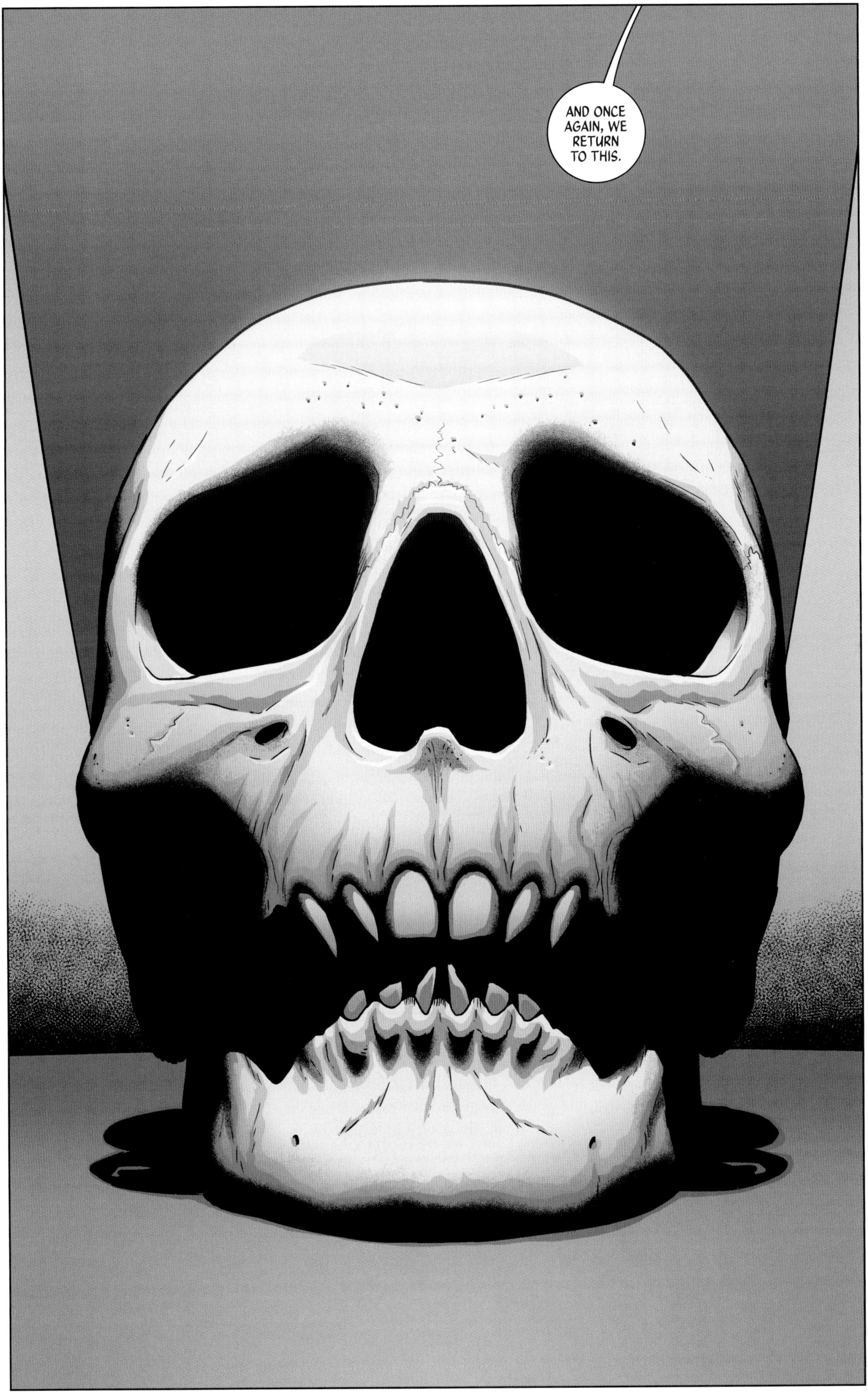
AND ONCE AGAIN, WE RETURN TO THIS.

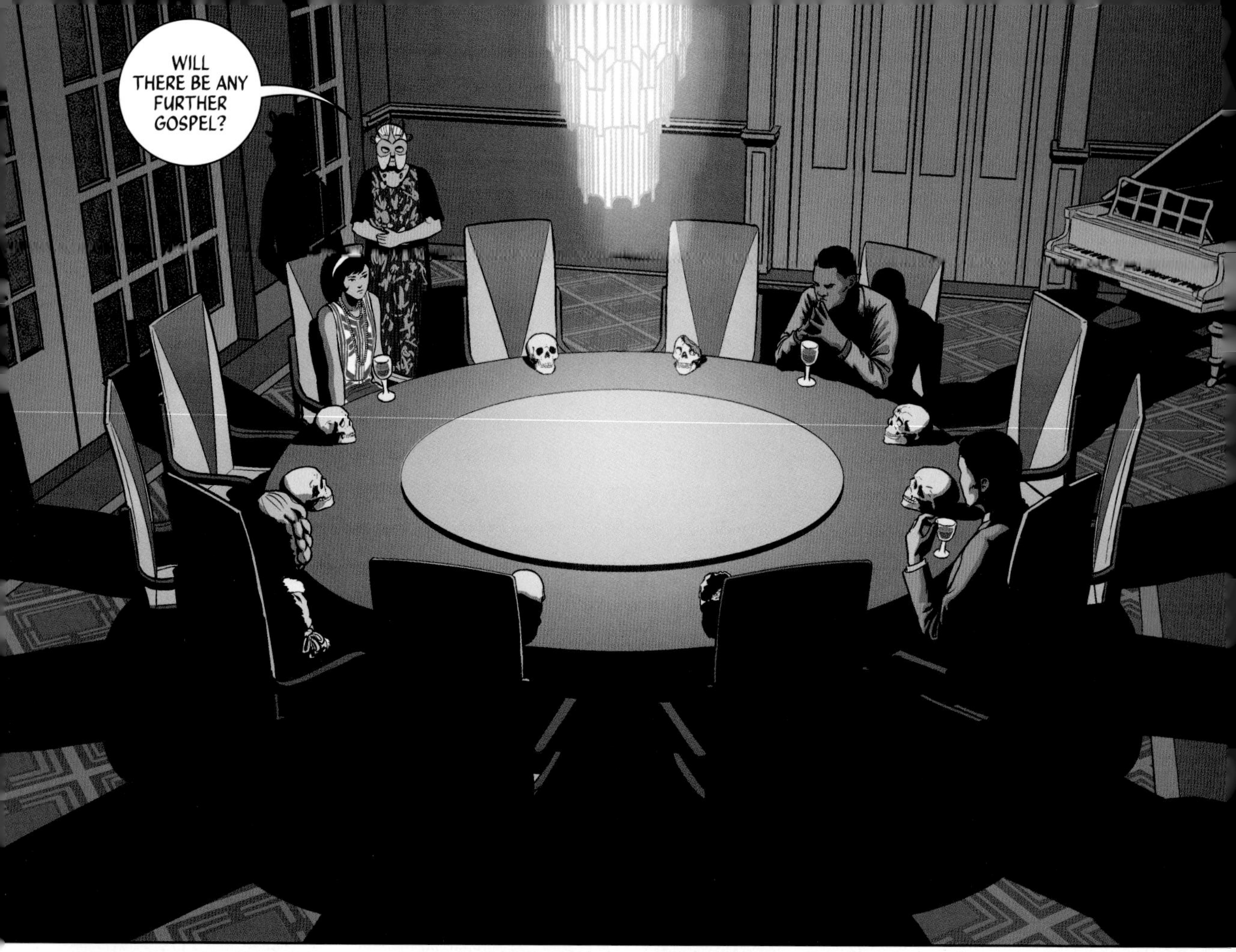
WILL THERE BE ANY FURTHER GOSPEL?
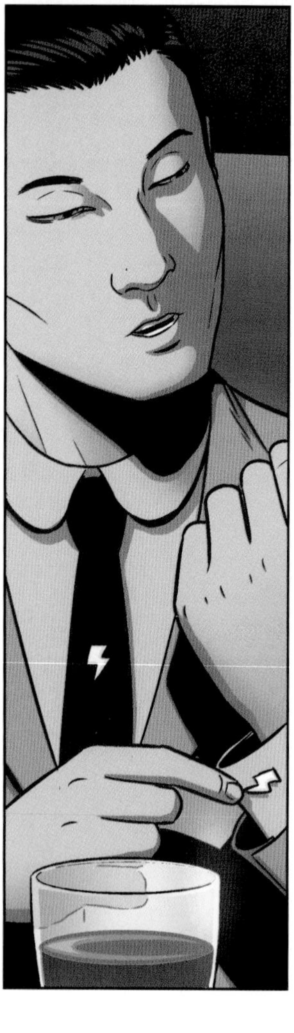
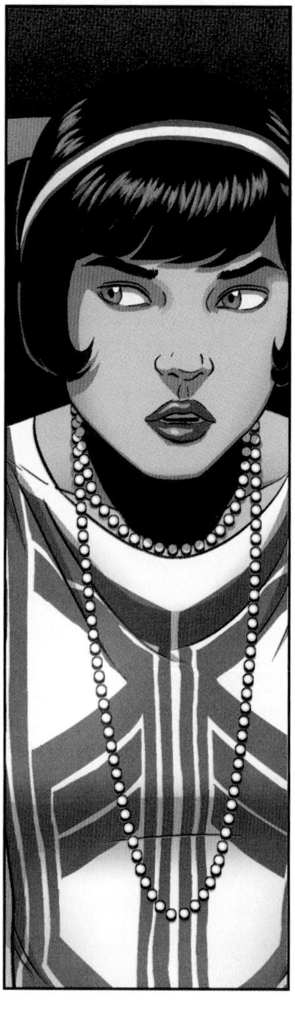
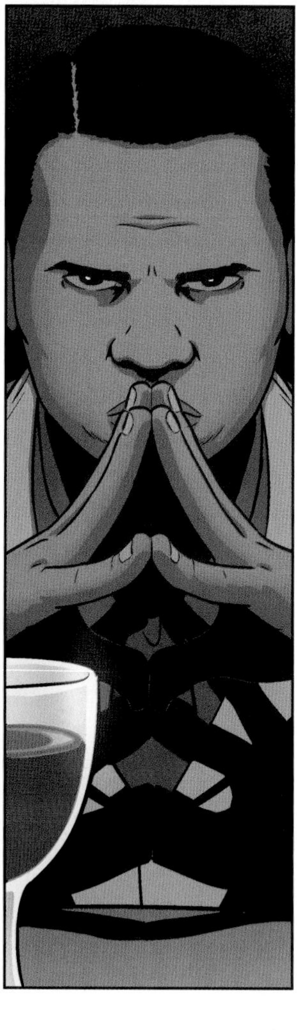
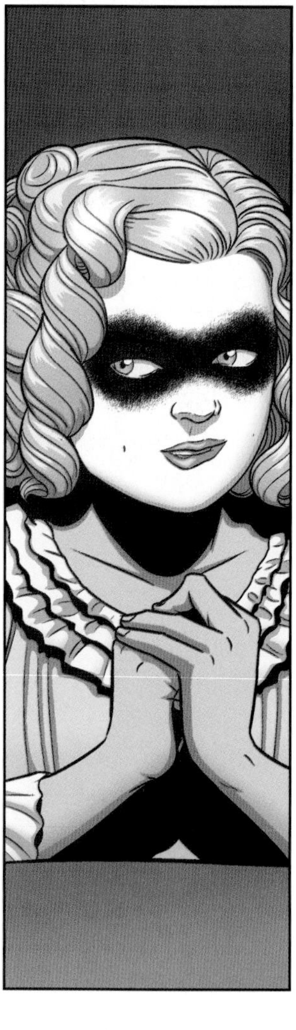

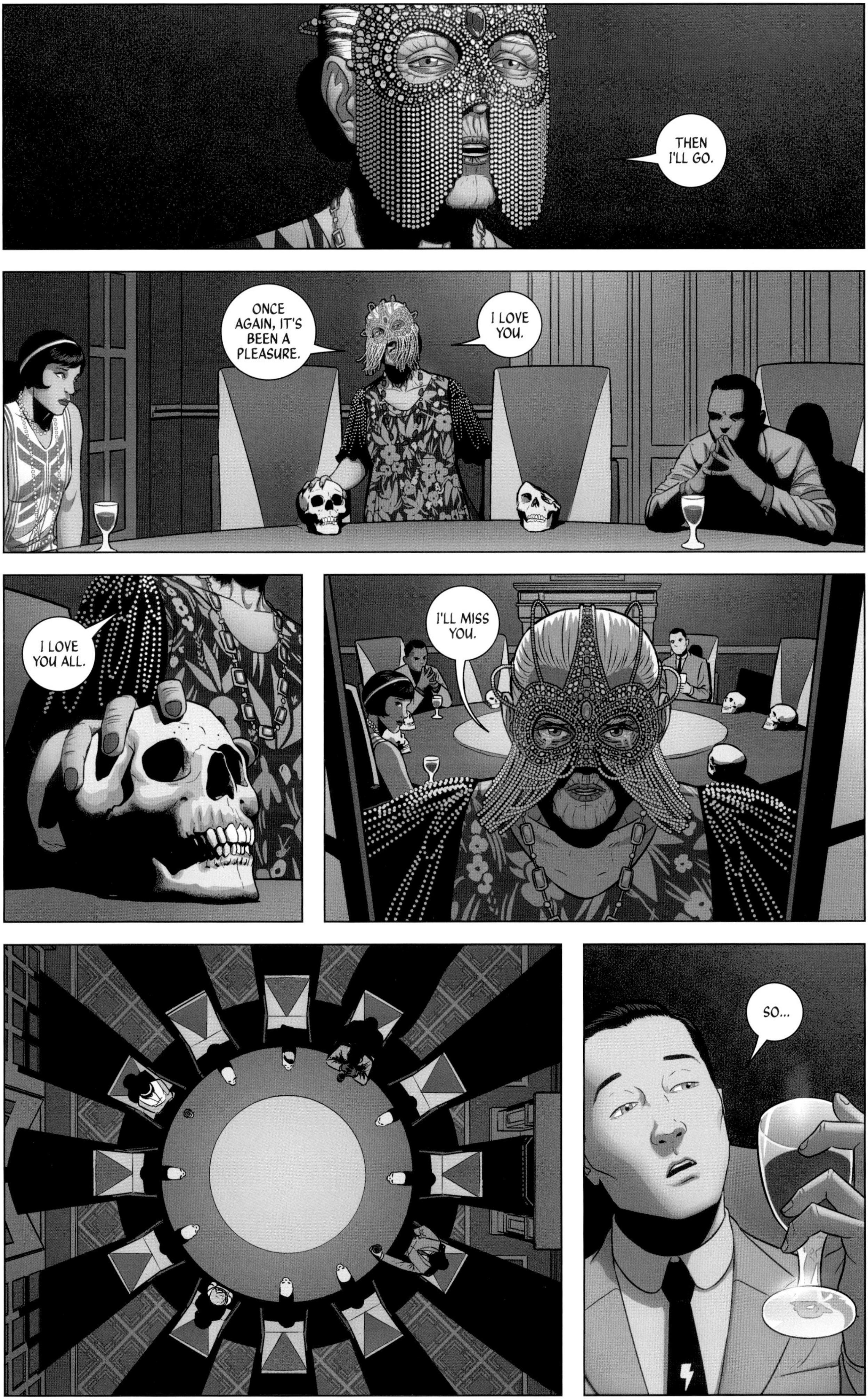
THEN I'LL GO.
ONCE AGAIN, IT'S BEEN A PLEASURE.
I LOVE YOU.
I LOVE YOU ALL.
I'LL MISS YOU.
SO...

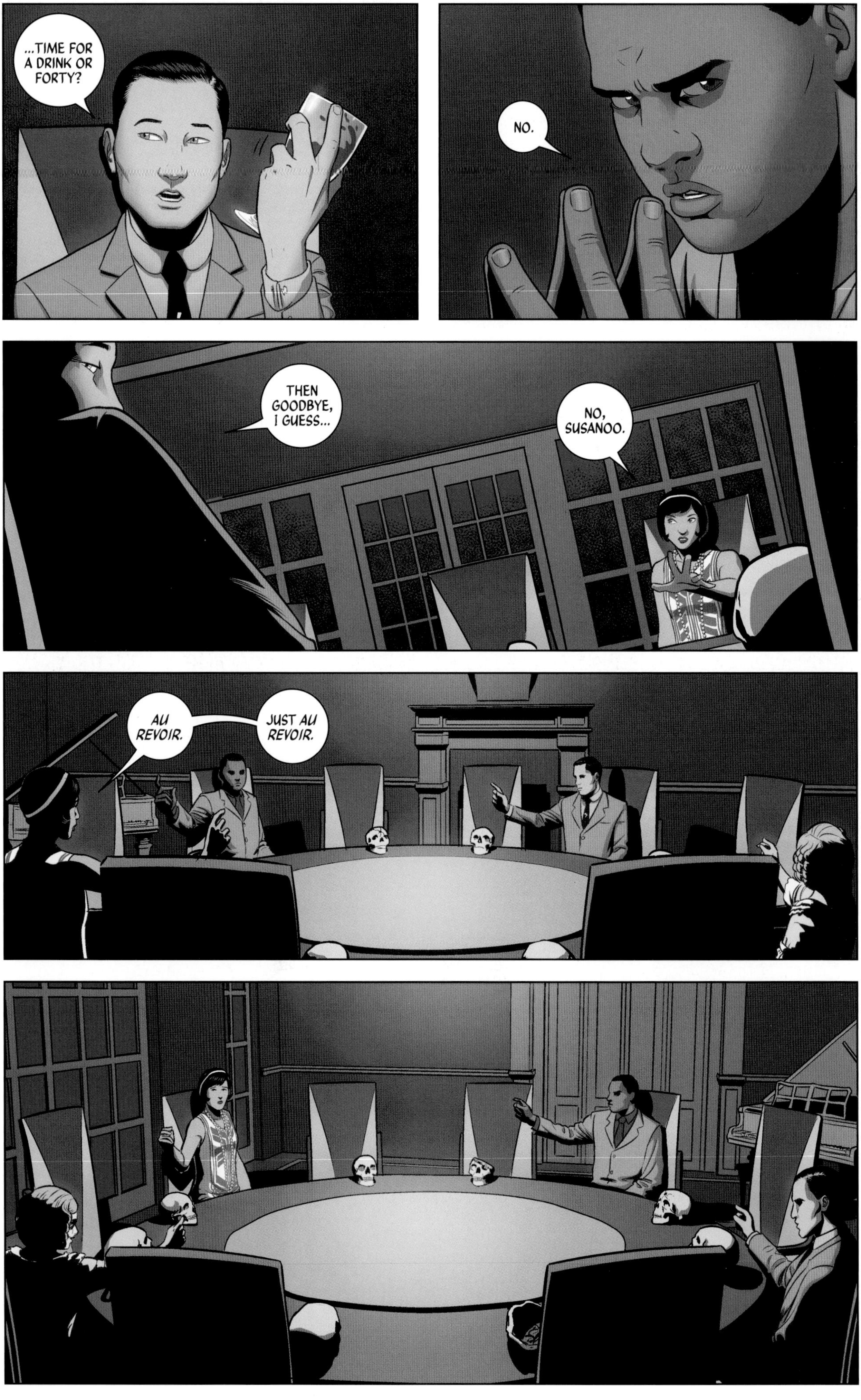
...TIME FOR A DRINK OR FORTY?
NO.
THEN GOODBYE, I GUESS...
NO, SUSANOO.
AU REVOIR.
JUST AU REVOIR.

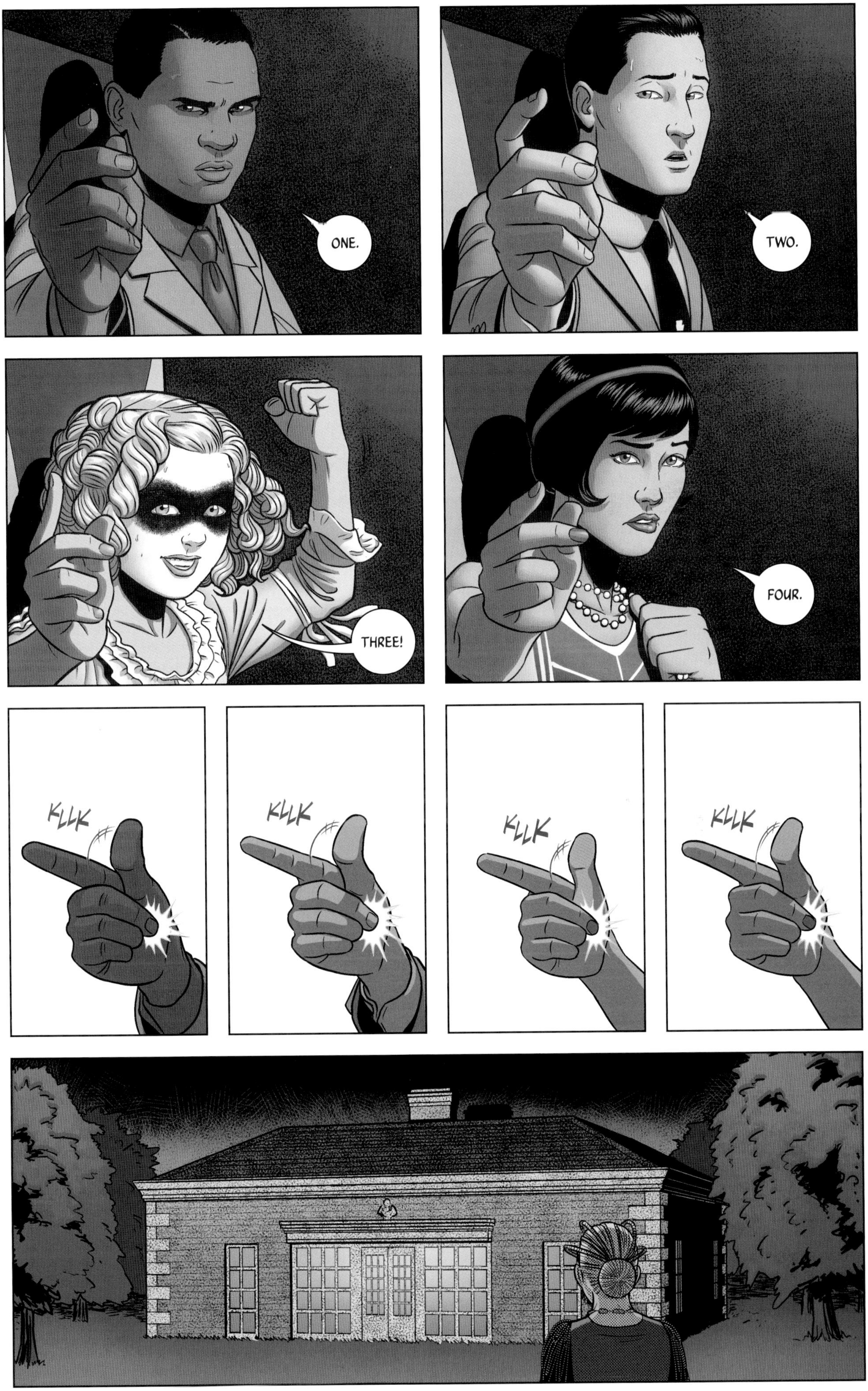
ONE.
TWO.
THREE!
FOUR.
KLLK
KLLK
KLLK
KLLK

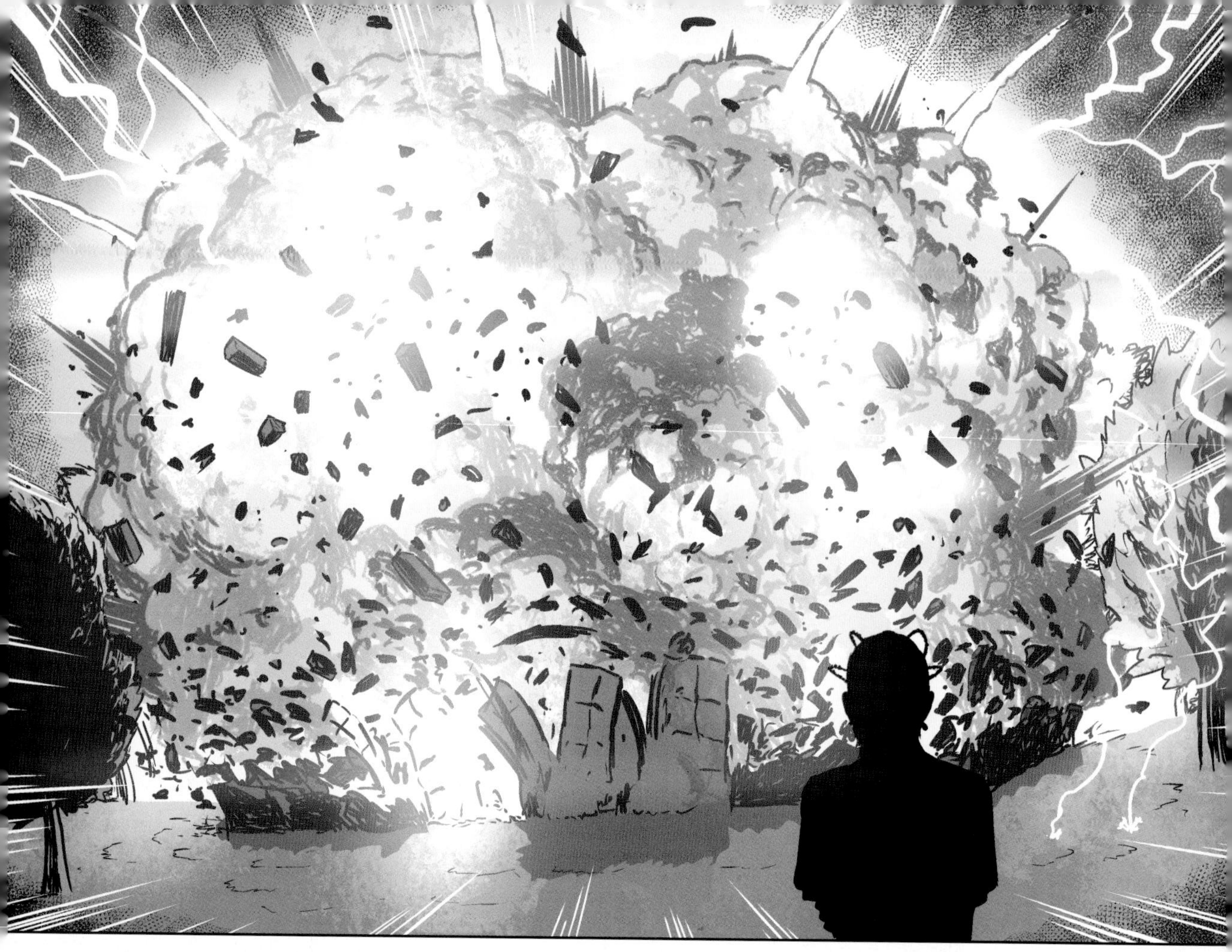
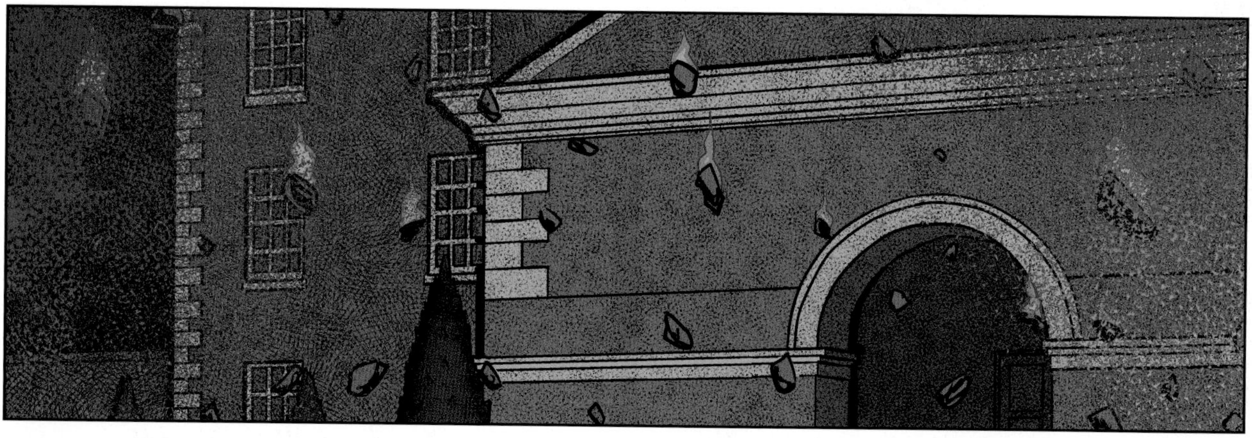
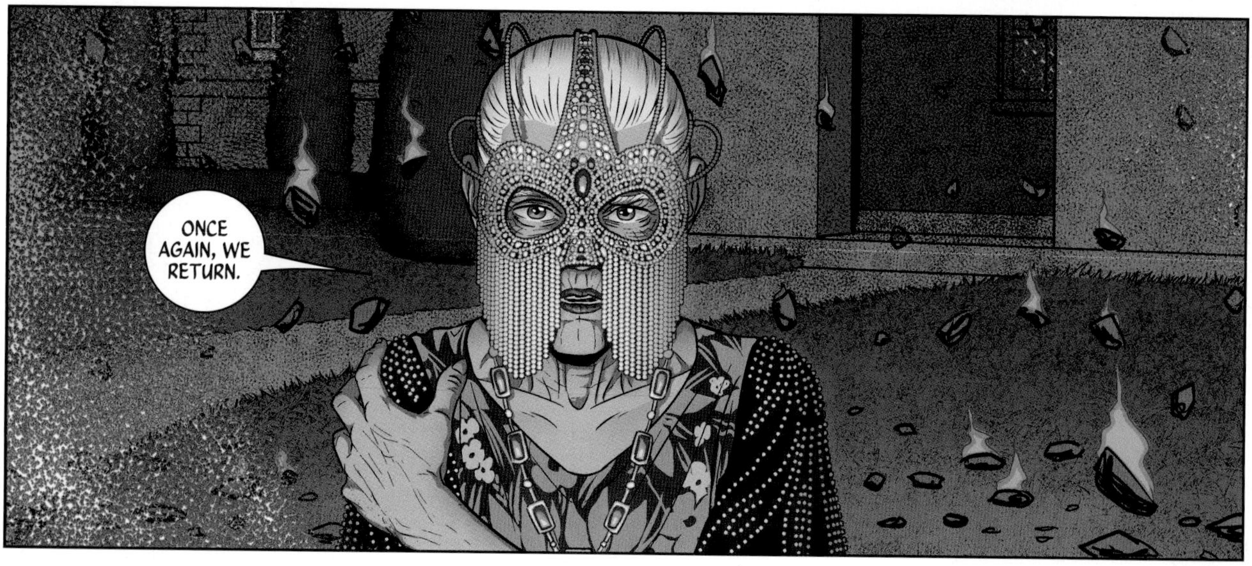
ONCE AGAIN, WE RETURN.

1-2-3-4

1 JANUARY 2014

BROCKLEY,
SOUTH LONDON.

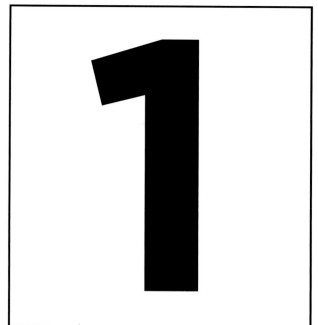

1

It's not that I'm afraid my parents wouldn't approve.

I'm afraid they *would.*

I want this to be all mine.

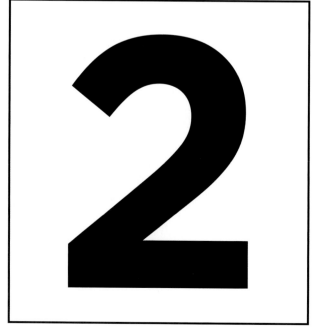

2

Amaterasu's only been around for a couple of weeks.

How many of these girls have even *seen* her?

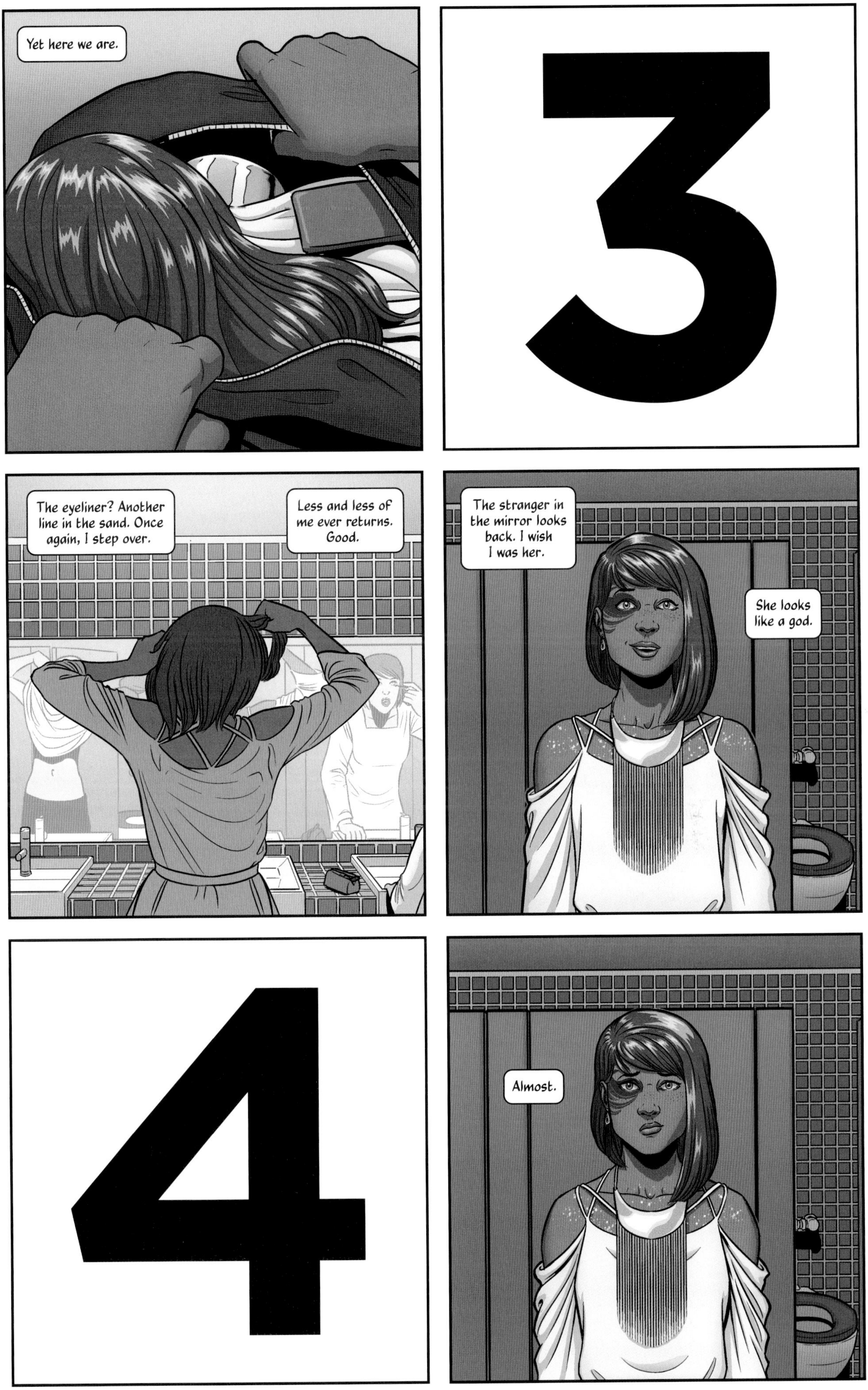
Yet here we are.
3
The eyeliner? Another line in the sand. Once again, I step over.
Less and less of me ever returns. Good.
The stranger in the mirror looks back. I wish I was her.
She looks like a god.
4
Almost.

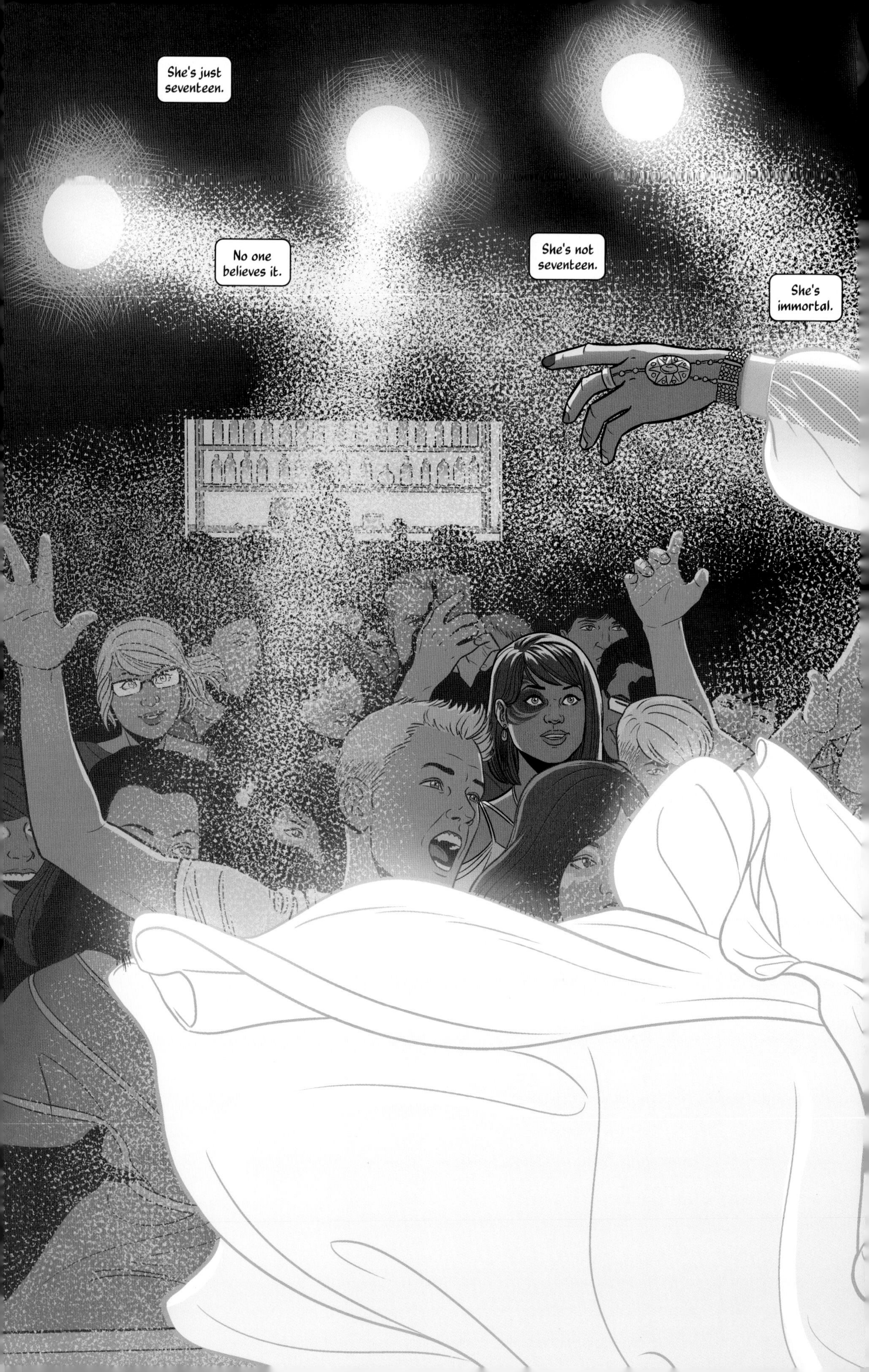
She's just seventeen.
No one believes it.
She's not seventeen.
She's immortal.

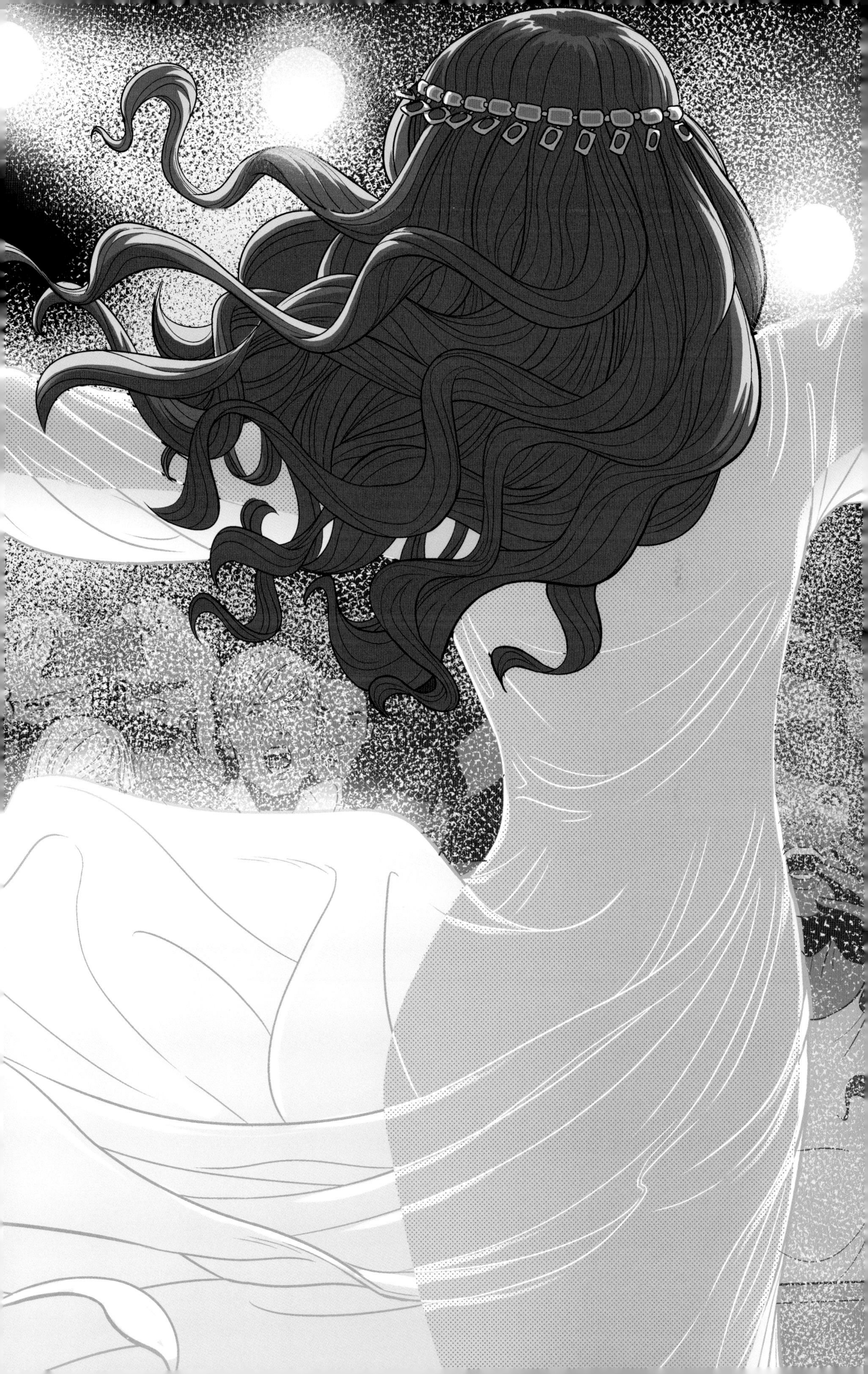

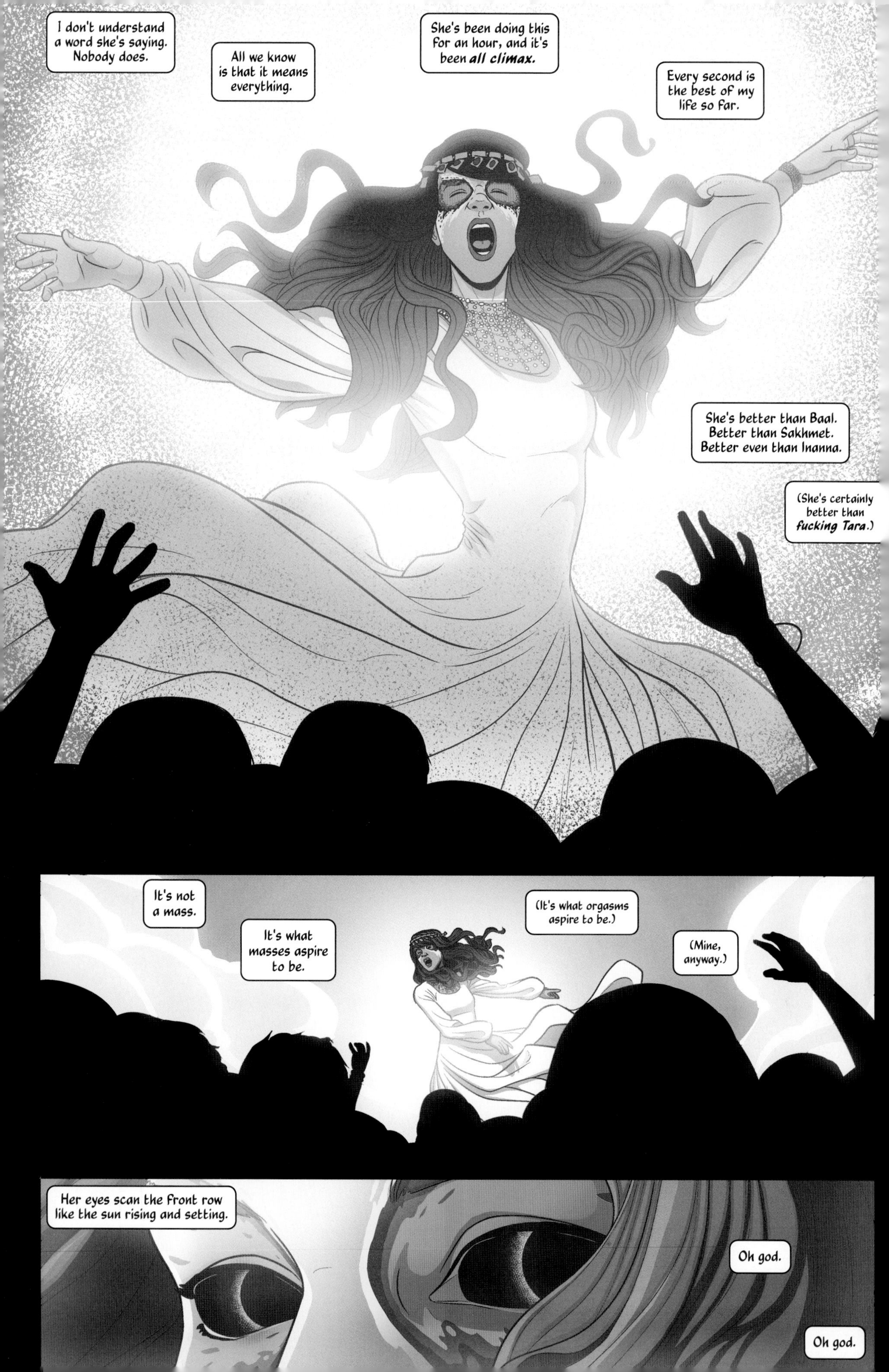
I don't understand a word she's saying. Nobody does.
All we know is that it means everything.
She's been doing this for an hour, and it's been ***all climax.***
Every second is the best of my life so far.
She's better than Baal. Better than Sakhmet. Better even than Inanna.
(She's certainly better than ***fucking Tara.***)
It's not a mass.
It's what masses aspire to be.
(It's what orgasms aspire to be.)
(Mine, anyway.)
Her eyes scan the front row like the sun rising and setting.
Oh god.
Oh god.

The girl to my left passes out, hyperventilating.

The boy to my right falls to his knees, cum leaking from his crotch.

She's not even looking at *them.*

She's looking at *me.* I swear, she's looking at me.

She smiles.

At me.

Infinity passes.

I'm blessed, I'm blessed, oh so blessed...

And it's not enough.

A moment of hubris.

"I want everything you have."

And then I'm gone.

(Best gig ever, FYI.)

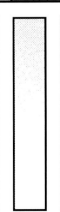

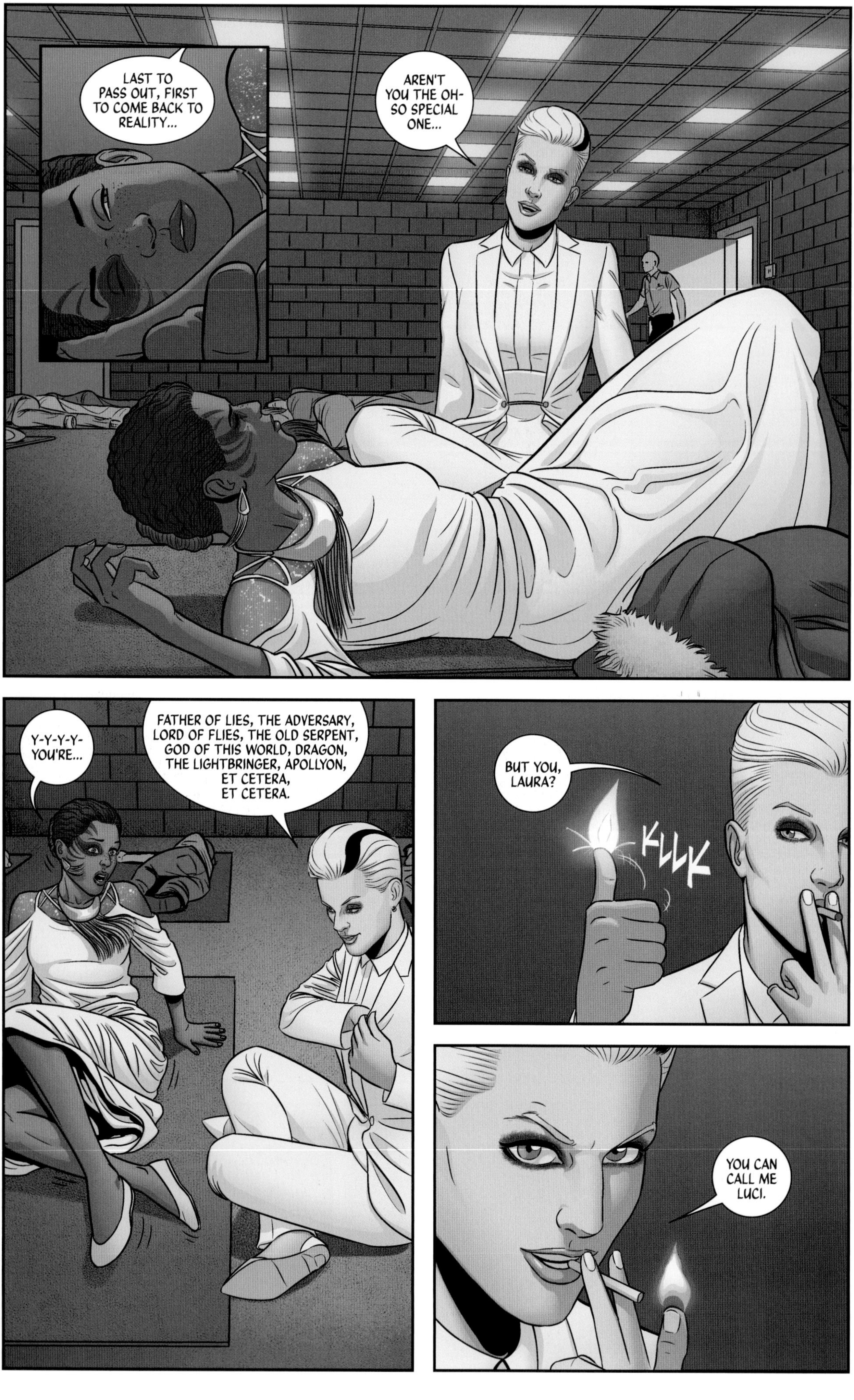

LAST TO PASS OUT, FIRST TO COME BACK TO REALITY...
AREN'T YOU THE OH-SO SPECIAL ONE...
Y-Y-Y-Y-YOU'RE...
FATHER OF LIES, THE ADVERSARY, LORD OF FLIES, THE OLD SERPENT, GOD OF THIS WORLD, DRAGON, THE LIGHTBRINGER, APOLLYON, ET CETERA, ET CETERA.
BUT YOU, LAURA?
KLLK
YOU CAN CALL ME LUCI.

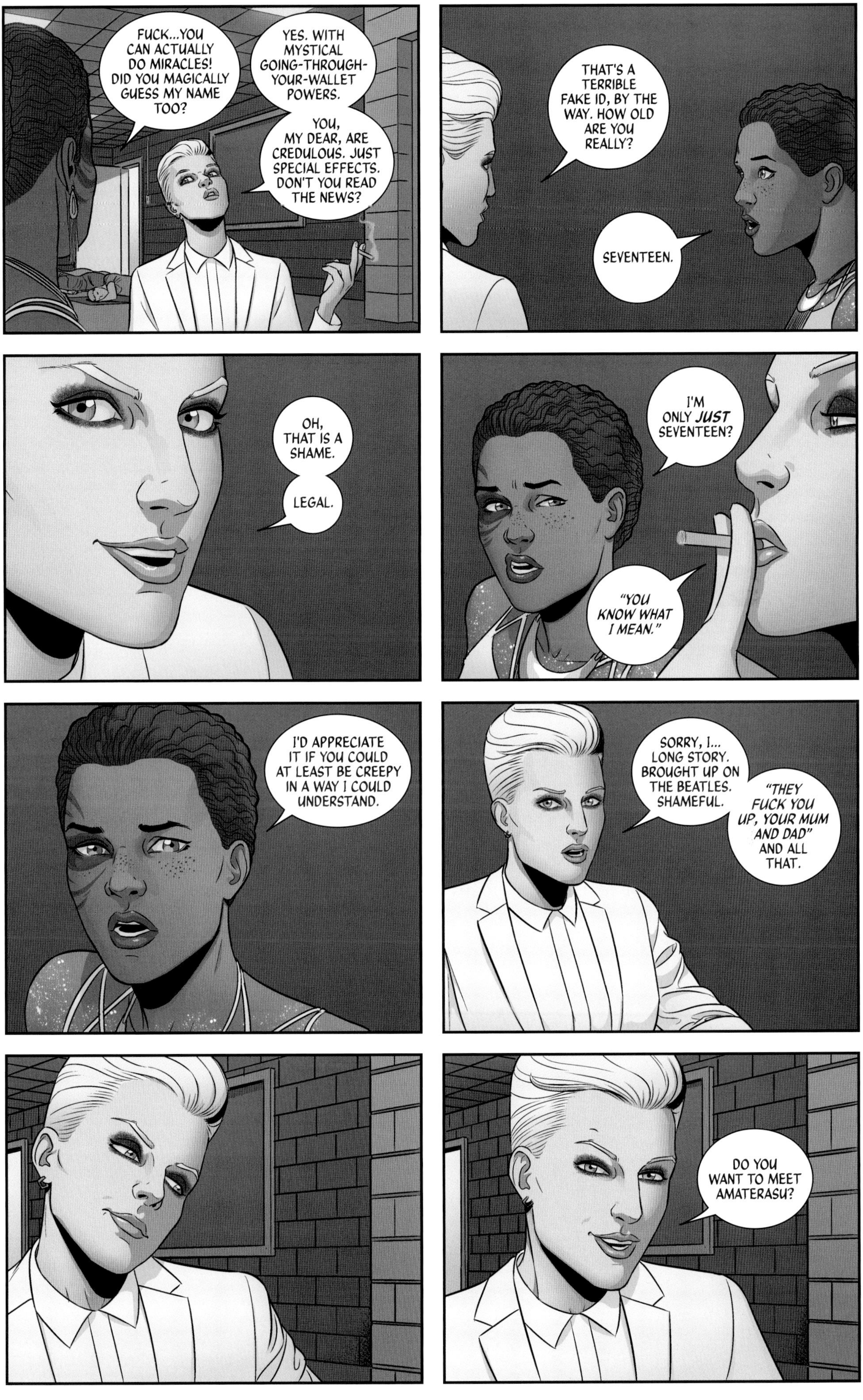
FUCK...YOU CAN ACTUALLY DO MIRACLES! DID YOU MAGICALLY GUESS MY NAME TOO?
YES. WITH MYSTICAL GOING-THROUGH-YOUR-WALLET POWERS.
YOU, MY DEAR, ARE CREDULOUS. JUST SPECIAL EFFECTS. DON'T YOU READ THE NEWS?
THAT'S A TERRIBLE FAKE ID, BY THE WAY. HOW OLD ARE YOU REALLY?
SEVENTEEN.
OH, THAT IS A SHAME.
LEGAL.
I'M ONLY *JUST* SEVENTEEN?
"YOU KNOW WHAT I MEAN."
I'D APPRECIATE IT IF YOU COULD AT LEAST BE CREEPY IN A WAY I COULD UNDERSTAND.
SORRY, I... LONG STORY. BROUGHT UP ON THE BEATLES. SHAMEFUL.
"THEY FUCK YOU UP, YOUR MUM AND DAD" AND ALL THAT.
DO YOU WANT TO MEET AMATERASU?

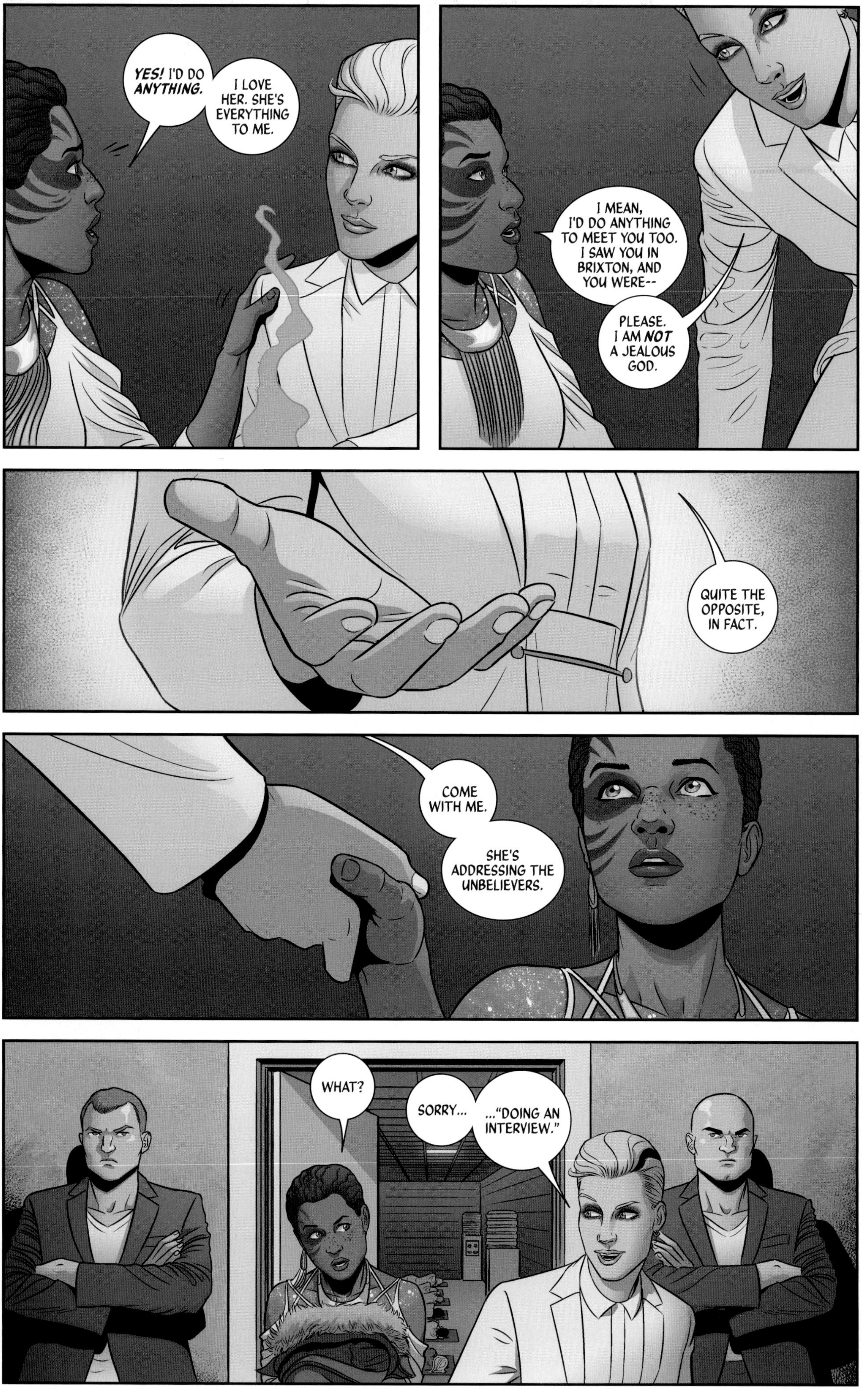
YES! I'D DO ***ANYTHING.***
I LOVE HER. SHE'S EVERYTHING TO ME.
I MEAN, I'D DO ANYTHING TO MEET YOU TOO. I SAW YOU IN BRIXTON, AND YOU WERE--
PLEASE. I AM ***NOT*** A JEALOUS GOD.
QUITE THE OPPOSITE, IN FACT.
COME WITH ME.
SHE'S ADDRESSING THE UNBELIEVERS.
WHAT?
SORRY...
..."DOING AN INTERVIEW."

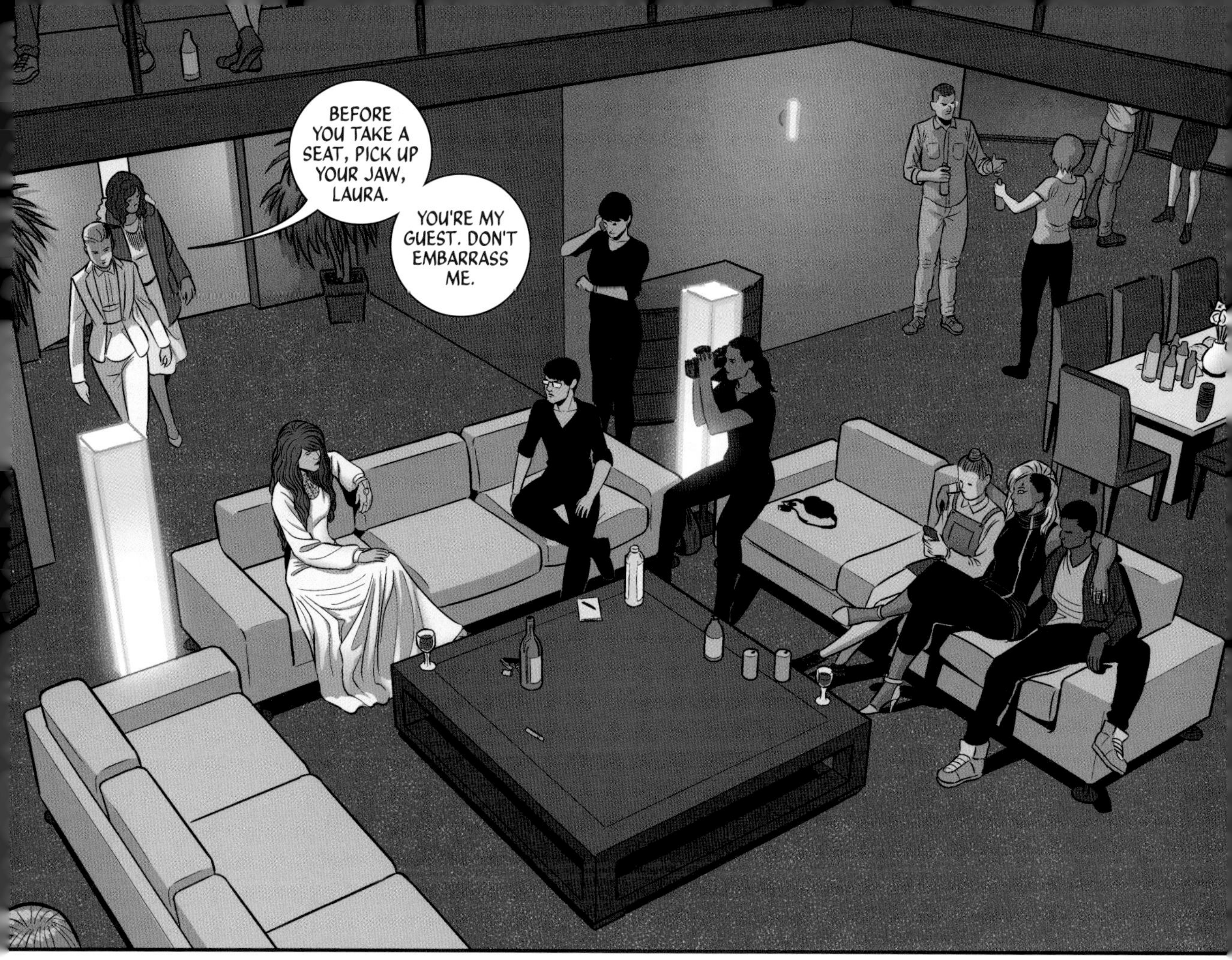
BEFORE YOU TAKE A SEAT, PICK UP YOUR JAW, LAURA.
YOU'RE MY GUEST. DON'T EMBARRASS ME.

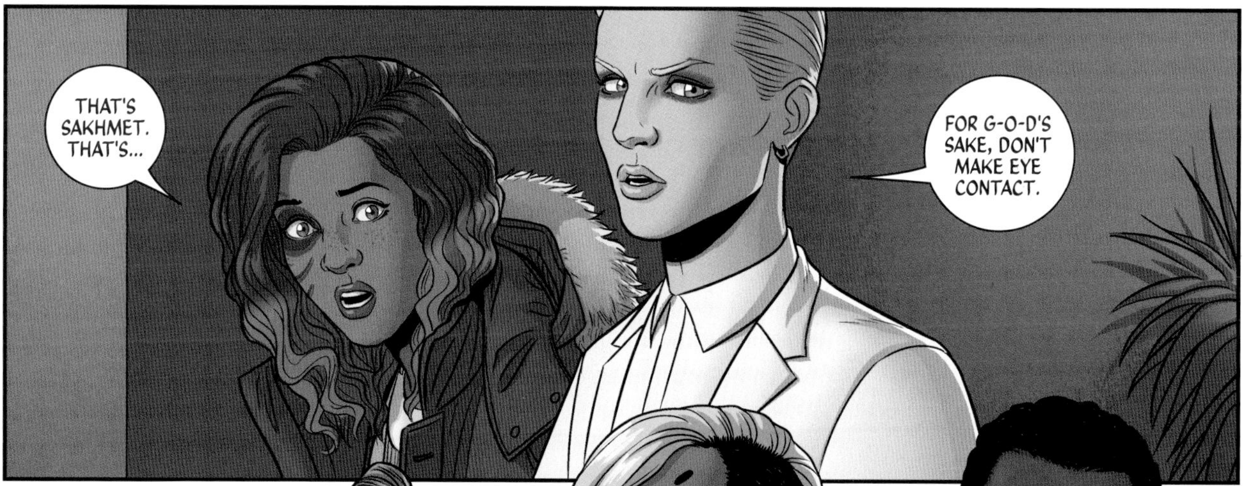
THAT'S SAKHMET. THAT'S...
FOR G-O-D'S SAKE, DON'T MAKE EYE CONTACT.

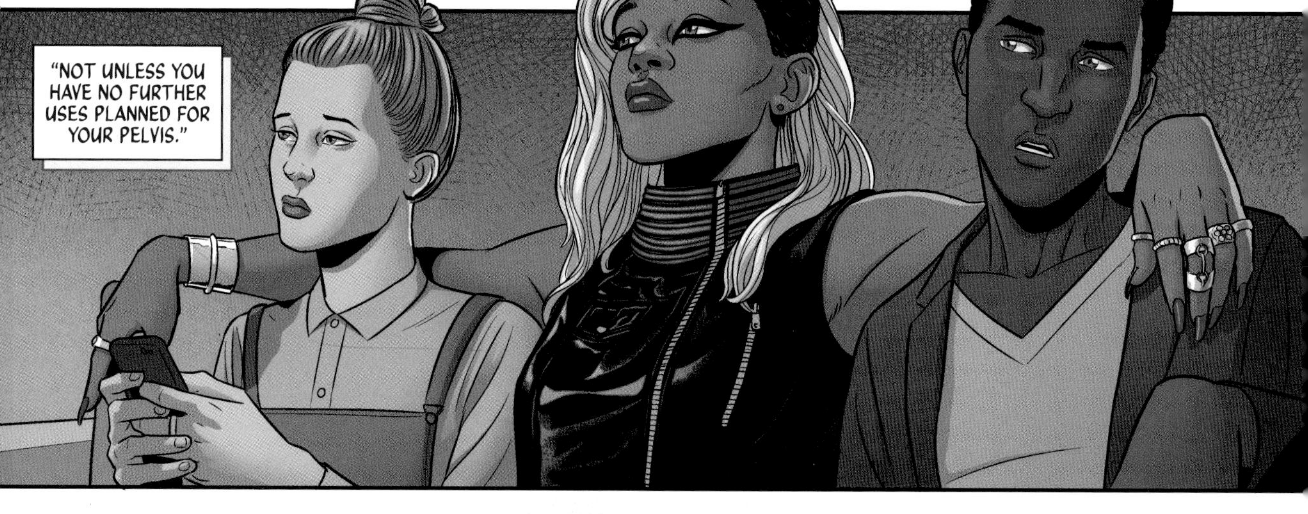
"NOT UNLESS YOU HAVE NO FURTHER USES PLANNED FOR YOUR PELVIS."

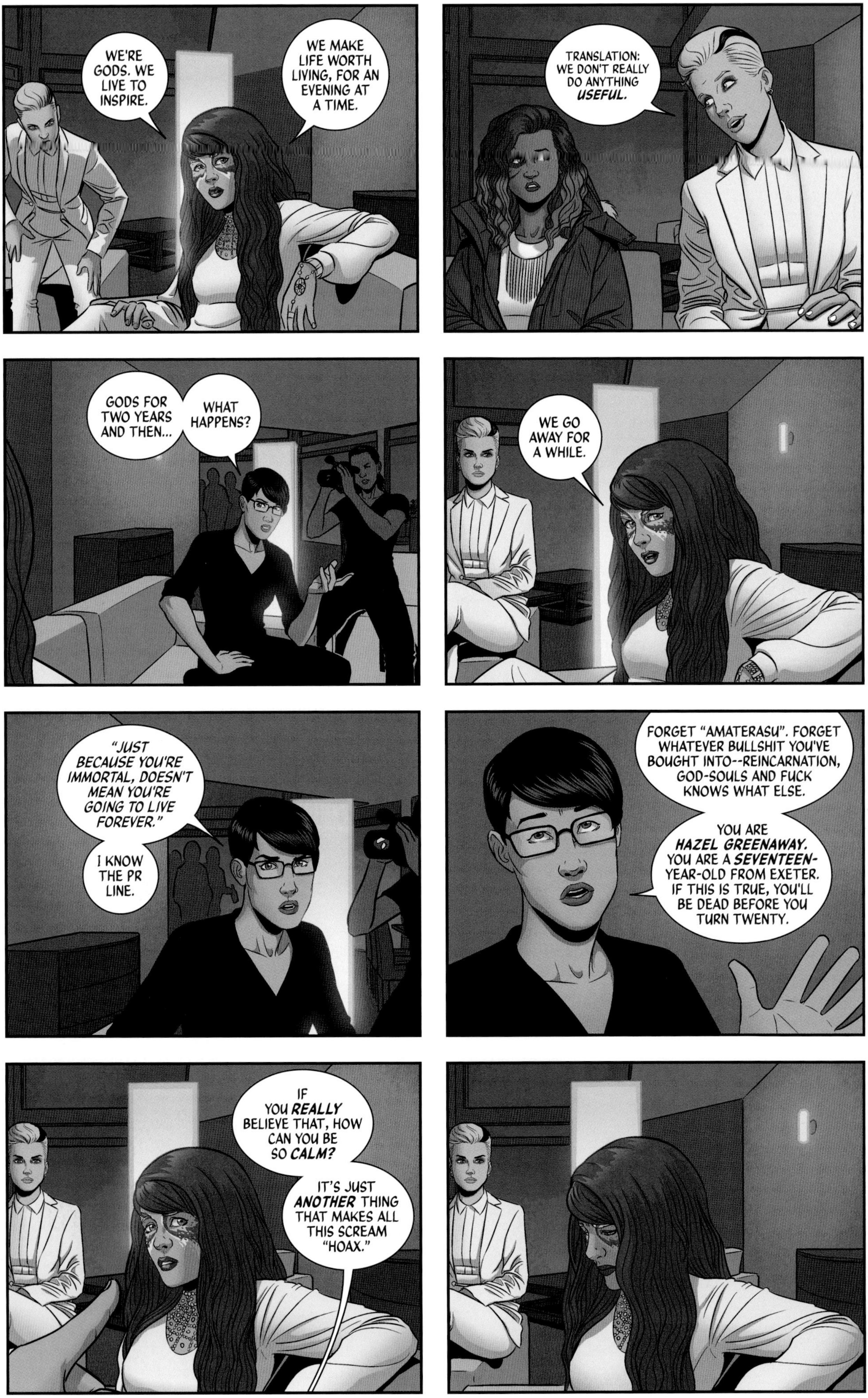

WE'RE GODS. WE LIVE TO INSPIRE.
WE MAKE LIFE WORTH LIVING, FOR AN EVENING AT A TIME.
TRANSLATION: WE DON'T REALLY DO ANYTHING ***USEFUL.***
GODS FOR TWO YEARS AND THEN...
WHAT HAPPENS?
WE GO AWAY FOR A WHILE.
"JUST BECAUSE YOU'RE IMMORTAL, DOESN'T MEAN YOU'RE GOING TO LIVE FOREVER."
I KNOW THE PR LINE.
FORGET "AMATERASU". FORGET WHATEVER BULLSHIT YOU'VE BOUGHT INTO--REINCARNATION, GOD-SOULS AND FUCK KNOWS WHAT ELSE.
YOU ARE ***HAZEL GREENAWAY.*** YOU ARE A ***SEVENTEEN-***YEAR-OLD FROM EXETER. IF THIS IS TRUE, YOU'LL BE DEAD BEFORE YOU TURN TWENTY.
IF YOU ***REALLY*** BELIEVE THAT, HOW CAN YOU BE SO ***CALM?***
IT'S JUST ***ANOTHER*** THING THAT MAKES ALL THIS SCREAM "HOAX."

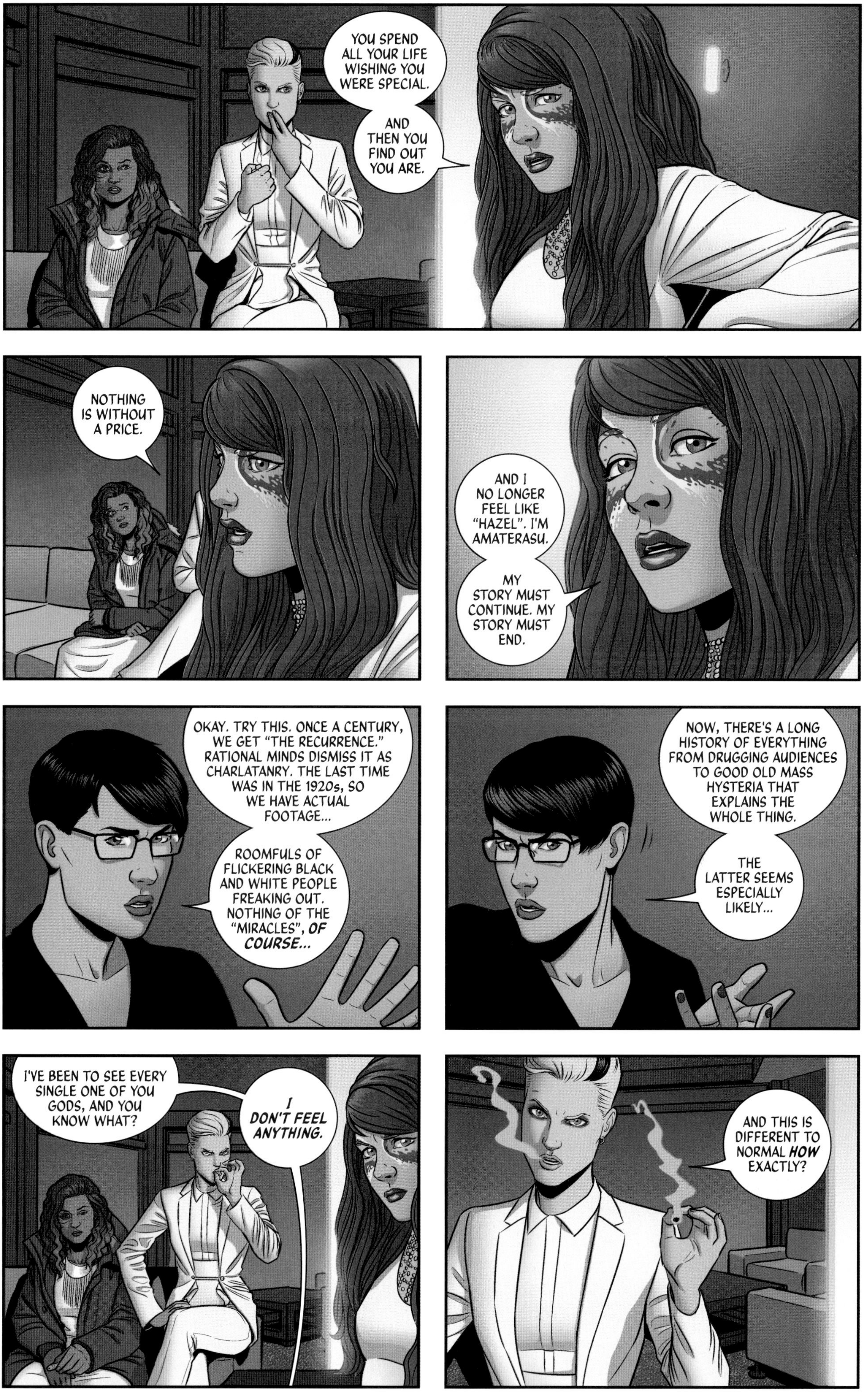
YOU SPEND ALL YOUR LIFE WISHING YOU WERE SPECIAL.
AND THEN YOU FIND OUT YOU ARE.
NOTHING IS WITHOUT A PRICE.
AND I NO LONGER FEEL LIKE "HAZEL". I'M AMATERASU.
MY STORY MUST CONTINUE. MY STORY MUST END.
OKAY. TRY THIS. ONCE A CENTURY, WE GET "THE RECURRENCE." RATIONAL MINDS DISMISS IT AS CHARLATANRY. THE LAST TIME WAS IN THE 1920s, SO WE HAVE ACTUAL FOOTAGE...
ROOMFULS OF FLICKERING BLACK AND WHITE PEOPLE FREAKING OUT. NOTHING OF THE "MIRACLES", OF COURSE...
NOW, THERE'S A LONG HISTORY OF EVERYTHING FROM DRUGGING AUDIENCES TO GOOD OLD MASS HYSTERIA THAT EXPLAINS THE WHOLE THING.
THE LATTER SEEMS ESPECIALLY LIKELY...
I'VE BEEN TO SEE EVERY SINGLE ONE OF YOU GODS, AND YOU KNOW WHAT?
I DON'T FEEL ANYTHING.
AND THIS IS DIFFERENT TO NORMAL HOW EXACTLY?

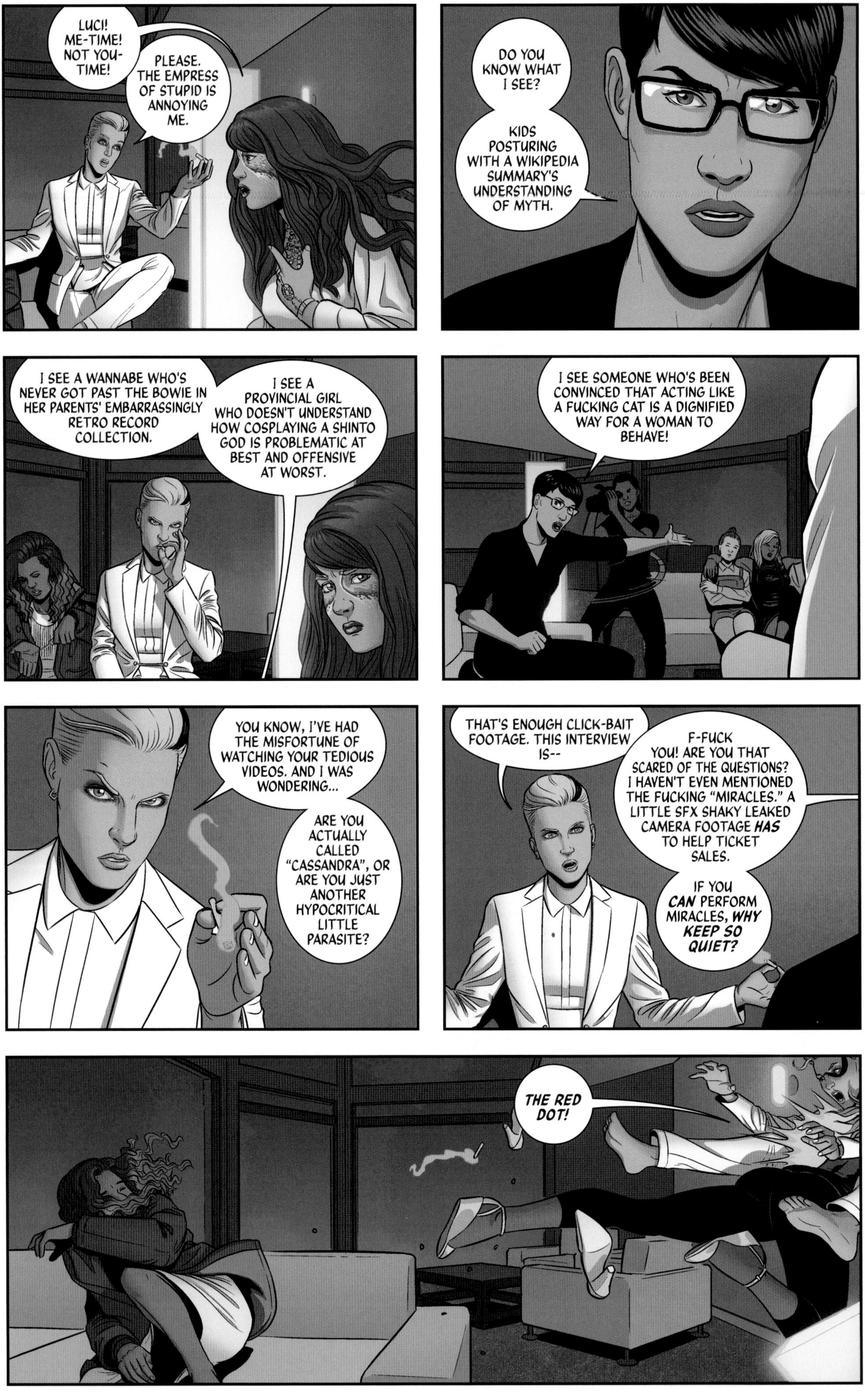
LUCI! ME-TIME! NOT YOU-TIME!
PLEASE. THE EMPRESS OF STUPID IS ANNOYING ME.
DO YOU KNOW WHAT I SEE?
KIDS POSTURING WITH A WIKIPEDIA SUMMARY'S UNDERSTANDING OF MYTH.
I SEE A WANNABE WHO'S NEVER GOT PAST THE BOWIE IN HER PARENTS' EMBARRASSINGLY RETRO RECORD COLLECTION.
I SEE A PROVINCIAL GIRL WHO DOESN'T UNDERSTAND HOW COSPLAYING A SHINTO GOD IS PROBLEMATIC AT BEST AND OFFENSIVE AT WORST.
I SEE SOMEONE WHO'S BEEN CONVINCED THAT ACTING LIKE A FUCKING CAT IS A DIGNIFIED WAY FOR A WOMAN TO BEHAVE!
YOU KNOW, I'VE HAD THE MISFORTUNE OF WATCHING YOUR TEDIOUS VIDEOS. AND I WAS WONDERING...
ARE YOU ACTUALLY CALLED "CASSANDRA", OR ARE YOU JUST ANOTHER HYPOCRITICAL LITTLE PARASITE?
THAT'S ENOUGH CLICK-BAIT FOOTAGE. THIS INTERVIEW IS--
F-FUCK YOU! ARE YOU THAT SCARED OF THE QUESTIONS? I HAVEN'T EVEN MENTIONED THE FUCKING "MIRACLES." A LITTLE SFX SHAKY LEAKED CAMERA FOOTAGE ***HAS*** TO HELP TICKET SALES.
IF YOU ***CAN*** PERFORM MIRACLES, ***WHY KEEP SO QUIET?***
THE RED DOT!

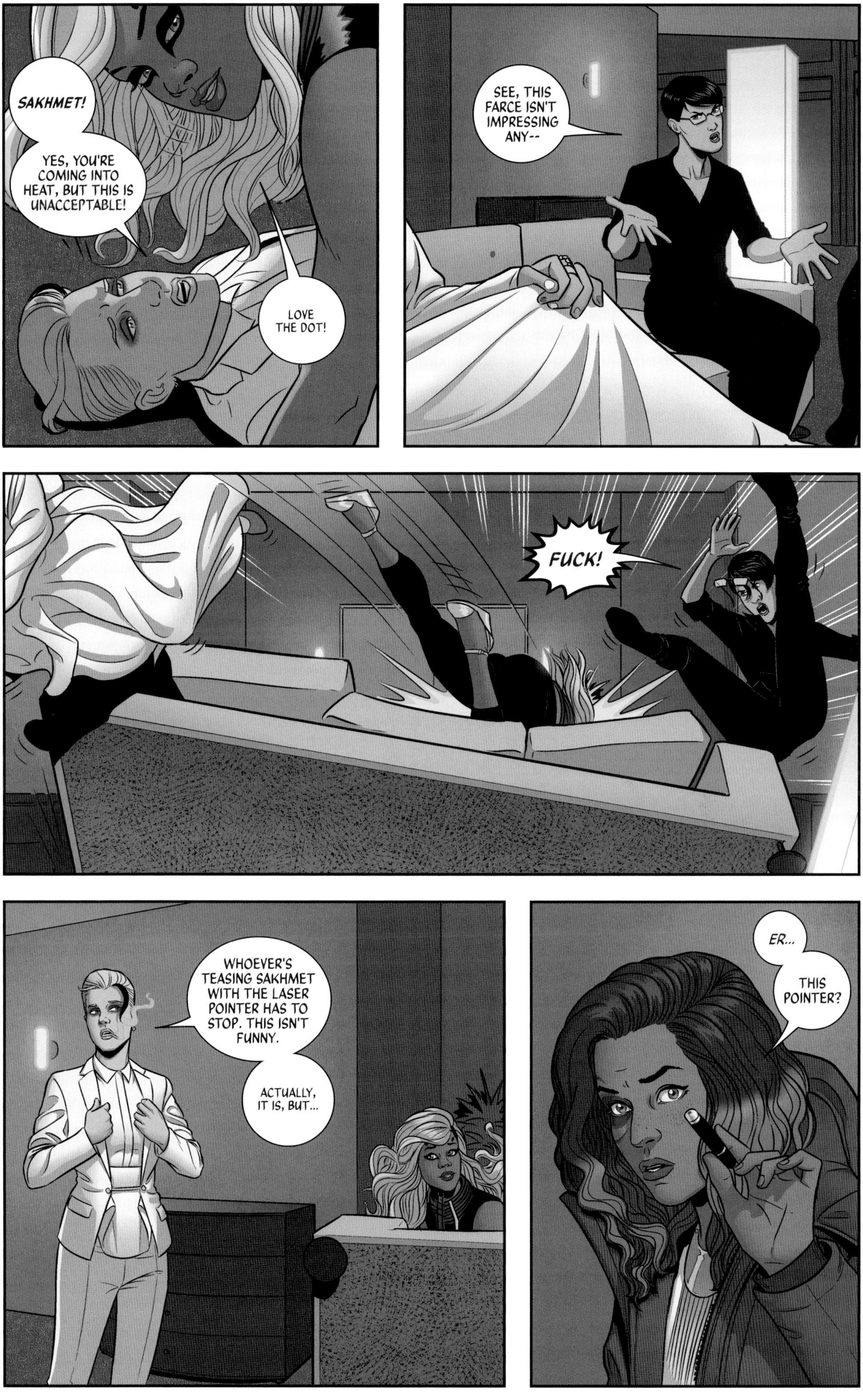
SAKHMET!
YES, YOU'RE COMING INTO HEAT, BUT THIS IS UNACCEPTABLE!
LOVE THE DOT!
SEE, THIS FARCE ISN'T IMPRESSING ANY--
FUCK!
WHOEVER'S TEASING SAKHMET WITH THE LASER POINTER HAS TO STOP. THIS ISN'T FUNNY.
ACTUALLY, IT IS, BUT...
ER...
THIS POINTER?

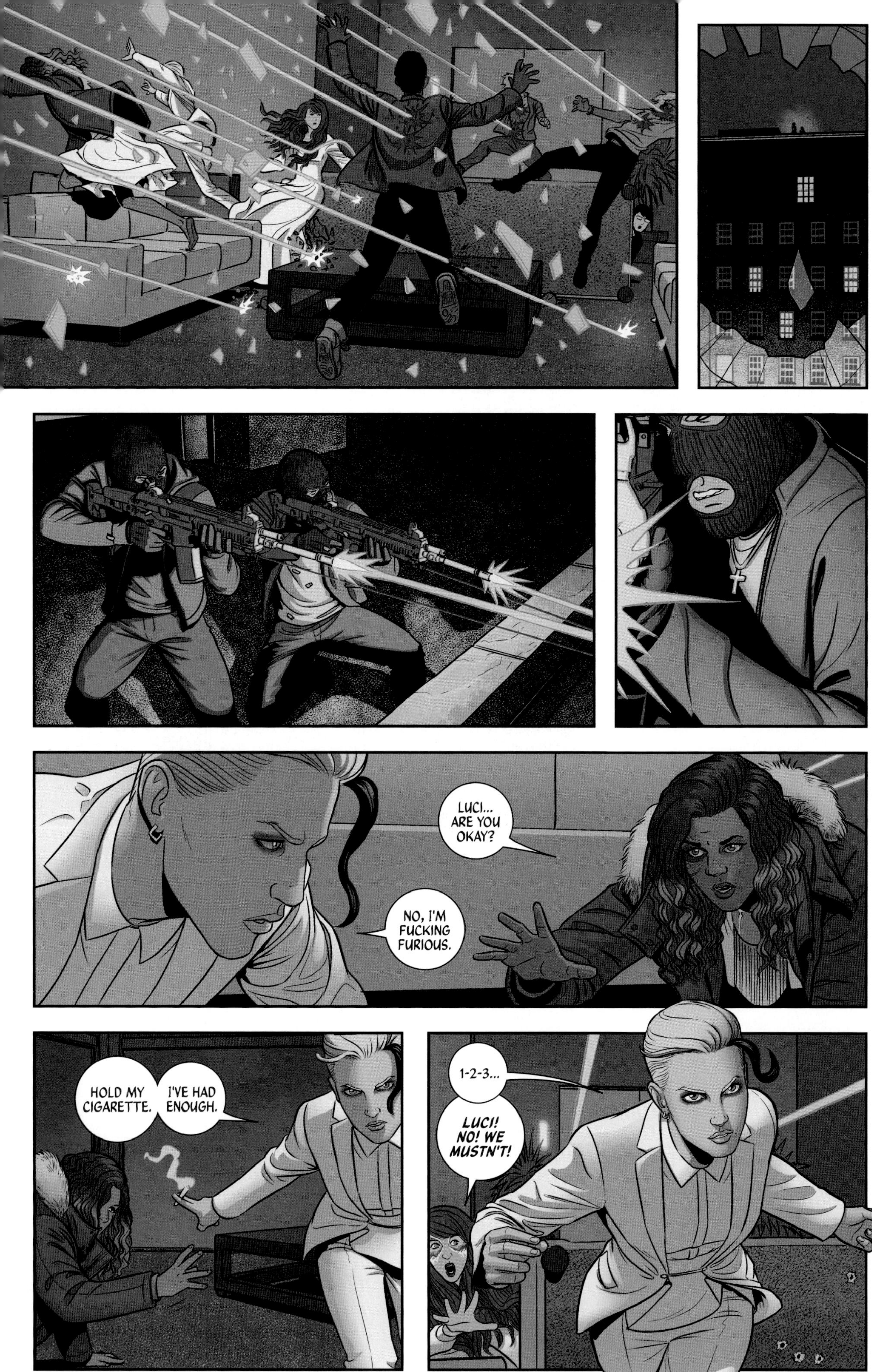
LUCI... ARE YOU OKAY?
NO, I'M FUCKING FURIOUS.
HOLD MY CIGARETTE.
I'VE HAD ENOUGH.
1-2-3...
LUCI! NO! WE MUSTN'T!

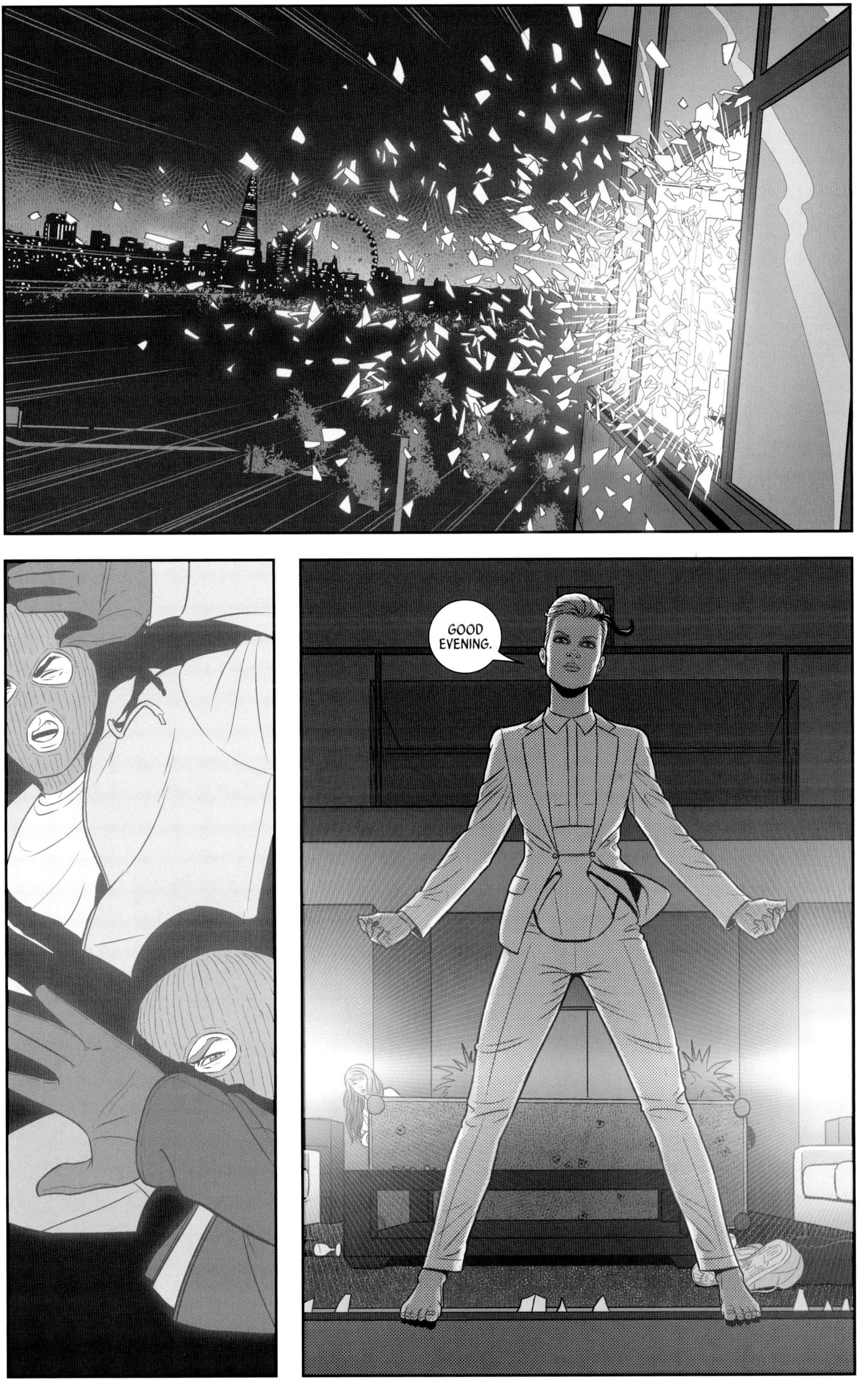
GOOD EVENING.

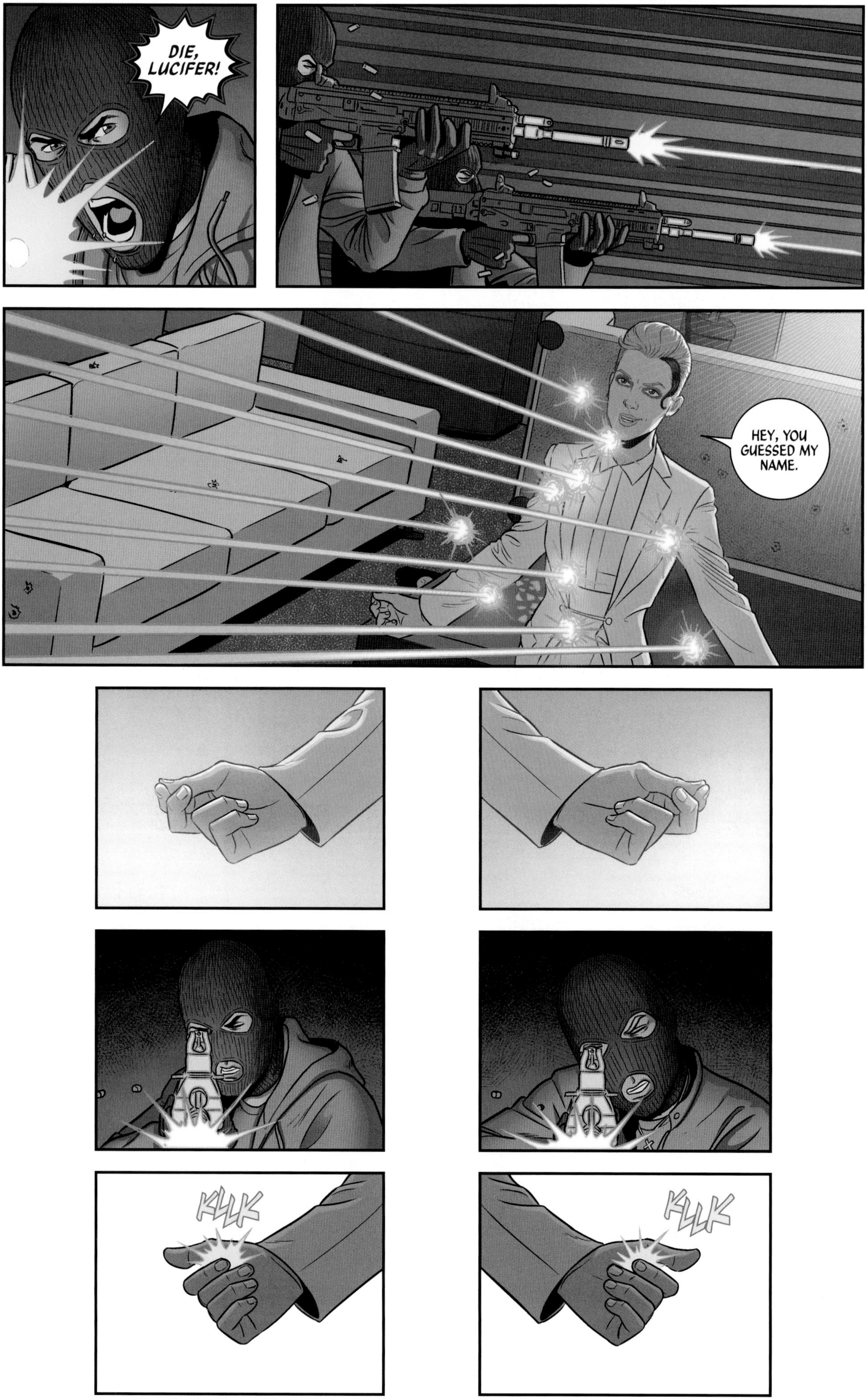
DIE, LUCIFER!
HEY, YOU GUESSED MY NAME.
KLLK
KLLK

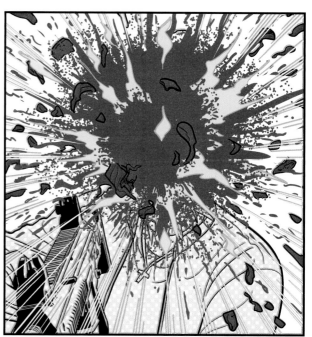

WHY WOULD WE BE SO COY WITH THE MIRACLES, CASSANDRA?

...MAYBE WE *DIDN'T* WANT TO SCARE THE SHIT OUT OF YOU?

When the police turned up, Luci went calmly.

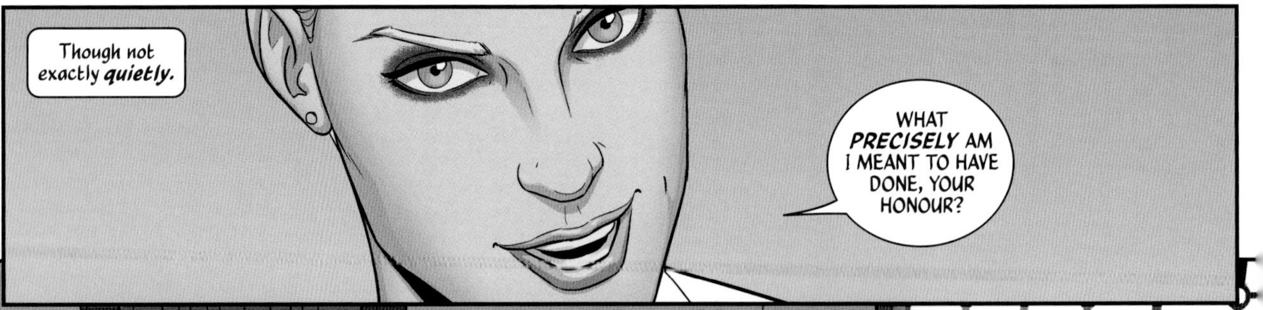
Though not exactly *quietly.*
WHAT *PRECISELY* AM I MEANT TO HAVE DONE, YOUR HONOUR?

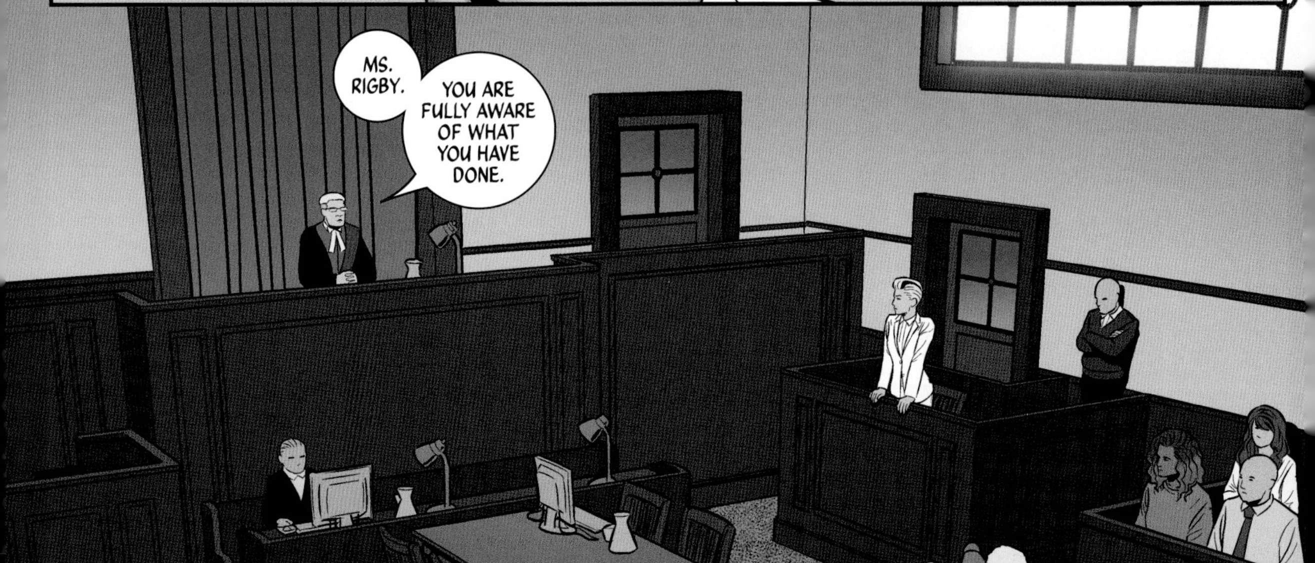
MS. RIGBY.
YOU ARE FULLY AWARE OF WHAT YOU HAVE DONE.

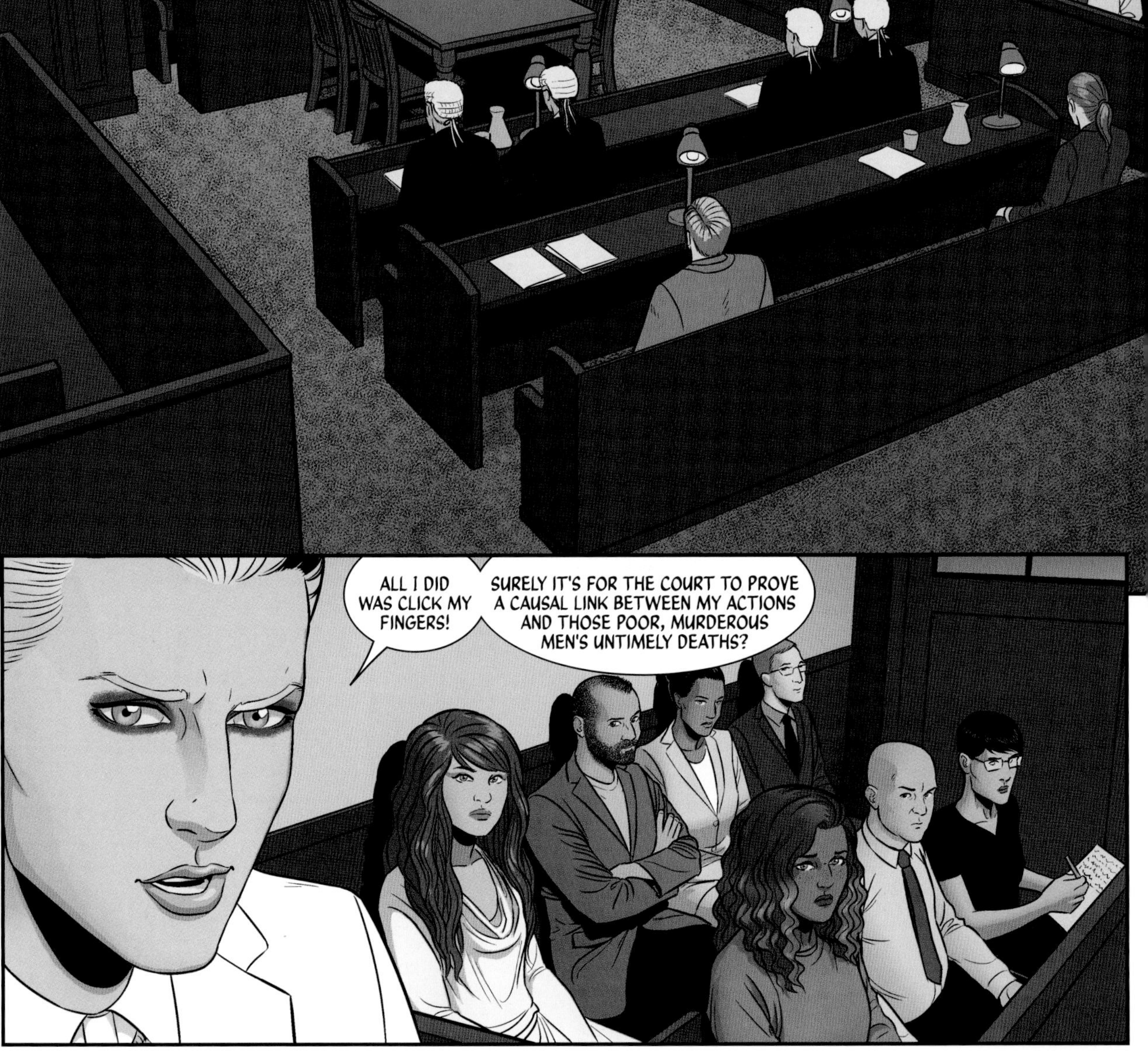
ALL I DID WAS CLICK MY FINGERS!
SURELY IT'S FOR THE COURT TO PROVE A CAUSAL LINK BETWEEN MY ACTIONS AND THOSE POOR, MURDEROUS MEN'S UNTIMELY DEATHS?

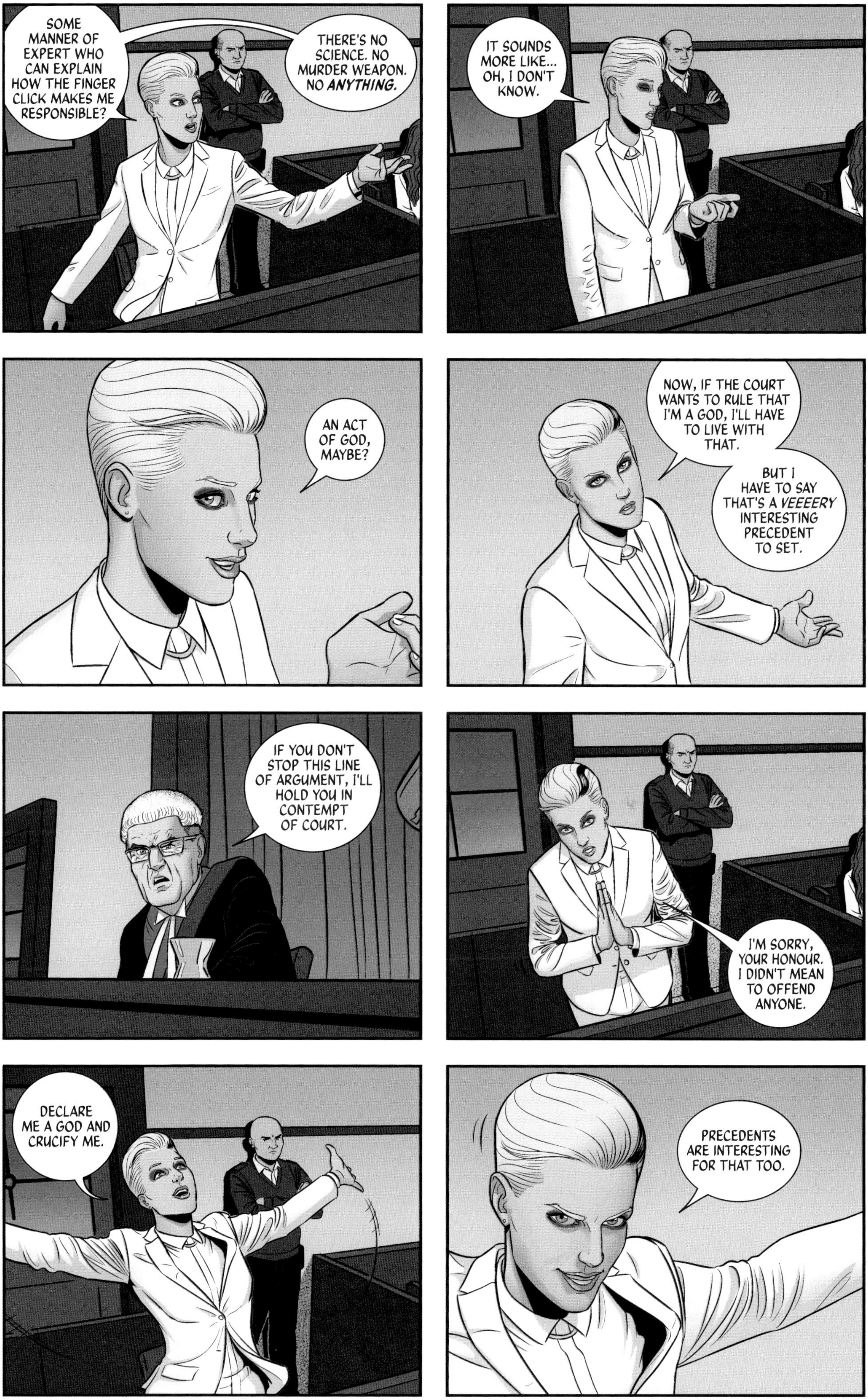
SOME MANNER OF EXPERT WHO CAN EXPLAIN HOW THE FINGER CLICK MAKES ME RESPONSIBLE?
THERE'S NO SCIENCE. NO MURDER WEAPON. NO *ANYTHING.*
IT SOUNDS MORE LIKE... OH, I DON'T KNOW.
AN ACT OF GOD, MAYBE?
NOW, IF THE COURT WANTS TO RULE THAT I'M A GOD, I'LL HAVE TO LIVE WITH THAT.
BUT I HAVE TO SAY THAT'S A *VEEEERY* INTERESTING PRECEDENT TO SET.
IF YOU DON'T STOP THIS LINE OF ARGUMENT, I'LL HOLD YOU IN CONTEMPT OF COURT.
I'M SORRY, YOUR HONOUR. I DIDN'T MEAN TO OFFEND ANYONE.
DECLARE ME A GOD AND CRUCIFY ME.
PRECEDENTS ARE INTERESTING FOR THAT TOO.

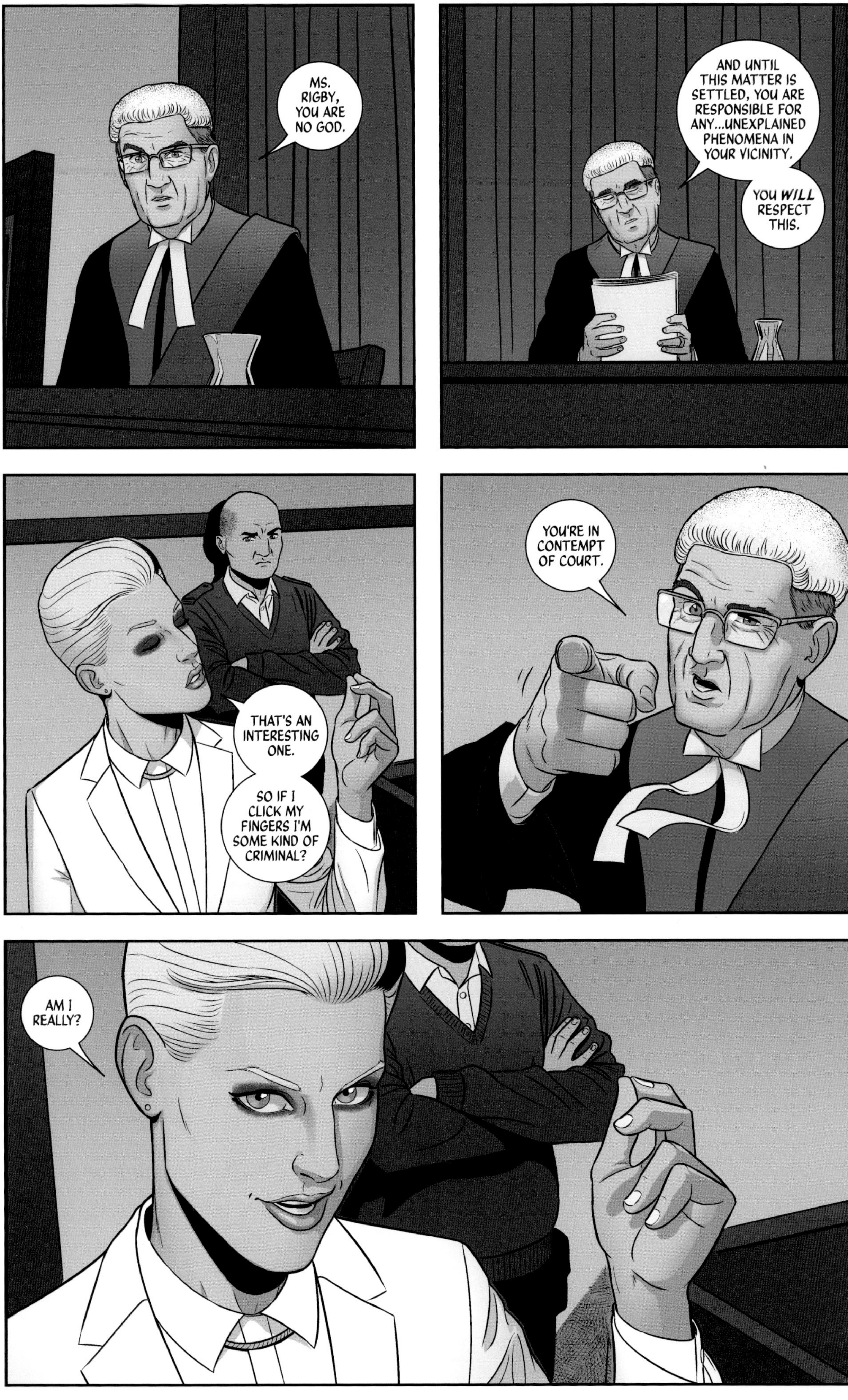
MS. RIGBY, YOU ARE NO GOD.
AND UNTIL THIS MATTER IS SETTLED, YOU ARE RESPONSIBLE FOR ANY...UNEXPLAINED PHENOMENA IN YOUR VICINITY.
YOU WILL RESPECT THIS.
THAT'S AN INTERESTING ONE.
SO IF I CLICK MY FINGERS I'M SOME KIND OF CRIMINAL?
YOU'RE IN CONTEMPT OF COURT.
AM I REALLY?

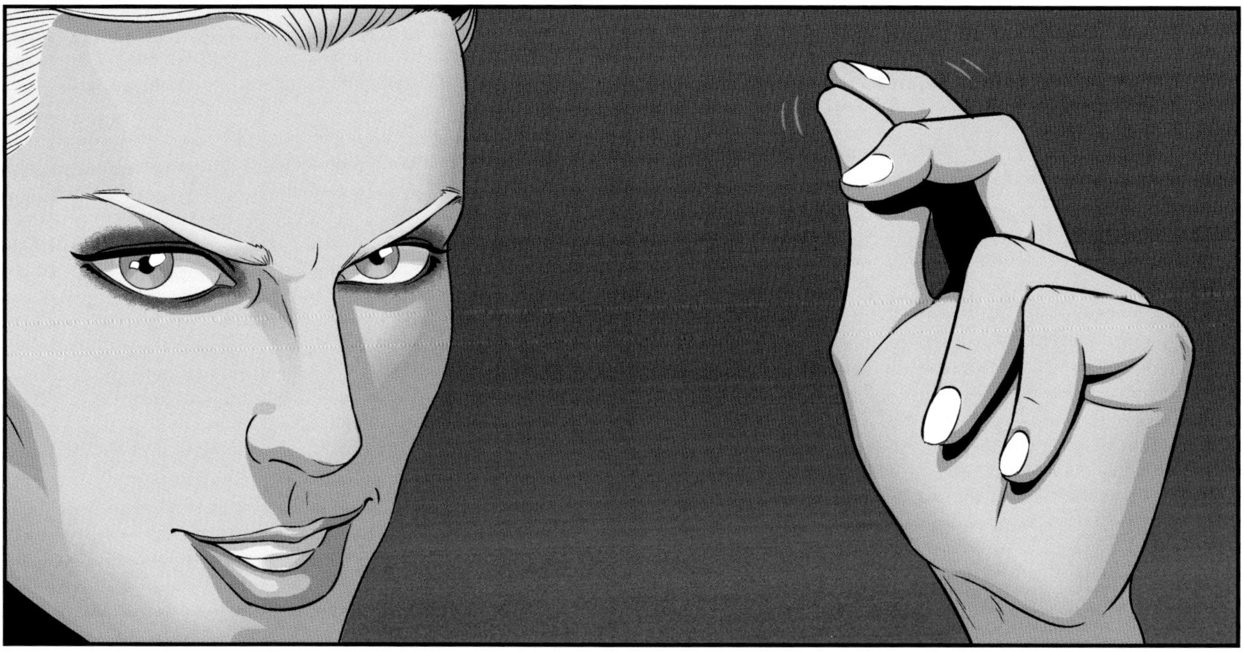

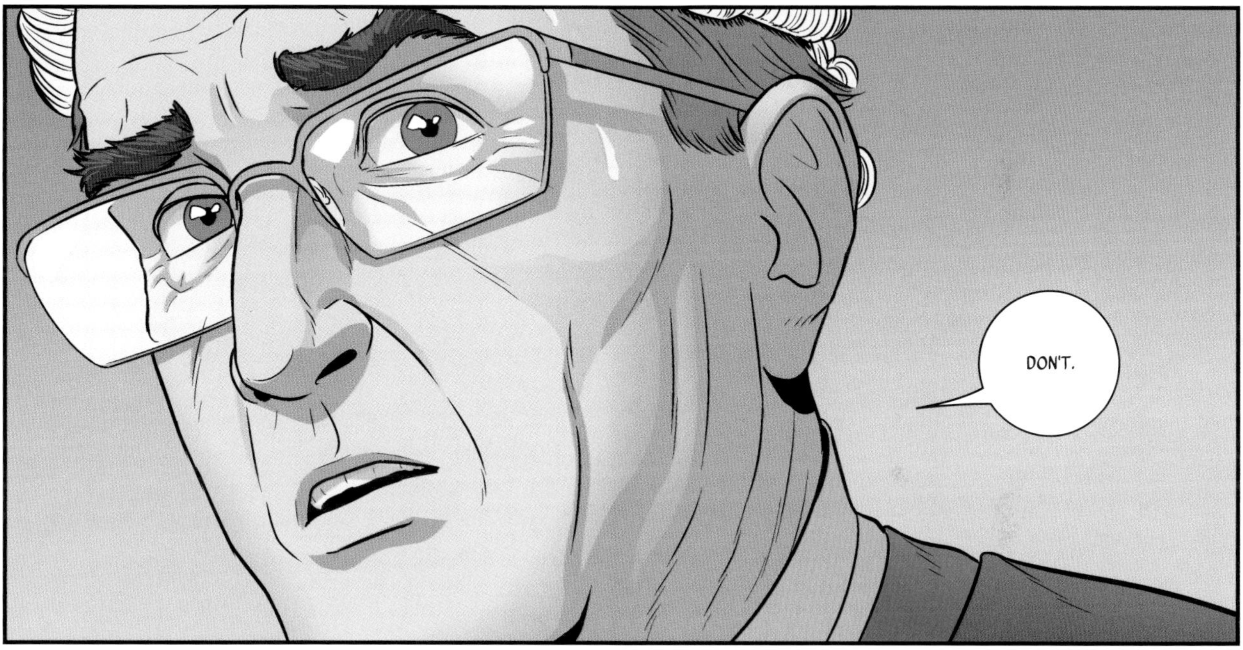
DON'T.

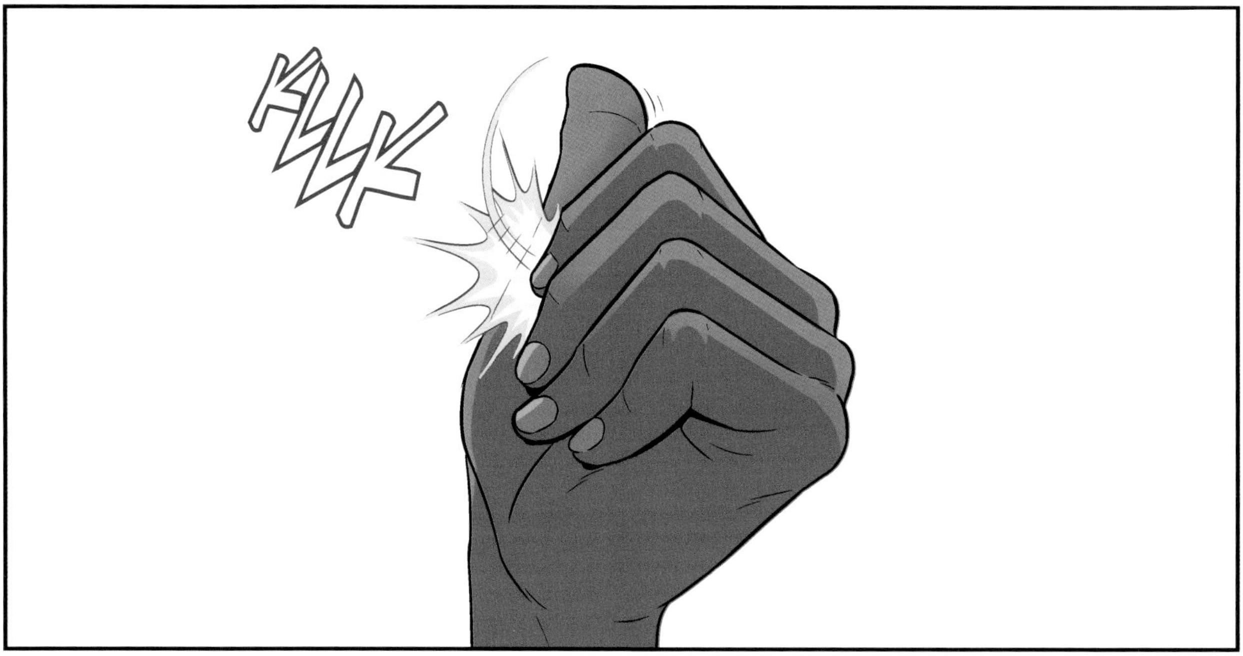
KLLK

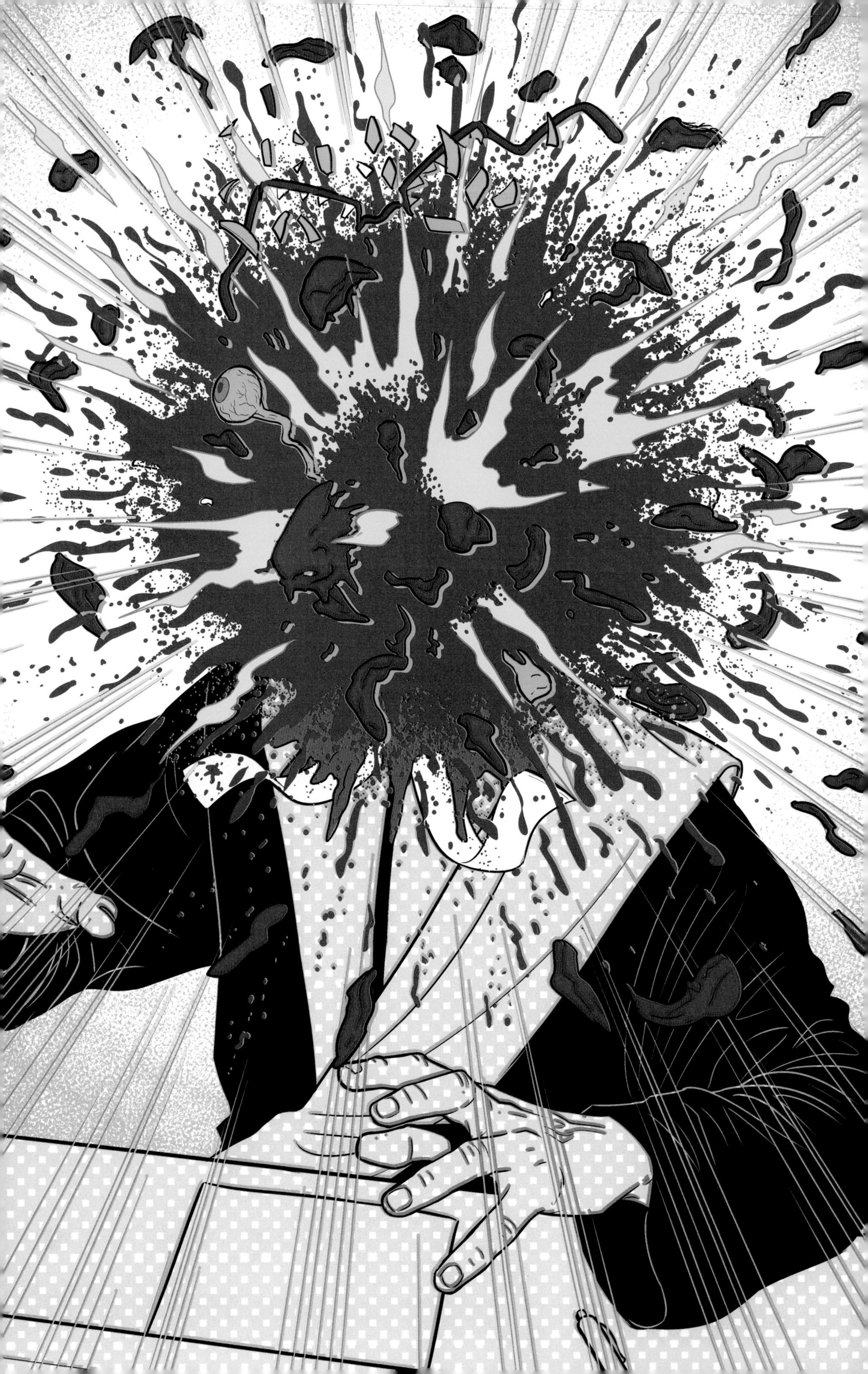

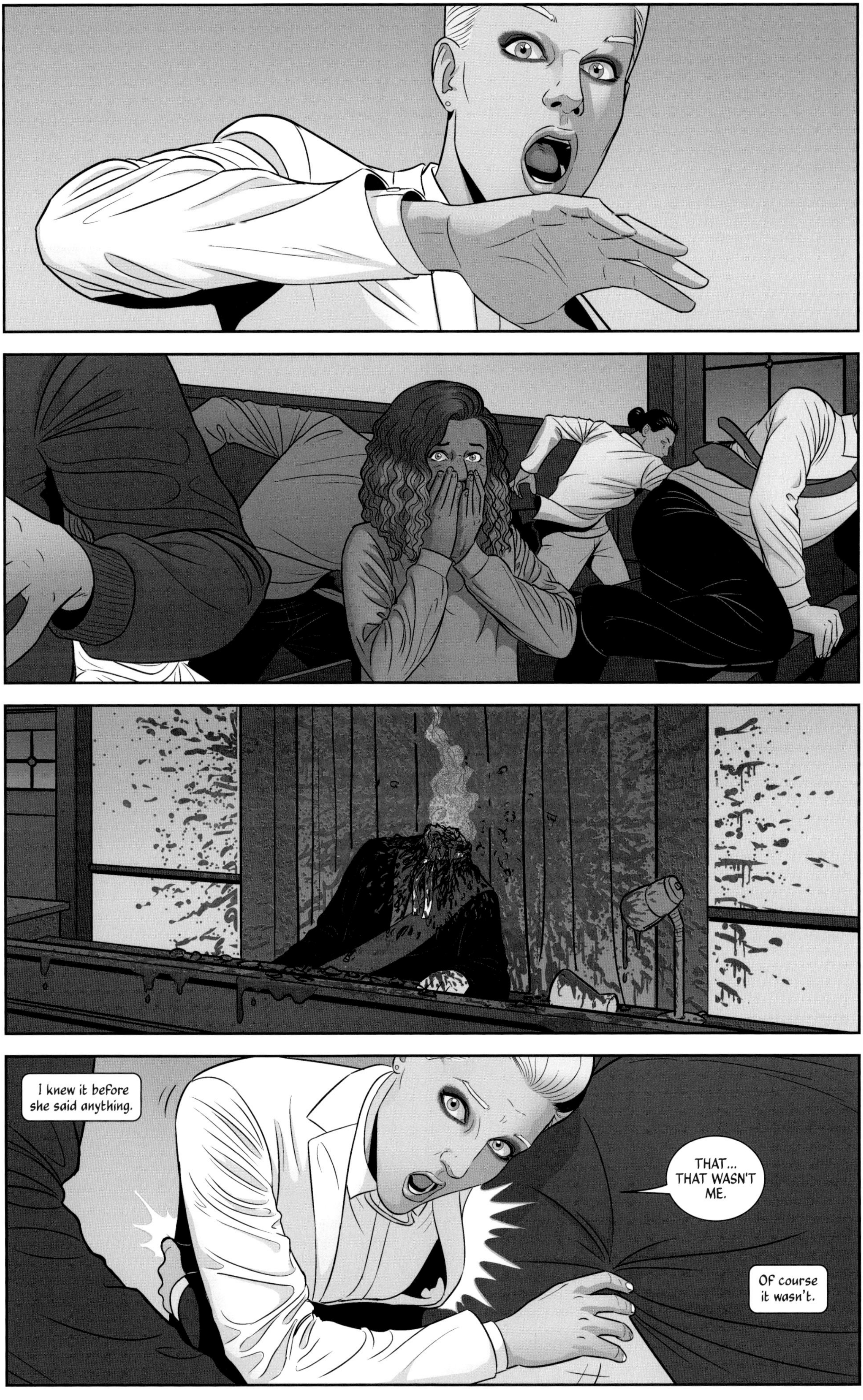
I knew it before she said anything.
THAT... THAT WASN'T ME.
Of course it wasn't.

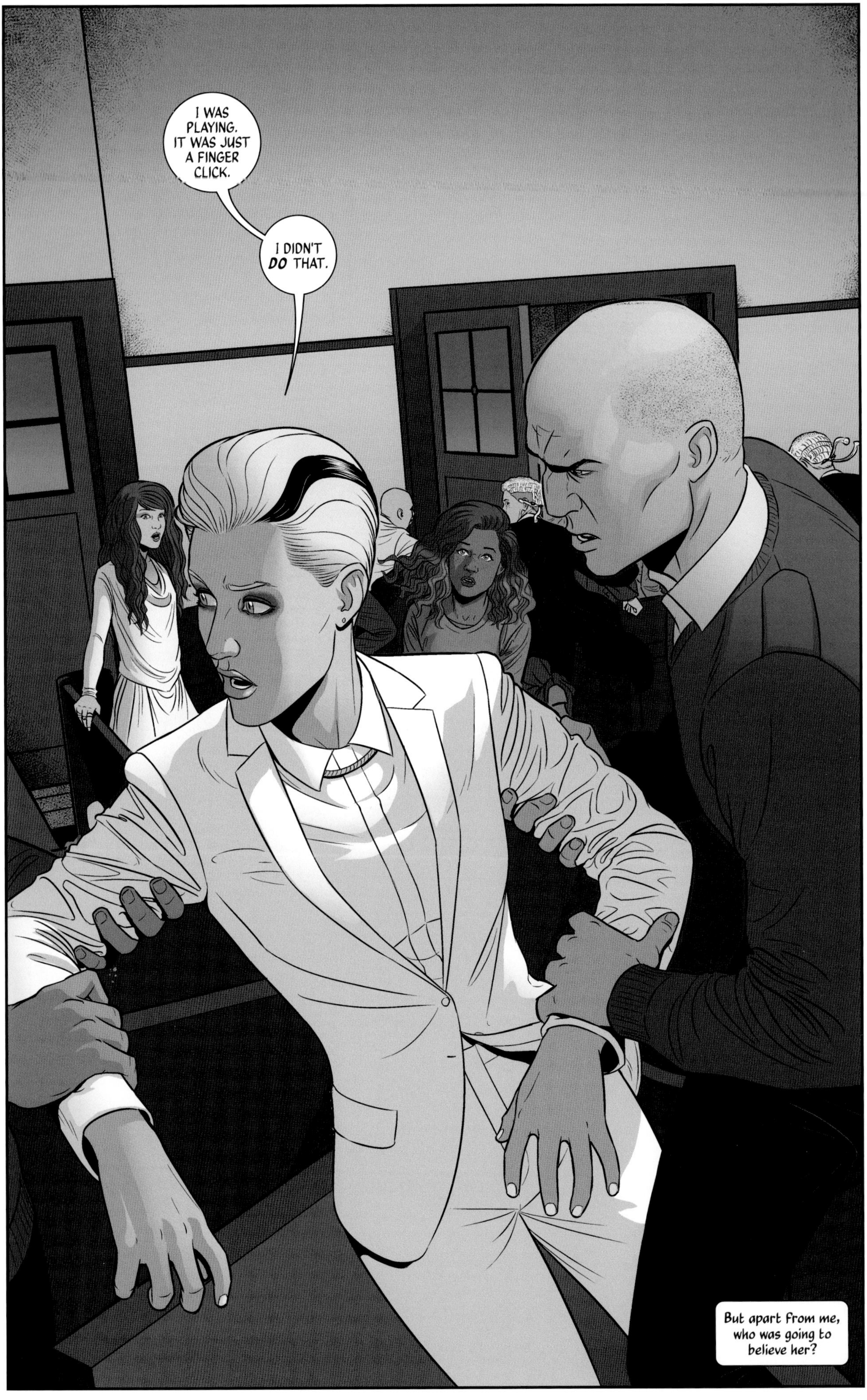
I WAS PLAYING. IT WAS JUST A FINGER CLICK.
I DIDN'T DO THAT.
But apart from me, who was going to believe her?

THE
WICKED
+
THE DIVINE

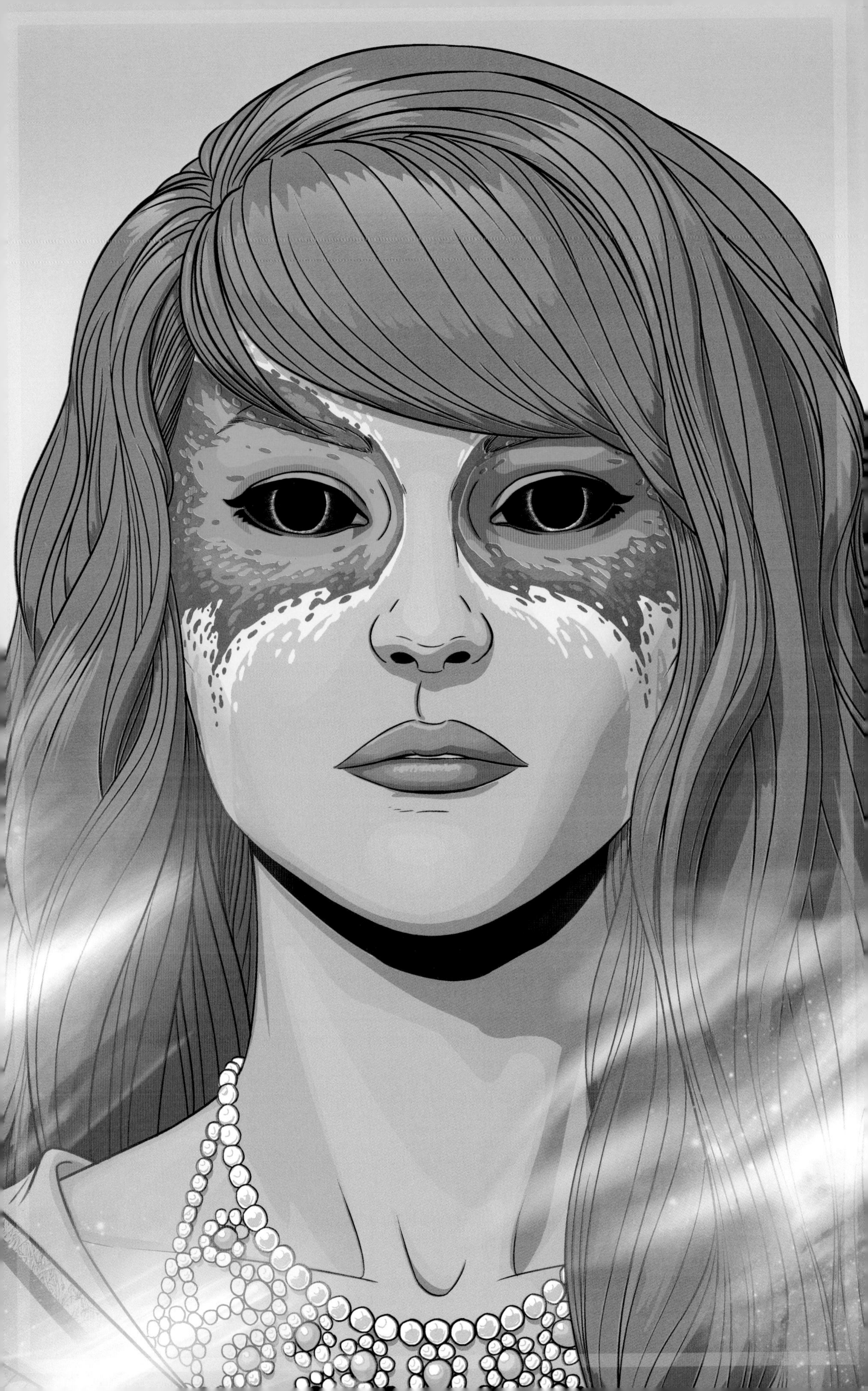

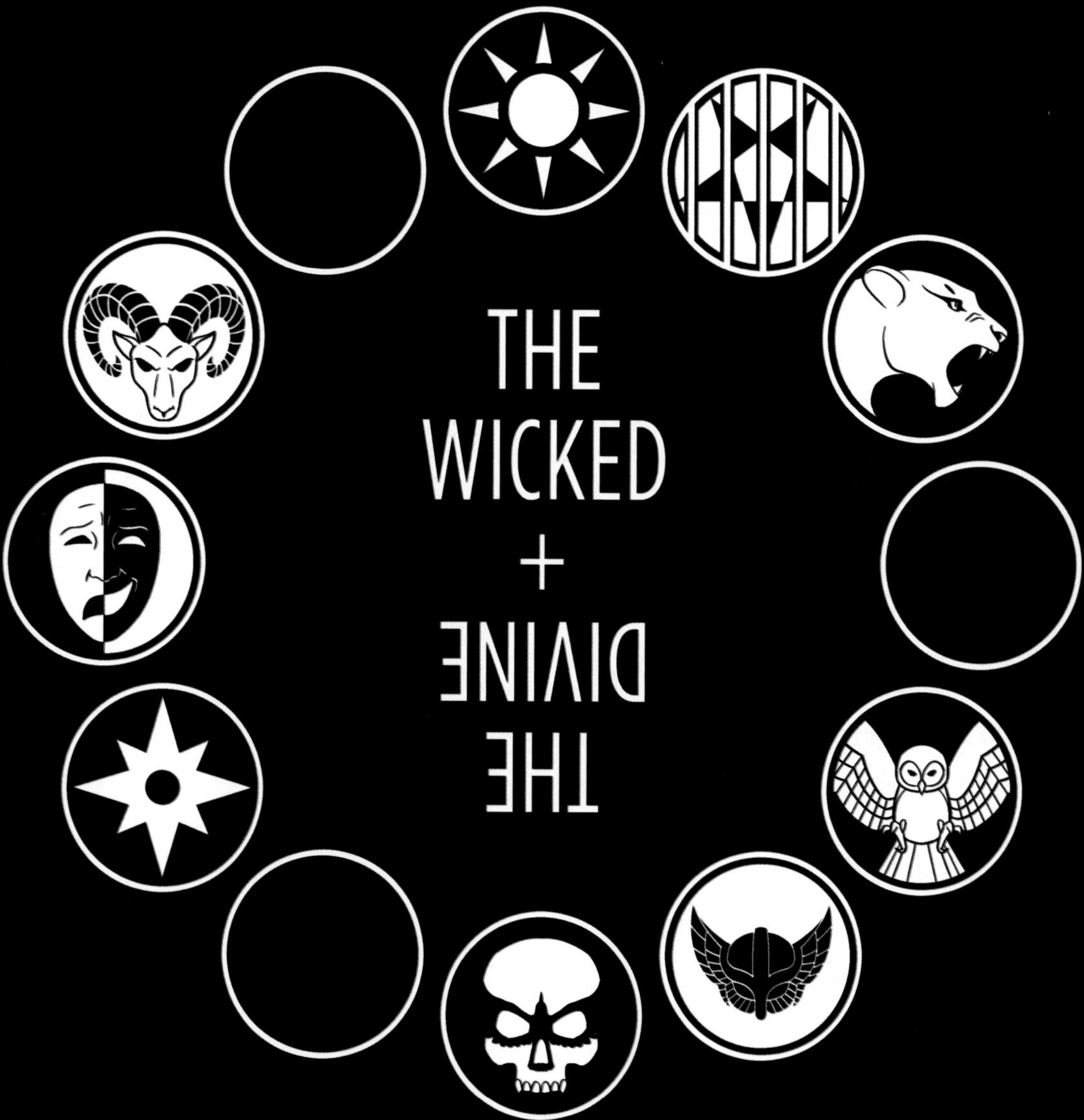
THE
WICKED
+
THE
DIVINE

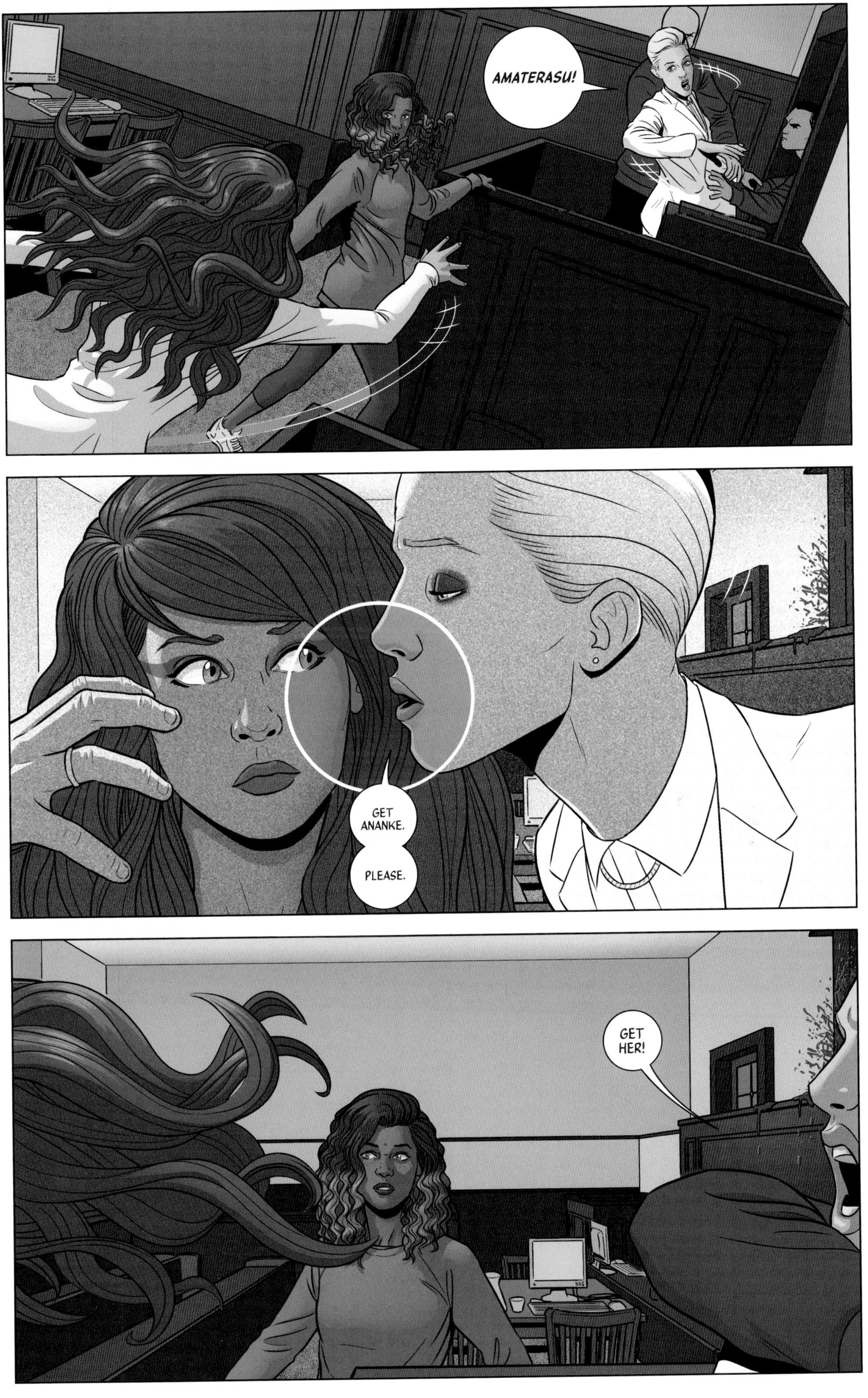
AMATERASU!
GET ANANKE.
PLEASE.
GET HER!

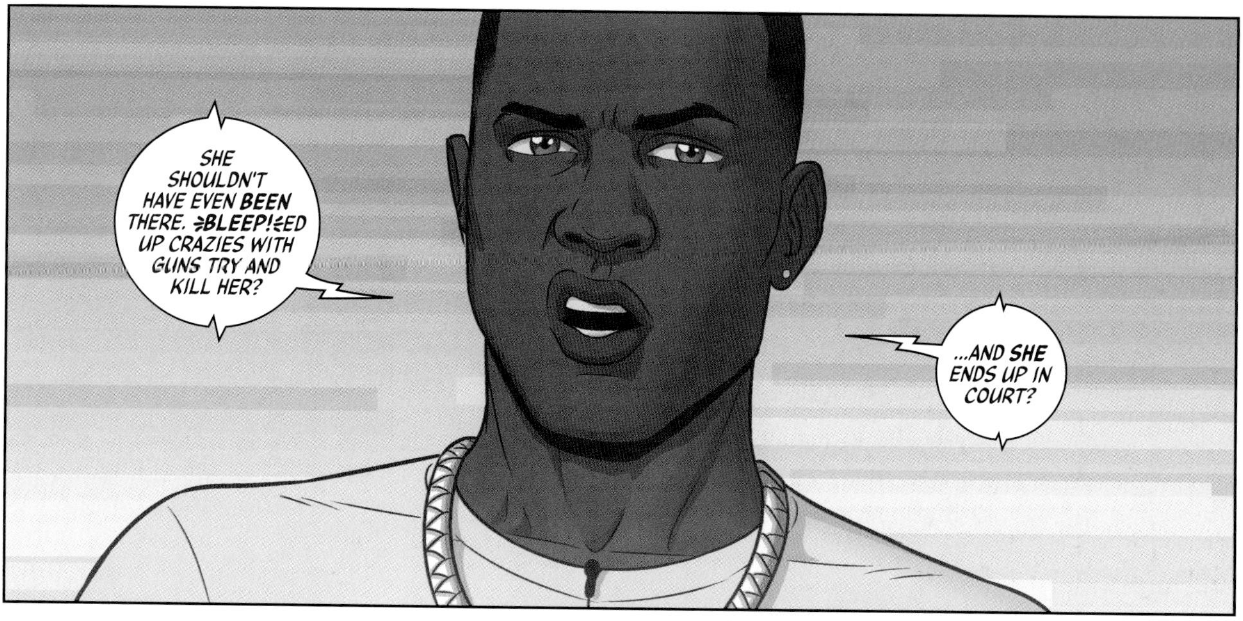
SHE SHOULDN'T HAVE EVEN BEEN THERE. ≯BLEEP!≮ED UP CRAZIES WITH GUNS TRY AND KILL HER?
...AND SHE ENDS UP IN COURT?
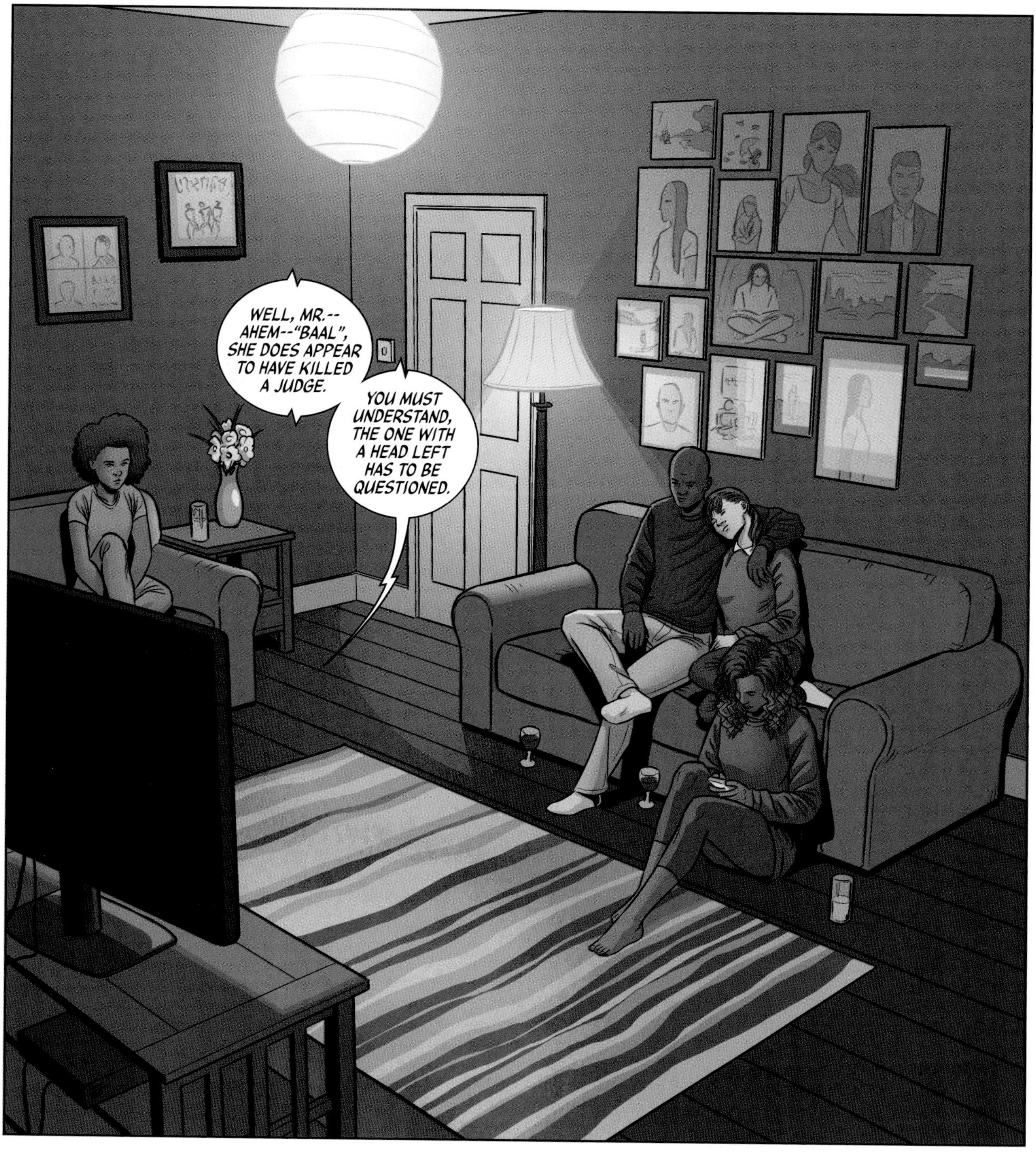
WELL, MR.-- AHEM--"BAAL", SHE DOES APPEAR TO HAVE KILLED A JUDGE.
YOU MUST UNDERSTAND, THE ONE WITH A HEAD LEFT HAS TO BE QUESTIONED.

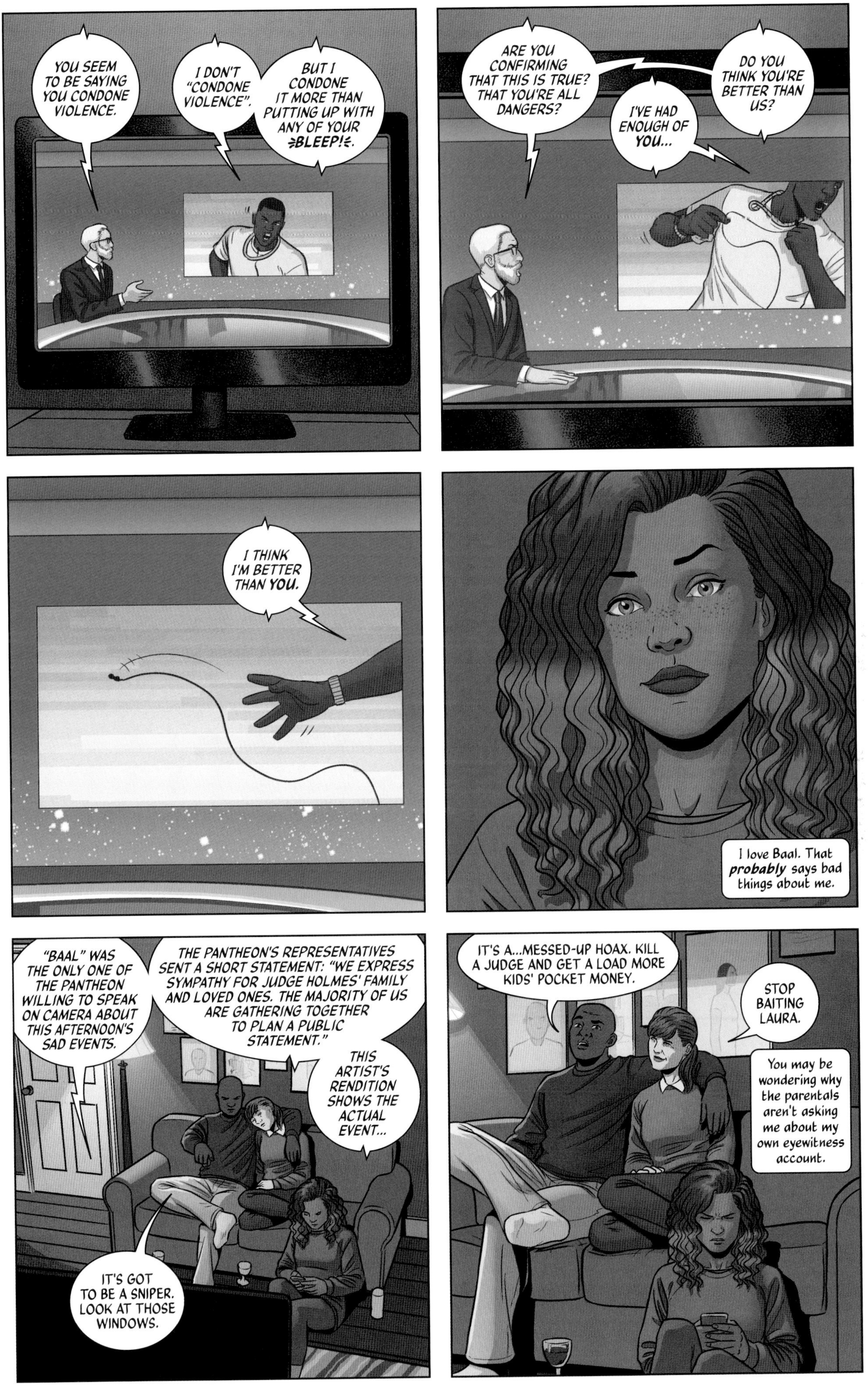
YOU SEEM TO BE SAYING YOU CONDONE VIOLENCE.
I DON'T "CONDONE VIOLENCE".
BUT I CONDONE IT MORE THAN PUTTING UP WITH ANY OF YOUR *BLEEP!*.
ARE YOU CONFIRMING THAT THIS IS TRUE? THAT YOU'RE ALL DANGERS?
DO YOU THINK YOU'RE BETTER THAN US?
I'VE HAD ENOUGH OF **YOU...**
I THINK I'M BETTER THAN **YOU.**
I love Baal. That ***probably*** says bad things about me.
"BAAL" WAS THE ONLY ONE OF THE PANTHEON WILLING TO SPEAK ON CAMERA ABOUT THIS AFTERNOON'S SAD EVENTS.
THE PANTHEON'S REPRESENTATIVES SENT A SHORT STATEMENT: "WE EXPRESS SYMPATHY FOR JUDGE HOLMES' FAMILY AND LOVED ONES. THE MAJORITY OF US ARE GATHERING TOGETHER TO PLAN A PUBLIC STATEMENT."
THIS ARTIST'S RENDITION SHOWS THE ACTUAL EVENT...
IT'S GOT TO BE A SNIPER. LOOK AT THOSE WINDOWS.
IT'S A...MESSED-UP HOAX. KILL A JUDGE AND GET A LOAD MORE KIDS' POCKET MONEY.
STOP BAITING LAURA.
You may be wondering why the parentals aren't asking me about my own eyewitness account.

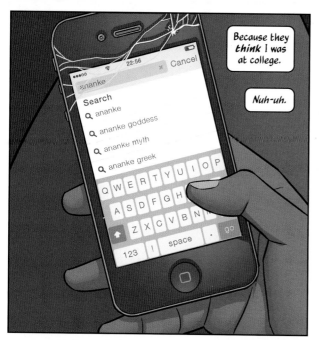

22:56
ananke
Cancel
Search
ananke
ananke goddess
ananke myth
ananke greek
Because they *think* I was at college.
Nuh-uh.
22:56
en.m.wikipedia.org
Ananke (mythology)
This article is about the mythological figure. For Jupiter's moon, see Ananke (moon).
In Greek Mythology, Ananke (From the noun Ἀνάγκη meaning "force, constraint, necessity") was the personification of necessity. Present at the beginning of time she was the absolute ruler of all destiny and fate, for both gods and mortals.
Hmm.
22:56
lucifer "the recurrence"
Cancel
Search
ananke lucifer "the recurrence"
22.57
ananke lucifer "the recurrence"
Search results
SITE WITH NO RELEVANCE
Blah blah blah...
ANOTHER SITE WITH NO RELEVANCE
Yet more blah...
AM I GOING TO HAVE TO GO ONTO THE SECOND PAGE OF SEARCH RESULTS? OH GOD. NO.
This is turning into homework...

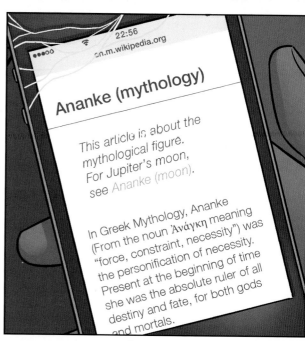

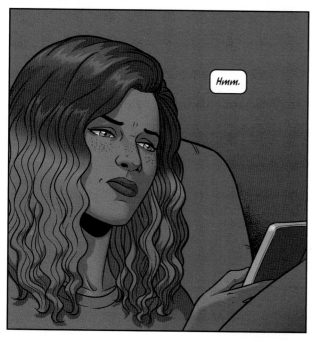

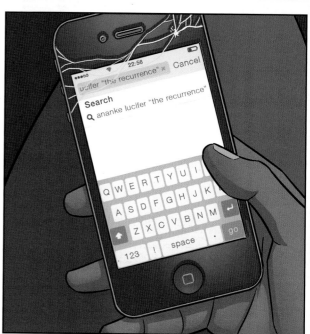

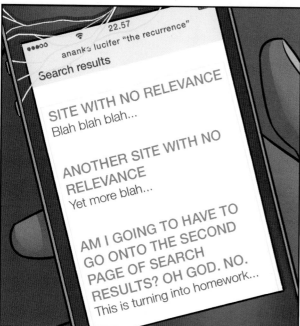

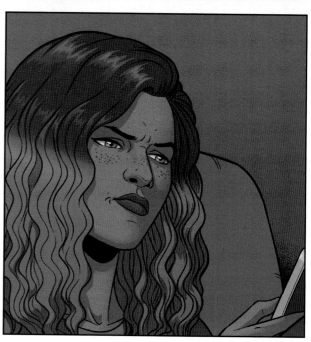

THE NO-PINKIE
PINKIE SWEAR

ONE WEEK LATER

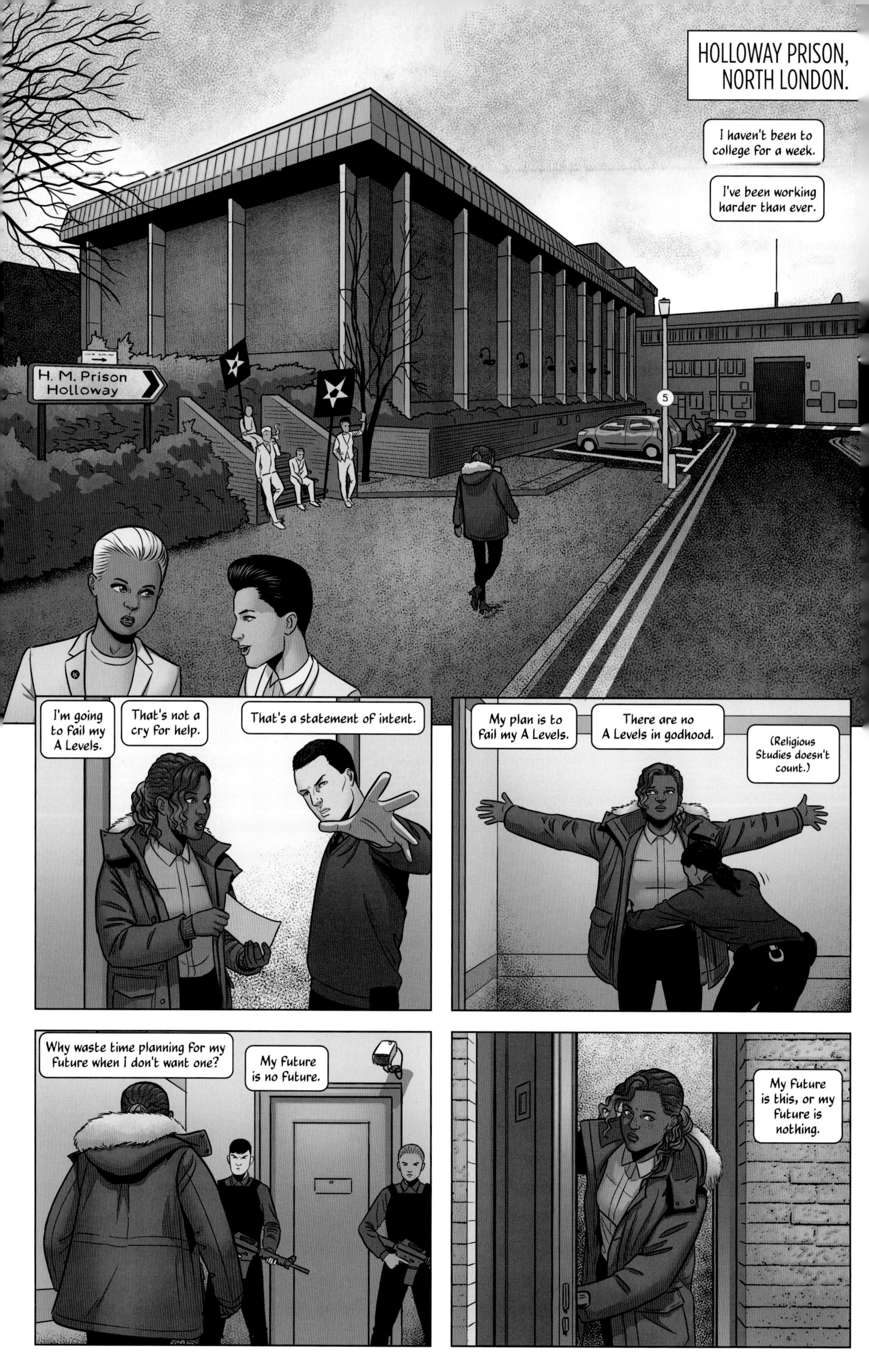
HOLLOWAY PRISON, NORTH LONDON.
I haven't been to college for a week.
I've been working harder than ever.
H. M. Prison Holloway
I'm going to fail my A Levels.
That's not a cry for help.
That's a statement of intent.
My plan is to fail my A Levels.
There are no A Levels in godhood.
(Religious Studies doesn't count.)
Why waste time planning for my future when I don't want one?
My future is no future.
My future is this, or my future is nothing.

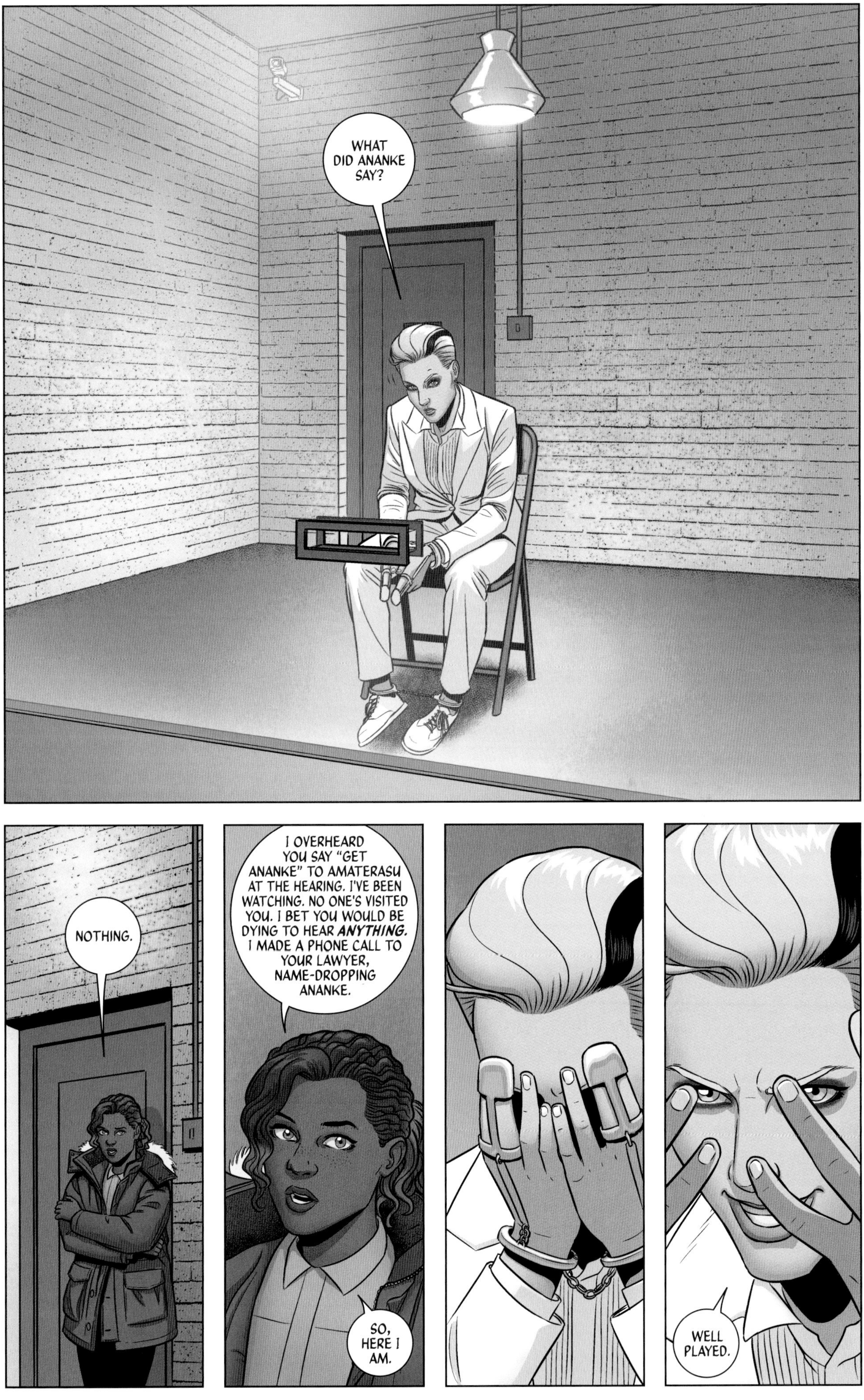
WHAT DID ANANKE SAY?
NOTHING.
I OVERHEARD YOU SAY "GET ANANKE" TO AMATERASU AT THE HEARING. I'VE BEEN WATCHING. NO ONE'S VISITED YOU. I BET YOU WOULD BE DYING TO HEAR ***ANYTHING.*** I MADE A PHONE CALL TO YOUR LAWYER, NAME-DROPPING ANANKE.
SO, HERE I AM.
WELL PLAYED.

YOU'RE THE GIRL I TOOK BACKSTAGE AT THE LITTLE SUN GOD'S PERFORMANCE, AREN'T YOU?

YUP.

NOW, I KNOW YOU MUST FEEL TERRIBLY TEASED WE DIDN'T CONSUMMATE OUR FLIRTATION, BUT THIS SCREEN MAKES IT SOMEWHAT TRICKY. INTANGIBLE CUNNILINGUS IS BEYOND EVEN *MY* ABILITIES.

THAT SAID, I'VE NEVER TRIED. THEY *DO* SAY I HAVE A WICKED TONGUE...

DO YOU HAVE A CIGARETTE? OR COCAINE?

IDEALLY COCAINE?

NUH-UH.

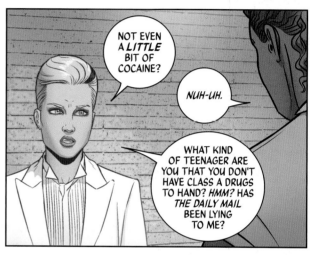

NOT EVEN A *LITTLE* BIT OF COCAINE?

NUH-UH.

WHAT KIND OF TEENAGER ARE YOU THAT YOU DON'T HAVE CLASS A DRUGS TO HAND? HMM? HAS *THE DAILY MAIL* BEEN LYING TO ME?

WHO IS ANANKE?

IF YOU TELL ME, I'LL FIND HER. I WANT TO HELP.

HEH. YOU KNOW THE STORY. TWELVE GODS, REINCARNATE, NINETY YEARS, *ET CETERA.*

A SAD, SAD STORY OF LIVES WASTED BEING TRULY DIVINE.

SHE'S THE ONE WHO BREAKS THE WONDERFUL NEWS.

SHE'S THE ONE WE DON'T TALK ABOUT.

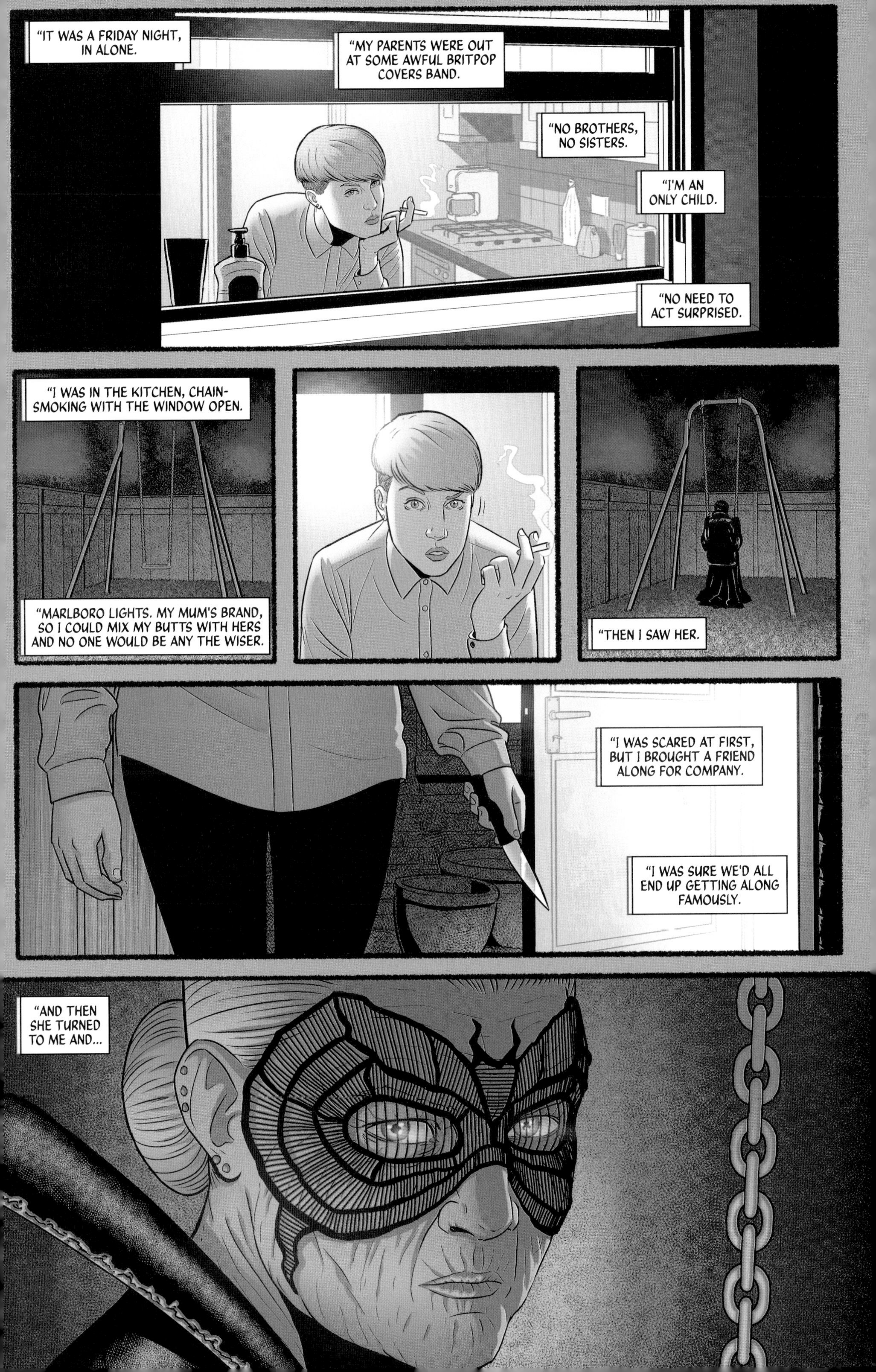
"IT WAS A FRIDAY NIGHT, IN ALONE.
"MY PARENTS WERE OUT AT SOME AWFUL BRITPOP COVERS BAND.
"NO BROTHERS, NO SISTERS.
"I'M AN ONLY CHILD.
"NO NEED TO ACT SURPRISED.
"I WAS IN THE KITCHEN, CHAIN-SMOKING WITH THE WINDOW OPEN.
"MARLBORO LIGHTS. MY MUM'S BRAND, SO I COULD MIX MY BUTTS WITH HERS AND NO ONE WOULD BE ANY THE WISER.
"THEN I SAW HER.
"I WAS SCARED AT FIRST, BUT I BROUGHT A FRIEND ALONG FOR COMPANY.
"I WAS SURE WE'D ALL END UP GETTING ALONG FAMOUSLY.
"AND THEN SHE TURNED TO ME AND...

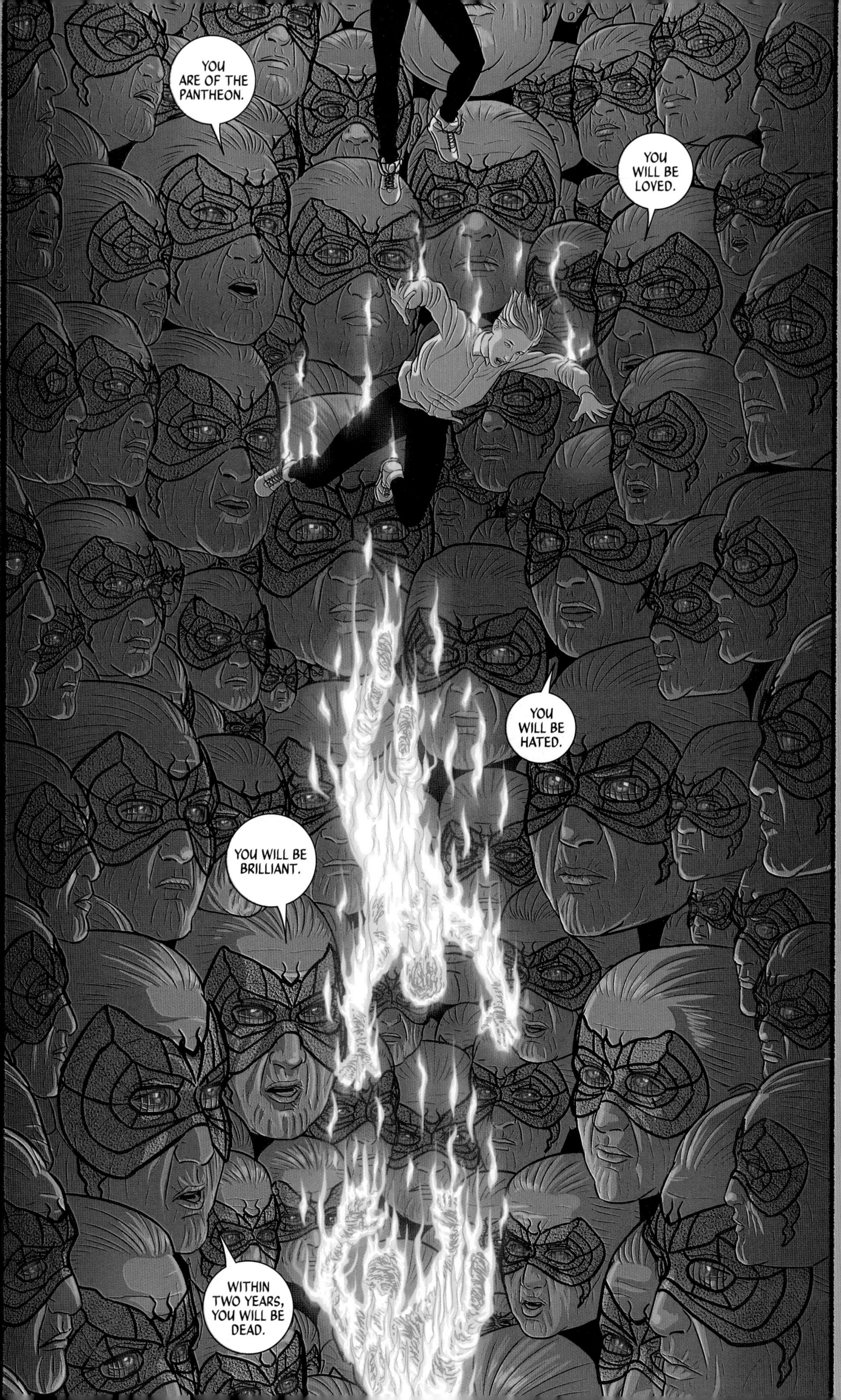
YOU ARE OF THE PANTHEON.
YOU WILL BE LOVED.
YOU WILL BE HATED.
YOU WILL BE BRILLIANT.
WITHIN TWO YEARS, YOU WILL BE DEAD.

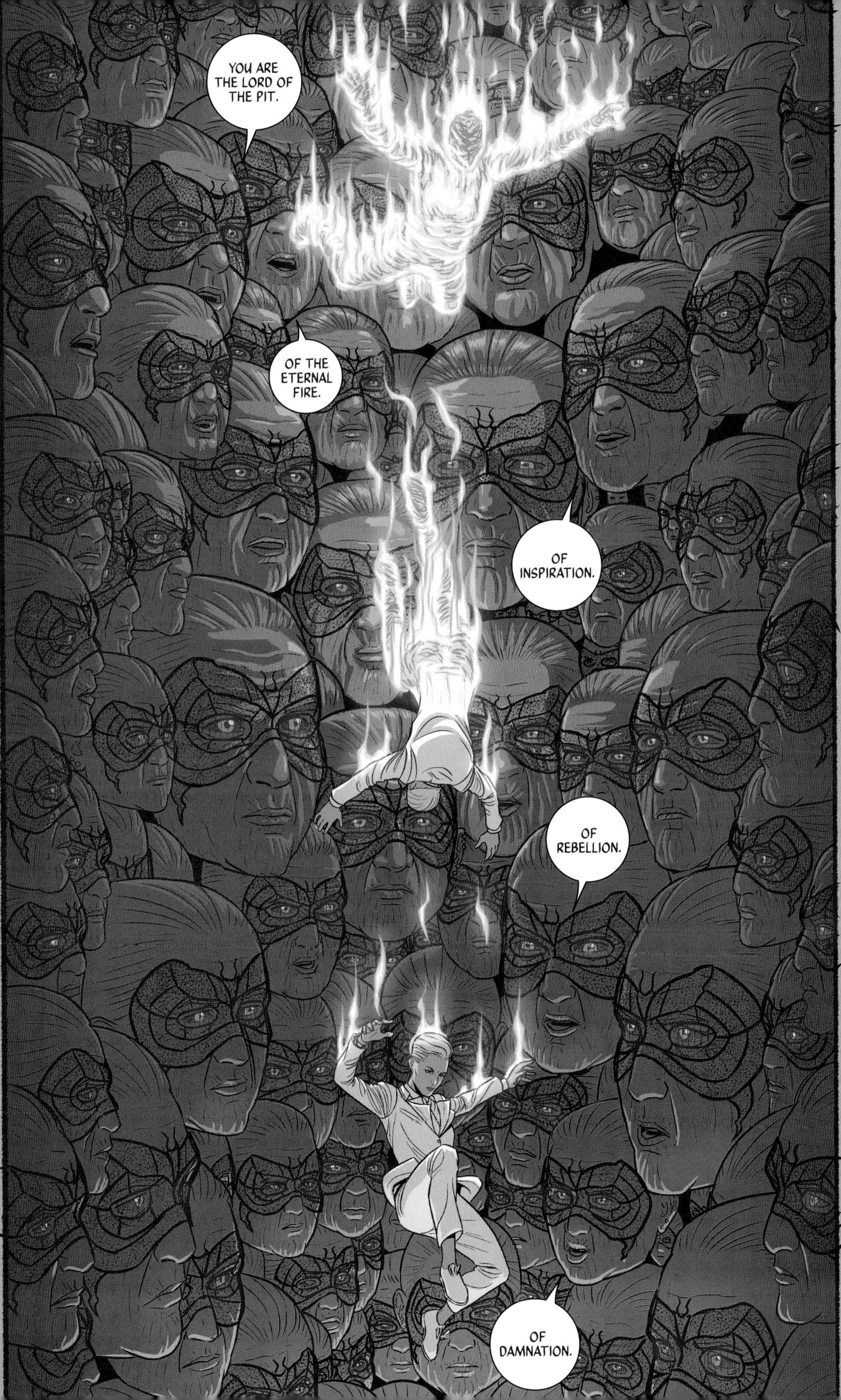
YOU ARE THE LORD OF THE PIT.
OF THE ETERNAL FIRE.
OF INSPIRATION.
OF REBELLION.
OF DAMNATION.

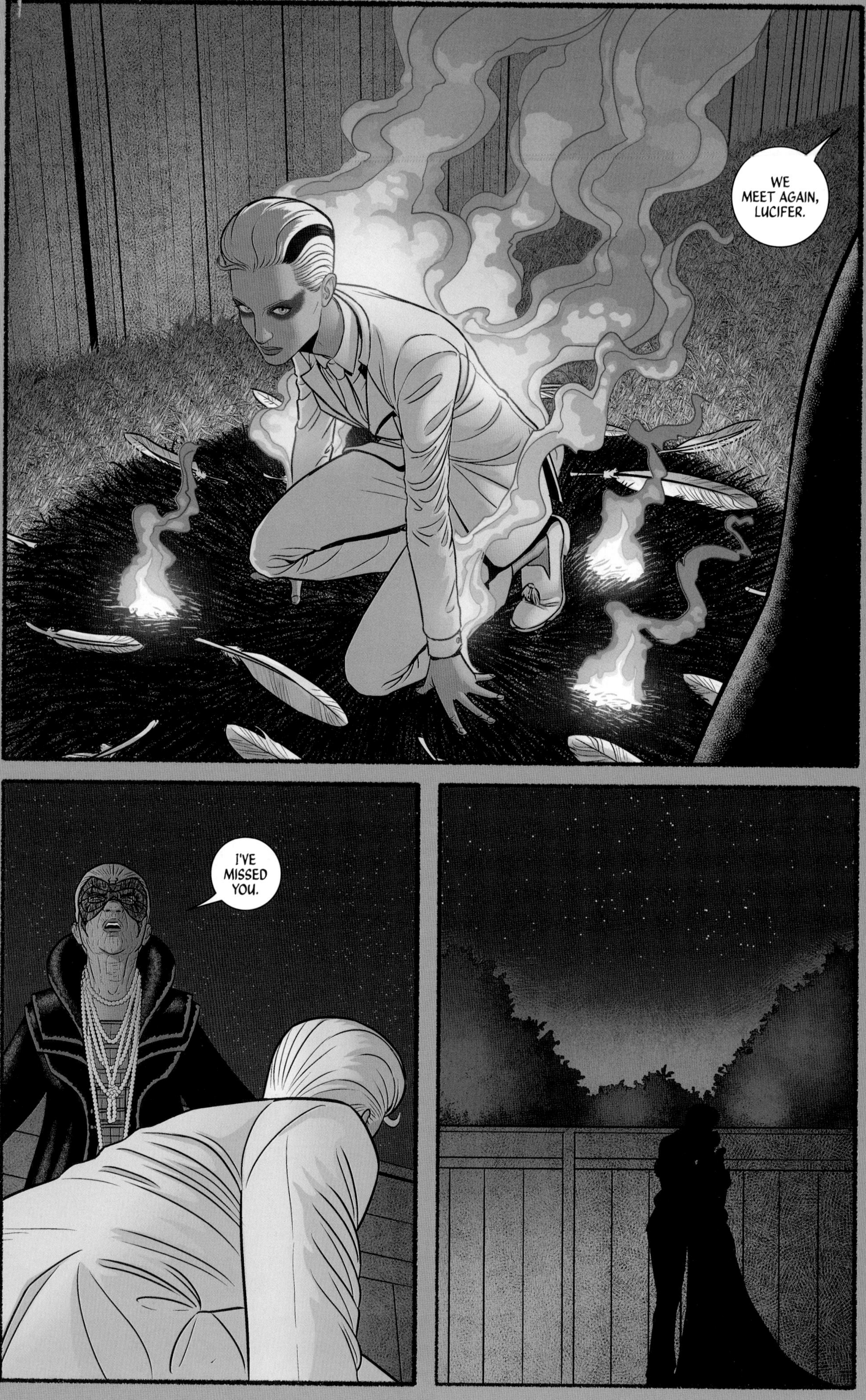
WE MEET AGAIN, LUCIFER.
I'VE MISSED YOU.

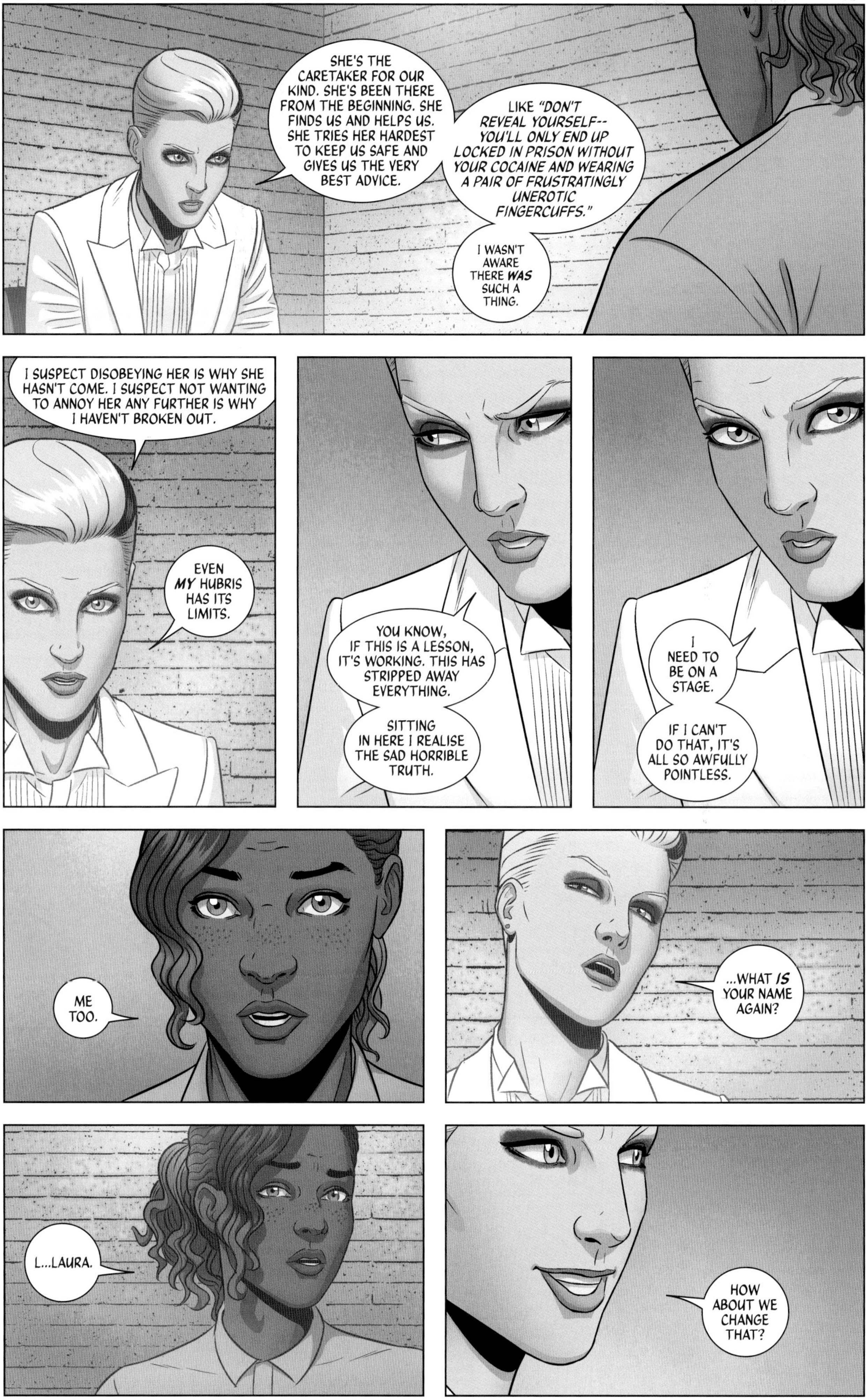
SHE'S THE CARETAKER FOR OUR KIND. SHE'S BEEN THERE FROM THE BEGINNING. SHE FINDS US AND HELPS US. SHE TRIES HER HARDEST TO KEEP US SAFE AND GIVES US THE VERY BEST ADVICE.
LIKE *"DON'T REVEAL YOURSELF-- YOU'LL ONLY END UP LOCKED IN PRISON WITHOUT YOUR COCAINE AND WEARING A PAIR OF FRUSTRATINGLY UNEROTIC FINGERCUFFS."*
I WASN'T AWARE THERE ***WAS*** SUCH A THING.
I SUSPECT DISOBEYING HER IS WHY SHE HASN'T COME. I SUSPECT NOT WANTING TO ANNOY HER ANY FURTHER IS WHY I HAVEN'T BROKEN OUT.
EVEN ***MY*** HUBRIS HAS ITS LIMITS.
YOU KNOW, IF THIS IS A LESSON, IT'S WORKING. THIS HAS STRIPPED AWAY EVERYTHING.
SITTING IN HERE I REALISE THE SAD HORRIBLE TRUTH.
I NEED TO BE ON A STAGE.
IF I CAN'T DO THAT, IT'S ALL SO AWFULLY POINTLESS.
ME TOO.
...WHAT ***IS*** YOUR NAME AGAIN?
L...LAURA.
HOW ABOUT WE CHANGE THAT?

LUCIFER IMPLIES DEMONS. I HAVE NONE AS OF YET, BUT I PROBABLY SHOULD INITIATE A FEW...

DAMNATION IS *DELIGHTFUL.* EVERYONE SHOULD TRY IT.

CAN YOU DO THAT? TURN ME INTO... SOMETHING LIKE YOU?

YES, OF COURSE I CAN. LOOK AT WODEN AND HIS CHEERILY RACIST ARMY OF ETHNIC MONO-CULTURED VALKYRIE FUCK BUDDIES.

I JUST HAVEN'T FOUND ANYONE WICKED ENOUGH TO DESERVE IT YET.

HELP ME AND THAT SOMEONE IS YOU.

I... WHY ME?

BECAUSE LUCIFER IS IN HELL. AND YOU'RE THE ONLY ONE WHO CAME.

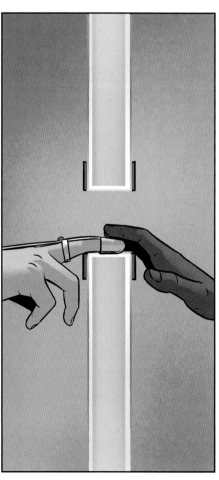

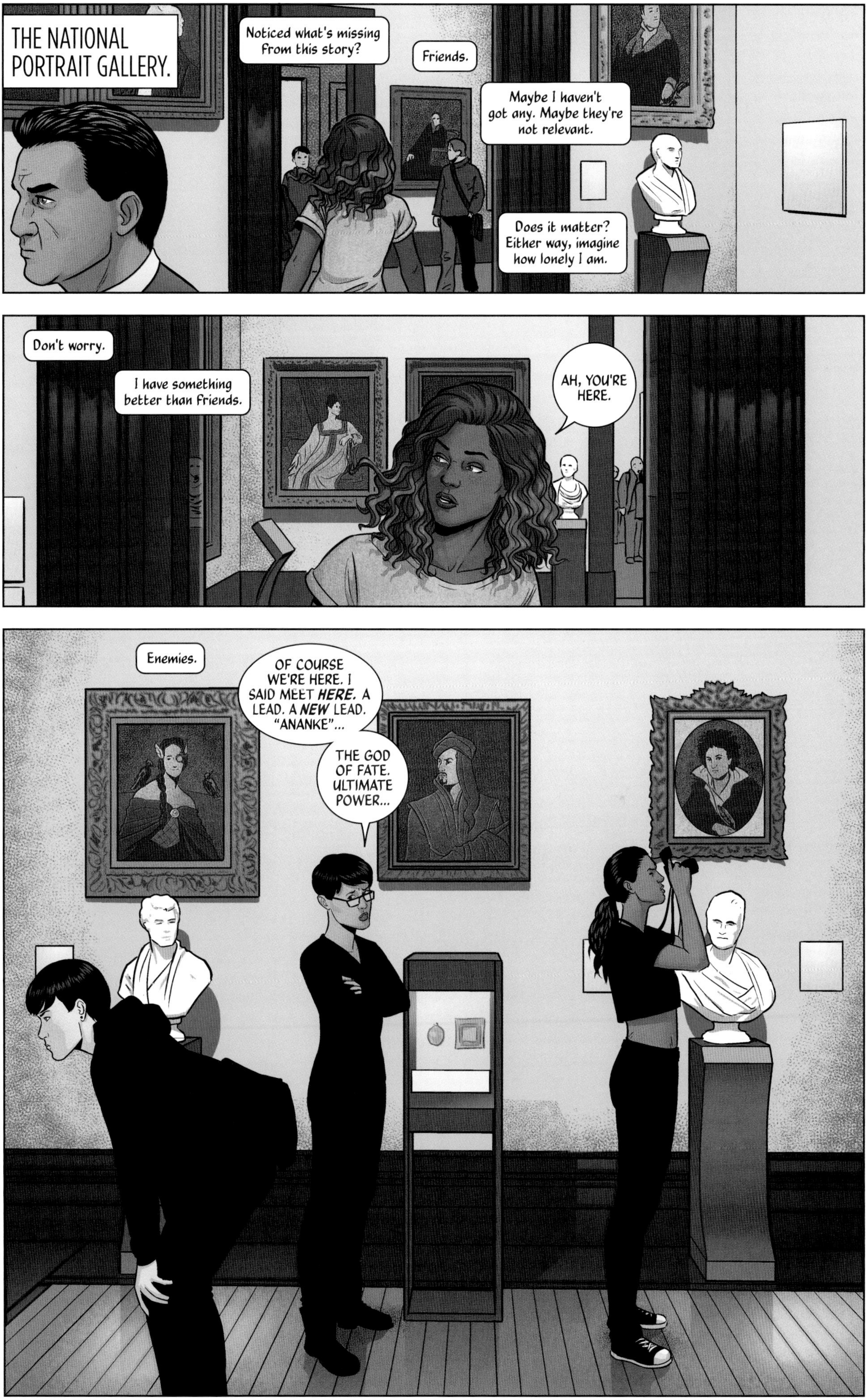
THE NATIONAL PORTRAIT GALLERY.
Noticed what's missing from this story?
Friends.
Maybe I haven't got any. Maybe they're not relevant.
Does it matter? Either way, imagine how lonely I am.
Don't worry.
I have something better than friends.
AH, YOU'RE HERE.
Enemies.
OF COURSE WE'RE HERE. I SAID MEET **HERE.** A LEAD. A **NEW** LEAD. "ANANKE"...
THE GOD OF FATE. ULTIMATE POWER...

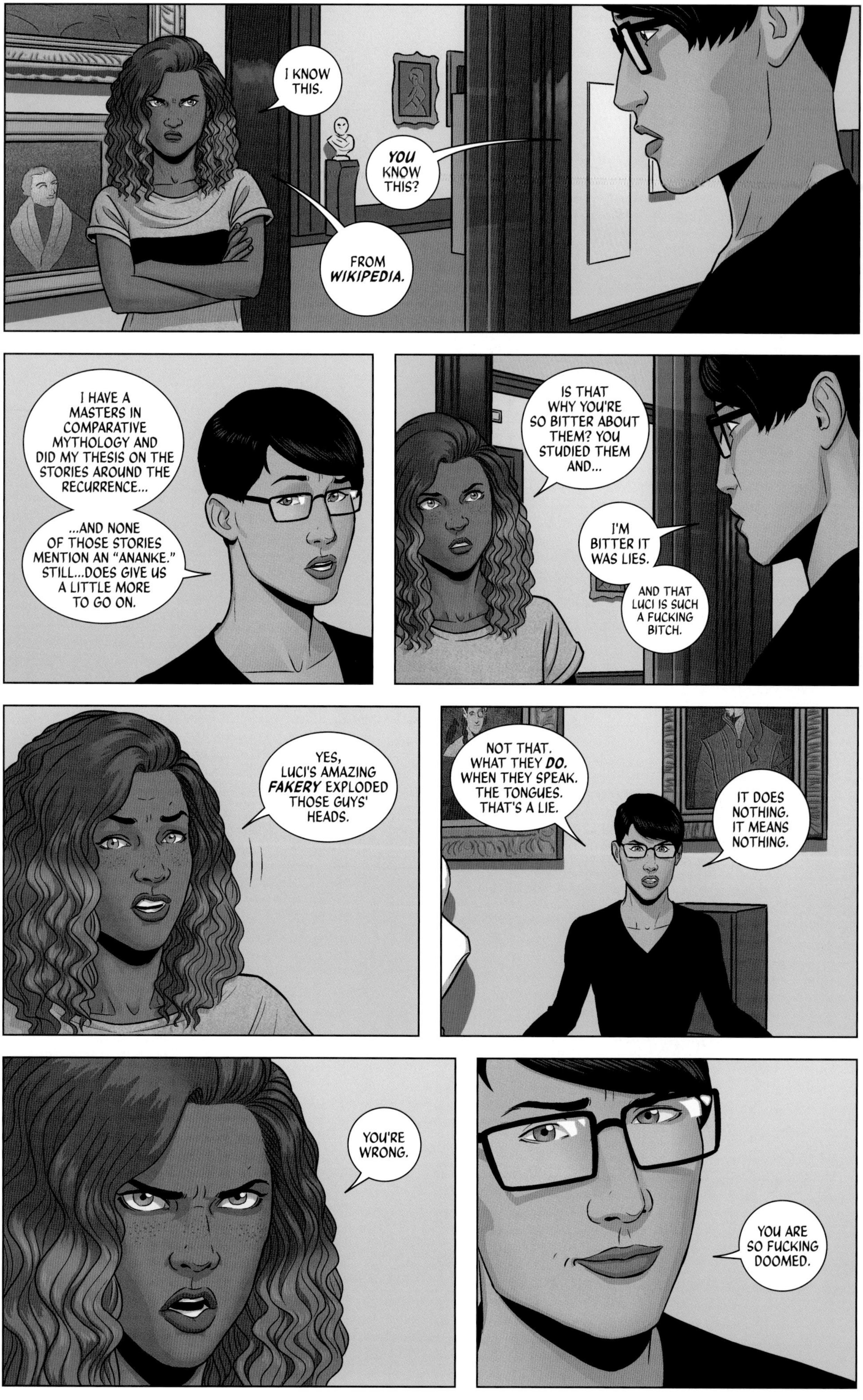
I KNOW THIS.
YOU KNOW THIS?
FROM *WIKIPEDIA.*
I HAVE A MASTERS IN COMPARATIVE MYTHOLOGY AND DID MY THESIS ON THE STORIES AROUND THE RECURRENCE...
...AND NONE OF THOSE STORIES MENTION AN "ANANKE." STILL...DOES GIVE US A LITTLE MORE TO GO ON.
IS THAT WHY YOU'RE SO BITTER ABOUT THEM? YOU STUDIED THEM AND...
I'M BITTER IT WAS LIES.
AND THAT LUCI IS SUCH A FUCKING BITCH.
YES, LUCI'S AMAZING *FAKERY* EXPLODED THOSE GUYS' HEADS.
NOT THAT. WHAT THEY *DO.* WHEN THEY SPEAK. THE TONGUES. THAT'S A LIE.
IT DOES NOTHING. IT MEANS NOTHING.
YOU'RE WRONG.
YOU ARE SO FUCKING DOOMED.

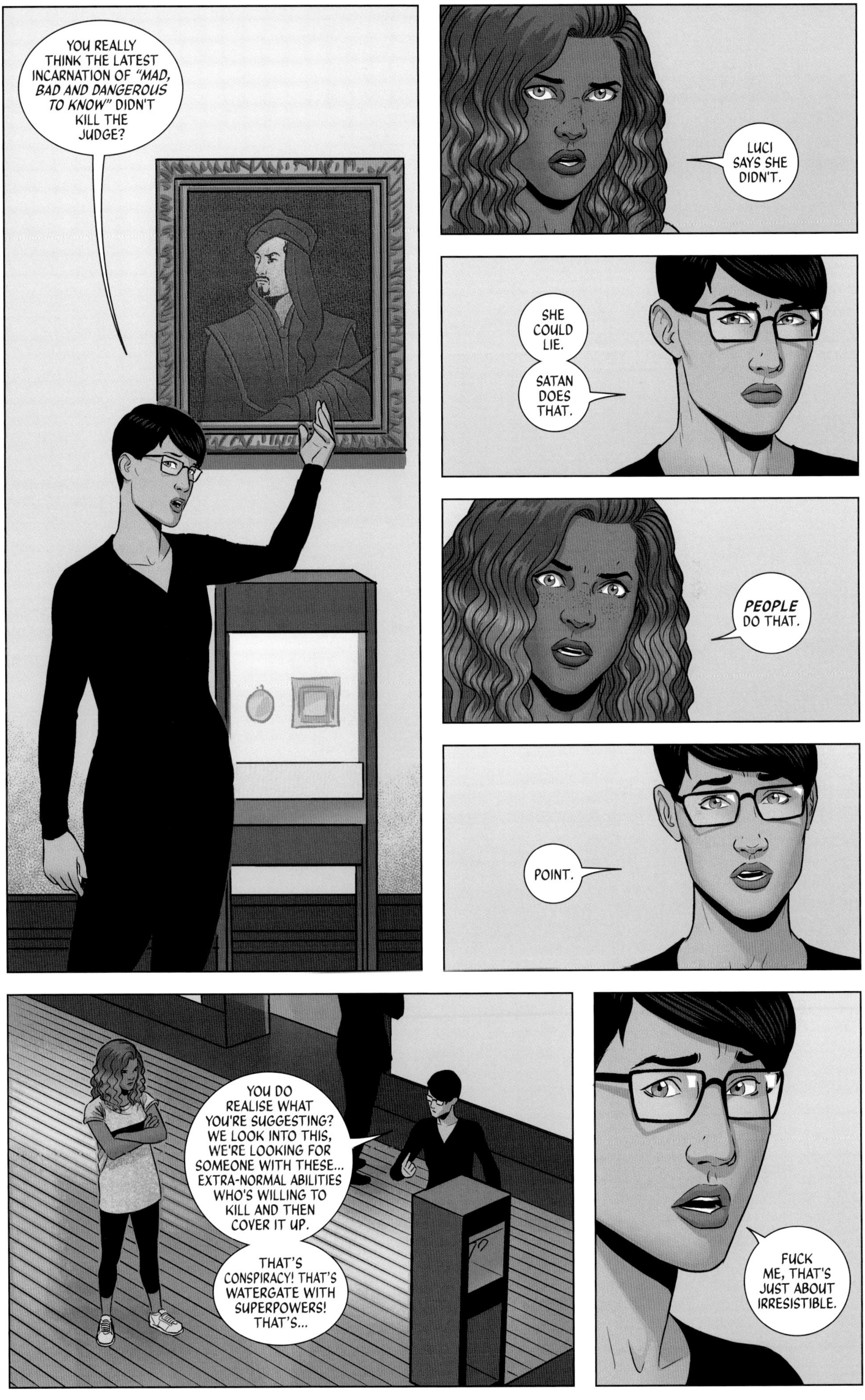
YOU REALLY THINK THE LATEST INCARNATION OF *"MAD, BAD AND DANGEROUS TO KNOW"* DIDN'T KILL THE JUDGE?
LUCI SAYS SHE DIDN'T.
SHE COULD LIE.
SATAN DOES THAT.
PEOPLE DO THAT.
POINT.
YOU DO REALISE WHAT YOU'RE SUGGESTING? WE LOOK INTO THIS, WE'RE LOOKING FOR SOMEONE WITH THESE... EXTRA-NORMAL ABILITIES WHO'S WILLING TO KILL AND THEN COVER IT UP.
THAT'S CONSPIRACY! THAT'S WATERGATE WITH SUPERPOWERS! THAT'S...
FUCK ME, THAT'S JUST ABOUT IRRESISTIBLE.

WE NEED TO HELP HER.

BUT WE DON'T EVEN KNOW WHAT ANY OF THEM COULD DO.

YOU DON'T, LITTLE MISS MY-FIRST-SEARCH-ENGINE. I HAVE A STUDENT LOAN'S WORTH OF THIS CRAP ROLLING AROUND UP HERE...

IT'S A FIRE GOD, OR SOMEONE WHO COULD ABSTRACTLY PLAY WITH FIRE, LIKE A SKY GOD. MAYBE SOME CHTHONIC...I MEAN *UNDERWORLD*... GODS TOO.

AMATERASU, WHO WAS *THERE*. BAAL, PROBABLY. SAKHMET, DEFINITELY. WODEN, INANNA, MINERVA, THE MORRIGAN... POSSIBLY.

TARA? WHO KNOWS ABOUT TARA? WE DON'T KNOW WHETHER SHE'S BUDDHIST, HINDU OR TARA FROM FUCKING *BUFFY*.

AND ANANKE.

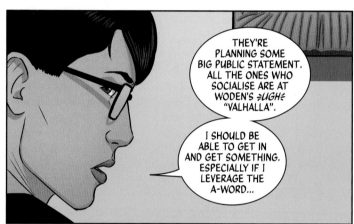

THEY'RE PLANNING SOME BIG PUBLIC STATEMENT. ALL THE ONES WHO SOCIALISE ARE AT WODEN'S ≥UGH≤ "VALHALLA".

I SHOULD BE ABLE TO GET IN AND GET SOMETHING. ESPECIALLY IF I LEVERAGE THE A-WORD...

OH, WOW--

I CAN GET *ME* IN.

YOU NEED TO GO TO THE OTHERS.

I CAN'T GET TO SEE TARA.

Fucking Tara.

SHE DOESN'T SEE ANYONE.

I WASN'T TALKING ABOUT TARA.

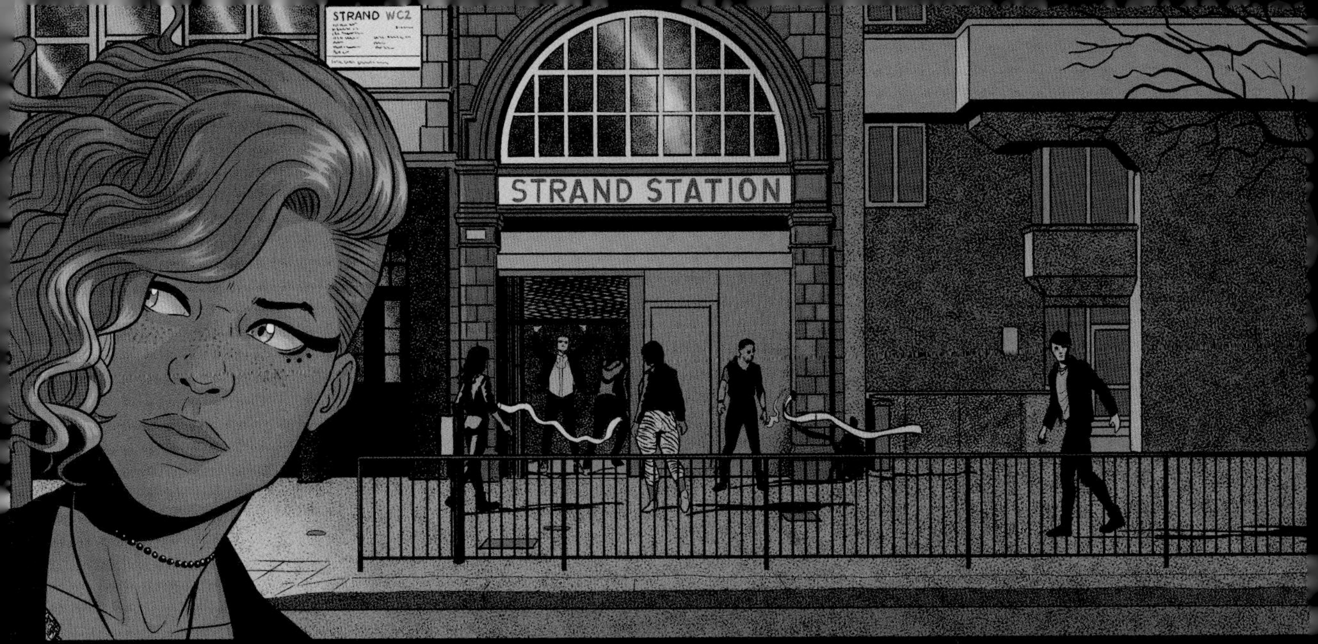
STRAND WC2
STRAND STATION

The Morrigan.

I've seen all the gods...

...except
The Morrigan.

I was at Baal's second gig,
in a warehouse in the middle of
nowhere (i.e. East London).

When Inanna did that
whole week in Camden,
I was crying in the front
row every night.

I've seen Lucifer in Brixton,
Minerva in a cinema in Shepherd's Bush,
Sakhmet at everywhere from Bethnal Green
to the O2, and fucking Tara in
the fucking West End.

I know the names of every
single one of Woden's Valkyries,
and have seen most of them.

But The Morrigan?

She's not like
the others.

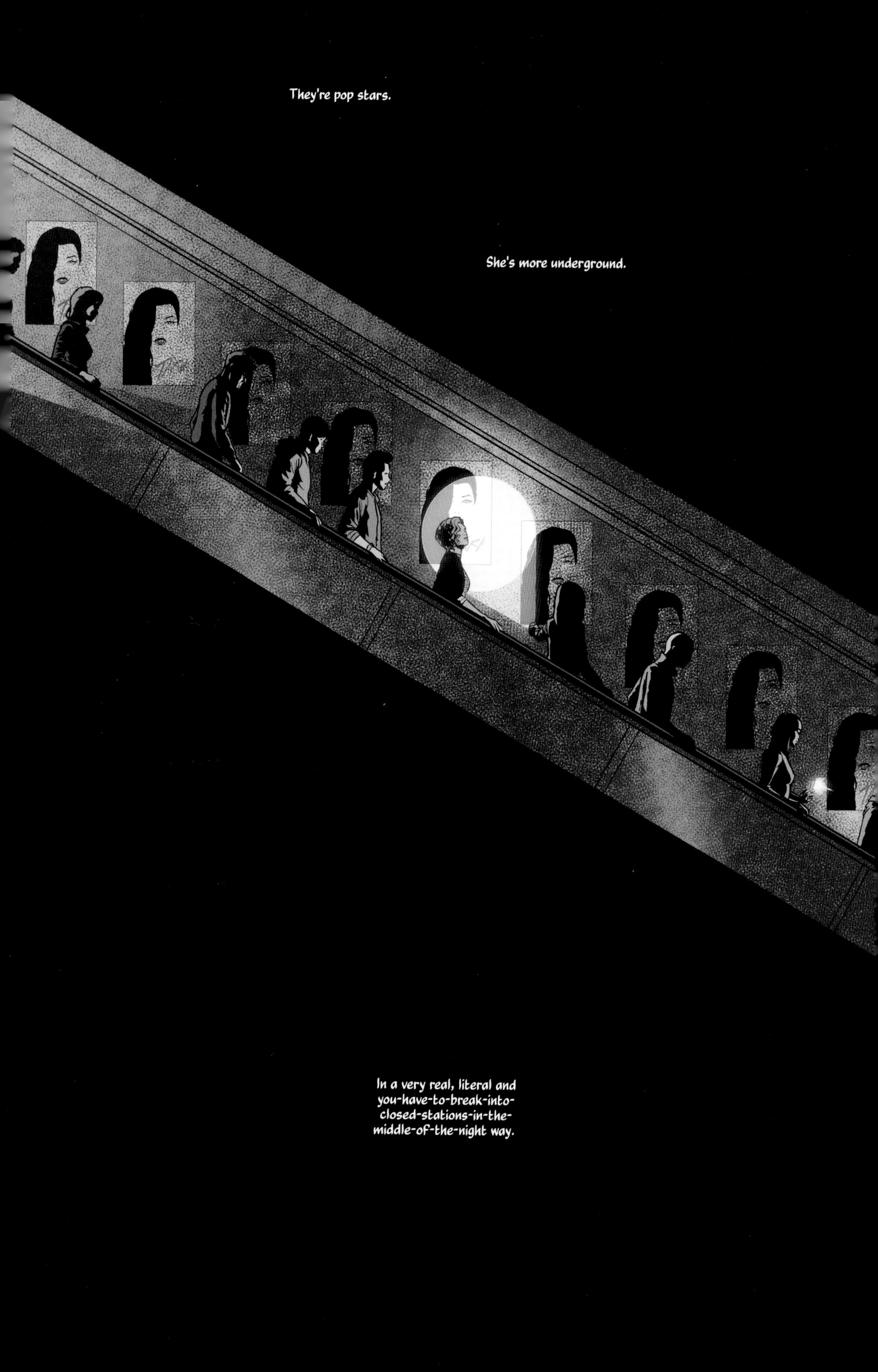
They're pop stars.
She's more underground.
In a very real, literal and you-have-to-break-into-closed-stations-in-the-middle-of-the-night way.

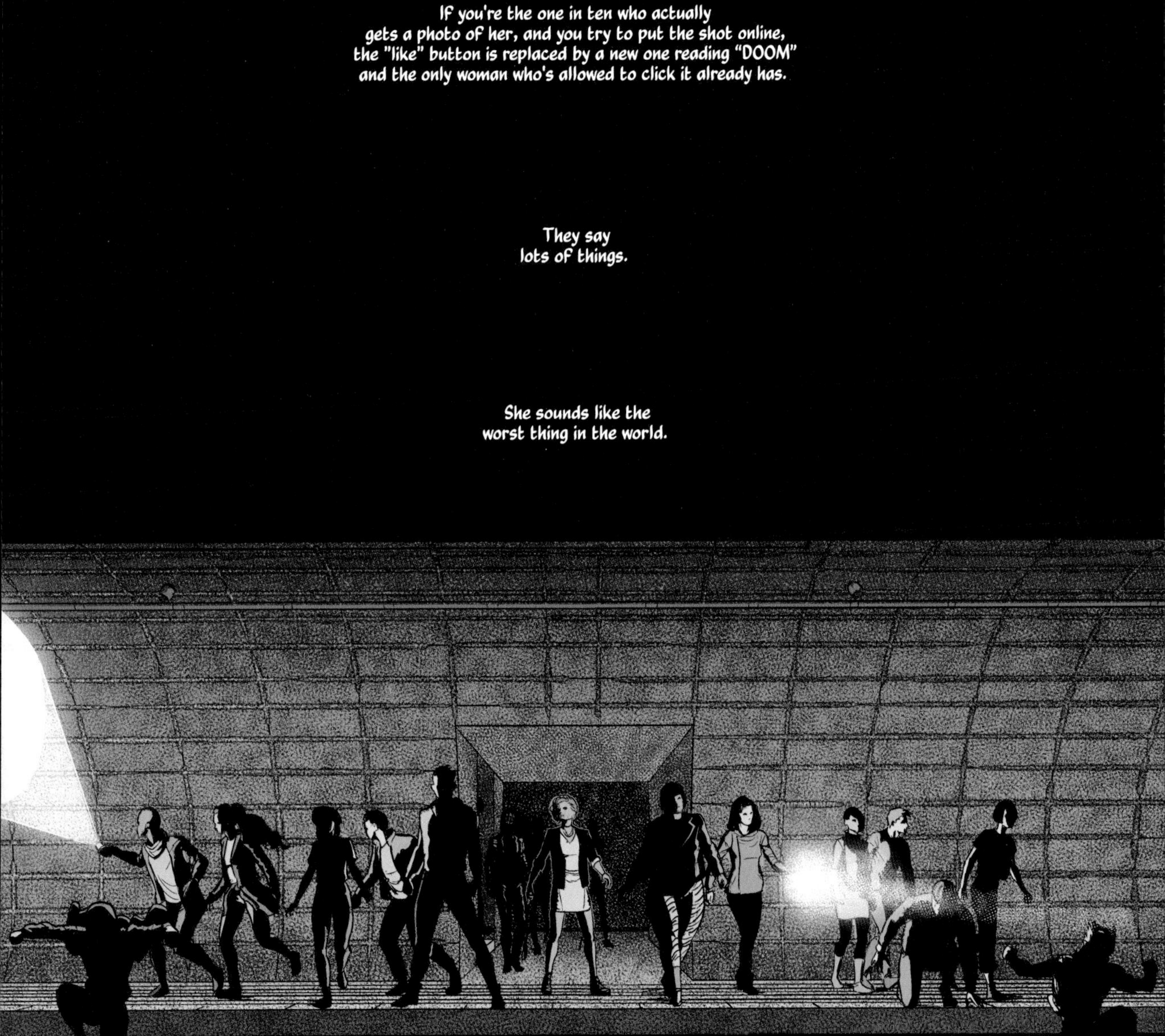
If you're the one in ten who actually gets a photo of her, and you try to put the shot online, the "like" button is replaced by a new one reading "DOOM" and the only woman who's allowed to click it already has.
They say lots of things.
She sounds like the worst thing in the world.

None of the crowd says her name.

They don't say *any* of The Morrigan's names.

It's not like she's only got the one.

All of them scare us.

But we still want to see her.

She's something special,
everyone says.

We just wait
and wait
and wait...

And after half an hour
someone says...

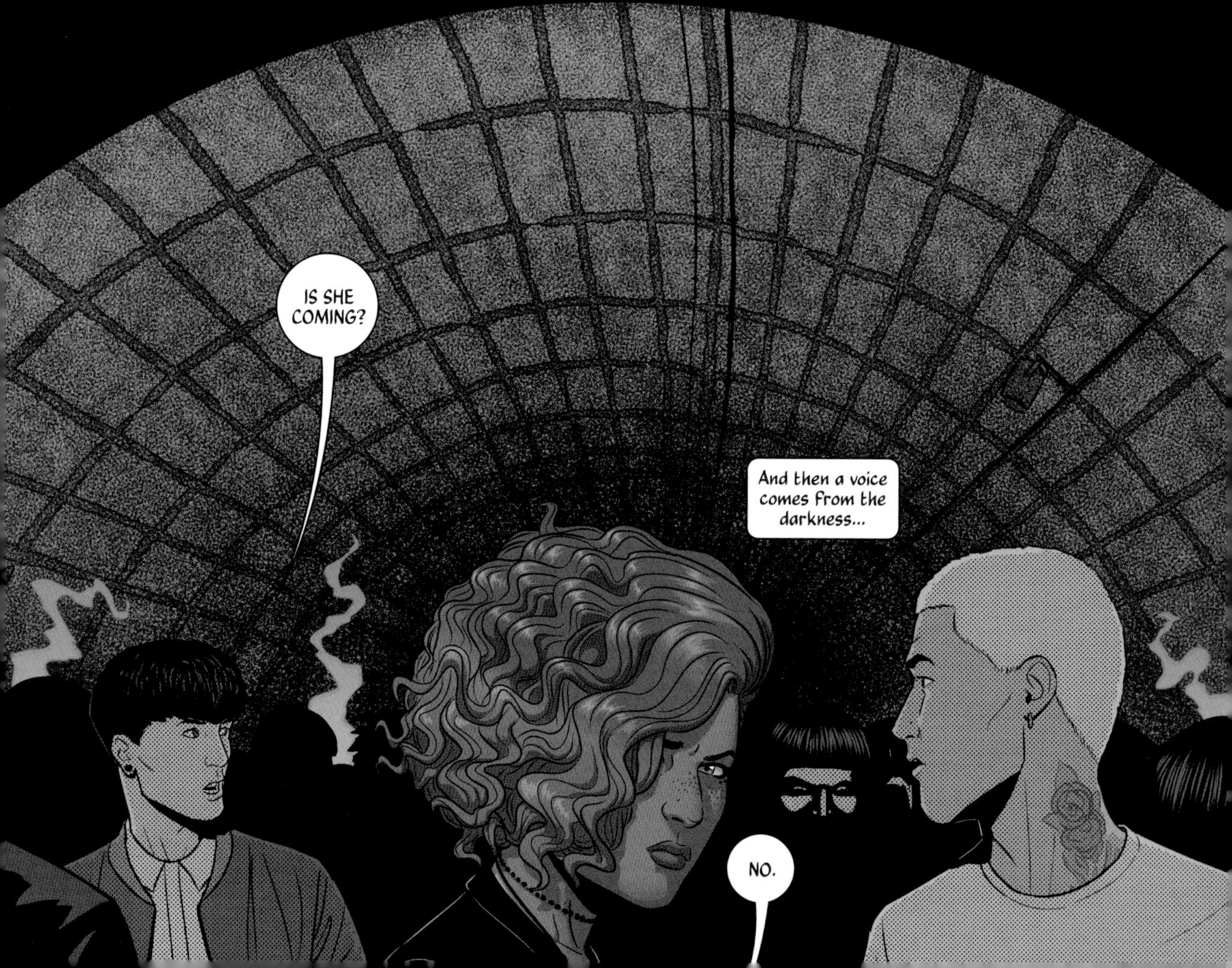
IS SHE COMING?
And then a voice comes from the darkness...
NO.

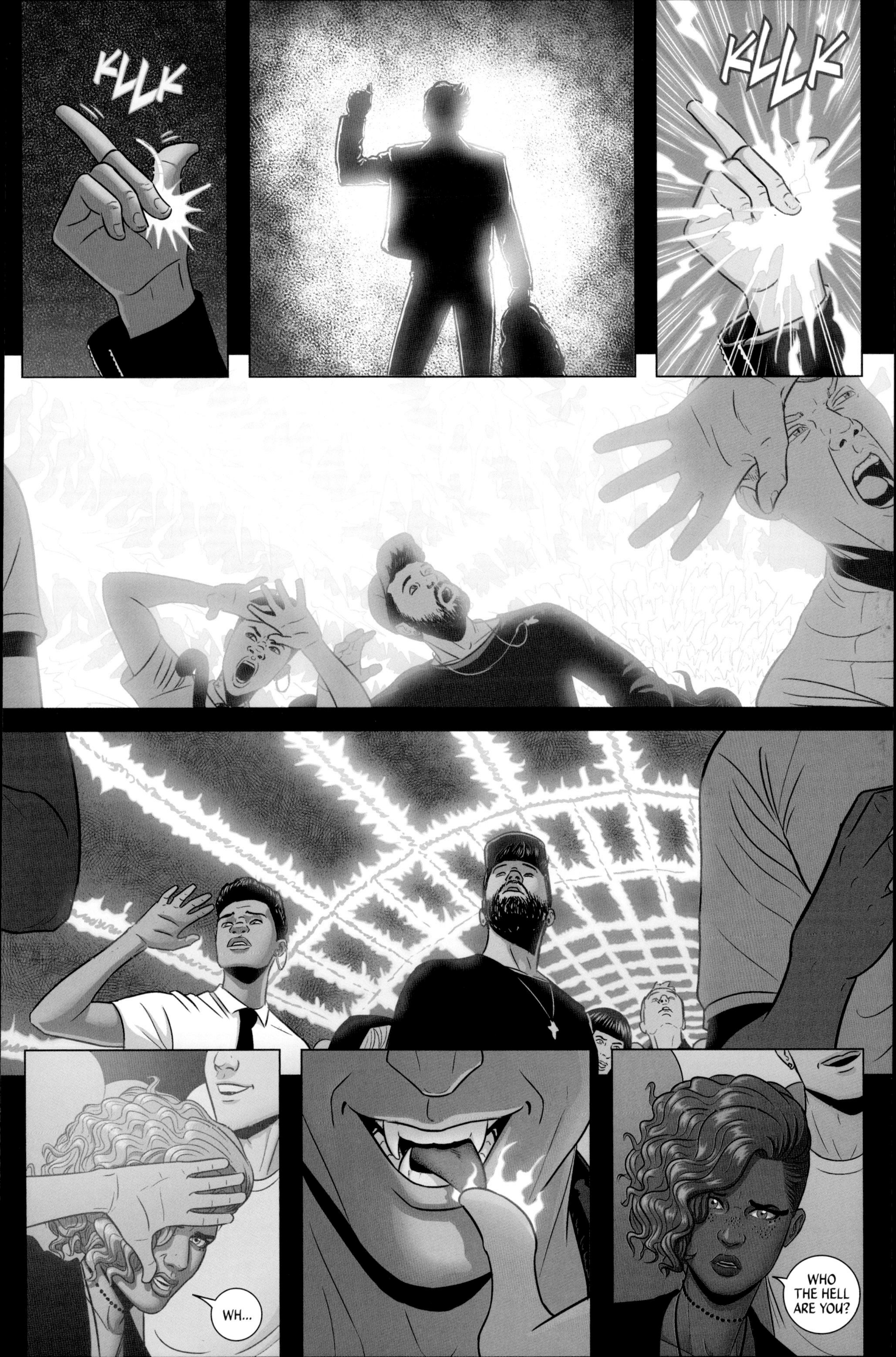
KLLK
KLLK
WH...
WHO THE HELL ARE YOU?

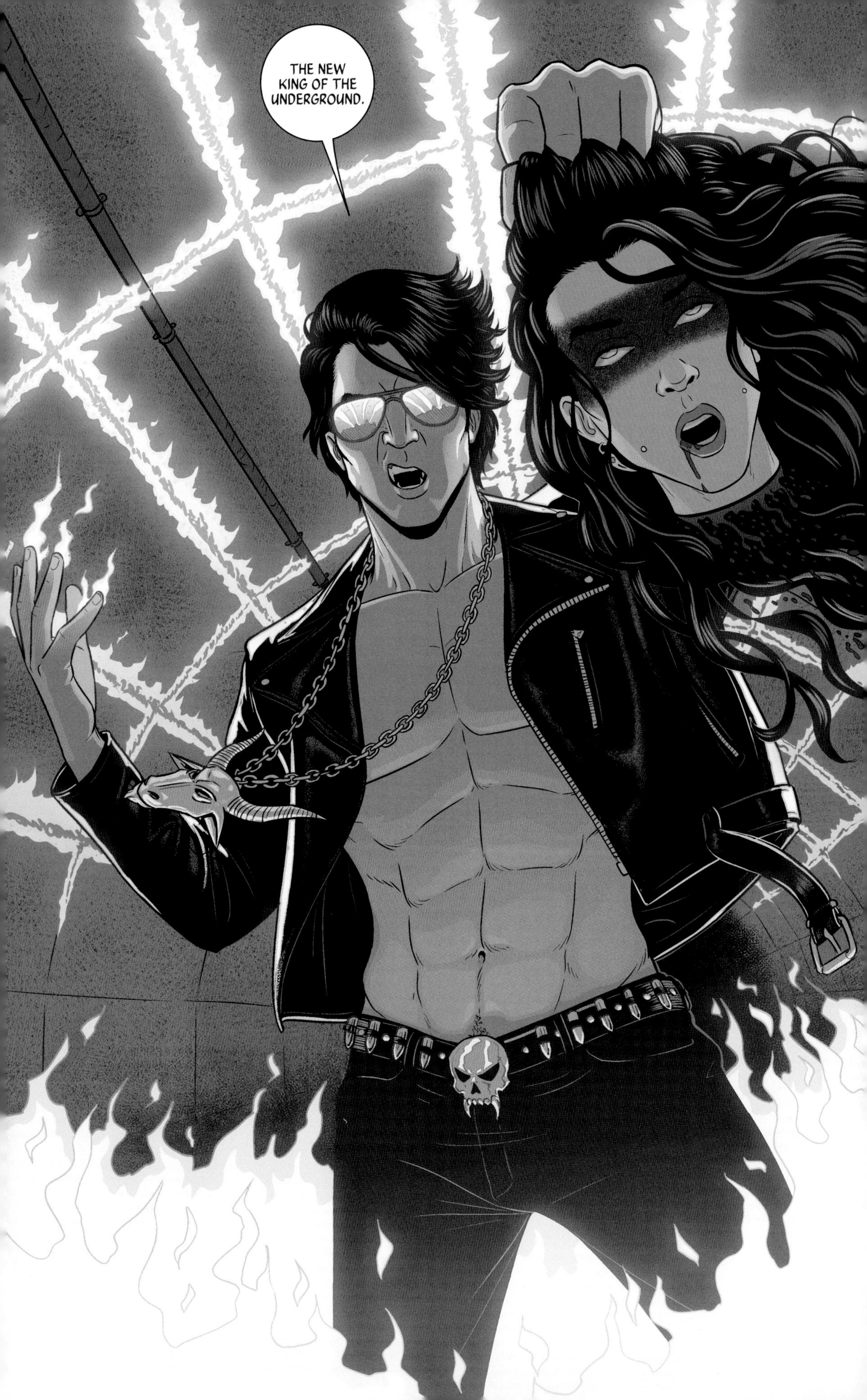
THE NEW KING OF THE UNDERGROUND.

"BAPHOMET"

10 JANUARY 2014

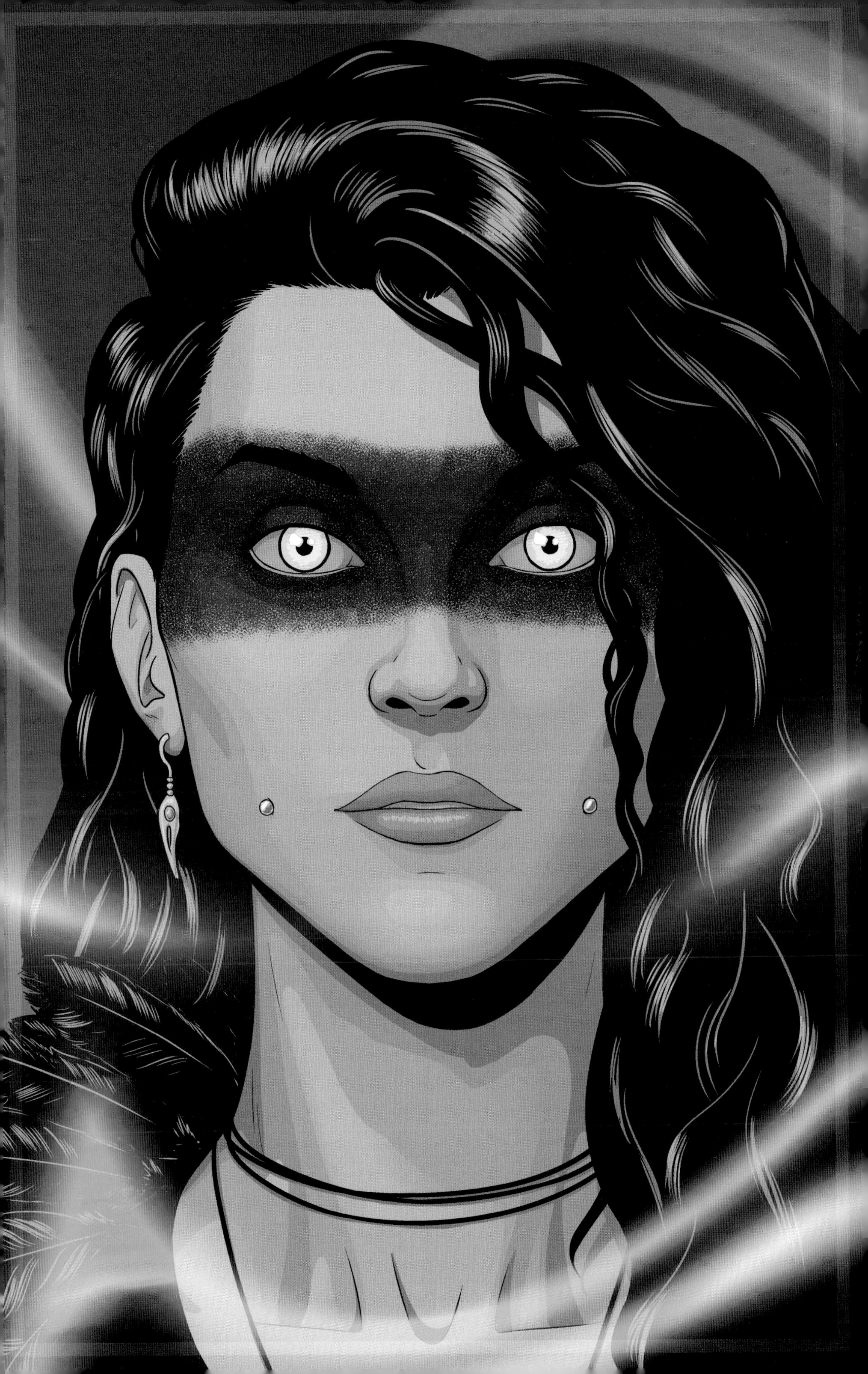

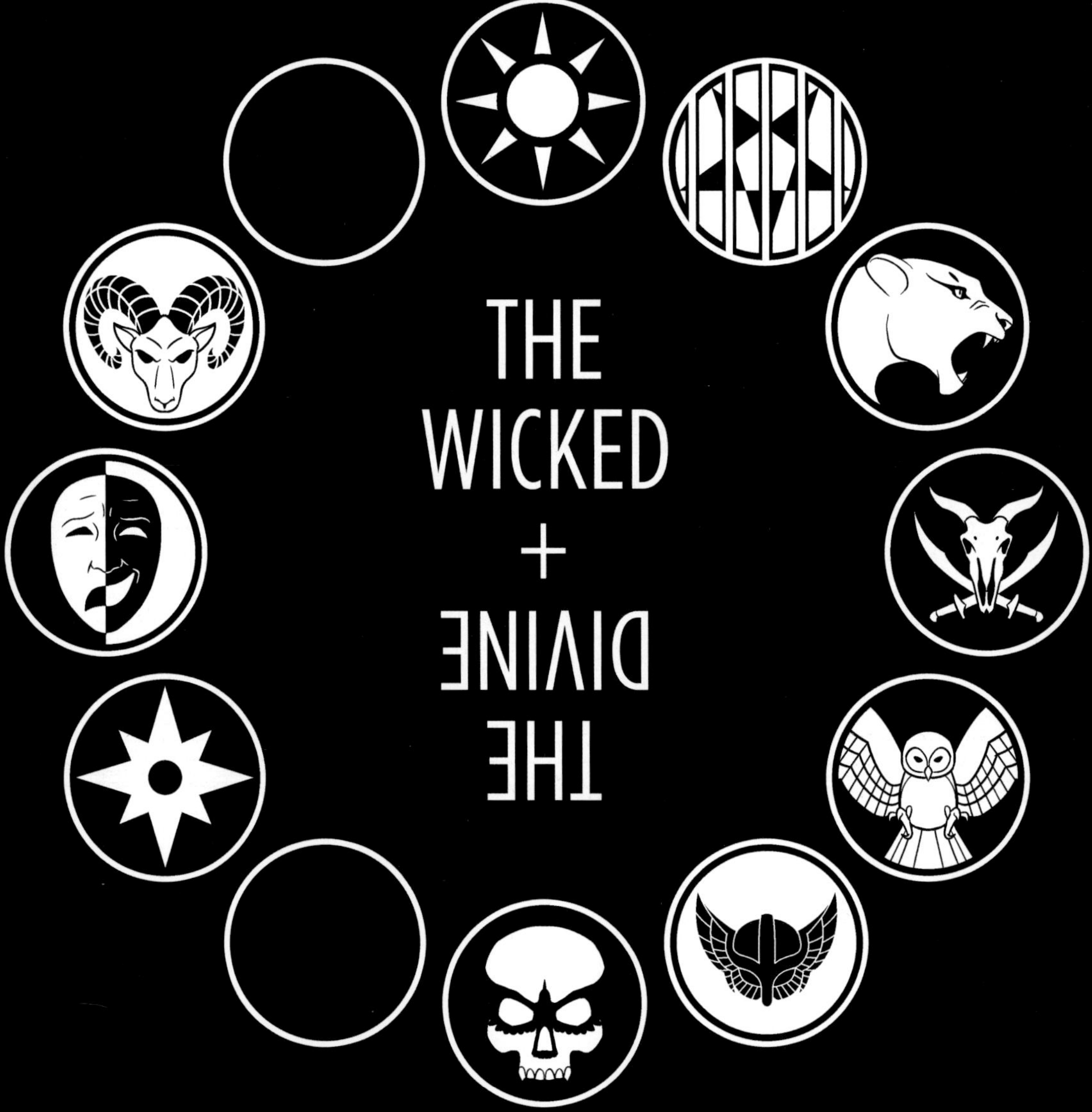
THE
WICKED
+
DIVINE
THE

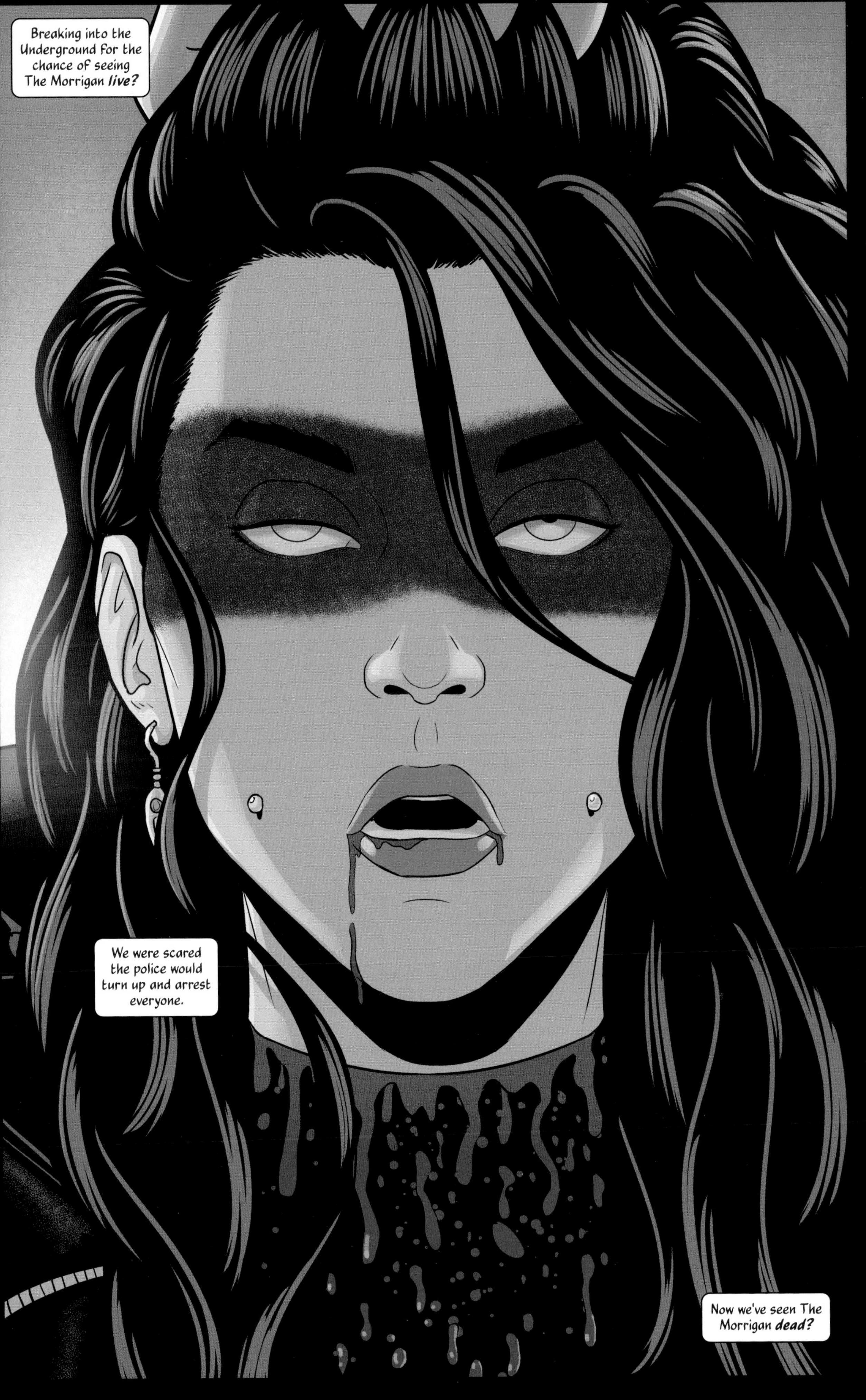

Breaking into the Underground for the chance of seeing The Morrigan *live?*
We were scared the police would turn up and arrest everyone.
Now we've seen The Morrigan ***dead?***

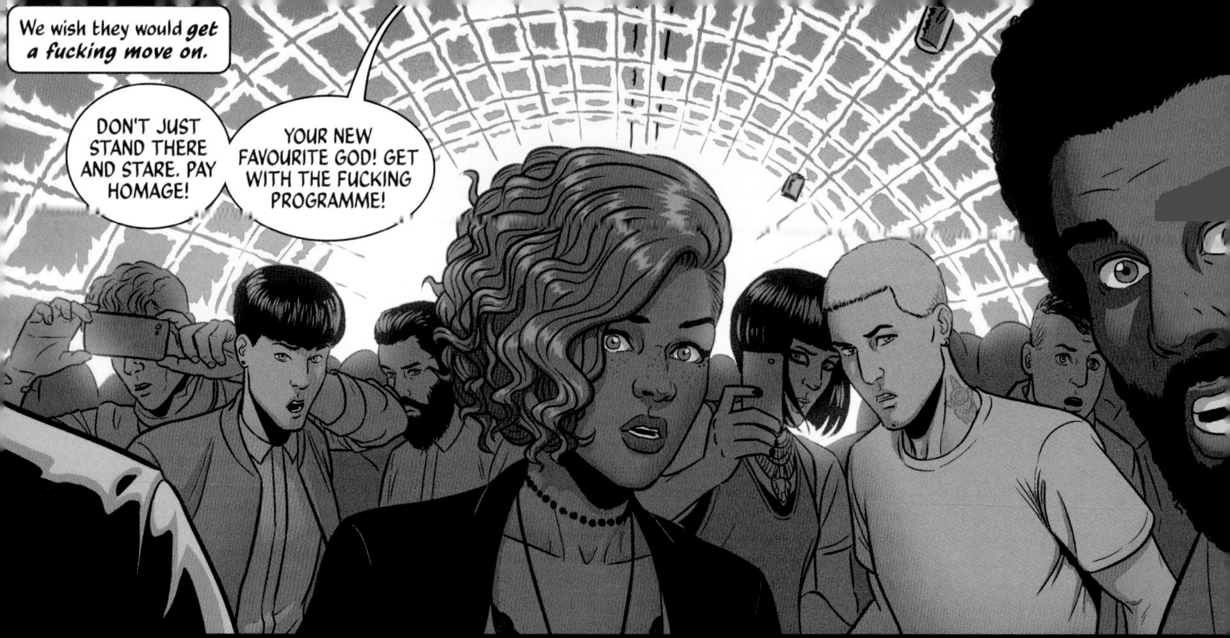
We wish they would *get a fucking move on.*
DON'T JUST STAND THERE AND STARE. PAY HOMAGE!
YOUR NEW FAVOURITE GOD! GET WITH THE FUCKING PROGRAMME!

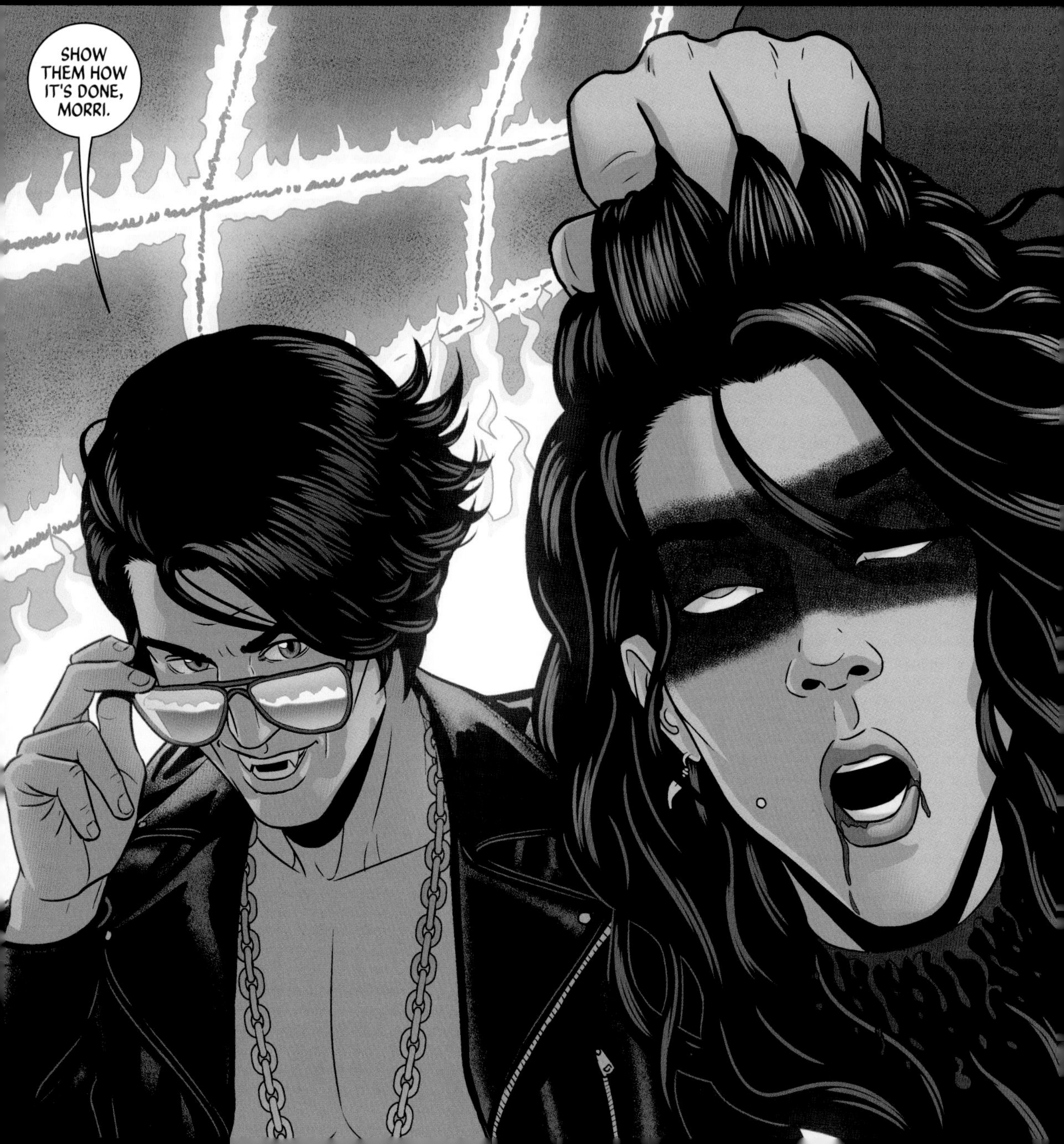
SHOW THEM HOW IT'S DONE, MORRI.

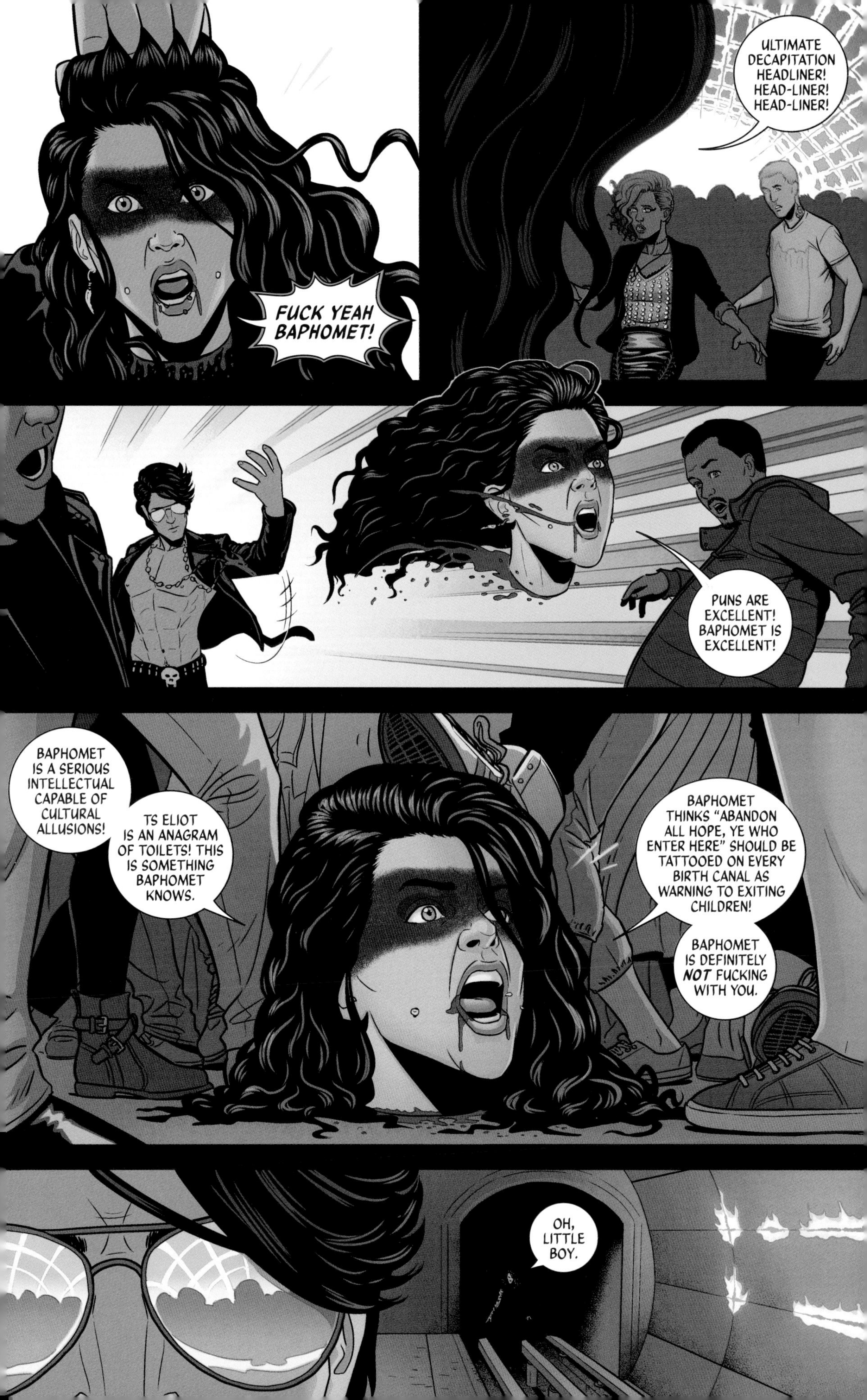
FUCK YEAH BAPHOMET!
ULTIMATE DECAPITATION HEADLINER! HEAD-LINER! HEAD-LINER!
PUNS ARE EXCELLENT! BAPHOMET IS EXCELLENT!
BAPHOMET IS A SERIOUS INTELLECTUAL CAPABLE OF CULTURAL ALLUSIONS!
TS ELIOT IS AN ANAGRAM OF TOILETS! THIS IS SOMETHING BAPHOMET KNOWS.
BAPHOMET THINKS "ABANDON ALL HOPE, YE WHO ENTER HERE" SHOULD BE TATTOOED ON EVERY BIRTH CANAL AS WARNING TO EXITING CHILDREN!
BAPHOMET IS DEFINITELY NOT FUCKING WITH YOU.
OH, LITTLE BOY.

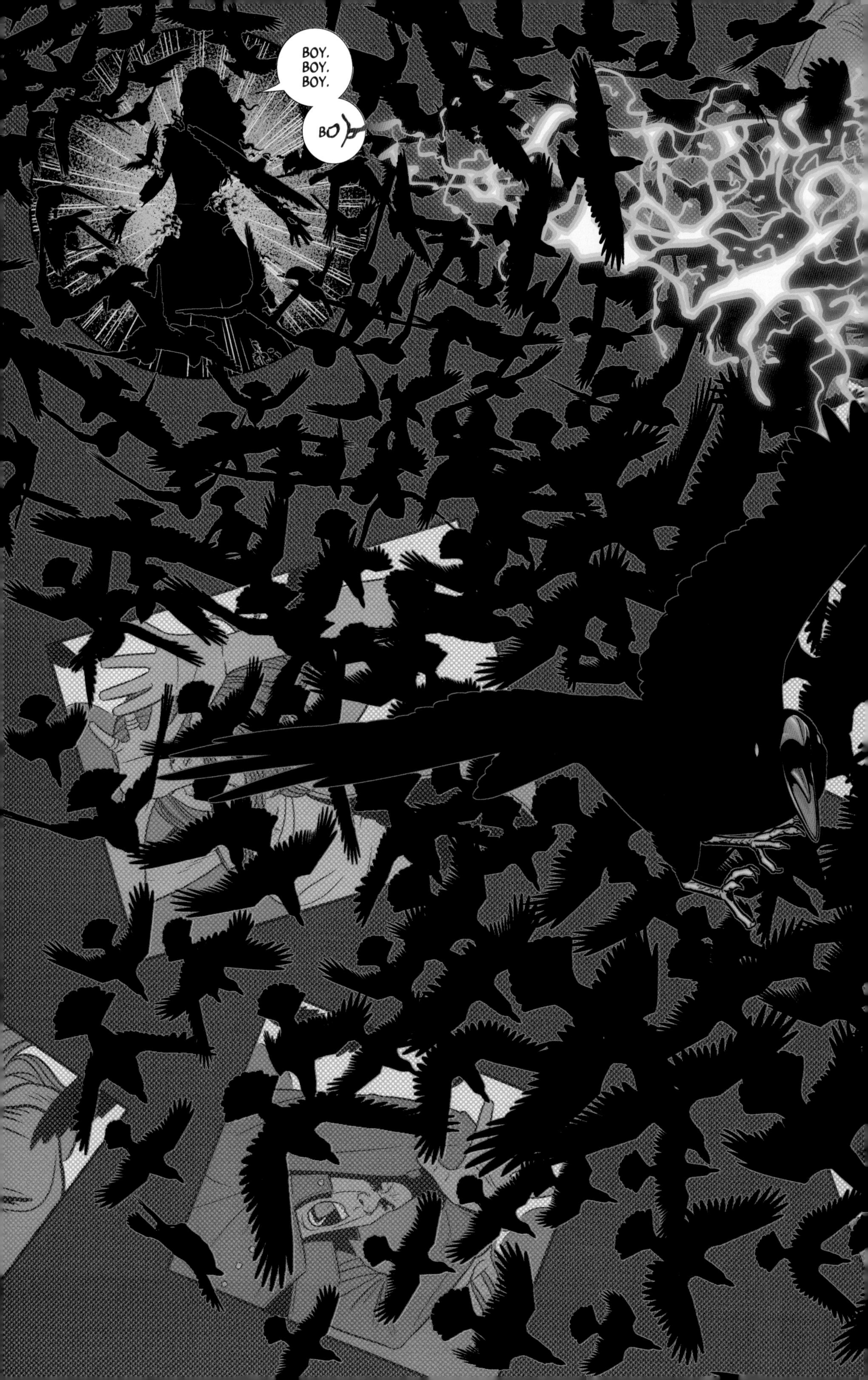
BOY.
BOY.
BOY.
BO

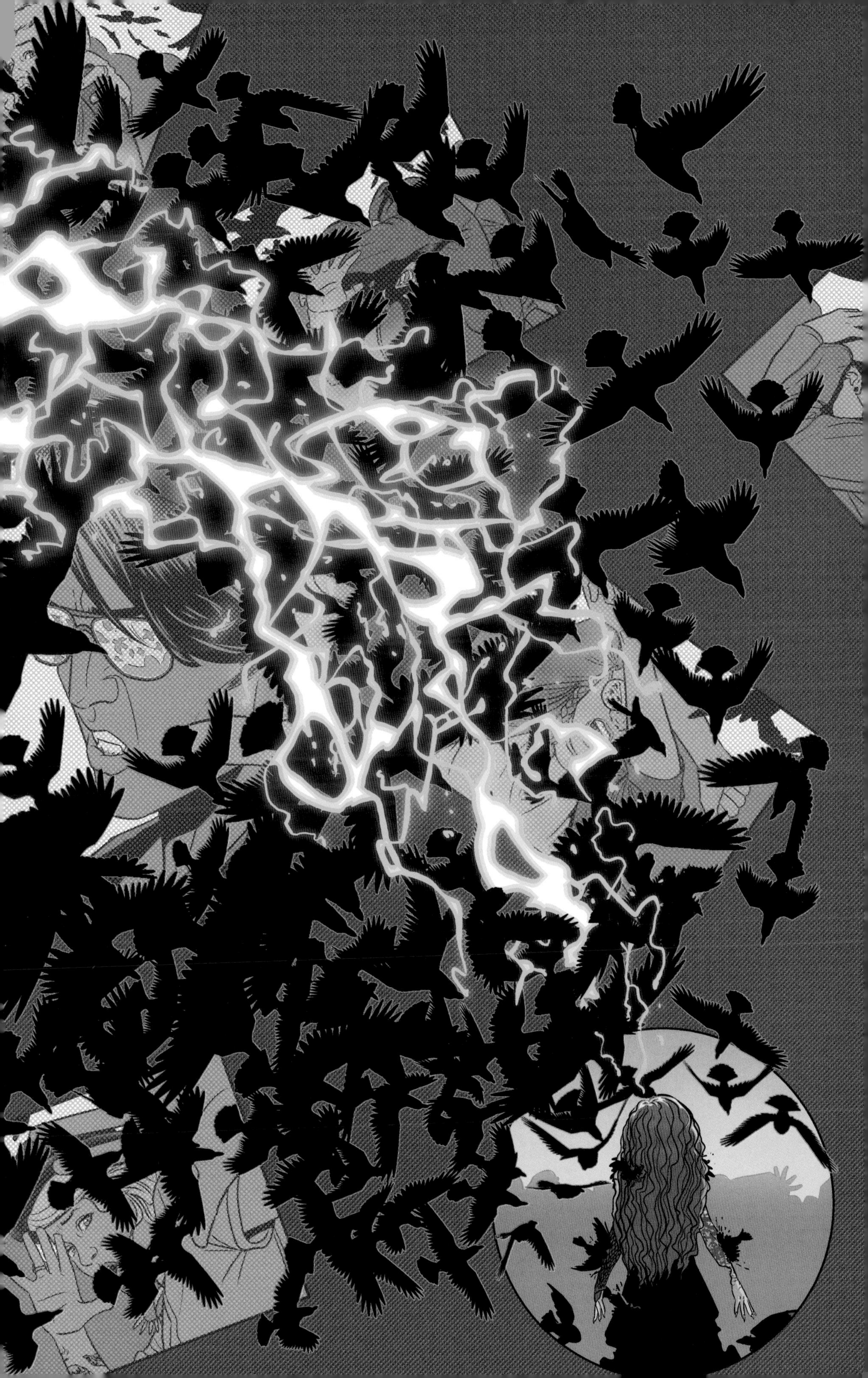

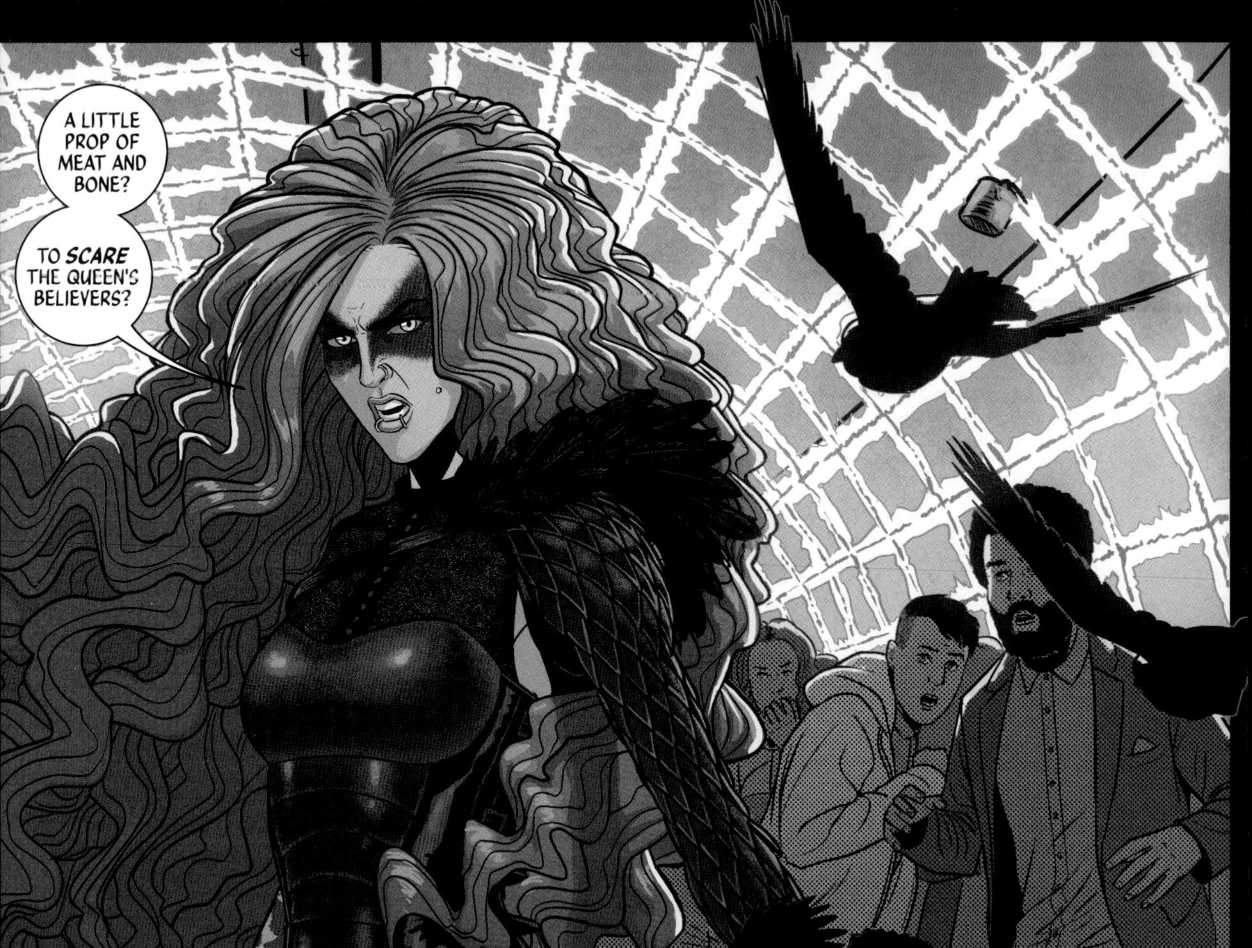
A LITTLE PROP OF MEAT AND BONE?
TO *SCARE* THE QUEEN'S BELIEVERS?
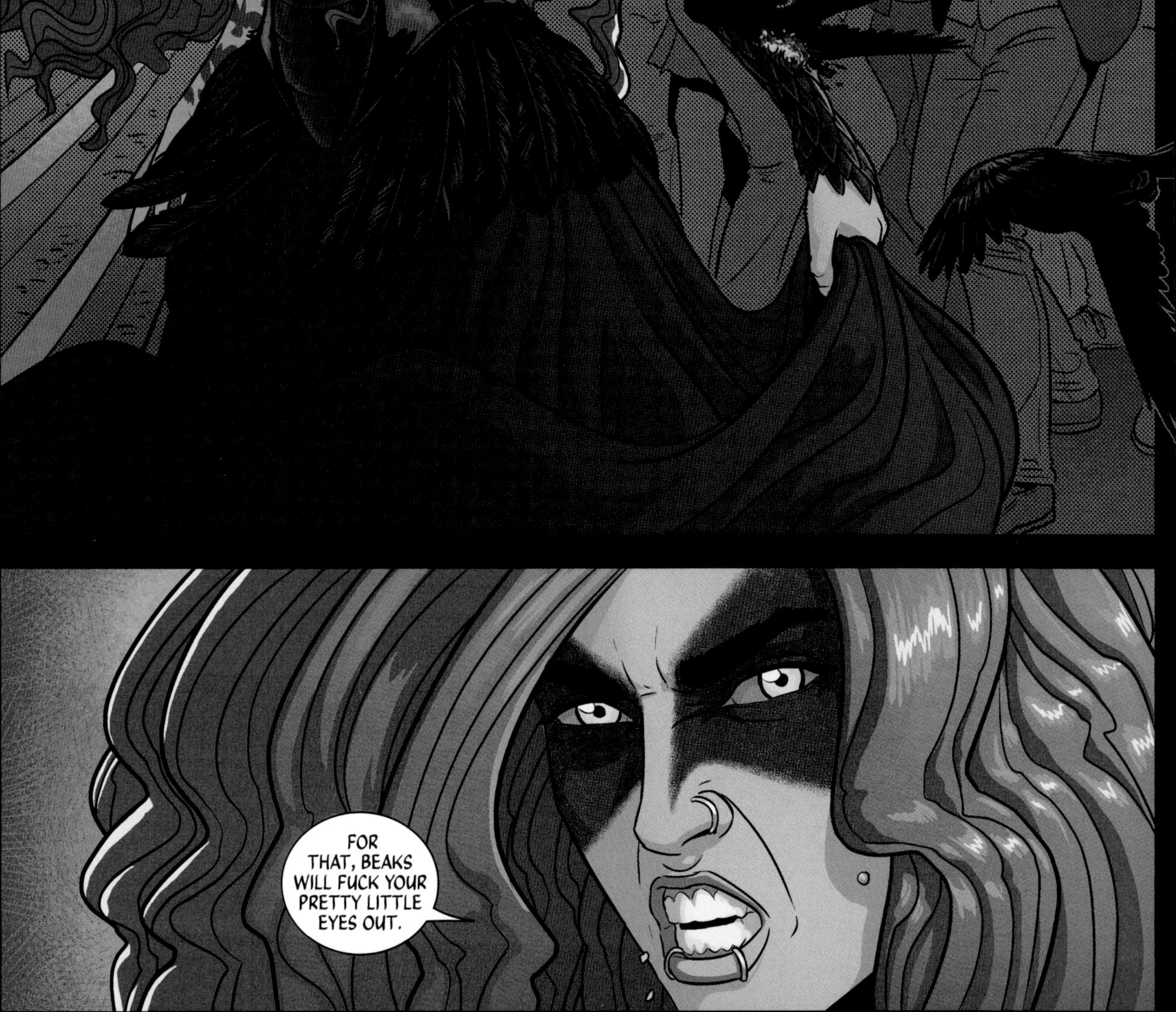
FOR THAT, BEAKS WILL FUCK YOUR PRETTY LITTLE EYES OUT.

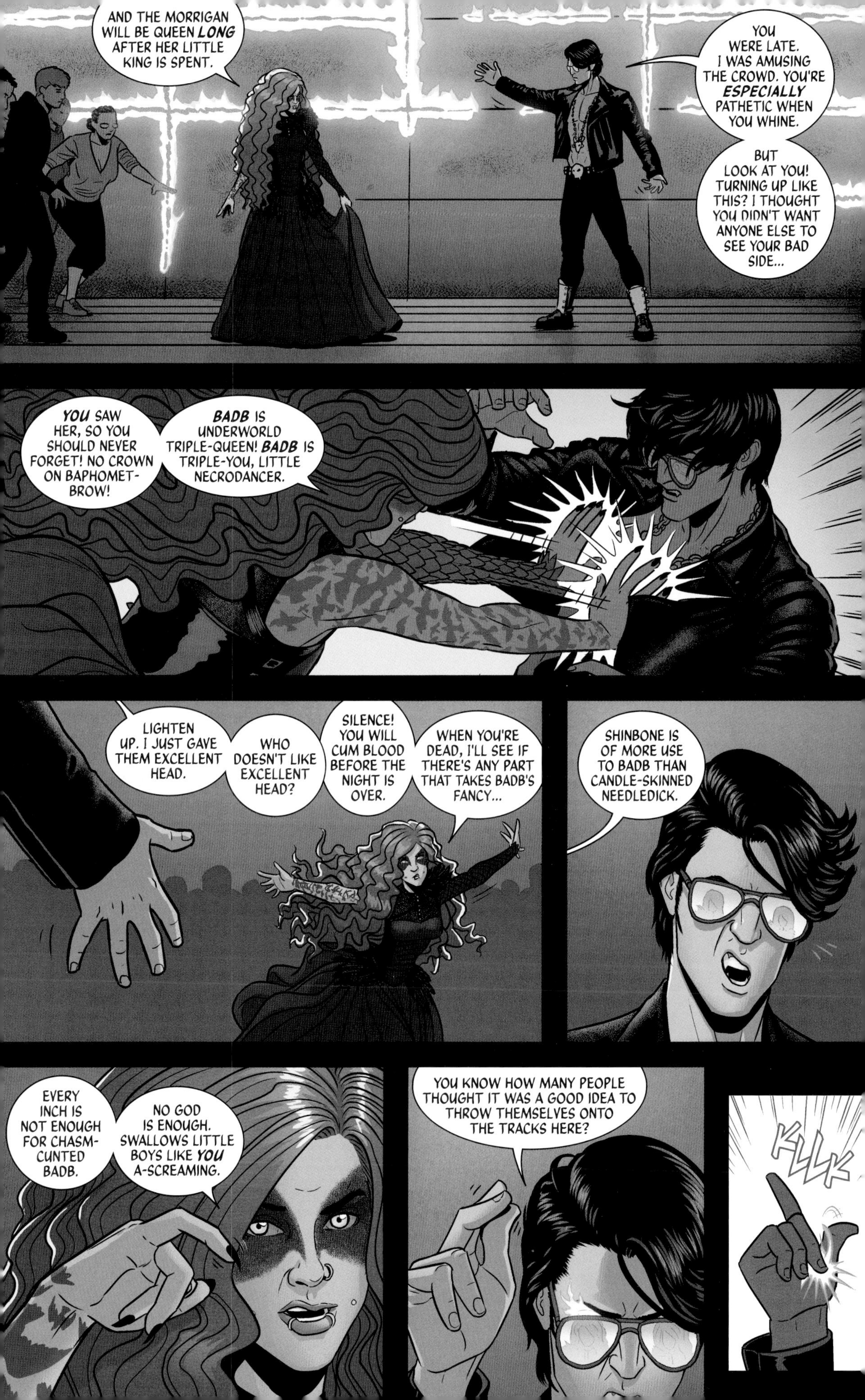
AND THE MORRIGAN WILL BE QUEEN **LONG** AFTER HER LITTLE KING IS SPENT.
YOU WERE LATE. I WAS AMUSING THE CROWD. YOU'RE **ESPECIALLY** PATHETIC WHEN YOU WHINE.
BUT LOOK AT YOU! TURNING UP LIKE THIS? I THOUGHT YOU DIDN'T WANT ANYONE ELSE TO SEE YOUR BAD SIDE...
YOU SAW HER, SO YOU SHOULD NEVER FORGET! NO CROWN ON BAPHOMET-BROW!
BADB IS UNDERWORLD TRIPLE-QUEEN! **BADB** IS TRIPLE-YOU, LITTLE NECRODANCER.
LIGHTEN UP. I JUST GAVE THEM EXCELLENT HEAD.
WHO DOESN'T LIKE EXCELLENT HEAD?
SILENCE! YOU WILL CUM BLOOD BEFORE THE NIGHT IS OVER.
WHEN YOU'RE DEAD, I'LL SEE IF THERE'S ANY PART THAT TAKES BADB'S FANCY...
SHINBONE IS OF MORE USE TO BADB THAN CANDLE-SKINNED NEEDLEDICK.
EVERY INCH IS NOT ENOUGH FOR CHASM-CUNTED BADB.
NO GOD IS ENOUGH. SWALLOWS LITTLE BOYS LIKE **YOU** A-SCREAMING.
YOU KNOW HOW MANY PEOPLE THOUGHT IT WAS A GOOD IDEA TO THROW THEMSELVES ONTO THE TRACKS HERE?
KLLK

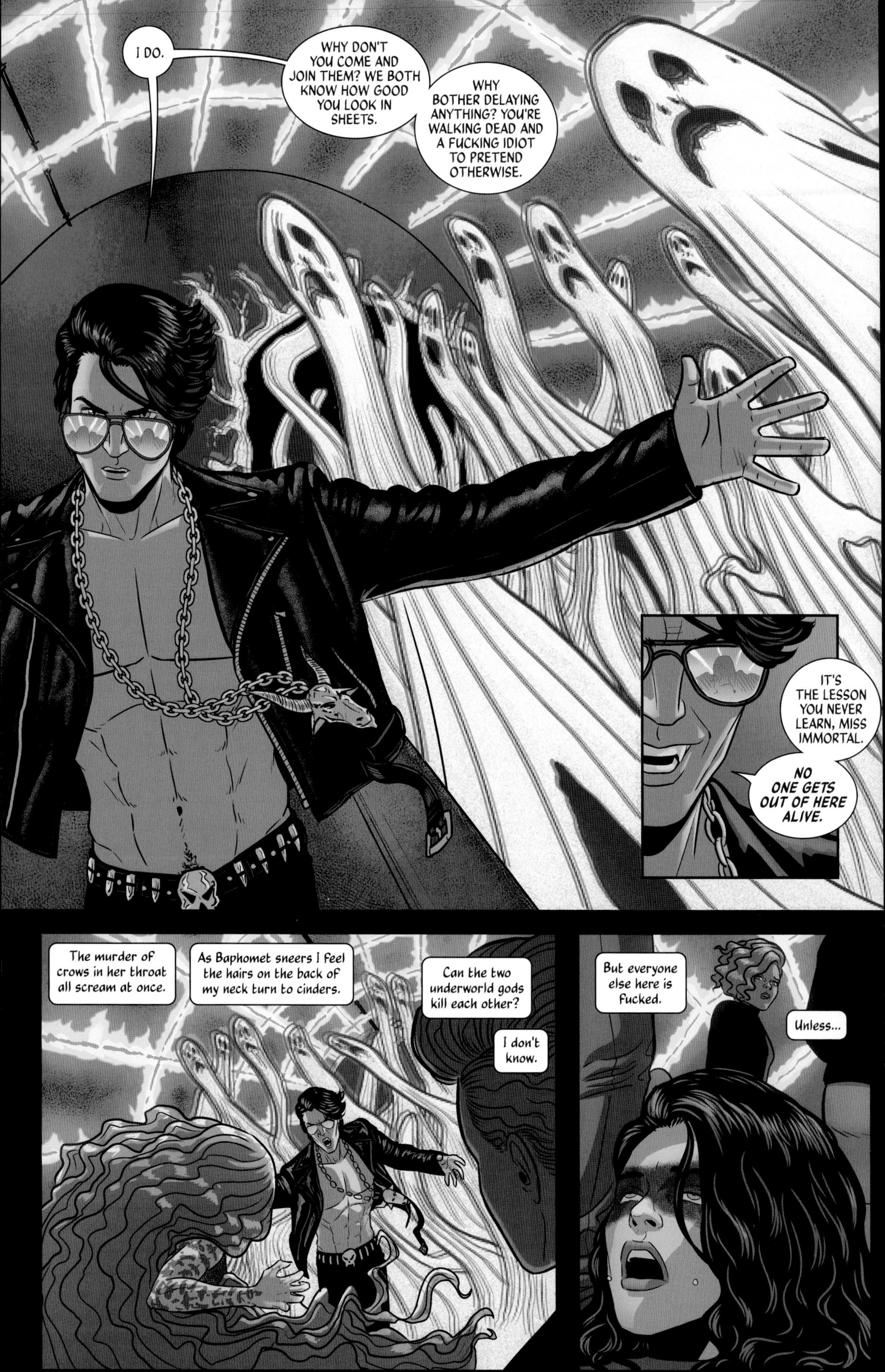
I DO.
WHY DON'T YOU COME AND JOIN THEM? WE BOTH KNOW HOW GOOD YOU LOOK IN SHEETS.
WHY BOTHER DELAYING ANYTHING? YOU'RE WALKING DEAD AND A FUCKING IDIOT TO PRETEND OTHERWISE.
IT'S THE LESSON YOU NEVER LEARN, MISS IMMORTAL.
NO ONE GETS OUT OF HERE ALIVE.
The murder of crows in her throat all scream at once.
As Baphomet sneers I feel the hairs on the back of my neck turn to cinders.
Can the two underworld gods kill each other?
I don't know.
But everyone else here is fucked.
Unless...

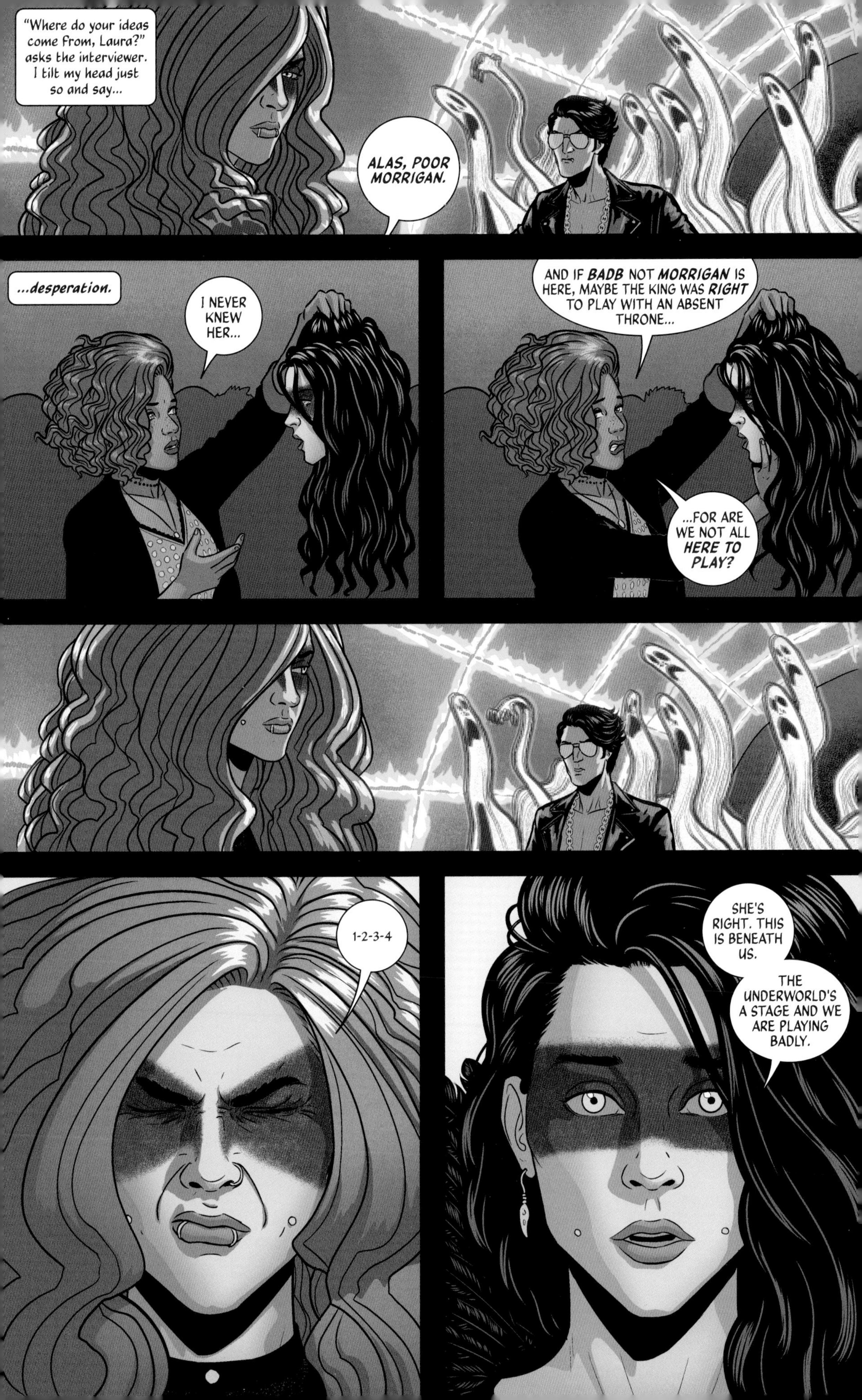
"Where do your ideas come from, Laura?" asks the interviewer. I tilt my head just so and say...
ALAS, POOR MORRIGAN.
...desperation.
I NEVER KNEW HER...
AND IF BADB NOT MORRIGAN IS HERE, MAYBE THE KING WAS RIGHT TO PLAY WITH AN ABSENT THRONE...
...FOR ARE WE NOT ALL HERE TO PLAY?
1-2-3-4
SHE'S RIGHT. THIS IS BENEATH US.
THE UNDERWORLD'S A STAGE AND WE ARE PLAYING BADLY.

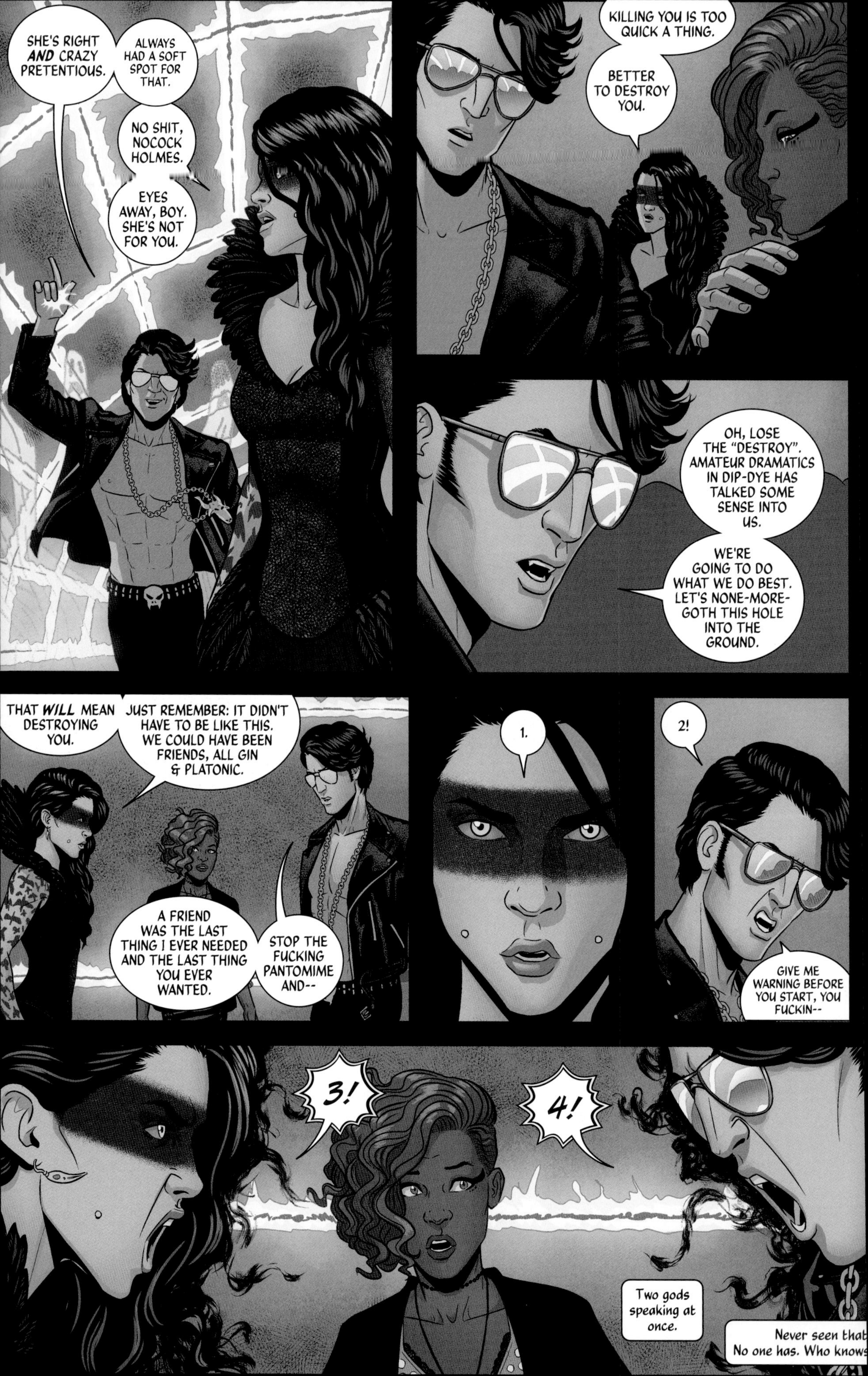
SHE'S RIGHT **AND** CRAZY PRETENTIOUS.
ALWAYS HAD A SOFT SPOT FOR THAT.
NO SHIT, NOCOCK HOLMES.
EYES AWAY, BOY. SHE'S NOT FOR YOU.
KILLING YOU IS TOO QUICK A THING.
BETTER TO DESTROY YOU.
OH, LOSE THE "DESTROY". AMATEUR DRAMATICS IN DIP-DYE HAS TALKED SOME SENSE INTO US.
WE'RE GOING TO DO WHAT WE DO BEST. LET'S NONE-MORE-GOTH THIS HOLE INTO THE GROUND.
THAT **WILL** MEAN DESTROYING YOU.
JUST REMEMBER: IT DIDN'T HAVE TO BE LIKE THIS. WE COULD HAVE BEEN FRIENDS, ALL GIN & PLATONIC.
A FRIEND WAS THE LAST THING I EVER NEEDED AND THE LAST THING YOU EVER WANTED.
STOP THE FUCKING PANTOMIME AND--
1.
2!
GIVE ME WARNING BEFORE YOU START, YOU FUCKIN--
3!
4!
Two gods speaking at once.
Never seen that
No one has. Who knows

This

is going to

(fuck)

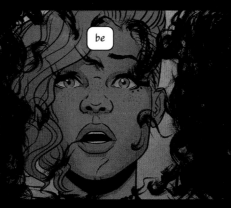

be

We're all going
to die.

We're all going
to die.

We're all going
to die.

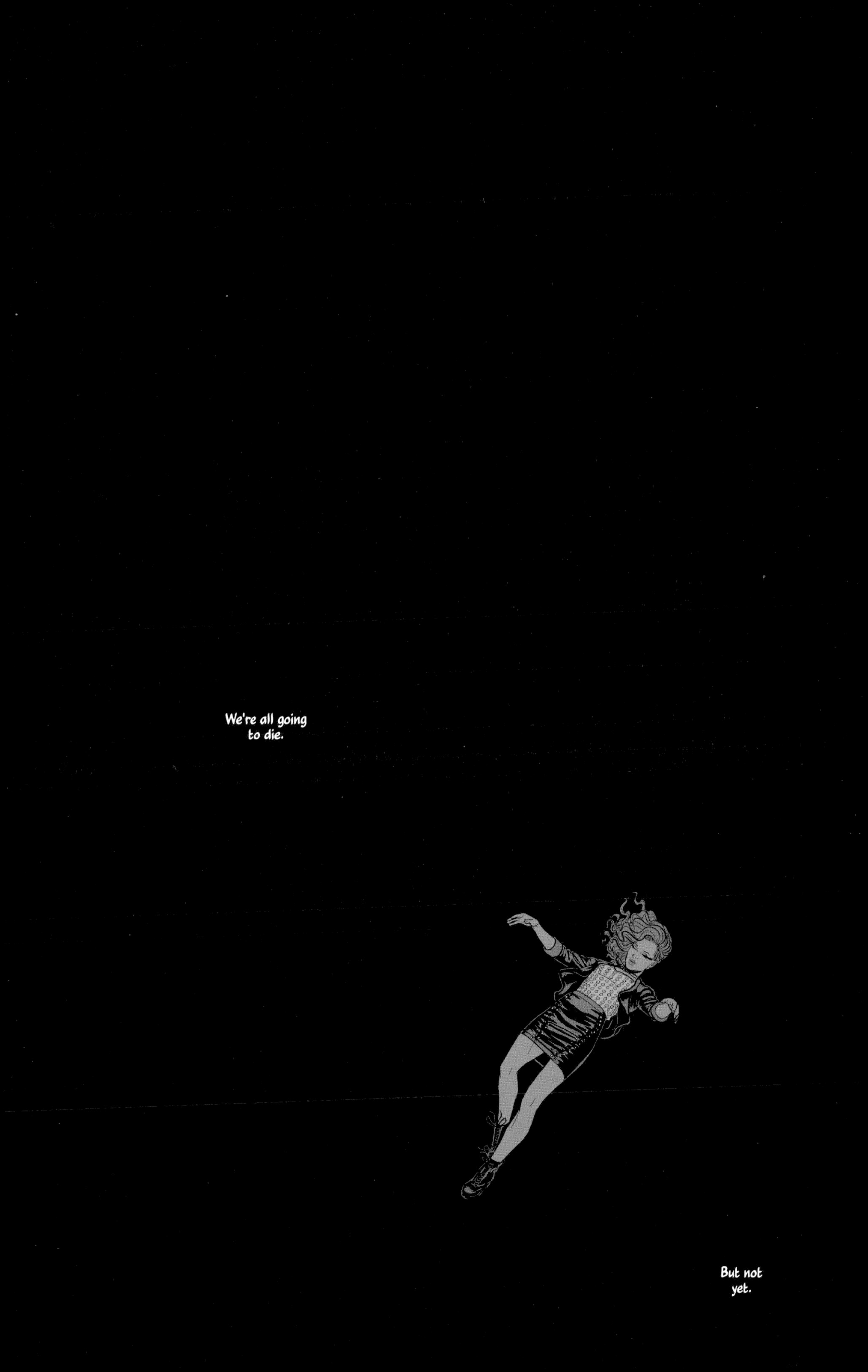
We're all going to die.
But not yet.

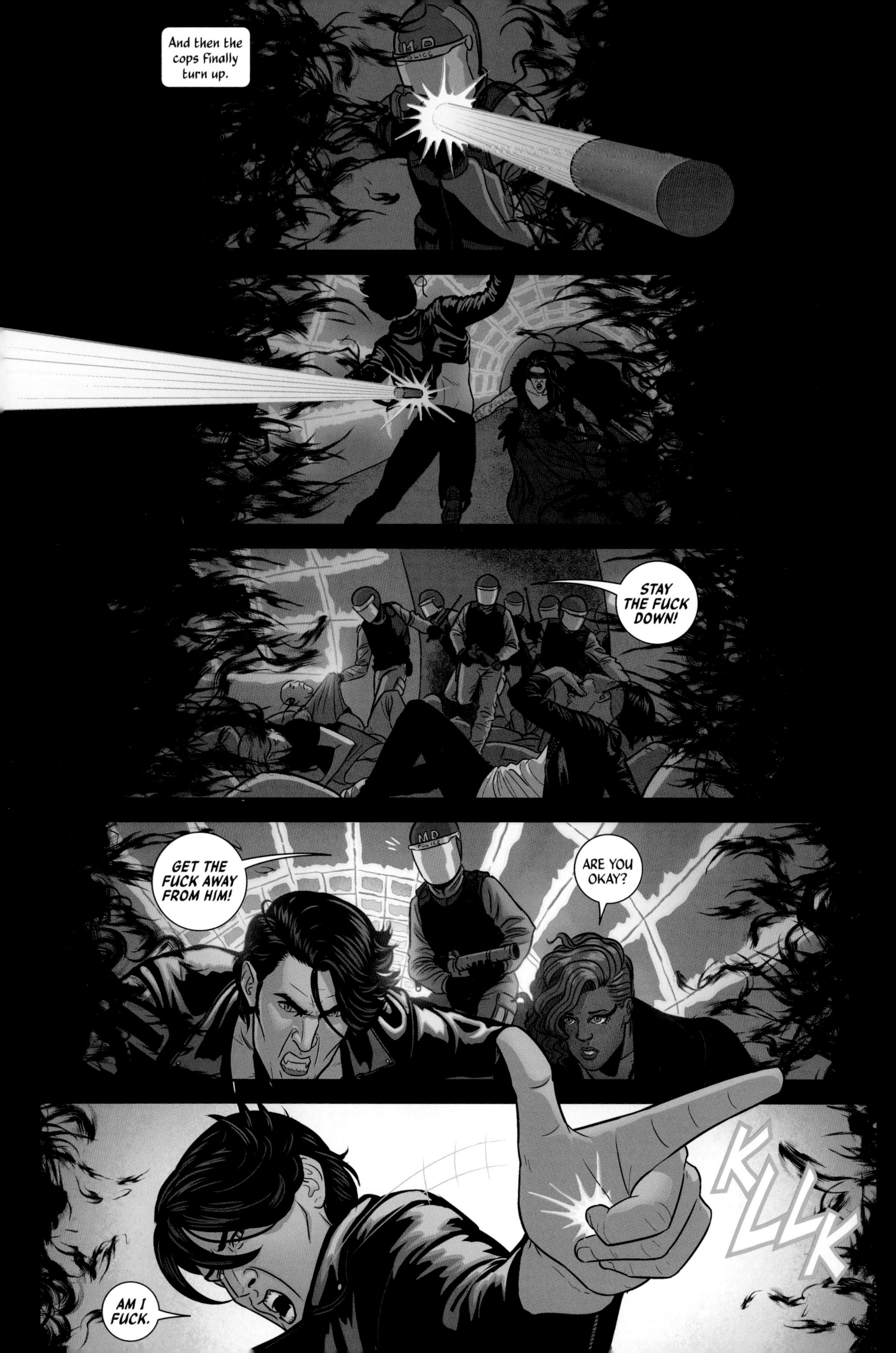
And then the cops finally turn up.
STAY THE FUCK DOWN!
GET THE FUCK AWAY FROM HIM!
ARE YOU OKAY?
AM I FUCK.
KLLK

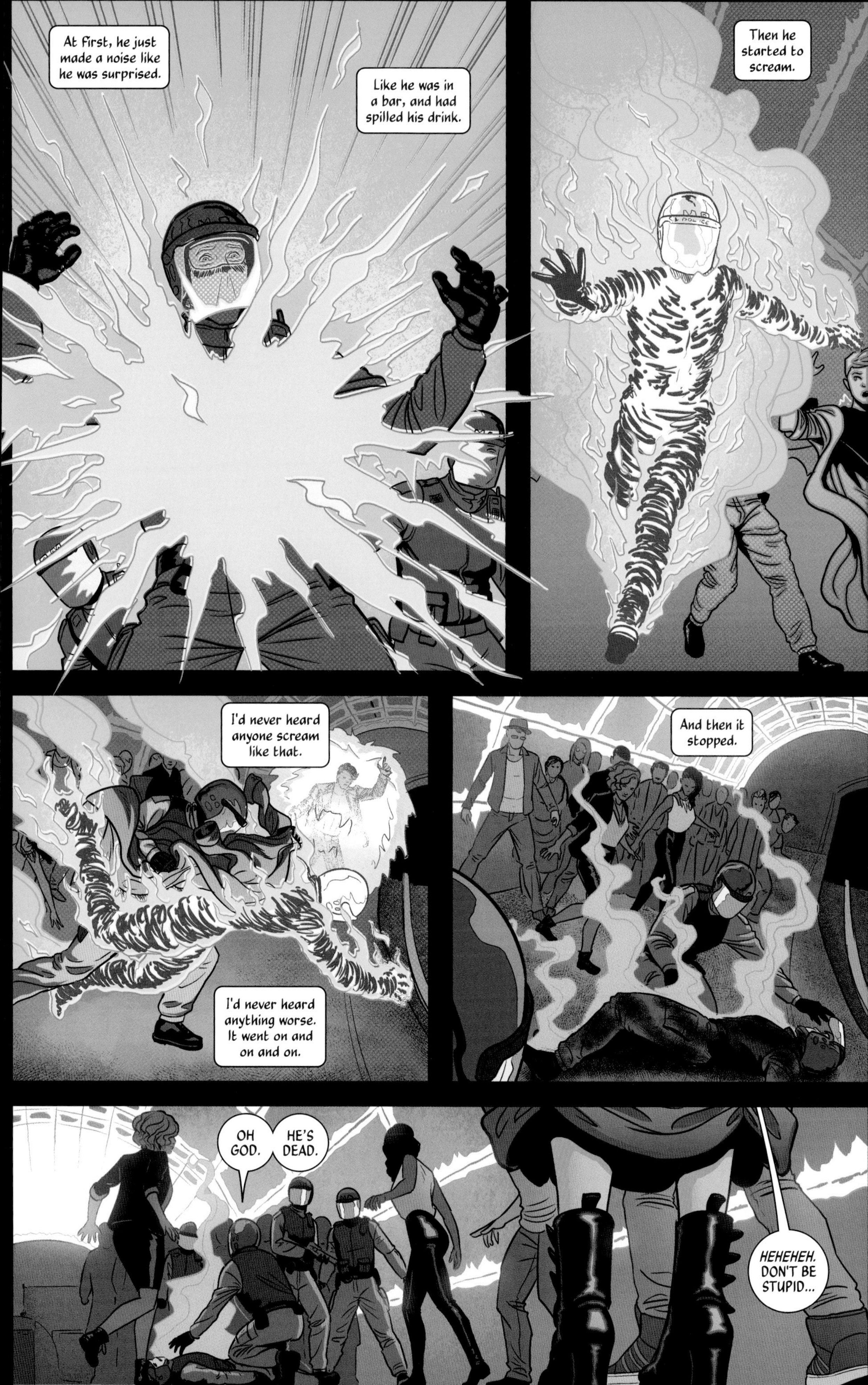
At first, he just made a noise like he was surprised.
Like he was in a bar, and had spilled his drink.
Then he started to scream.
I'd never heard anyone scream like that.
I'd never heard anything worse. It went on and on and on.
And then it stopped.
OH GOD.
HE'S DEAD.
HEHEHEH. DON'T BE STUPID...

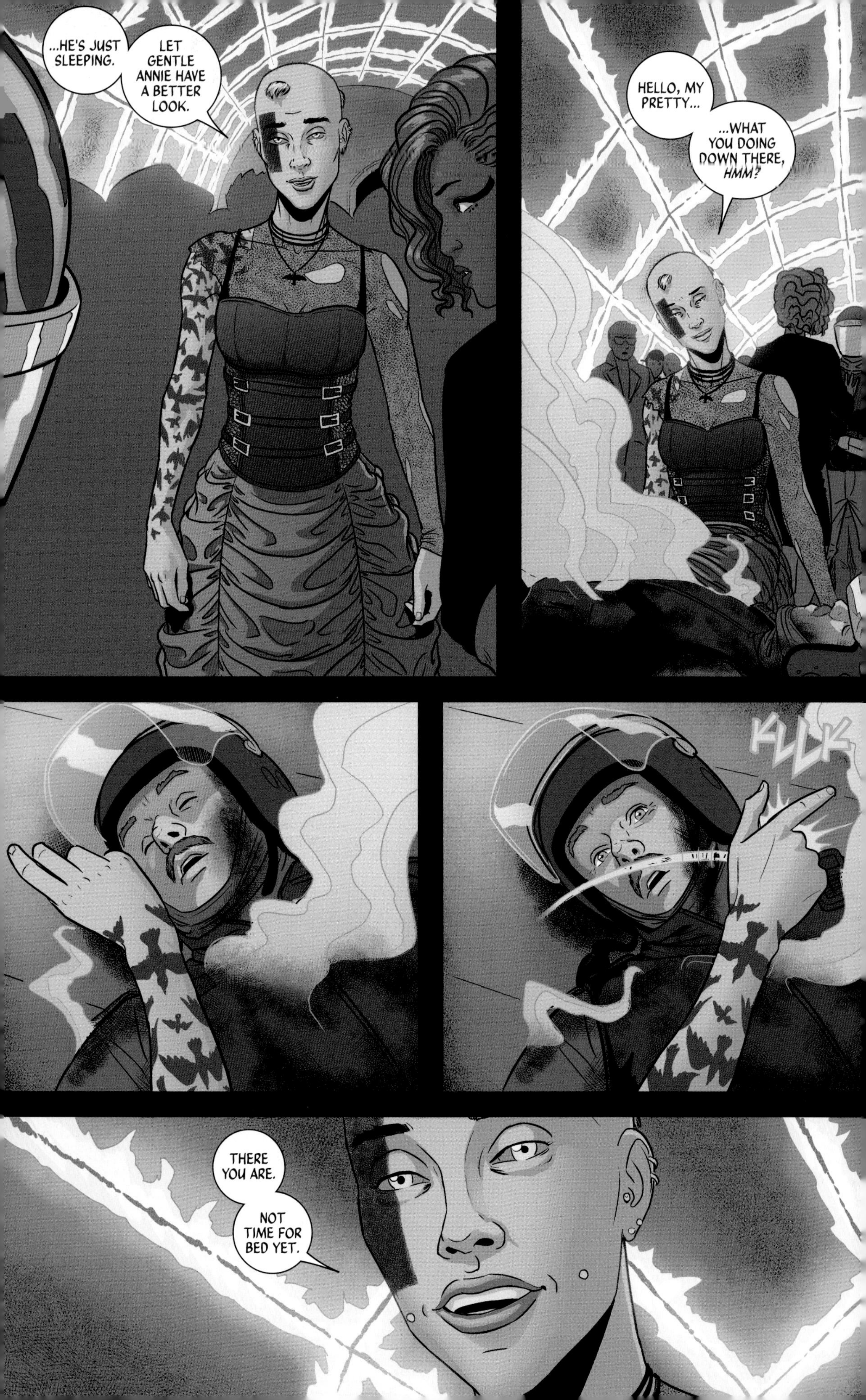
...HE'S JUST SLEEPING.
LET GENTLE ANNIE HAVE A BETTER LOOK.
HELLO, MY PRETTY...
...WHAT YOU DOING DOWN THERE, *HMM?*
KLLK
THERE YOU ARE.
NOT TIME FOR BED YET.

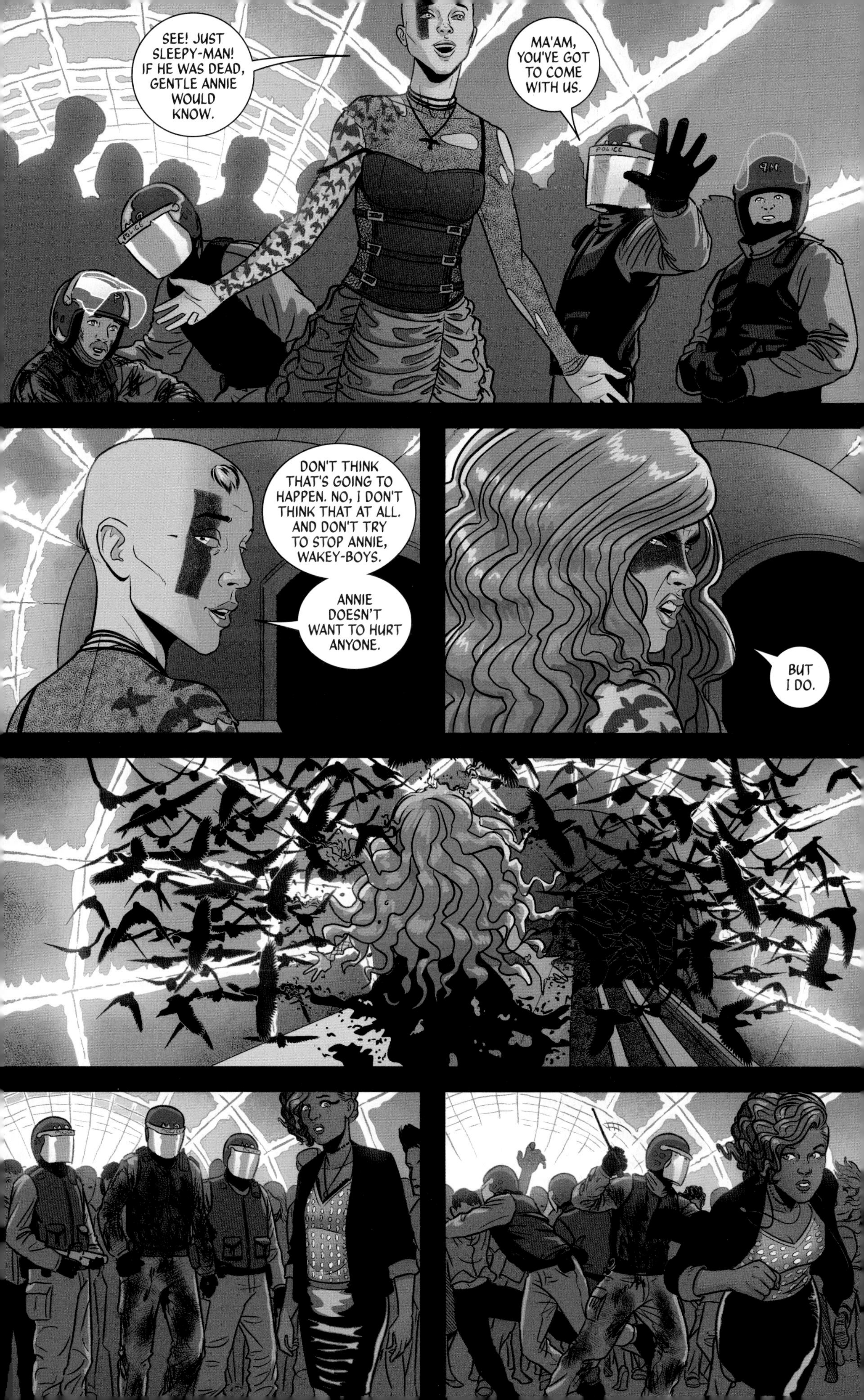
SEE! JUST SLEEPY-MAN! IF HE WAS DEAD, GENTLE ANNIE WOULD KNOW.
MA'AM, YOU'VE GOT TO COME WITH US.
DON'T THINK THAT'S GOING TO HAPPEN. NO, I DON'T THINK THAT AT ALL. AND DON'T TRY TO STOP ANNIE, WAKEY-BOYS.
ANNIE DOESN'T WANT TO HURT ANYONE.
BUT I DO.

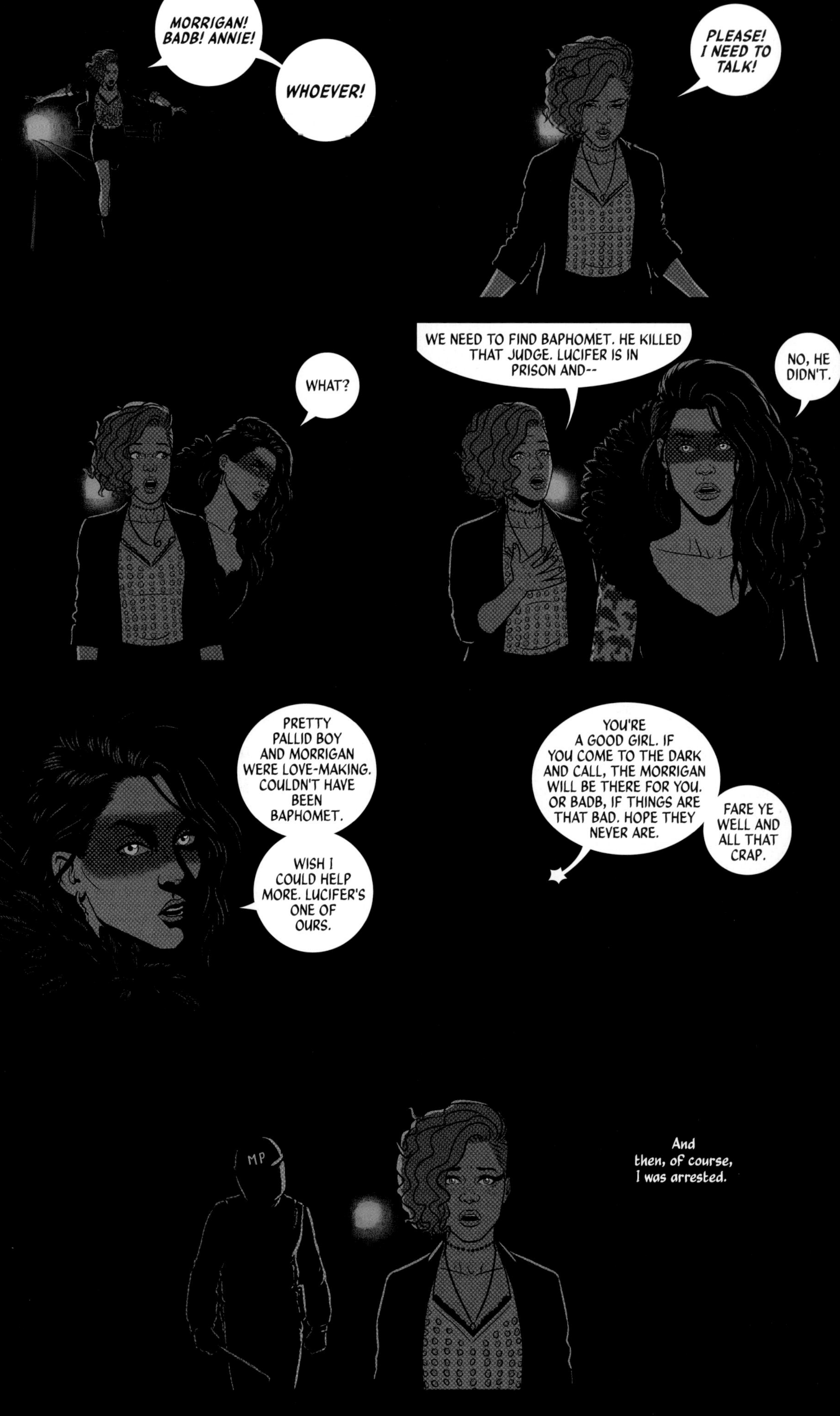
MORRIGAN! BADB! ANNIE!
WHOEVER!
PLEASE! I NEED TO TALK!
WHAT?
WE NEED TO FIND BAPHOMET. HE KILLED THAT JUDGE. LUCIFER IS IN PRISON AND--
NO, HE DIDN'T.
PRETTY PALLID BOY AND MORRIGAN WERE LOVE-MAKING. COULDN'T HAVE BEEN BAPHOMET.
WISH I COULD HELP MORE. LUCIFER'S ONE OF OURS.
YOU'RE A GOOD GIRL. IF YOU COME TO THE DARK AND CALL, THE MORRIGAN WILL BE THERE FOR YOU. OR BADB, IF THINGS ARE THAT BAD. HOPE THEY NEVER ARE.
FARE YE WELL AND ALL THAT CRAP.
MP
And then, of course, I was arrested.

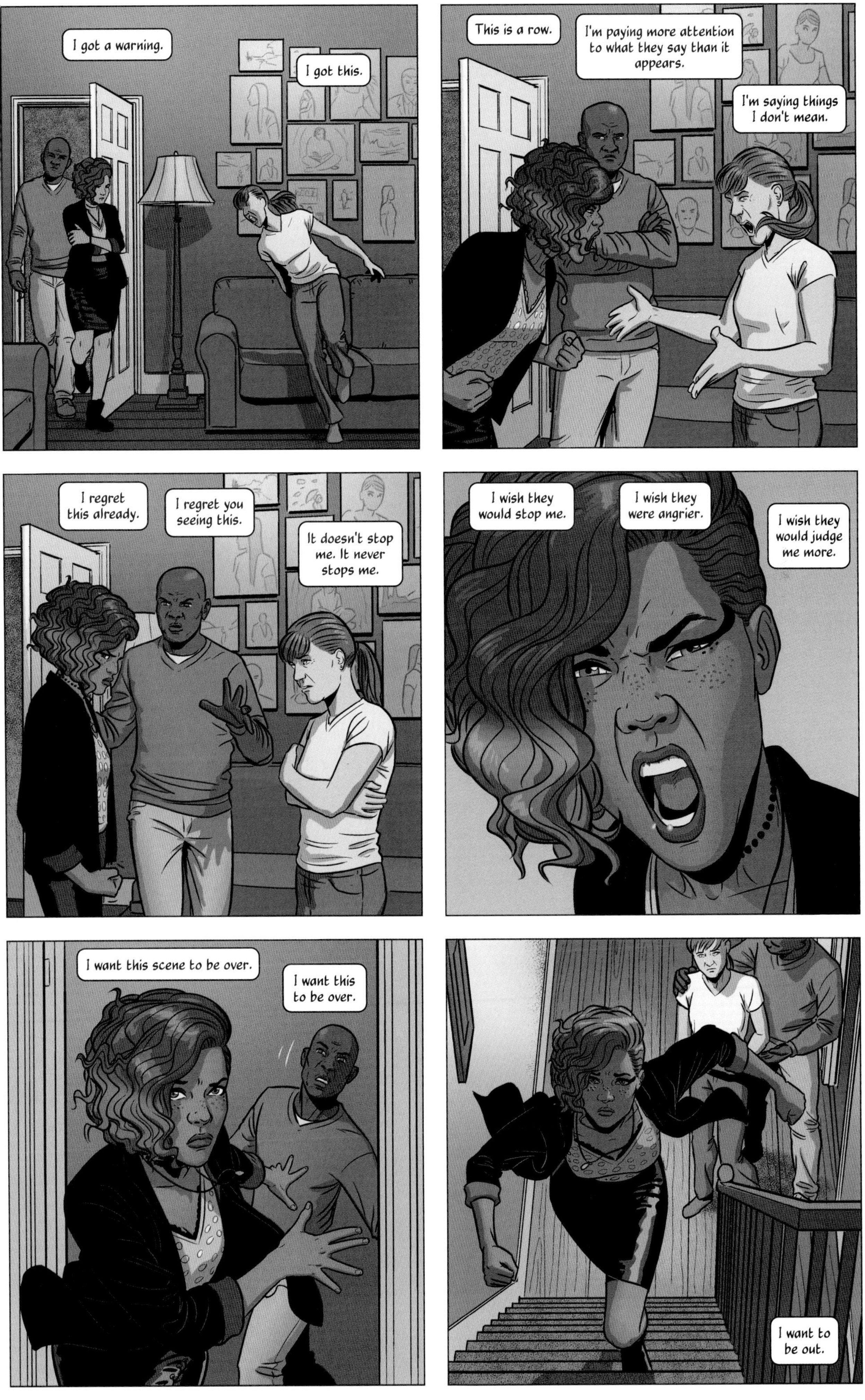
I got a warning.
I got this.
This is a row.
I'm paying more attention to what they say than it appears.
I'm saying things I don't mean.
I regret this already.
I regret you seeing this.
It doesn't stop me. It never stops me.
I wish they would stop me.
I wish they were angrier.
I wish they would judge me more.
I want this scene to be over.
I want this to be over.
I want to be out.

CHTHONIC
HOMESICK BLUES

10 JANUARY 2014

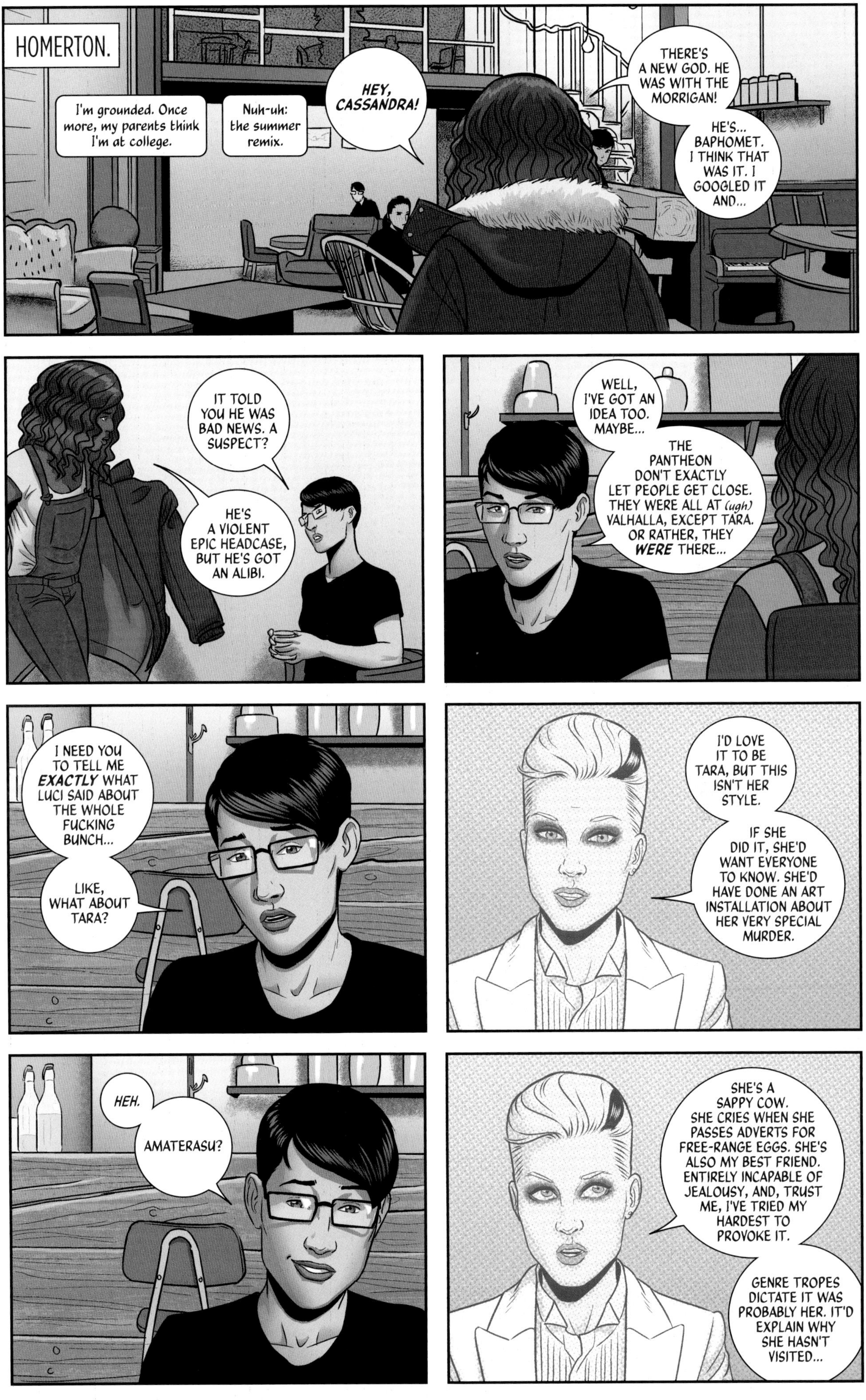
HOMERTON.
I'm grounded. Once more, my parents think I'm at college.
Nuh-uh: the summer remix.
HEY, CASSANDRA!
THERE'S A NEW GOD. HE WAS WITH THE MORRIGAN!
HE'S... BAPHOMET. I THINK THAT WAS IT. I GOOGLED IT AND...
IT TOLD YOU HE WAS BAD NEWS. A SUSPECT?
HE'S A VIOLENT EPIC HEADCASE, BUT HE'S GOT AN ALIBI.
WELL, I'VE GOT AN IDEA TOO. MAYBE...
THE PANTHEON DON'T EXACTLY LET PEOPLE GET CLOSE. THEY WERE ALL AT *(ugh)* VALHALLA, EXCEPT TARA. OR RATHER, THEY ***WERE*** THERE...
I NEED YOU TO TELL ME ***EXACTLY*** WHAT LUCI SAID ABOUT THE WHOLE FUCKING BUNCH...
LIKE, WHAT ABOUT TARA?
I'D LOVE IT TO BE TARA, BUT THIS ISN'T HER STYLE.
IF SHE DID IT, SHE'D WANT EVERYONE TO KNOW. SHE'D HAVE DONE AN ART INSTALLATION ABOUT HER VERY SPECIAL MURDER.
HEH.
AMATERASU?
SHE'S A SAPPY COW. SHE CRIES WHEN SHE PASSES ADVERTS FOR FREE-RANGE EGGS. SHE'S ALSO MY BEST FRIEND. ENTIRELY INCAPABLE OF JEALOUSY, AND, TRUST ME, I'VE TRIED MY HARDEST TO PROVOKE IT.
GENRE TROPES DICTATE IT WAS PROBABLY HER. IT'D EXPLAIN WHY SHE HASN'T VISITED...

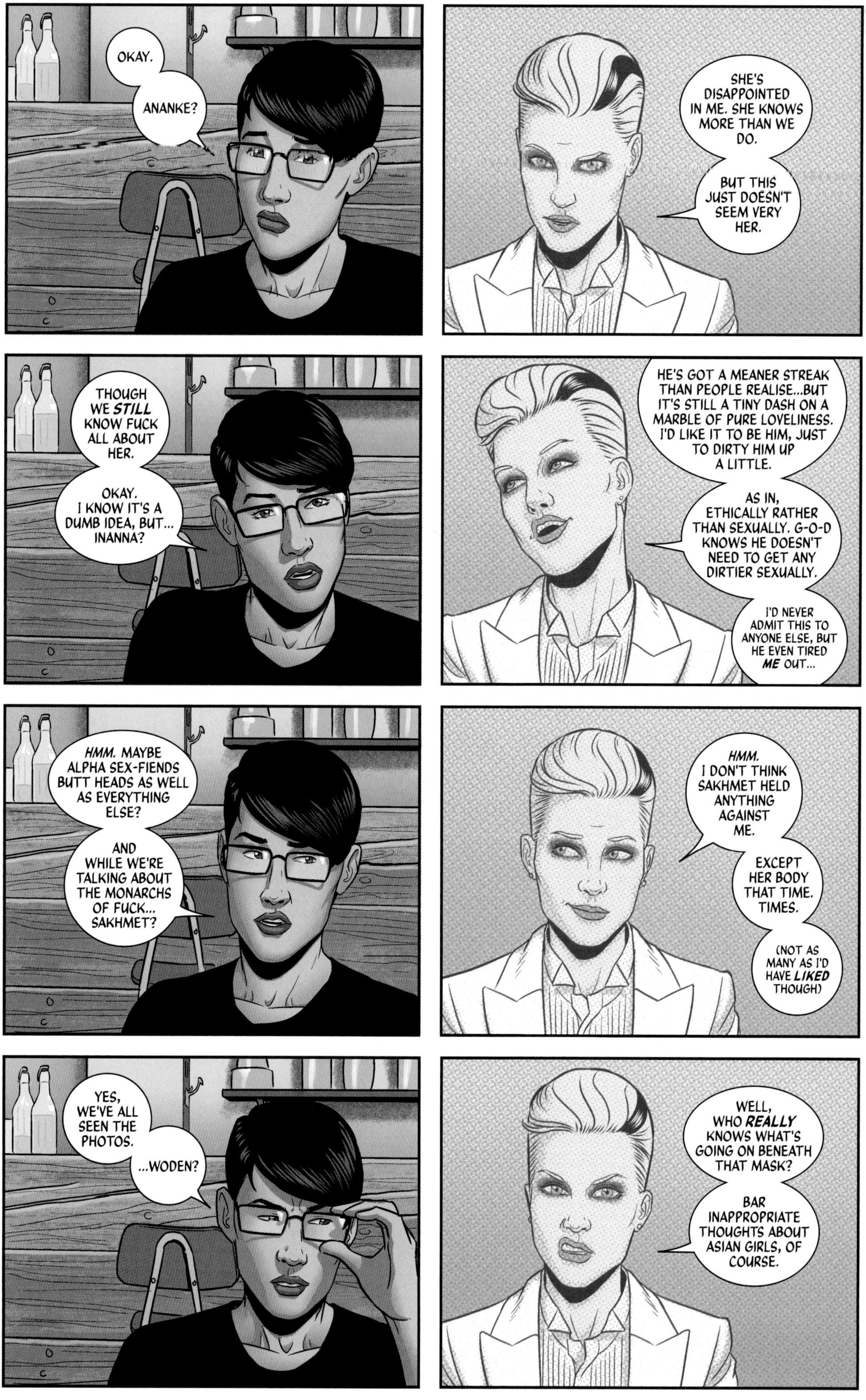

OKAY.
ANANKE?
SHE'S DISAPPOINTED IN ME. SHE KNOWS MORE THAN WE DO.
BUT THIS JUST DOESN'T SEEM VERY HER.
THOUGH WE *STILL* KNOW FUCK ALL ABOUT HER.
OKAY. I KNOW IT'S A DUMB IDEA, BUT... INANNA?
HE'S GOT A MEANER STREAK THAN PEOPLE REALISE...BUT IT'S STILL A TINY DASH ON A MARBLE OF PURE LOVELINESS. I'D LIKE IT TO BE HIM, JUST TO DIRTY HIM UP A LITTLE.
AS IN, ETHICALLY RATHER THAN SEXUALLY. G-O-D KNOWS HE DOESN'T NEED TO GET ANY DIRTIER SEXUALLY.
I'D NEVER ADMIT THIS TO ANYONE ELSE, BUT HE EVEN TIRED *ME* OUT...
HMM. MAYBE ALPHA SEX-FIENDS BUTT HEADS AS WELL AS EVERYTHING ELSE?
AND WHILE WE'RE TALKING ABOUT THE MONARCHS OF FUCK... SAKHMET?
HMM. I DON'T THINK SAKHMET HELD ANYTHING AGAINST ME.
EXCEPT HER BODY THAT TIME. TIMES.
(NOT AS MANY AS I'D HAVE *LIKED* THOUGH)
YES, WE'VE ALL SEEN THE PHOTOS.
...WODEN?
WELL, WHO *REALLY* KNOWS WHAT'S GOING ON BENEATH THAT MASK?
BAR INAPPROPRIATE THOUGHTS ABOUT ASIAN GIRLS, OF COURSE.

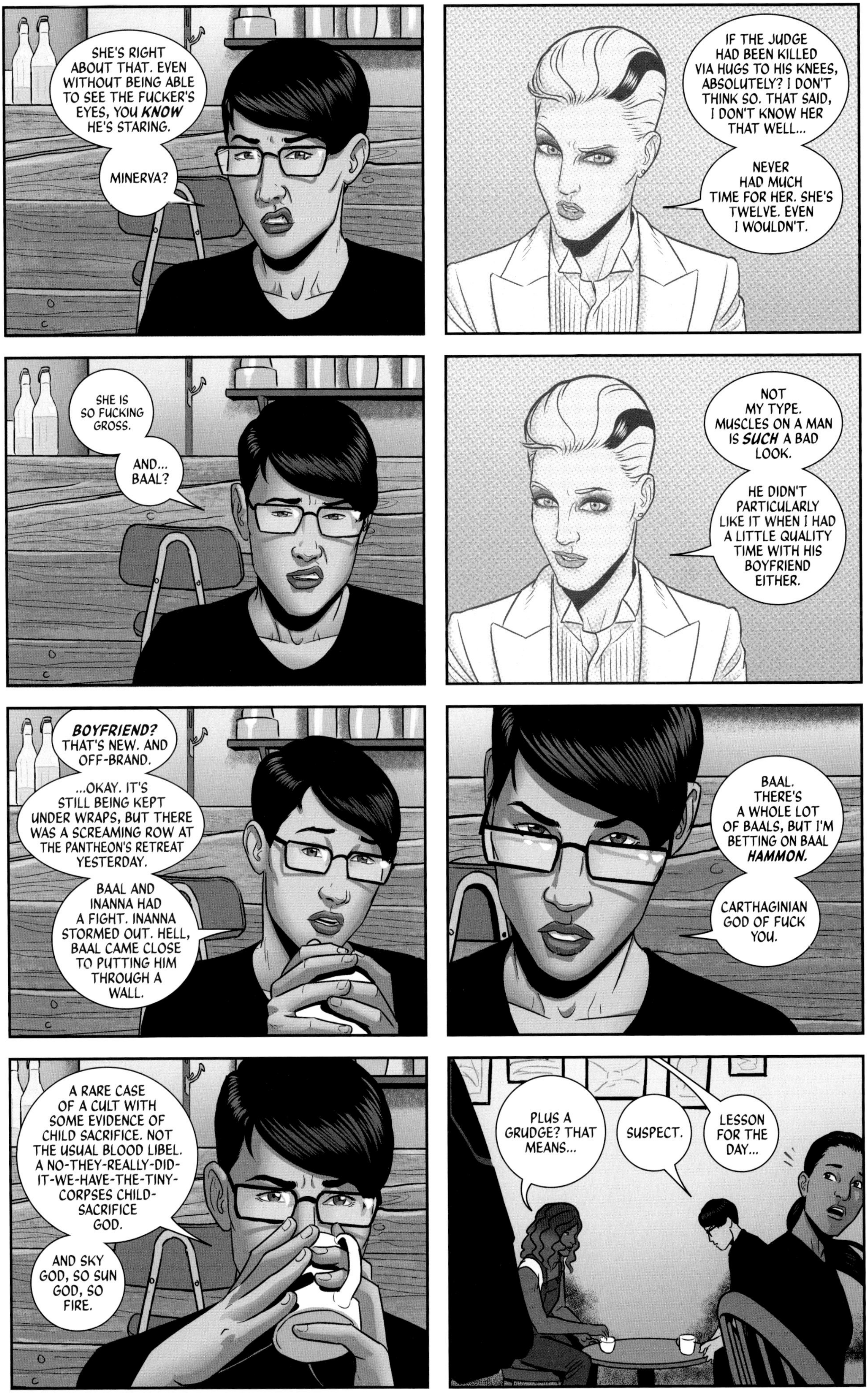
SHE'S RIGHT ABOUT THAT. EVEN WITHOUT BEING ABLE TO SEE THE FUCKER'S EYES, YOU **KNOW** HE'S STARING.
MINERVA?
IF THE JUDGE HAD BEEN KILLED VIA HUGS TO HIS KNEES, ABSOLUTELY? I DON'T THINK SO. THAT SAID, I DON'T KNOW HER THAT WELL...
NEVER HAD MUCH TIME FOR HER. SHE'S TWELVE. EVEN I WOULDN'T.
SHE IS SO FUCKING GROSS.
AND... BAAL?
NOT MY TYPE. MUSCLES ON A MAN IS **SUCH** A BAD LOOK.
HE DIDN'T PARTICULARLY LIKE IT WHEN I HAD A LITTLE QUALITY TIME WITH HIS BOYFRIEND EITHER.
BOYFRIEND? THAT'S NEW. AND OFF-BRAND.
...OKAY. IT'S STILL BEING KEPT UNDER WRAPS, BUT THERE WAS A SCREAMING ROW AT THE PANTHEON'S RETREAT YESTERDAY.
BAAL AND INANNA HAD A FIGHT. INANNA STORMED OUT. HELL, BAAL CAME CLOSE TO PUTTING HIM THROUGH A WALL.
BAAL. THERE'S A WHOLE LOT OF BAALS, BUT I'M BETTING ON BAAL **HAMMON.**
CARTHAGINIAN GOD OF FUCK YOU.
A RARE CASE OF A CULT WITH SOME EVIDENCE OF CHILD SACRIFICE. NOT THE USUAL BLOOD LIBEL. A NO-THEY-REALLY-DID-IT-WE-HAVE-THE-TINY-CORPSES CHILD-SACRIFICE GOD.
AND SKY GOD, SO SUN GOD, SO FIRE.
LESSON FOR THE DAY...
SUSPECT.
PLUS A GRUDGE? THAT MEANS...

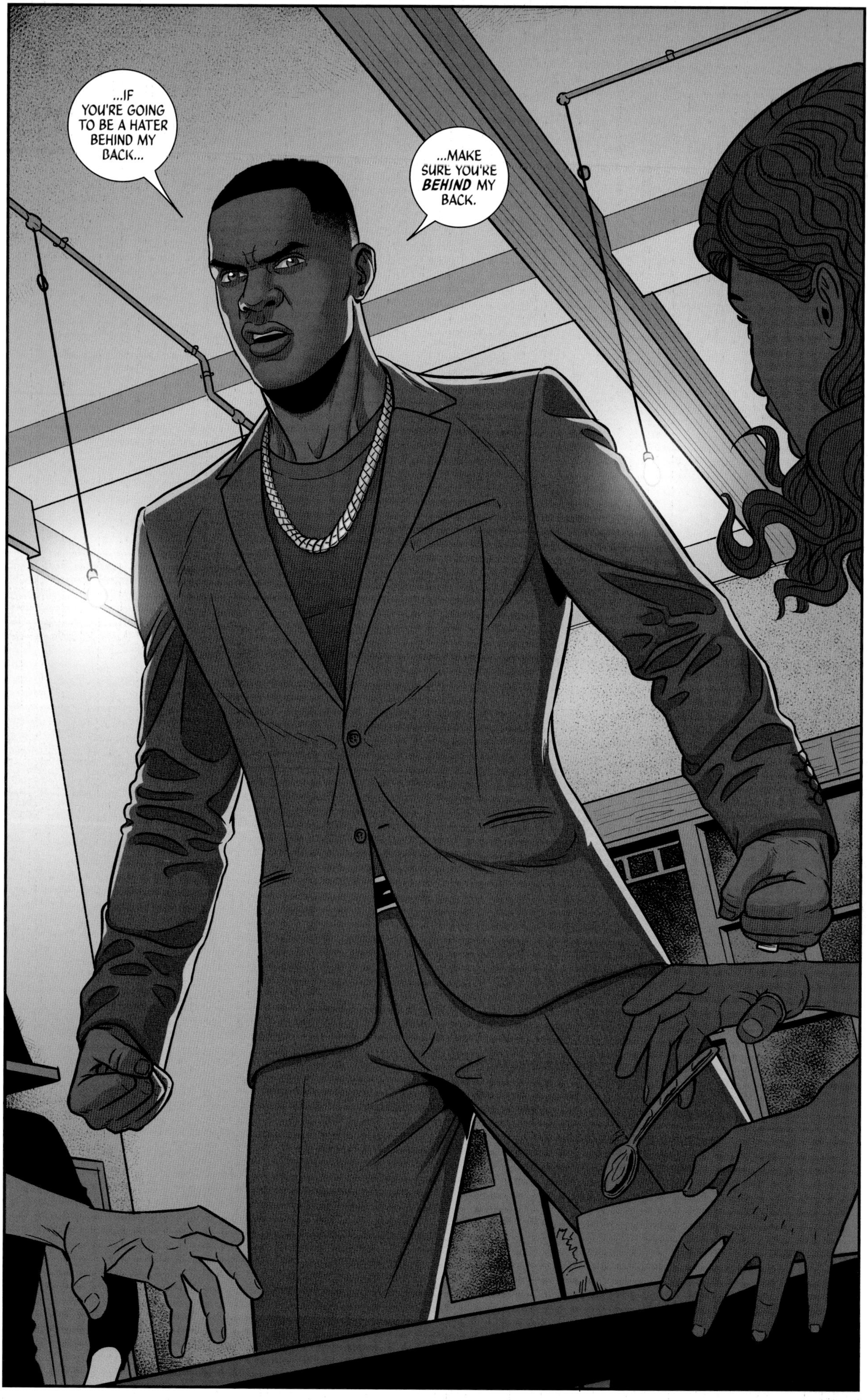
...IF YOU'RE GOING TO BE A HATER BEHIND MY BACK...
...MAKE SURE YOU'RE *BEHIND* MY BACK.

REVENGE IS THE
MOST IMPORTANT
MEAL OF THE DAY

10 JANUARY 2014

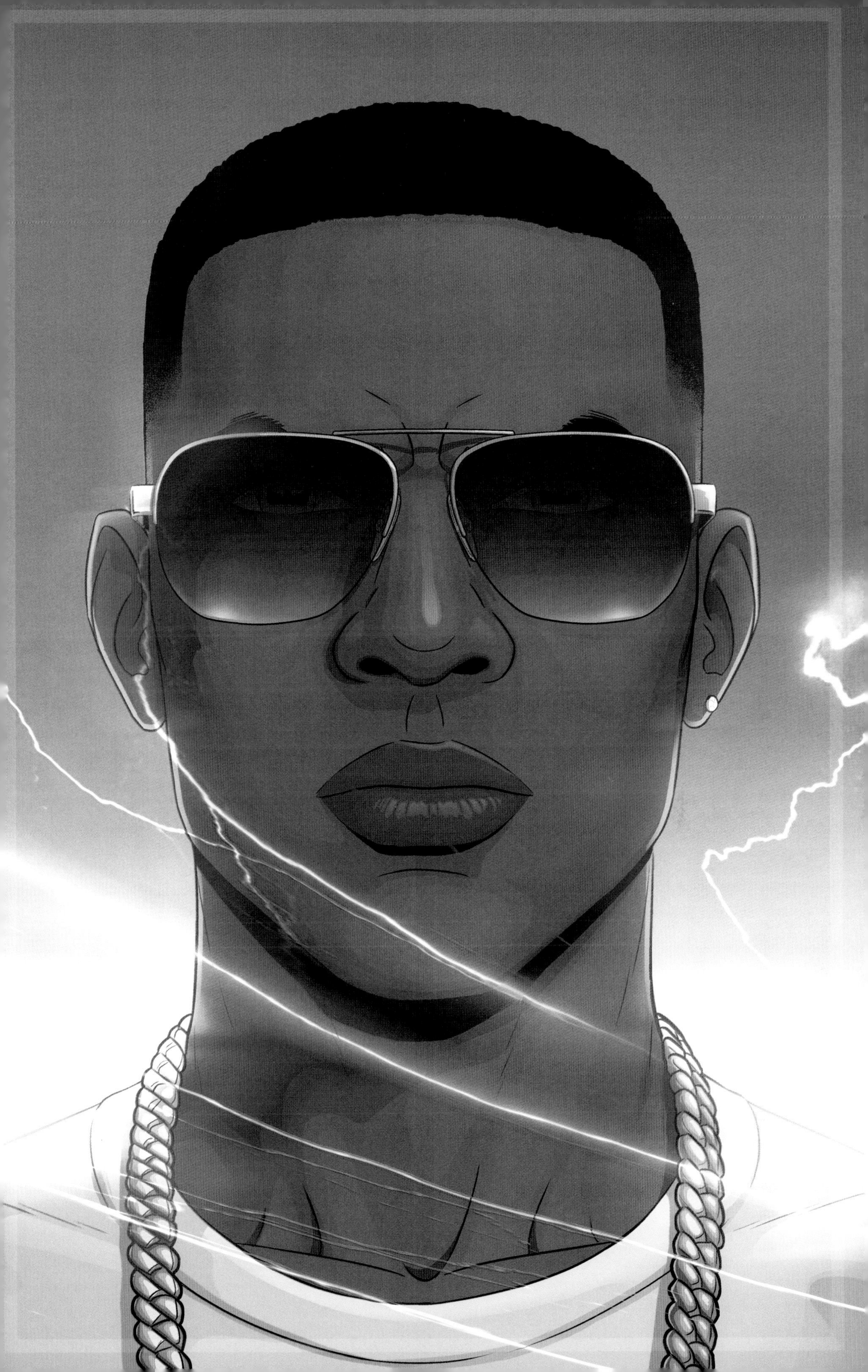

THE
WICKED
+
THE DIVINE

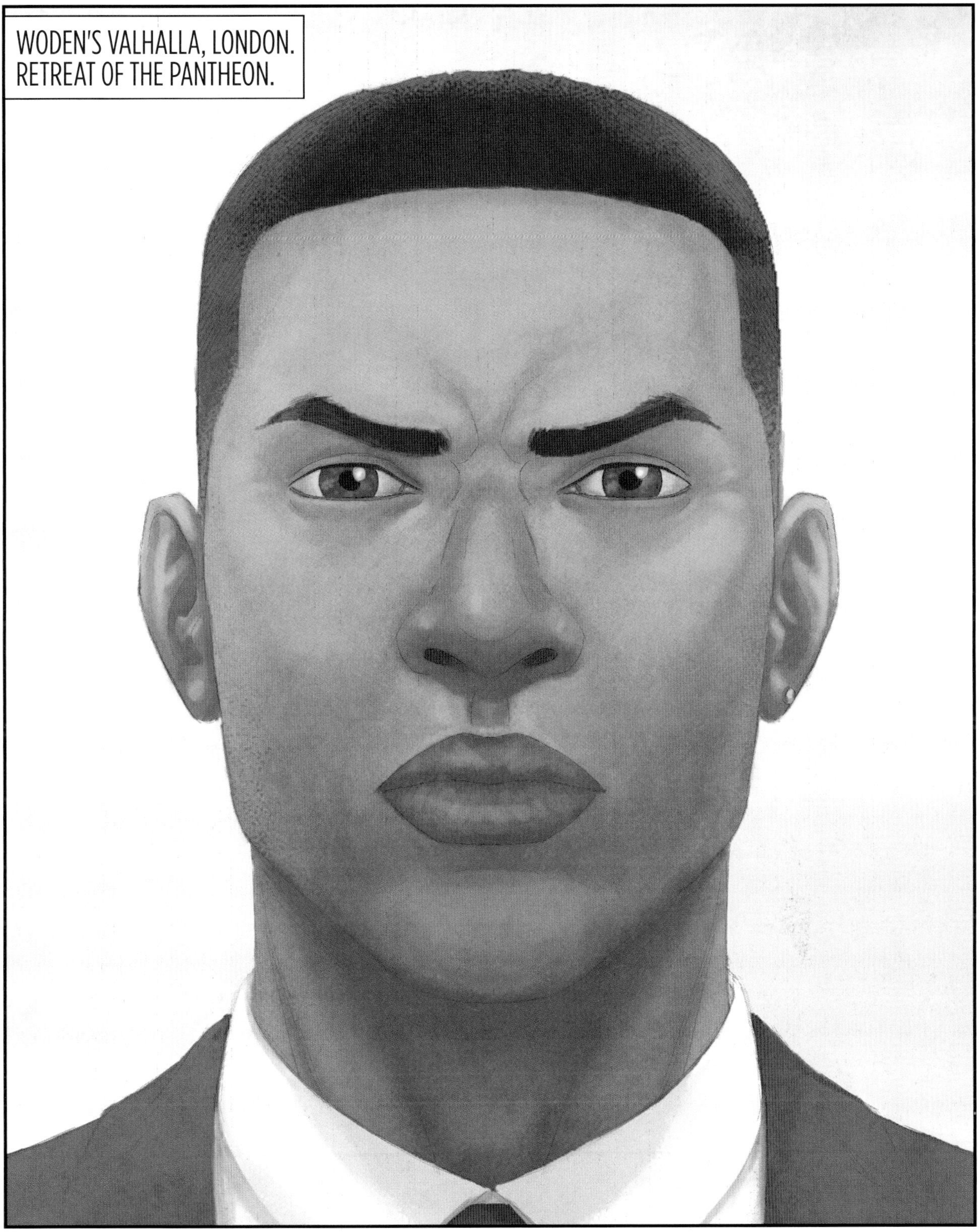
WODEN'S VALHALLA, LONDON. RETREAT OF THE PANTHEON.

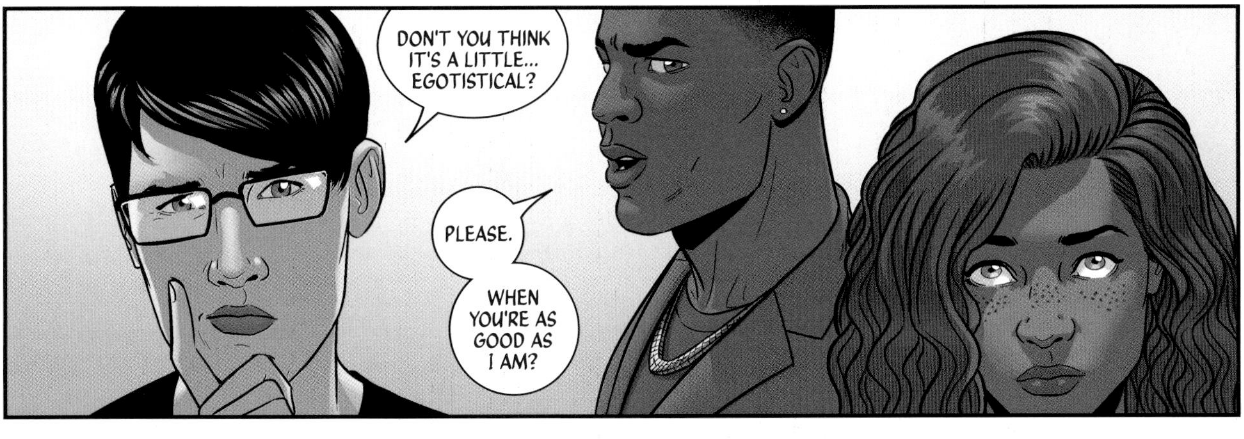
DON'T YOU THINK IT'S A LITTLE... EGOTISTICAL?
PLEASE.
WHEN YOU'RE AS GOOD AS I AM?

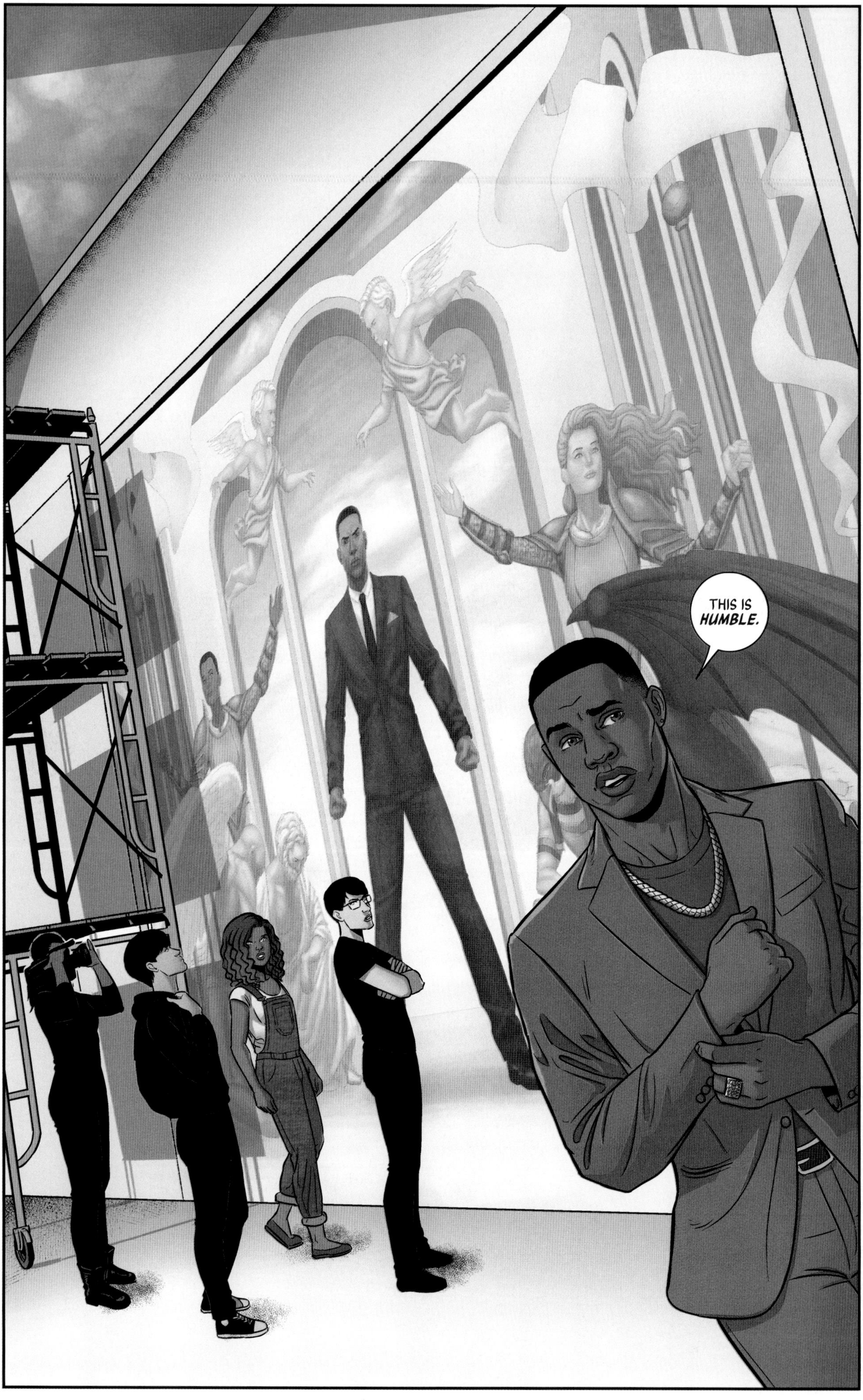
THIS IS *HUMBLE.*

THE IMMORAL OF THE TALE

10 JANUARY 2014

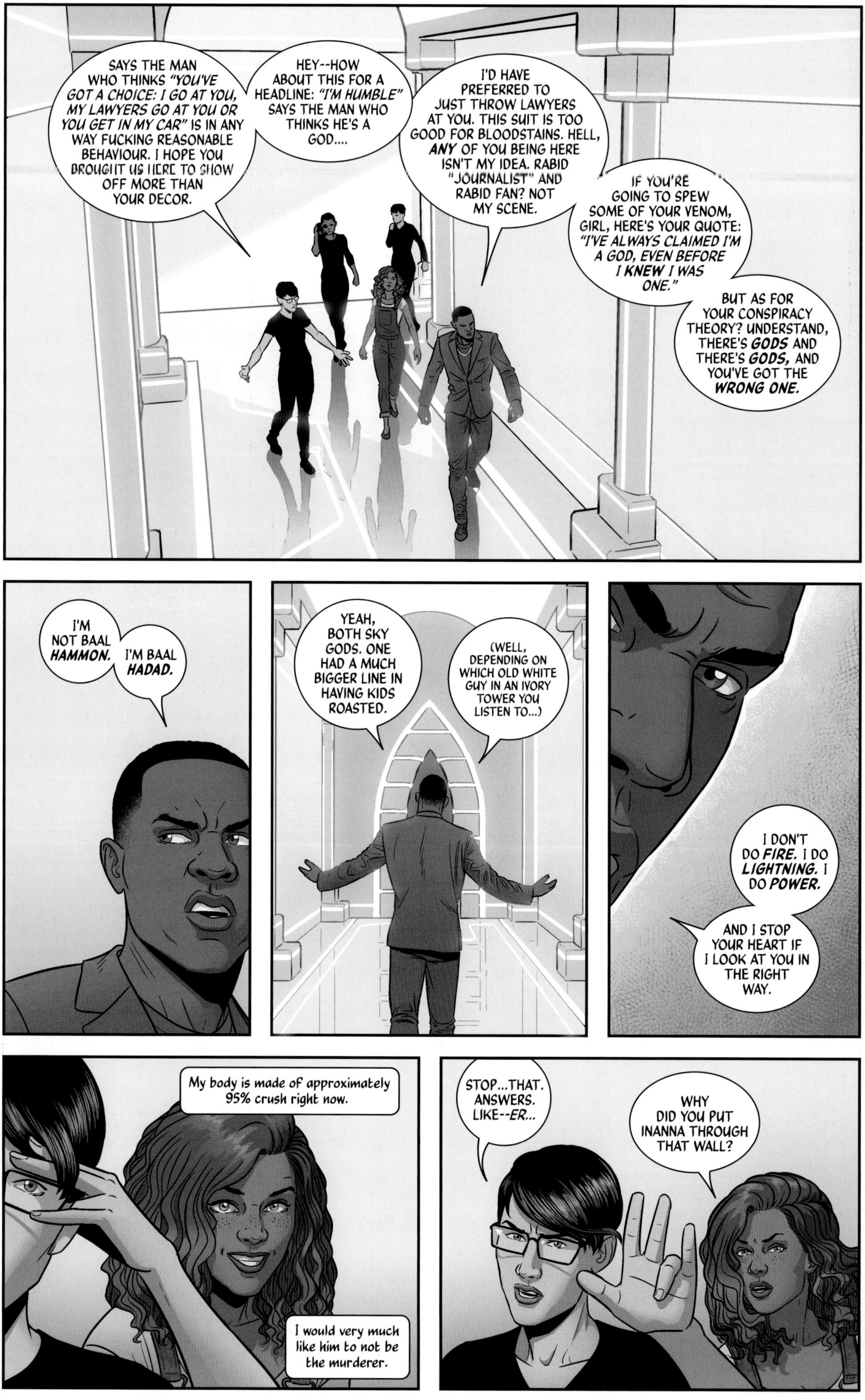
SAYS THE MAN WHO THINKS "YOU'VE GOT A CHOICE: I GO AT YOU, MY LAWYERS GO AT YOU OR YOU GET IN MY CAR" IS IN ANY WAY FUCKING REASONABLE BEHAVIOUR. I HOPE YOU BROUGHT US HERE TO SHOW OFF MORE THAN YOUR DECOR.
HEY--HOW ABOUT THIS FOR A HEADLINE: "I'M HUMBLE" SAYS THE MAN WHO THINKS HE'S A GOD....
I'D HAVE PREFERRED TO JUST THROW LAWYERS AT YOU. THIS SUIT IS TOO GOOD FOR BLOODSTAINS. HELL, ANY OF YOU BEING HERE ISN'T MY IDEA. RABID "JOURNALIST" AND RABID FAN? NOT MY SCENE.
IF YOU'RE GOING TO SPEW SOME OF YOUR VENOM, GIRL, HERE'S YOUR QUOTE: "I'VE ALWAYS CLAIMED I'M A GOD, EVEN BEFORE I KNEW I WAS ONE."
BUT AS FOR YOUR CONSPIRACY THEORY? UNDERSTAND, THERE'S GODS AND THERE'S GODS, AND YOU'VE GOT THE WRONG ONE.
I'M NOT BAAL HAMMON.
I'M BAAL HADAD.
YEAH, BOTH SKY GODS. ONE HAD A MUCH BIGGER LINE IN HAVING KIDS ROASTED.
(WELL, DEPENDING ON WHICH OLD WHITE GUY IN AN IVORY TOWER YOU LISTEN TO...)
I DON'T DO FIRE. I DO LIGHTNING. I DO POWER.
AND I STOP YOUR HEART IF I LOOK AT YOU IN THE RIGHT WAY.
My body is made of approximately 95% crush right now.
I would very much like him to not be the murderer.
STOP...THAT. ANSWERS. LIKE--ER...
WHY DID YOU PUT INANNA THROUGH THAT WALL?

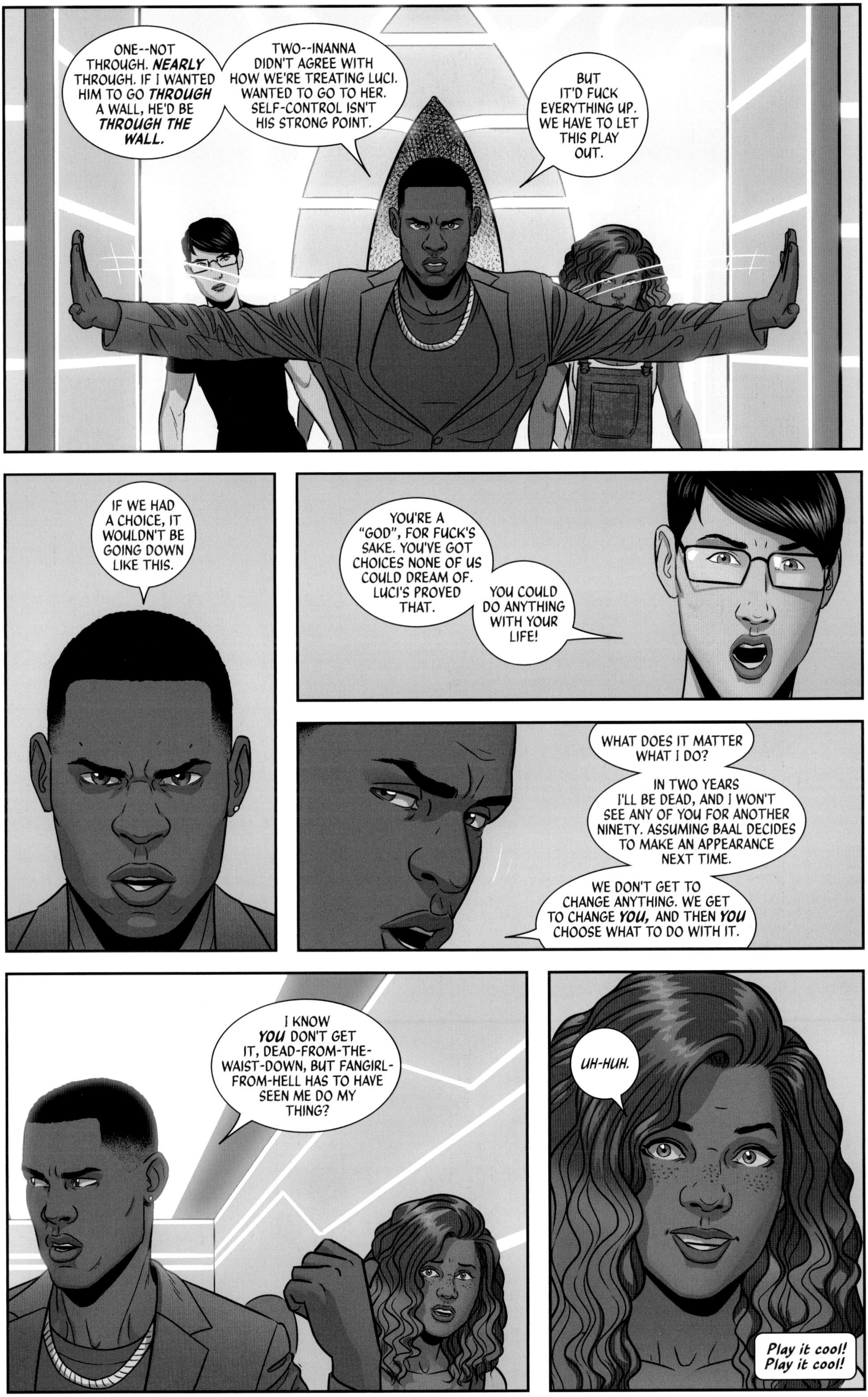
ONE--NOT THROUGH. NEARLY THROUGH. IF I WANTED HIM TO GO THROUGH A WALL, HE'D BE THROUGH THE WALL.
TWO--INANNA DIDN'T AGREE WITH HOW WE'RE TREATING LUCI. WANTED TO GO TO HER. SELF-CONTROL ISN'T HIS STRONG POINT.
BUT IT'D FUCK EVERYTHING UP. WE HAVE TO LET THIS PLAY OUT.
IF WE HAD A CHOICE, IT WOULDN'T BE GOING DOWN LIKE THIS.
YOU'RE A "GOD", FOR FUCK'S SAKE. YOU'VE GOT CHOICES NONE OF US COULD DREAM OF. LUCI'S PROVED THAT.
YOU COULD DO ANYTHING WITH YOUR LIFE!
WHAT DOES IT MATTER WHAT I DO?
IN TWO YEARS I'LL BE DEAD, AND I WON'T SEE ANY OF YOU FOR ANOTHER NINETY. ASSUMING BAAL DECIDES TO MAKE AN APPEARANCE NEXT TIME.
WE DON'T GET TO CHANGE ANYTHING. WE GET TO CHANGE YOU, AND THEN YOU CHOOSE WHAT TO DO WITH IT.
I KNOW YOU DON'T GET IT, DEAD-FROM-THE-WAIST-DOWN, BUT FANGIRL-FROM-HELL HAS TO HAVE SEEN ME DO MY THING?
UH-HUH.
Play it cool! Play it cool!

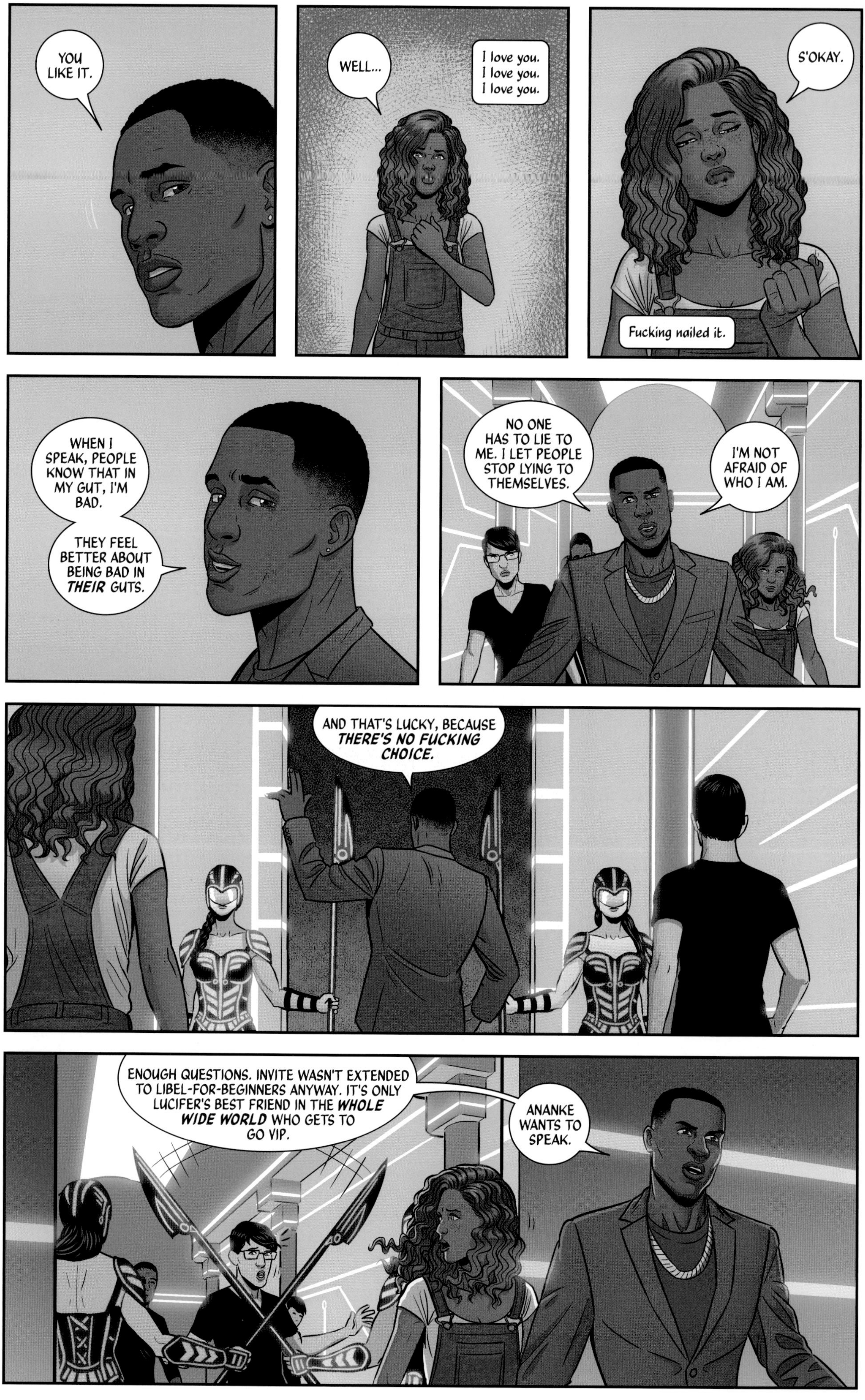
YOU LIKE IT.
WELL...
I love you. I love you. I love you.
S'OKAY.
Fucking nailed it.
WHEN I SPEAK, PEOPLE KNOW THAT IN MY GUT, I'M BAD.
THEY FEEL BETTER ABOUT BEING BAD IN *THEIR* GUTS.
NO ONE HAS TO LIE TO ME. I LET PEOPLE STOP LYING TO THEMSELVES.
I'M NOT AFRAID OF WHO I AM.
AND THAT'S LUCKY, BECAUSE *THERE'S NO FUCKING CHOICE.*
ENOUGH QUESTIONS. INVITE WASN'T EXTENDED TO LIBEL-FOR-BEGINNERS ANYWAY. IT'S ONLY LUCIFER'S BEST FRIEND IN THE *WHOLE WIDE WORLD* WHO GETS TO GO VIP.
ANANKE WANTS TO SPEAK.

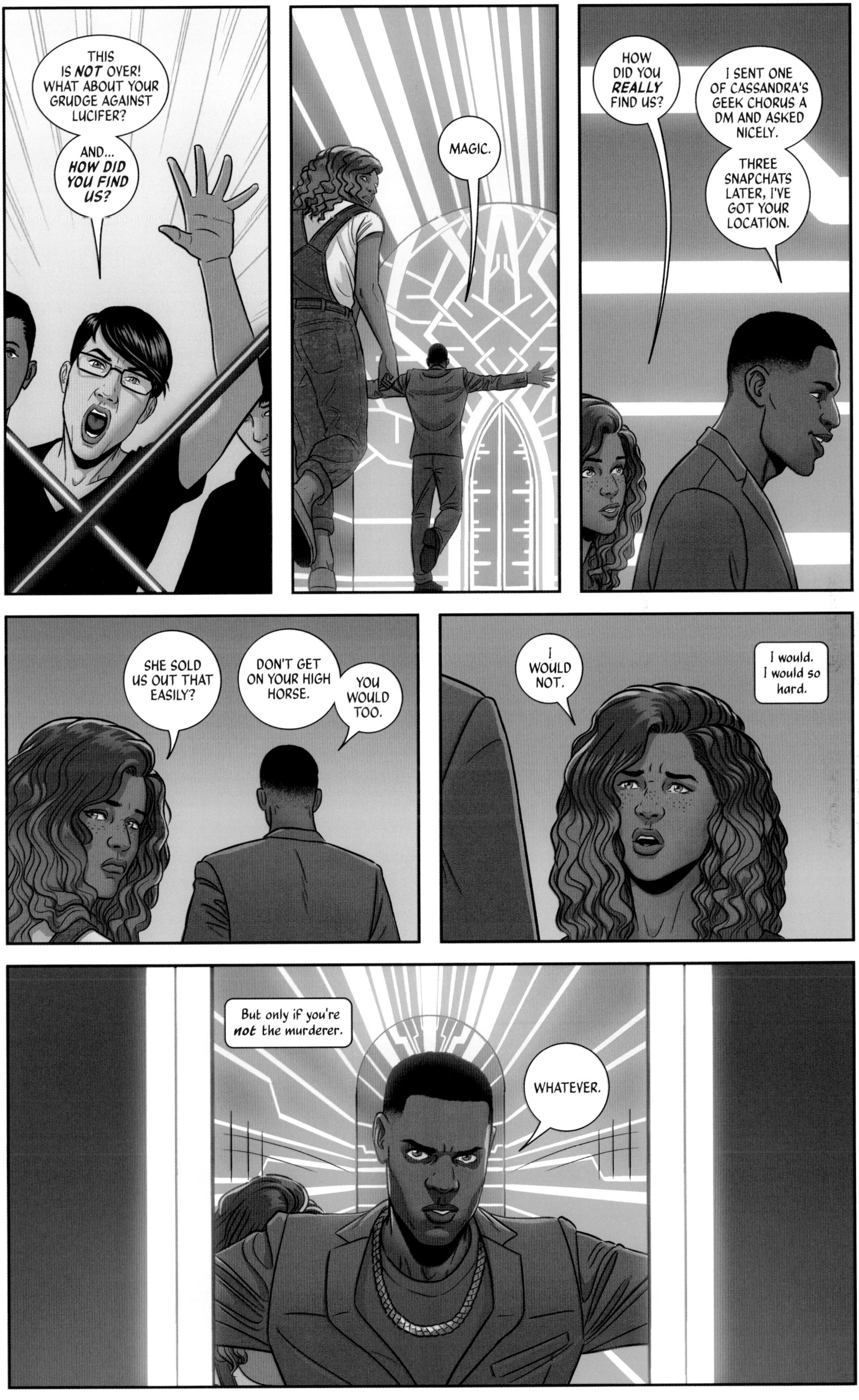
THIS IS **NOT** OVER! WHAT ABOUT YOUR GRUDGE AGAINST LUCIFER?
AND... ***HOW DID YOU FIND US?***
MAGIC.
HOW DID YOU ***REALLY*** FIND US?
I SENT ONE OF CASSANDRA'S GEEK CHORUS A DM AND ASKED NICELY.
THREE SNAPCHATS LATER, I'VE GOT YOUR LOCATION.
SHE SOLD US OUT THAT EASILY?
DON'T GET ON YOUR HIGH HORSE.
YOU WOULD TOO.
I WOULD NOT.
I would. I would so hard.
But only if you're ***not*** the murderer.
WHATEVER.

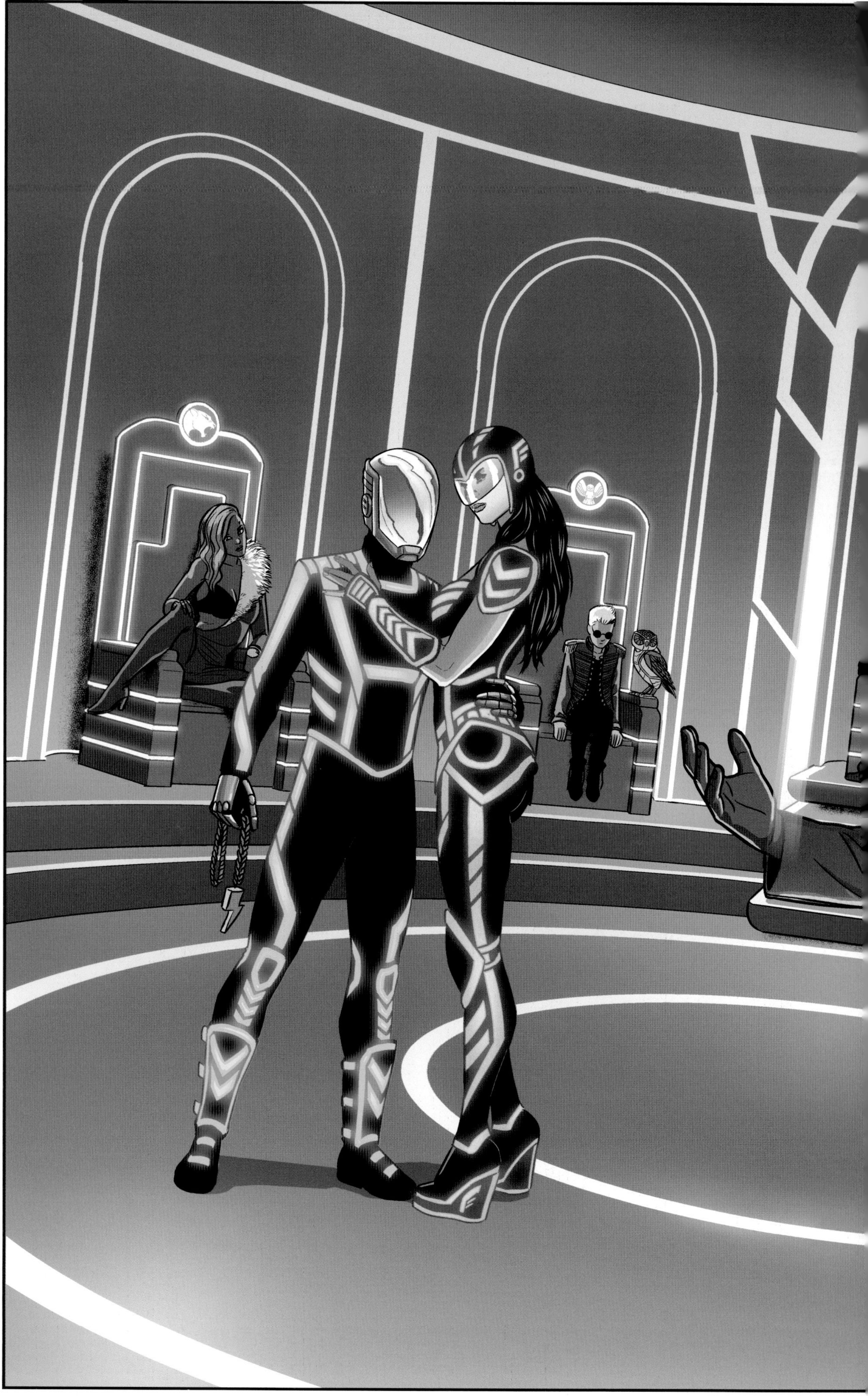

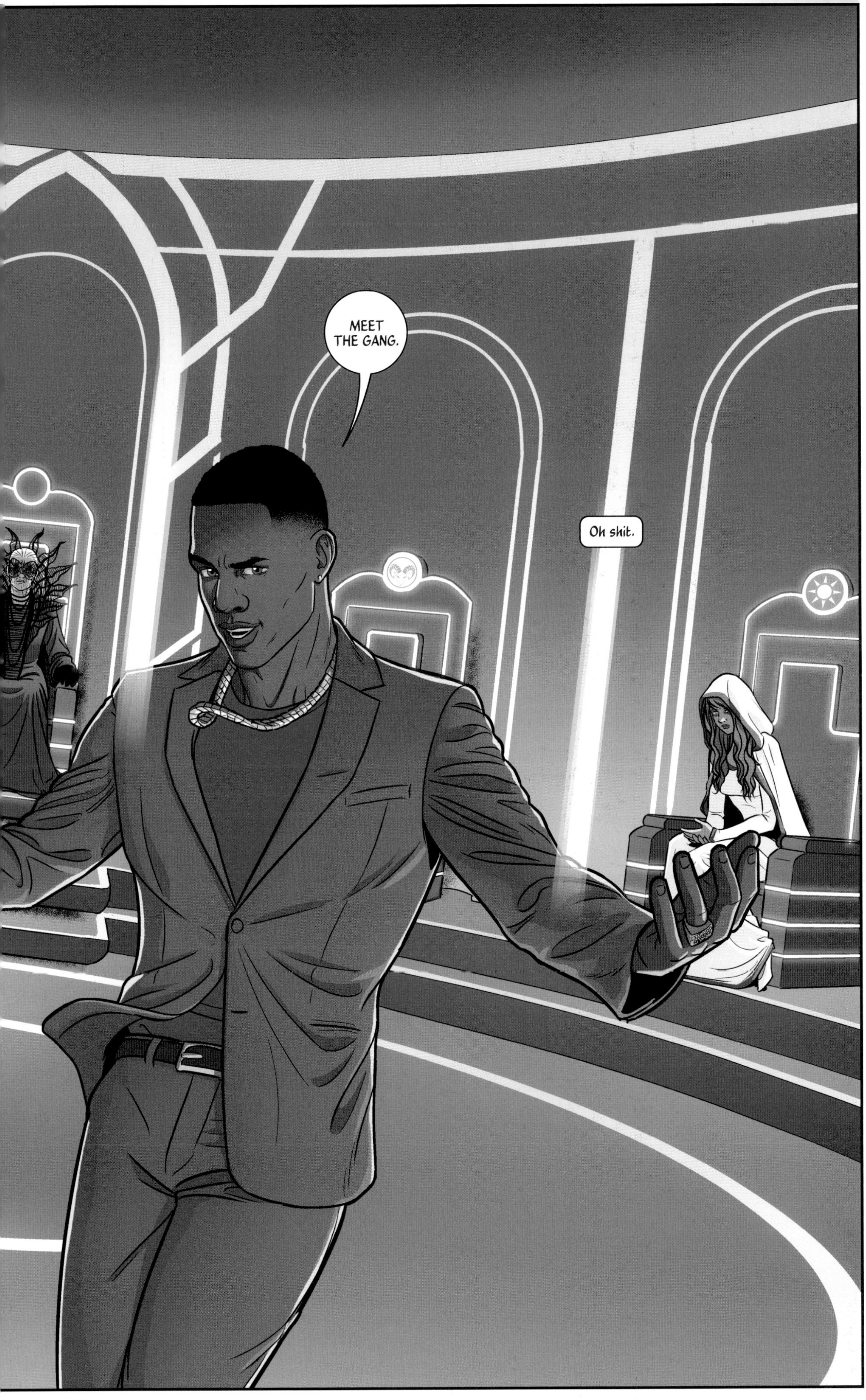
MEET THE GANG.
Oh shit.

I'm trying to not hyperventilate.

I'm failing.

FINISHED THESE UP.

SWEET.

I am made of fail.

My superpower is fail.

Just look at them...

Sakhmet sprawls, barely awake, eyes lazily stirring towards Woden's valkyrie.

Minerva looks even smaller out of costume, sitting next to what she *still* claims is a prototype Owlphone from a Silicon Roundabout start-up.

Ananke looks like dust made flesh.

Baal has already forgotten I exist.

Amaterasu waves a little hello. It's as strange, wonderful and petrifying as the sun winking at you.

And me?

I am fail girl.

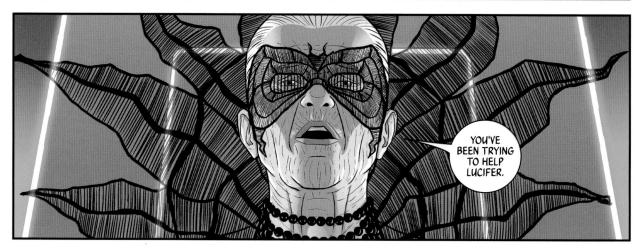

YOU'VE BEEN TRYING TO HELP LUCIFER.

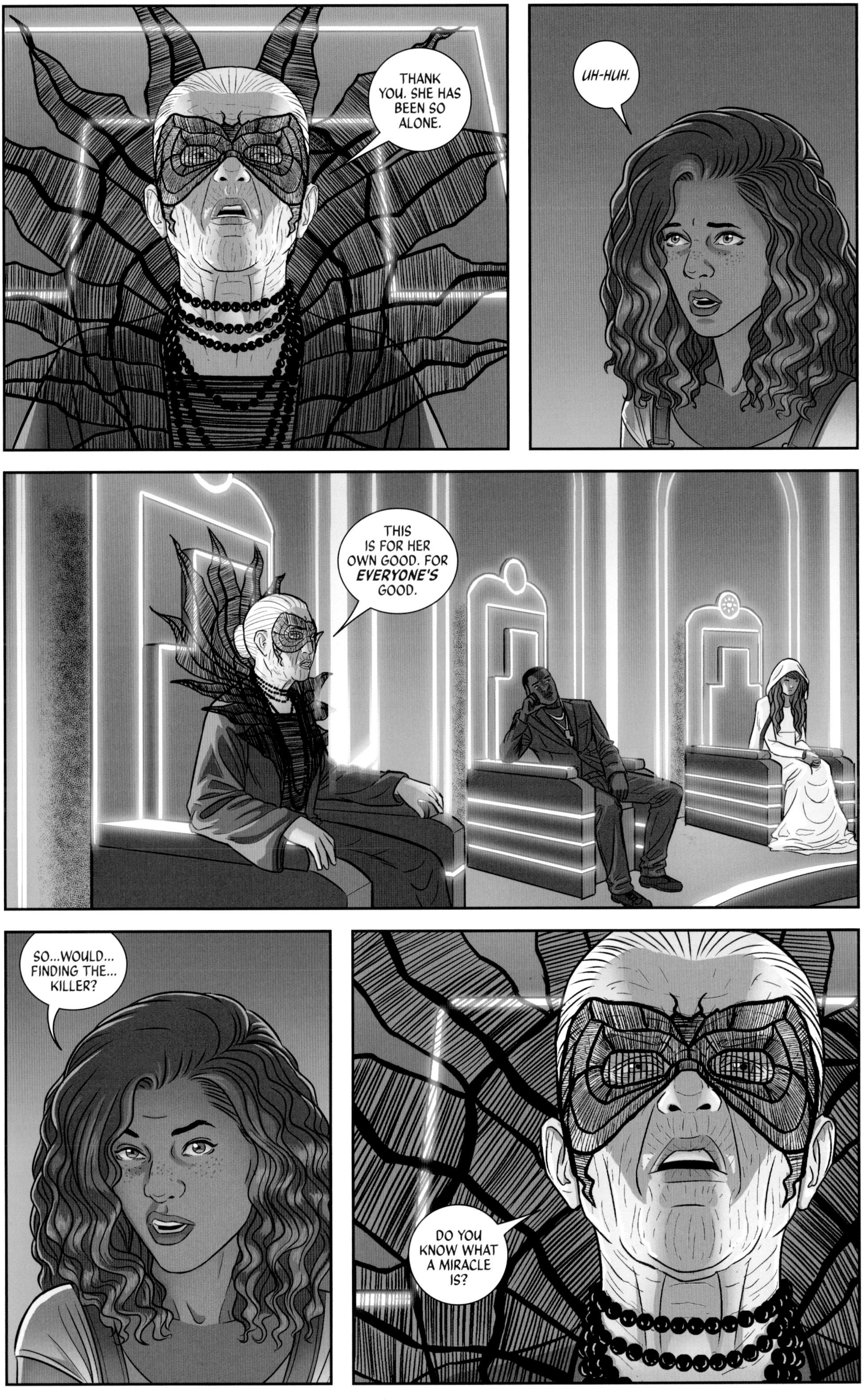
THANK YOU. SHE HAS BEEN SO ALONE.
UH-HUH.
THIS IS FOR HER OWN GOOD. FOR **EVERYONE'S** GOOD.
SO...WOULD... FINDING THE... KILLER?
DO YOU KNOW WHAT A MIRACLE IS?

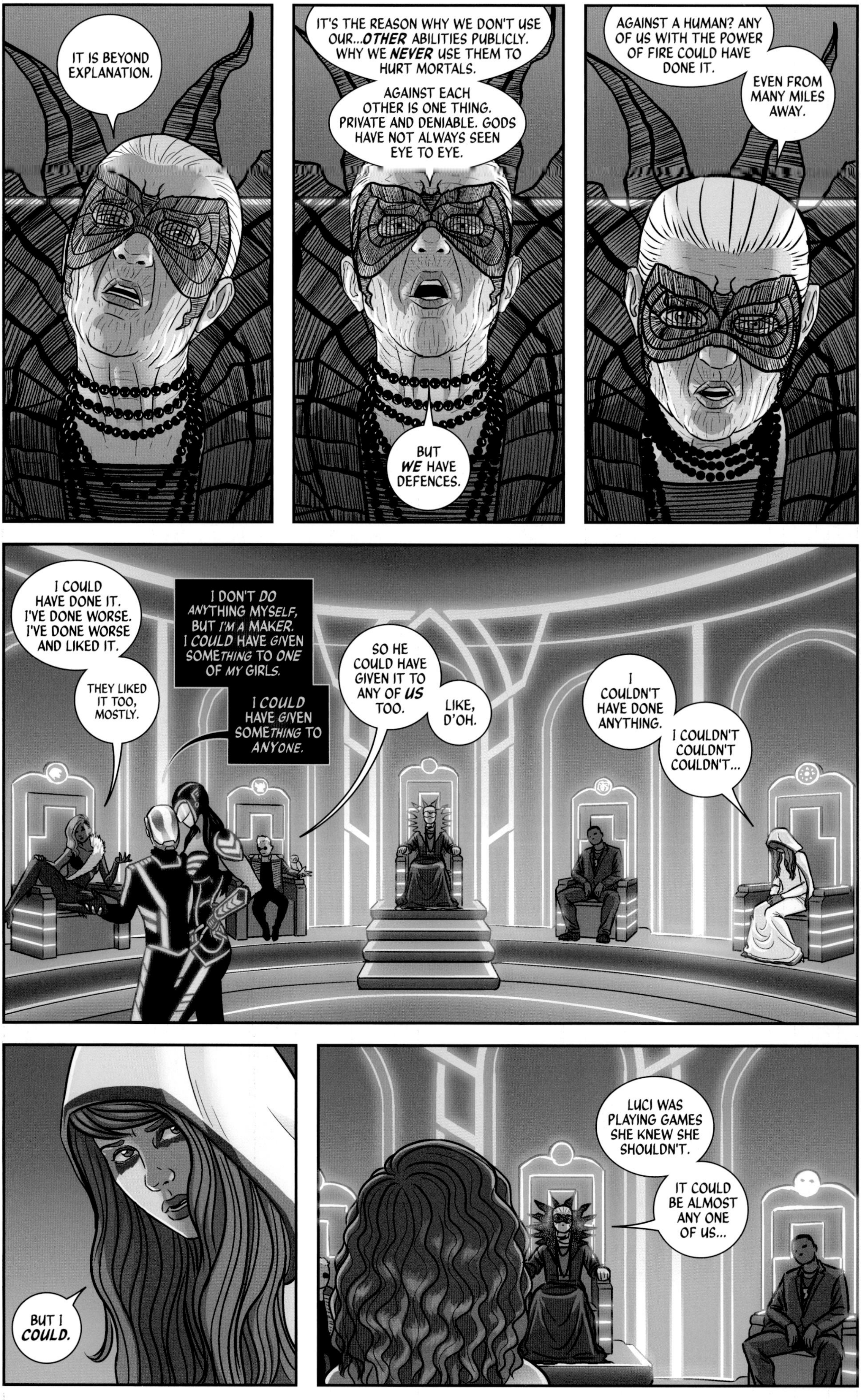
IT IS BEYOND EXPLANATION.
IT'S THE REASON WHY WE DON'T USE OUR...**OTHER** ABILITIES PUBLICLY. WHY WE **NEVER** USE THEM TO HURT MORTALS.
AGAINST EACH OTHER IS ONE THING. PRIVATE AND DENIABLE. GODS HAVE NOT ALWAYS SEEN EYE TO EYE.
BUT **WE** HAVE DEFENCES.
AGAINST A HUMAN? ANY OF US WITH THE POWER OF FIRE COULD HAVE DONE IT.
EVEN FROM MANY MILES AWAY.
I COULD HAVE DONE IT. I'VE DONE WORSE. I'VE DONE WORSE AND LIKED IT.
THEY LIKED IT TOO, MOSTLY.
I DON'T *DO* ANYTHING MY*SELF*, BUT *I'M* A MAKER. I *COULD* HAVE *GIVEN* SOME*THING* TO *ONE* OF *MY GIRLS*.
I *COULD* HAVE *GIVEN* SOME*THING* TO *ANYONE*.
SO HE COULD HAVE GIVEN IT TO ANY OF **US** TOO.
LIKE, D'OH.
I COULDN'T HAVE DONE ANYTHING.
I COULDN'T COULDN'T COULDN'T...
BUT I **COULD.**
LUCI WAS PLAYING GAMES SHE KNEW SHE SHOULDN'T.
IT COULD BE ALMOST ANY ONE OF US...

...OR IT COULD JUST HAVE BEEN QUEEN BITCH ALL ALONG.

WE DON'T OPENLY ACT ON HUMANS BECAUSE *THIS* IS HOW IT ENDS UP.

WE ARE BEYOND THEM. WE CAN ONLY POLICE OURSELVES.

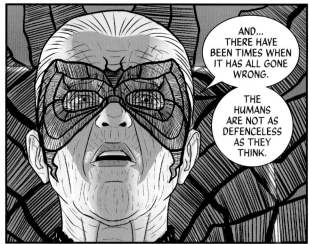

AND... THERE HAVE BEEN TIMES WHEN IT HAS ALL GONE WRONG.

THE HUMANS ARE NOT AS DEFENCELESS AS THEY THINK.

SO LUCIFER HAS TO STAY IN *HER CELL* UNTIL THE KILLER *IS* FOUND. *THEY* COULD *STILL* SLIP *UP*. WE'RE NOT *ALL THAT* SMART.

UNTIL THEN: IT *KEEPS HER* SAFE. IT *KEEPS US* ALL SAFE.

LUCIFER HAS *ALWAYS* HAD TROUBLE BELIEVING IN THE GODS, INCLUDING HERSELF. WE MUST MAKE THE WORLD UNDERSTAND HOW UNLIKE THE REST OF THE PANTHEON THE GREAT REBEL IS.

OTHERWISE THIS RISKS BEING THE LAST RECURRENCE... AND INSPIRATION WILL LEAVE THE WORLD FOREVER. HUMANITY WOULD NOT REALISE WHAT IT HAD LOST UNTIL IT WAS GONE.

SHE STAYS IN PRISON AS LONG AS IS REQUIRED.

AND IF IT'S TO THE END OF THIS CYCLE...

...THEN AT LEAST WE'LL ALL GET TO PLAY NEXT TIME.

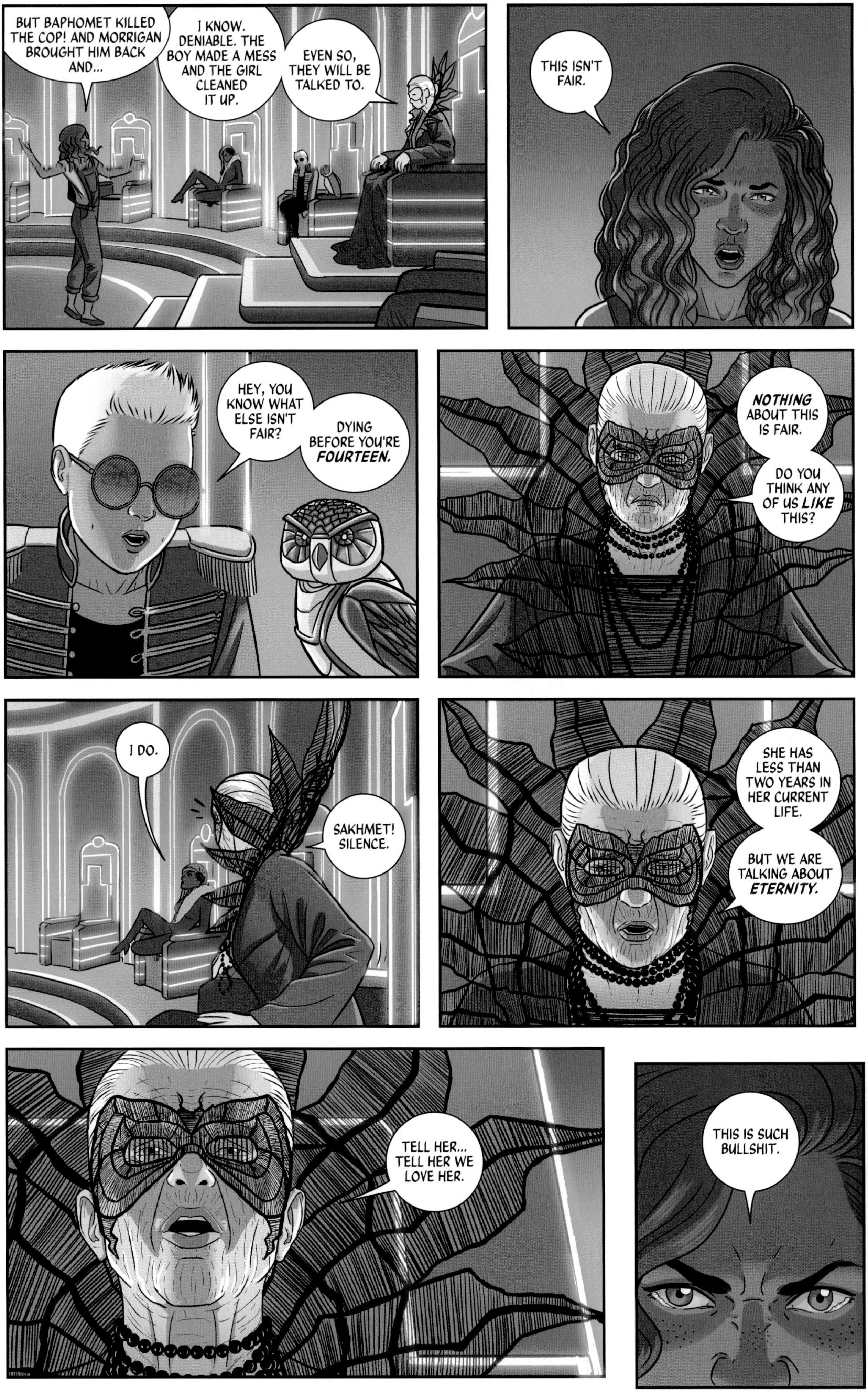
BUT BAPHOMET KILLED THE COP! AND MORRIGAN BROUGHT HIM BACK AND...
I KNOW. DENIABLE. THE BOY MADE A MESS AND THE GIRL CLEANED IT UP.
EVEN SO, THEY WILL BE TALKED TO.
THIS ISN'T FAIR.
HEY, YOU KNOW WHAT ELSE ISN'T FAIR?
DYING BEFORE YOU'RE ***FOURTEEN.***
NOTHING ABOUT THIS IS FAIR.
DO YOU THINK ANY OF US ***LIKE*** THIS?
I DO.
SAKHMET! SILENCE.
SHE HAS LESS THAN TWO YEARS IN HER CURRENT LIFE.
BUT WE ARE TALKING ABOUT ***ETERNITY.***
TELL HER... TELL HER WE LOVE HER.
THIS IS SUCH BULLSHIT.

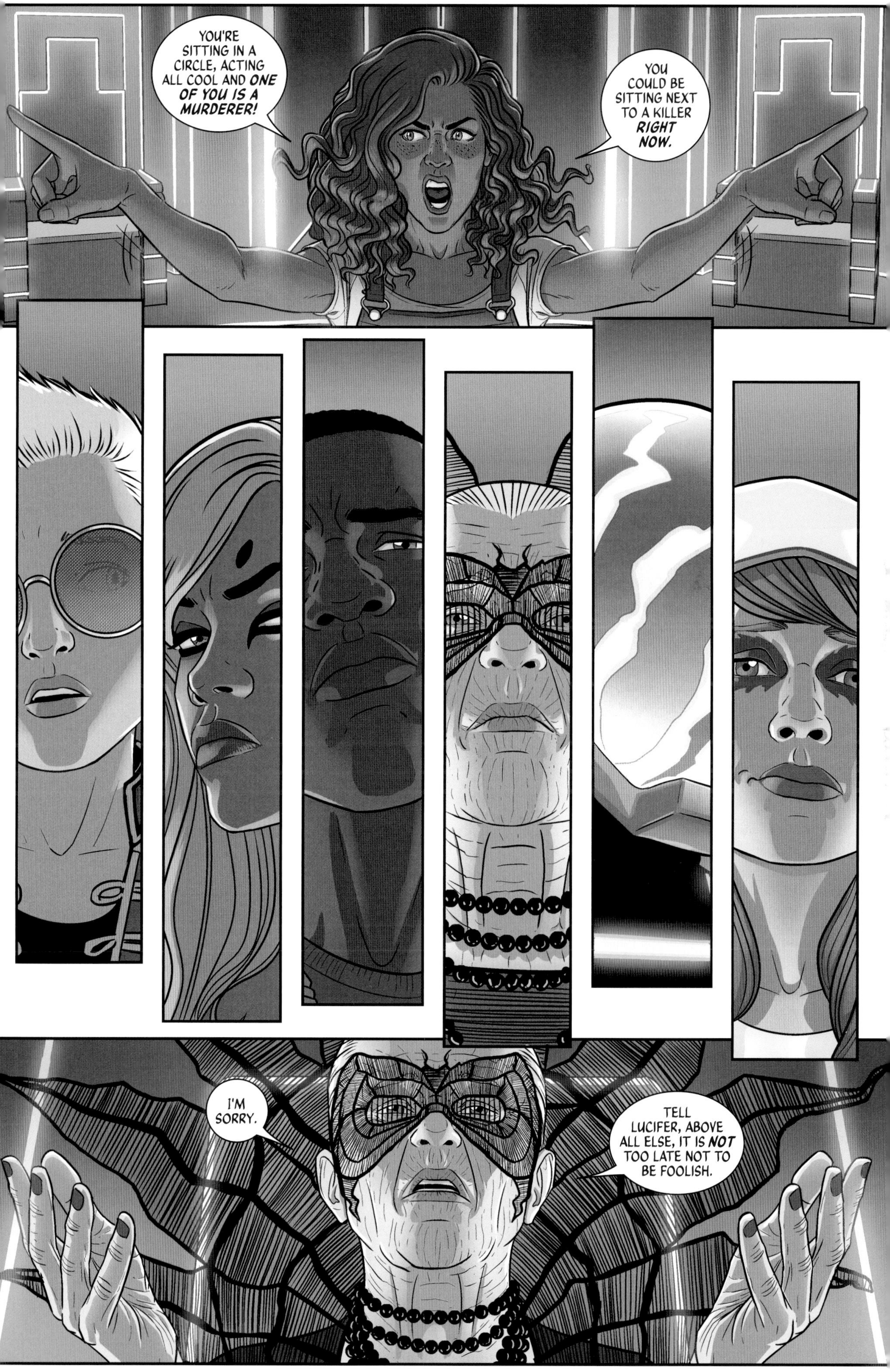
YOU'RE SITTING IN A CIRCLE, ACTING ALL COOL AND ONE OF YOU IS A MURDERER!
YOU COULD BE SITTING NEXT TO A KILLER RIGHT NOW.
I'M SORRY.
TELL LUCIFER, ABOVE ALL ELSE, IT IS NOT TOO LATE NOT TO BE FOOLISH.

IT'S GOING
TO BE OKAY

11 JANUARY 2014

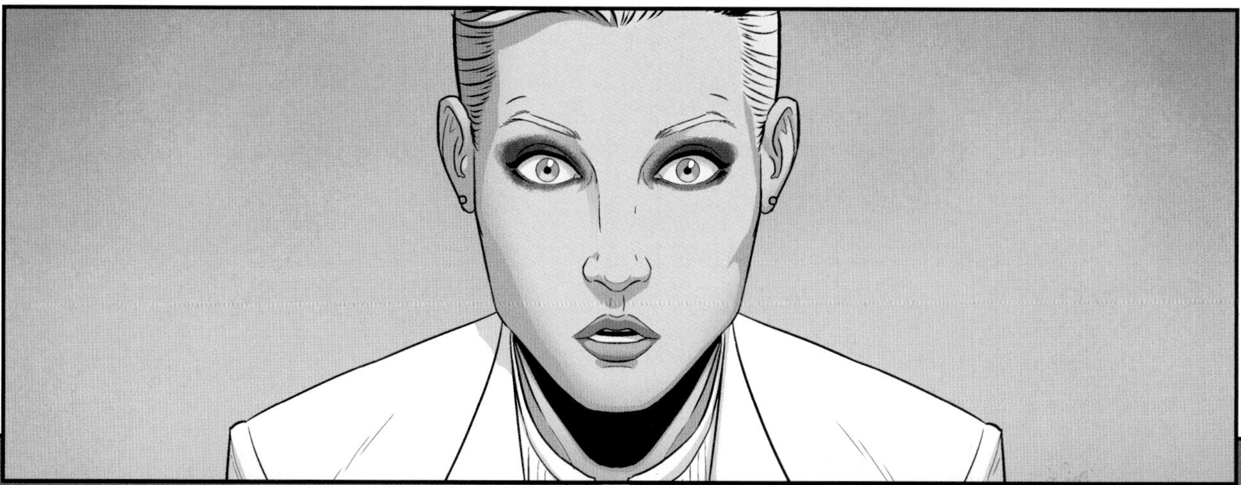

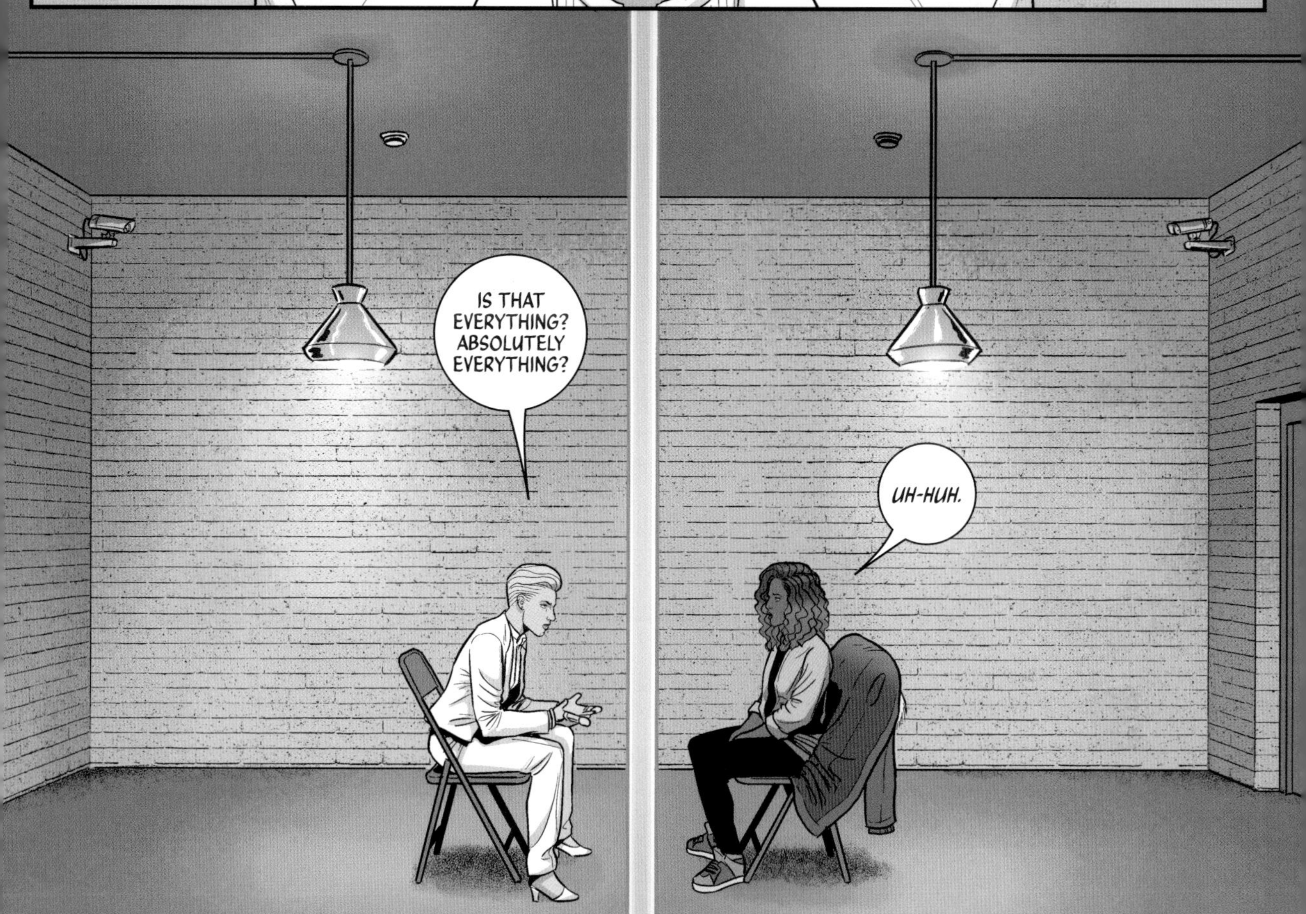
IS THAT EVERYTHING? ABSOLUTELY EVERYTHING?
UH-HUH.

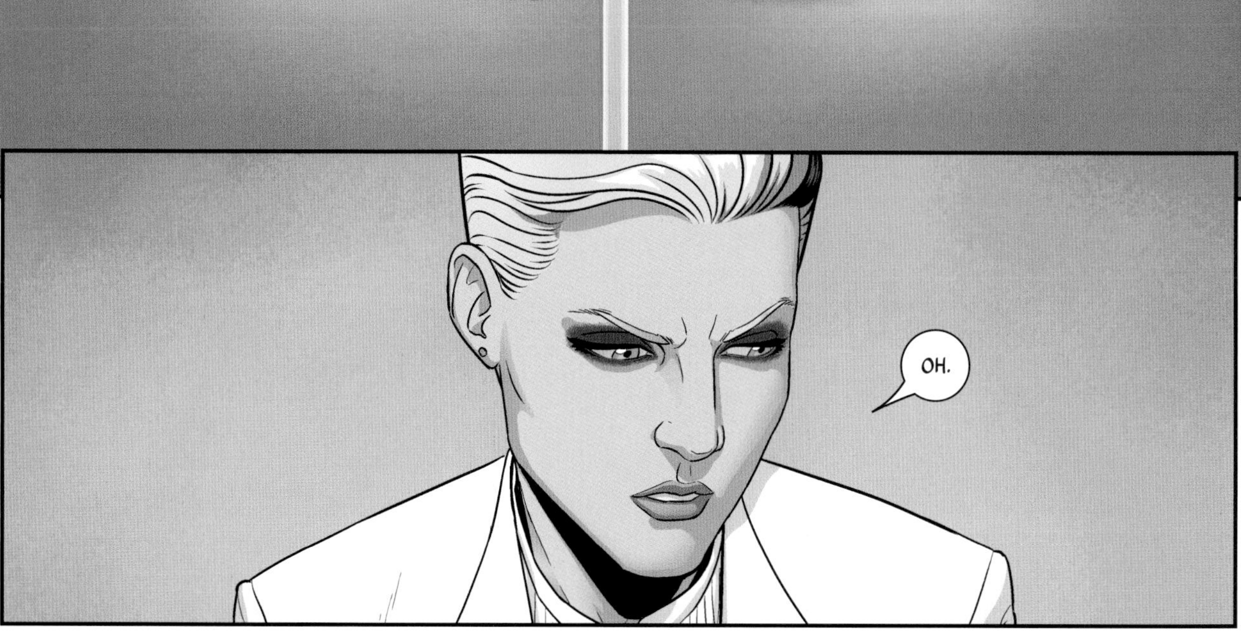
OH.

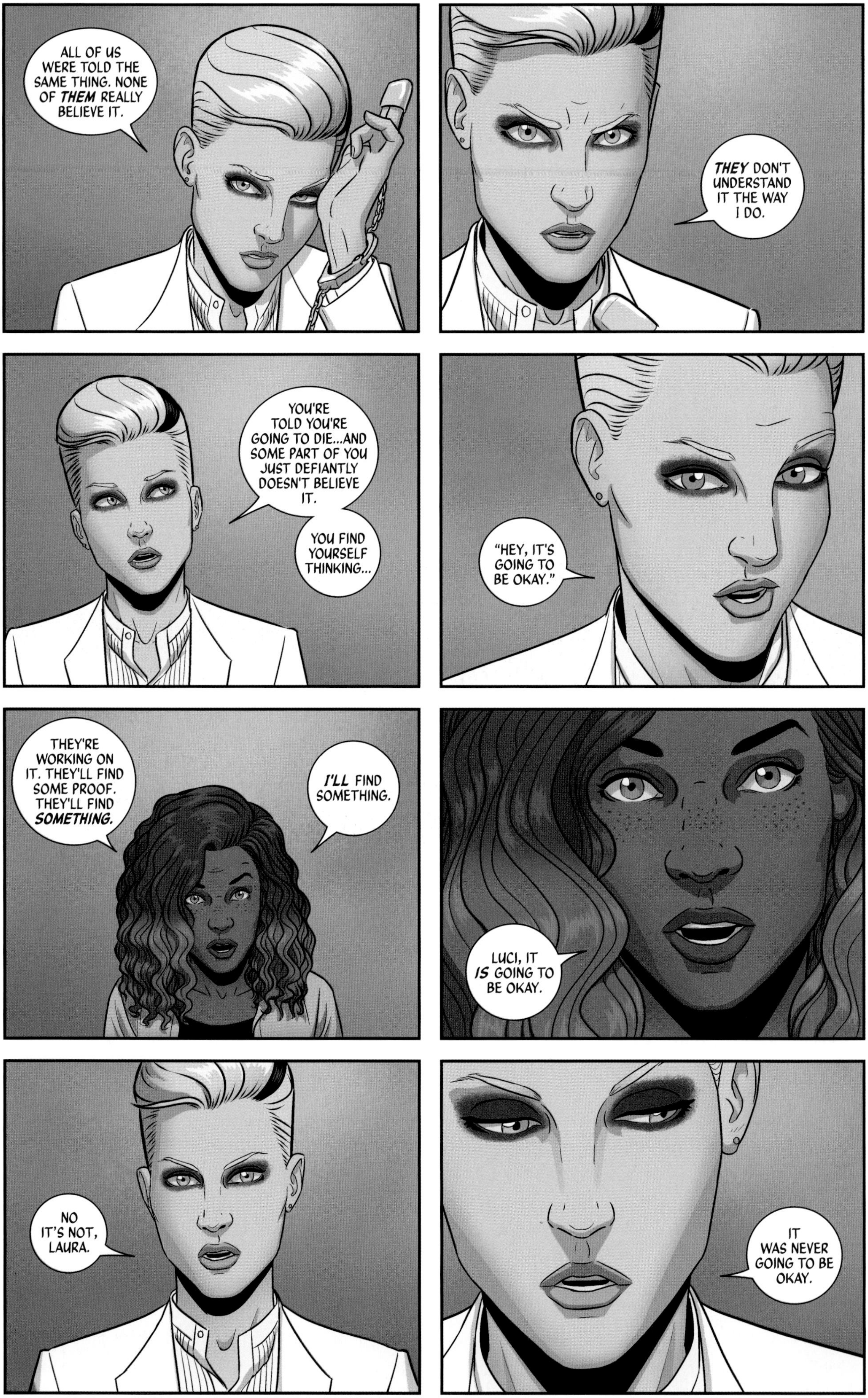
ALL OF US WERE TOLD THE SAME THING. NONE OF *THEM* REALLY BELIEVE IT.
THEY DON'T UNDERSTAND IT THE WAY I DO.
YOU'RE TOLD YOU'RE GOING TO DIE...AND SOME PART OF YOU JUST DEFIANTLY DOESN'T BELIEVE IT.
YOU FIND YOURSELF THINKING...
"HEY, IT'S GOING TO BE OKAY."
THEY'RE WORKING ON IT. THEY'LL FIND SOME PROOF. THEY'LL FIND *SOMETHING.*
I'LL FIND SOMETHING.
LUCI, IT *IS* GOING TO BE OKAY.
NO IT'S NOT, LAURA.
IT WAS NEVER GOING TO BE OKAY.

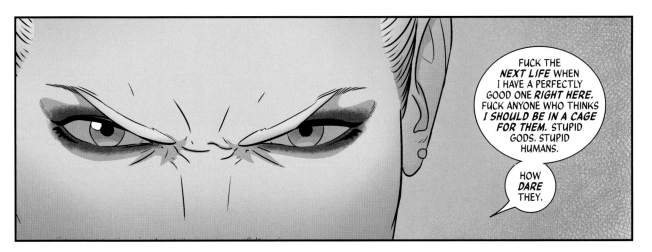

FUCK THE *NEXT LIFE* WHEN I HAVE A PERFECTLY GOOD ONE *RIGHT HERE.* FUCK ANYONE WHO THINKS *I SHOULD BE IN A CAGE FOR THEM.* STUPID GODS. STUPID HUMANS.

HOW *DARE* THEY.

WHAT ARE YOU GOING TO DO?

NOW, LAURA, I'VE GIVEN UP HOPE FOR THE COCAINE...

BUT DO YOU HAVE CIGARETTES *THIS TIME?*

UH-HUH.

EXCELLENT.

1-2-3-4.

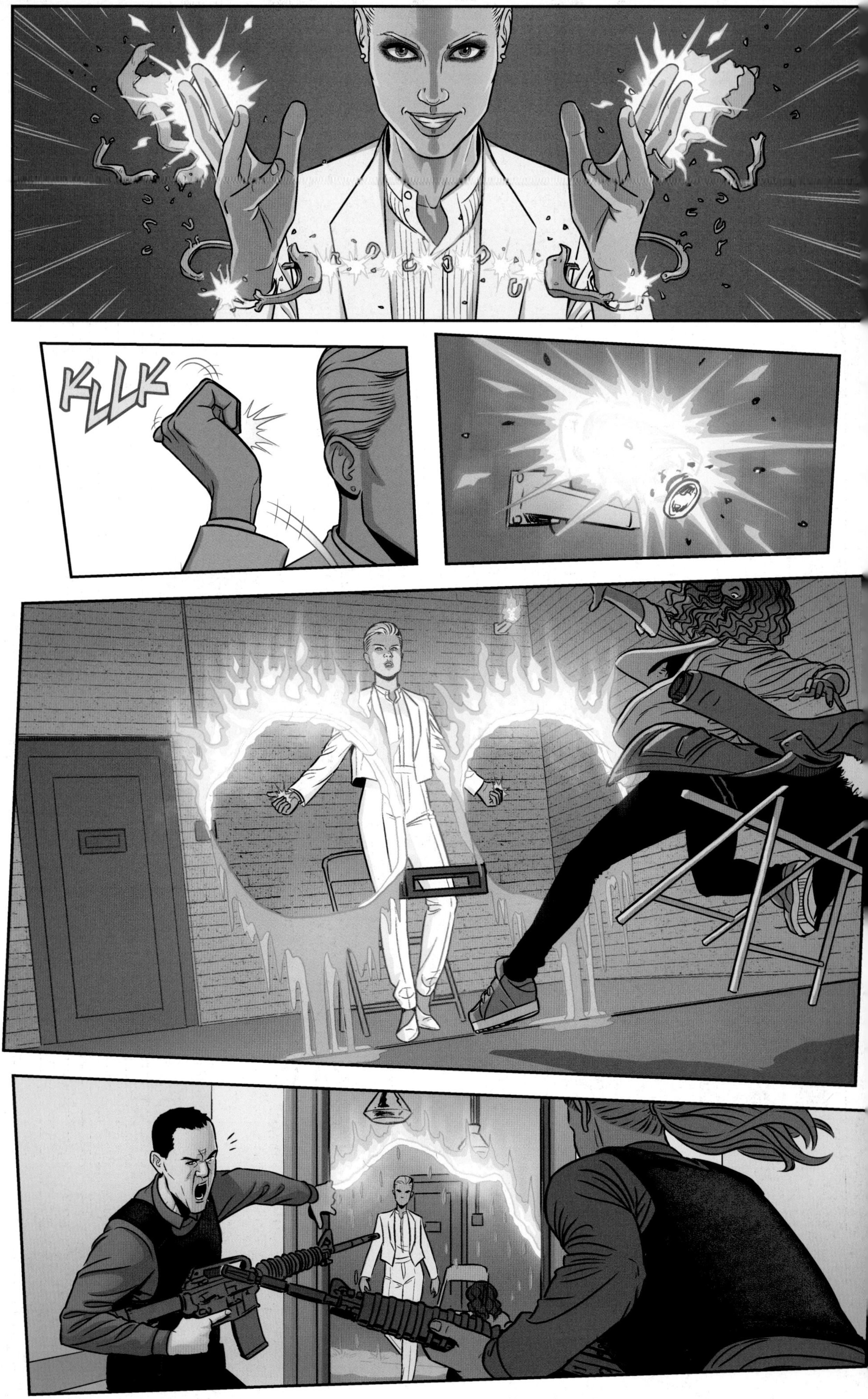
KLLK

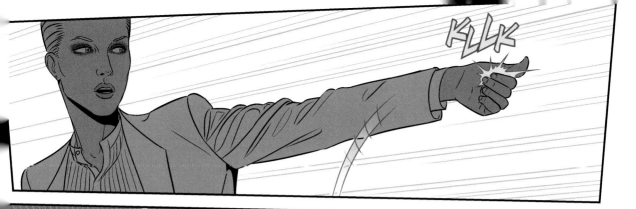

KLLK

WHAT AM I GOING TO DO?

I'M GOING TO SMOKE.

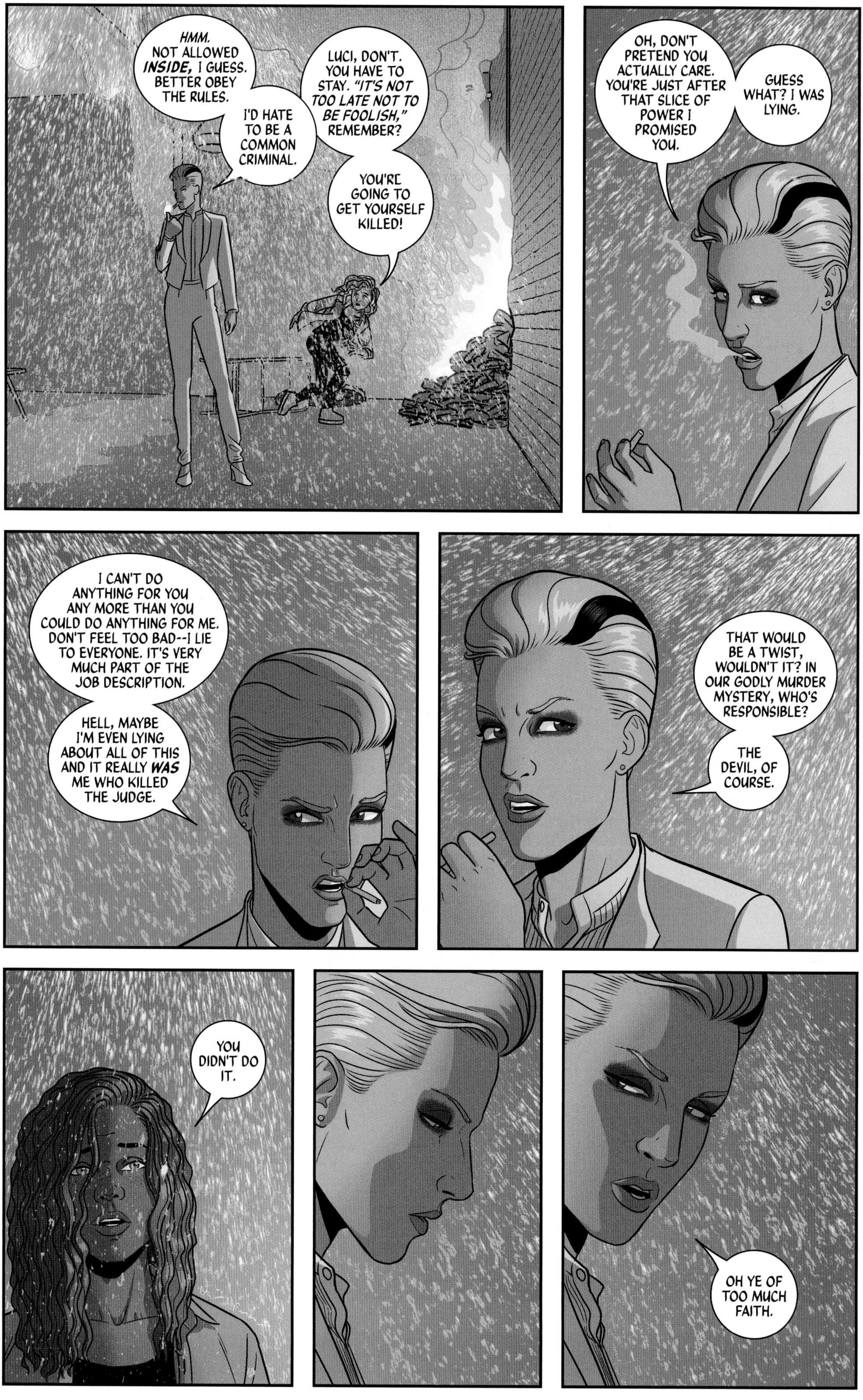
HMM. NOT ALLOWED *INSIDE,* I GUESS. BETTER OBEY THE RULES.
I'D HATE TO BE A COMMON CRIMINAL.
LUCI, DON'T. YOU HAVE TO STAY. *"IT'S NOT TOO LATE NOT TO BE FOOLISH,"* REMEMBER?
YOU'RE GOING TO GET YOURSELF KILLED!
OH, DON'T PRETEND YOU ACTUALLY CARE. YOU'RE JUST AFTER THAT SLICE OF POWER I PROMISED YOU.
GUESS WHAT? I WAS LYING.
I CAN'T DO ANYTHING FOR YOU ANY MORE THAN YOU COULD DO ANYTHING FOR ME. DON'T FEEL TOO BAD--I LIE TO EVERYONE. IT'S VERY MUCH PART OF THE JOB DESCRIPTION.
HELL, MAYBE I'M EVEN LYING ABOUT ALL OF THIS AND IT REALLY ***WAS*** ME WHO KILLED THE JUDGE.
THAT WOULD BE A TWIST, WOULDN'T IT? IN OUR GODLY MURDER MYSTERY, WHO'S RESPONSIBLE?
THE DEVIL, OF COURSE.
YOU DIDN'T DO IT.
OH YE OF TOO MUCH FAITH.

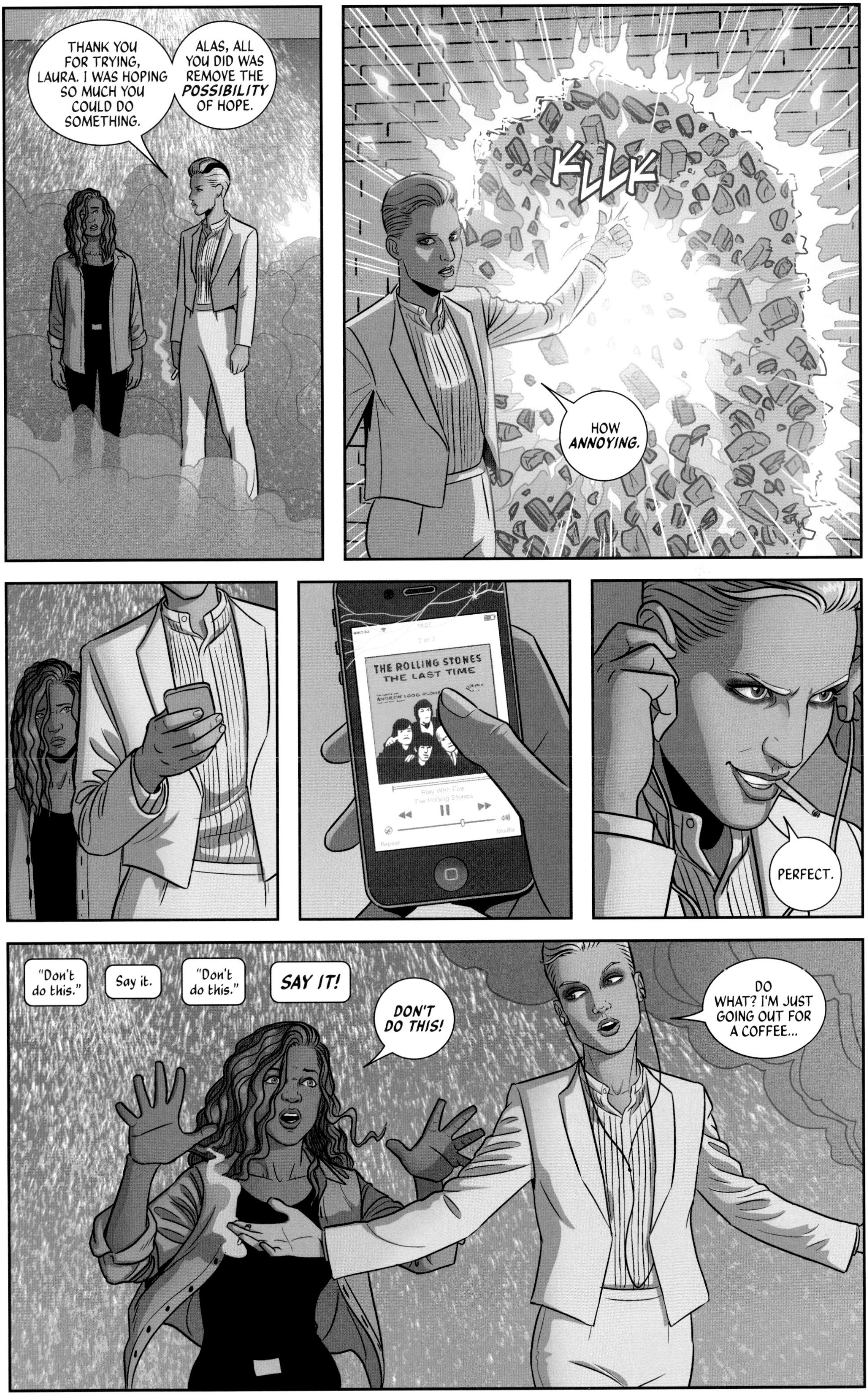
THANK YOU FOR TRYING, LAURA. I WAS HOPING SO MUCH YOU COULD DO SOMETHING.
ALAS, ALL YOU DID WAS REMOVE THE *POSSIBILITY* OF HOPE.
KLLK
HOW *ANNOYING.*
THE ROLLING STONES
THE LAST TIME
Play With Fire
The Rolling Stones
PERFECT.
"Don't do this."
Say it.
"Don't do this."
SAY IT!
DON'T DO THIS!
DO WHAT? I'M JUST GOING OUT FOR A COFFEE...

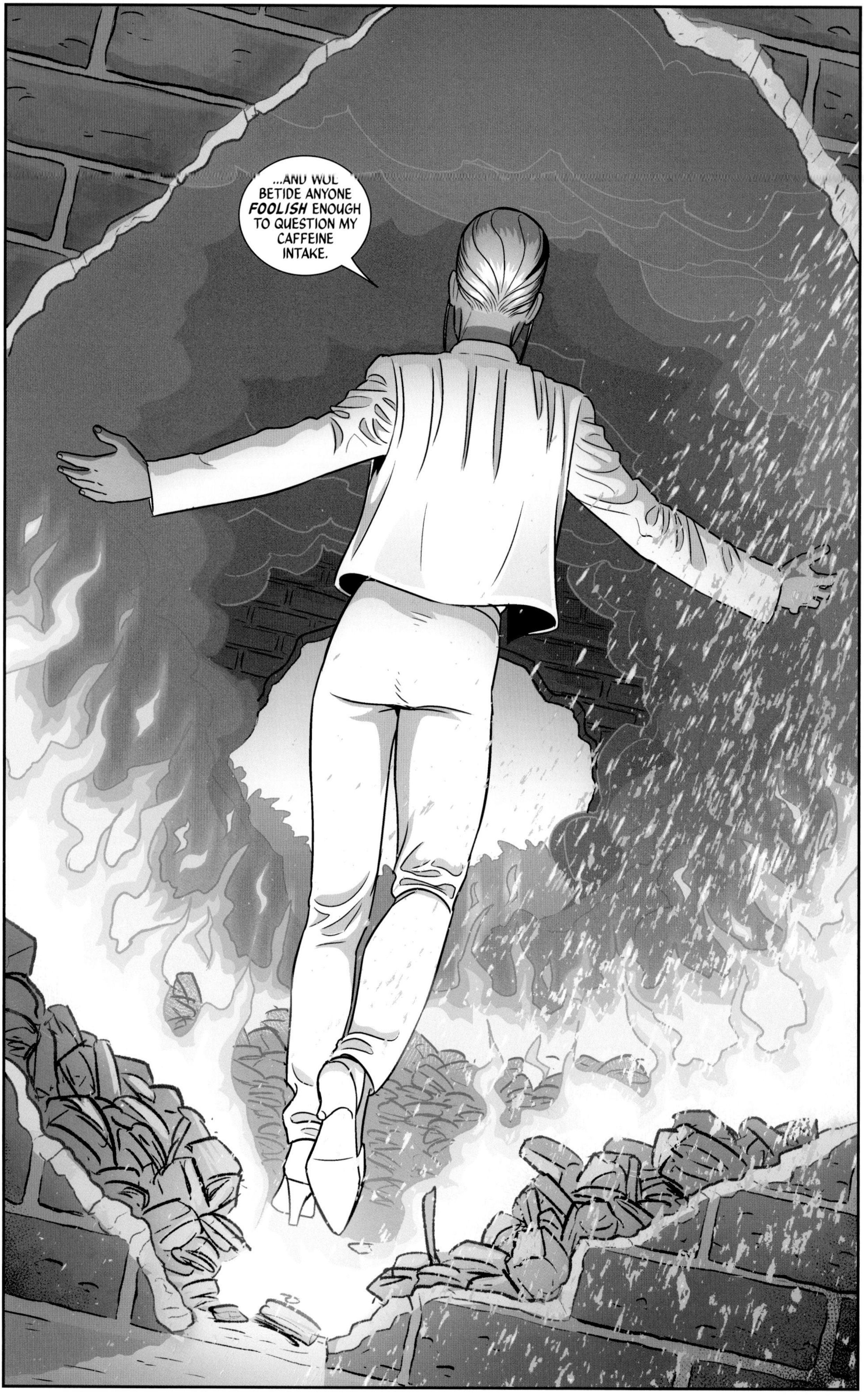
...AND WOE BETIDE ANYONE *FOOLISH* ENOUGH TO QUESTION MY CAFFEINE INTAKE.

THE
WICKED
+
THE
DIVINE

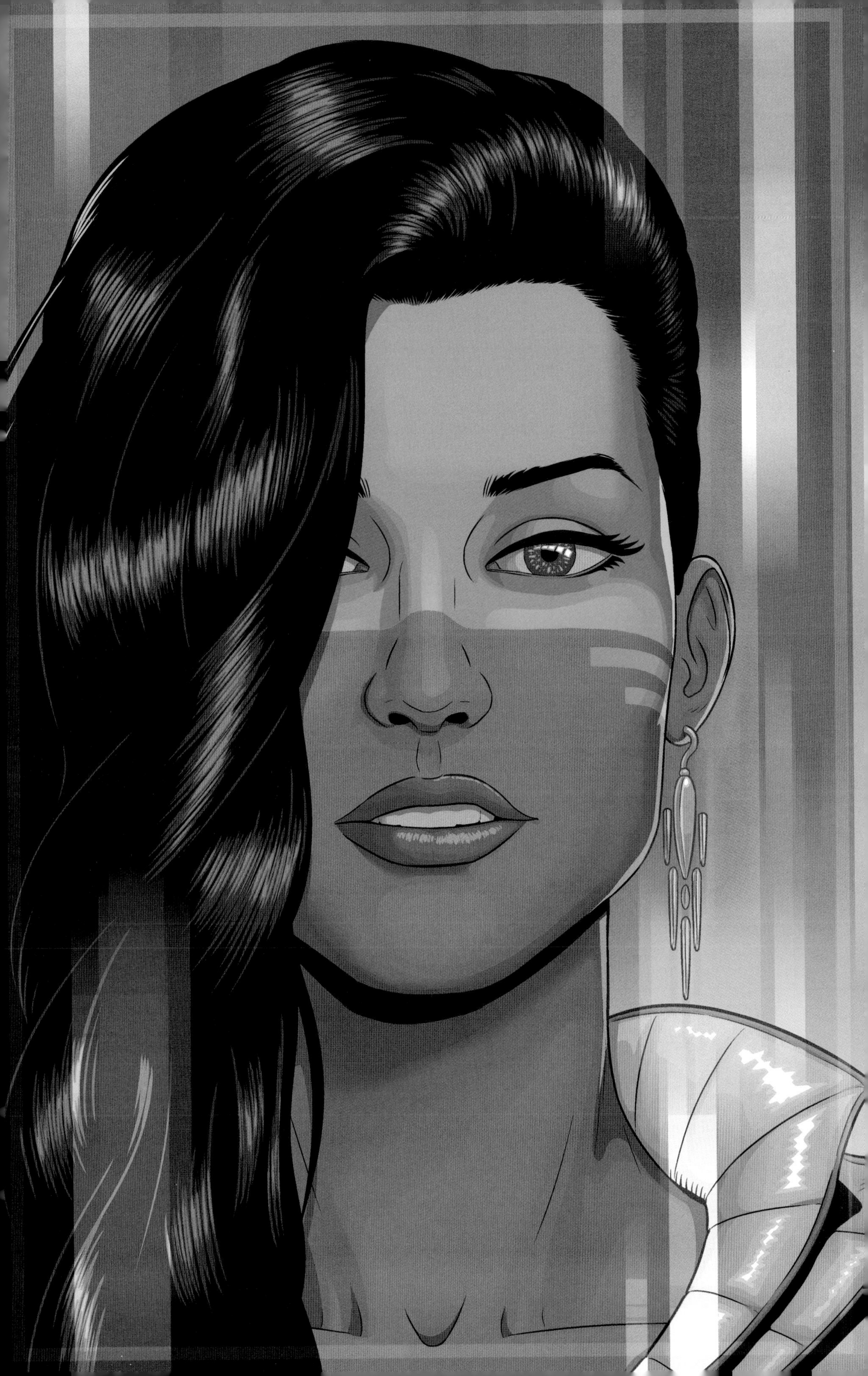

THE
WICKED
+
ƎNIVID
THE

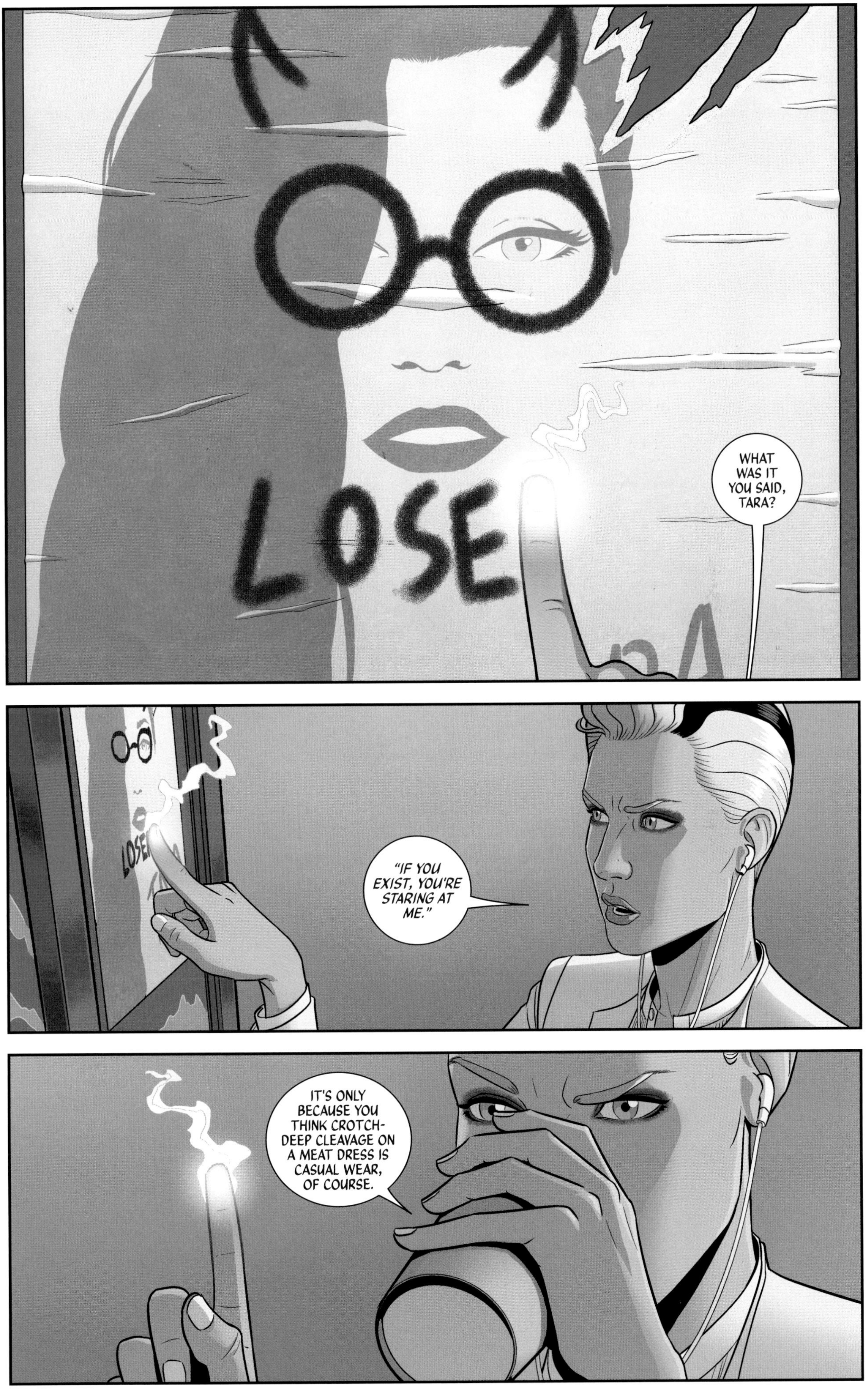
WHAT WAS IT YOU SAID, TARA?
"IF YOU EXIST, YOU'RE STARING AT ME."
IT'S ONLY BECAUSE YOU THINK CROTCH-DEEP CLEAVAGE ON A MEAT DRESS IS CASUAL WEAR, OF COURSE.

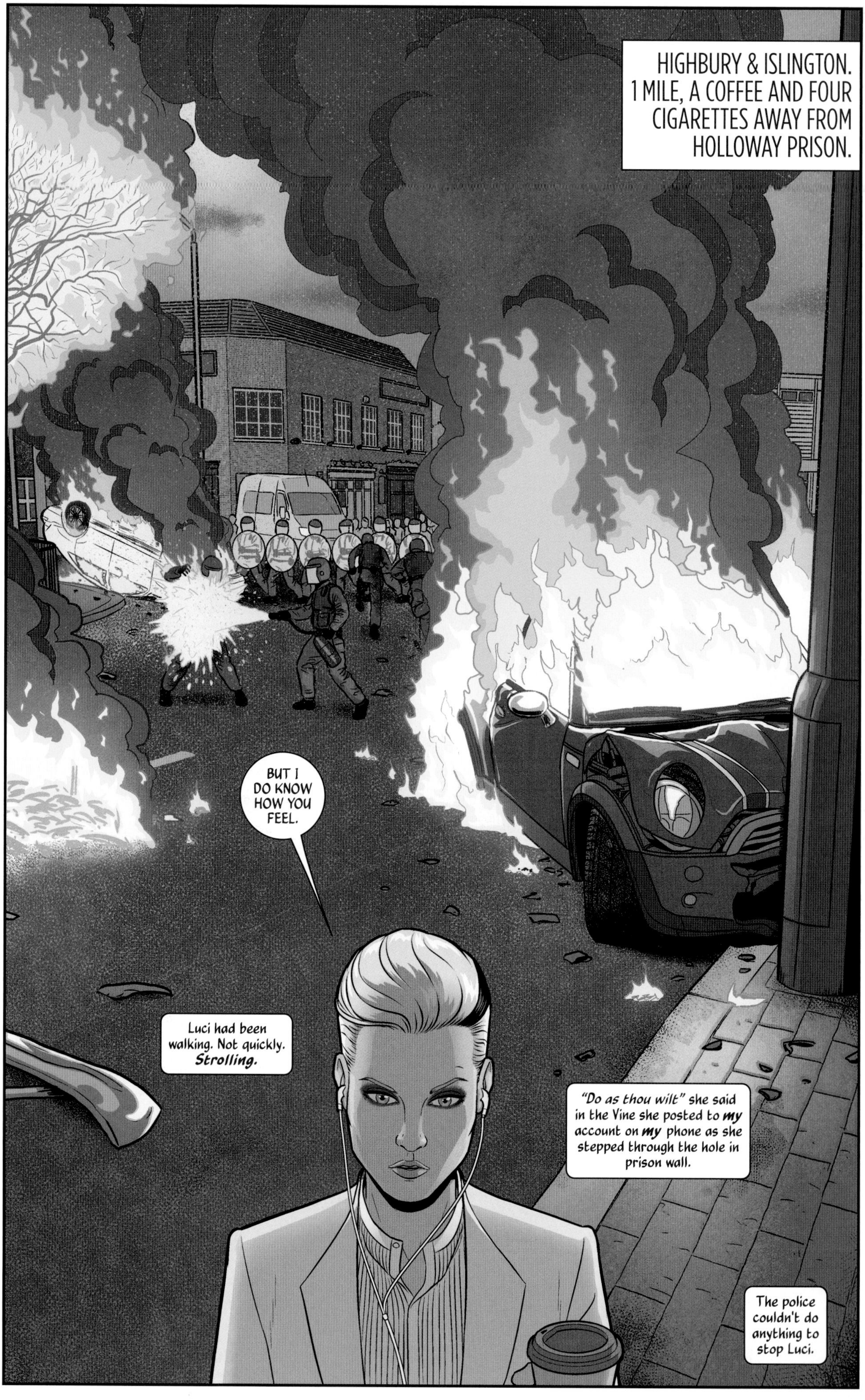

HIGHBURY & ISLINGTON. 1 MILE, A COFFEE AND FOUR CIGARETTES AWAY FROM HOLLOWAY PRISON.
BUT I DO KNOW HOW YOU FEEL.
Luci had been walking. Not quickly. ***Strolling.***
"Do as thou wilt" she said in the Vine she posted to ***my*** account on ***my*** phone as she stepped through the hole in prison wall.
The police couldn't do anything to stop Luci.

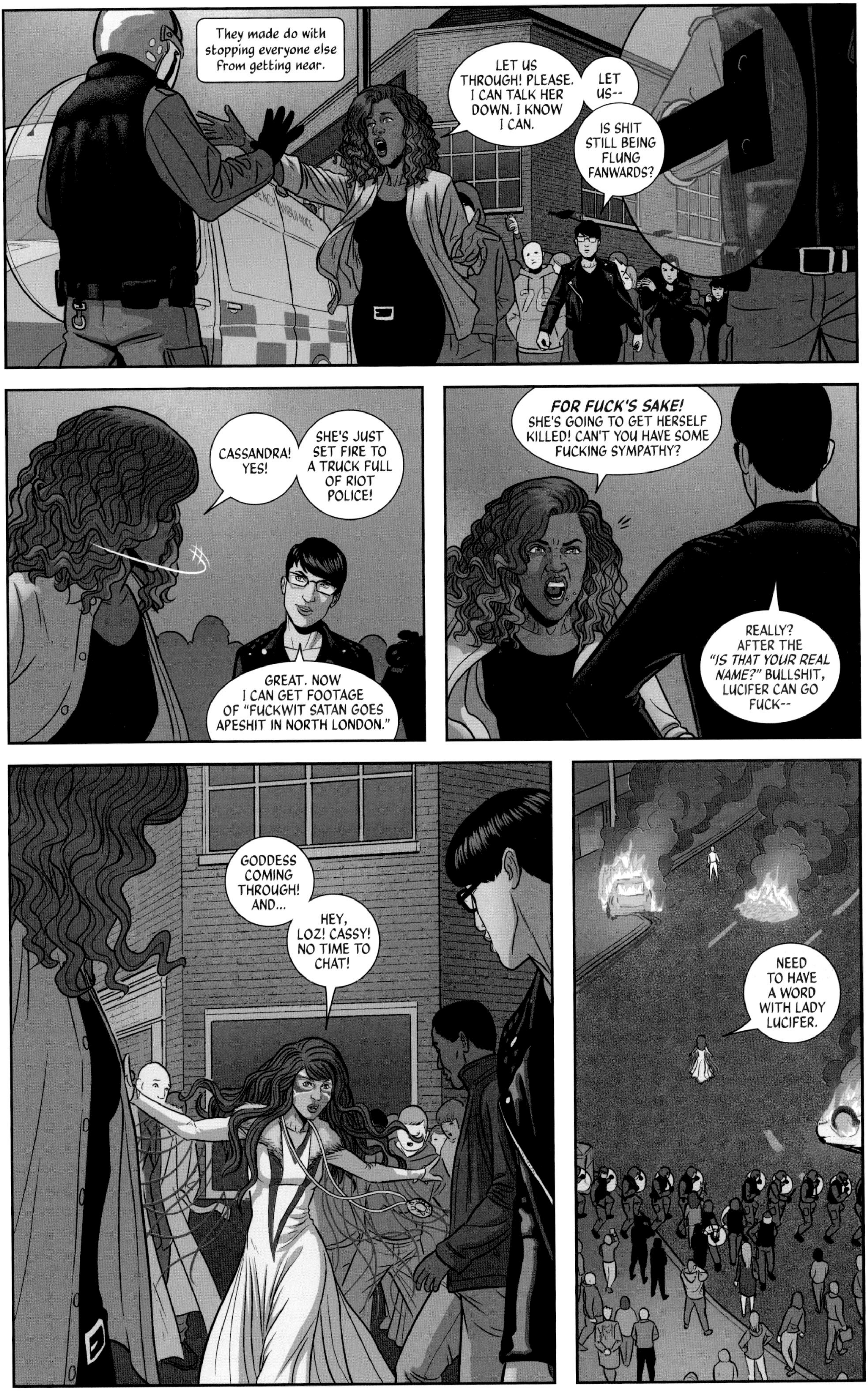
They made do with stopping everyone else from getting near.
LET US THROUGH! PLEASE. I CAN TALK HER DOWN. I KNOW I CAN.
LET US--
IS SHIT STILL BEING FLUNG FANWARDS?
CASSANDRA! YES!
SHE'S JUST SET FIRE TO A TRUCK FULL OF RIOT POLICE!
GREAT. NOW I CAN GET FOOTAGE OF "FUCKWIT SATAN GOES APESHIT IN NORTH LONDON."
FOR FUCK'S SAKE! SHE'S GOING TO GET HERSELF KILLED! CAN'T YOU HAVE SOME FUCKING SYMPATHY?
REALLY? AFTER THE "IS THAT YOUR REAL NAME?" BULLSHIT, LUCIFER CAN GO FUCK--
GODDESS COMING THROUGH! AND...
HEY, LOZ! CASSY! NO TIME TO CHAT!
NEED TO HAVE A WORD WITH LADY LUCIFER.

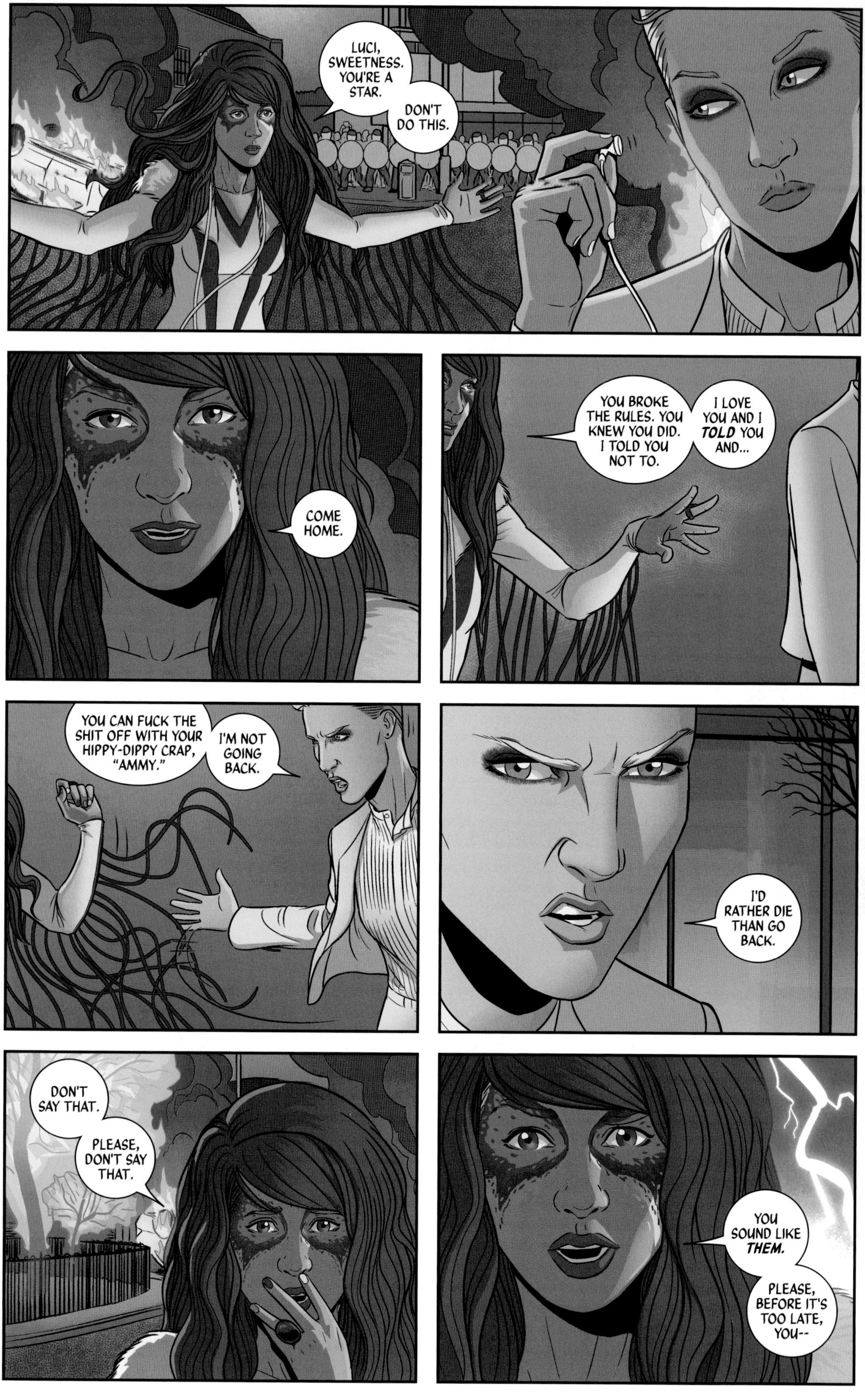
LUCI, SWEETNESS. YOU'RE A STAR.
DON'T DO THIS.
COME HOME.
YOU BROKE THE RULES. YOU KNEW YOU DID. I TOLD YOU NOT TO.
I LOVE YOU AND I ***TOLD*** YOU AND...
YOU CAN FUCK THE SHIT OFF WITH YOUR HIPPY-DIPPY CRAP, "AMMY."
I'M NOT GOING BACK.
I'D RATHER DIE THAN GO BACK.
DON'T SAY THAT.
PLEASE, DON'T SAY THAT.
YOU SOUND LIKE ***THEM.***
PLEASE, BEFORE IT'S TOO LATE, YOU--

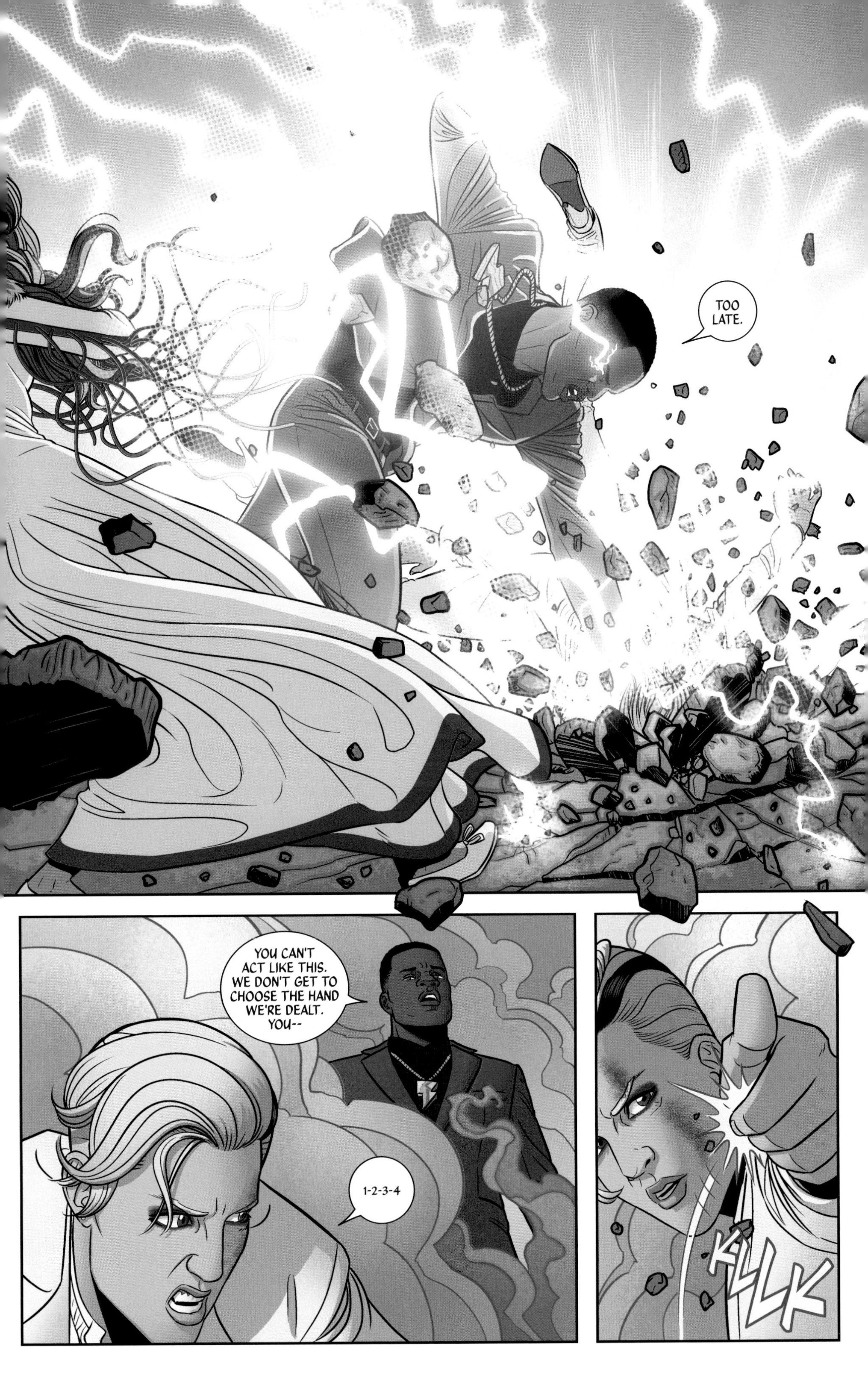
TOO LATE.
YOU CAN'T ACT LIKE THIS. WE DON'T GET TO CHOOSE THE HAND WE'RE DEALT. YOU--
1-2-3-4
KLLK

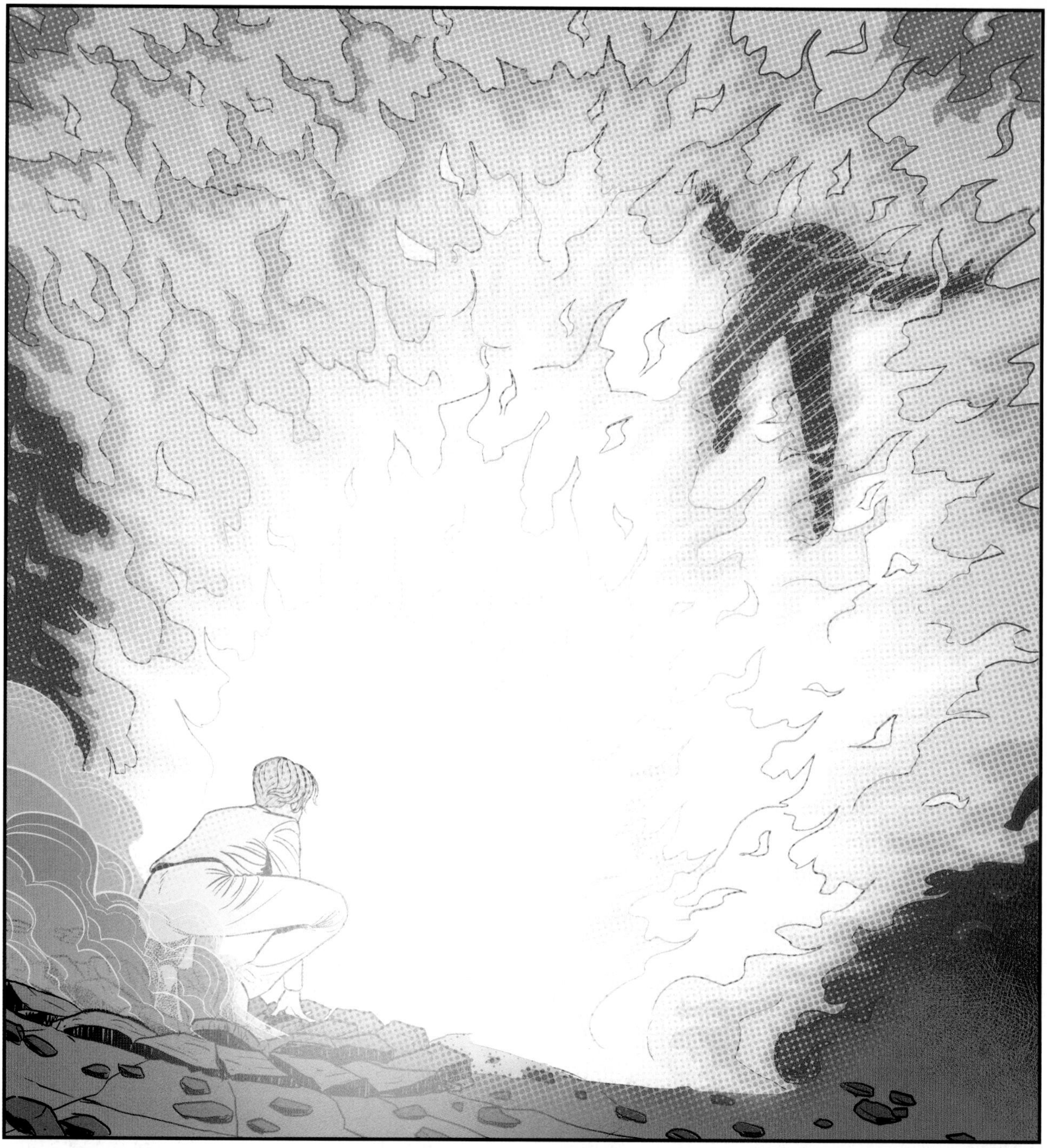

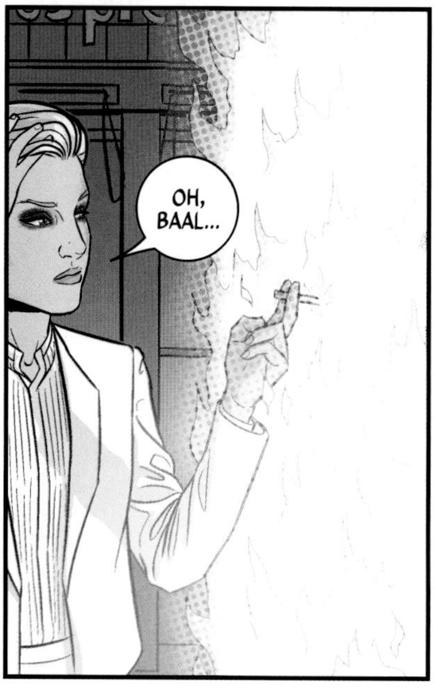
OH, BAAL...

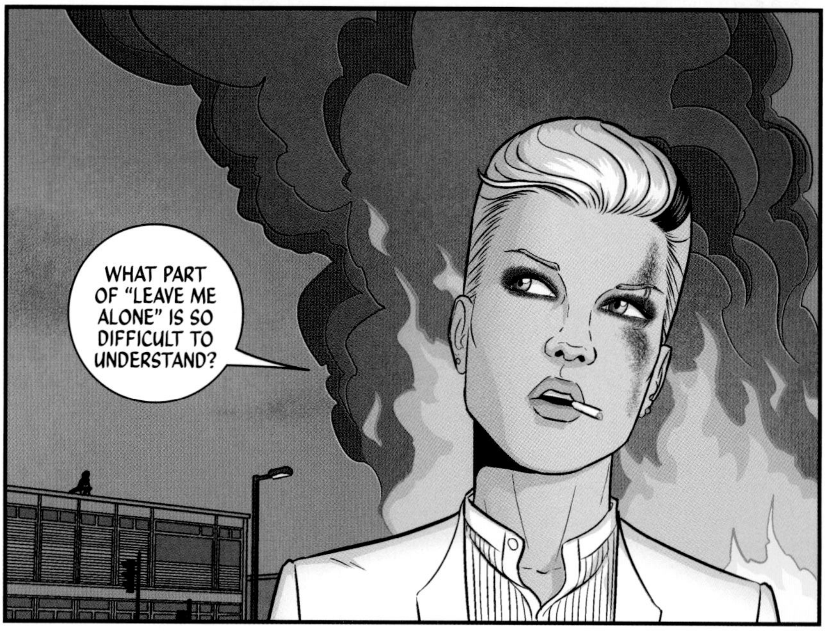
WHAT PART OF "LEAVE ME ALONE" IS SO DIFFICULT TO UNDERSTAND?

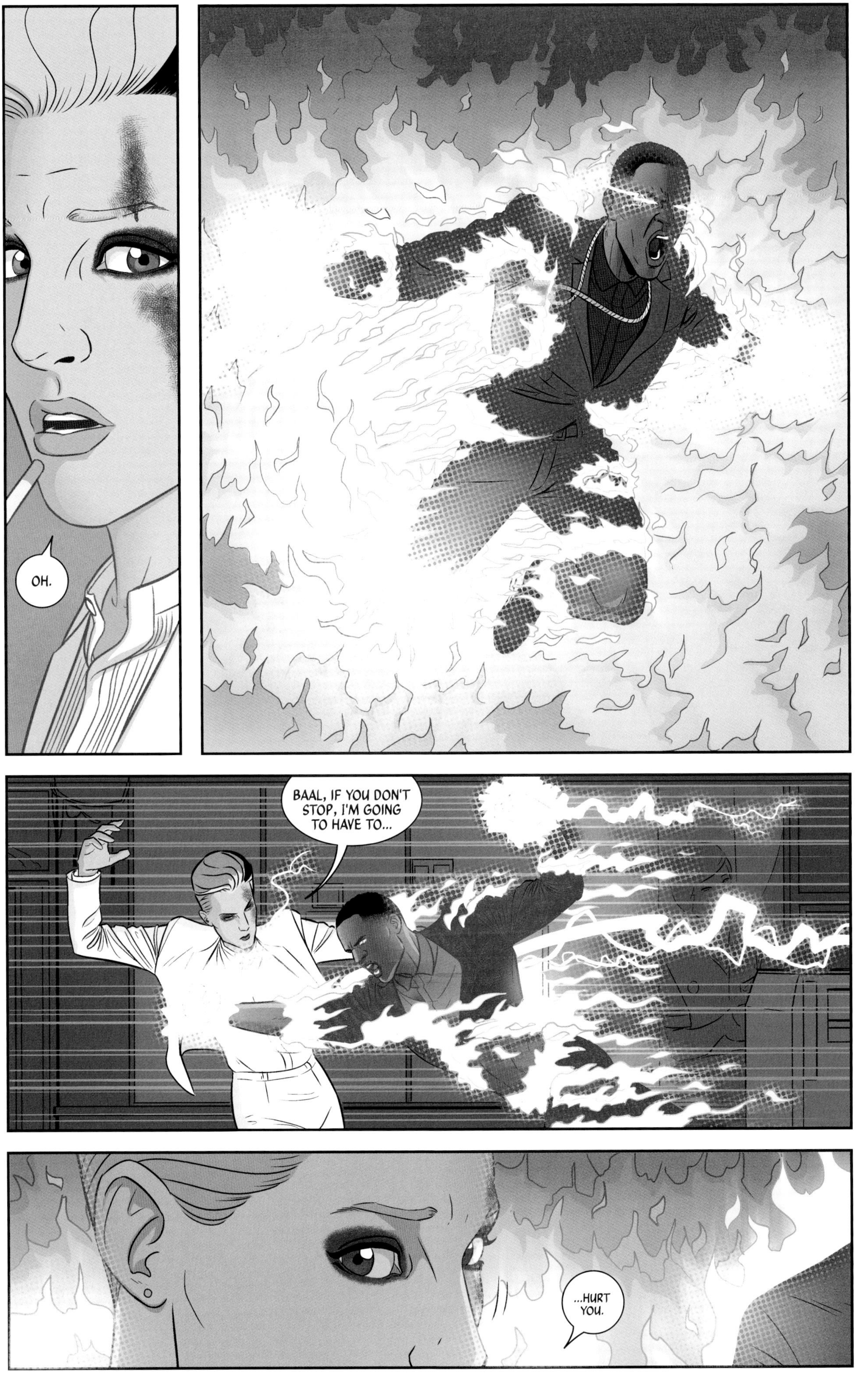
OH.
BAAL, IF YOU DON'T STOP, I'M GOING TO HAVE TO...
...HURT YOU.

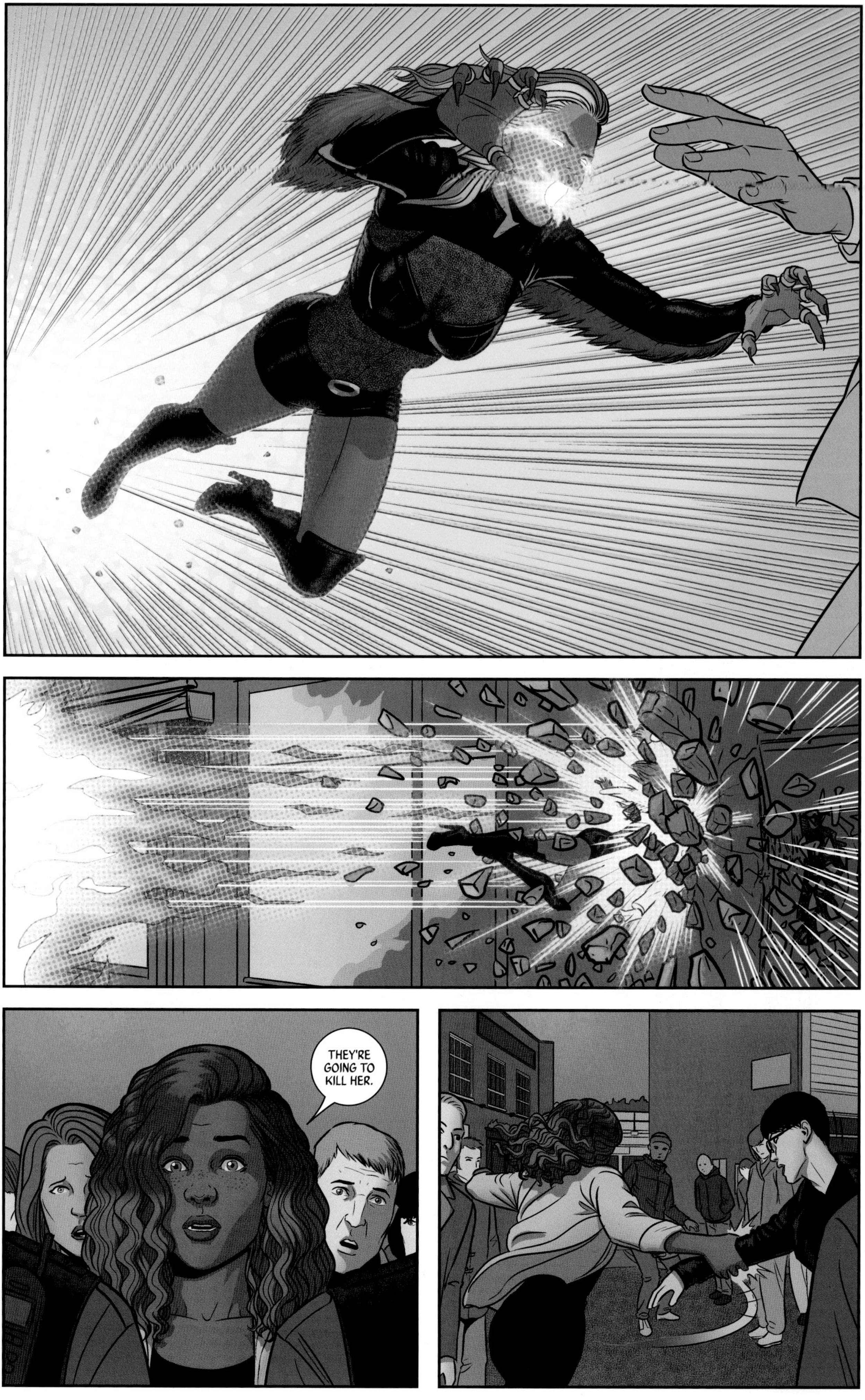
THEY'RE GOING TO KILL HER.

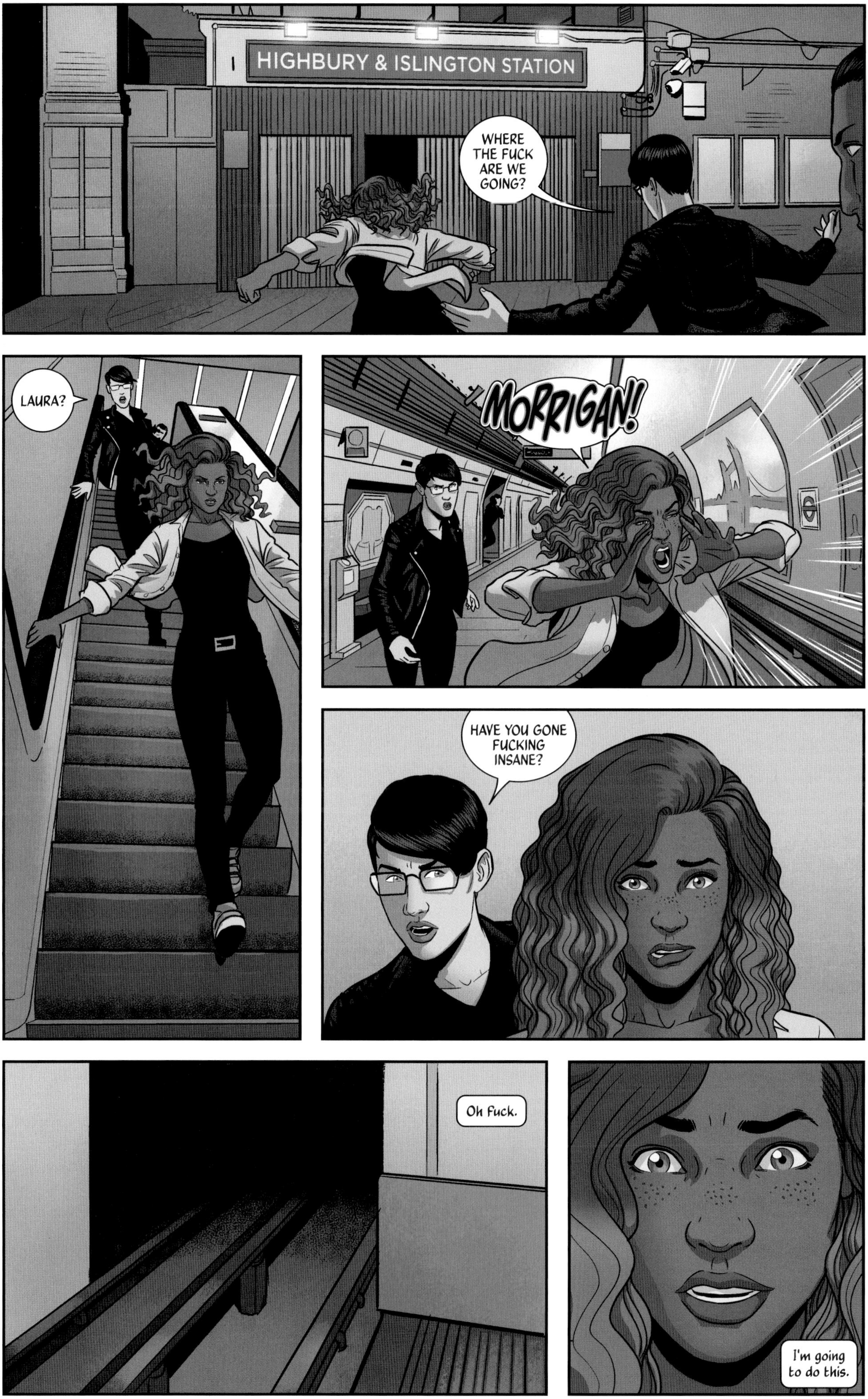
HIGHBURY & ISLINGTON STATION
WHERE THE FUCK ARE WE GOING?
LAURA?
MORRIGAN!
HAVE YOU GONE FUCKING INSANE?
Oh fuck.
I'm going to do this.

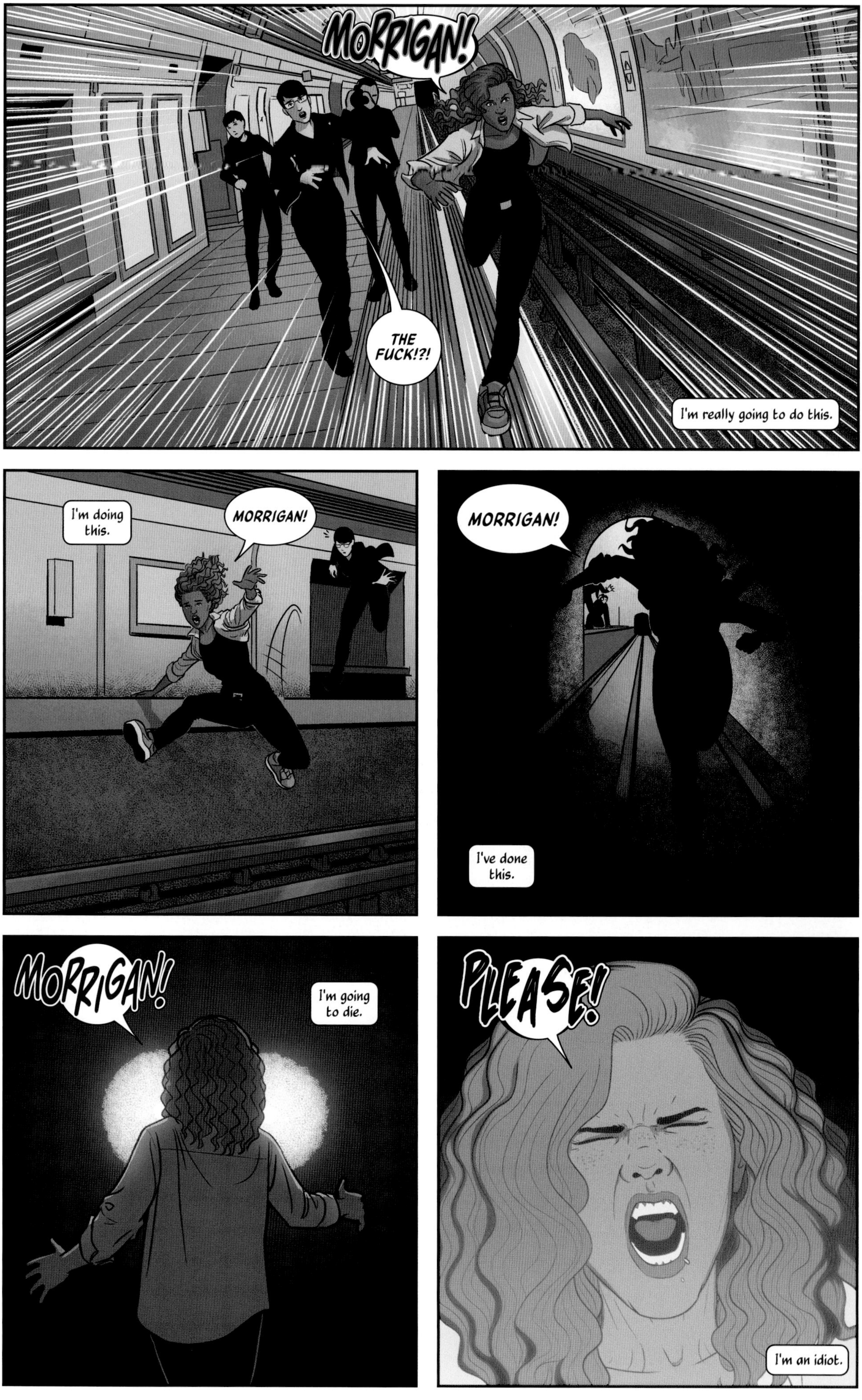
MORRIGAN!
THE FUCK!?!
I'm really going to do this.
I'm doing this.
MORRIGAN!
MORRIGAN!
I've done this.
MORRIGAN!
I'm going to die.
PLEASE!
I'm an idiot.

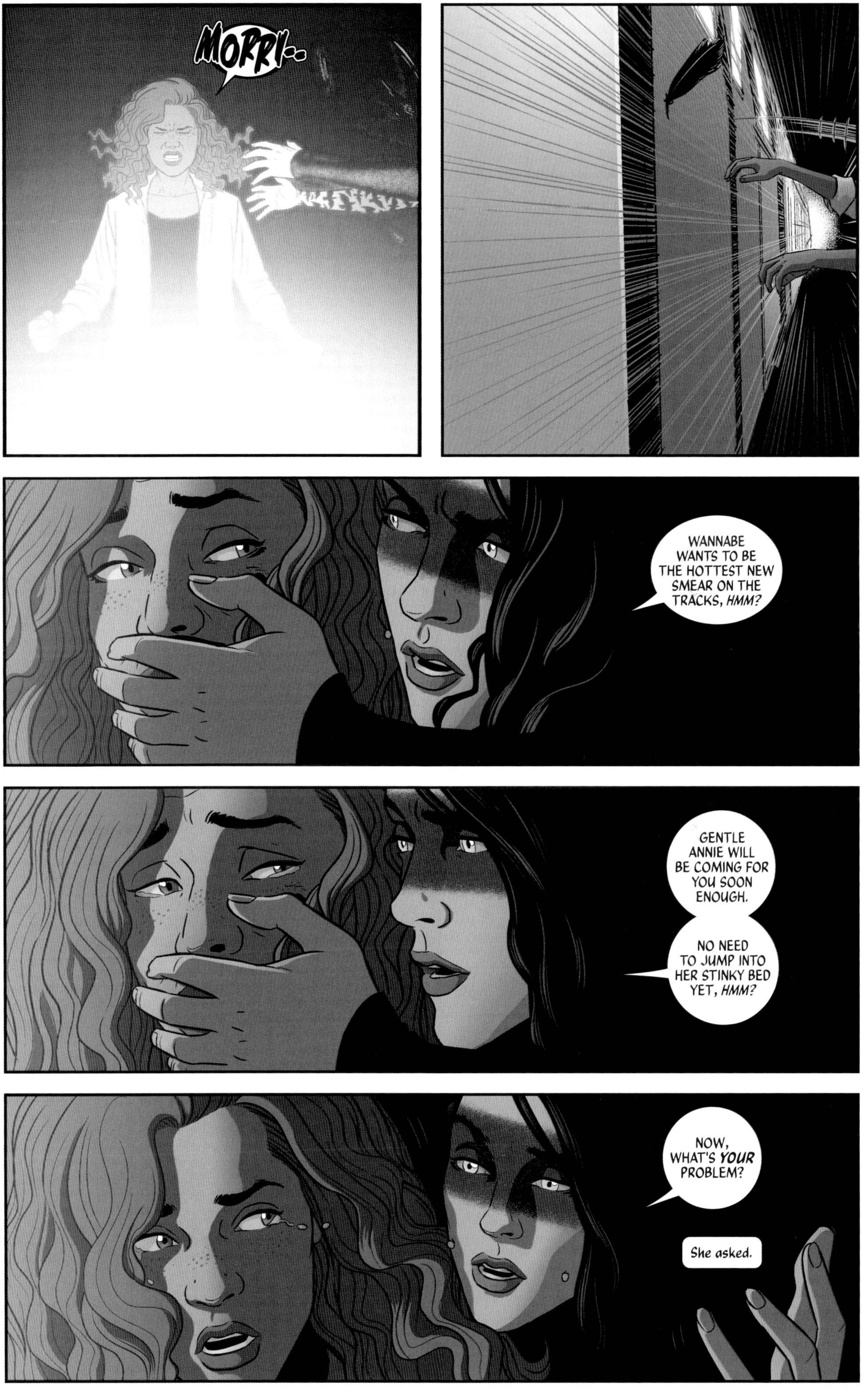
MORRI-..
WANNABE WANTS TO BE THE HOTTEST NEW SMEAR ON THE TRACKS, *HMM?*
GENTLE ANNIE WILL BE COMING FOR YOU SOON ENOUGH.
NO NEED TO JUMP INTO HER STINKY BED YET, *HMM?*
NOW, WHAT'S ***YOUR*** PROBLEM?
She asked.

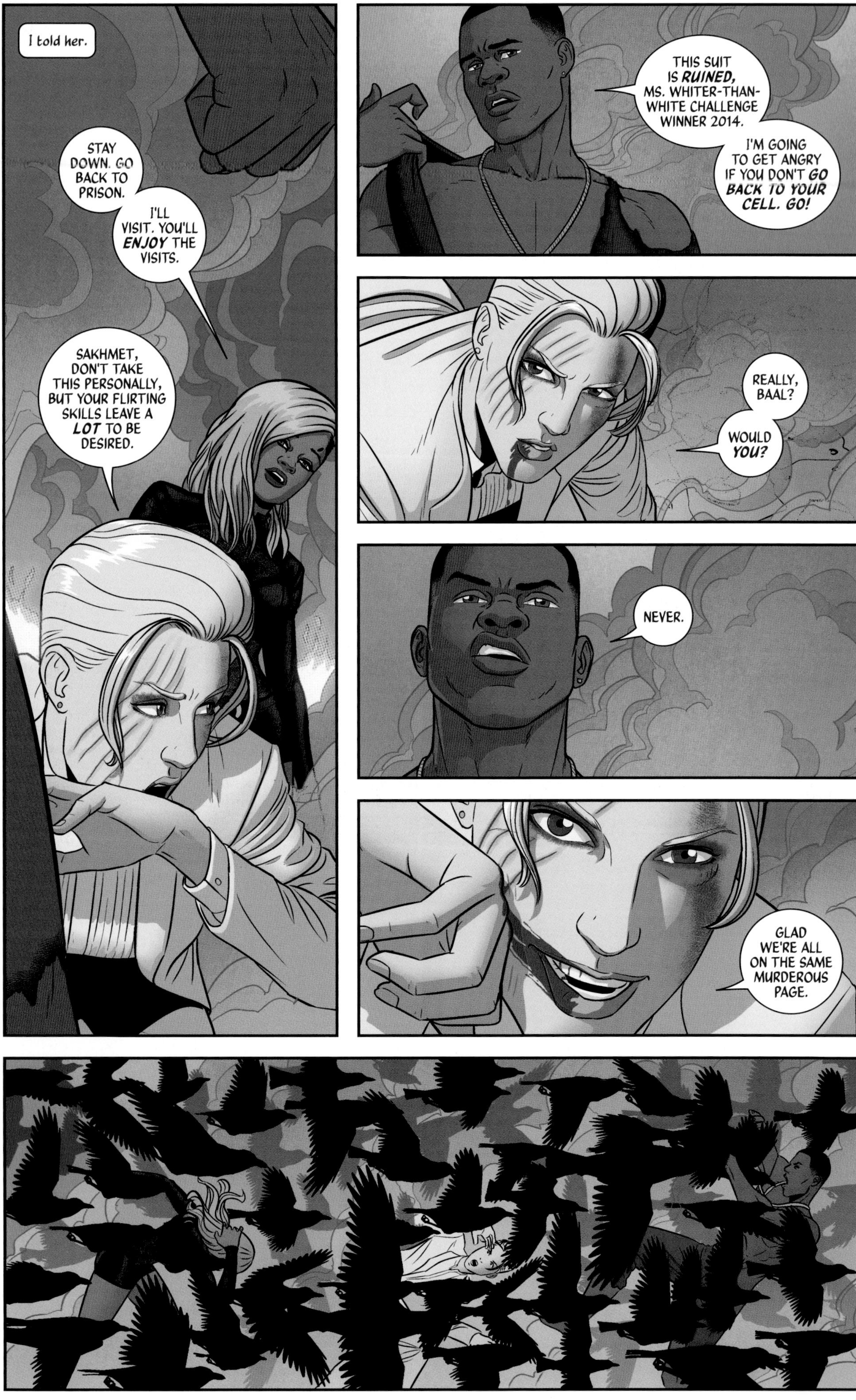
I told her.
STAY DOWN. GO BACK TO PRISON.
I'LL VISIT. YOU'LL ENJOY THE VISITS.
SAKHMET, DON'T TAKE THIS PERSONALLY, BUT YOUR FLIRTING SKILLS LEAVE A LOT TO BE DESIRED.
THIS SUIT IS RUINED, MS. WHITER-THAN-WHITE CHALLENGE WINNER 2014.
I'M GOING TO GET ANGRY IF YOU DON'T GO BACK TO YOUR CELL. GO!
REALLY, BAAL?
WOULD YOU?
NEVER.
GLAD WE'RE ALL ON THE SAME MURDEROUS PAGE.

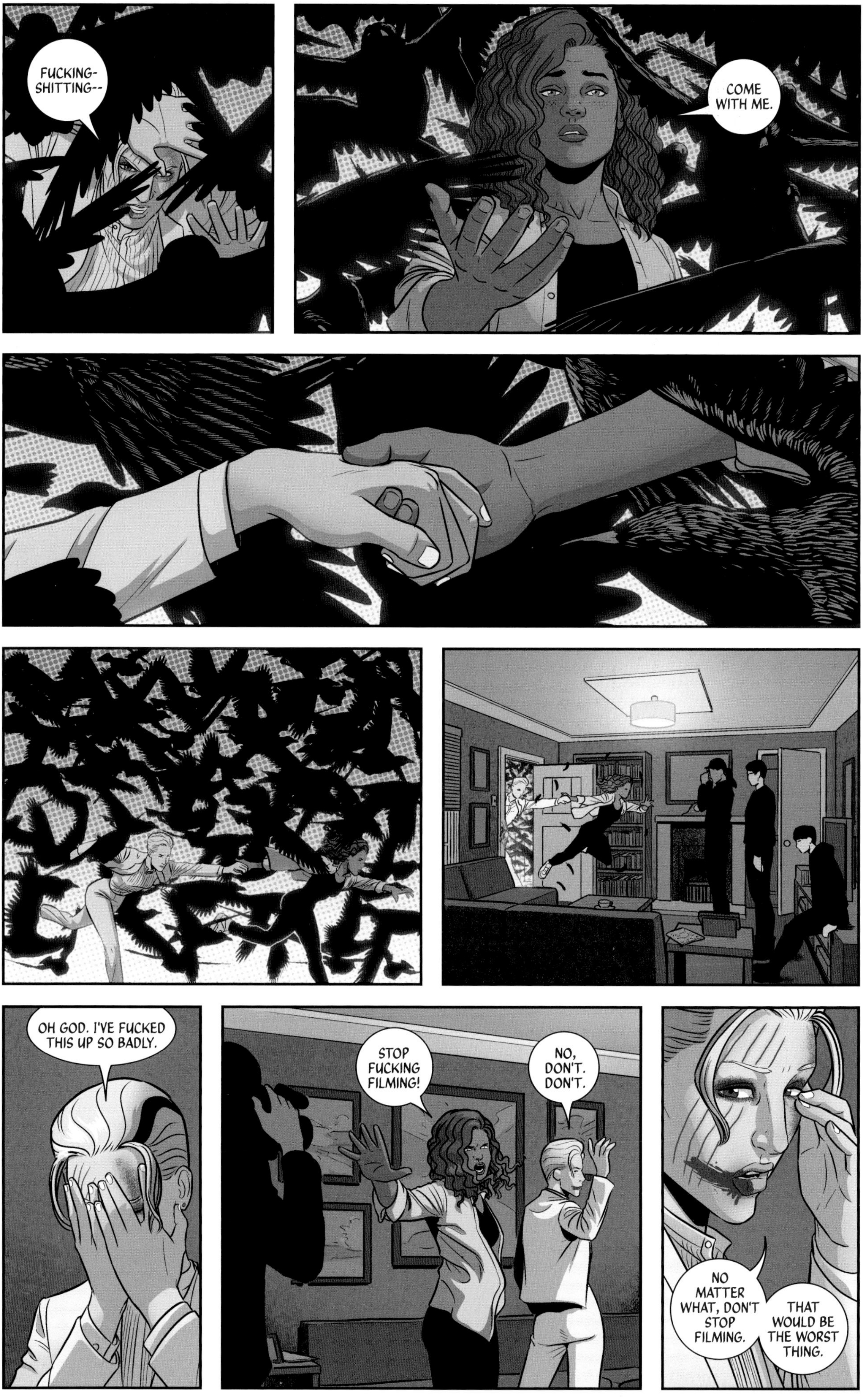
FUCKING-SHITTING--
COME WITH ME.
OH GOD. I'VE FUCKED THIS UP SO BADLY.
STOP FUCKING FILMING!
NO, DON'T. DON'T.
NO MATTER WHAT, DON'T STOP FILMING.
THAT WOULD BE THE WORST THING.

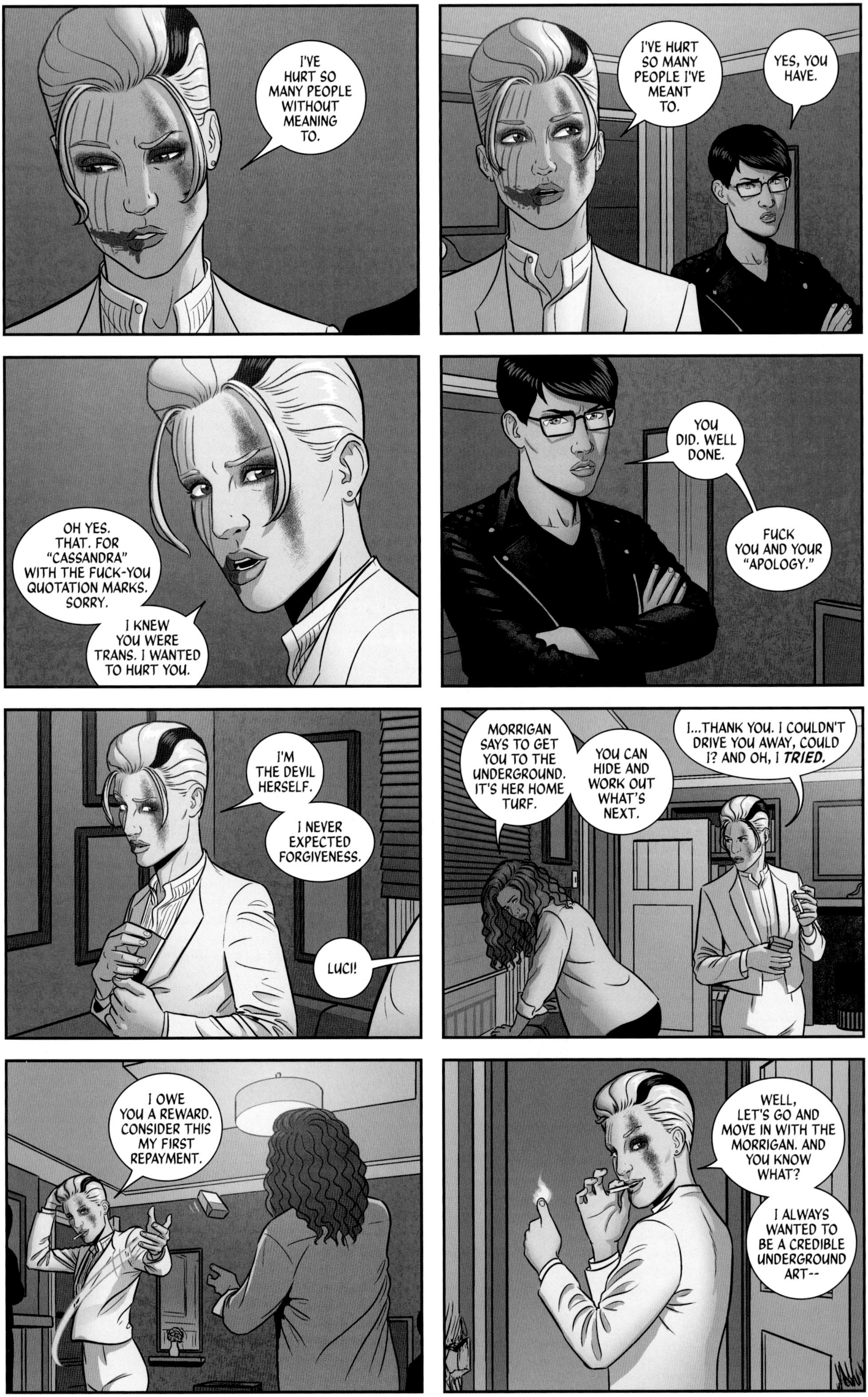
I'VE HURT SO MANY PEOPLE WITHOUT MEANING TO.
I'VE HURT SO MANY PEOPLE I'VE MEANT TO.
YES, YOU HAVE.
OH YES. THAT. FOR "CASSANDRA" WITH THE FUCK-YOU QUOTATION MARKS. SORRY.
I KNEW YOU WERE TRANS. I WANTED TO HURT YOU.
YOU DID. WELL DONE.
FUCK YOU AND YOUR "APOLOGY."
I'M THE DEVIL HERSELF.
I NEVER EXPECTED FORGIVENESS.
LUCI!
MORRIGAN SAYS TO GET YOU TO THE UNDERGROUND. IT'S HER HOME TURF.
YOU CAN HIDE AND WORK OUT WHAT'S NEXT.
I...THANK YOU. I COULDN'T DRIVE YOU AWAY, COULD I? AND OH, I *TRIED.*
I OWE YOU A REWARD. CONSIDER THIS MY FIRST REPAYMENT.
WELL, LET'S GO AND MOVE IN WITH THE MORRIGAN. AND YOU KNOW WHAT?
I ALWAYS WANTED TO BE A CREDIBLE UNDERGROUND ART--

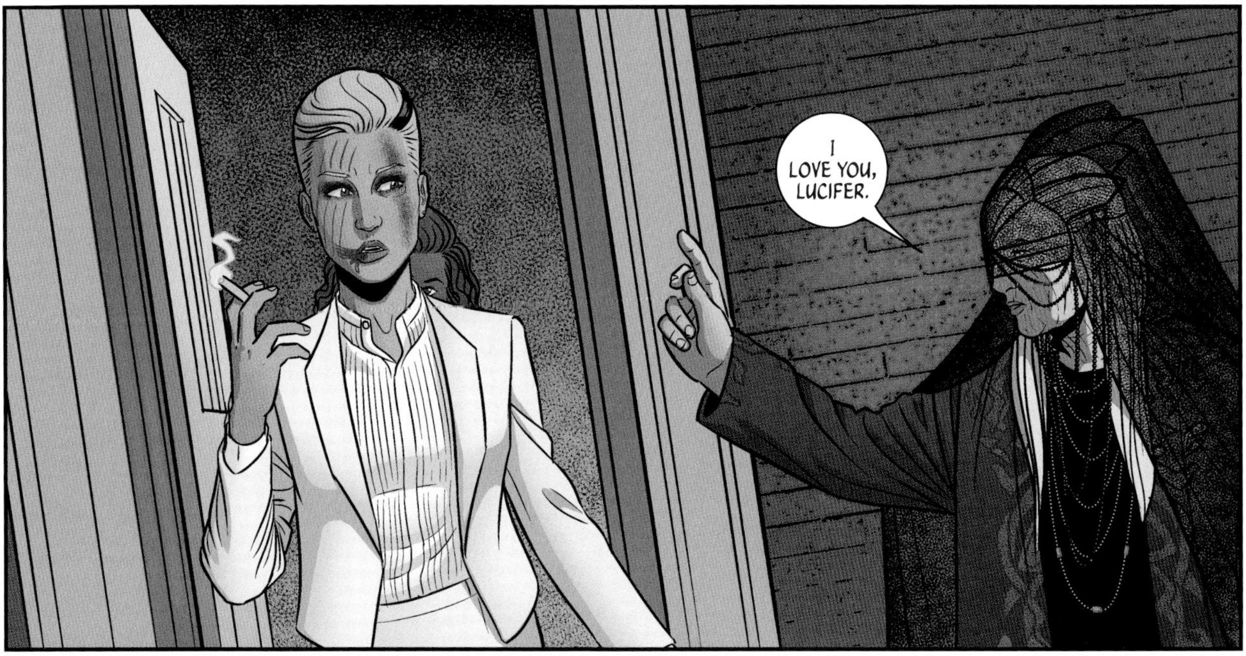
I LOVE YOU, LUCIFER.
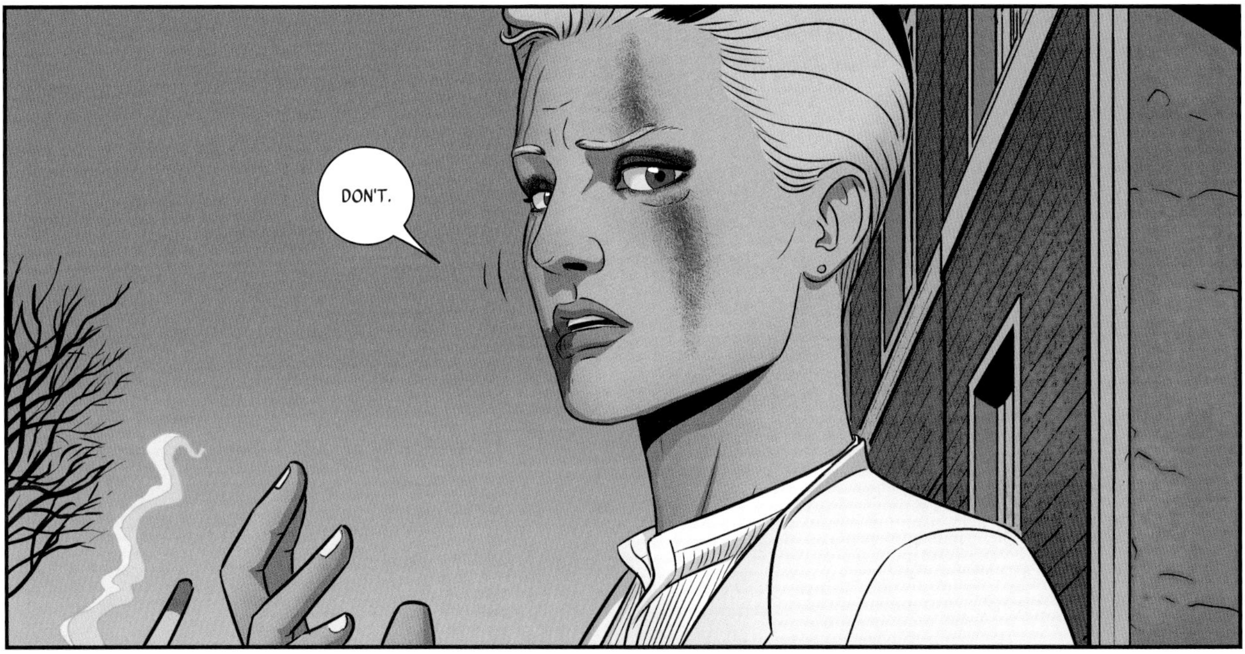
DON'T.
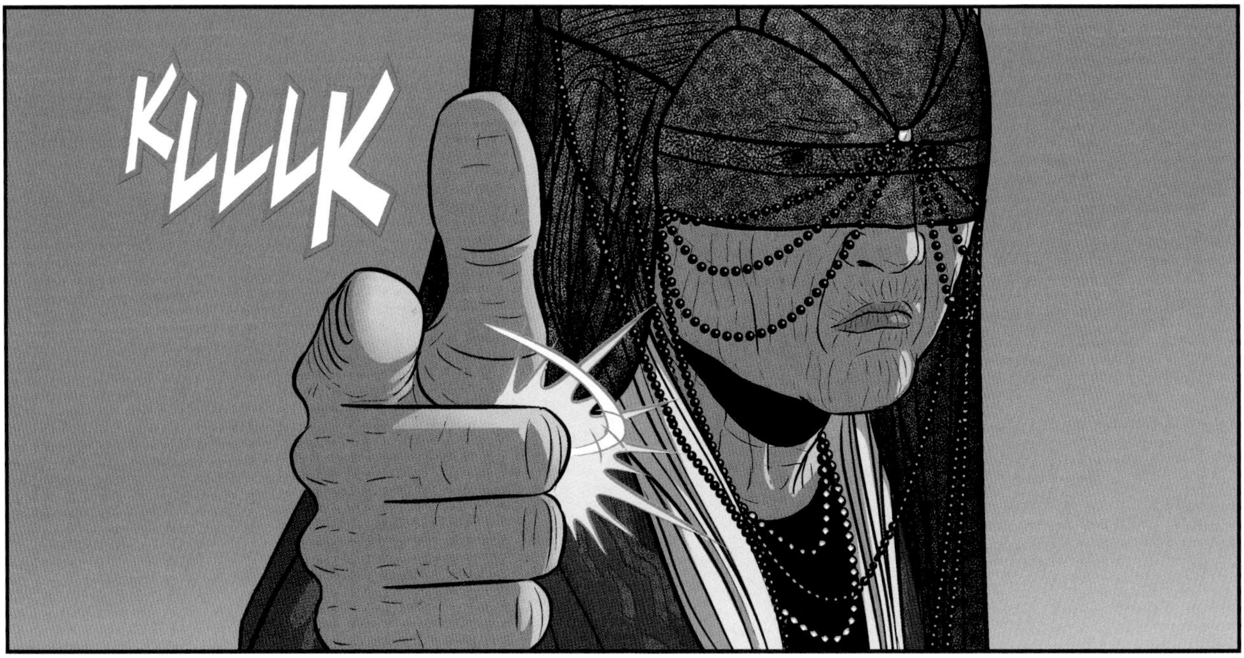
KLLLK

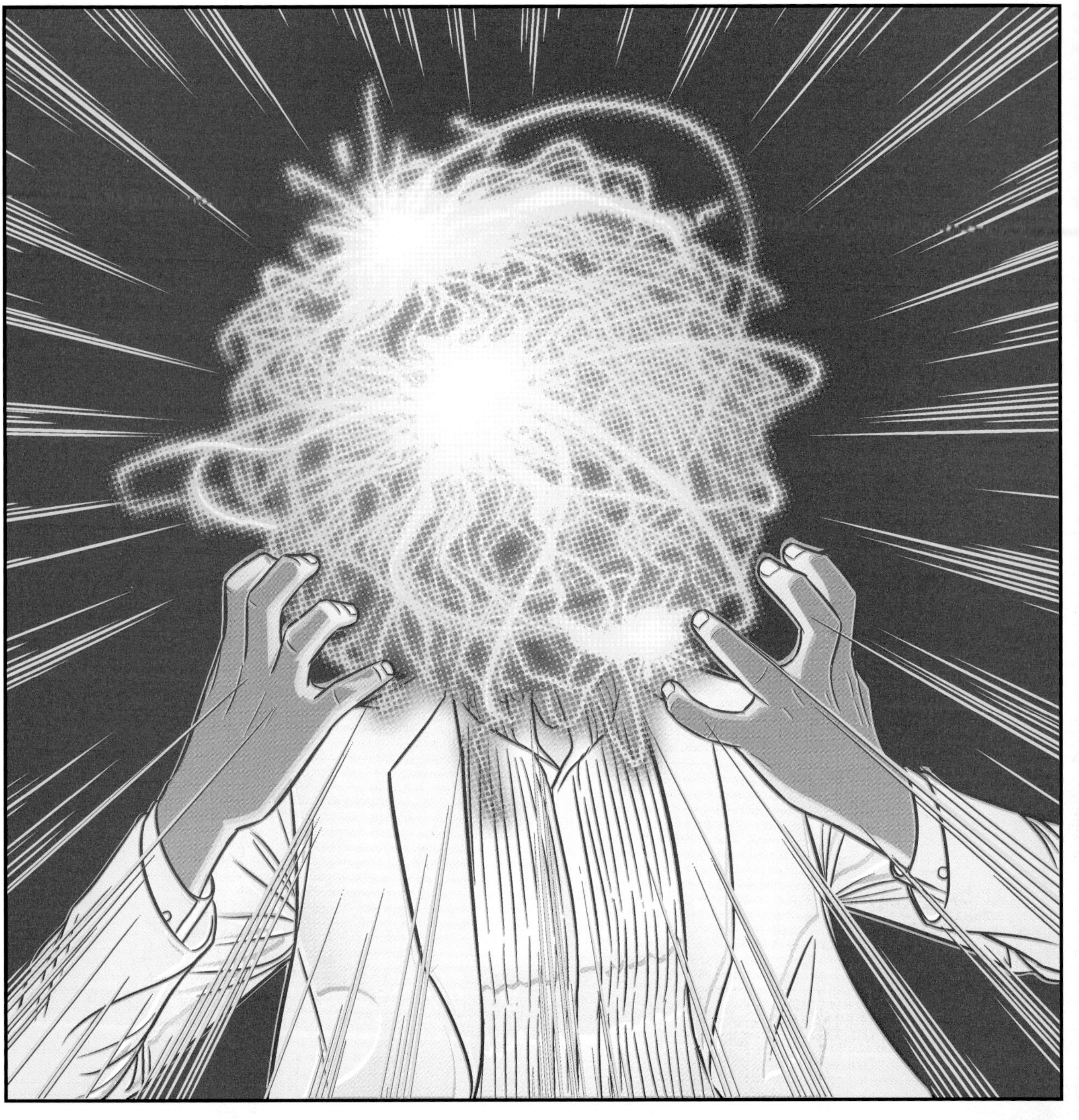
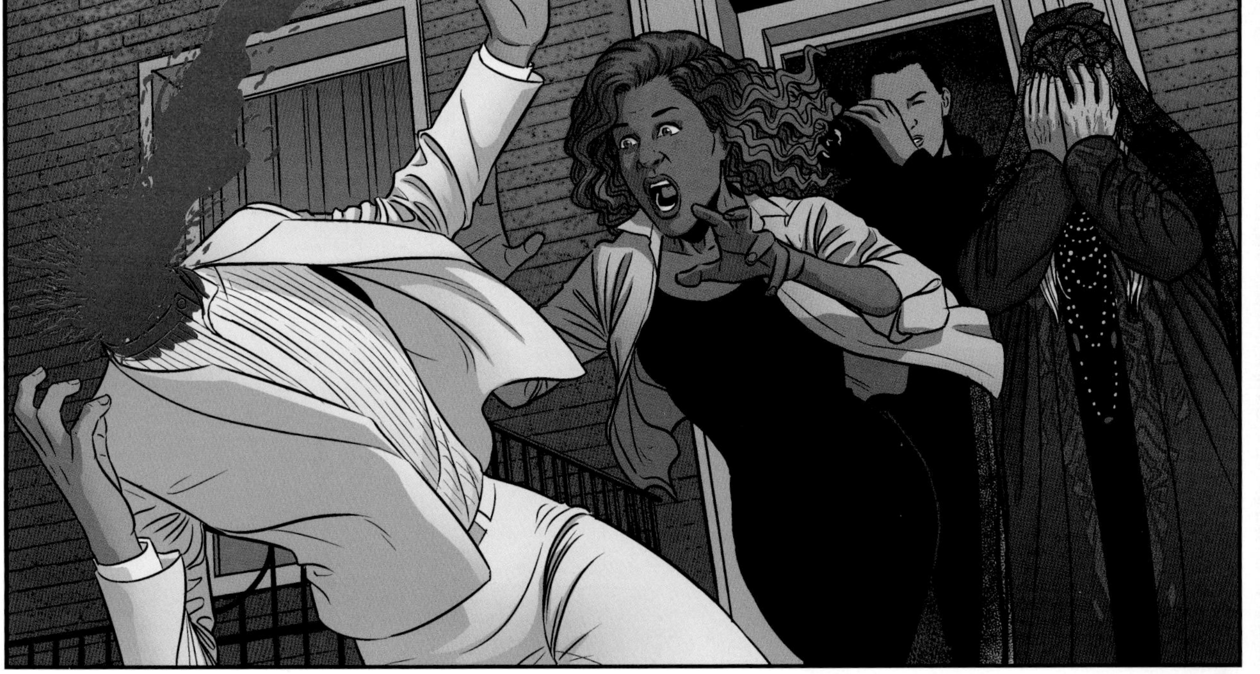

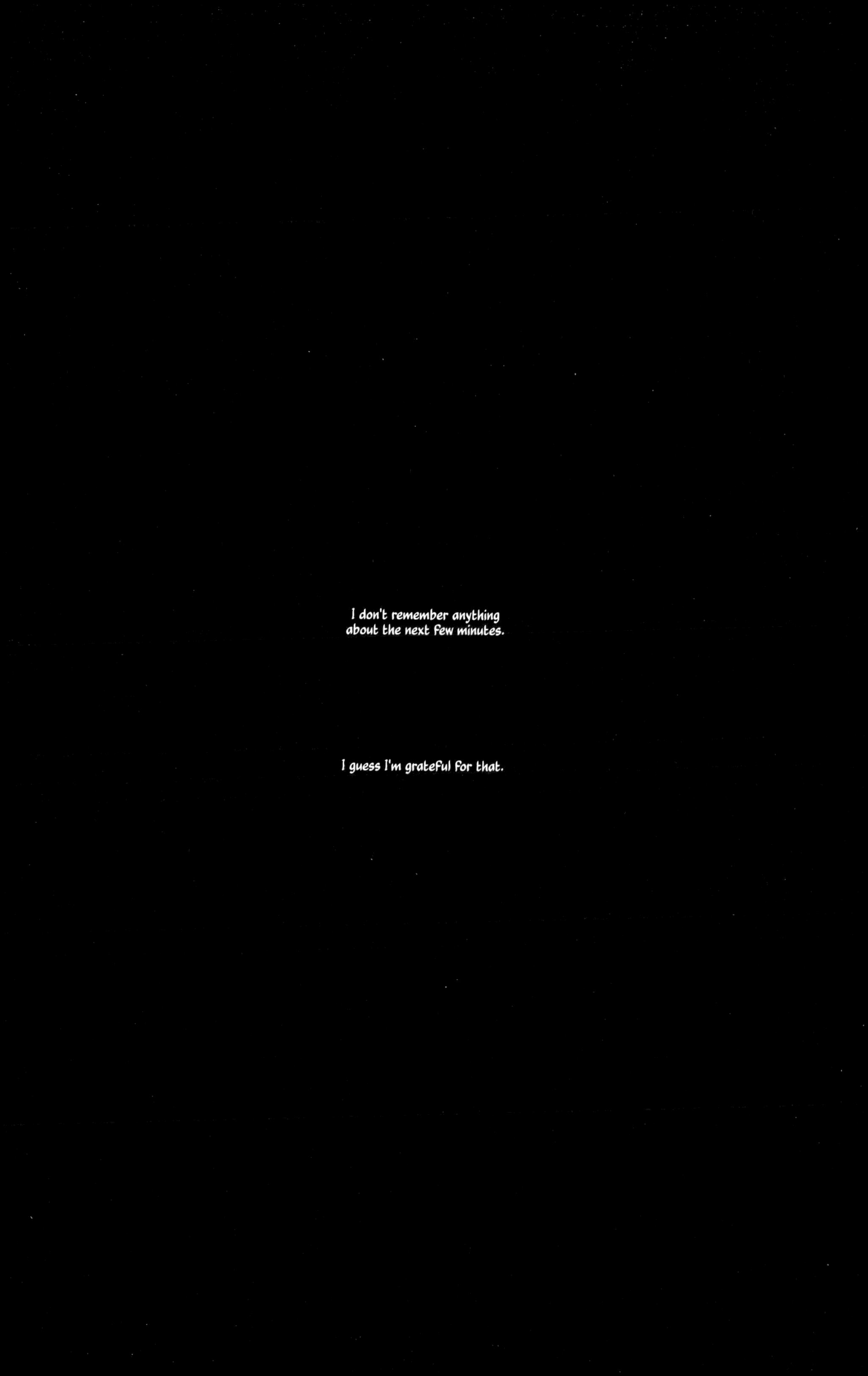
I don't remember anything about the next few minutes.
I guess I'm grateful for that.

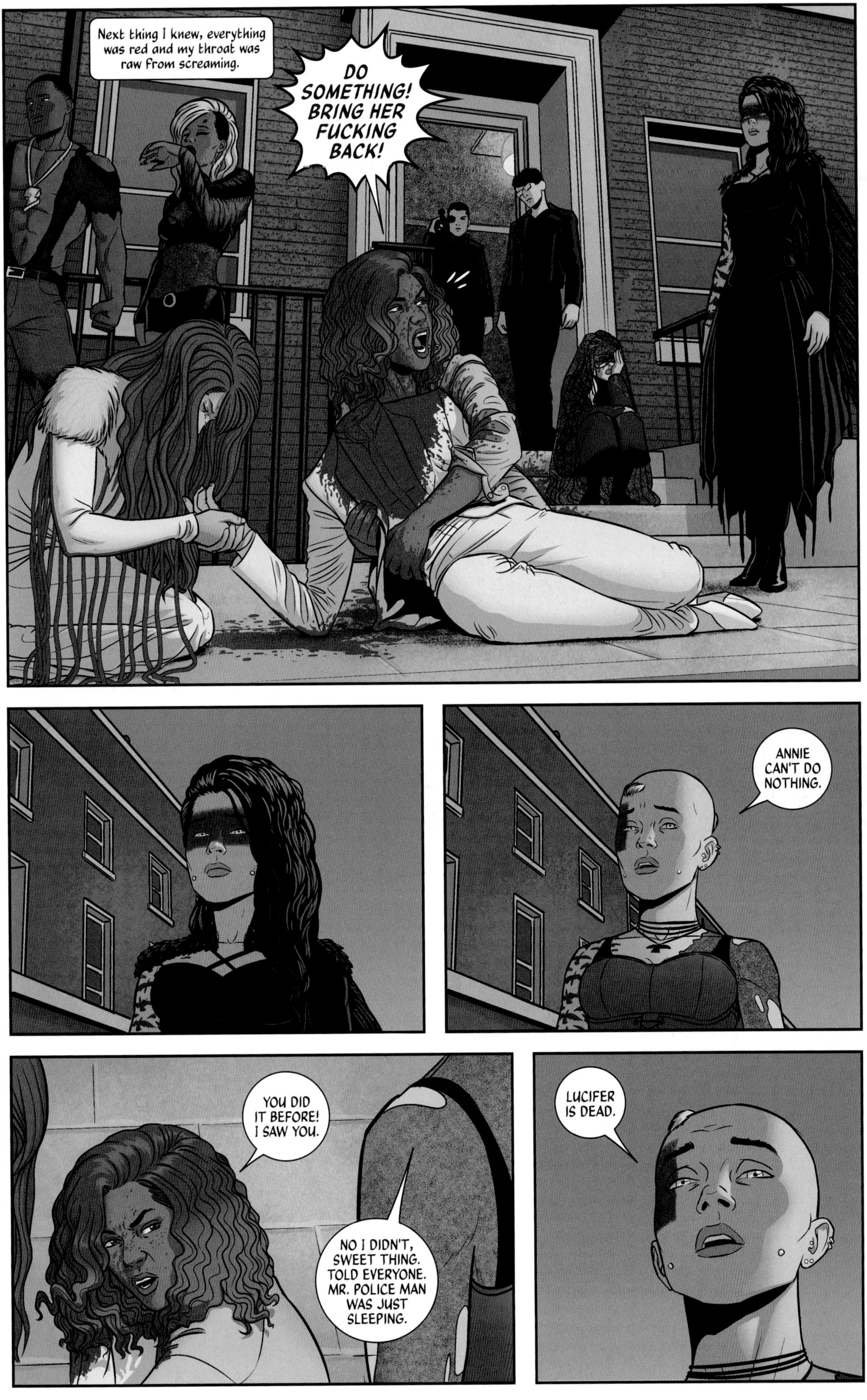
Next thing I knew, everything was red and my throat was raw from screaming.
DO SOMETHING! BRING HER FUCKING BACK!
ANNIE CAN'T DO NOTHING.
YOU DID IT BEFORE! I SAW YOU.
NO I DIDN'T, SWEET THING. TOLD EVERYONE. MR. POLICE MAN WAS JUST SLEEPING.
LUCIFER IS DEAD.

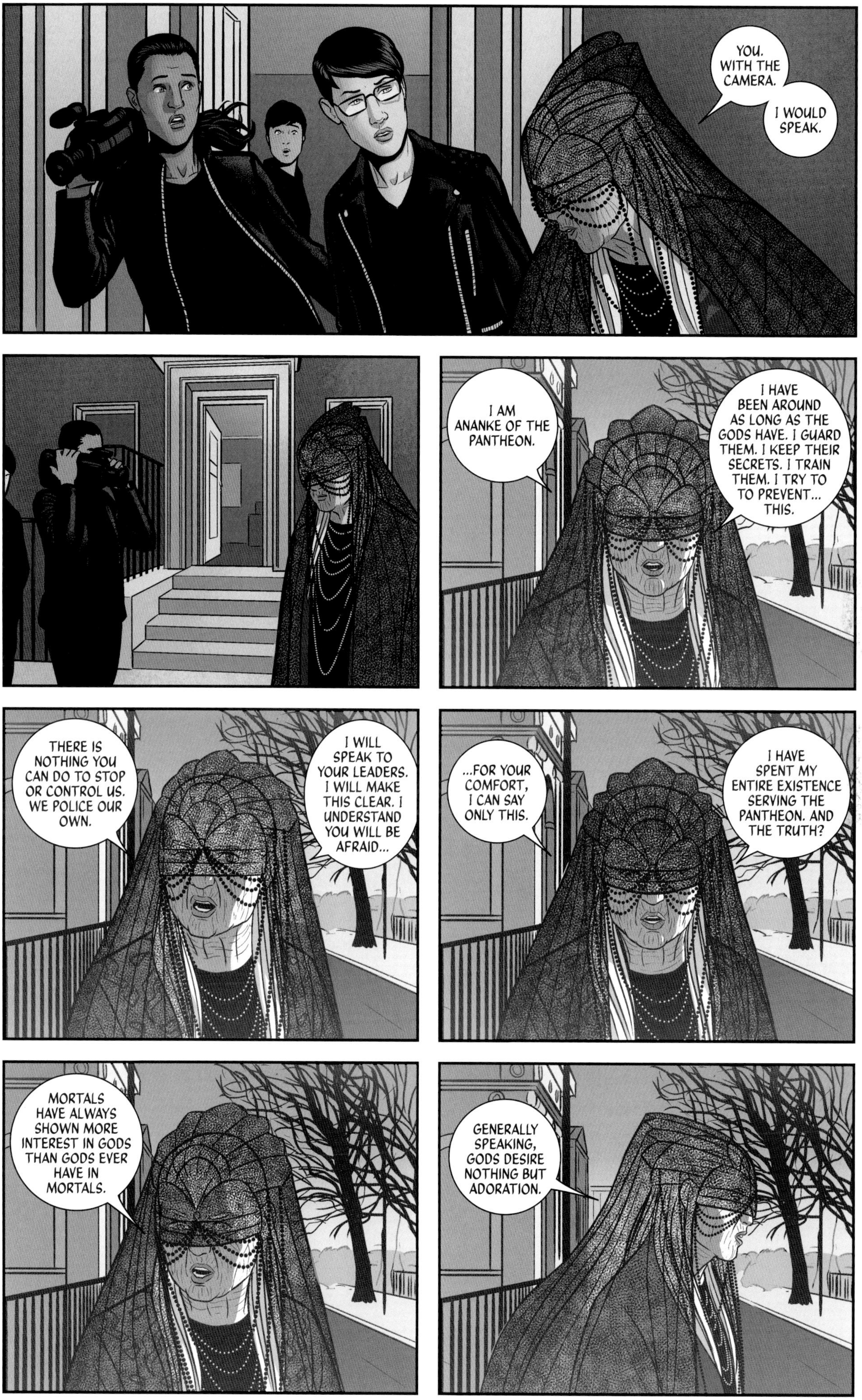
YOU. WITH THE CAMERA.
I WOULD SPEAK.
I AM ANANKE OF THE PANTHEON.
I HAVE BEEN AROUND AS LONG AS THE GODS HAVE. I GUARD THEM. I KEEP THEIR SECRETS. I TRAIN THEM. I TRY TO TO PREVENT... THIS.
THERE IS NOTHING YOU CAN DO TO STOP OR CONTROL US. WE POLICE OUR OWN.
I WILL SPEAK TO YOUR LEADERS. I WILL MAKE THIS CLEAR. I UNDERSTAND YOU WILL BE AFRAID...
...FOR YOUR COMFORT, I CAN SAY ONLY THIS.
I HAVE SPENT MY ENTIRE EXISTENCE SERVING THE PANTHEON. AND THE TRUTH?
MORTALS HAVE ALWAYS SHOWN MORE INTEREST IN GODS THAN GODS EVER HAVE IN MORTALS.
GENERALLY SPEAKING, GODS DESIRE NOTHING BUT ADORATION.

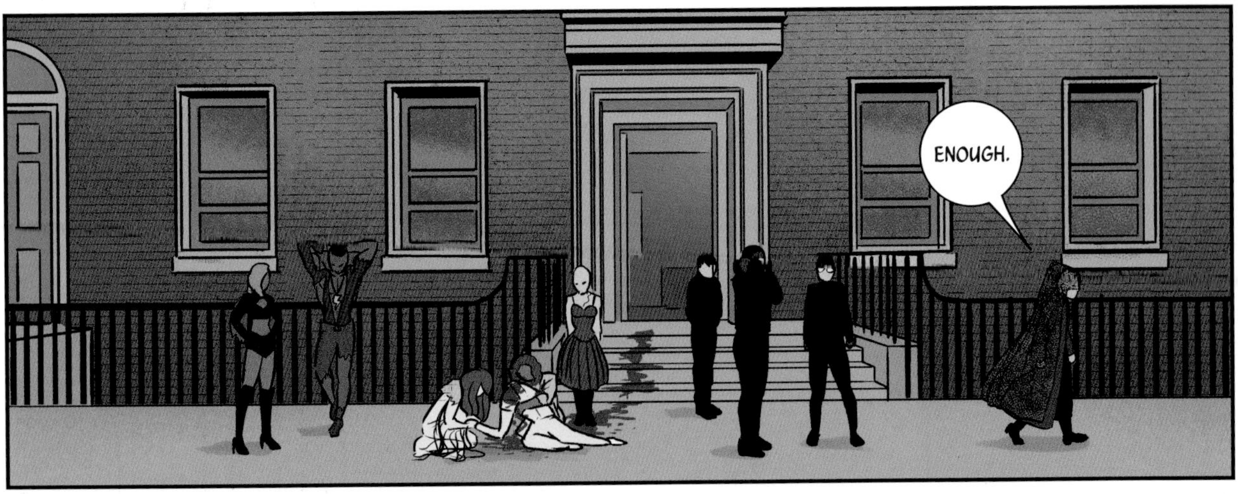
ENOUGH.
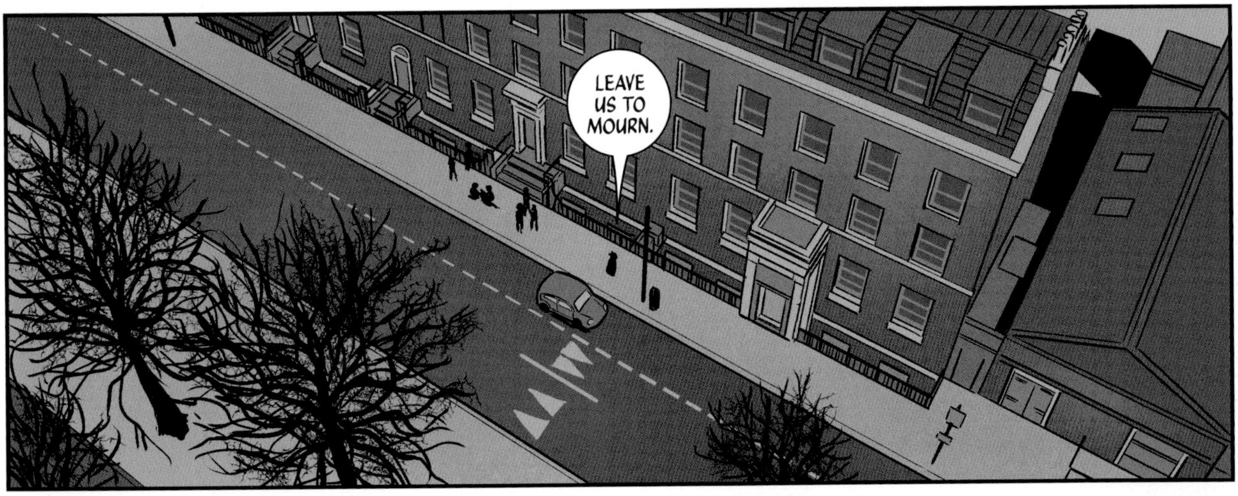
LEAVE US TO MOURN.
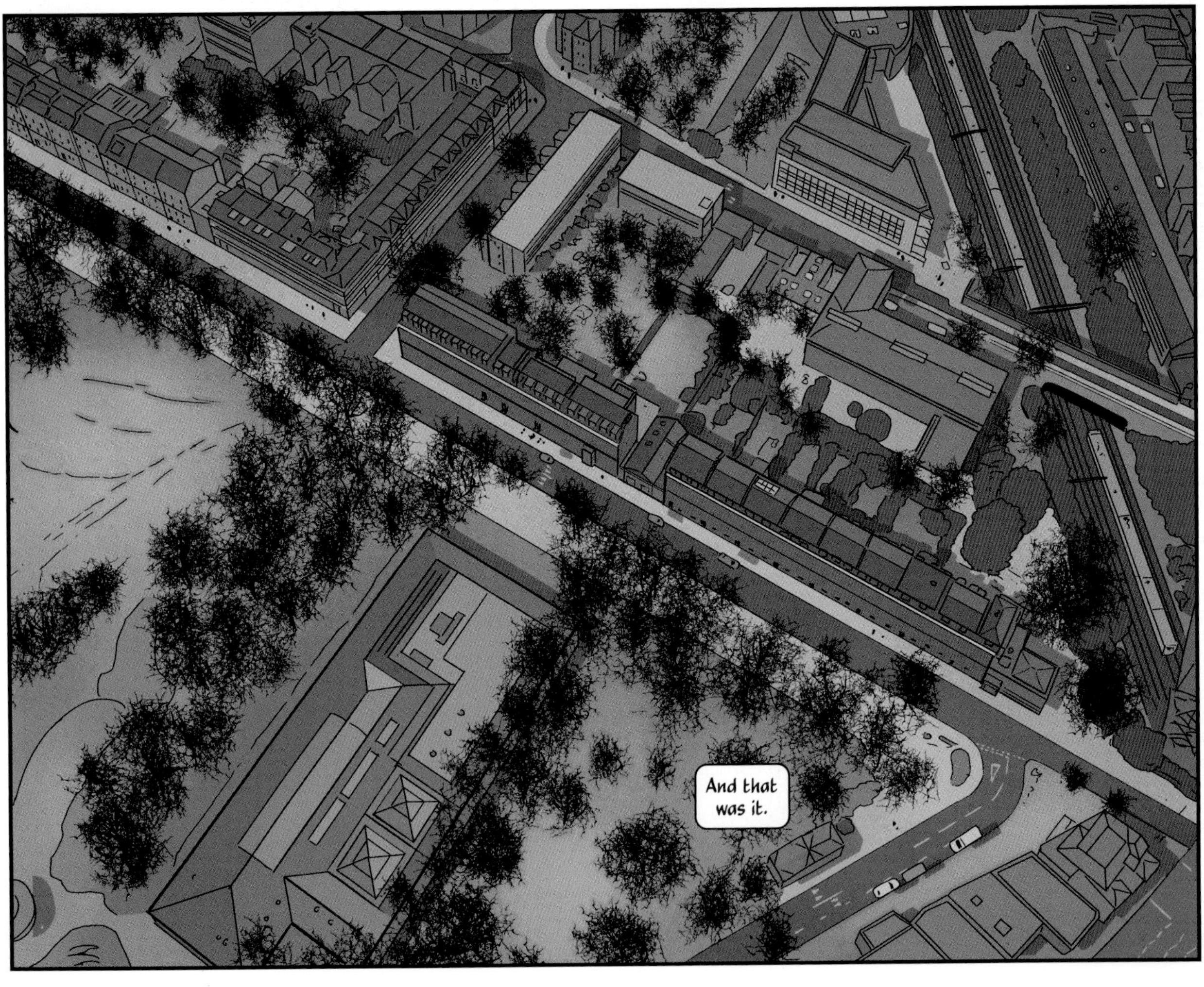
And that was it.

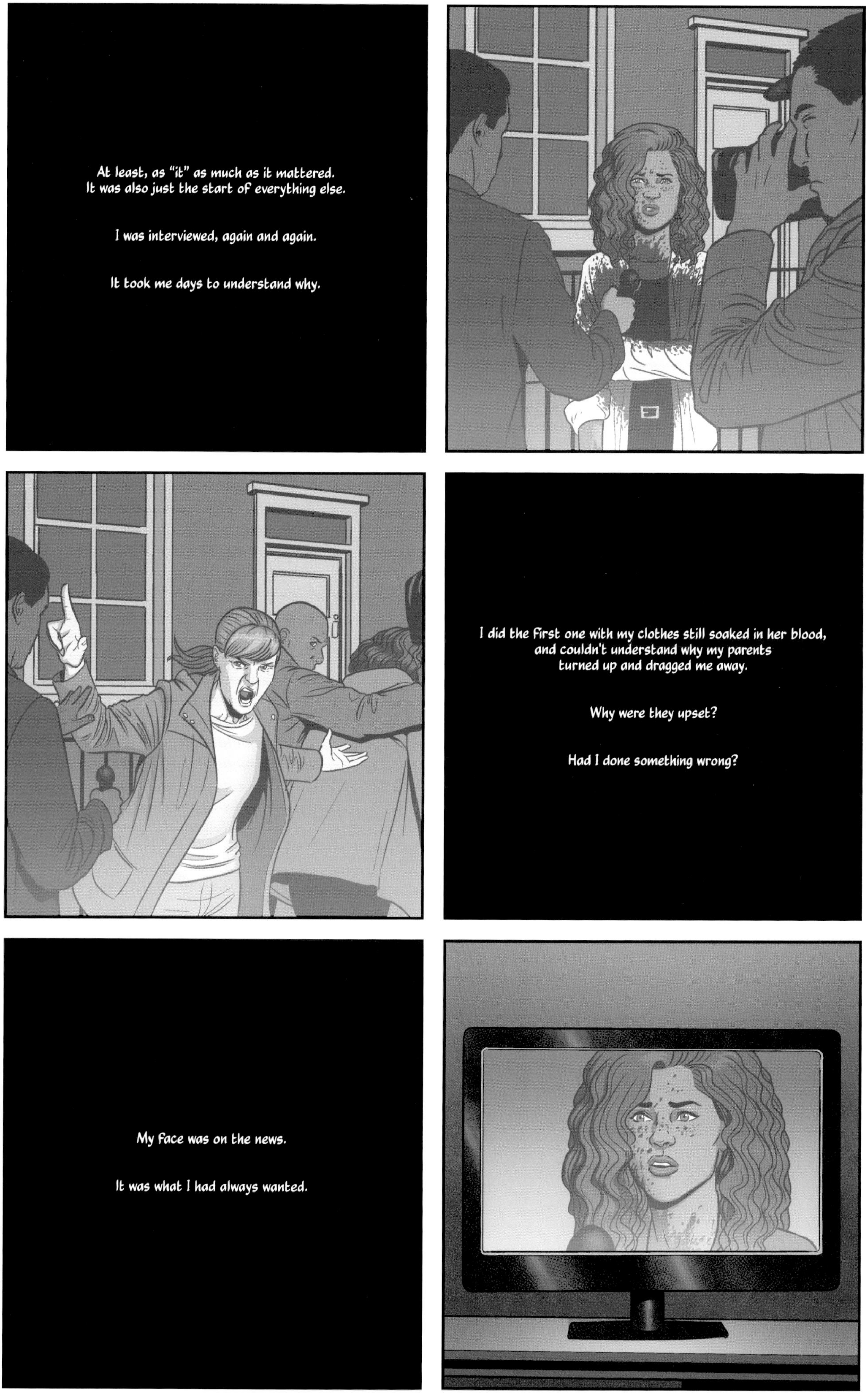
At least, as "it" as much as it mattered.
It was also just the start of everything else.
I was interviewed, again and again.
It took me days to understand why.
I did the first one with my clothes still soaked in her blood, and couldn't understand why my parents turned up and dragged me away.
Why were they upset?
Had I done something wrong?
My face was on the news.
It was what I had always wanted.

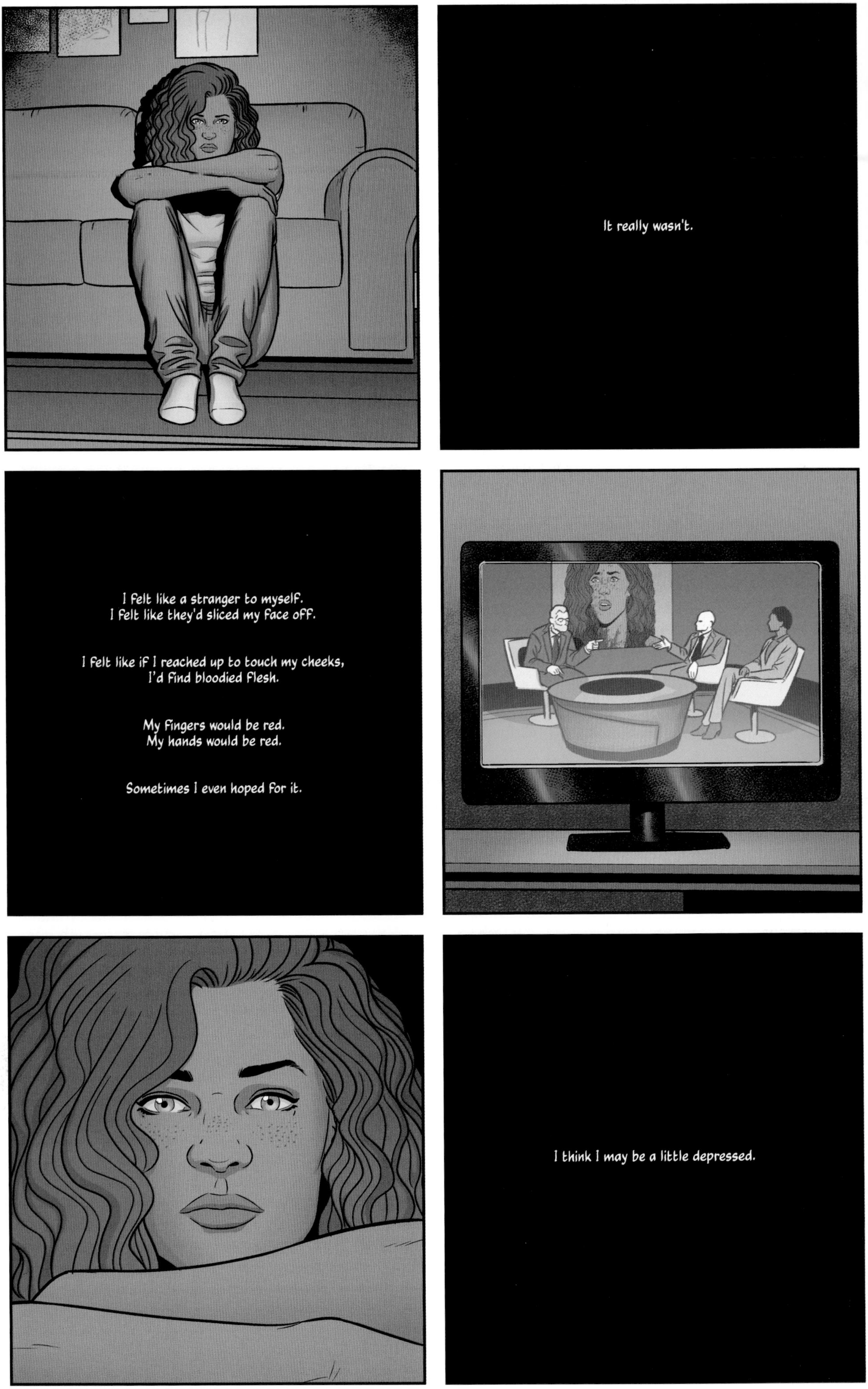
It really wasn't.
I felt like a stranger to myself.
I felt like they'd sliced my face off.
I felt like if I reached up to touch my cheeks,
I'd find bloodied flesh.
My fingers would be red.
My hands would be red.
Sometimes I even hoped for it.
I think I may be a little depressed.

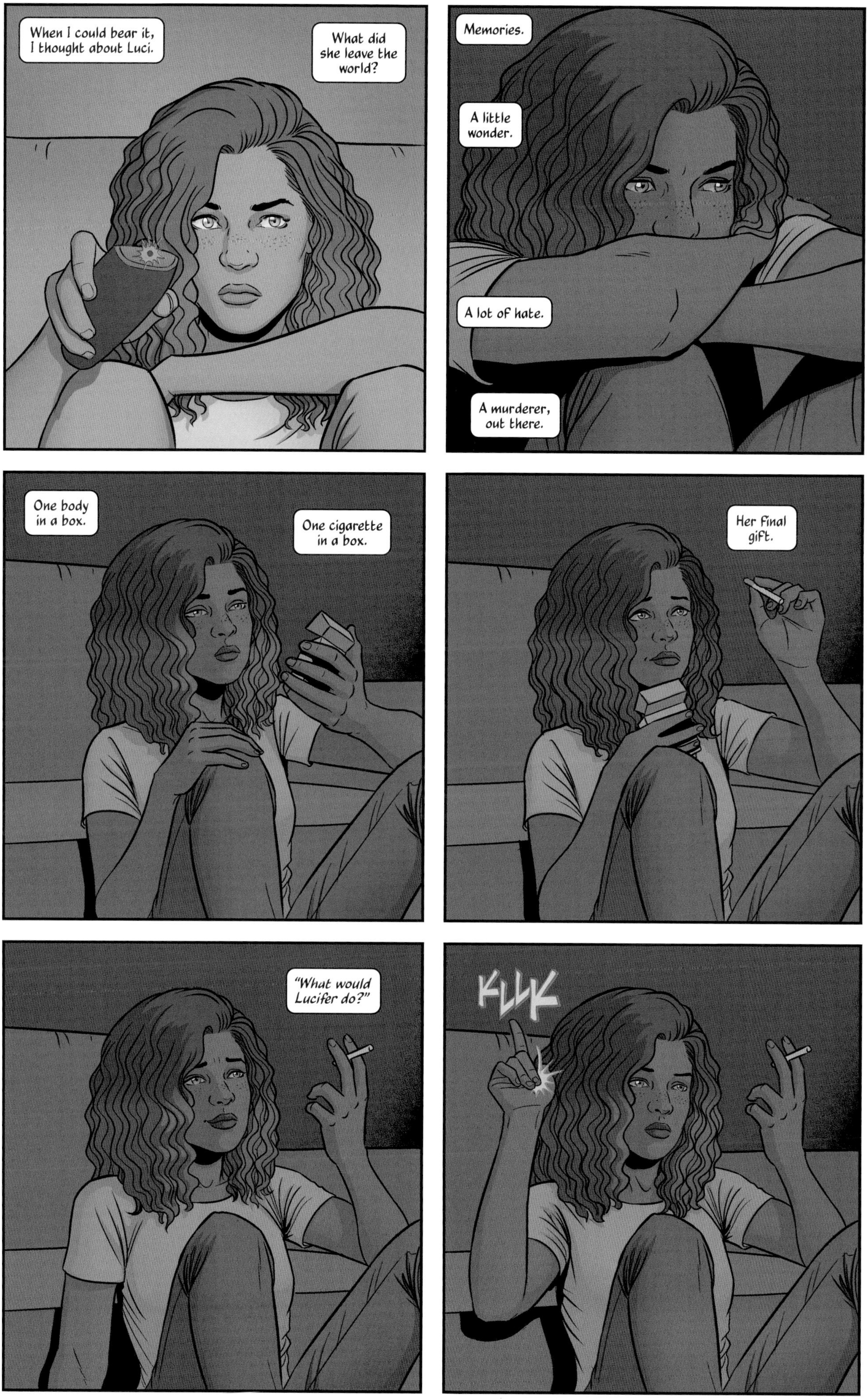
When I could bear it, I thought about Luci.
What did she leave the world?
Memories.
A little wonder.
A lot of hate.
A murderer, out there.
One body in a box.
One cigarette in a box.
Her final gift.
"What would Lucifer do?"
KLLK

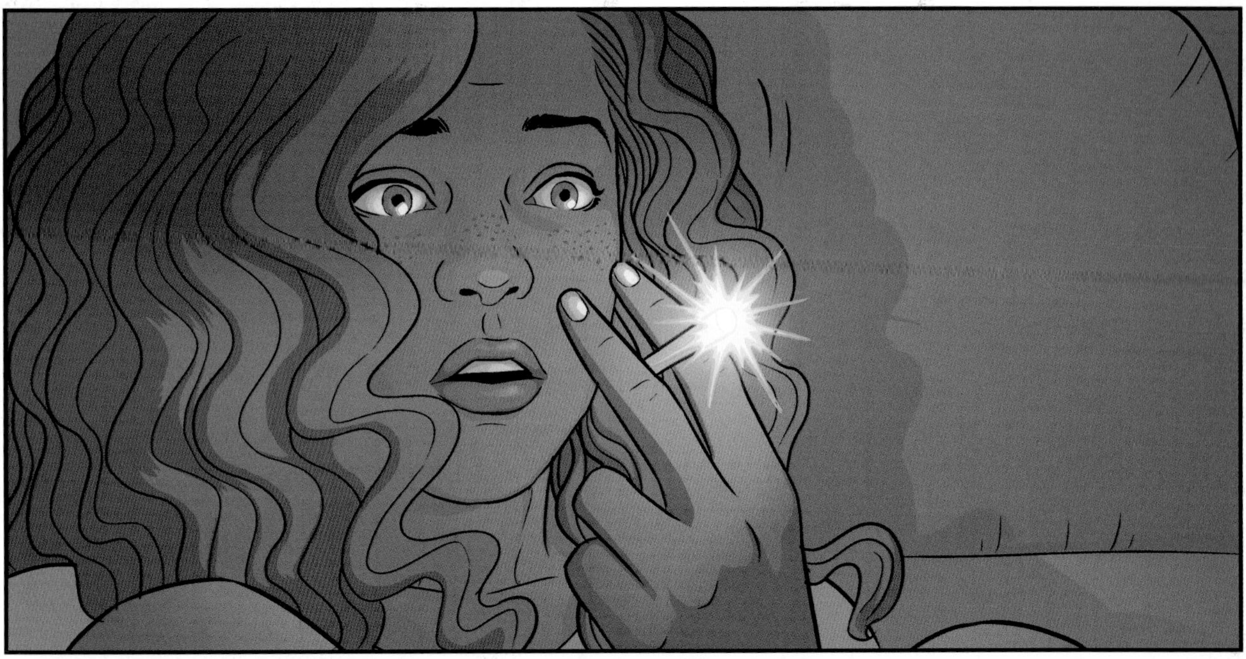
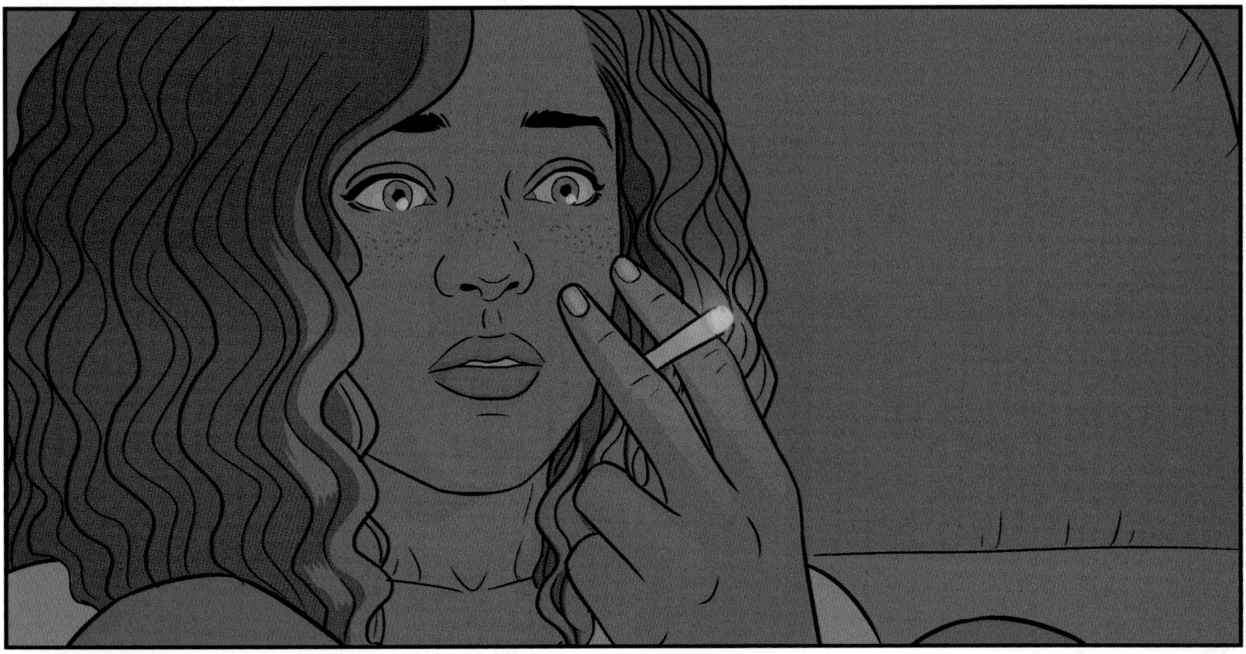
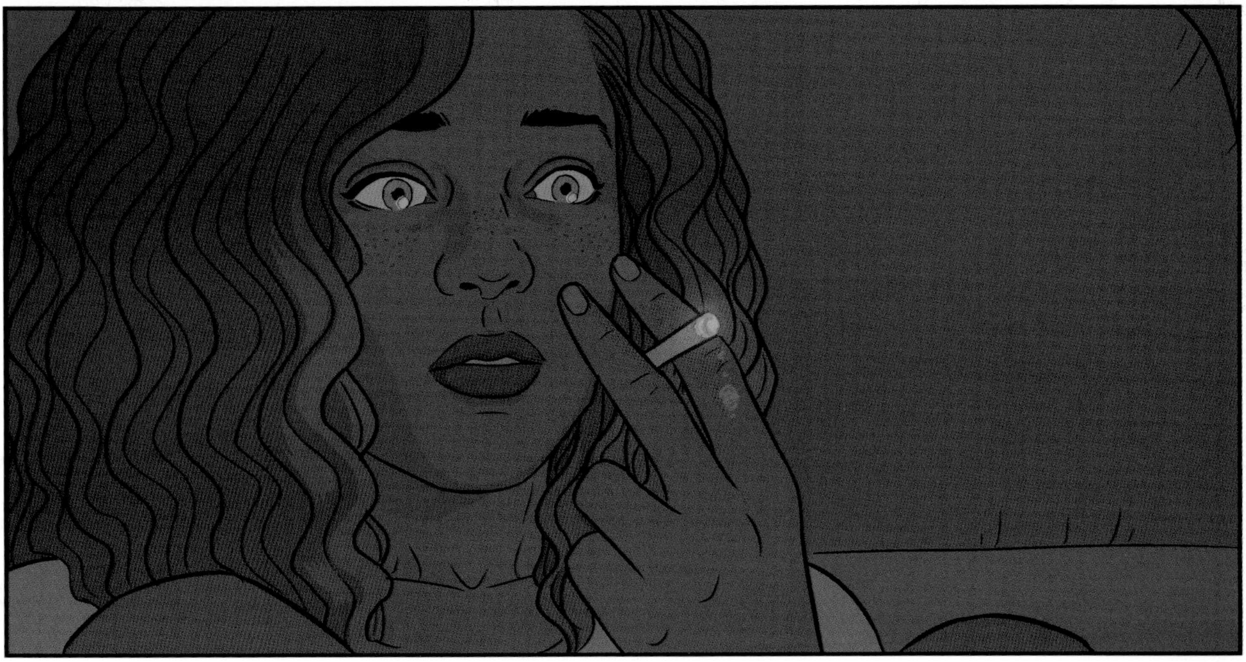

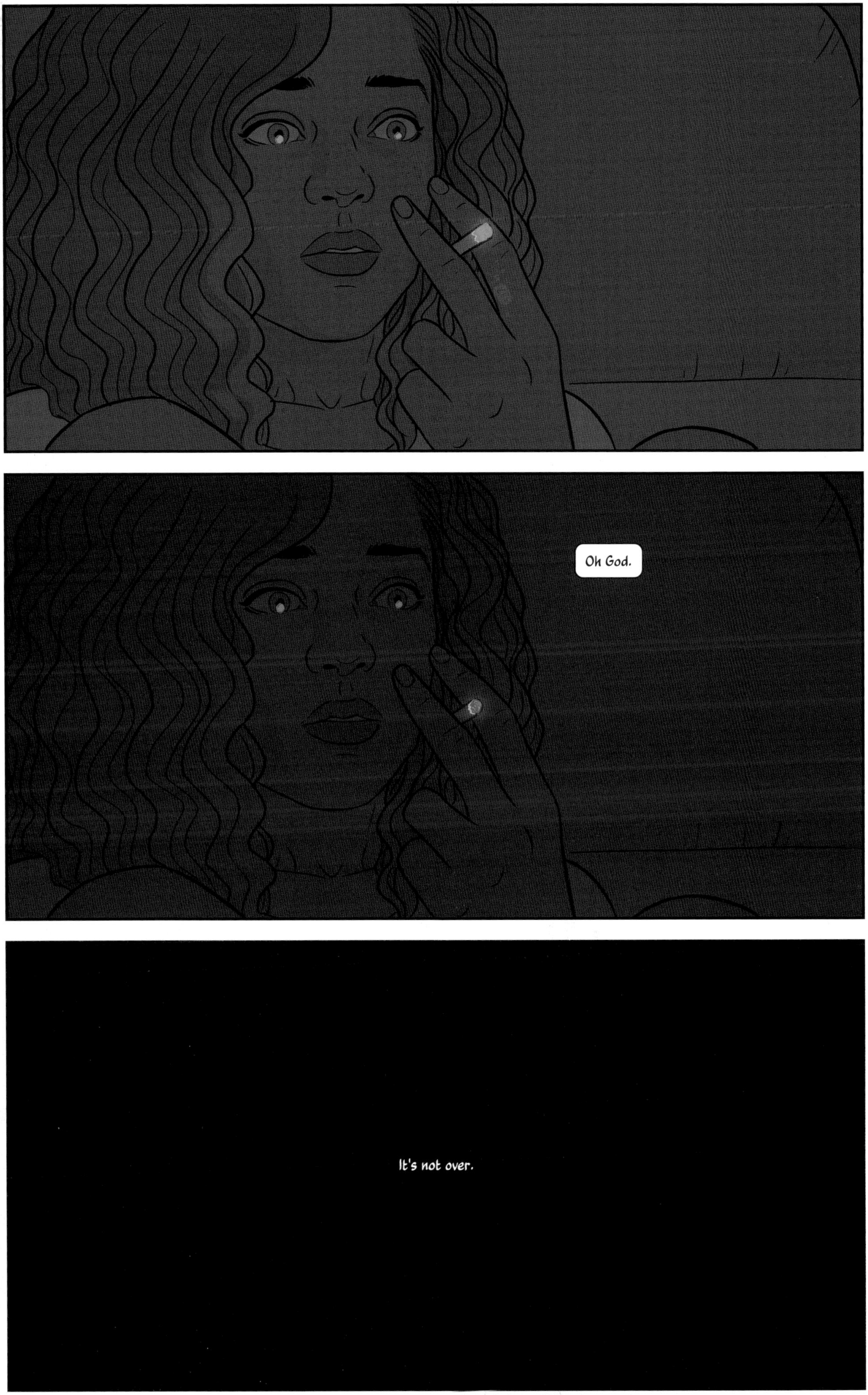
Oh God.
It's not over.

SYMPATHY

19 JANUARY 2014

THE

WICKED

+

THE DIVINE

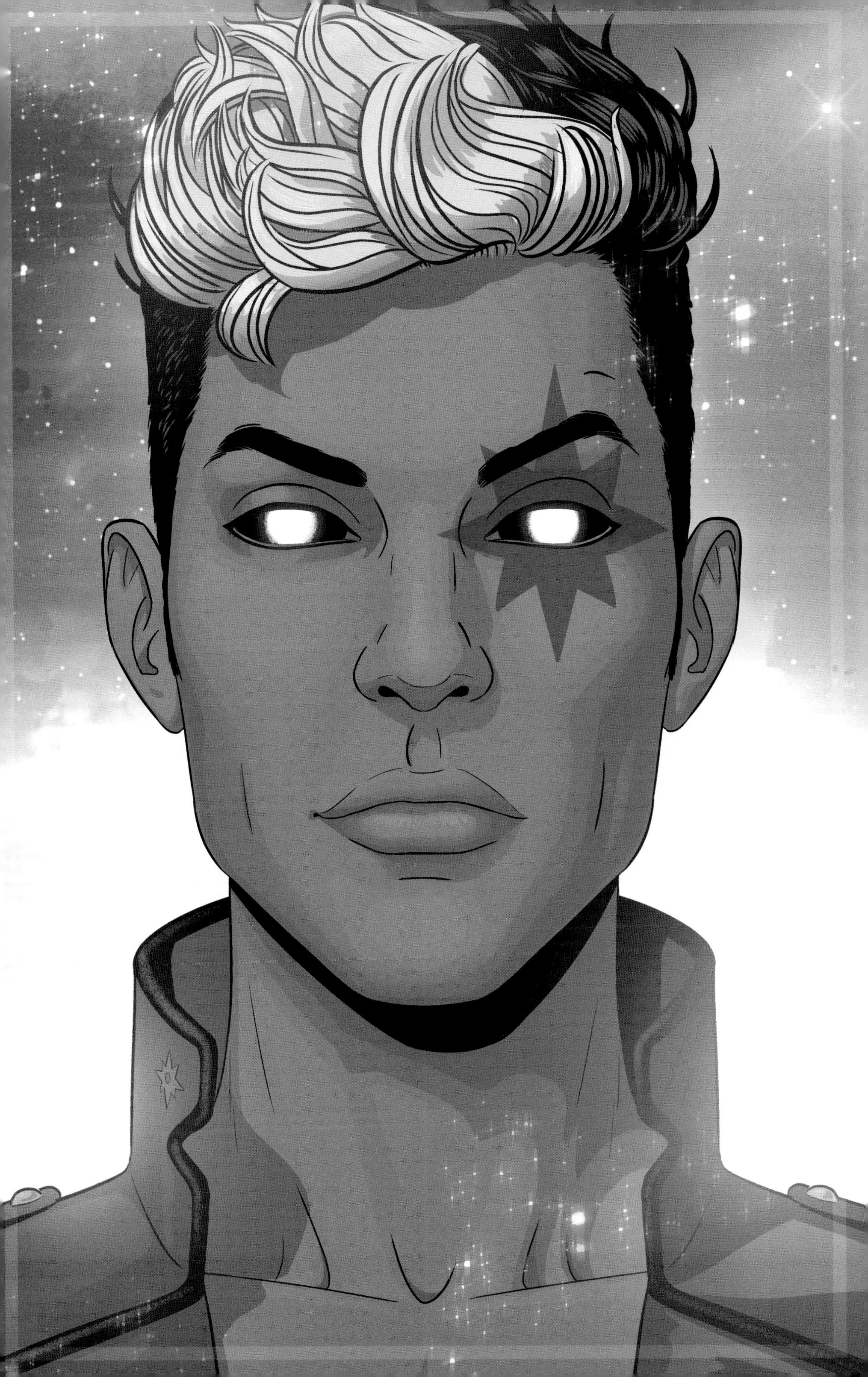

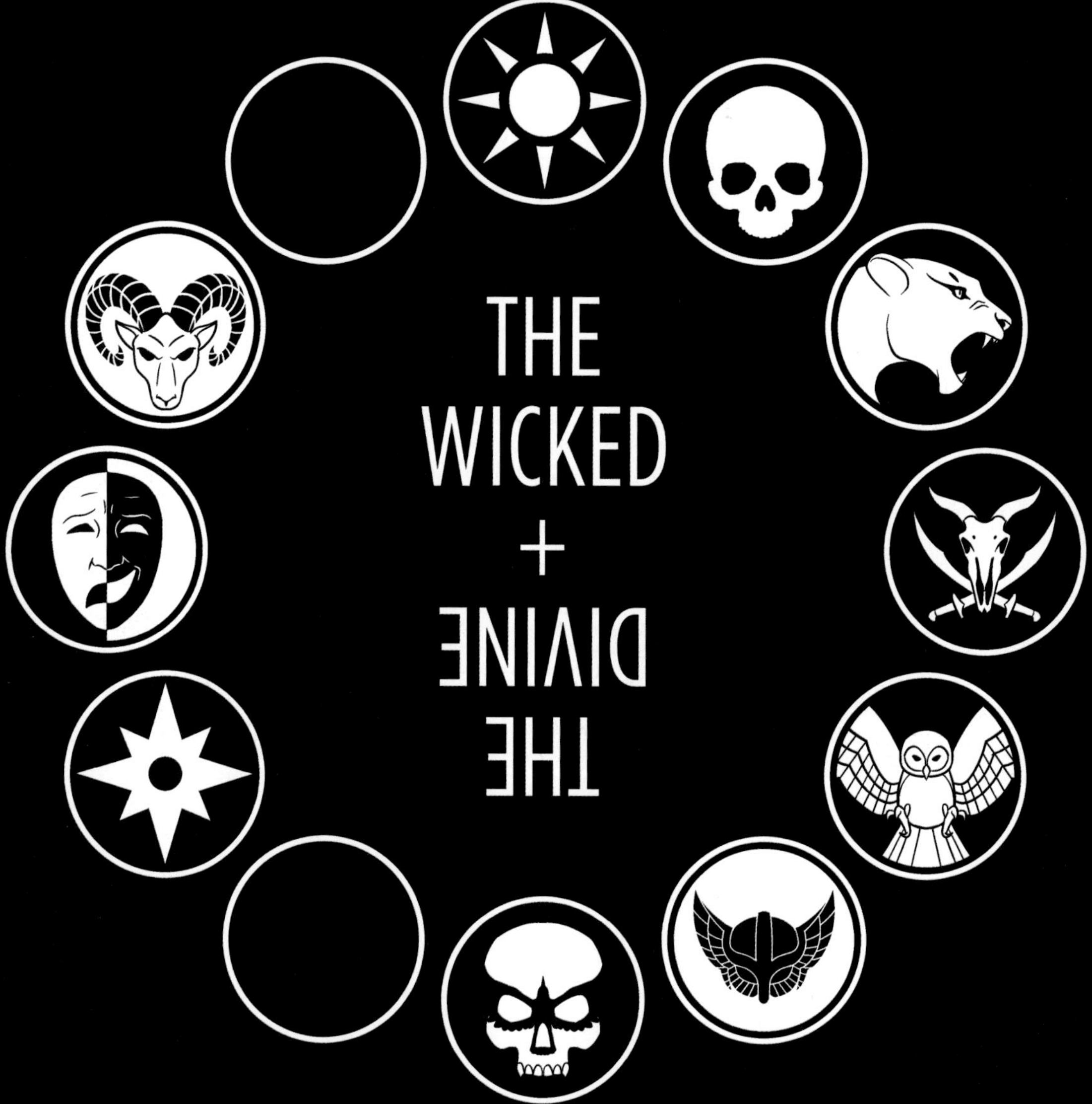
THE
WICKED
+
THE
DIVINE

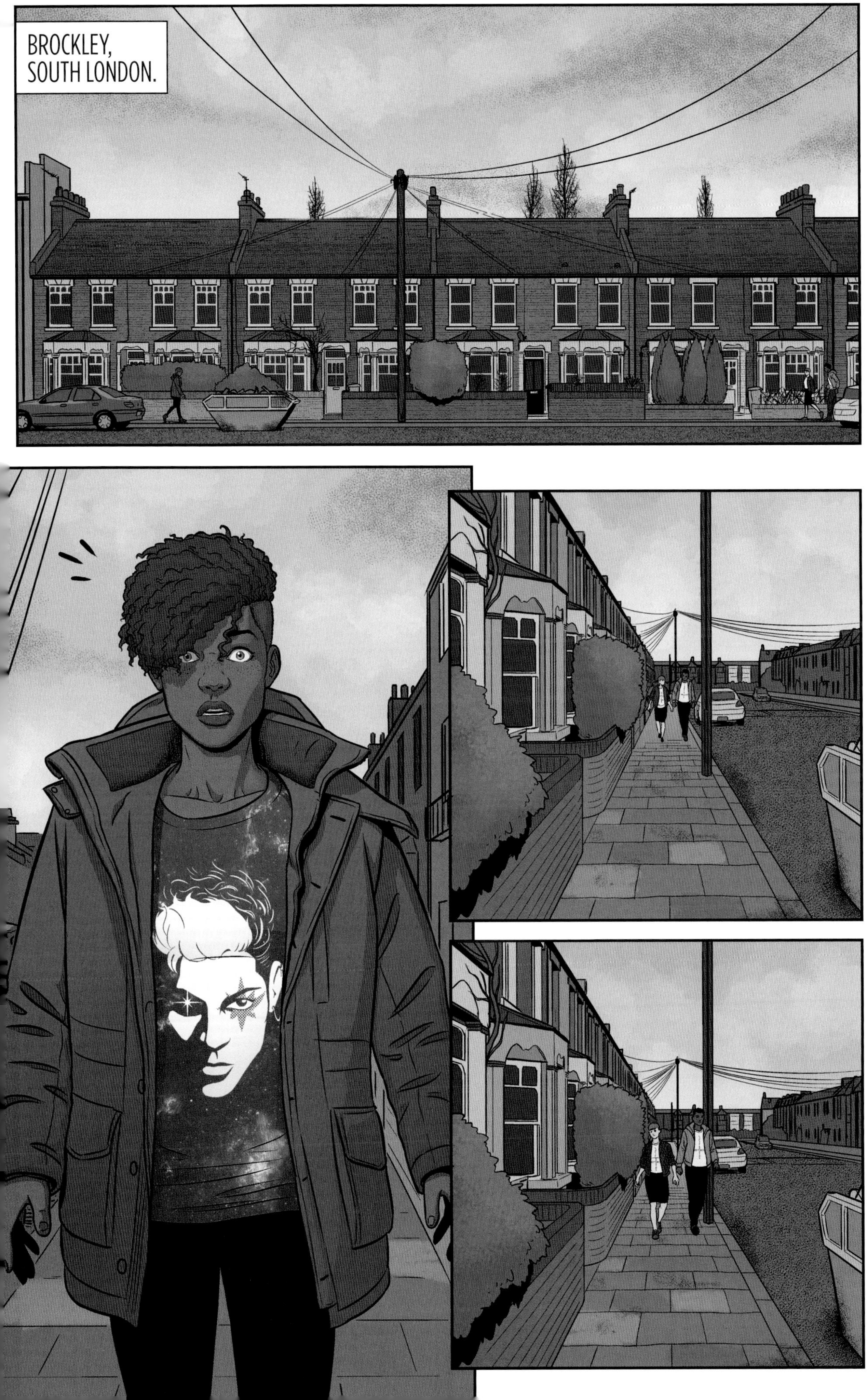
BROCKLEY, SOUTH LONDON.

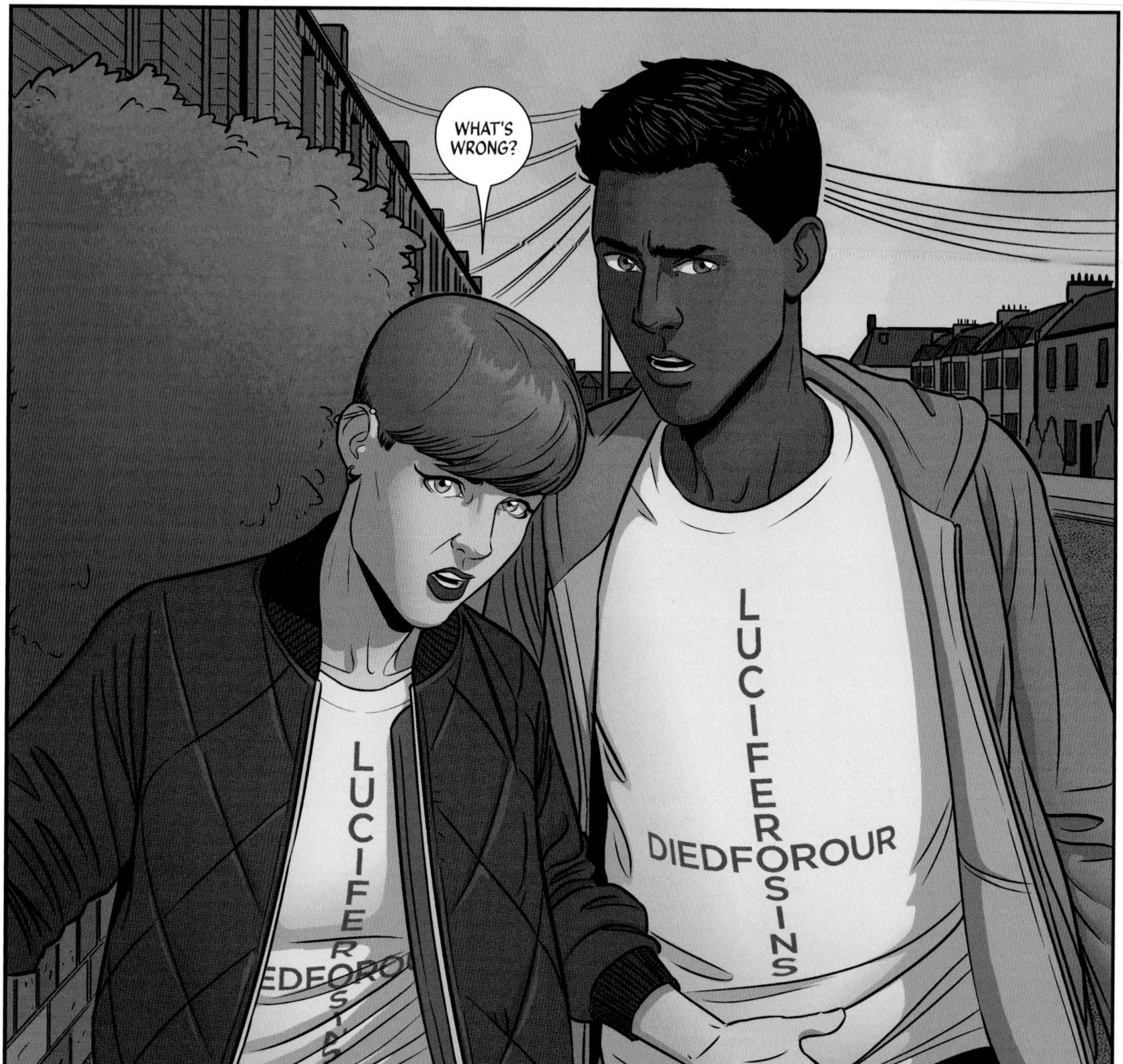
WHAT'S WRONG?
LUCIFEROSINS
DIEDFOROUR

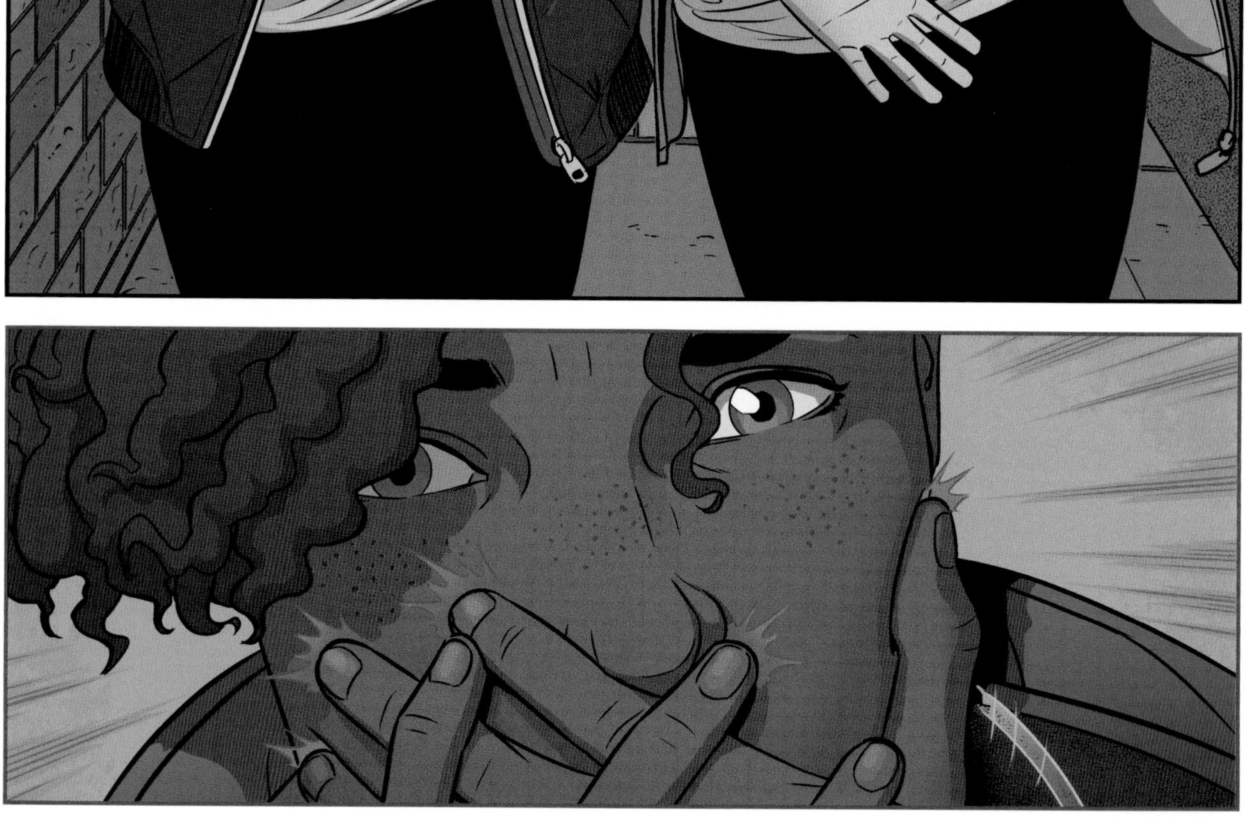

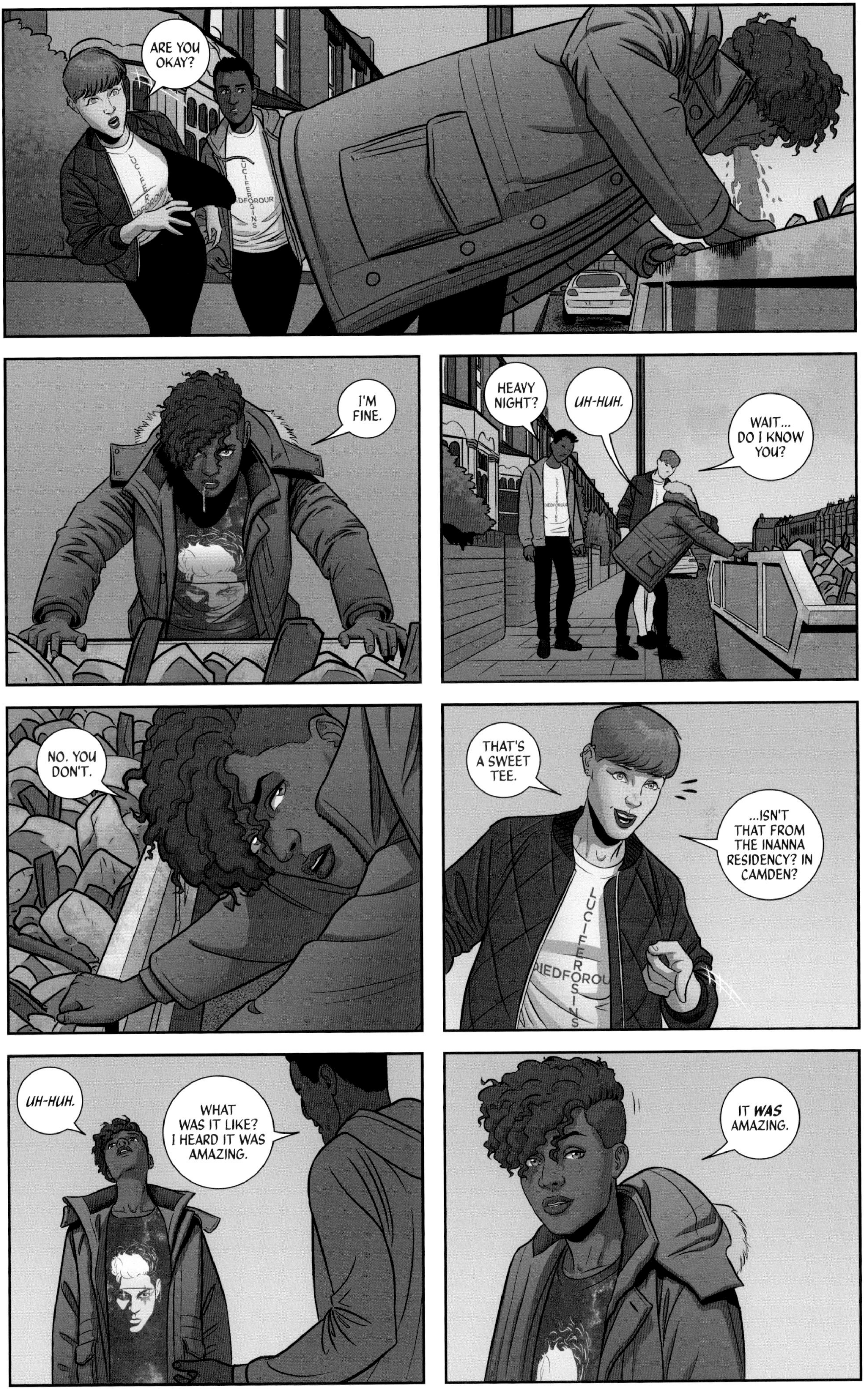
ARE YOU OKAY?
I'M FINE.
HEAVY NIGHT?
UH-HUH.
WAIT... DO I KNOW YOU?
NO. YOU DON'T.
THAT'S A SWEET TEE.
...ISN'T THAT FROM THE INANNA RESIDENCY? IN CAMDEN?
UH-HUH.
WHAT WAS IT LIKE? I HEARD IT WAS AMAZING.
IT **WAS** AMAZING.

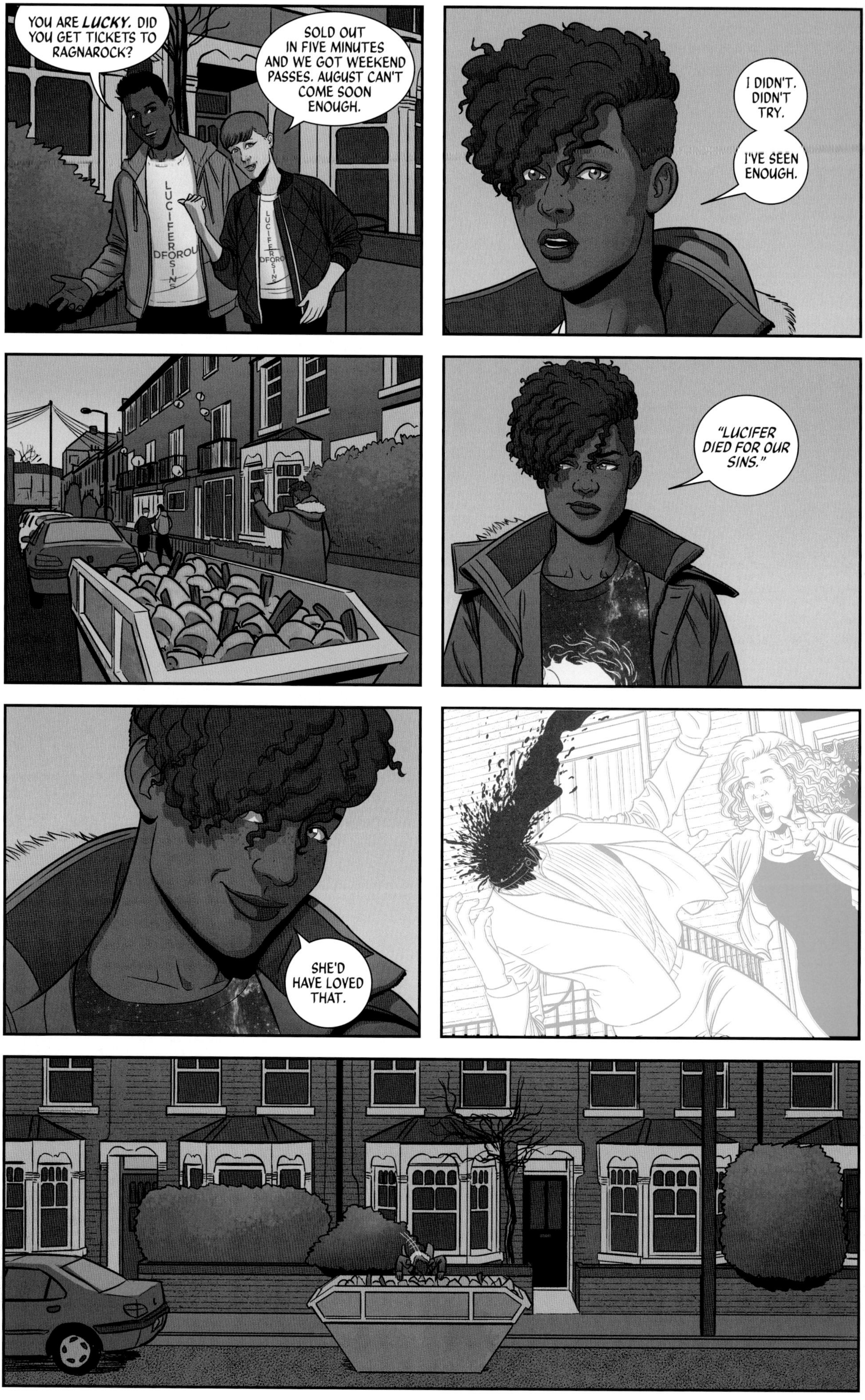
YOU ARE **LUCKY.** DID YOU GET TICKETS TO RAGNAROCK?
SOLD OUT IN FIVE MINUTES AND WE GOT WEEKEND PASSES. AUGUST CAN'T COME SOON ENOUGH.
I DIDN'T. DIDN'T TRY.
I'VE SEEN ENOUGH.
"LUCIFER DIED FOR OUR SINS."
SHE'D HAVE LOVED THAT.

HUMAN TRASH

28 FEBRUARY 2014

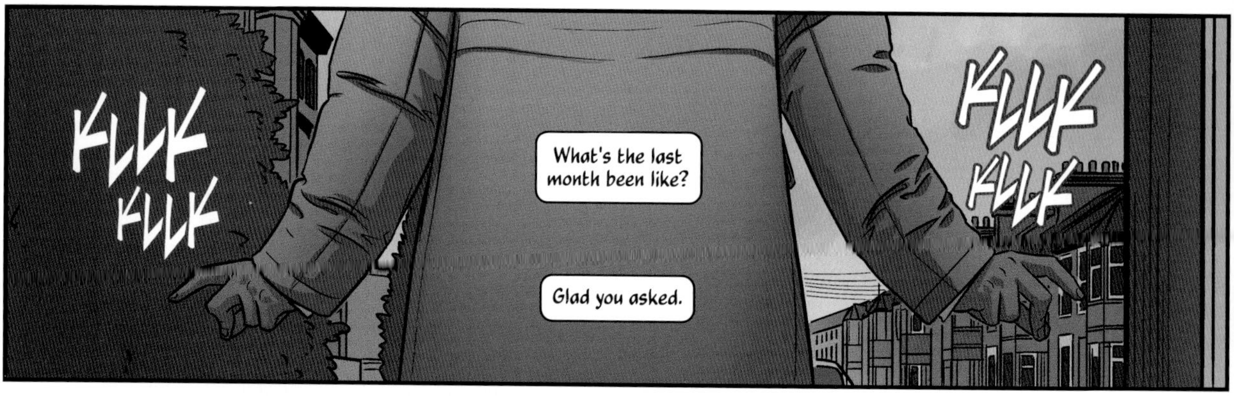
KLLK
KLLK
What's the last month been like?
Glad you asked.
KLLK
KLLK

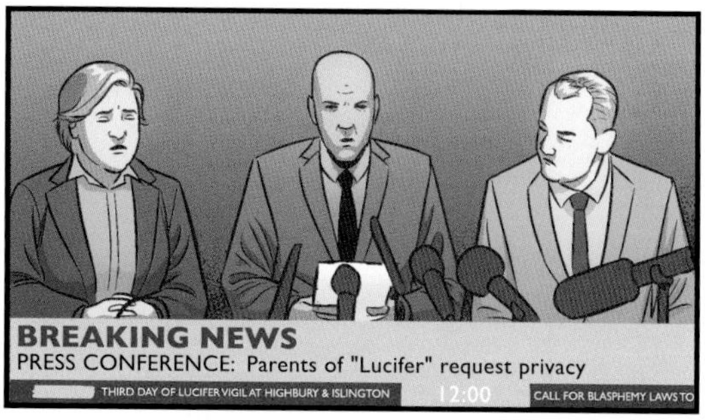
BREAKING NEWS
PRESS CONFERENCE: Parents of "Lucifer" request privacy
THIRD DAY OF LUCIFER VIGIL AT HIGHBURY & ISLINGTON
12:00
CALL FOR BLASPHEMY LAWS TO

"THE FUNERAL WILL BE HELD
AT AN UNDISCLOSED LOCATION.
WE REQUEST PRIVACY
AT THIS DIFFICULT TIME.

"FOR ALL THE CLAIMS THAT
SHE WAS A GOD, SHE WAS
ALSO OUR LITTLE GIRL."

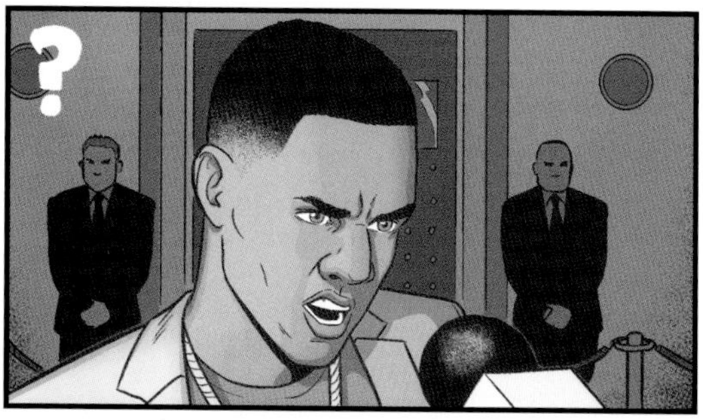
?

"NO, I DIDN'T GO TO THE *[BLEEP]* FUNERAL.
THE LAST THING HER FAMILY NEEDS IS SEEING
ANYONE WHO WAS BEATING ON THEIR
NOW-DEAD-DAUGHTER STANDING THERE
IN HIS BEST ALEXANDER McQUEEN.

"WHAT THE *[BLEEP]*
IS ***WRONG*** WITH YOU?"

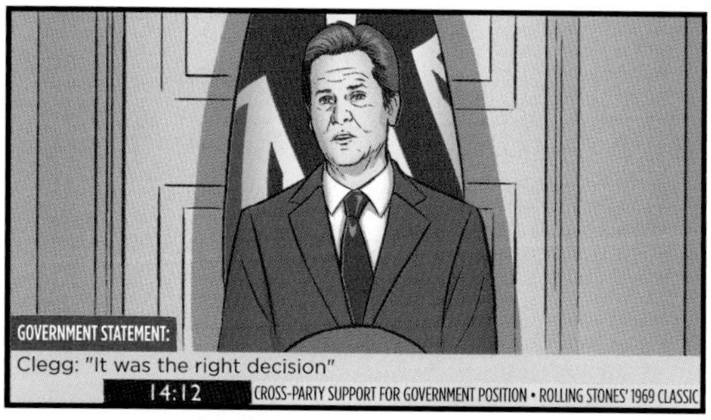
GOVERNMENT STATEMENT:
Clegg: "It was the right decision"
14:12
CROSS-PARTY SUPPORT FOR GOVERNMENT POSITION • ROLLING STONES' 1969 CLASSIC

"WHILE THIS GOVERNMENT CANNOT
OFFER THANKS TO THE PANTHEON
FOR ITS ACTIONS, THE INFORMATION
'ANANKE' SHARED HAS CONVINCED
US THAT THE SAD DEATH OF THIS
YOUNG GIRL WAS THE ONLY
SOLUTION TO THE SITUATION.

"IN ACTING SO SWIFTLY,
MANY LIVES WERE SAVED.
IT WAS THE RIGHT DECISION."

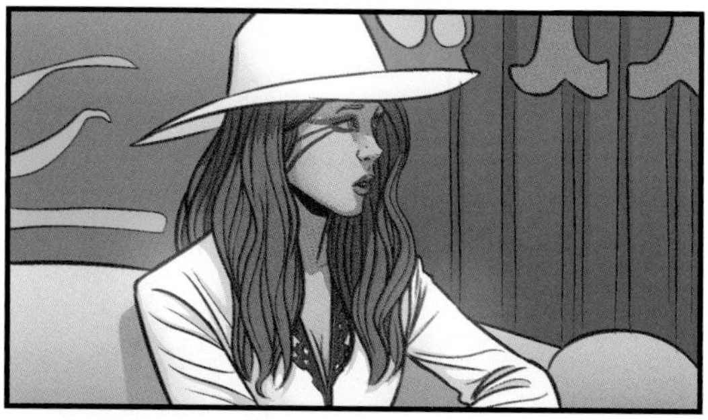

"I CRY FOR HER EVERY NIGHT.
I CRY EVERY MORNING.

"THE ONLY COMFORT IS THAT I KNOW
I'LL BE SEEING HER AGAIN SOON.
IT MAY BE NINETY YEARS FOR YOU,
BUT FOR US, IT'S LESS THAN TWO."

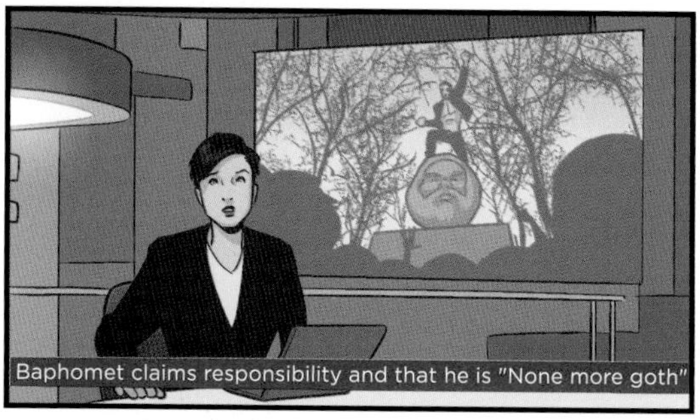
Baphomet claims responsibility and that he is "None more goth"

"LAST NIGHT, HIGHGATE CEMETERY
WAS THE SCENE OF A 'VALENTINE'S
DAY MASCARA.' EYEWITNESSES
REPORT SCENES OF THE ANIMATED
DEAD DANCING WITH THE LIVING.

"THE *'GOD'* BAPHOMET,
STILL WANTED BY THE POLICE,
HAS CLAIMED RESPONSIBILITY."

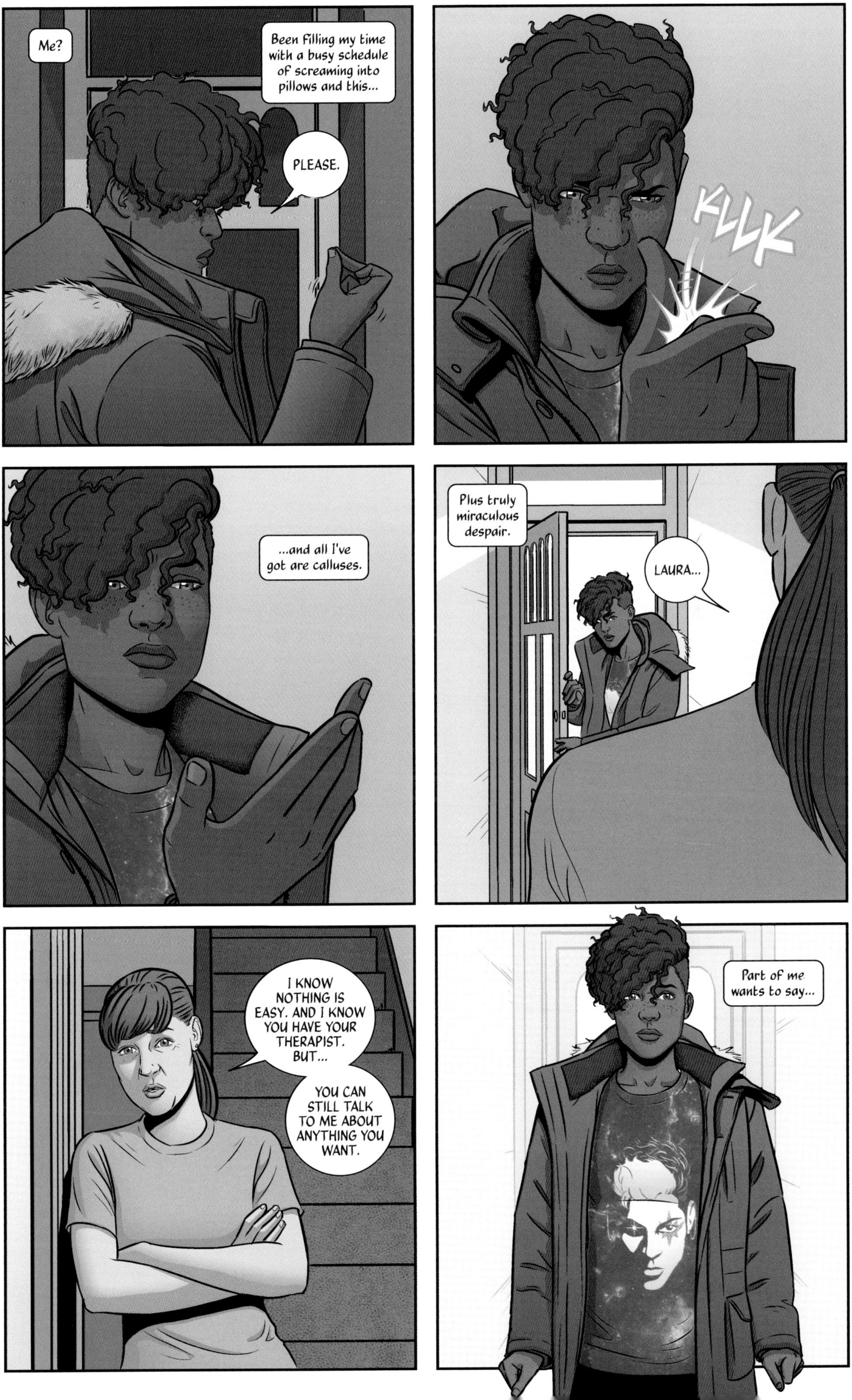
Me?
Been filling my time with a busy schedule of screaming into pillows and this...
PLEASE.
KLLK
...and all I've got are calluses.
Plus truly miraculous despair.
LAURA...
I KNOW NOTHING IS EASY. AND I KNOW YOU HAVE YOUR THERAPIST. BUT...
YOU CAN STILL TALK TO ME ABOUT ANYTHING YOU WANT.
Part of me wants to say...

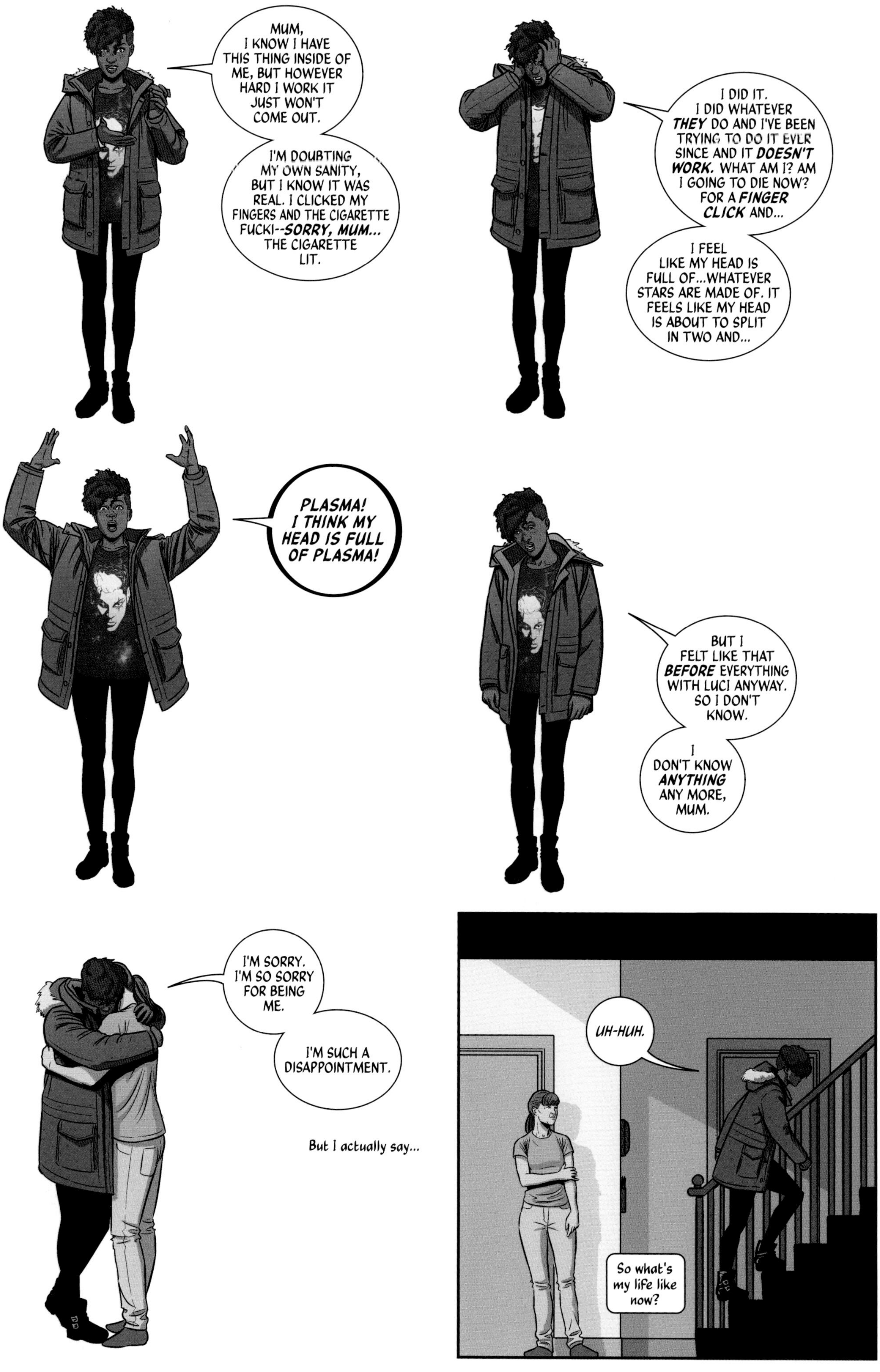
MUM, I KNOW I HAVE THIS THING INSIDE OF ME, BUT HOWEVER HARD I WORK IT JUST WON'T COME OUT.
I'M DOUBTING MY OWN SANITY, BUT I KNOW IT WAS REAL. I CLICKED MY FINGERS AND THE CIGARETTE FUCKI--*SORRY, MUM...* THE CIGARETTE LIT.
I DID IT. I DID WHATEVER *THEY* DO AND I'VE BEEN TRYING TO DO IT EVER SINCE AND IT *DOESN'T WORK.* WHAT AM I? AM I GOING TO DIE NOW? FOR A *FINGER CLICK* AND...
I FEEL LIKE MY HEAD IS FULL OF...WHATEVER STARS ARE MADE OF. IT FEELS LIKE MY HEAD IS ABOUT TO SPLIT IN TWO AND...
PLASMA! I THINK MY HEAD IS FULL OF PLASMA!
BUT I FELT LIKE THAT *BEFORE* EVERYTHING WITH LUCI ANYWAY. SO I DON'T KNOW.
I DON'T KNOW *ANYTHING* ANY MORE, MUM.
I'M SORRY. I'M SO SORRY FOR BEING ME.
I'M SUCH A DISAPPOINTMENT.
But I actually say...
UH-HUH.
So what's my life like now?

THE LIFE OF LAURA WILSON, AGED SEVENTEEN AND THREE QUARTERS.

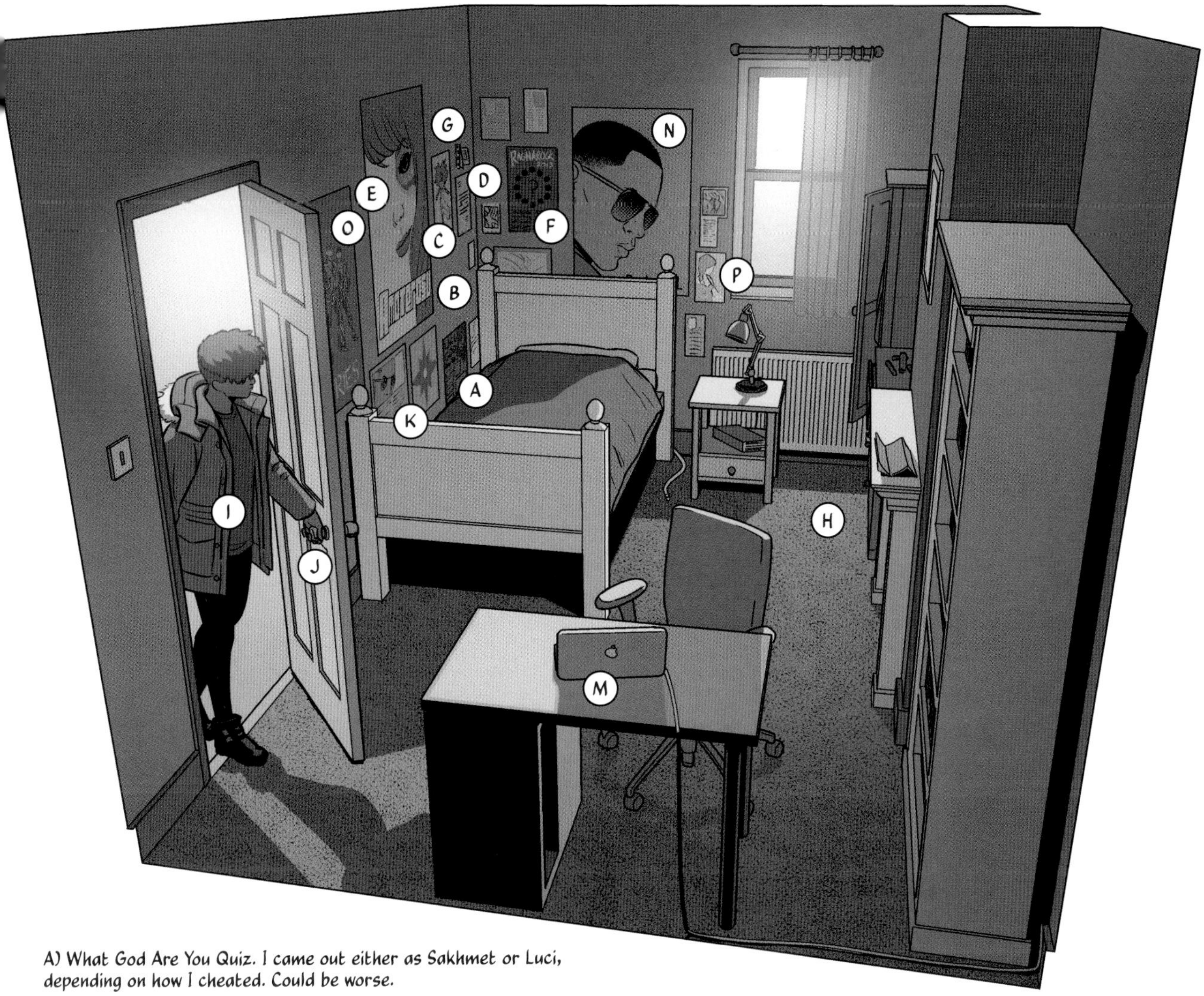
G
N
D
E
O
C
F
B
P
A
K
I
H
J
M

A) What God Are You Quiz. I came out either as Sakhmet or Luci, depending on how I cheated. Could be worse.

B) Suspicious gap. Couldn't bear Luci's poster there. Couldn't bear putting anything in its place.

C) Flyposter. Stolen from down the road near the venue the day before I saw Amaterasu.

D) I wrote to Brunhilde when she was kicked out of The Valkyries. She wrote back. That was kind of amazing.

E) Fan art poster. Bought from the land of online.

F) From last year's Ragnarock. August 15th, so before The Recurrence. Absolutely tiny. I was one of the youngest people there. This year's will be bigger than Glastonbury.

G) Photos of old friends from school. Some have called me. More than I expected. I'm...grateful? I think I am.

H) My floor's messier in real life. Pictured like this as I'm in denial.

I) 17-year-old girl with no life.

J) Unrelentingly unmiraculous fingertips.

K) Handed out to the crowd after Inanna's residency. Mine got crumpled. This has been carefully and lovingly ironed.

L) The cigarette box and the dog-end are hidden here. I can't throw them away, but I don't want mum to think I'm smoking.

M) Second-hand. Or possibly third-hand.

N) Still have a lot of inappropriate naked feelings about Baal. Still hope he isn't the murderer.

O) Valkyries, in their original line-up.

P) I draw the gods occasionally. This is the best I ever managed. It's Sakhmet, though here she looks more like Rihanna.

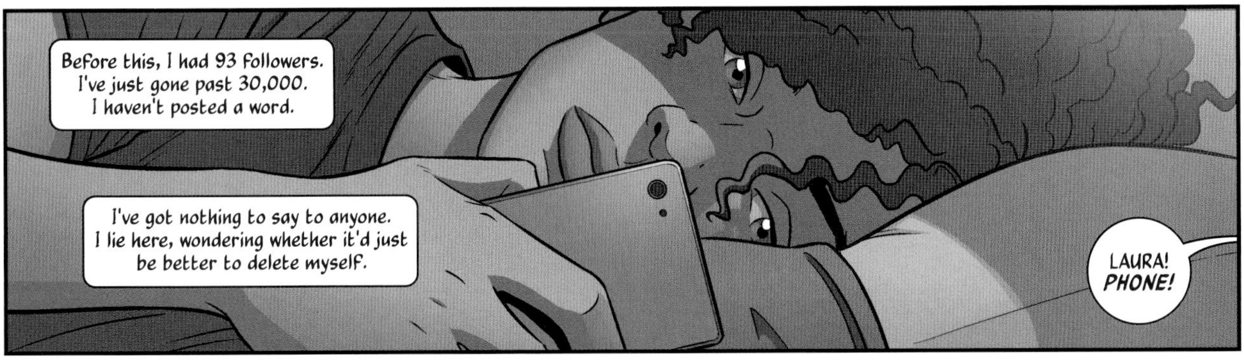
Before this, I had 93 followers. I've just gone past 30,000. I haven't posted a word.
I've got nothing to say to anyone. I lie here, wondering whether it'd just be better to delete myself.
LAURA! PHONE!

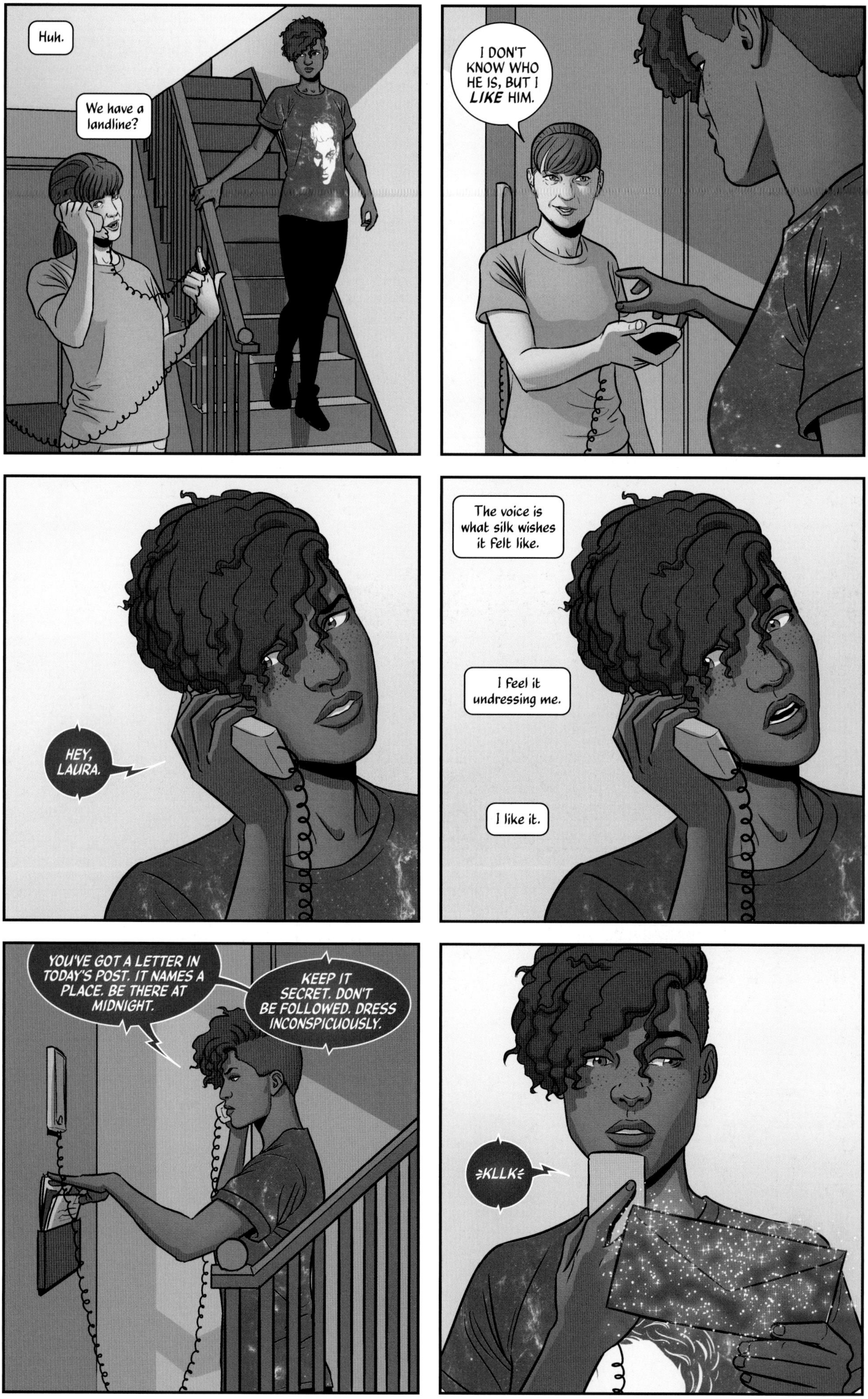
Huh.
We have a landline?
I DON'T KNOW WHO HE IS, BUT I *LIKE* HIM.
HEY, LAURA.
The voice is what silk wishes it felt like.
I feel it undressing me.
I like it.
YOU'VE GOT A LETTER IN TODAY'S POST. IT NAMES A PLACE. BE THERE AT MIDNIGHT.
KEEP IT SECRET. DON'T BE FOLLOWED. DRESS INCONSPICUOUSLY.
KLLK

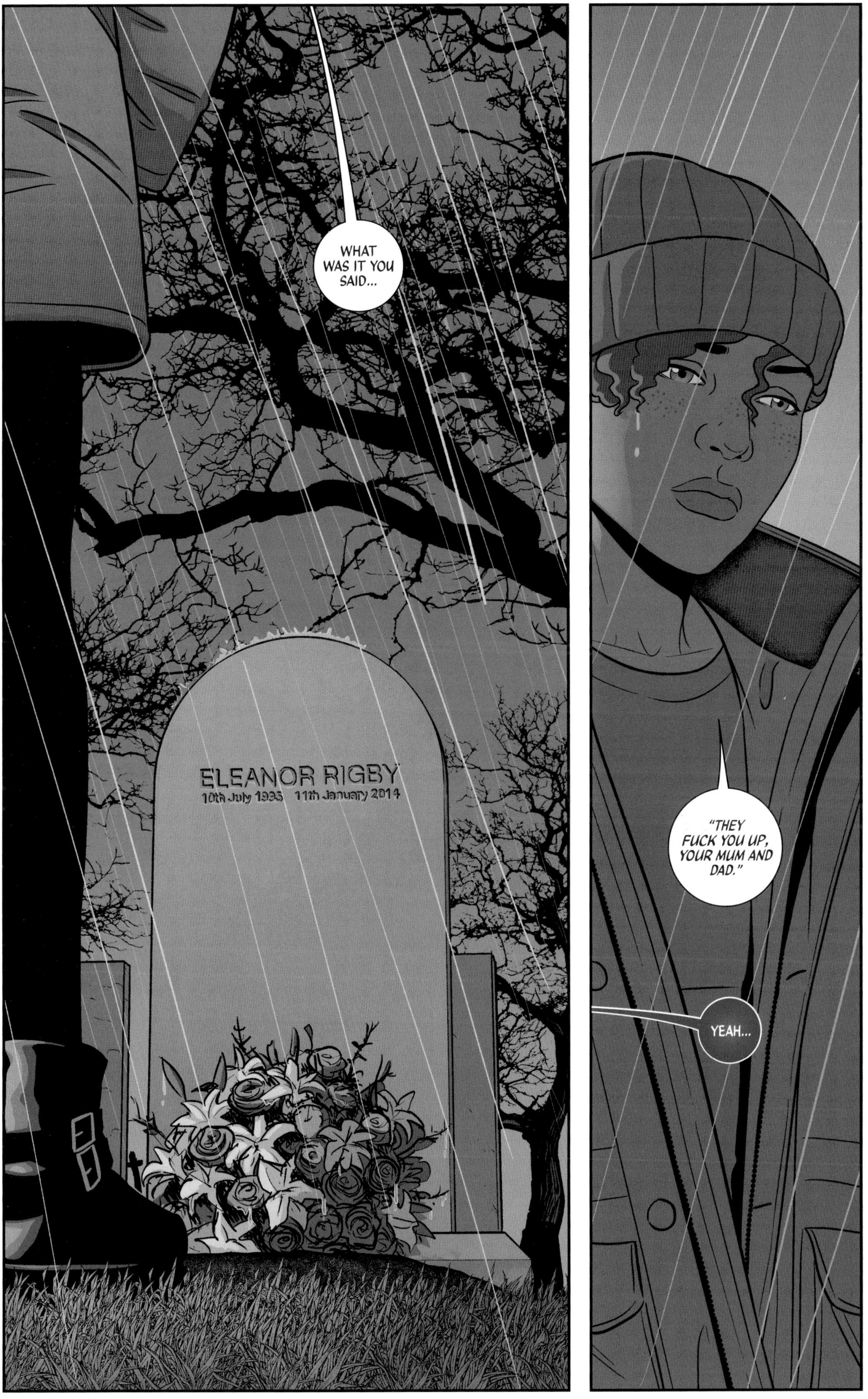
WHAT WAS IT YOU SAID...
ELEANOR RIGBY
10th July 1995 11th January 2014
"THEY FUCK YOU UP, YOUR MUM AND DAD."
YEAH...

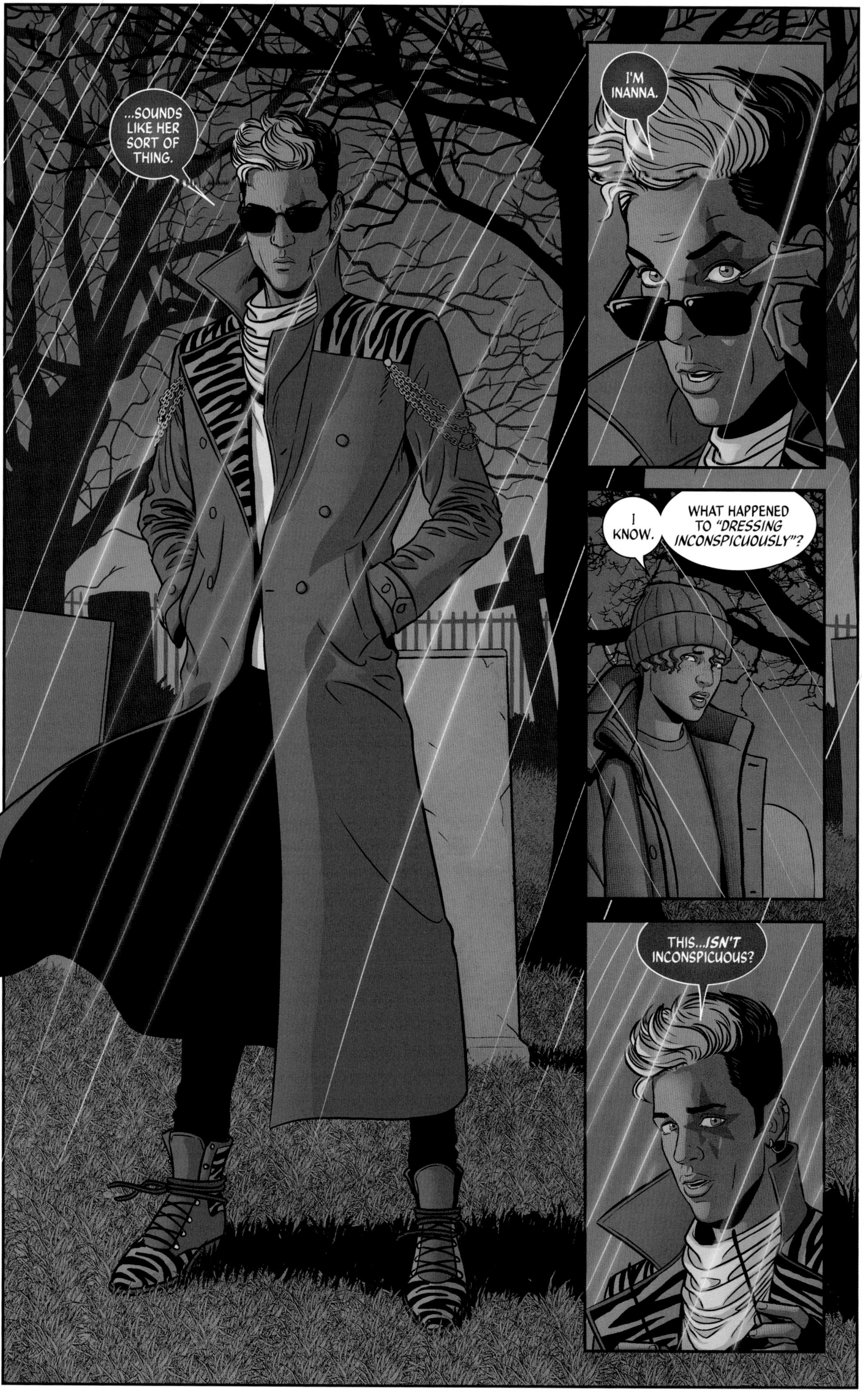
...SOUNDS LIKE HER SORT OF THING.
I'M INANNA.
I KNOW.
WHAT HAPPENED TO "DRESSING INCONSPICUOUSLY"?
THIS...ISN'T INCONSPICUOUS?

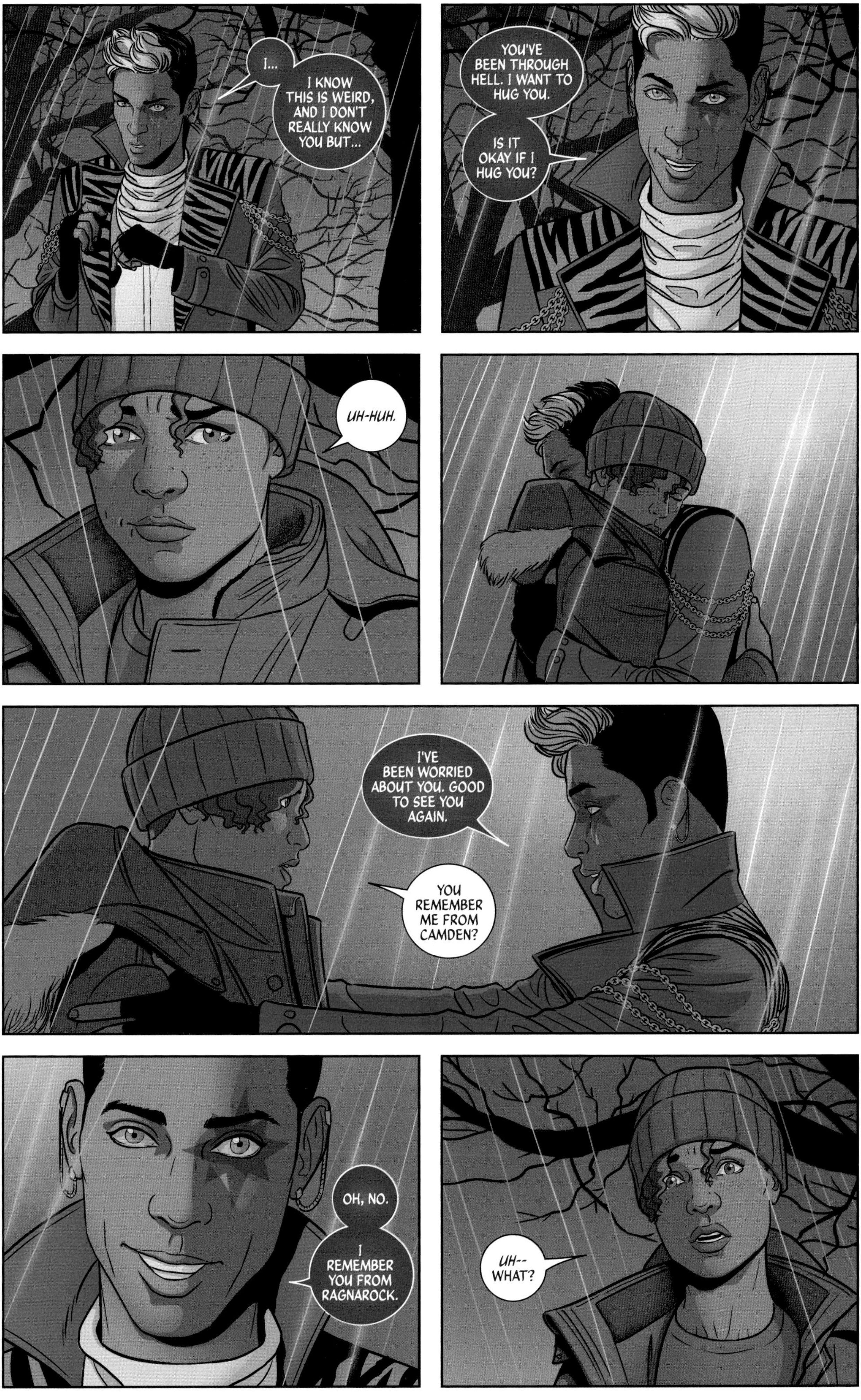
I...
I KNOW THIS IS WEIRD, AND I DON'T REALLY KNOW YOU BUT...
YOU'VE BEEN THROUGH HELL. I WANT TO HUG YOU.
IS IT OKAY IF I HUG YOU?
UH-HUH.
I'VE BEEN WORRIED ABOUT YOU. GOOD TO SEE YOU AGAIN.
YOU REMEMBER ME FROM CAMDEN?
OH, NO.
I REMEMBER YOU FROM RAGNAROCK.
UH-- WHAT?

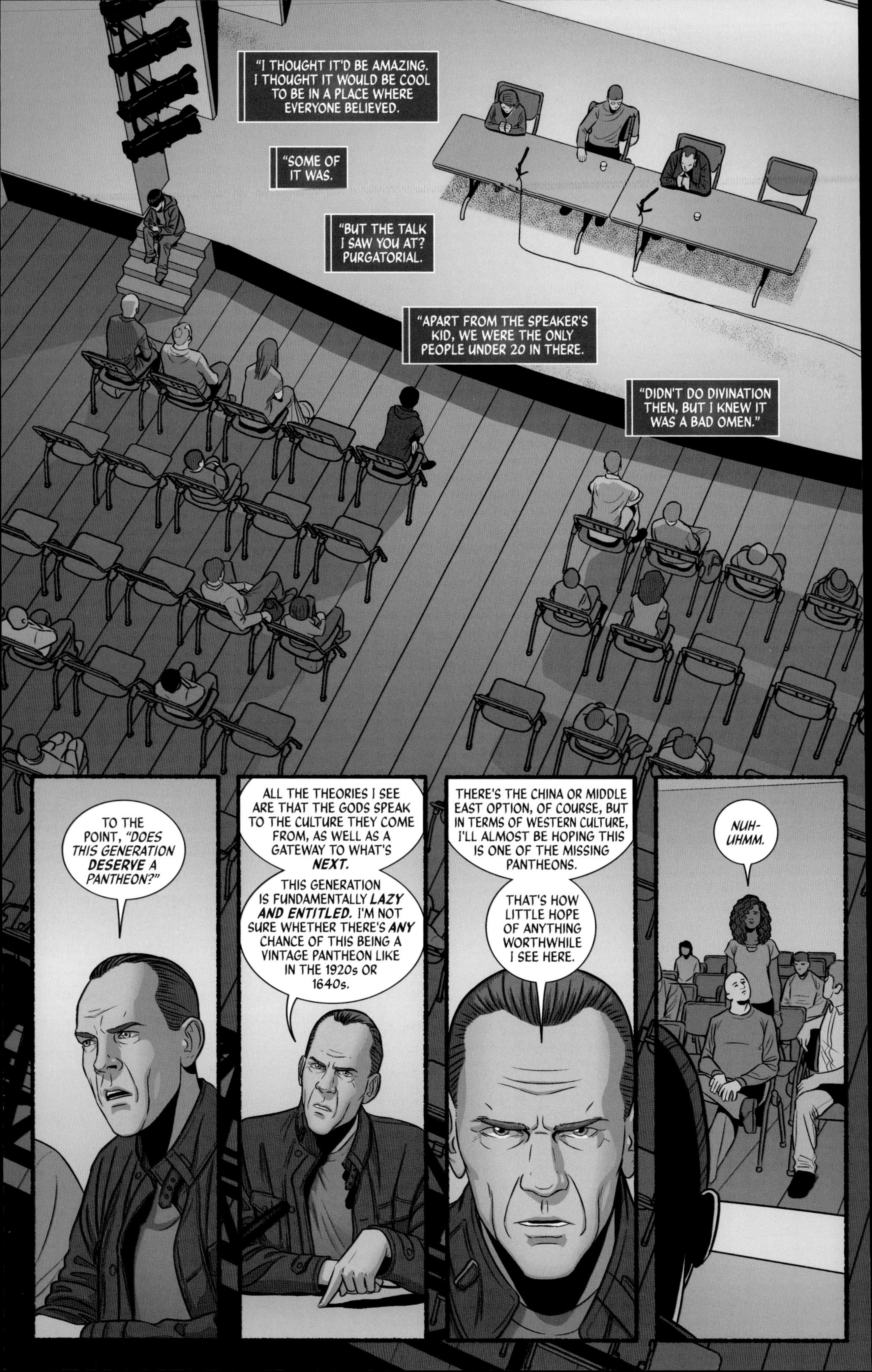
"I THOUGHT IT'D BE AMAZING. I THOUGHT IT WOULD BE COOL TO BE IN A PLACE WHERE EVERYONE BELIEVED.
"SOME OF IT WAS.
"BUT THE TALK I SAW YOU AT? PURGATORIAL.
"APART FROM THE SPEAKER'S KID, WE WERE THE ONLY PEOPLE UNDER 20 IN THERE.
"DIDN'T DO DIVINATION THEN, BUT I KNEW IT WAS A BAD OMEN."
TO THE POINT, *"DOES THIS GENERATION **DESERVE** A PANTHEON?"*
ALL THE THEORIES I SEE ARE THAT THE GODS SPEAK TO THE CULTURE THEY COME FROM, AS WELL AS A GATEWAY TO WHAT'S ***NEXT.***
THIS GENERATION IS FUNDAMENTALLY ***LAZY AND ENTITLED.*** I'M NOT SURE WHETHER THERE'S ***ANY*** CHANCE OF THIS BEING A VINTAGE PANTHEON LIKE IN THE 1920s OR 1640s.
THERE'S THE CHINA OR MIDDLE EAST OPTION, OF COURSE, BUT IN TERMS OF WESTERN CULTURE, I'LL ALMOST BE HOPING THIS IS ONE OF THE MISSING PANTHEONS.
THAT'S HOW LITTLE HOPE OF ANYTHING WORTHWHILE I SEE HERE.
NUH-UHMM.

YOU'RE ONLY SEEING CYCLES. LIKE...WHAT'S HAPPENED *BEFORE.* YOU DON'T KNOW ANYTHING ABOUT WHAT CAN HAPPEN *NOW.*

YOU HAVE NO FAITH. YOU DON'T *BELIEVE.*

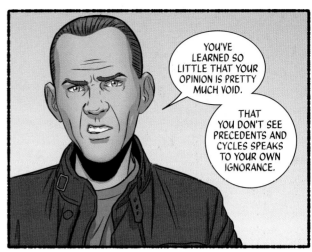

YOU'VE LEARNED SO LITTLE THAT YOUR OPINION IS PRETTY MUCH VOID.

THAT YOU DON'T SEE PRECEDENTS AND CYCLES SPEAKS TO YOUR OWN IGNORANCE.

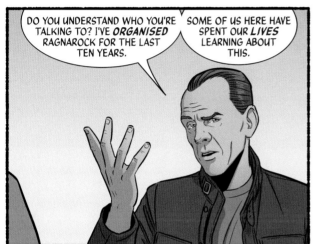

DO YOU UNDERSTAND WHO YOU'RE TALKING TO? I'VE *ORGANISED* RAGNAROCK FOR THE LAST TEN YEARS.

SOME OF US HERE HAVE SPENT OUR *LIVES* LEARNING ABOUT THIS.

YOU'VE LEARNED SO MUCH YOU KNOW *NOTHING.*

THANKS FOR THE EVIDENCE SUPPORTING MY POSITION. JUST LOOK AT YOU.

YOU DON'T *DESERVE* A PANTHEON.

LET'S TALK IN TWO YEARS.

YOU WERE FEARLESS.

NUH-UH. JUST ANGRY. I WENT OUTSIDE AND STOLE CIGARETTES UNTIL I STOPPED SHAKING. I'D NEVER EVEN SMOKED BEFORE...

...I'M SORRY, I DON'T REMEMBER YOU.

"YOU WOULDN'T THEN. MY GO-TO COSPLAY WAS WALLPAPER."

"EVERYTHING CHANGED AFTER ANANKE'S VISIT..."

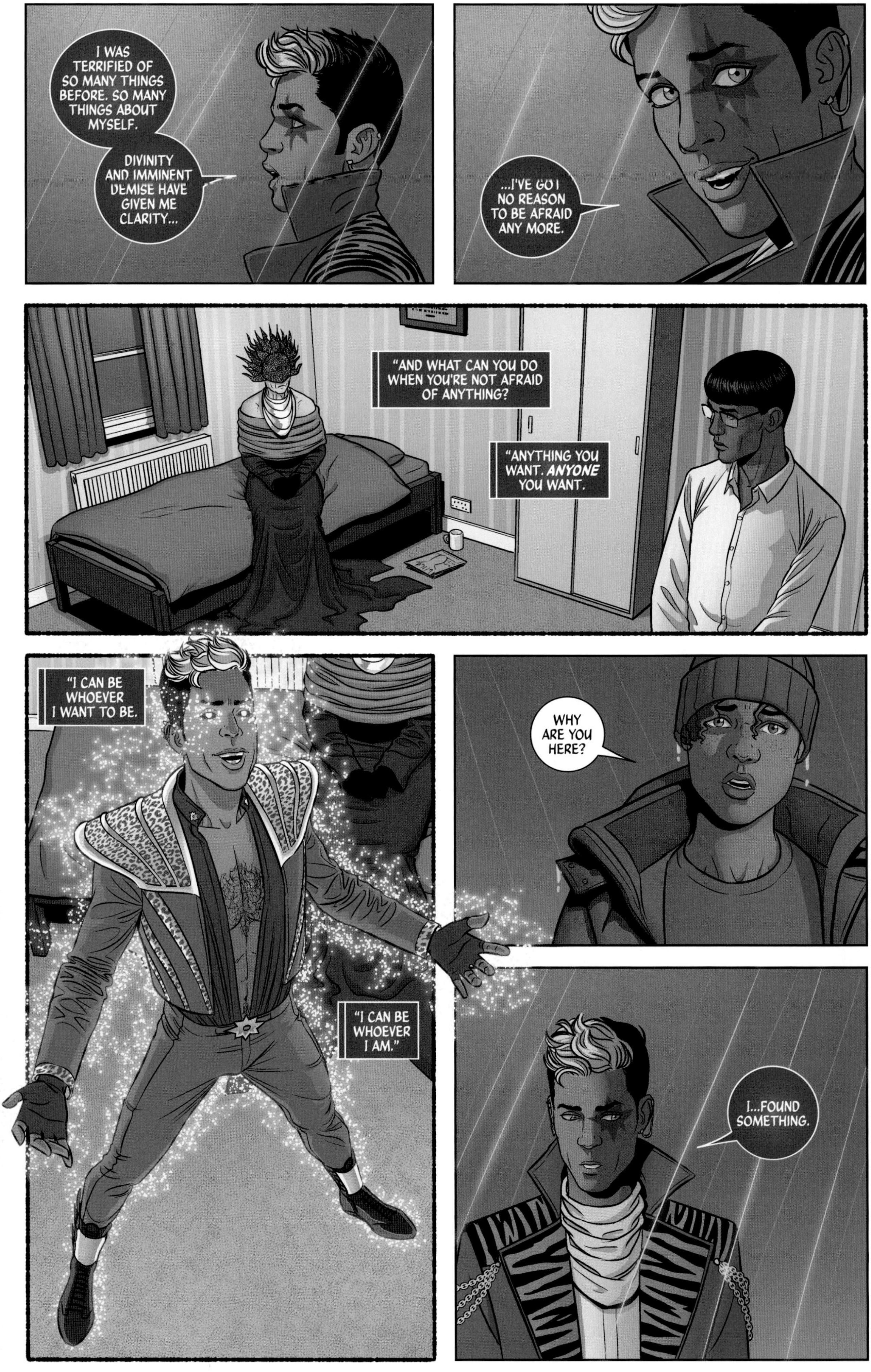
I WAS TERRIFIED OF SO MANY THINGS BEFORE. SO MANY THINGS ABOUT MYSELF.
DIVINITY AND IMMINENT DEMISE HAVE GIVEN ME CLARITY...
...I'VE GOT NO REASON TO BE AFRAID ANY MORE.
"AND WHAT CAN YOU DO WHEN YOU'RE NOT AFRAID OF ANYTHING?
"ANYTHING YOU WANT. ANYONE YOU WANT.
"I CAN BE WHOEVER I WANT TO BE.
"I CAN BE WHOEVER I AM."
WHY ARE YOU HERE?
I...FOUND SOMETHING.

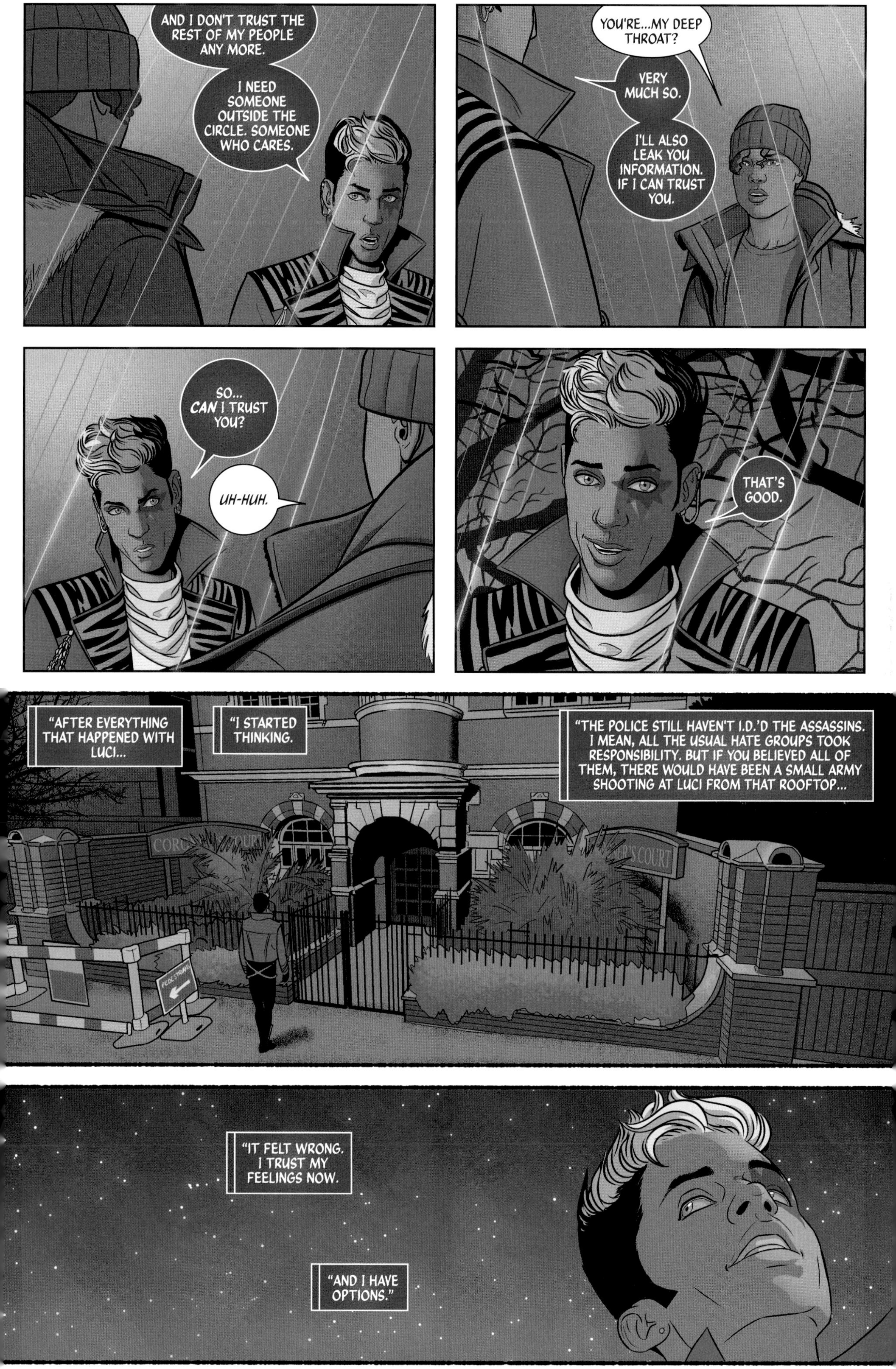
AND I DON'T TRUST THE REST OF MY PEOPLE ANY MORE.
I NEED SOMEONE OUTSIDE THE CIRCLE. SOMEONE WHO CARES.
YOU'RE...MY DEEP THROAT?
VERY MUCH SO.
I'LL ALSO LEAK YOU INFORMATION. IF I CAN TRUST YOU.
SO... *CAN* I TRUST YOU?
UH-HUH.
THAT'S GOOD.
"AFTER EVERYTHING THAT HAPPENED WITH LUCI...
"I STARTED THINKING.
"THE POLICE STILL HAVEN'T I.D.'D THE ASSASSINS. I MEAN, ALL THE USUAL HATE GROUPS TOOK RESPONSIBILITY. BUT IF YOU BELIEVED ALL OF THEM, THERE WOULD HAVE BEEN A SMALL ARMY SHOOTING AT LUCI FROM THAT ROOFTOP...
PEDESTRIANS
"IT FELT WRONG. I TRUST MY FEELINGS NOW.
"AND I HAVE OPTIONS."

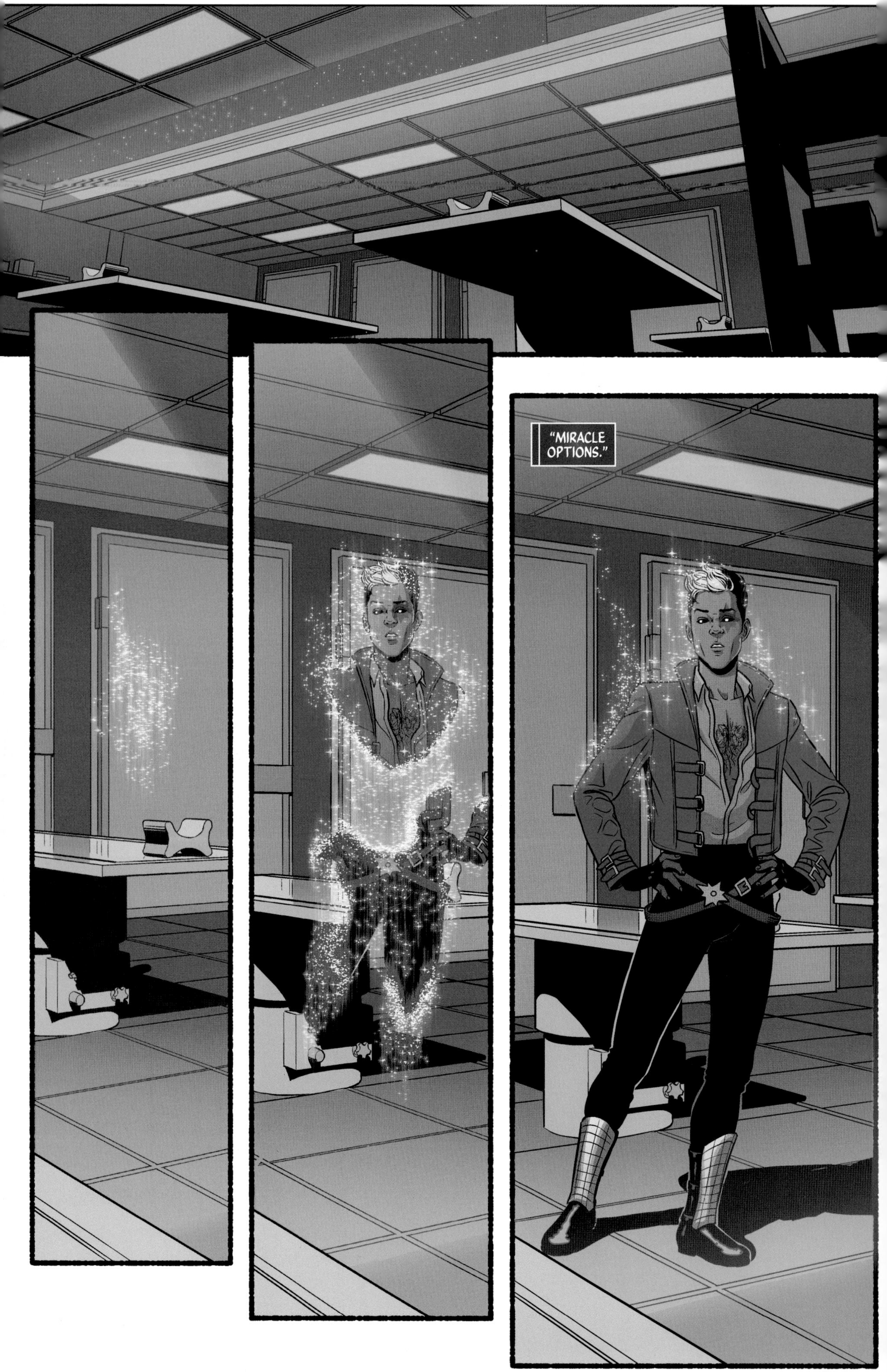
"MIRACLE OPTIONS."

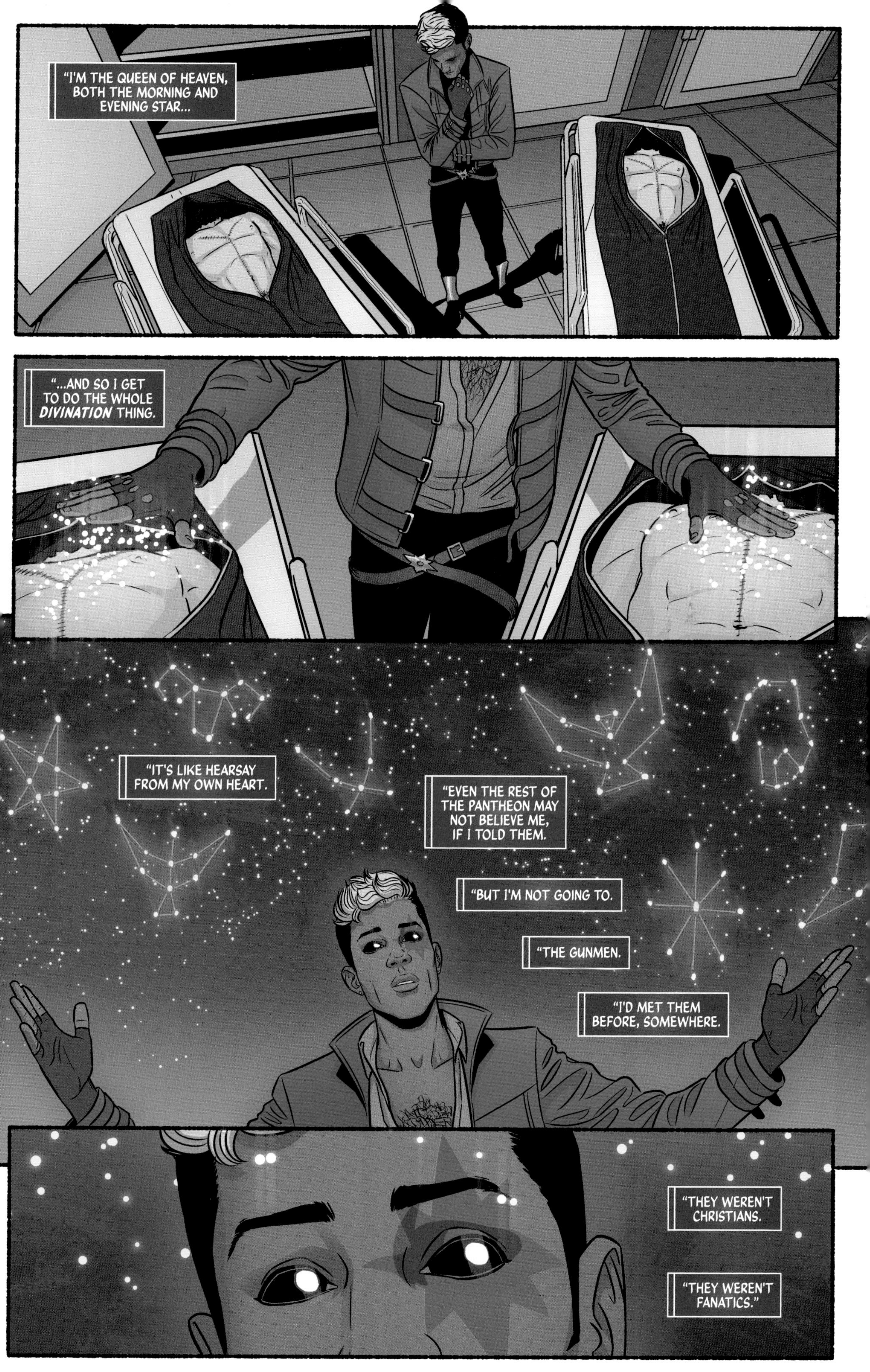
"I'M THE QUEEN OF HEAVEN, BOTH THE MORNING AND EVENING STAR...
"...AND SO I GET TO DO THE WHOLE *DIVINATION* THING.
"IT'S LIKE HEARSAY FROM MY OWN HEART.
"EVEN THE REST OF THE PANTHEON MAY NOT BELIEVE ME, IF I TOLD THEM.
"BUT I'M NOT GOING TO.
"THE GUNMEN.
"I'D MET THEM BEFORE, SOMEWHERE.
"THEY WEREN'T CHRISTIANS.
"THEY WEREN'T FANATICS."

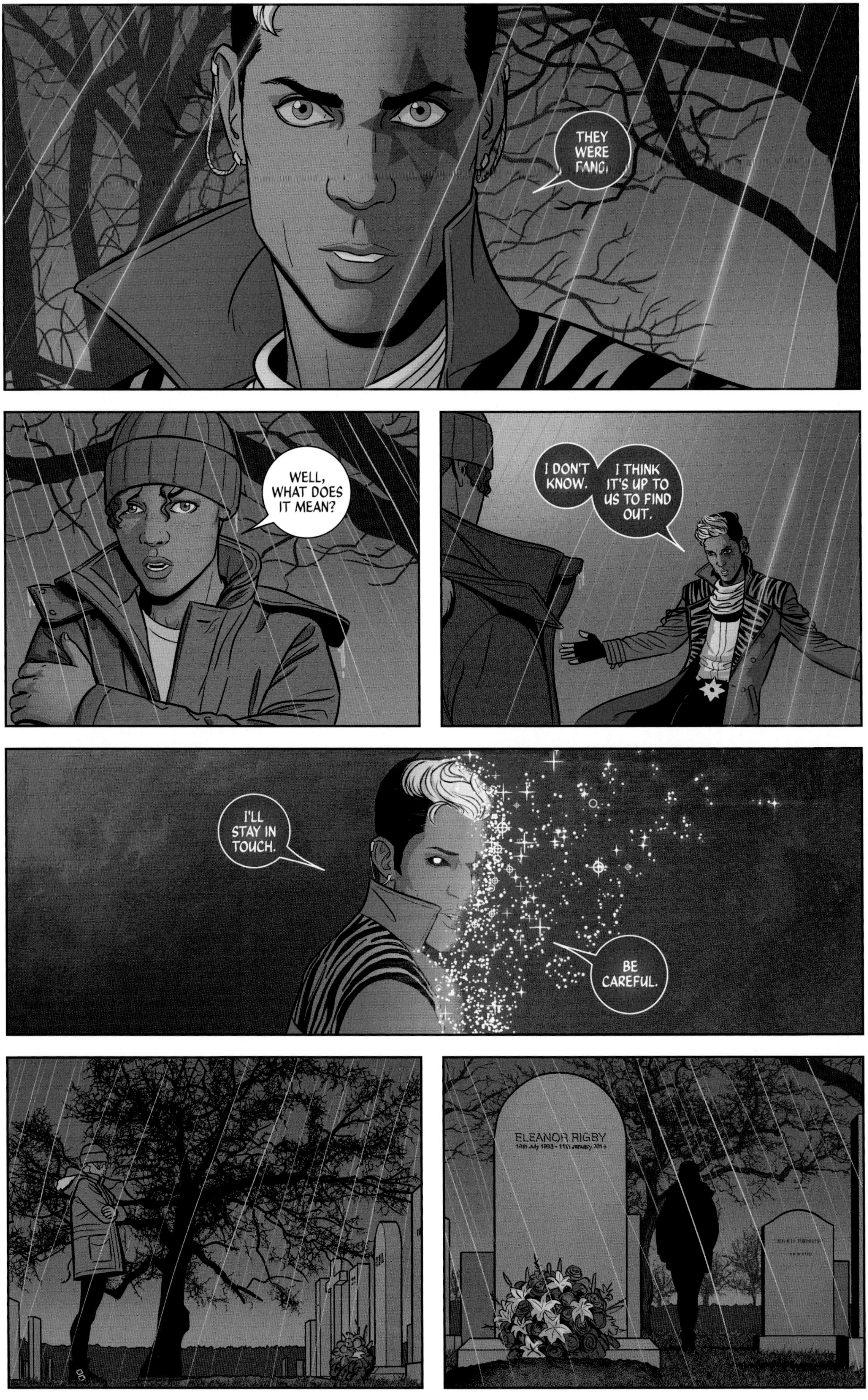
THEY WERE FANG.
WELL, WHAT DOES IT MEAN?
I DON'T KNOW.
I THINK IT'S UP TO US TO FIND OUT.
I'LL STAY IN TOUCH.
BE CAREFUL.
ELEANOR RIGBY

Fuck it.

Hey! I want to do some cons, gigs whatever. Will speak. Anyone want me?

Fuck it.

Hey! I want to do some con, whatever. Will speak. Anyone want me?

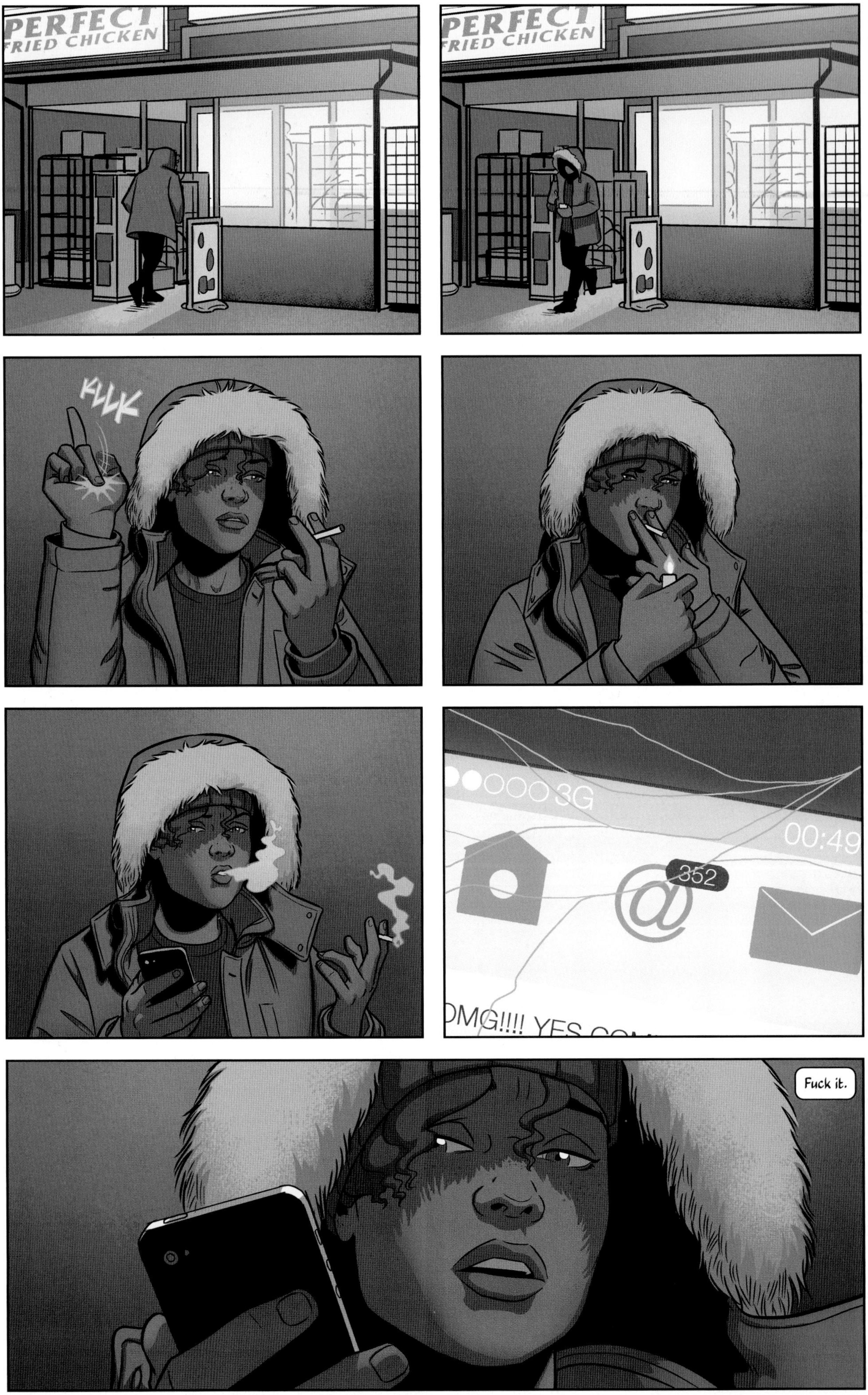
PERFECT FRIED CHICKEN
PERFECT FRIED CHICKEN
3G
00:49
352
OMG!!!! YES COM
Fuck it.

ABANDON
ALL HOPE

1 MARCH 2014

7

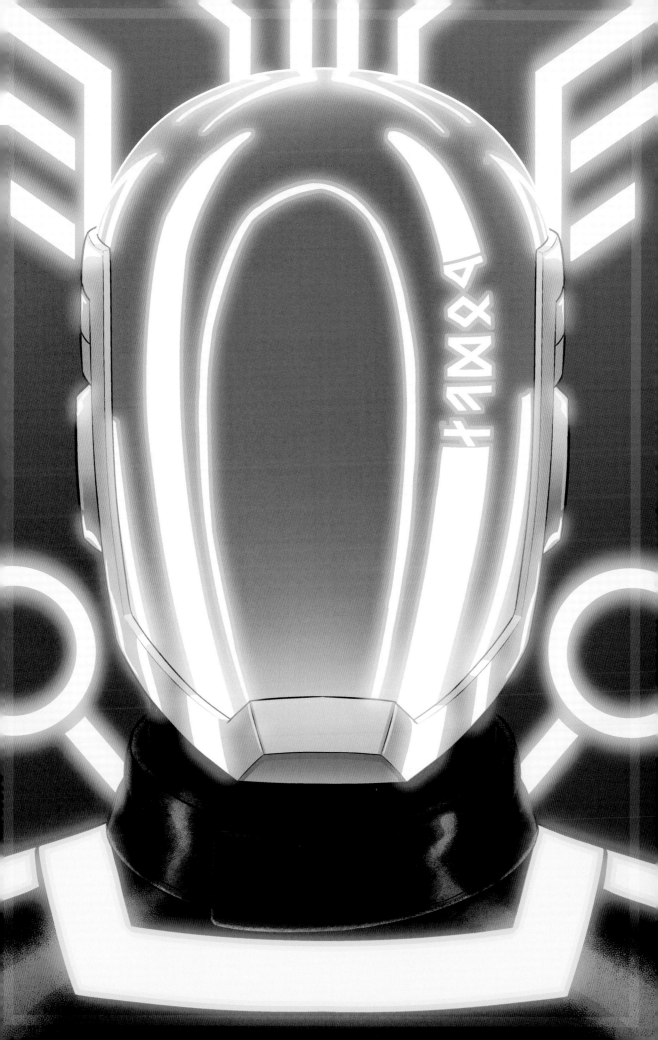

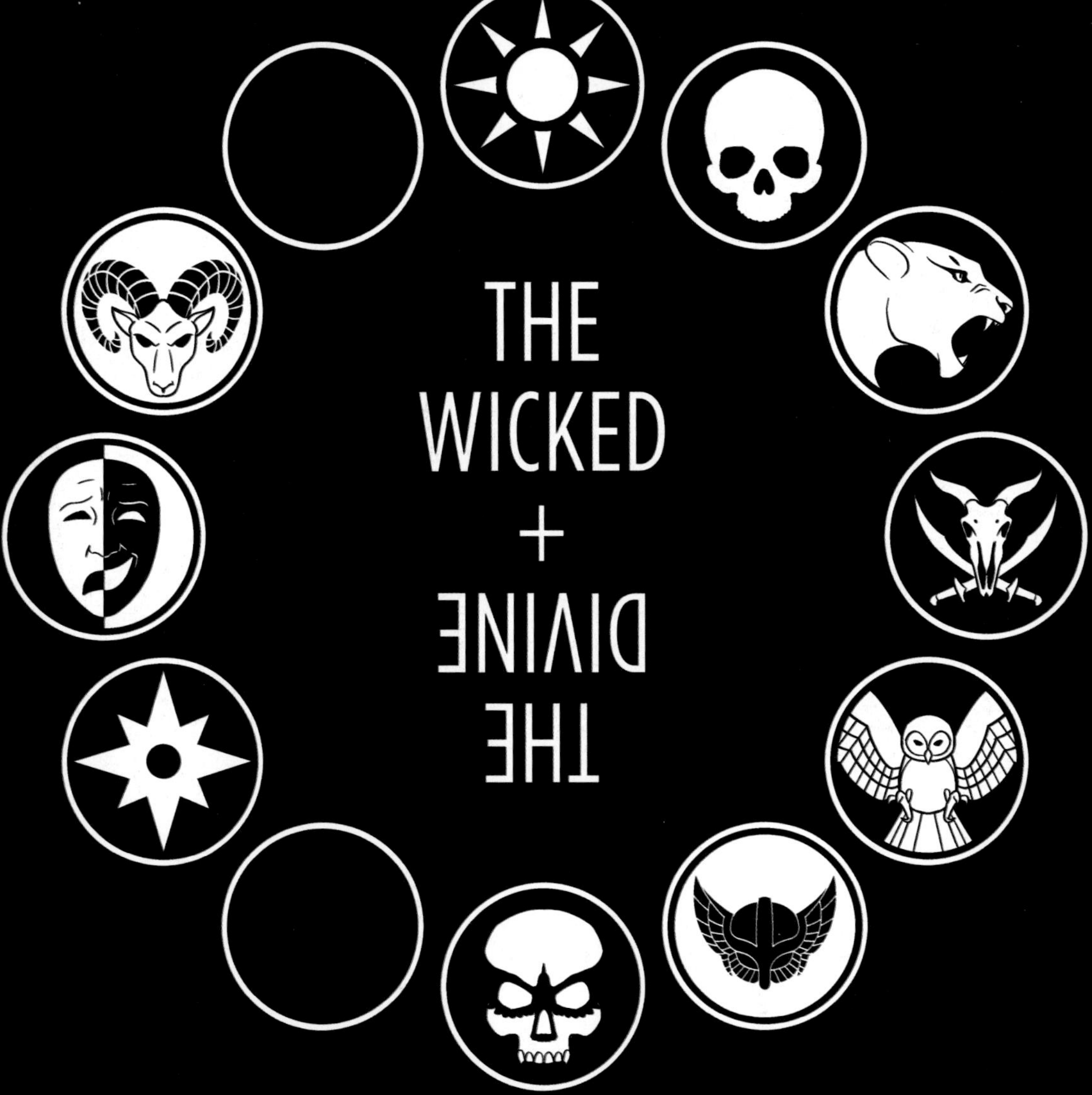
THE WICKED
+
THE DIVINE

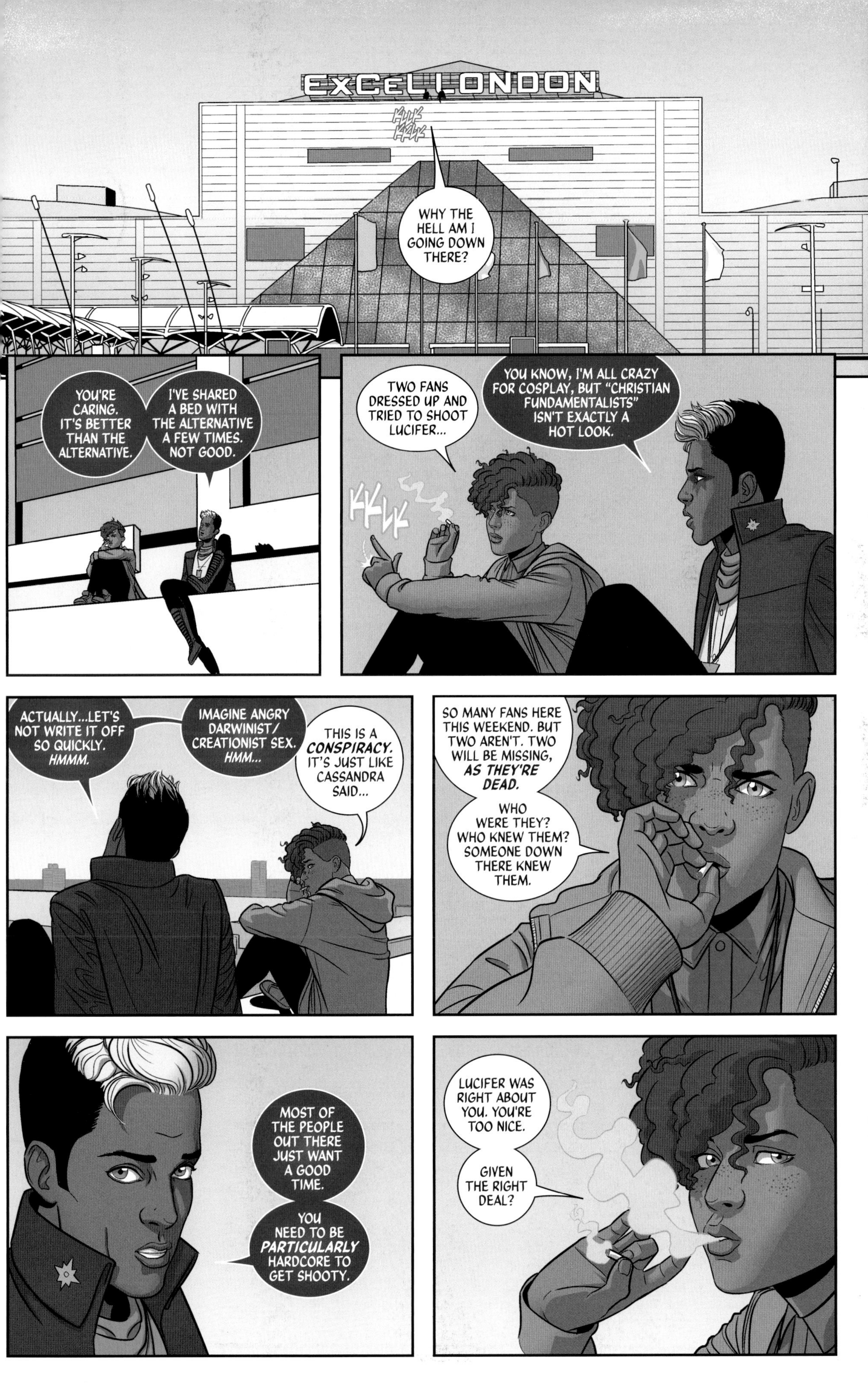
EXCEL LONDON
WHY THE HELL AM I GOING DOWN THERE?
YOU'RE CARING. IT'S BETTER THAN THE ALTERNATIVE.
I'VE SHARED A BED WITH THE ALTERNATIVE A FEW TIMES. NOT GOOD.
TWO FANS DRESSED UP AND TRIED TO SHOOT LUCIFER...
YOU KNOW, I'M ALL CRAZY FOR COSPLAY, BUT "CHRISTIAN FUNDAMENTALISTS" ISN'T EXACTLY A HOT LOOK.
ACTUALLY...LET'S NOT WRITE IT OFF SO QUICKLY. *HMMM.*
IMAGINE ANGRY DARWINIST/ CREATIONIST SEX. *HMM...*
THIS IS A ***CONSPIRACY.*** IT'S JUST LIKE CASSANDRA SAID...
SO MANY FANS HERE THIS WEEKEND. BUT TWO AREN'T. TWO WILL BE MISSING, ***AS THEY'RE DEAD.***
WHO WERE THEY? WHO KNEW THEM? SOMEONE DOWN THERE KNEW THEM.
MOST OF THE PEOPLE OUT THERE JUST WANT A GOOD TIME.
YOU NEED TO BE ***PARTICULARLY*** HARDCORE TO GET SHOOTY.
LUCIFER WAS RIGHT ABOUT YOU. YOU'RE TOO NICE.
GIVEN THE RIGHT DEAL?

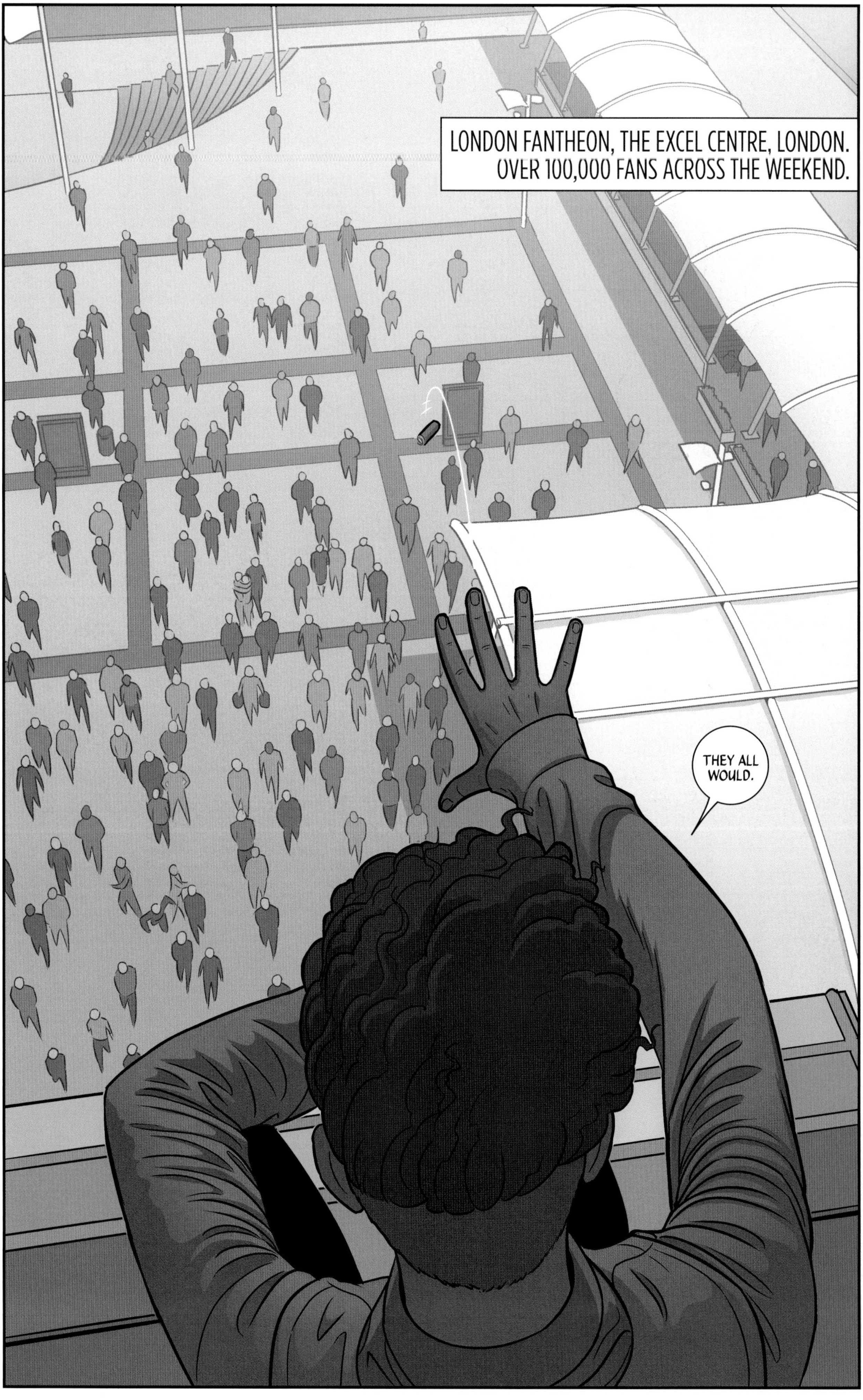
LONDON FANTHEON, THE EXCEL CENTRE, LONDON.
OVER 100,000 FANS ACROSS THE WEEKEND.
THEY ALL WOULD.

AWKWARD
CONVERSATION

12 APRIL 2014

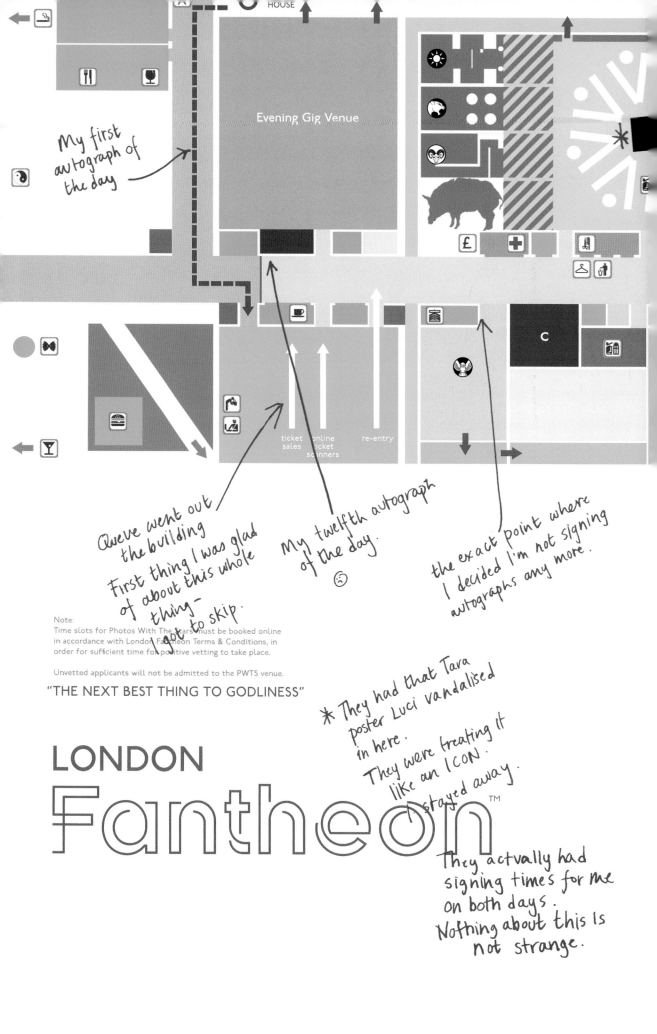

HOUSE
Evening Gig Venue
My first autograph of the day
C
ticket sales
online ticket scanners
re-entry

Queue went out the building

First thing I was glad of about this whole thing - I got to skip.

My twelfth autograph of the day. ☹

the exact point where I decided I'm not signing autographs any more.

Note:
Time slots for Photos With The Stars must be booked online in accordance with London Fantheon Terms & Conditions, in order for sufficient time for positive vetting to take place.

Unvetted applicants will not be admitted to the PWTS venue.

"THE NEXT BEST THING TO GODLINESS"

* They had that Tara poster Luci vandalised in here.
They were treating it like an ICON.
I stayed away.

LONDON
Fantheon™

They actually had signing times for me on both days.
Nothing about this is not strange.

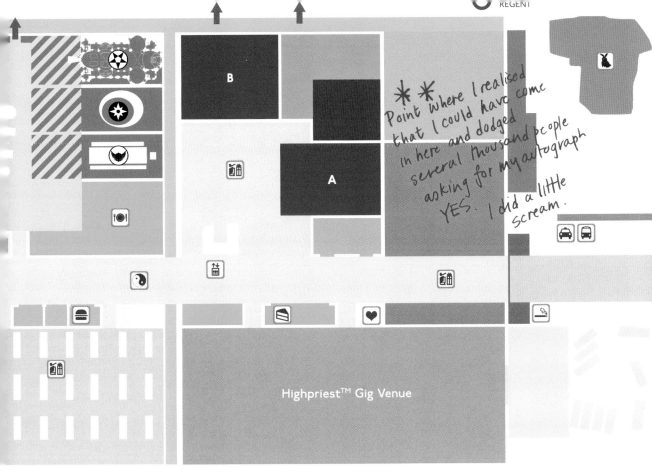
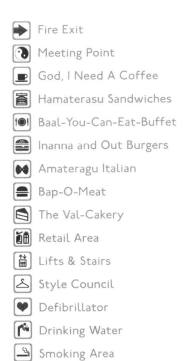

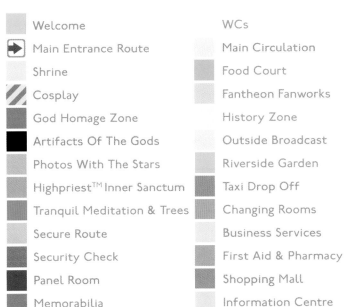

Welcome	WCs	Fire Exit
Main Entrance Route	Main Circulation	Meeting Point
Shrine	Food Court	God, I Need A Coffee
Cosplay	Fantheon Fanworks	Hamaterasu Sandwiches
God Homage Zone	History Zone	Baal-You-Can-Eat-Buffet
Artifacts Of The Gods	Outside Broadcast	Inanna and Out Burgers
Photos With The Stars	Riverside Garden	Amateragu Italian
Highpriest™ Inner Sanctum	Taxi Drop Off	Bap-O-Meat
Tranquil Meditation & Trees	Changing Rooms	The Val-Cakery
Secure Route	Business Services	Retail Area
Security Check	First Aid & Pharmacy	Lifts & Stairs
Panel Room	Shopping Mall	Style Council
Memorabilia	Information Centre	Defibrillator
Press Lounge	Gods' Private Hotel	Drinking Water
VIP Zone	VIP Drop Off	Smoking Area
Gig Space	External Area	ATM
	Family Space (becomes Recovery Room from 7pm onwards)	

2015 art & design: alison sampson
www.alisonsampsonart.tumblr.com

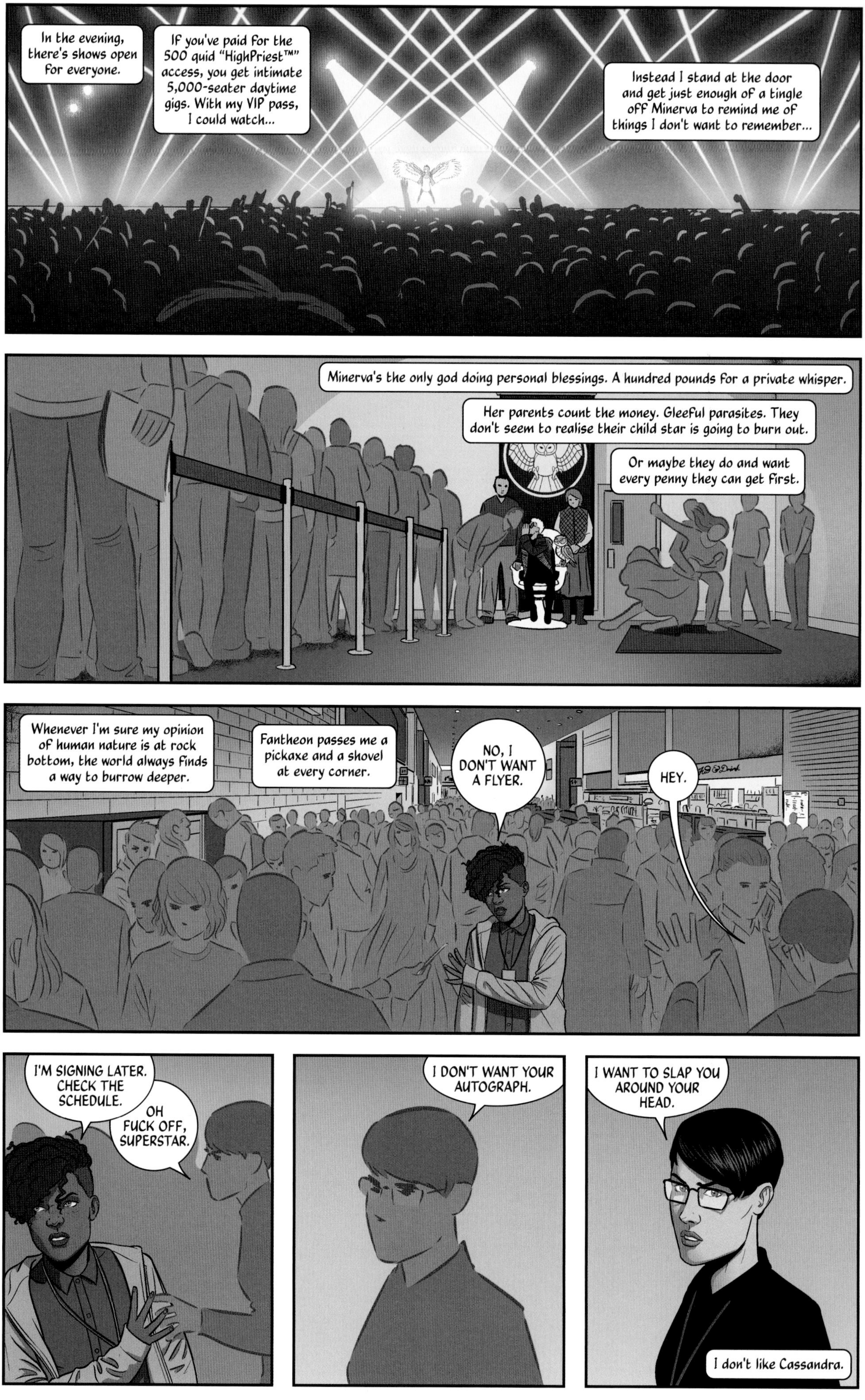
In the evening, there's shows open for everyone.
If you've paid for the 500 quid "HighPriest™" access, you get intimate 5,000-seater daytime gigs. With my VIP pass, I could watch...
Instead I stand at the door and get just enough of a tingle off Minerva to remind me of things I don't want to remember...
Minerva's the only god doing personal blessings. A hundred pounds for a private whisper.
Her parents count the money. Gleeful parasites. They don't seem to realise their child star is going to burn out.
Or maybe they do and want every penny they can get first.
Whenever I'm sure my opinion of human nature is at rock bottom, the world always finds a way to burrow deeper.
Fantheon passes me a pickaxe and a shovel at every corner.
NO, I DON'T WANT A FLYER.
HEY.
I'M SIGNING LATER. CHECK THE SCHEDULE.
OH FUCK OFF, SUPERSTAR.
I DON'T WANT YOUR AUTOGRAPH.
I WANT TO SLAP YOU AROUND YOUR HEAD.
I don't like Cassandra.

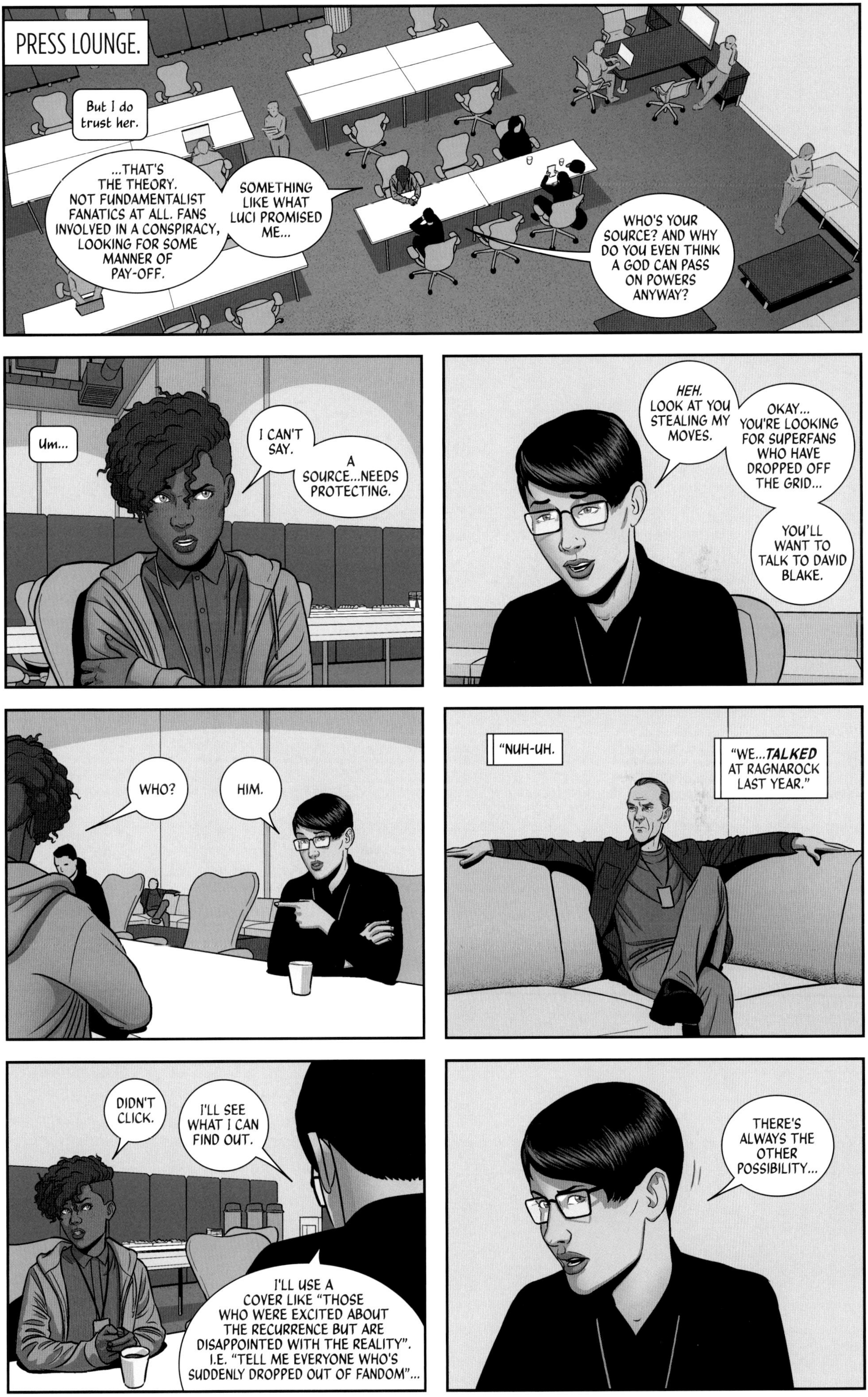
PRESS LOUNGE.
But I do trust her.
...THAT'S THE THEORY. NOT FUNDAMENTALIST FANATICS AT ALL. FANS INVOLVED IN A CONSPIRACY, LOOKING FOR SOME MANNER OF PAY-OFF.
SOMETHING LIKE WHAT LUCI PROMISED ME...
WHO'S YOUR SOURCE? AND WHY DO YOU EVEN THINK A GOD CAN PASS ON POWERS ANYWAY?
Um...
I CAN'T SAY.
A SOURCE...NEEDS PROTECTING.
HEH. LOOK AT YOU STEALING MY MOVES.
OKAY... YOU'RE LOOKING FOR SUPERFANS WHO HAVE DROPPED OFF THE GRID...
YOU'LL WANT TO TALK TO DAVID BLAKE.
WHO?
HIM.
"NUH-UH.
"WE...***TALKED*** AT RAGNAROCK LAST YEAR."
DIDN'T CLICK.
I'LL SEE WHAT I CAN FIND OUT.
I'LL USE A COVER LIKE "THOSE WHO WERE EXCITED ABOUT THE RECURRENCE BUT ARE DISAPPOINTED WITH THE REALITY". I.E. "TELL ME EVERYONE WHO'S SUDDENLY DROPPED OUT OF FANDOM"...
THERE'S ALWAYS THE OTHER POSSIBILITY...

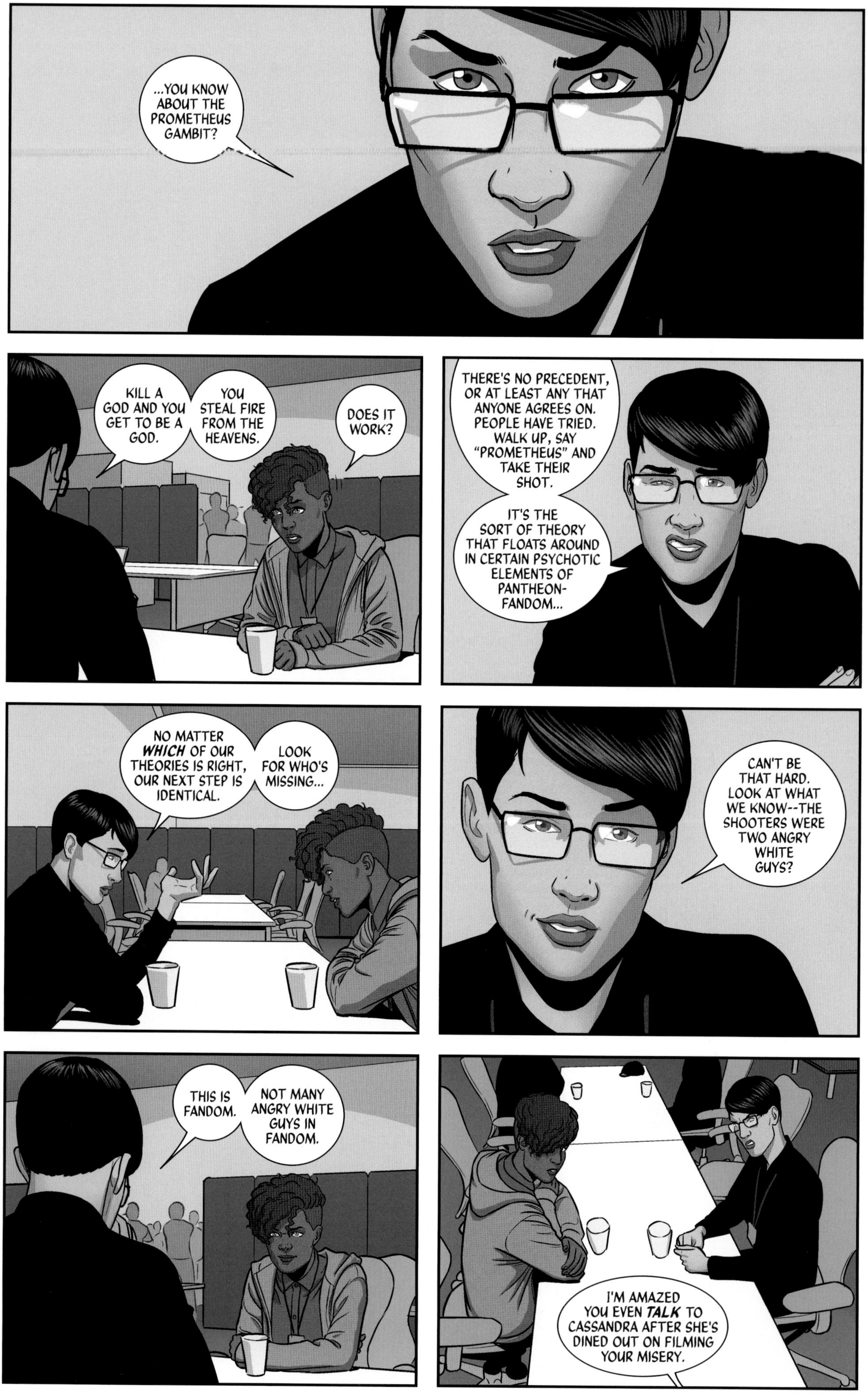
...YOU KNOW ABOUT THE PROMETHEUS GAMBIT?
KILL A GOD AND YOU GET TO BE A GOD.
YOU STEAL FIRE FROM THE HEAVENS.
DOES IT WORK?
THERE'S NO PRECEDENT, OR AT LEAST ANY THAT ANYONE AGREES ON. PEOPLE HAVE TRIED. WALK UP, SAY "PROMETHEUS" AND TAKE THEIR SHOT.
IT'S THE SORT OF THEORY THAT FLOATS AROUND IN CERTAIN PSYCHOTIC ELEMENTS OF PANTHEON-FANDOM...
NO MATTER ***WHICH*** OF OUR THEORIES IS RIGHT, OUR NEXT STEP IS IDENTICAL.
LOOK FOR WHO'S MISSING...
CAN'T BE THAT HARD. LOOK AT WHAT WE KNOW--THE SHOOTERS WERE TWO ANGRY WHITE GUYS?
THIS IS FANDOM.
NOT MANY ANGRY WHITE GUYS IN FANDOM.
I'M AMAZED YOU EVEN ***TALK*** TO CASSANDRA AFTER SHE'S DINED OUT ON FILMING YOUR MISERY.

WHICH PART OF *"YOU'RE FIRED, NEVER SPEAK TO ME AGAIN"* DON'T YOU UNDERSTAND, BETH?

HOW CAN YOU FIRE ME? THAT IMPLIES IT WAS A JOB. YOU WEREN'T EVEN PAYING.

BUT YOU'RE ROLLING IN YOUR BLOOD MONEY NOW THOUGH, AREN'T YOU?

FUCK YOU, BETH. YOU TOLD BAAL WHERE WE WERE.

YOU BLEW IT.

This is my fault. I told Cass.

Perhaps that was a mistake.

UH...NEED TO GET TO MY NEXT PANEL.

WE SHOULD GO.

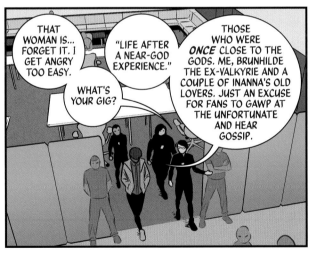

THAT WOMAN IS... FORGET IT. I GET ANGRY TOO EASY.

WHAT'S YOUR GIG?

"LIFE AFTER A NEAR-GOD EXPERIENCE."

THOSE WHO WERE *ONCE* CLOSE TO THE GODS. ME, BRUNHILDE THE EX-VALKYRIE AND A COUPLE OF INANNA'S OLD LOVERS. JUST AN EXCUSE FOR FANS TO GAWP AT THE UNFORTUNATE AND HEAR GOSSIP.

FANS. *HEH.* YOU KNOW WHAT THE WORD "FAN" DERIVES FROM?

FANATIC.

EVEN IF YOU'RE *RIGHT*, THE SHOOTERS WERE JUST ANOTHER KIND OF FANATIC.

YOU LIKE PATRONISING ME, DON'T YOU?

"UH-HUH."

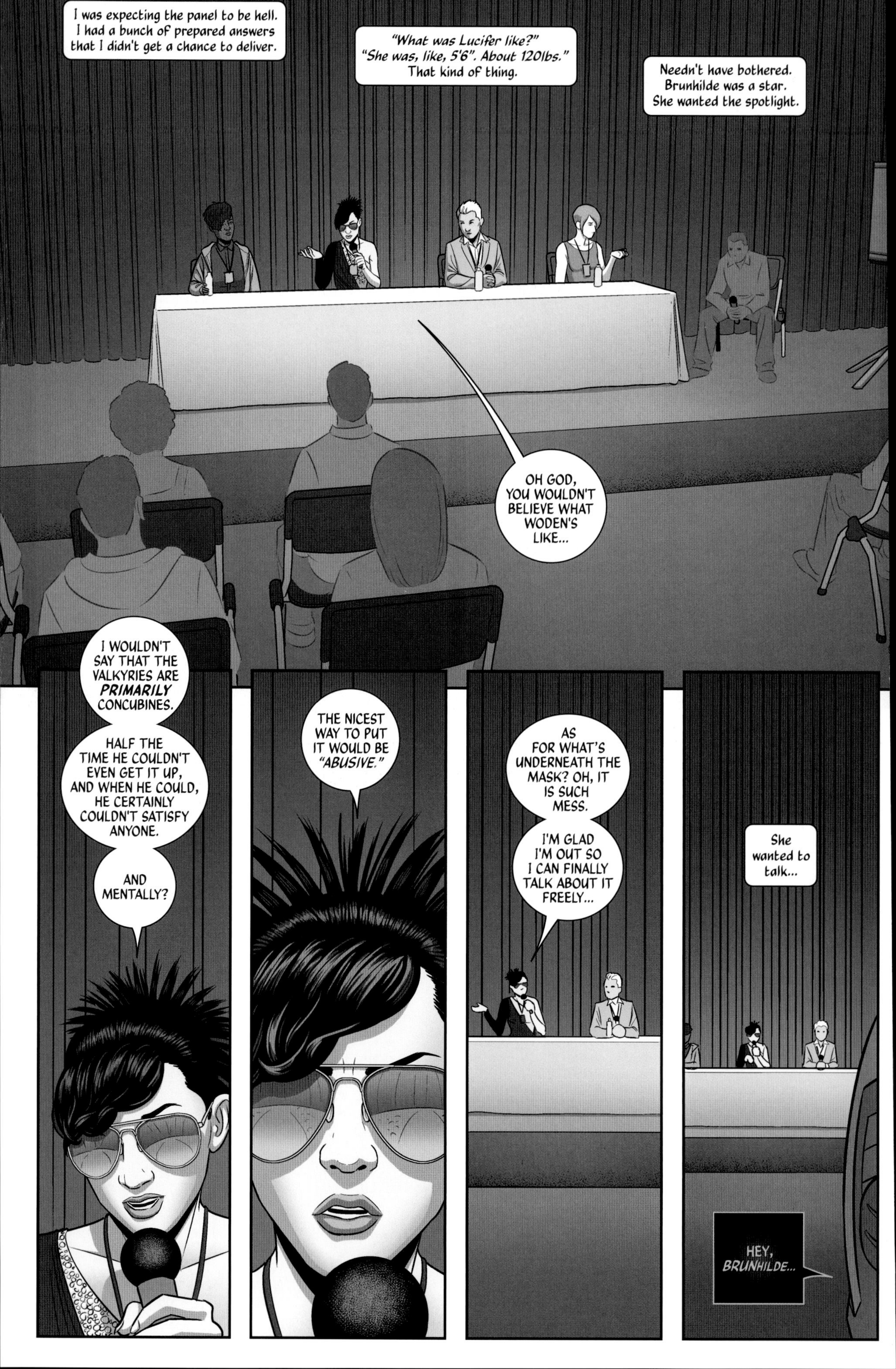
I was expecting the panel to be hell. I had a bunch of prepared answers that I didn't get a chance to deliver.
"What was Lucifer like?" "She was, like, 5'6". About 120lbs." That kind of thing.
Needn't have bothered. Brunhilde was a star. She wanted the spotlight.
OH GOD, YOU WOULDN'T BELIEVE WHAT WODEN'S LIKE...
I WOULDN'T SAY THAT THE VALKYRIES ARE *PRIMARILY* CONCUBINES.
HALF THE TIME HE COULDN'T EVEN GET IT UP, AND WHEN HE COULD, HE CERTAINLY COULDN'T SATISFY ANYONE.
AND MENTALLY?
THE NICEST WAY TO PUT IT WOULD BE *"ABUSIVE."*
AS FOR WHAT'S UNDERNEATH THE MASK? OH, IT IS SUCH MESS.
I'M GLAD I'M OUT SO I CAN FINALLY TALK ABOUT IT FREELY...
She wanted to talk...
HEY, *BRUNHILDE...*

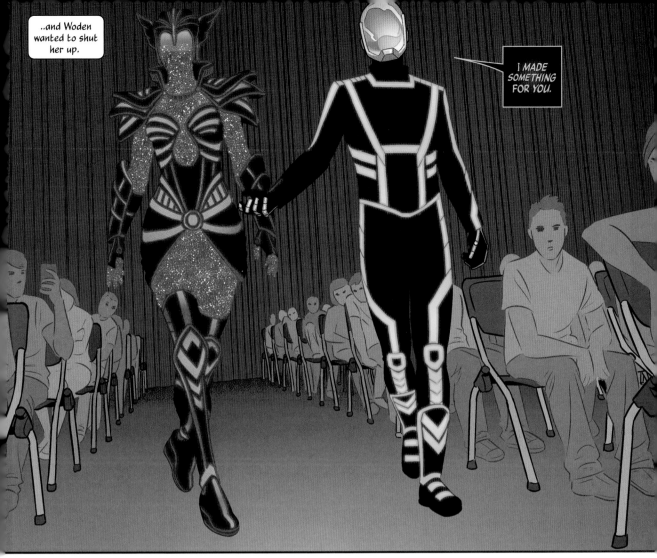

..and Woden wanted to shut her up.

I MADE SOMETHING FOR YOU.

I MISSED YOU. THE VALKYRIES AREN'T THE SAME.

ADMIT IT'S ALL LIES AND COME HOME.

YOU DON'T MEAN IT.

WOULD I HAVE MADE THIS FOR YOU IF I DIDN'T...

YOU KNOW IT'S NOT EASY.

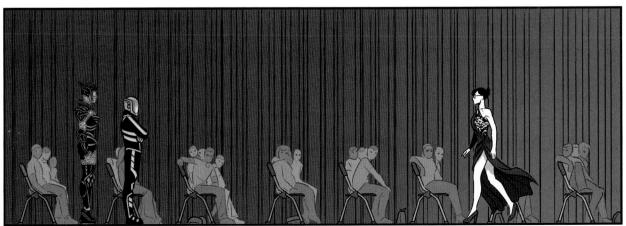

...DOES IT HAVE TO BE HERE?

IT DOES.

YOU KNOW I LOVE YOU, BUT I DON'T EXACTLY TRUST YOU ANY MORE.

IT WAS ALL LIES.

EVERY WORD OF IT.

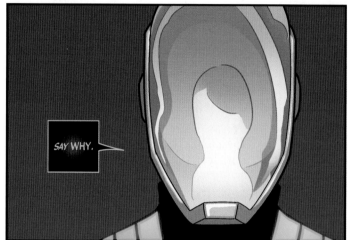

SAY WHY.

I WANTED TO GET BACK AT YOU FOR KICKING ME OUT.

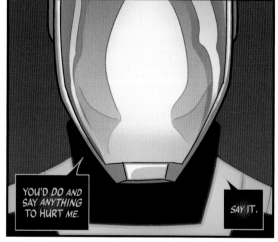

YOU'D DO AND SAY ANYTHING TO HURT ME.

SAY IT.

I'D DO AND SAY ANYTHING.

IT'S ALL I HAVE LEFT.

THANK YOU.

KLLK

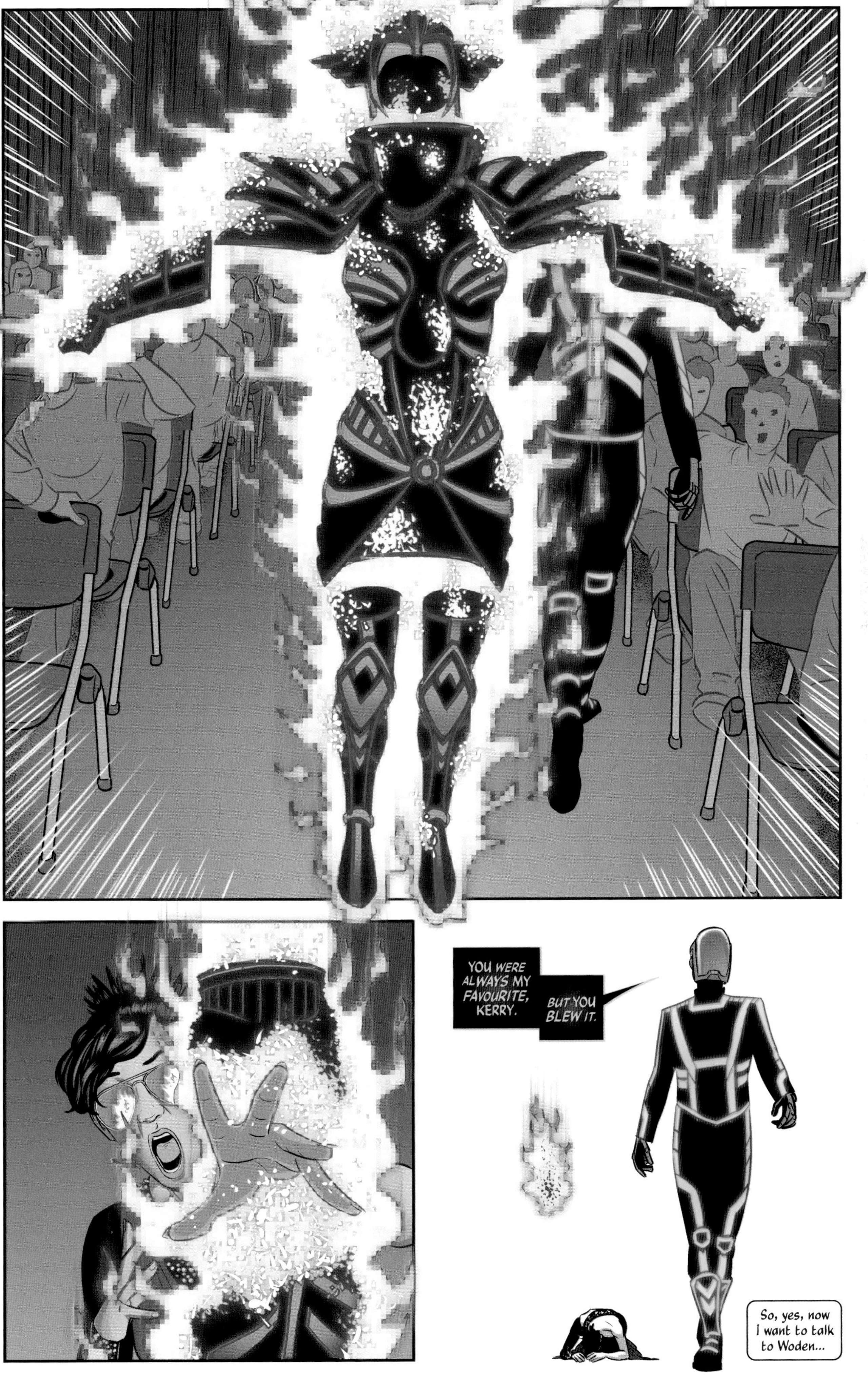
YOU WERE ALWAYS MY FAVOURITE, KERRY.
BUT YOU BLEW IT.
So, yes, now I want to talk to Woden...

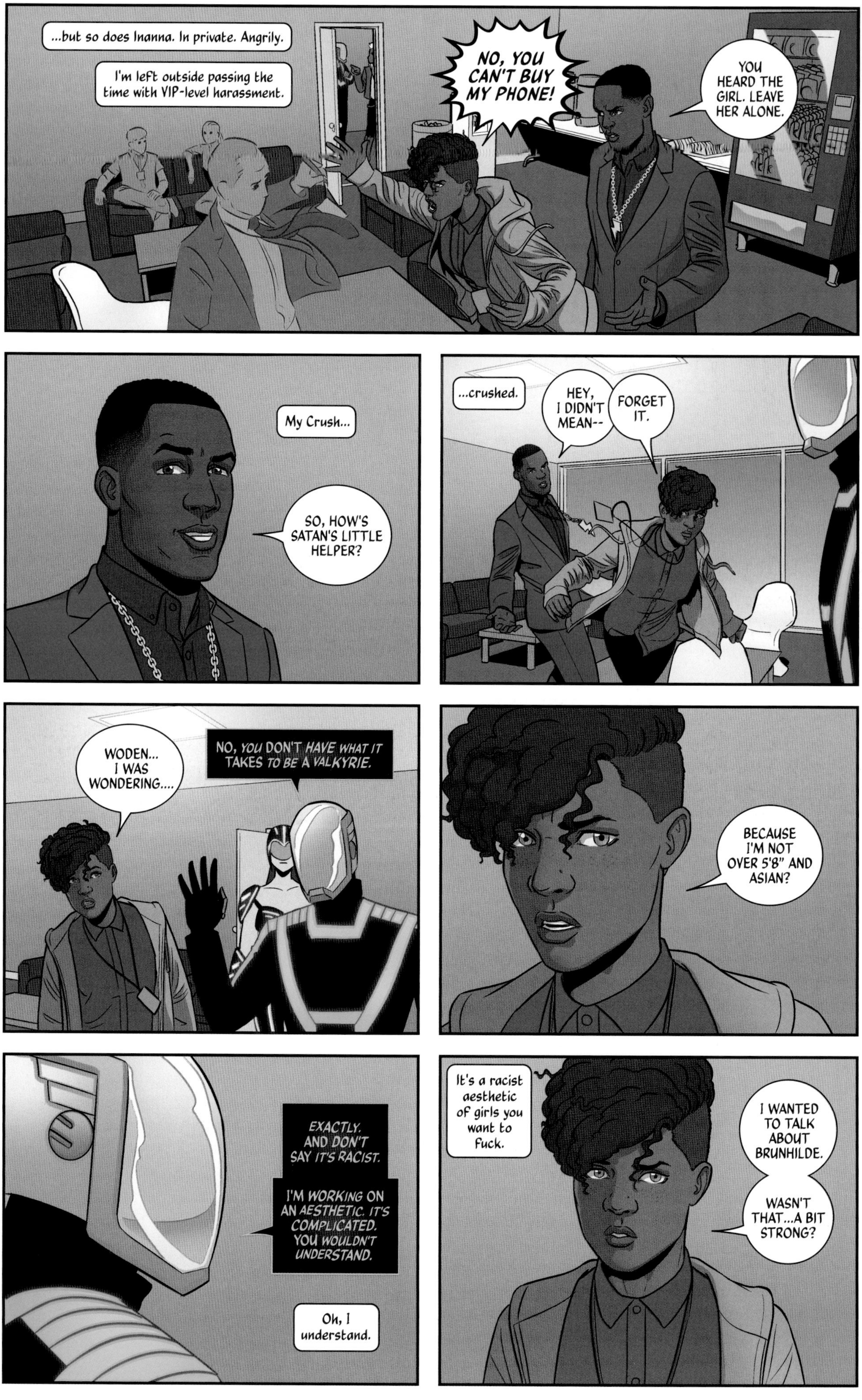
...but so does Inanna. In private. Angrily.
I'm left outside passing the time with VIP-level harassment.
NO, YOU CAN'T BUY MY PHONE!
YOU HEARD THE GIRL. LEAVE HER ALONE.
My Crush...
SO, HOW'S SATAN'S LITTLE HELPER?
...crushed.
HEY, I DIDN'T MEAN--
FORGET IT.
WODEN... I WAS WONDERING....
NO, YOU DON'T HAVE WHAT IT TAKES TO BE A VALKYRIE.
BECAUSE I'M NOT OVER 5'8" AND ASIAN?
EXACTLY. AND DON'T SAY IT'S RACIST.
I'M WORKING ON AN AESTHETIC. IT'S COMPLICATED. YOU WOULDN'T UNDERSTAND.
Oh, I understand.
It's a racist aesthetic of girls you want to fuck.
I WANTED TO TALK ABOUT BRUNHILDE.
WASN'T THAT...A BIT STRONG?

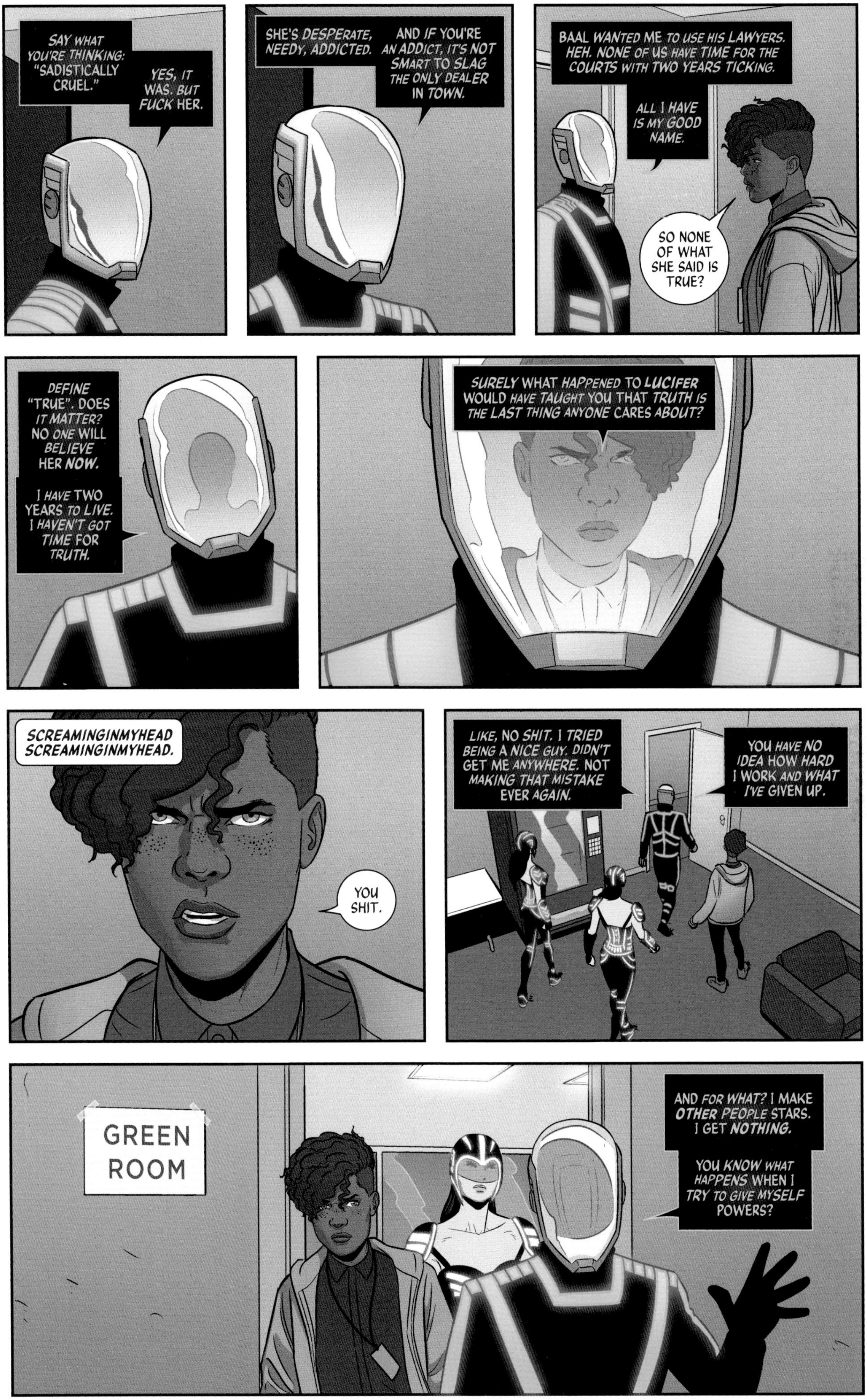
SAY WHAT YOU'RE THINKING: "SADISTICALLY CRUEL."
YES, IT WAS. BUT FUCK HER.
SHE'S DESPERATE, NEEDY, ADDICTED.
AND IF YOU'RE AN ADDICT, IT'S NOT SMART TO SLAG THE ONLY DEALER IN TOWN.
BAAL WANTED ME TO USE HIS LAWYERS. HEH. NONE OF US HAVE TIME FOR THE COURTS WITH TWO YEARS TICKING.
ALL I HAVE IS MY GOOD NAME.
SO NONE OF WHAT SHE SAID IS TRUE?
DEFINE "TRUE". DOES IT MATTER? NO ONE WILL BELIEVE HER NOW.
I HAVE TWO YEARS TO LIVE. I HAVEN'T GOT TIME FOR TRUTH.
SURELY WHAT HAPPENED TO LUCIFER WOULD HAVE TAUGHT YOU THAT TRUTH IS THE LAST THING ANYONE CARES ABOUT?
SCREAMINGINMYHEAD SCREAMINGINMYHEAD.
YOU SHIT.
LIKE, NO SHIT. I TRIED BEING A NICE GUY. DIDN'T GET ME ANYWHERE. NOT MAKING THAT MISTAKE EVER AGAIN.
YOU HAVE NO IDEA HOW HARD I WORK AND WHAT I'VE GIVEN UP.
GREEN ROOM
AND FOR WHAT? I MAKE OTHER PEOPLE STARS. I GET NOTHING.
YOU KNOW WHAT HAPPENS WHEN I TRY TO GIVE MYSELF POWERS?

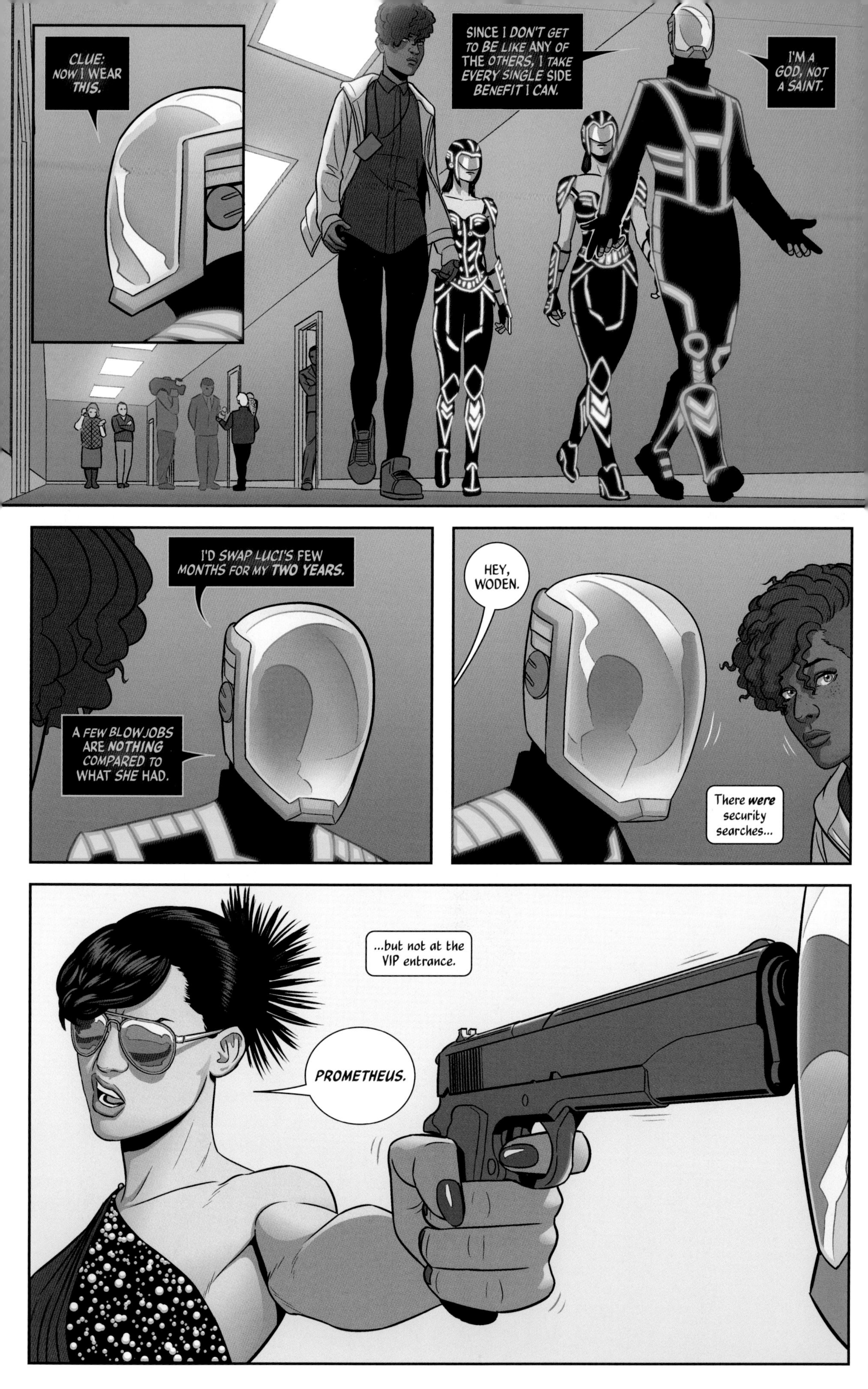
CLUE: NOW I WEAR THIS.
SINCE I DON'T GET TO BE LIKE ANY OF THE OTHERS, I TAKE EVERY SINGLE SIDE BENEFIT I CAN.
I'M A GOD, NOT A SAINT.
I'D SWAP LUCI'S FEW MONTHS FOR MY TWO YEARS.
A FEW BLOWJOBS ARE NOTHING COMPARED TO WHAT SHE HAD.
HEY, WODEN.
There were security searches...
...but not at the VIP entrance.
PROMETHEUS.

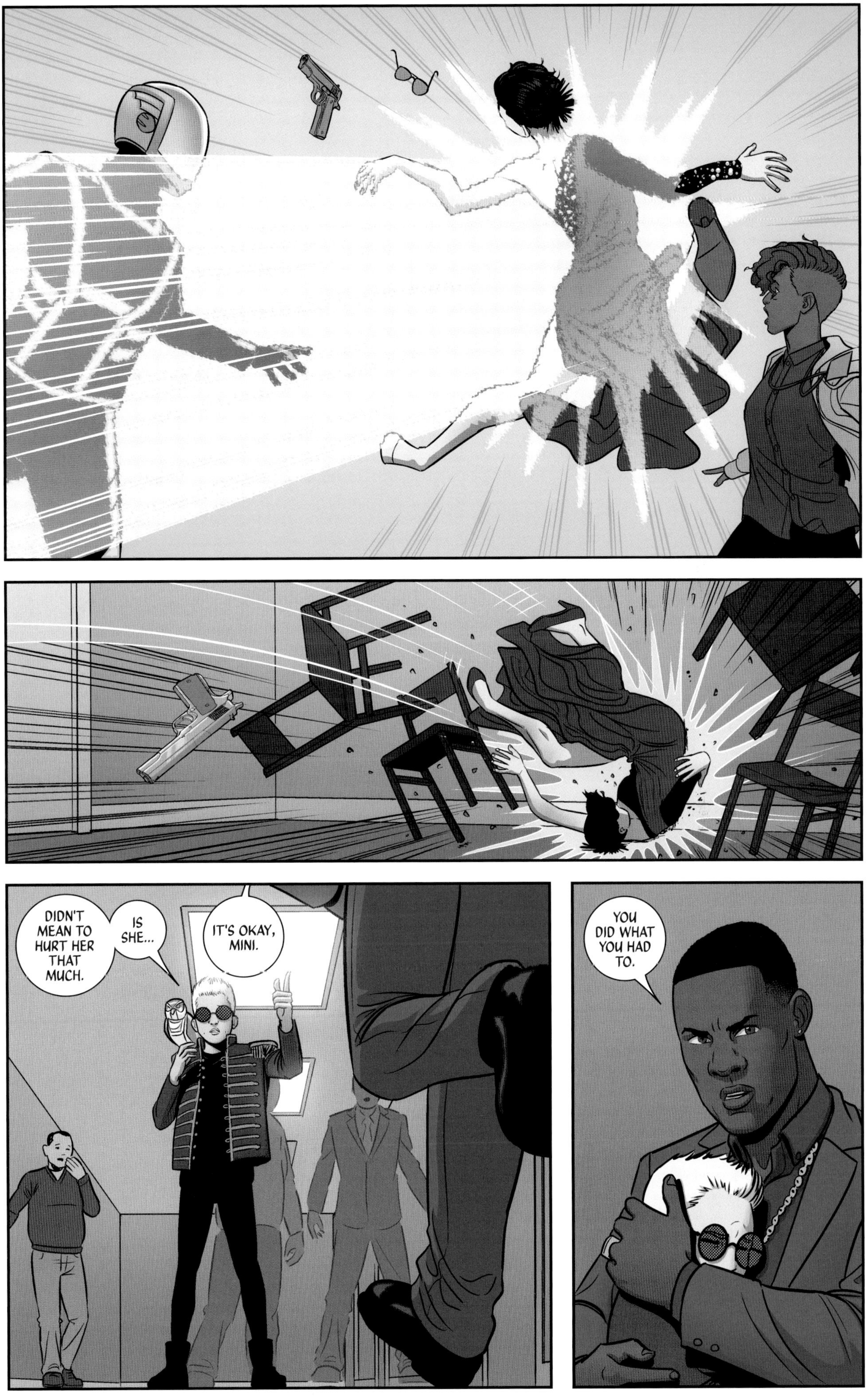
DIDN'T MEAN TO HURT HER THAT MUCH.
IS SHE...
IT'S OKAY, MINI.
YOU DID WHAT YOU HAD TO.

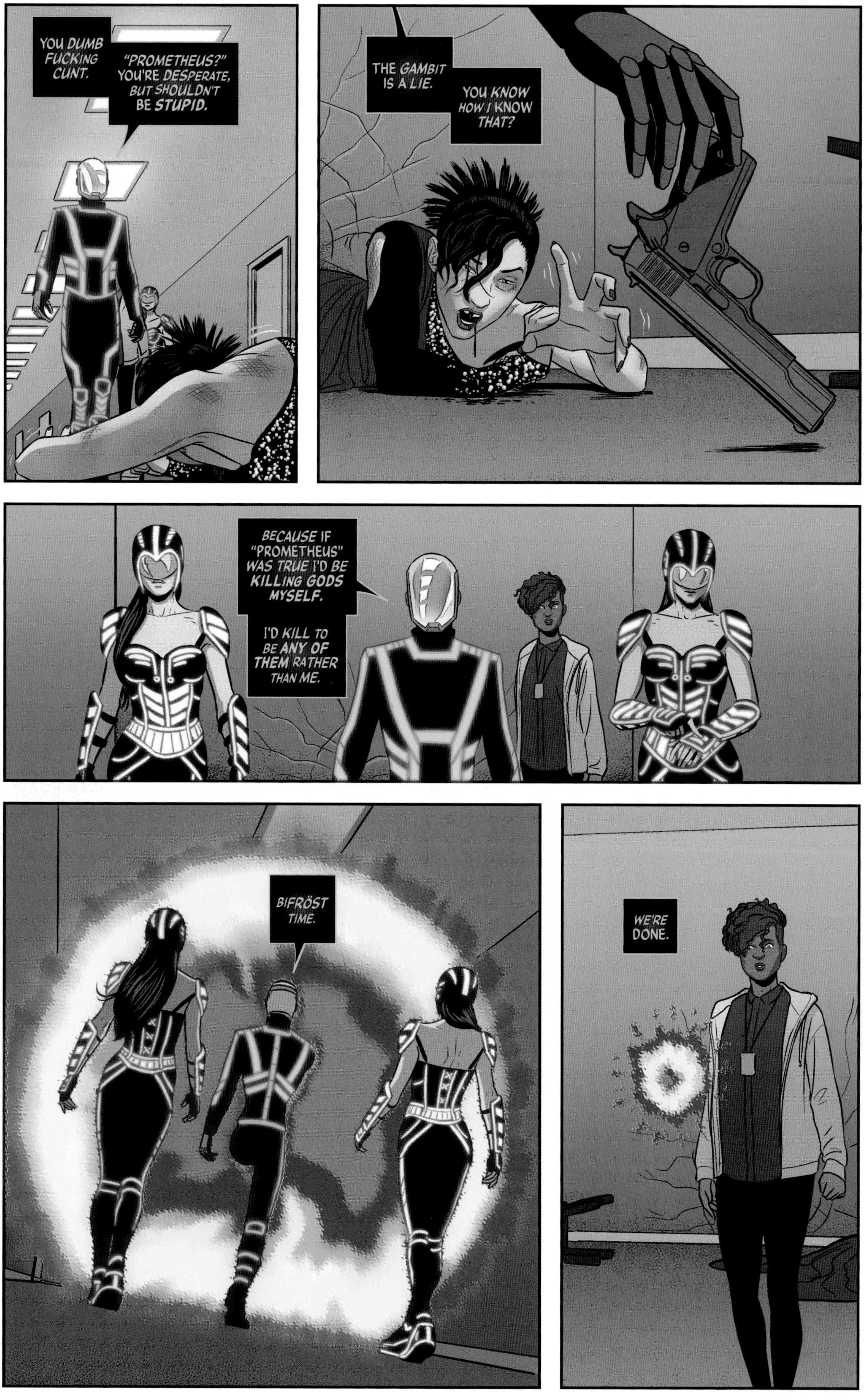
YOU DUMB FUCKING CUNT.
"PROMETHEUS?" YOU'RE DESPERATE, BUT SHOULDN'T BE STUPID.
THE GAMBIT IS A LIE.
YOU KNOW HOW I KNOW THAT?
BECAUSE IF "PROMETHEUS" WAS TRUE I'D BE KILLING GODS MYSELF.
I'D KILL TO BE ANY OF THEM RATHER THAN ME.
BIFRÖST TIME.
WE'RE DONE.

BAD
COMPANY

13 APRIL 2014

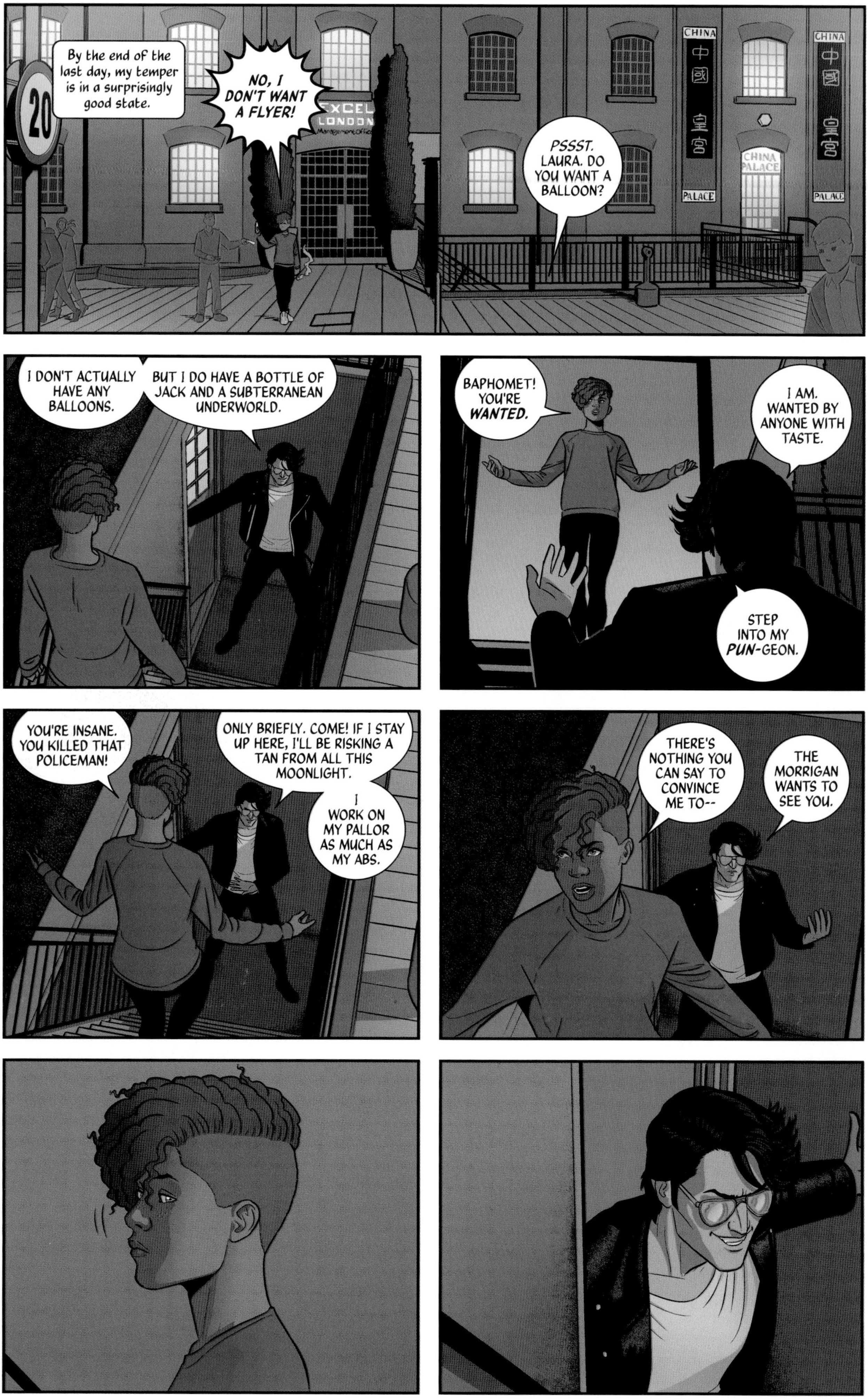
20
By the end of the last day, my temper is in a surprisingly good state.
NO, I DON'T WANT A FLYER!
PSSST. LAURA. DO YOU WANT A BALLOON?
CHINA 中國 皇宮 PALACE
CHINA PALACE
I DON'T ACTUALLY HAVE ANY BALLOONS.
BUT I DO HAVE A BOTTLE OF JACK AND A SUBTERRANEAN UNDERWORLD.
BAPHOMET! YOU'RE *WANTED.*
I AM. WANTED BY ANYONE WITH TASTE.
STEP INTO MY *PUN*-GEON.
YOU'RE INSANE. YOU KILLED THAT POLICEMAN!
ONLY BRIEFLY. COME! IF I STAY UP HERE, I'LL BE RISKING A TAN FROM ALL THIS MOONLIGHT.
I WORK ON MY PALLOR AS MUCH AS MY ABS.
THERE'S NOTHING YOU CAN SAY TO CONVINCE ME TO--
THE MORRIGAN WANTS TO SEE YOU.

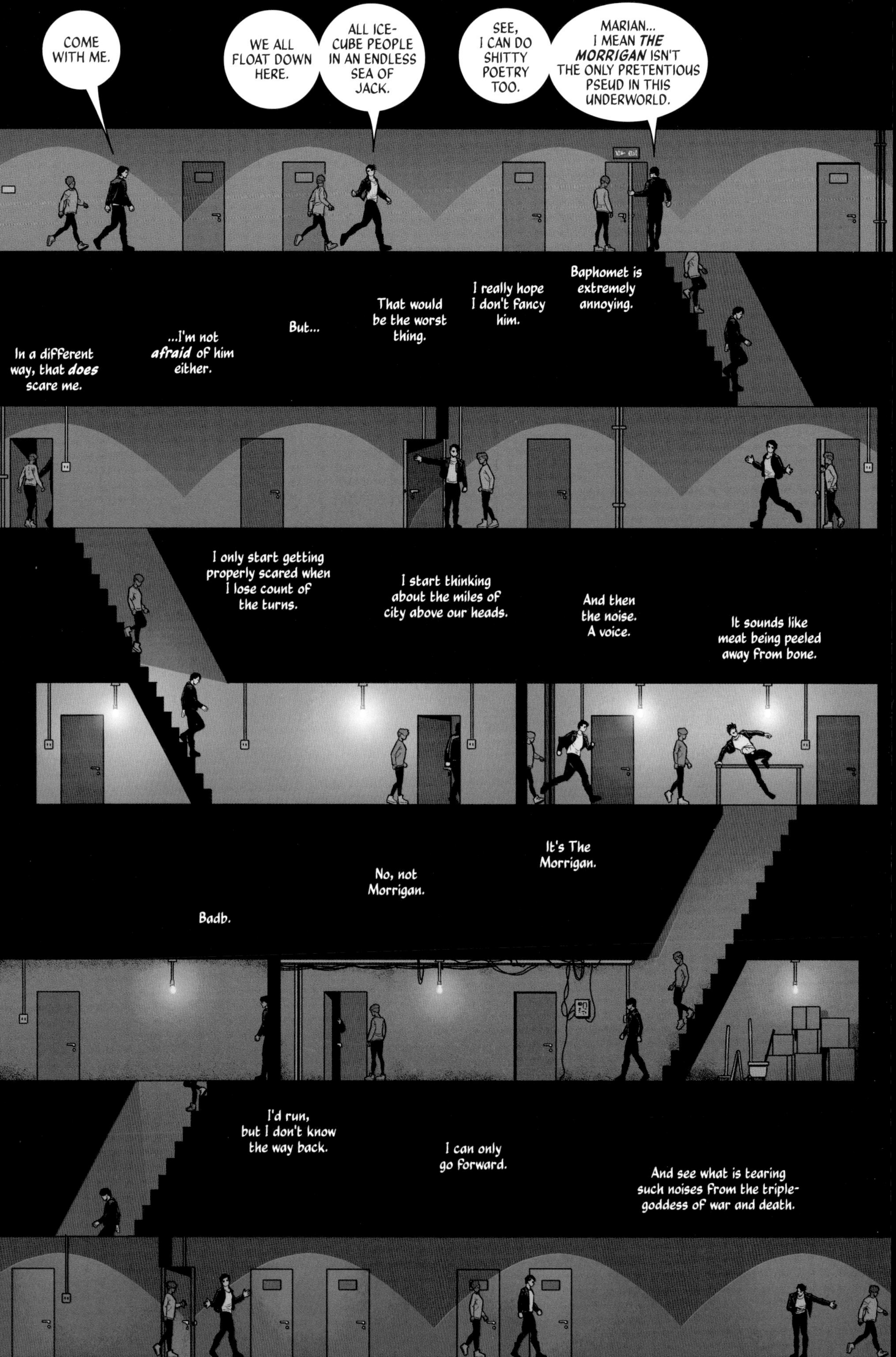
COME WITH ME.
WE ALL FLOAT DOWN HERE.
ALL ICE-CUBE PEOPLE IN AN ENDLESS SEA OF JACK.
SEE, I CAN DO SHITTY POETRY TOO.
MARIAN... I MEAN ***THE MORRIGAN*** ISN'T THE ONLY PRETENTIOUS PSEUD IN THIS UNDERWORLD.
Baphomet is extremely annoying.
I really hope I don't fancy him.
That would be the worst thing.
But...
...I'm not *afraid* of him either.
In a different way, that *does* scare me.
I only start getting properly scared when I lose count of the turns.
I start thinking about the miles of city above our heads.
And then the noise. A voice.
It sounds like meat being peeled away from bone.
It's The Morrigan.
No, not Morrigan.
Badb.
I'd run, but I don't know the way back.
I can only go forward.
And see what is tearing such noises from the triple-goddess of war and death.

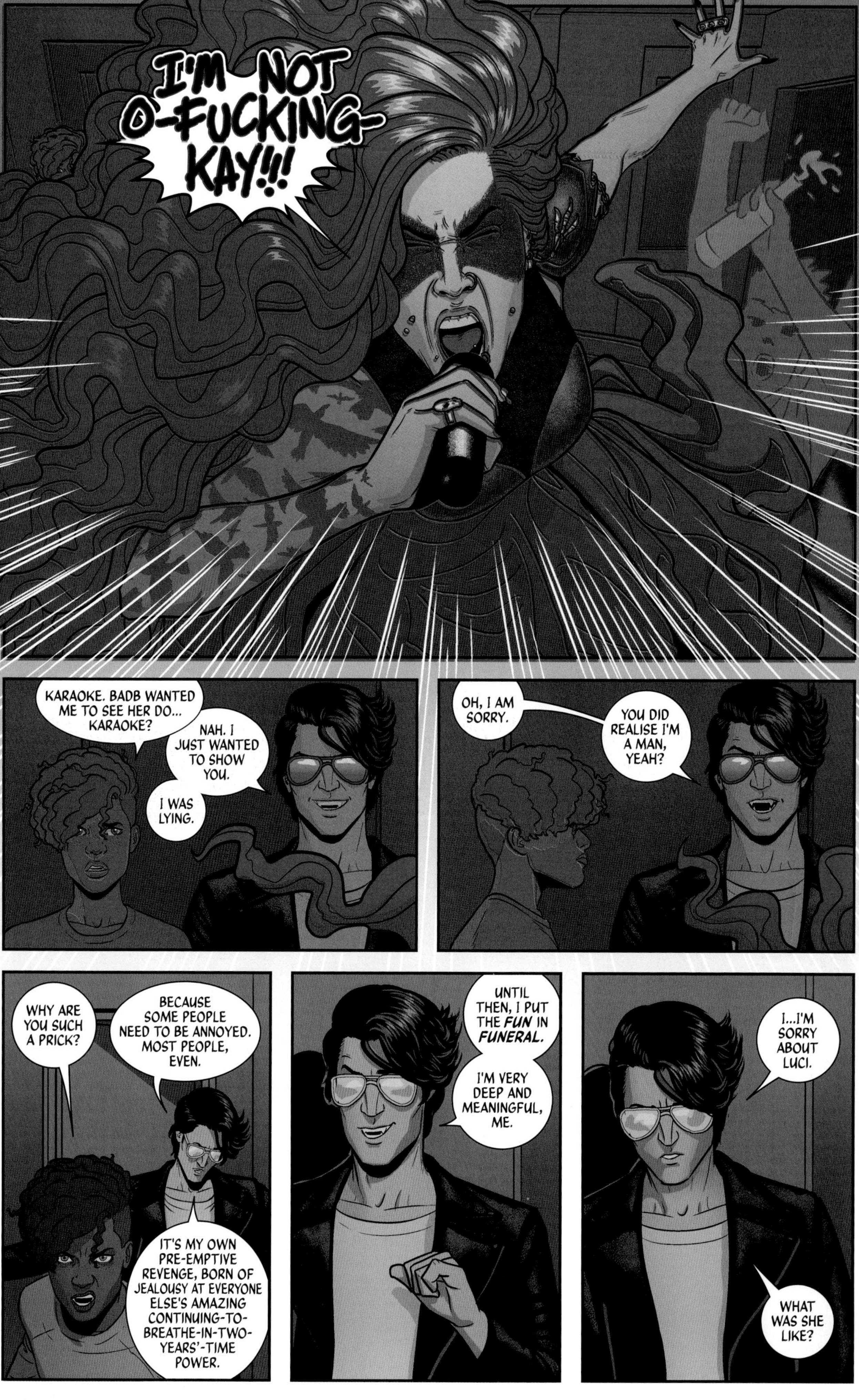
I'M NOT O-FUCKING-KAY!!!
KARAOKE. BADB WANTED ME TO SEE HER DO... KARAOKE?
NAH. I JUST WANTED TO SHOW YOU.
I WAS LYING.
OH, I AM SORRY.
YOU DID REALISE I'M A MAN, YEAH?
WHY ARE YOU SUCH A PRICK?
BECAUSE SOME PEOPLE NEED TO BE ANNOYED. MOST PEOPLE, EVEN.
IT'S MY OWN PRE-EMPTIVE REVENGE, BORN OF JEALOUSY AT EVERYONE ELSE'S AMAZING CONTINUING-TO-BREATHE-IN-TWO-YEARS'-TIME POWER.
UNTIL THEN, I PUT THE *FUN* IN *FUNERAL.*
I'M VERY DEEP AND MEANINGFUL, ME.
I...I'M SORRY ABOUT LUCI.
WHAT WAS SHE LIKE?

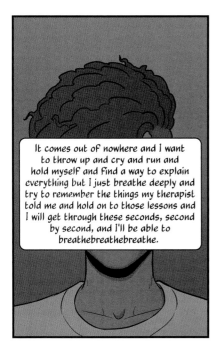

It comes out of nowhere and I want to throw up and cry and run and hold myself and find a way to explain everything but I just breathe deeply and try to remember the things my therapist told me and hold on to those lessons and I will get through these seconds, second by second, and I'll be able to breathebreathebreathe.

I HAVE TO GO.

LAURA. STOP.

YES, I LIED TO GET YOU DOWN HERE.

YOU'RE IN HELL. YOU NEED COMPANY.

MORRIGAN AND I AREN'T *GOOD* COMPANY.

BUT WE'RE GOOD *BAD* COMPANY.

AND WE'VE BEEN THERE.

I CAN'T SAY I CARE, BUT I DO UNDERSTAND.

PLUS-- I WASN'T LYING ABOUT THE JACK.

I can't think of a reason to say no.

It ends up being an awful evening.

I love it.

I don't want it to ever end.

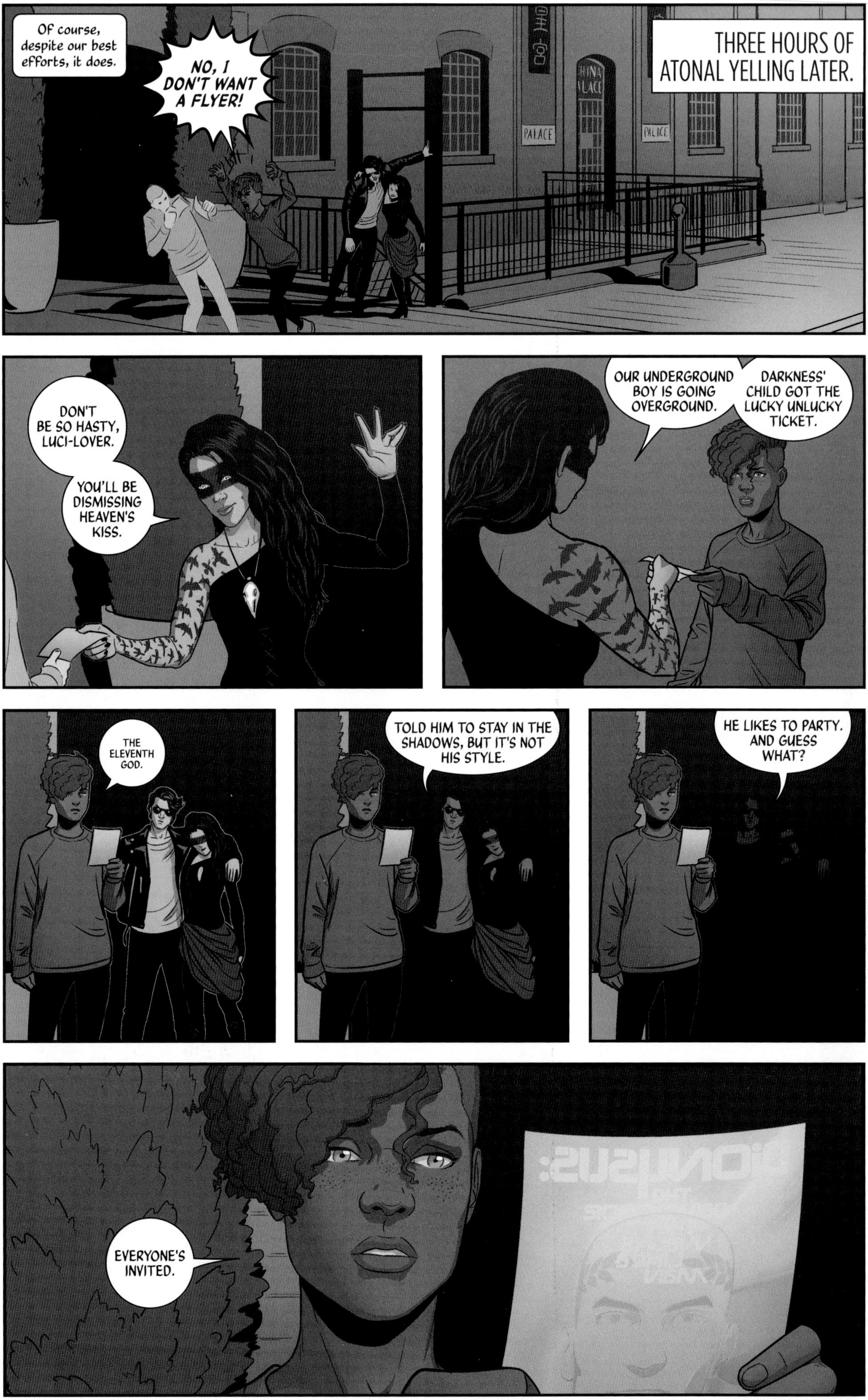

Of course, despite our best efforts, it does.
NO, I DON'T WANT A FLYER!
THREE HOURS OF ATONAL YELLING LATER.
DON'T BE SO HASTY, LUCI-LOVER.
YOU'LL BE DISMISSING HEAVEN'S KISS.
OUR UNDERGROUND BOY IS GOING OVERGROUND.
DARKNESS' CHILD GOT THE LUCKY UNLUCKY TICKET.
THE ELEVENTH GOD.
TOLD HIM TO STAY IN THE SHADOWS, BUT IT'S NOT HIS STYLE.
HE LIKES TO PARTY. AND GUESS WHAT?
EVERYONE'S INVITED.

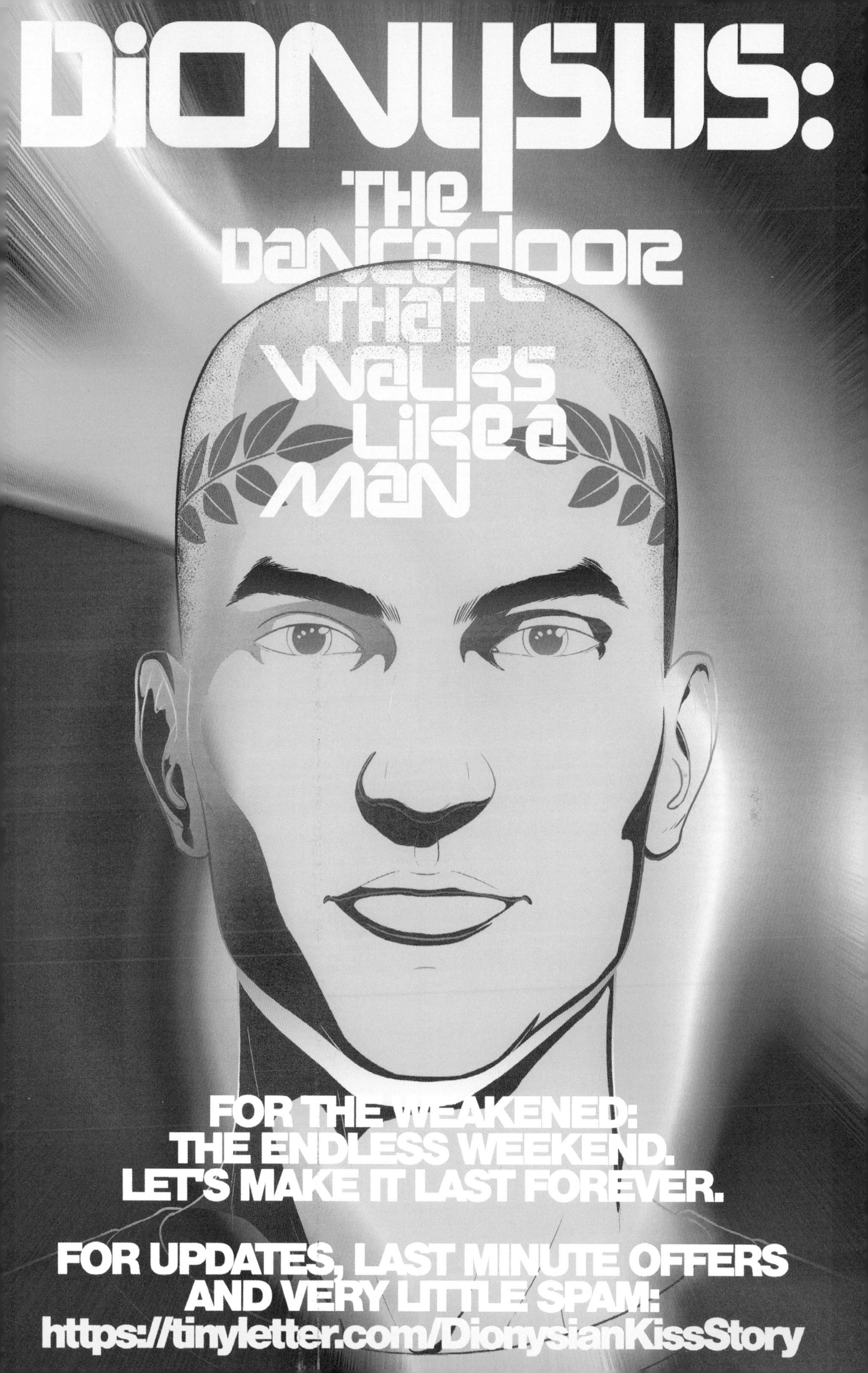
DIONYSUS:
THE DANCEFLOOR THAT WALKS LIKE A MAN
FOR THE WEAKENED:
THE ENDLESS WEEKEND.
LET'S MAKE IT LAST FOREVER.
FOR UPDATES, LAST MINUTE OFFERS
AND VERY LITTLE SPAM:
https://tinyletter.com/DionysianKissStory

DIONYSUS

14 APRIL 2014

THE
DIVINE

+

WICKED THE

THE WICKED

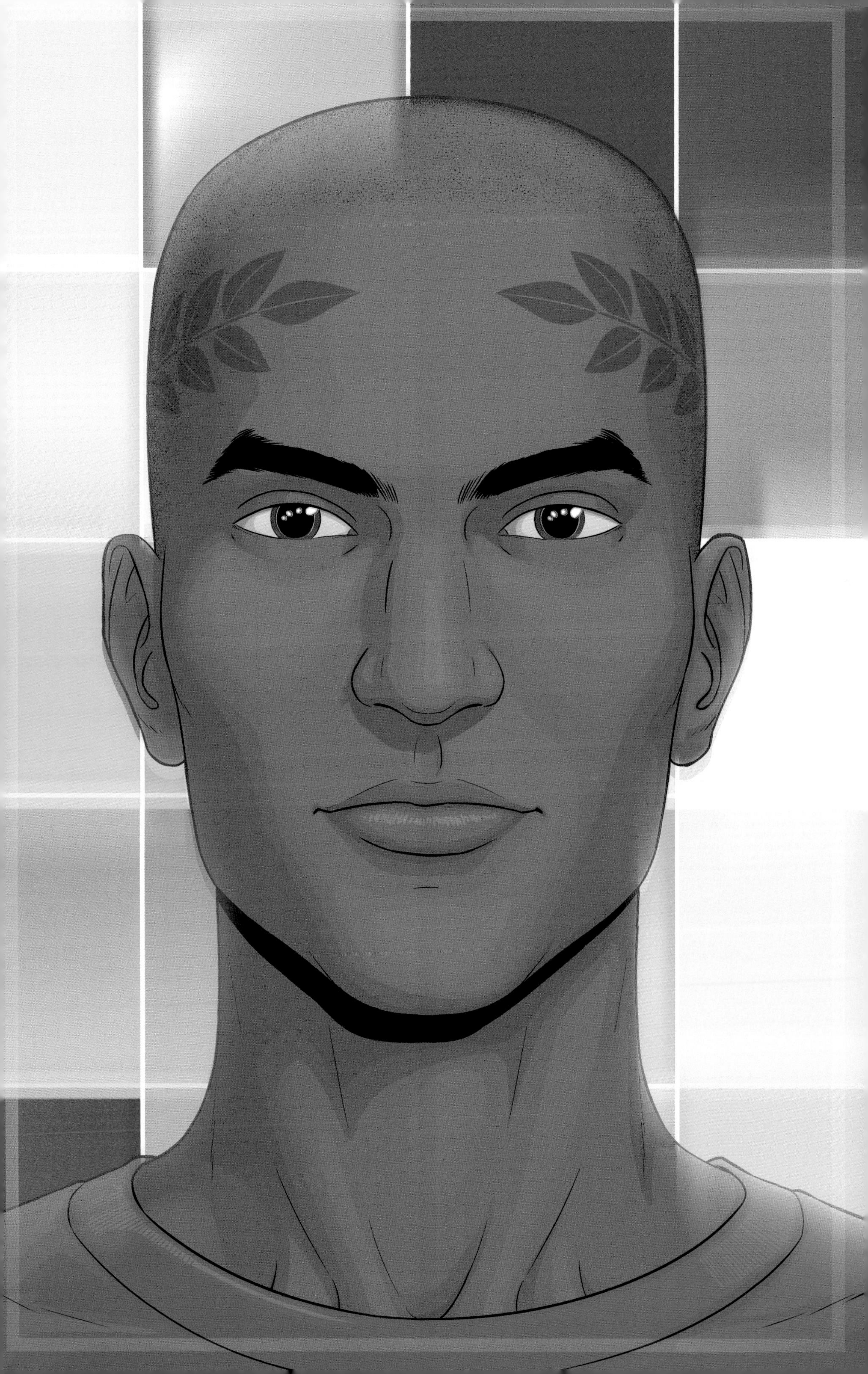

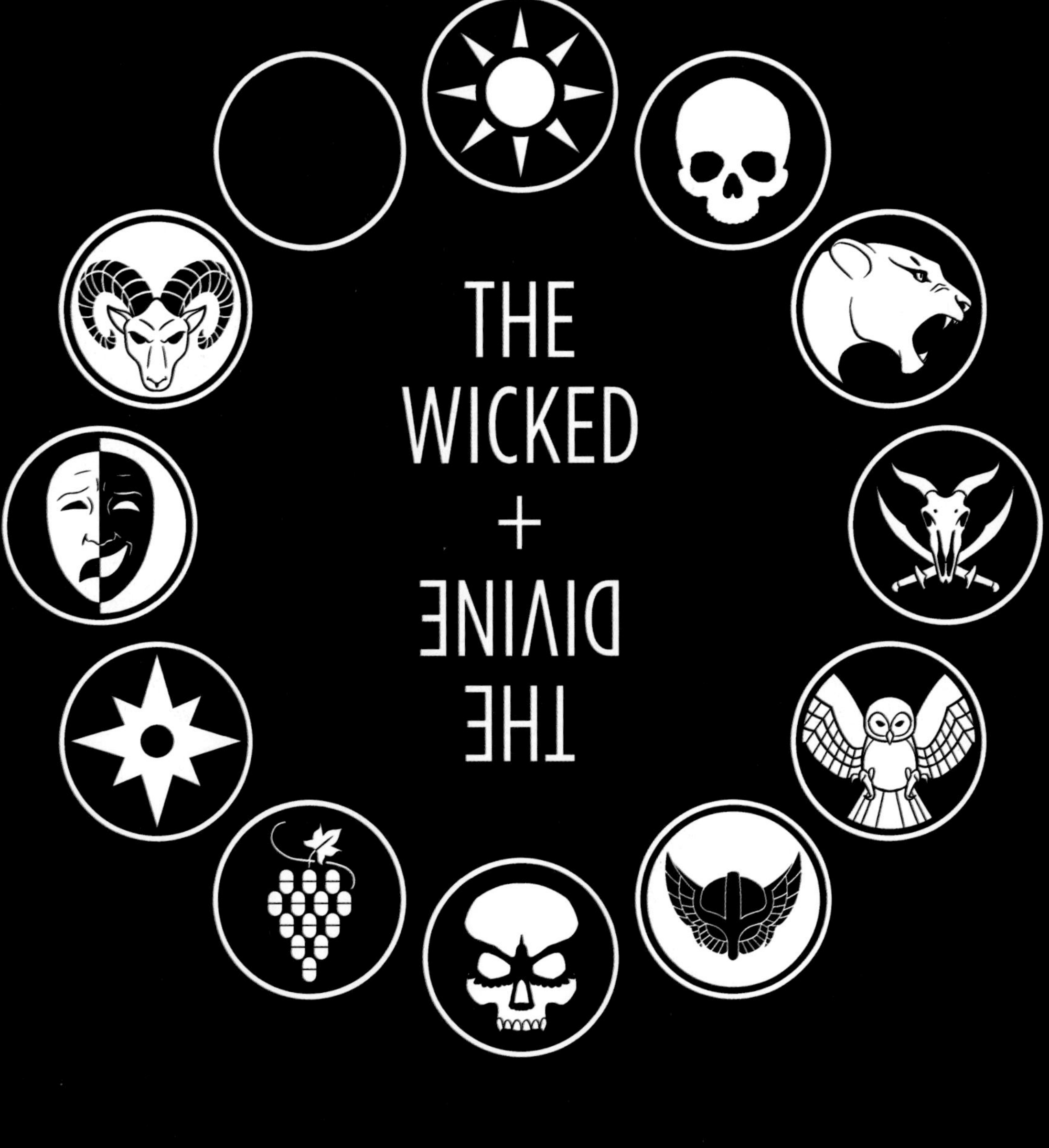
THE
WICKED
+
THE
DIVINE

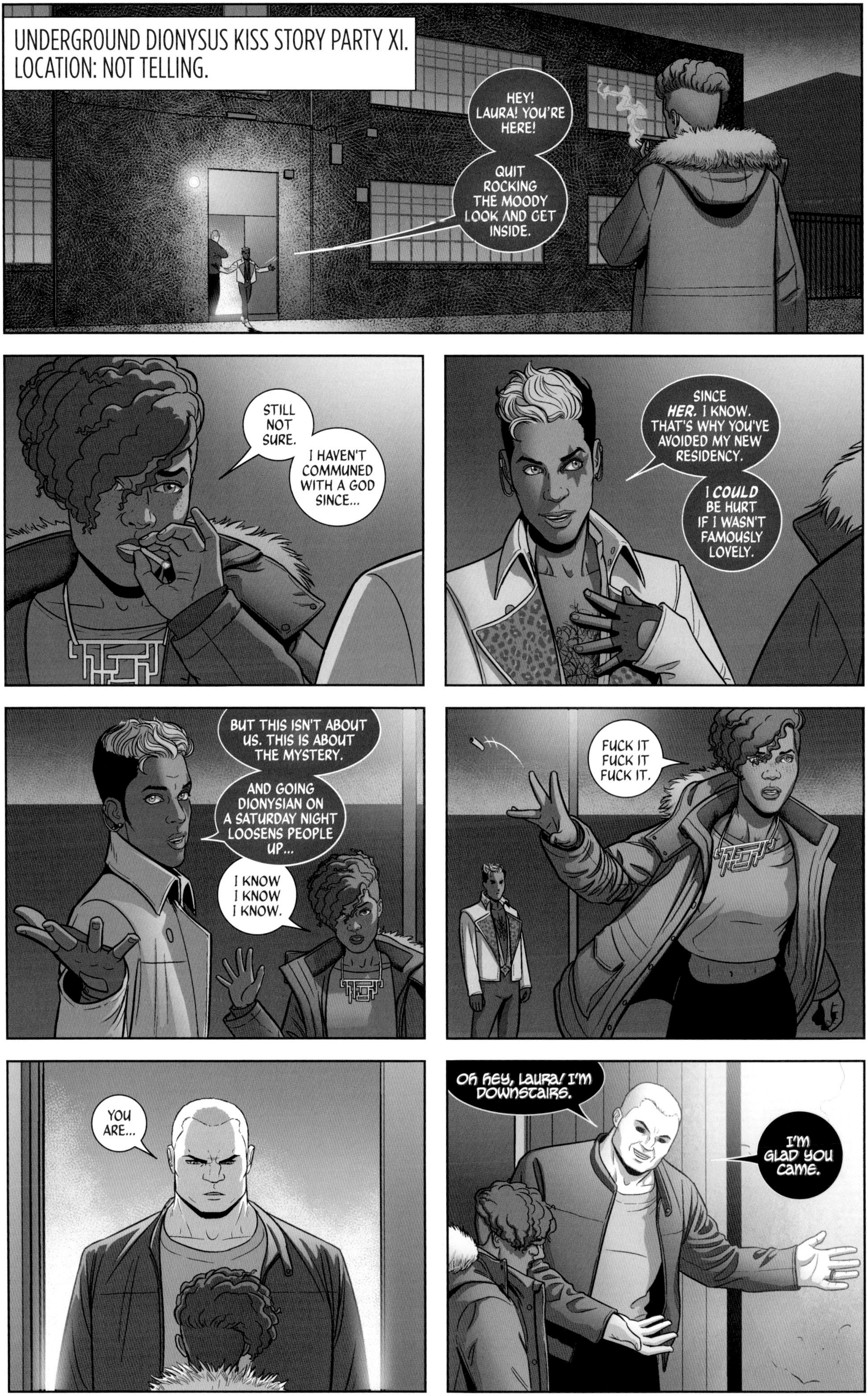
UNDERGROUND DIONYSUS KISS STORY PARTY XI.
LOCATION: NOT TELLING.
HEY! LAURA! YOU'RE HERE!
QUIT ROCKING THE MOODY LOOK AND GET INSIDE.
STILL NOT SURE.
I HAVEN'T COMMUNED WITH A GOD SINCE...
SINCE HER. I KNOW. THAT'S WHY YOU'VE AVOIDED MY NEW RESIDENCY.
I COULD BE HURT IF I WASN'T FAMOUSLY LOVELY.
BUT THIS ISN'T ABOUT US. THIS IS ABOUT THE MYSTERY.
AND GOING DIONYSIAN ON A SATURDAY NIGHT LOOSENS PEOPLE UP...
I KNOW I KNOW I KNOW.
FUCK IT FUCK IT FUCK IT.
YOU ARE...
OH HEY, LAURA! I'M DOWNSTAIRS.
I'M GLAD YOU CAME.

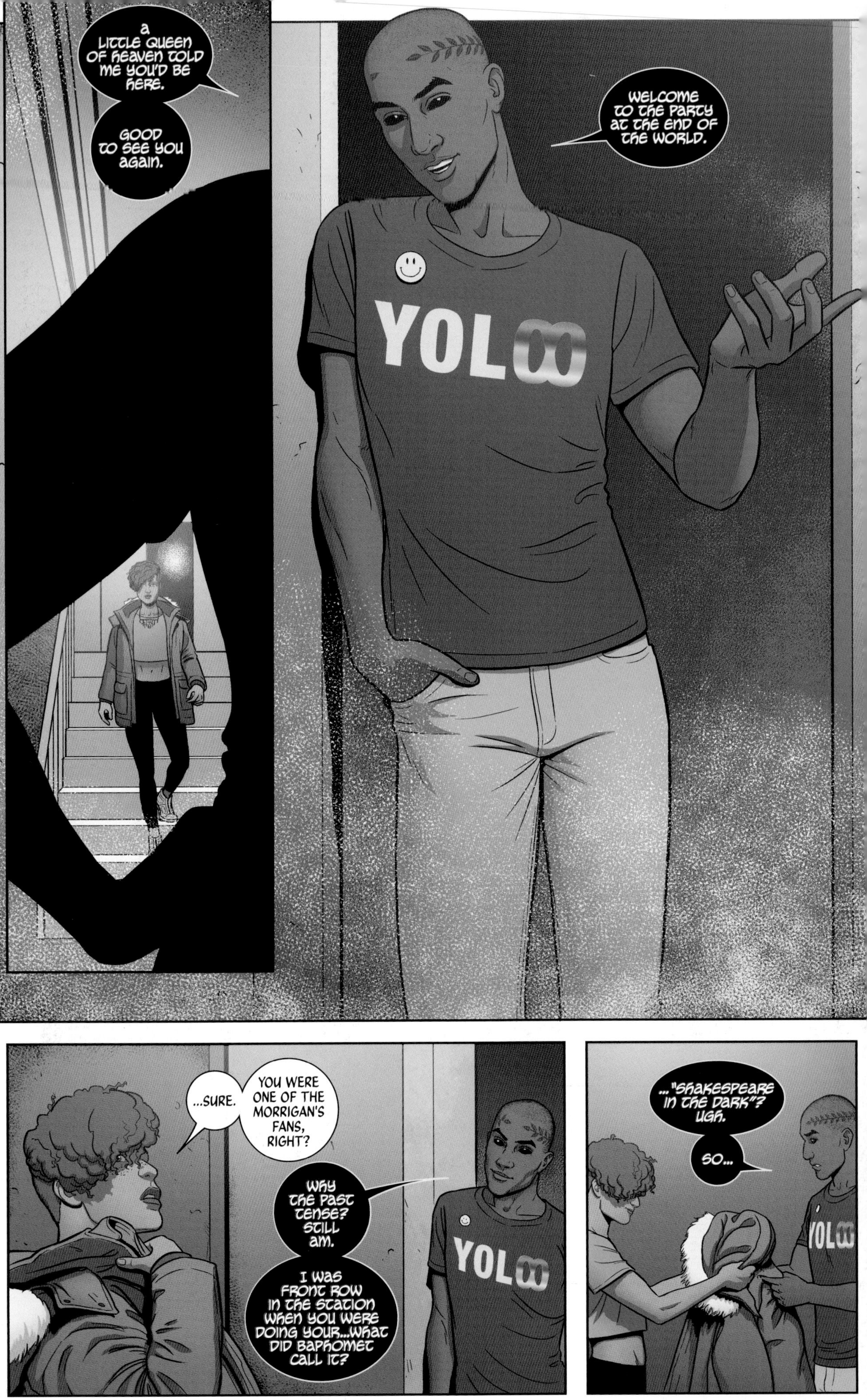

A LITTLE QUEEN OF HEAVEN TOLD ME YOU'D BE HERE.
GOOD TO SEE YOU AGAIN.
WELCOME TO THE PARTY AT THE END OF THE WORLD.
YOL∞
...SURE.
YOU WERE ONE OF THE MORRIGAN'S FANS, RIGHT?
WHY THE PAST TENSE? STILL AM.
I WAS FRONT ROW IN THE STATION WHEN YOU WERE DOING YOUR...WHAT DID BAPHOMET CALL IT?
YOL∞
..."SHAKESPEARE IN THE DARK"? UGH.
SO...
YOL∞

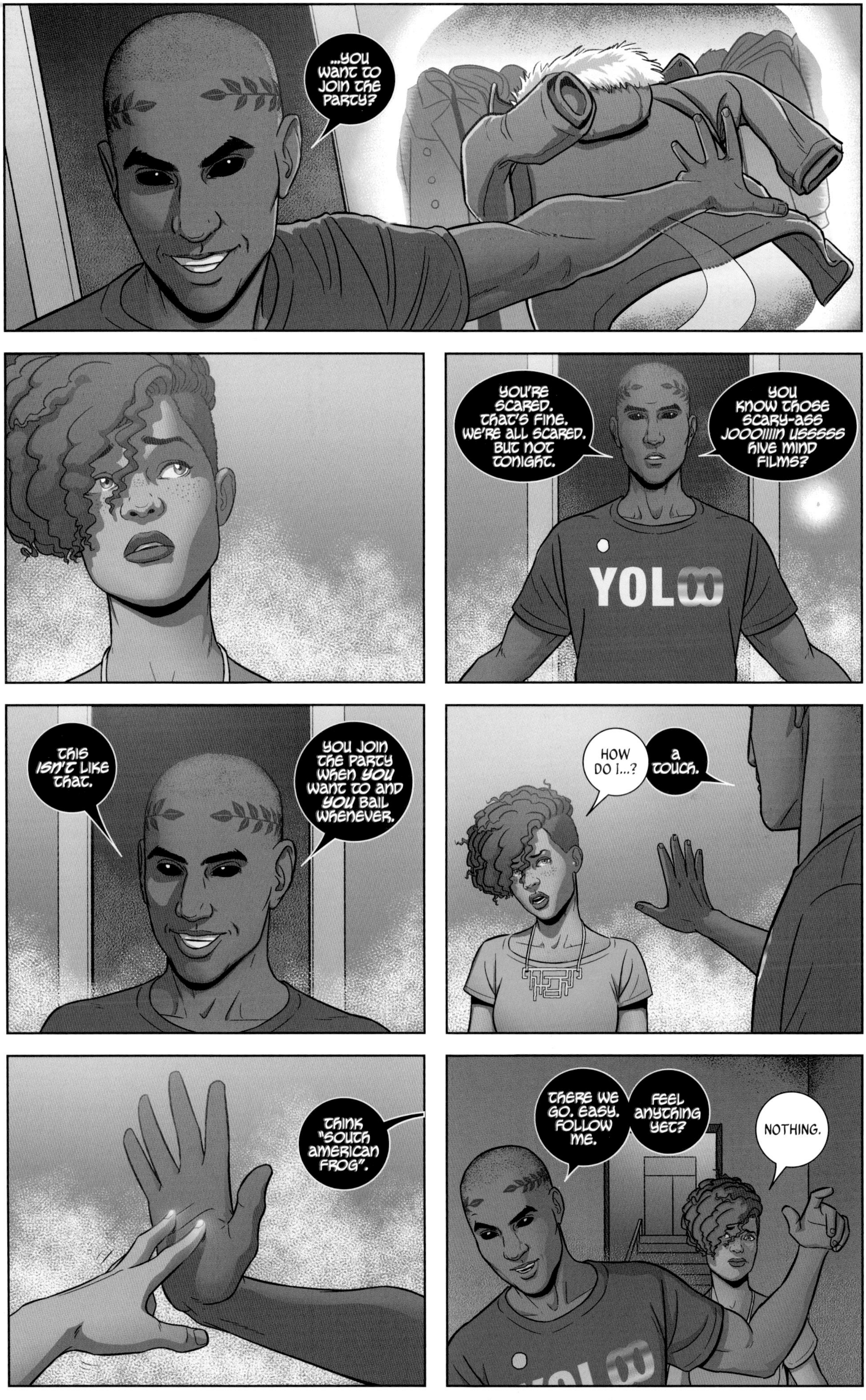
...YOU WANT TO JOIN THE PARTY?
YOU'RE SCARED. THAT'S FINE. WE'RE ALL SCARED. BUT NOT TONIGHT.
YOU KNOW THOSE SCARY-ASS JOOOIIIIN USSSSS HIVE MIND FILMS?
YOL∞
THIS ISN'T LIKE THAT.
YOU JOIN THE PARTY WHEN YOU WANT TO AND YOU BAIL WHENEVER.
HOW DO I...?
A TOUCH.
THINK "SOUTH AMERICAN FROG".
THERE WE GO. EASY. FOLLOW ME.
FEEL ANYTHING YET?
NOTHING.

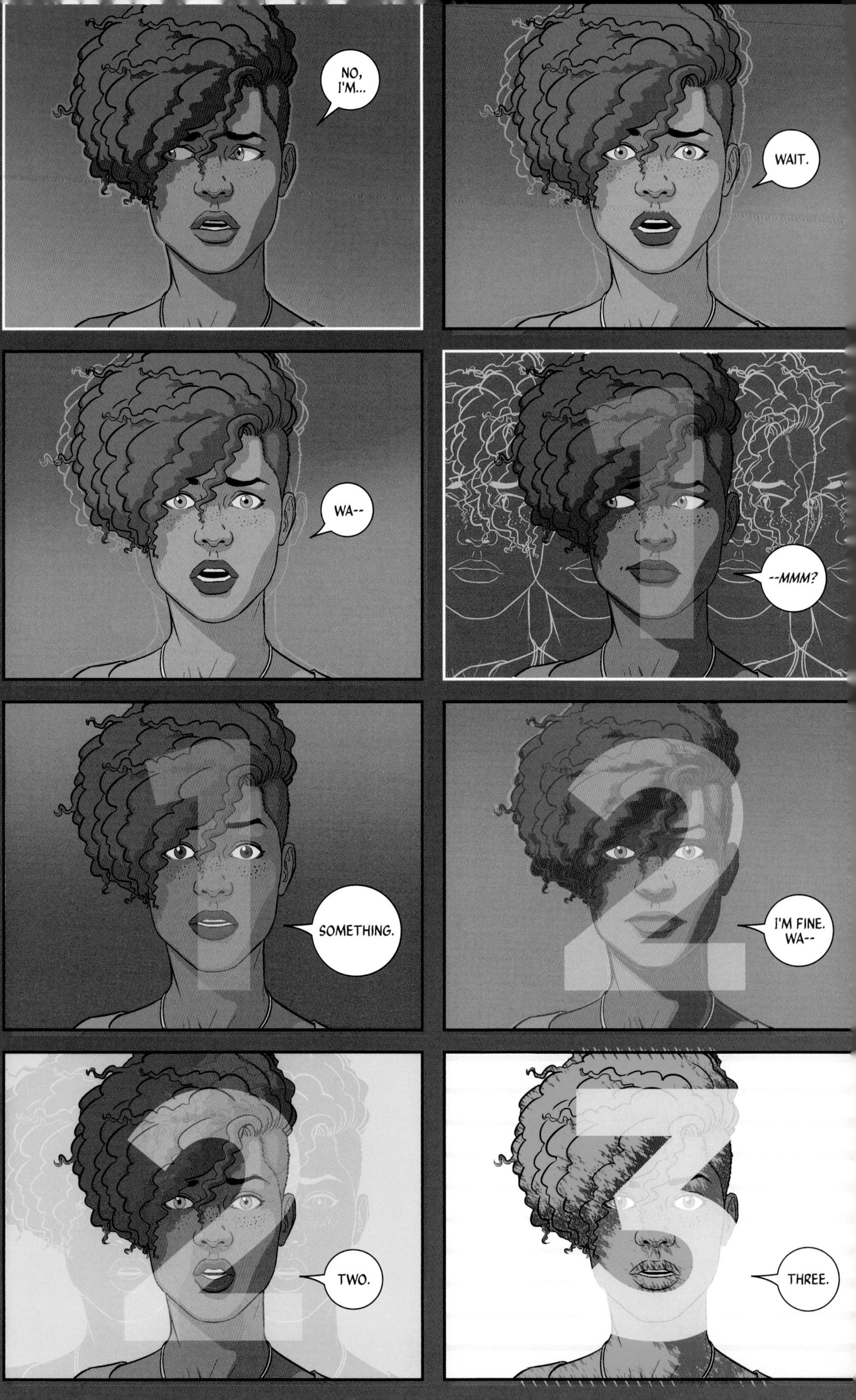

NO, I'M...
WAIT.
WA--
--MMM?
SOMETHING.
I'M FINE. WA--
TWO.
THREE.

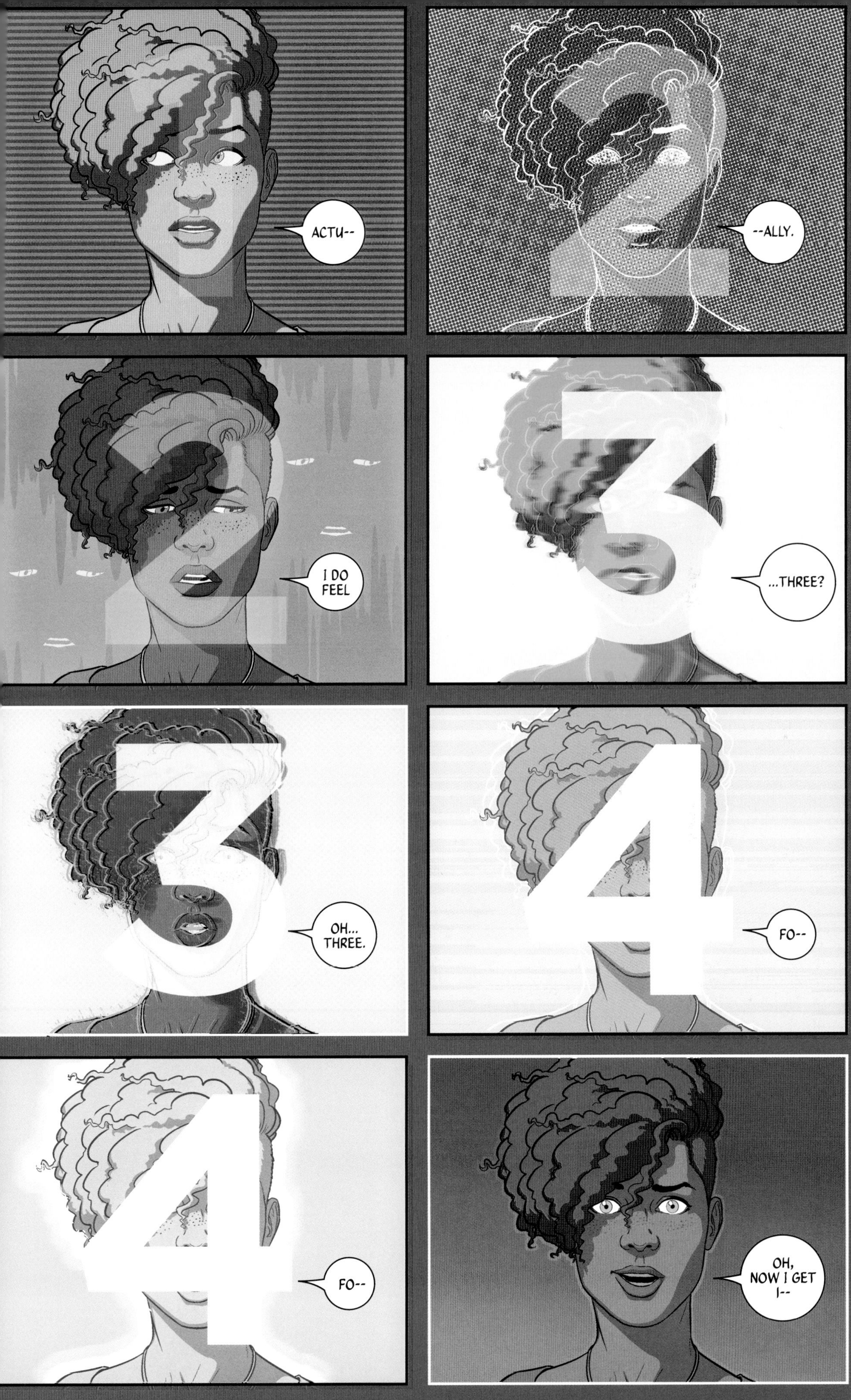
ACTU--
--ALLY.
I DO FEEL
...THREE?
OH... THREE.
FO--
FO--
OH, NOW I GET I--

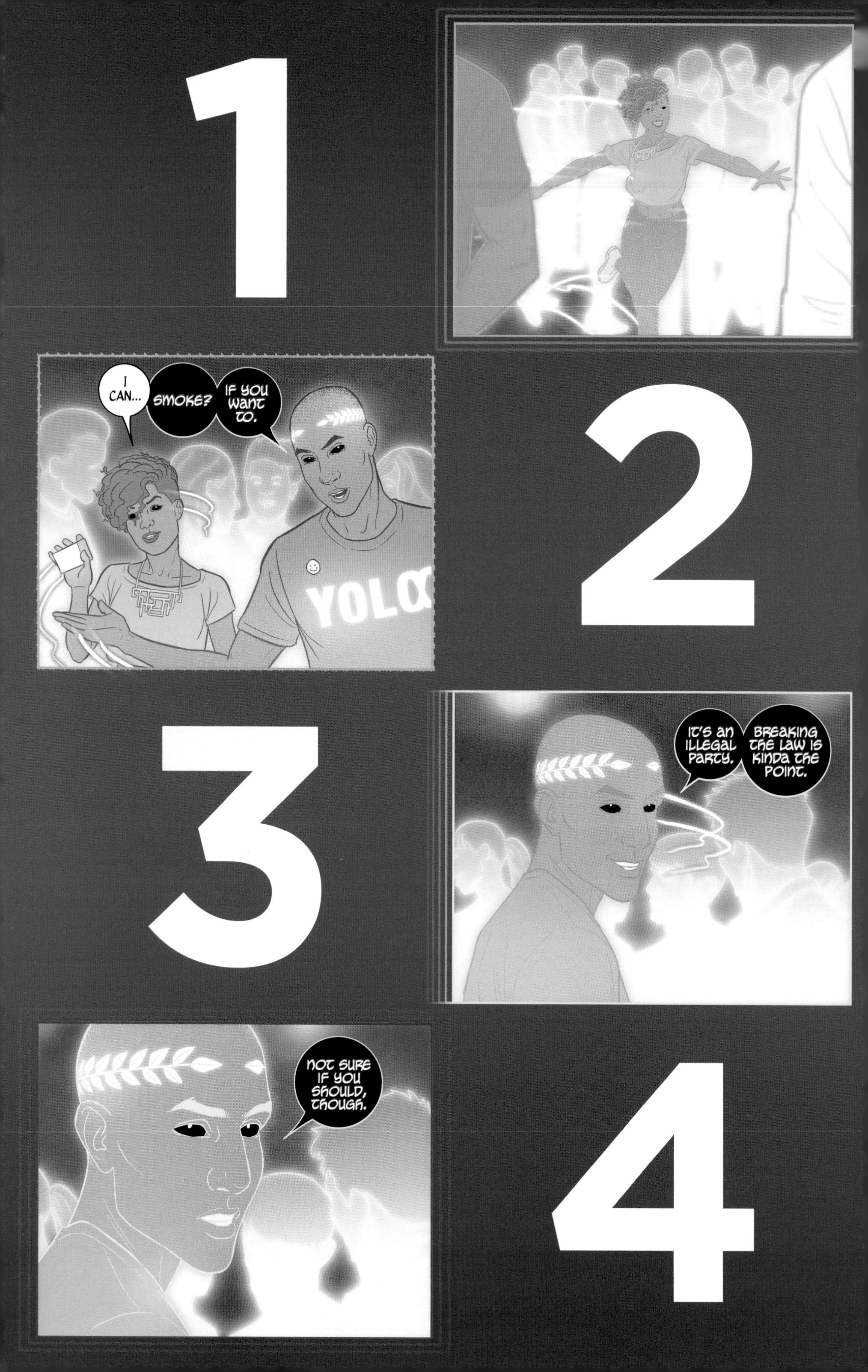
1
I CAN...
SMOKE?
IF YOU WANT TO.
2
3
IT'S AN ILLEGAL PARTY.
BREAKING THE LAW IS KINDA THE POINT.
NOT SURE IF YOU SHOULD, THOUGH.
4

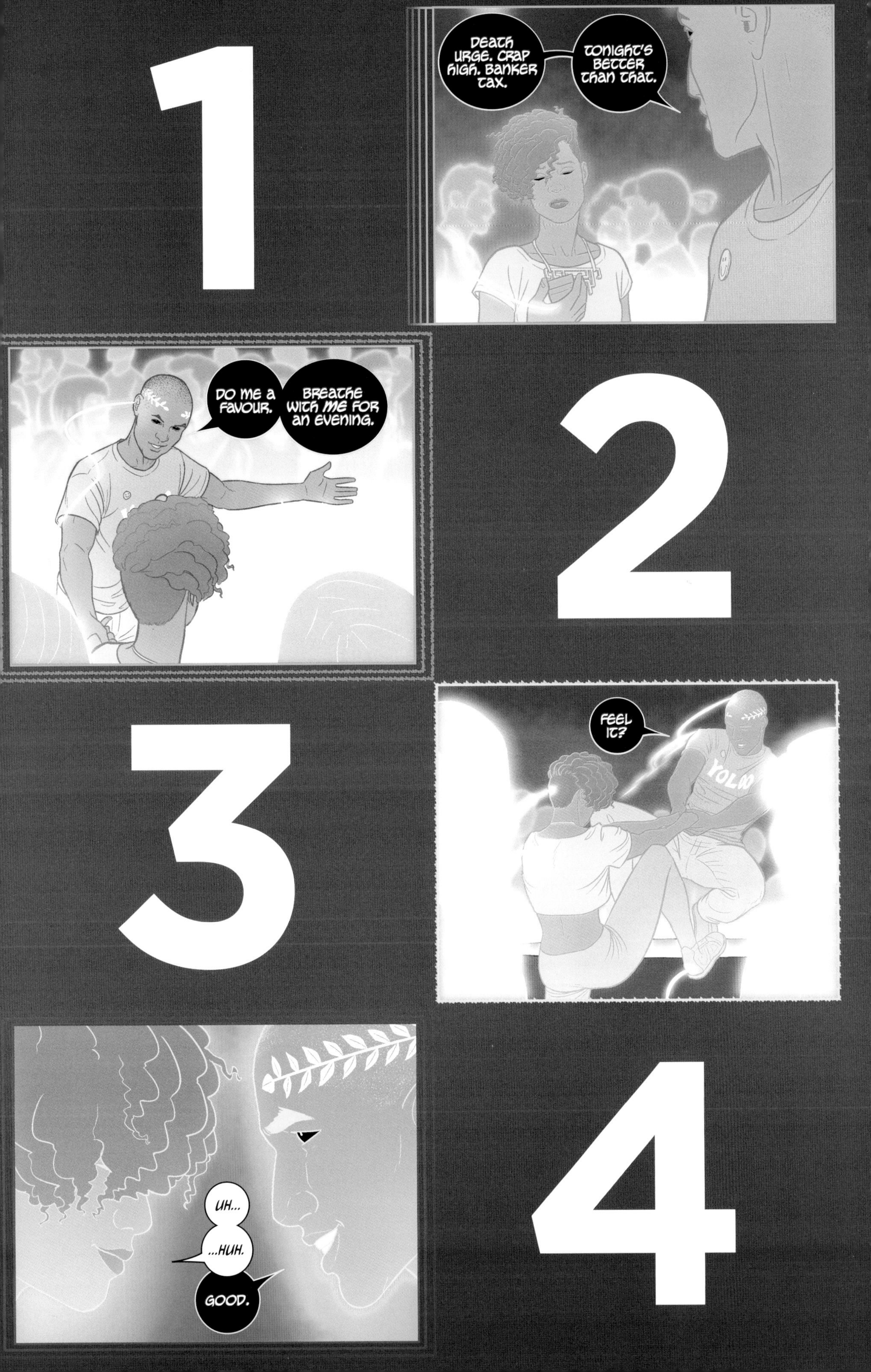
1
DEATH URGE. CRAP HIGH. BANKER TAX.
TONIGHT'S BETTER THAN THAT.
DO ME A FAVOUR.
BREATHE WITH *ME* FOR AN EVENING.
2
3
FEEL IT?
UH...
...HUH.
GOOD.
4

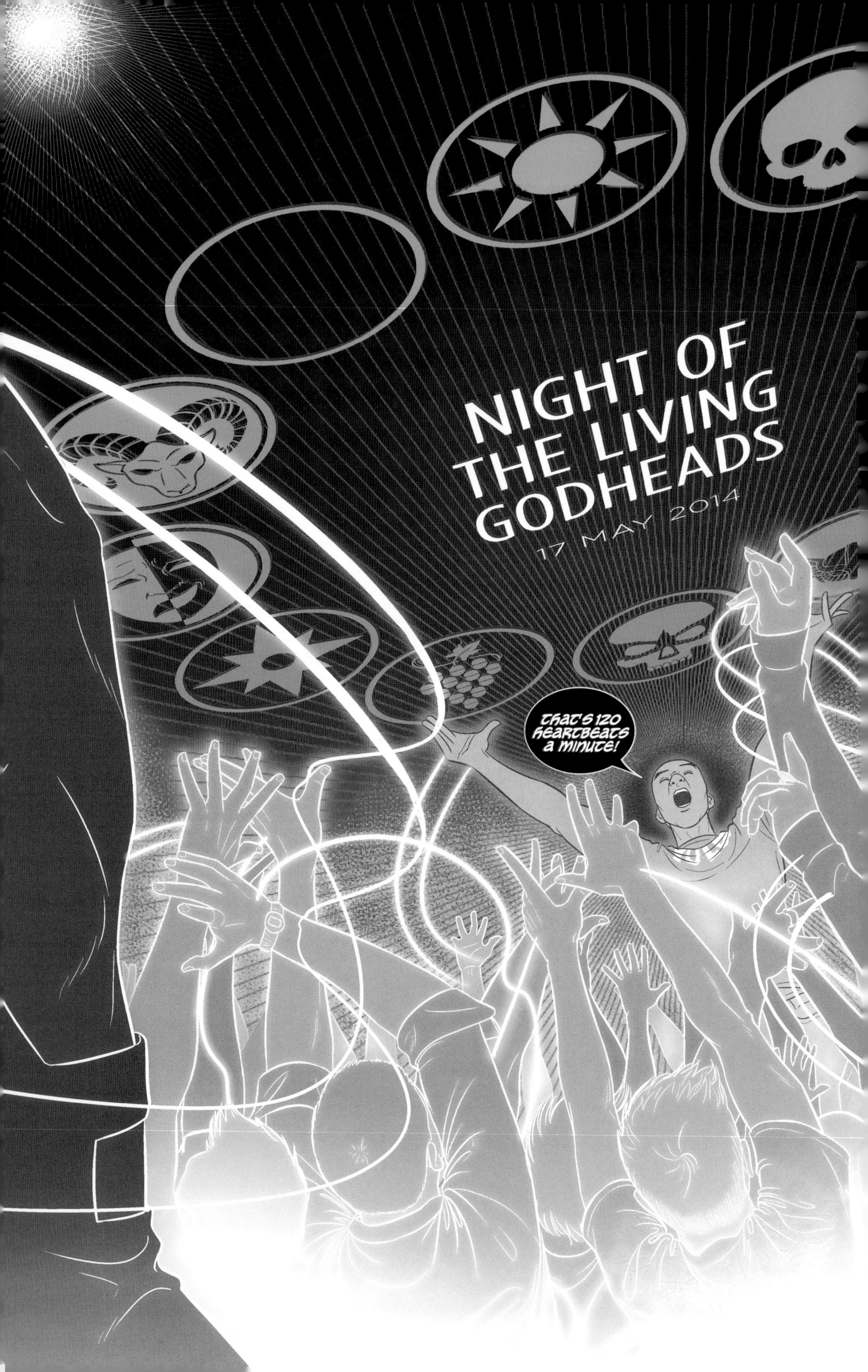
NIGHT OF THE LIVING GODHEADS
17 MAY 2014
THAT'S 120 HEARTBEATS A MINUTE!

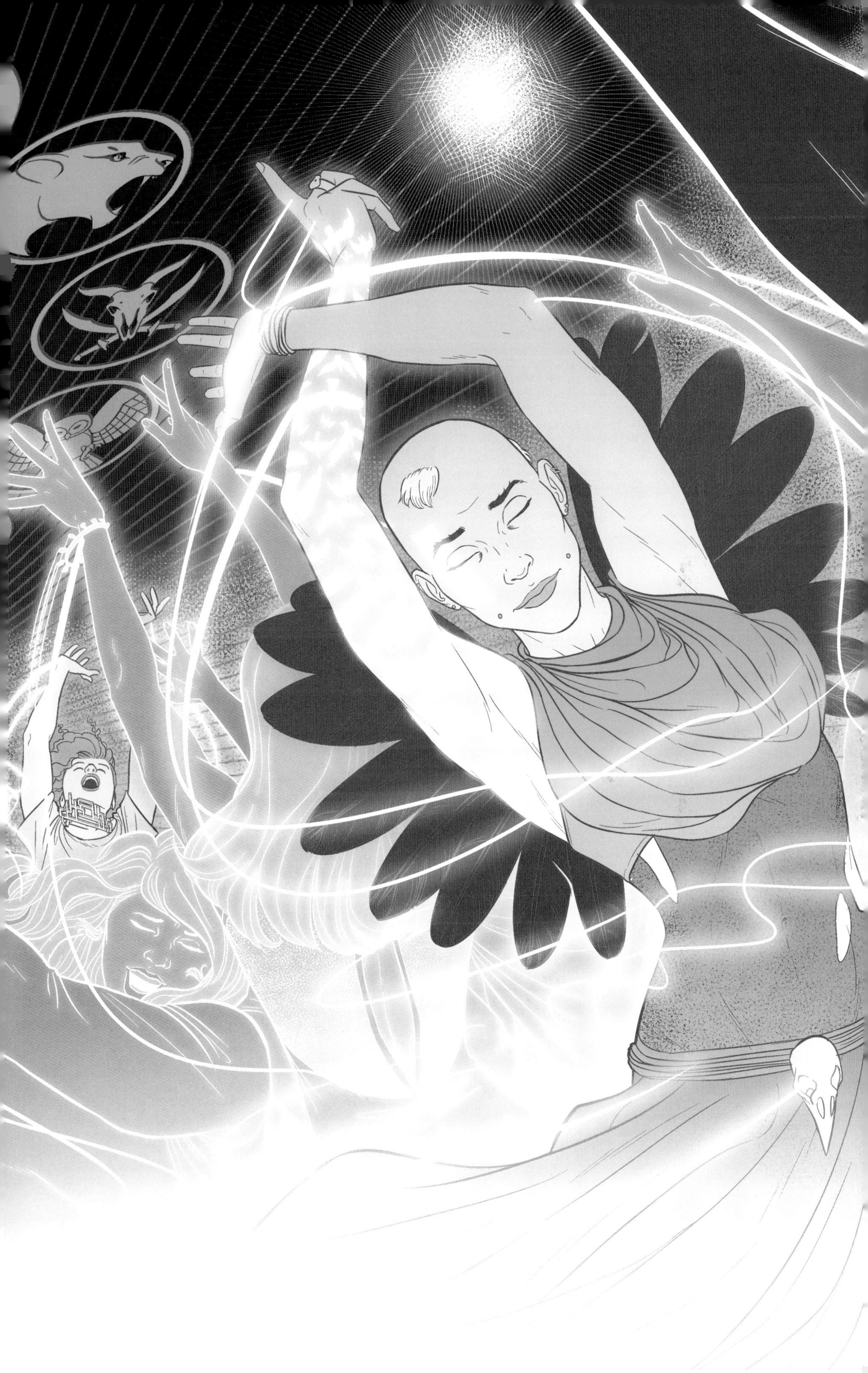

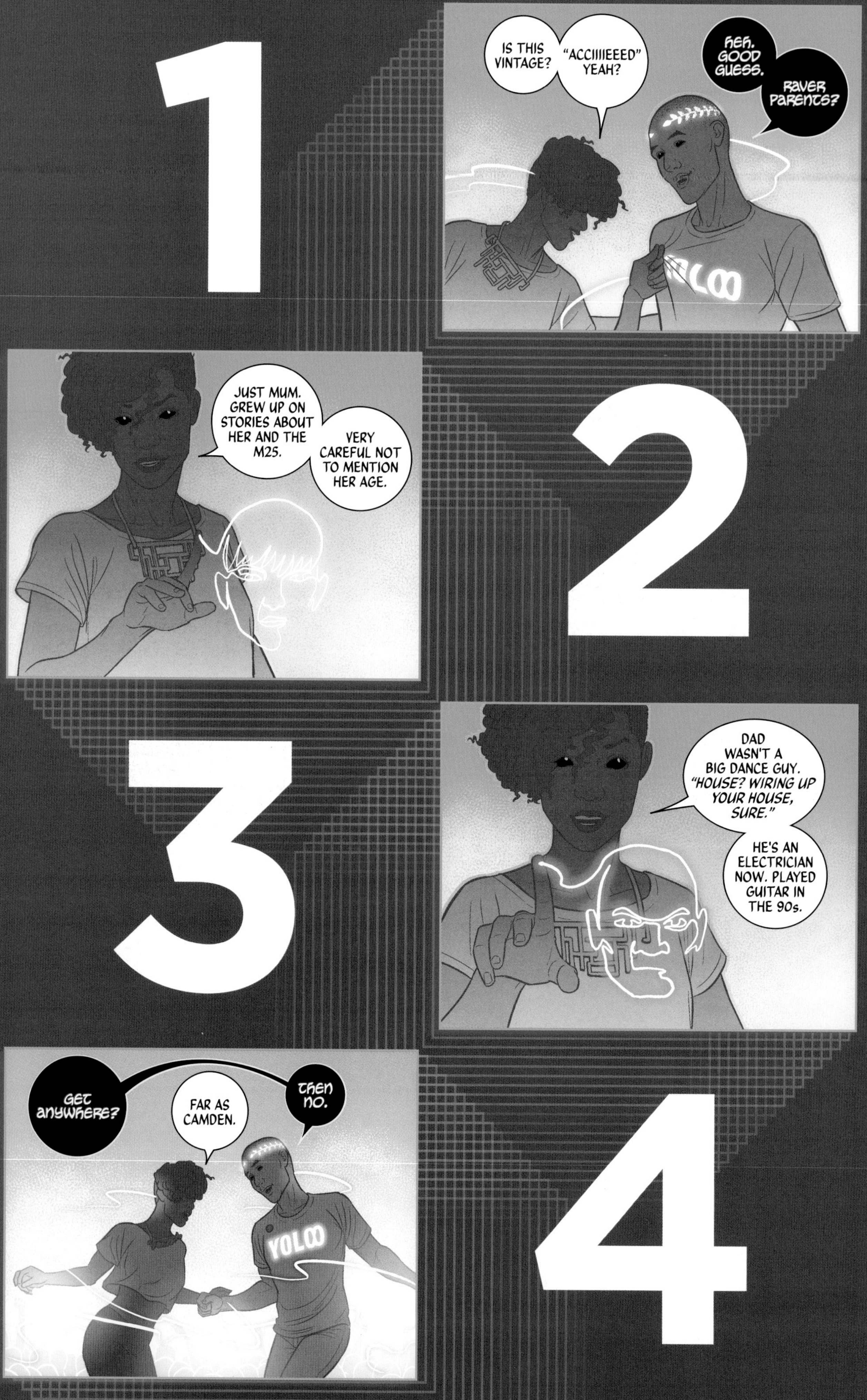
1
IS THIS VINTAGE?
"ACCIIIIEEED" YEAH?
HEH. GOOD GUESS.
RAVER PARENTS?
2
JUST MUM. GREW UP ON STORIES ABOUT HER AND THE M25.
VERY CAREFUL NOT TO MENTION HER AGE.
3
DAD WASN'T A BIG DANCE GUY. *"HOUSE? WIRING UP YOUR HOUSE, SURE."*
HE'S AN ELECTRICIAN NOW. PLAYED GUITAR IN THE 90s.
4
GET ANYWHERE?
FAR AS CAMDEN.
THEN NO.
YOLOO

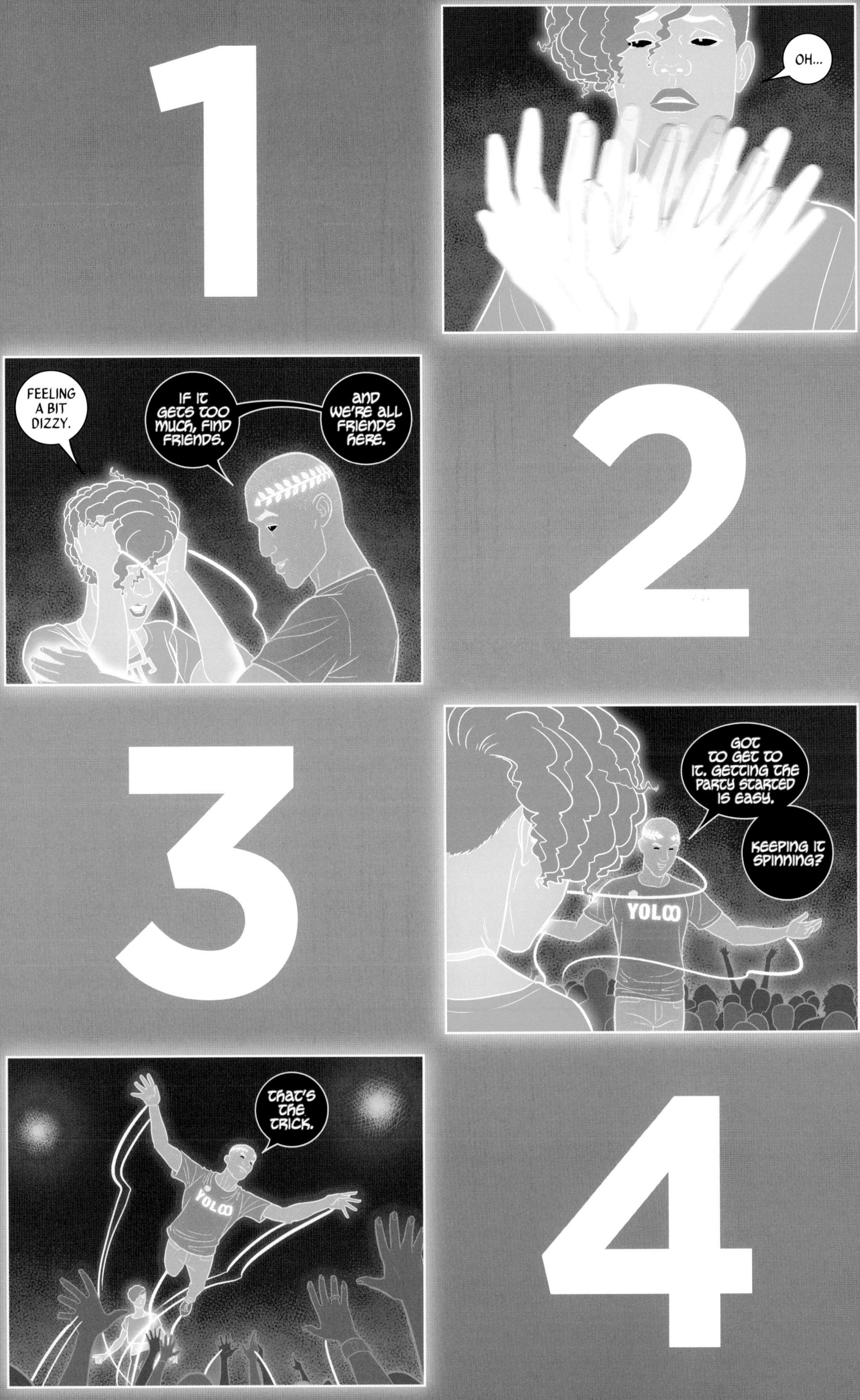
1
OH...
FEELING A BIT DIZZY.
IF IT GETS TOO MUCH, FIND FRIENDS.
AND WE'RE ALL FRIENDS HERE.
2
3
GOT TO GET TO IT. GETTING THE PARTY STARTED IS EASY.
KEEPING IT SPINNING?
THAT'S THE TRICK.
4

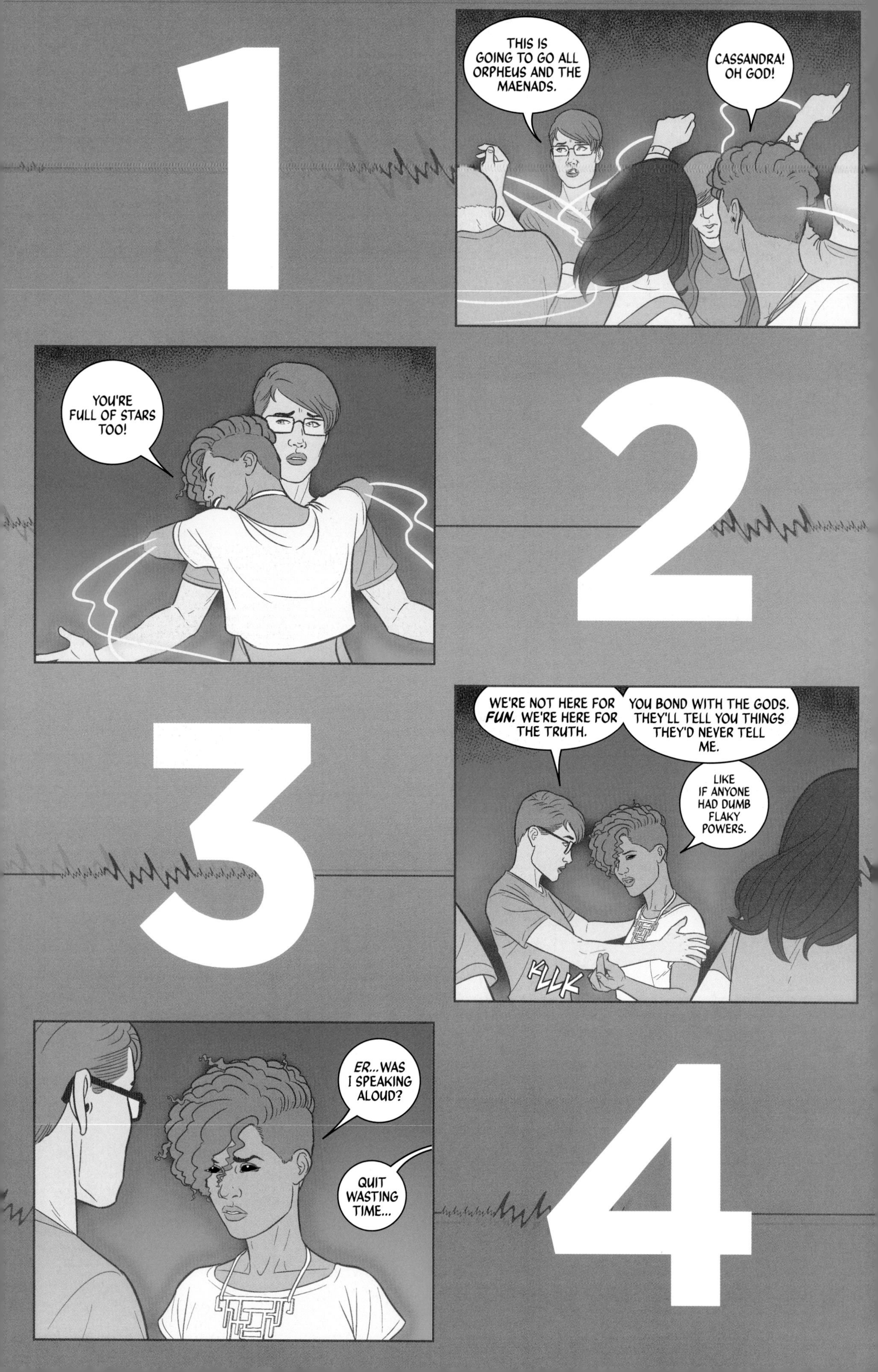
THIS IS GOING TO GO ALL ORPHEUS AND THE MAENADS.
CASSANDRA! OH GOD!
YOU'RE FULL OF STARS TOO!
WE'RE NOT HERE FOR *FUN.* WE'RE HERE FOR THE TRUTH.
YOU BOND WITH THE GODS. THEY'LL TELL YOU THINGS THEY'D NEVER TELL ME.
LIKE IF ANYONE HAD DUMB FLAKY POWERS.
KLLK
ER...WAS I SPEAKING ALOUD?
QUIT WASTING TIME...

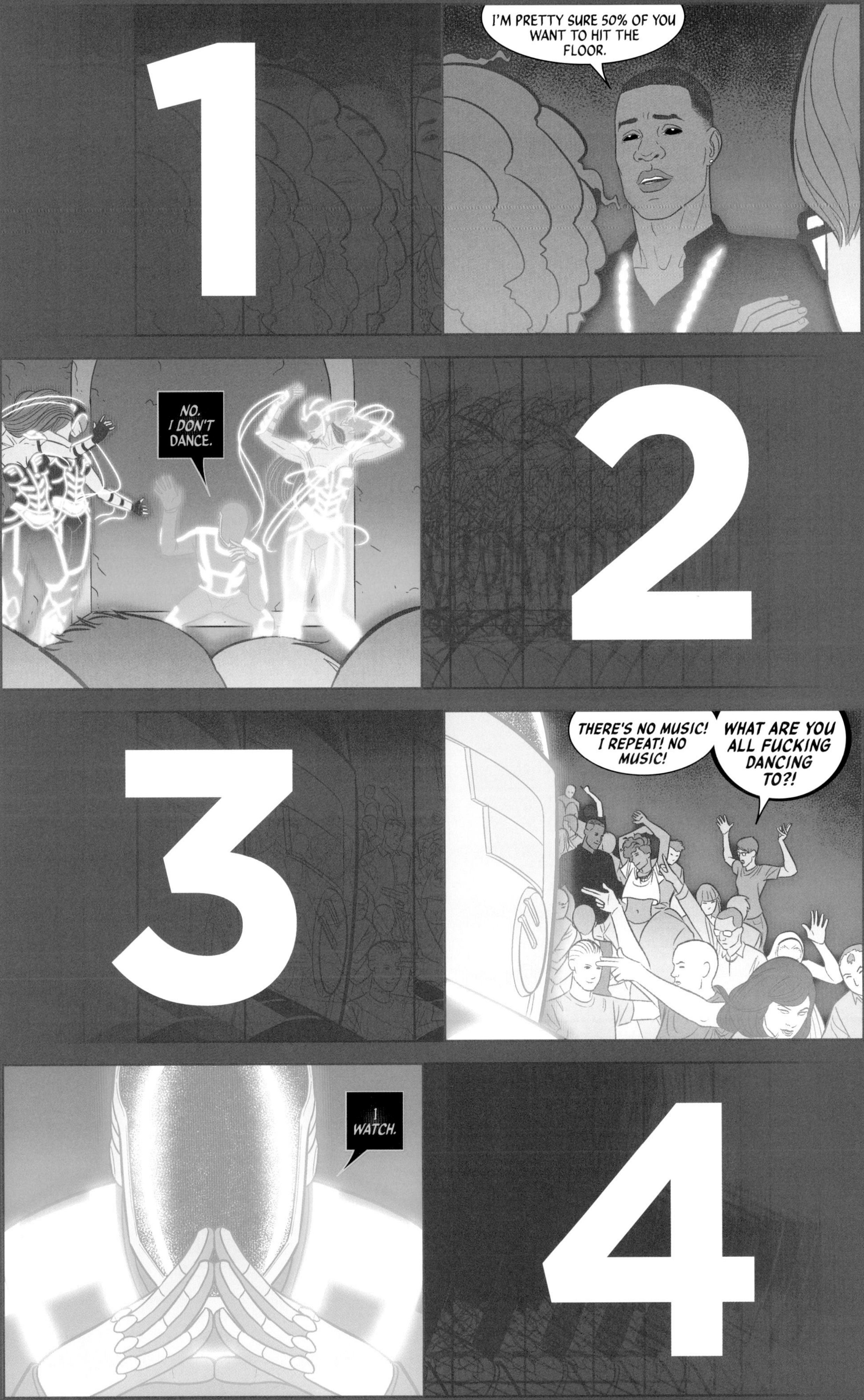
1
I'M PRETTY SURE 50% OF YOU WANT TO HIT THE FLOOR.
NO. I DON'T DANCE.
2
3
THERE'S NO MUSIC! I REPEAT! NO MUSIC!
WHAT ARE YOU ALL FUCKING DANCING TO?!
I WATCH.
4

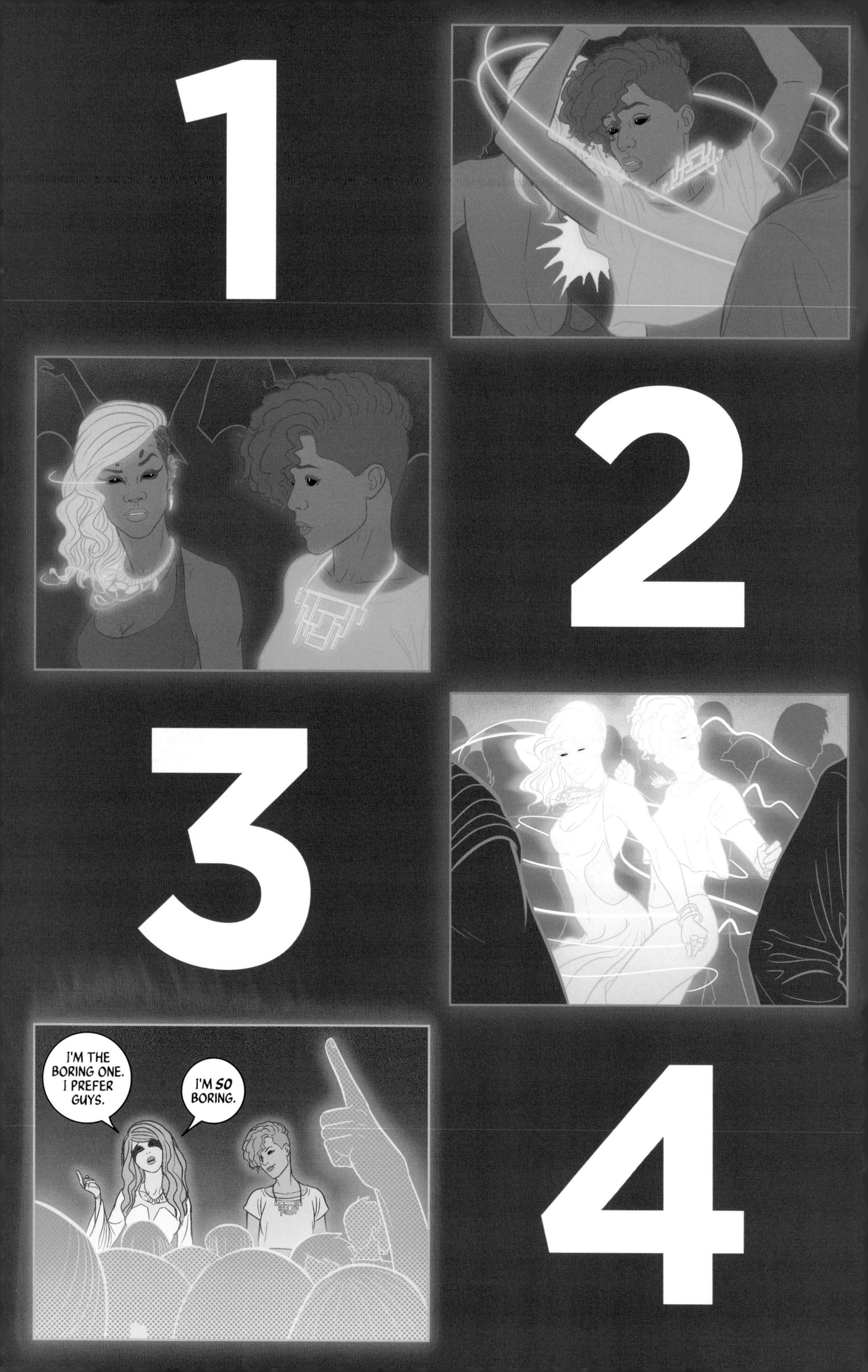
1
2
3
I'M THE BORING ONE. I PREFER GUYS.
I'M *SO* BORING.
4

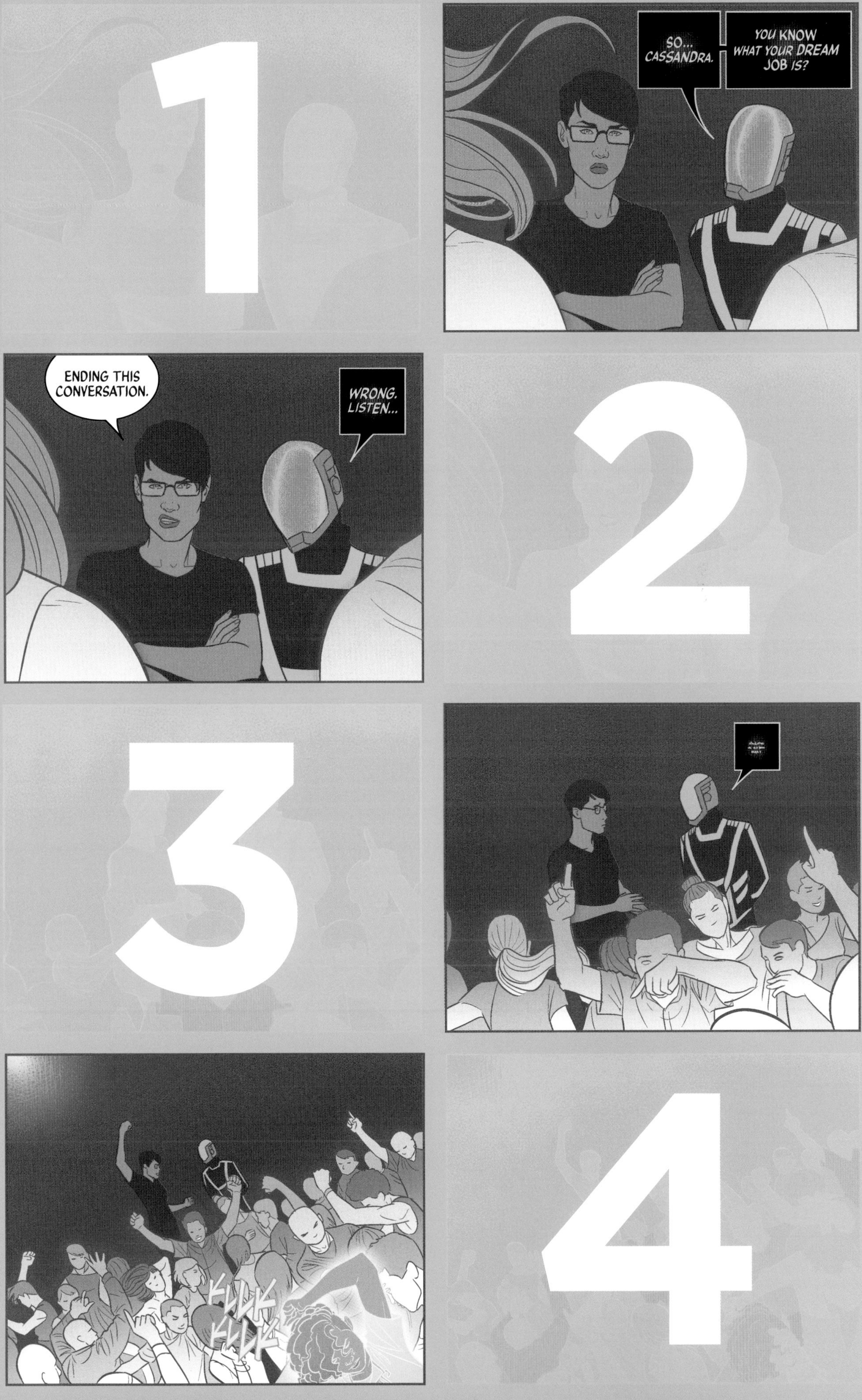
1
SO... CASSANDRA.
YOU KNOW WHAT YOUR DREAM JOB IS?
ENDING THIS CONVERSATION.
WRONG. LISTEN...
2
3
4
KLLK KLLK

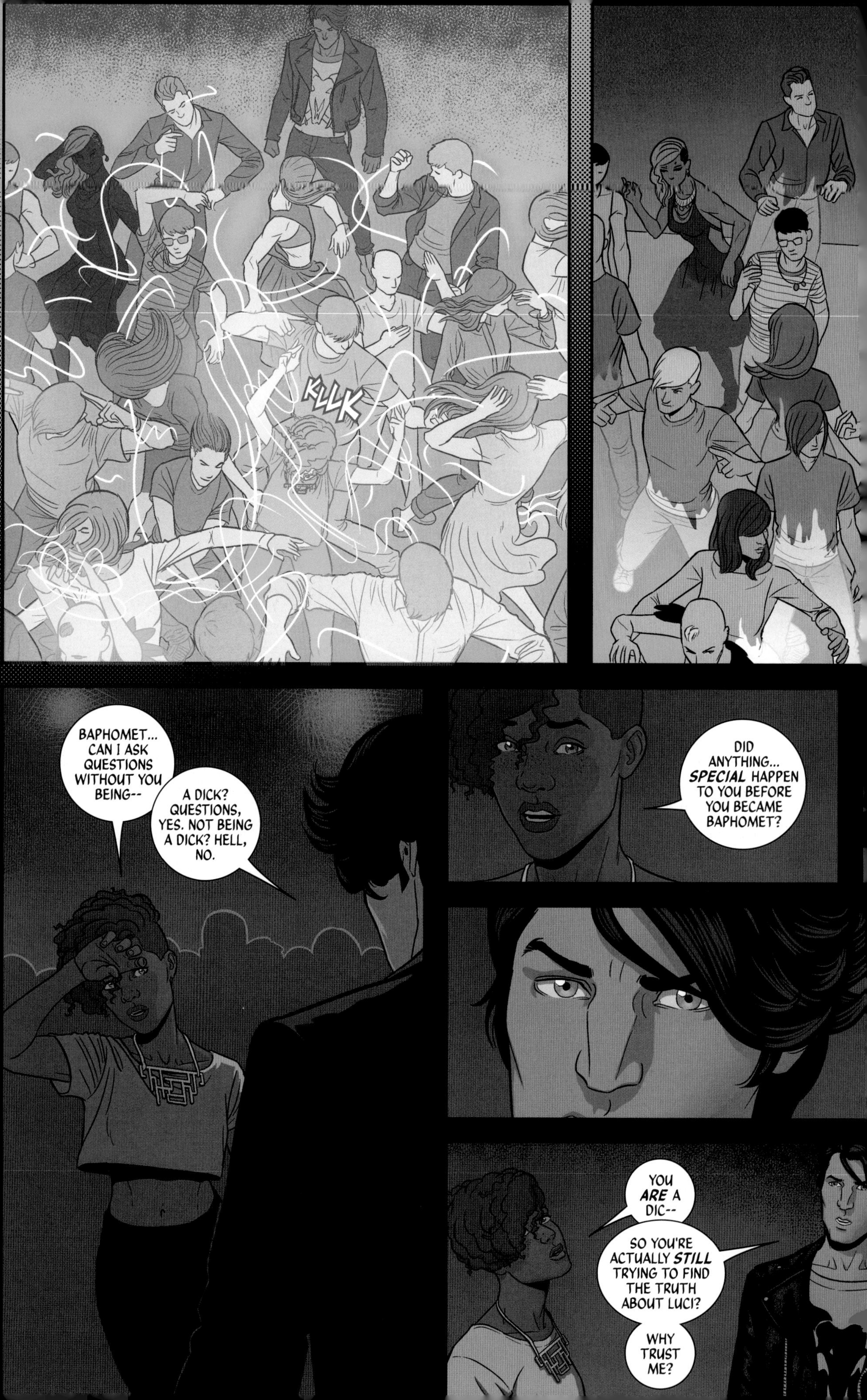
KLUK
BAPHOMET... CAN I ASK QUESTIONS WITHOUT YOU BEING--
A DICK? QUESTIONS, YES. NOT BEING A DICK? HELL, NO.
DID ANYTHING... **SPECIAL** HAPPEN TO YOU BEFORE YOU BECAME BAPHOMET?
YOU **ARE** A DIC--
SO YOU'RE ACTUALLY **STILL** TRYING TO FIND THE TRUTH ABOUT LUCI?
WHY TRUST ME?

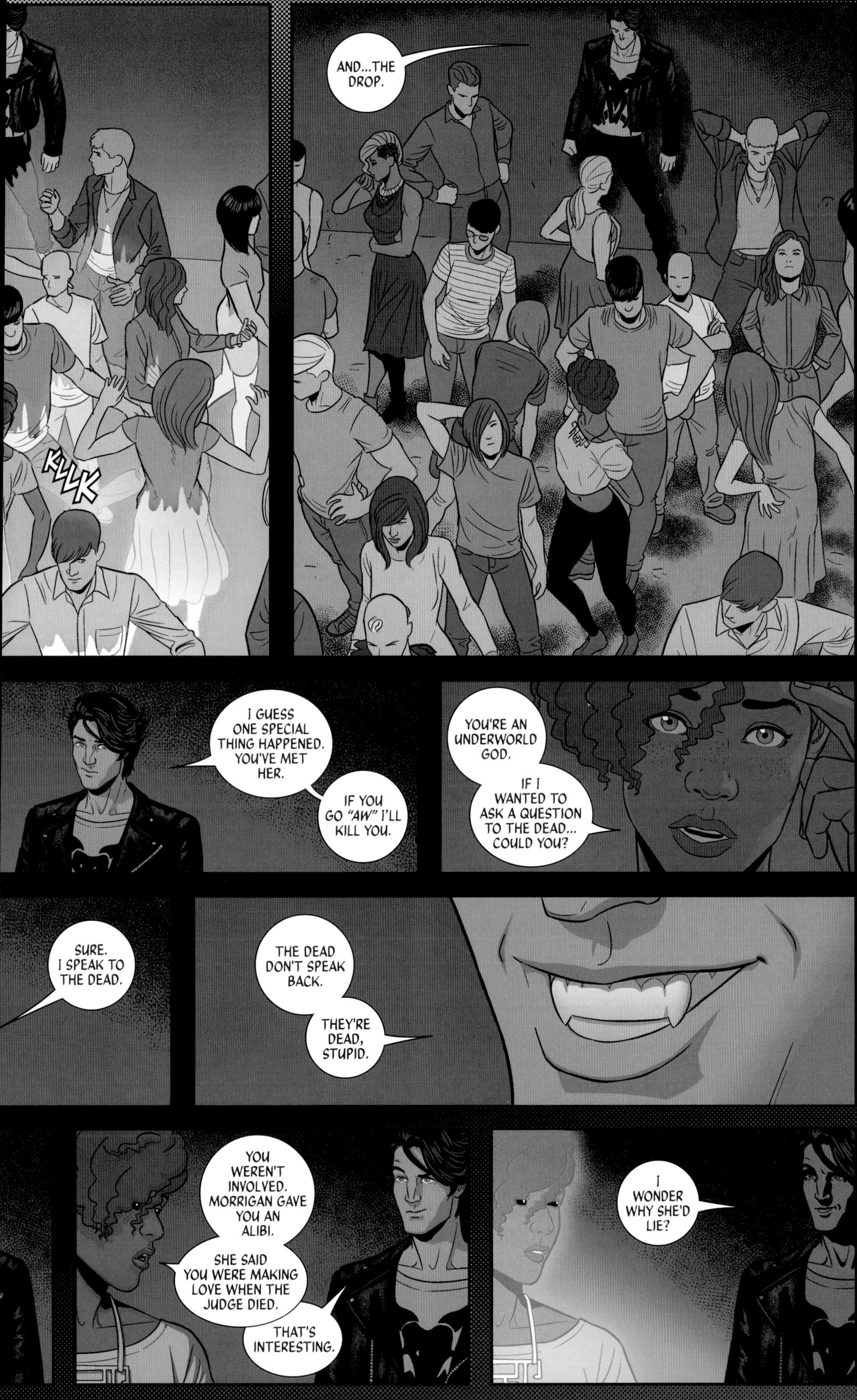
KLLK
AND...THE DROP.
I GUESS ONE SPECIAL THING HAPPENED. YOU'VE MET HER.
IF YOU GO "AW" I'LL KILL YOU.
YOU'RE AN UNDERWORLD GOD.
IF I WANTED TO ASK A QUESTION TO THE DEAD... COULD YOU?
SURE. I SPEAK TO THE DEAD.
THE DEAD DON'T SPEAK BACK.
THEY'RE DEAD, STUPID.
YOU WEREN'T INVOLVED. MORRIGAN GAVE YOU AN ALIBI.
SHE SAID YOU WERE MAKING LOVE WHEN THE JUDGE DIED.
THAT'S INTERESTING.
I WONDER WHY SHE'D LIE?

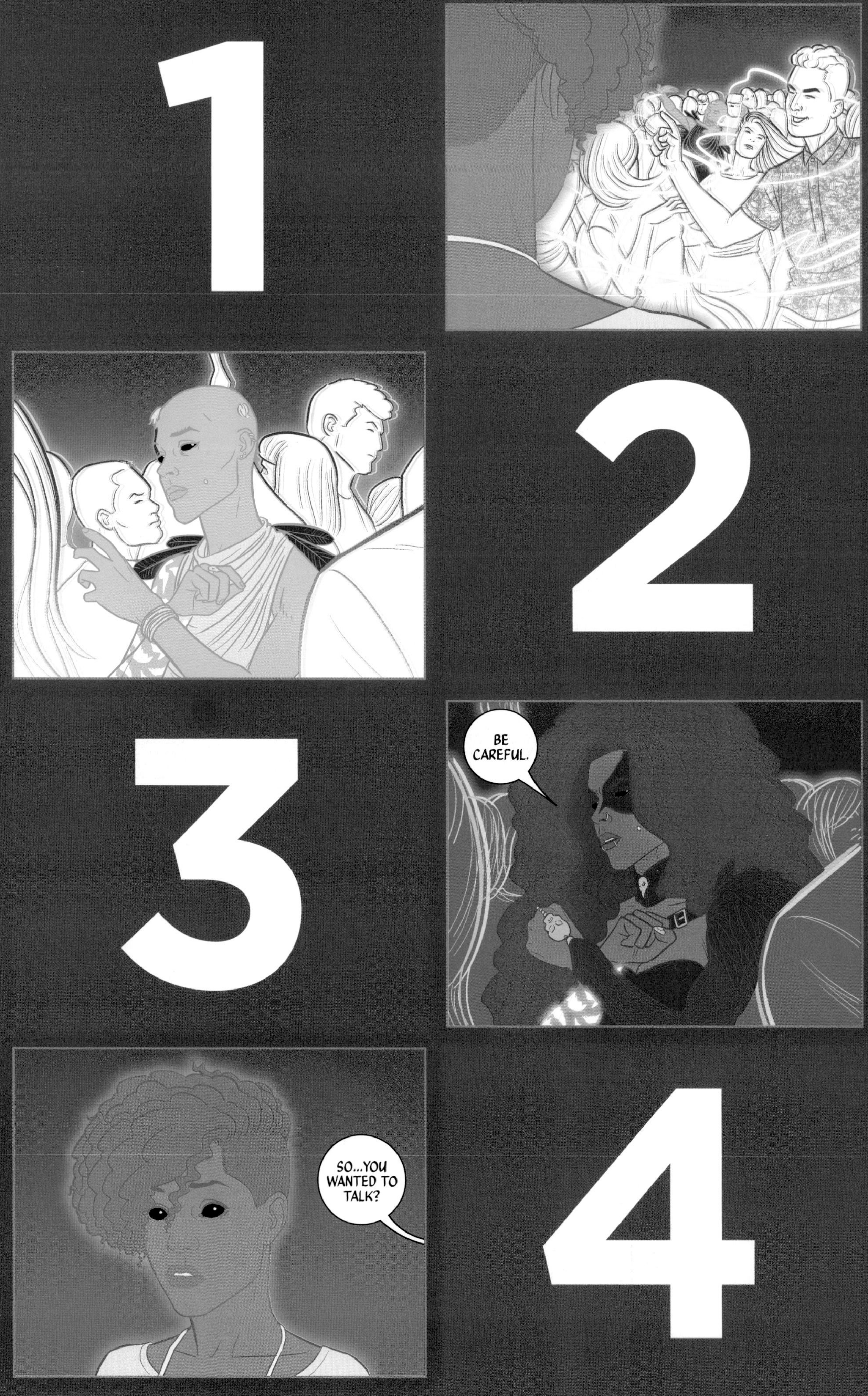
1
2
3
BE CAREFUL.
SO...YOU WANTED TO TALK?
4

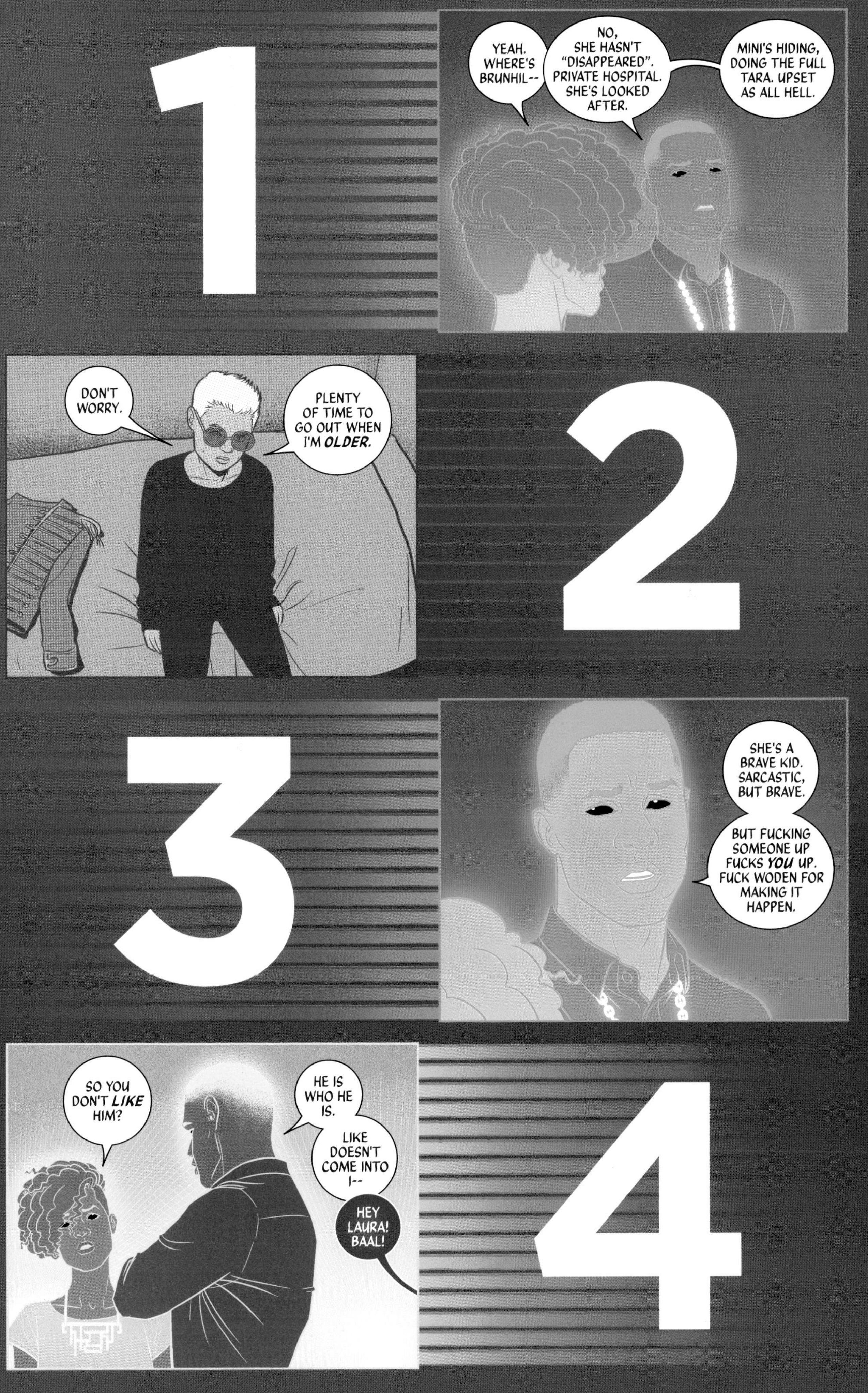
1
YEAH. WHERE'S BRUNHIL--
NO, SHE HASN'T "DISAPPEARED". PRIVATE HOSPITAL. SHE'S LOOKED AFTER.
MINI'S HIDING, DOING THE FULL TARA. UPSET AS ALL HELL.
DON'T WORRY.
PLENTY OF TIME TO GO OUT WHEN I'M *OLDER.*
2
3
SHE'S A BRAVE KID. SARCASTIC, BUT BRAVE.
BUT FUCKING SOMEONE UP FUCKS *YOU* UP. FUCK WODEN FOR MAKING IT HAPPEN.
SO YOU DON'T *LIKE* HIM?
HE IS WHO HE IS.
LIKE DOESN'T COME INTO I--
HEY LAURA! BAAL!
4

1

2

SO, SAFE TO SAY HE HASN'T ENTIRELY FORGIVEN ME YET.

I'M STILL A LITTLE SURPRISED. BAAL AND GUYS.

3

"GUY" IS A SMALL WORD, BUT I GUESS HE SAW ME LIKE THAT TOO.

I WAS HIS GATEWAY. I TOOK HIM INTO THE UNDERWORLD.

I TOOK HIM EVERYWHERE.

4

AND THEN YOU SLEPT WITH LUCI.

HOW DID SHE PUT IT?

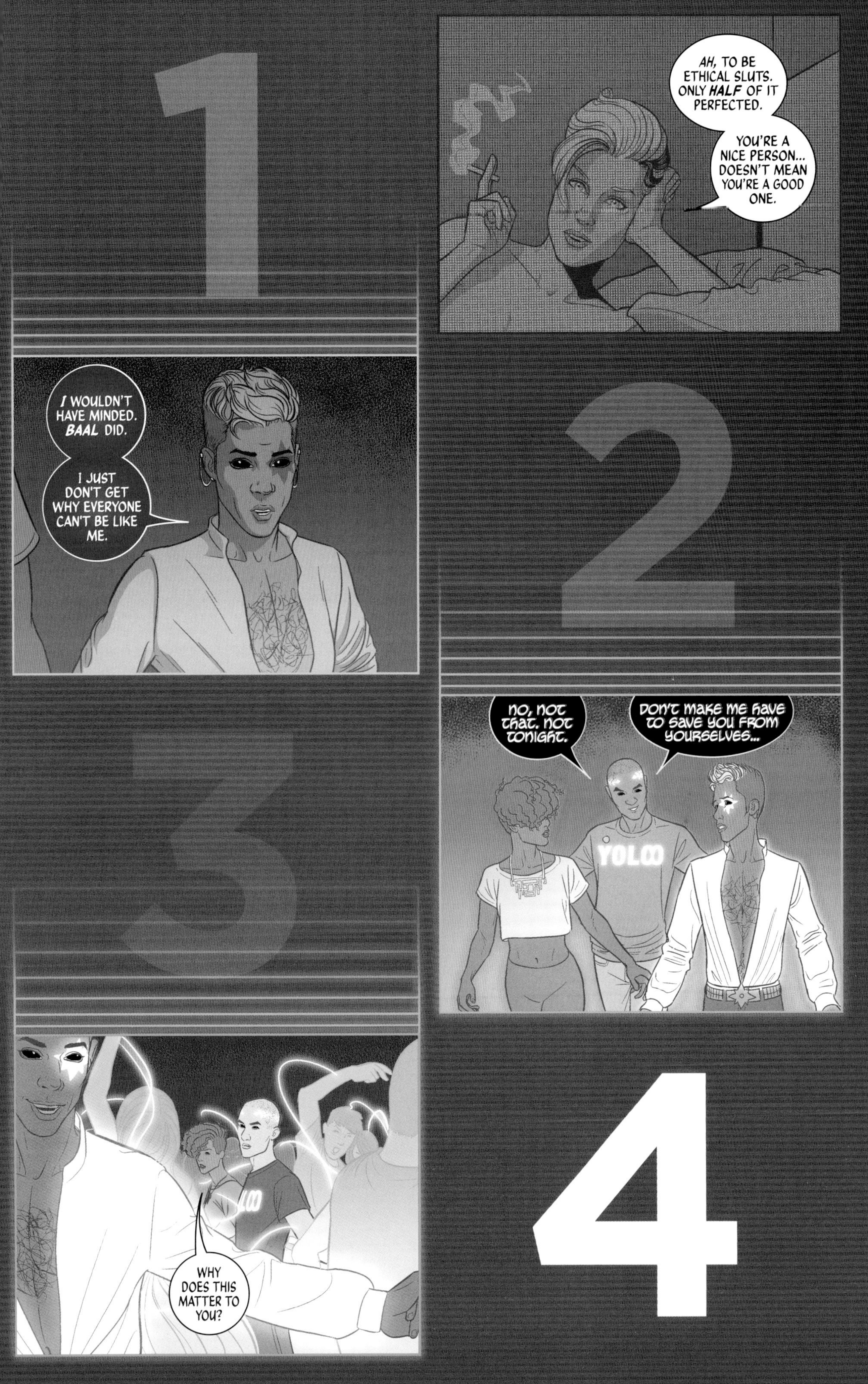
1
AH, TO BE ETHICAL SLUTS. ONLY HALF OF IT PERFECTED.
YOU'RE A NICE PERSON... DOESN'T MEAN YOU'RE A GOOD ONE.
I WOULDN'T HAVE MINDED. BAAL DID.
I JUST DON'T GET WHY EVERYONE CAN'T BE LIKE ME.
2
NO, NOT THAT. NOT TONIGHT.
DON'T MAKE ME HAVE TO SAVE YOU FROM YOURSELVES...
YOLO
3
WHY DOES THIS MATTER TO YOU?
4

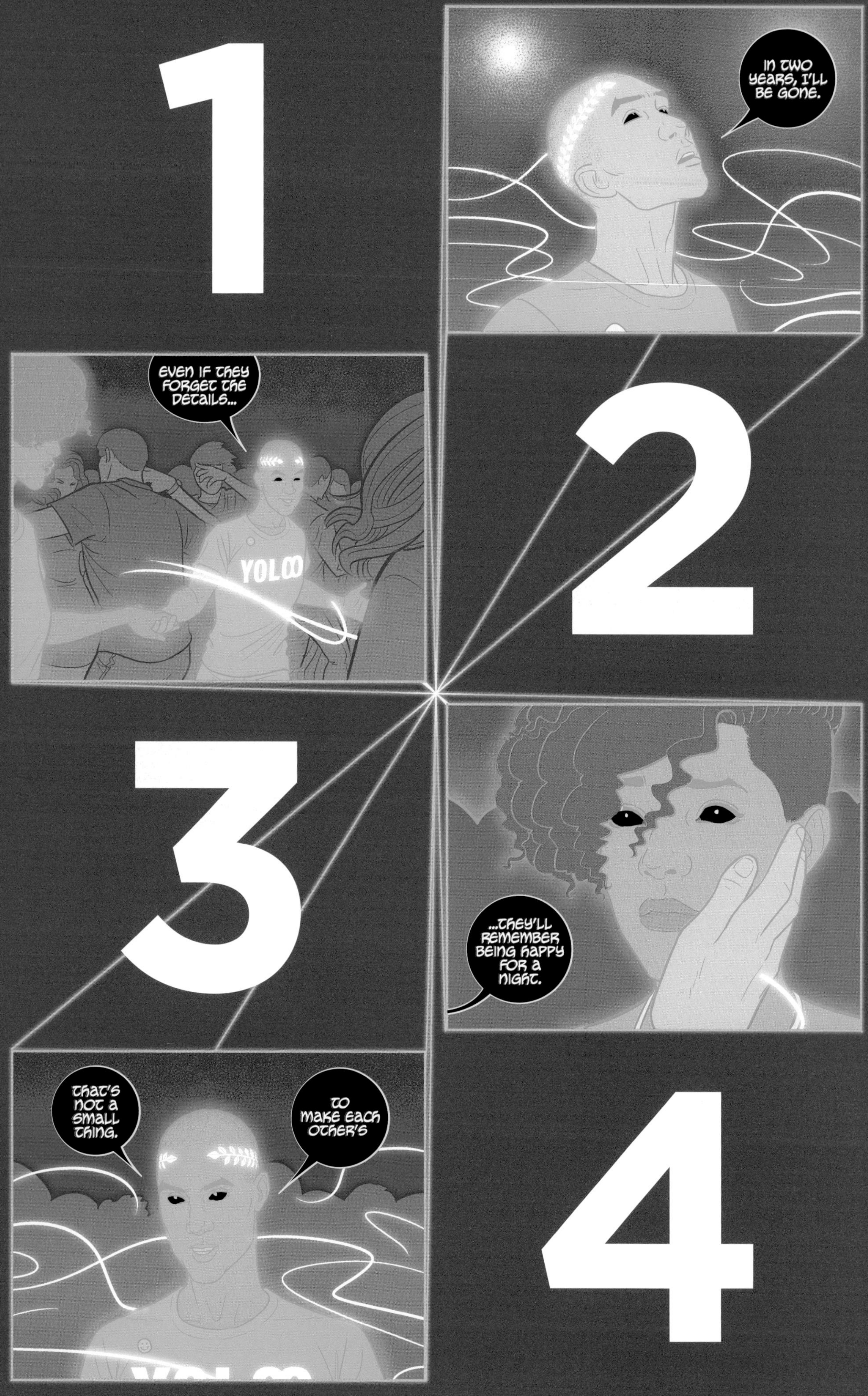
1
In two years, I'll be gone.
2
Even if they forget the details...
3
...they'll remember being happy for a night.
4
That's not a small thing.
To make each other's

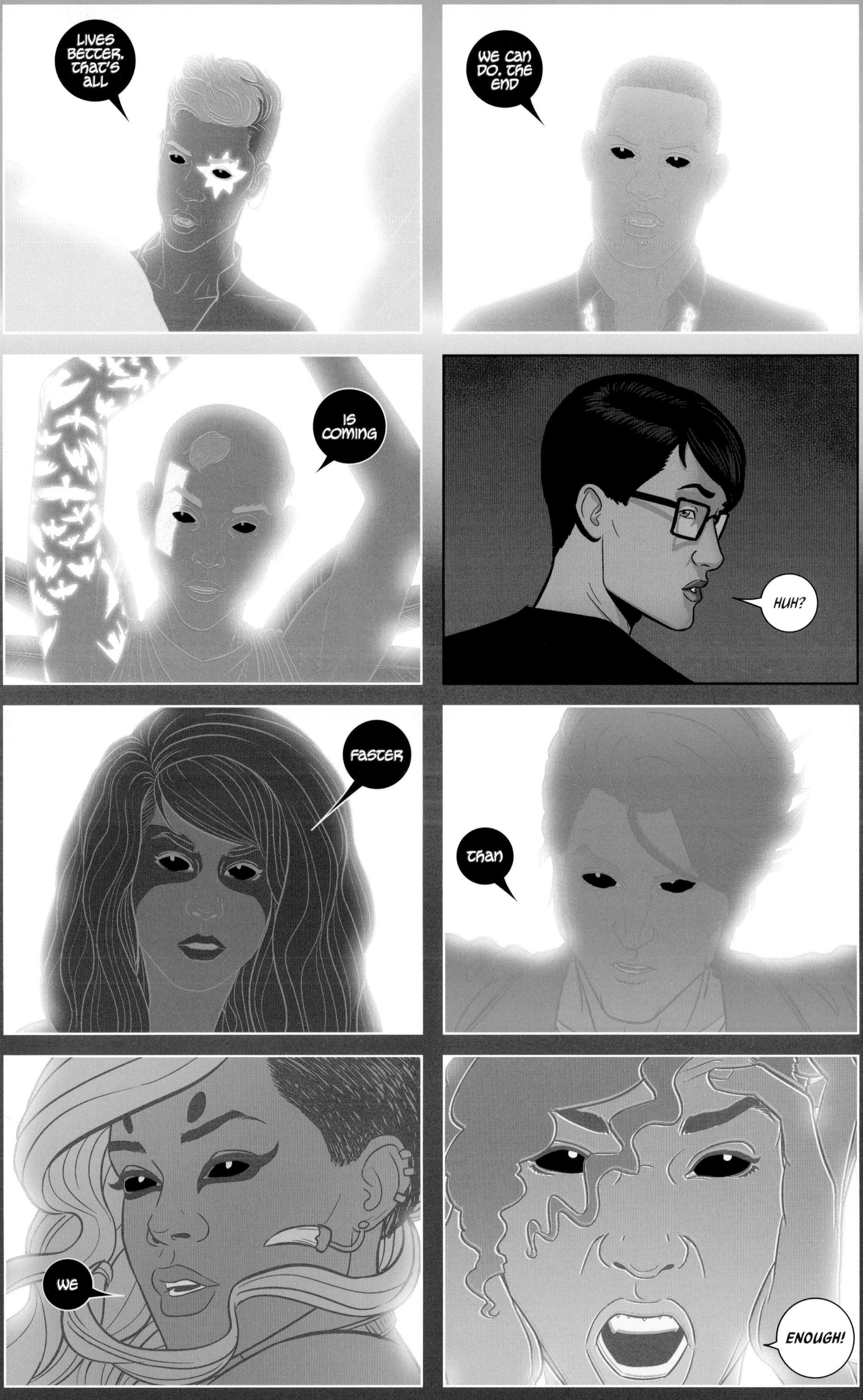
LIVES BETTER. THAT'S ALL
WE CAN DO. THE END
IS COMING
HUH?
FASTER
THAN
WE
ENOUGH!

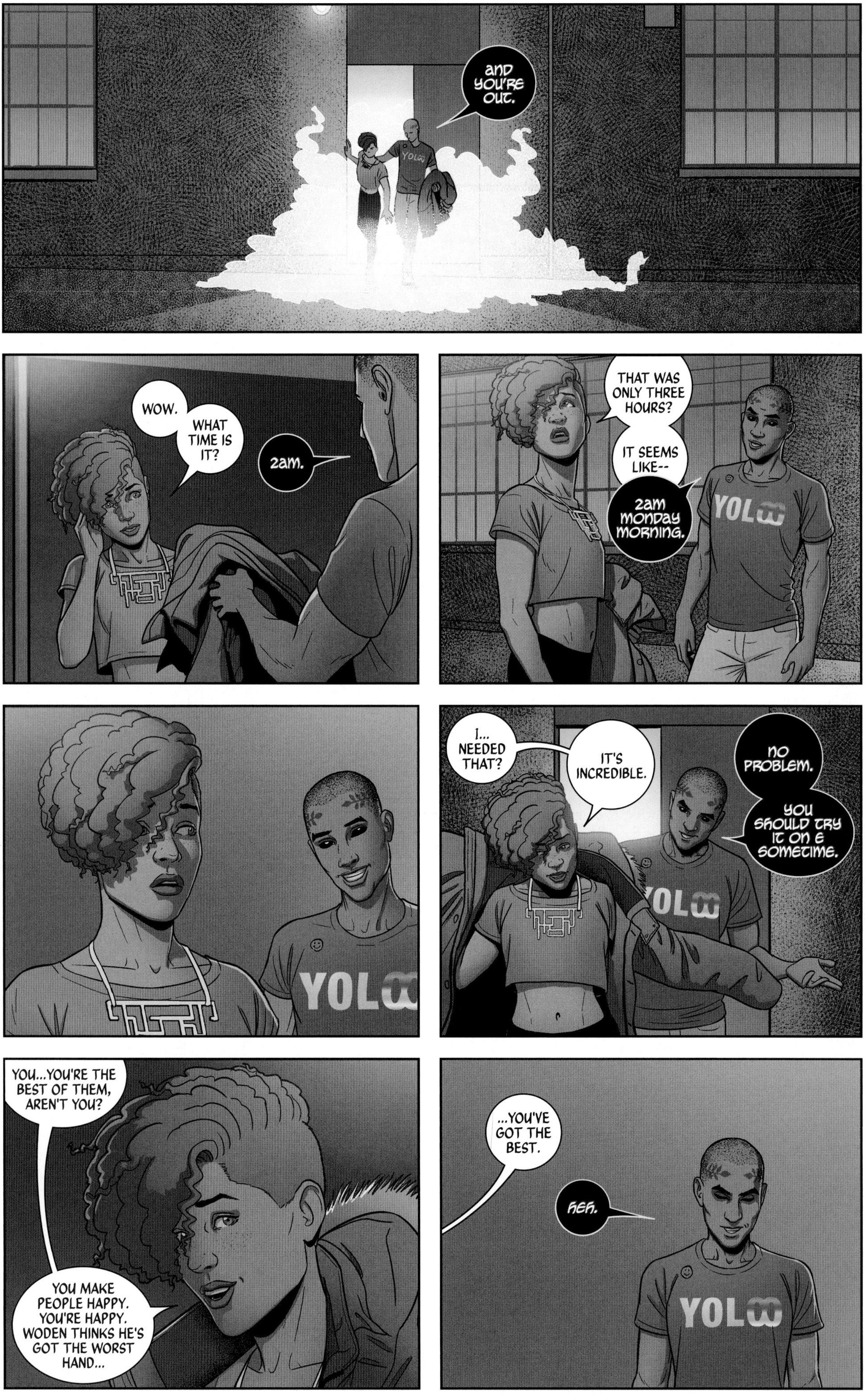
and you're out.
WOW.
WHAT TIME IS IT?
2am.
THAT WAS ONLY THREE HOURS?
IT SEEMS LIKE--
2am MONDAY MORNING.
I... NEEDED THAT?
IT'S INCREDIBLE.
no problem.
you should try it on E sometime.
YOU...YOU'RE THE BEST OF THEM, AREN'T YOU?
YOU MAKE PEOPLE HAPPY. YOU'RE HAPPY. WODEN THINKS HE'S GOT THE WORST HAND...
...YOU'VE GOT THE BEST.
Heh.

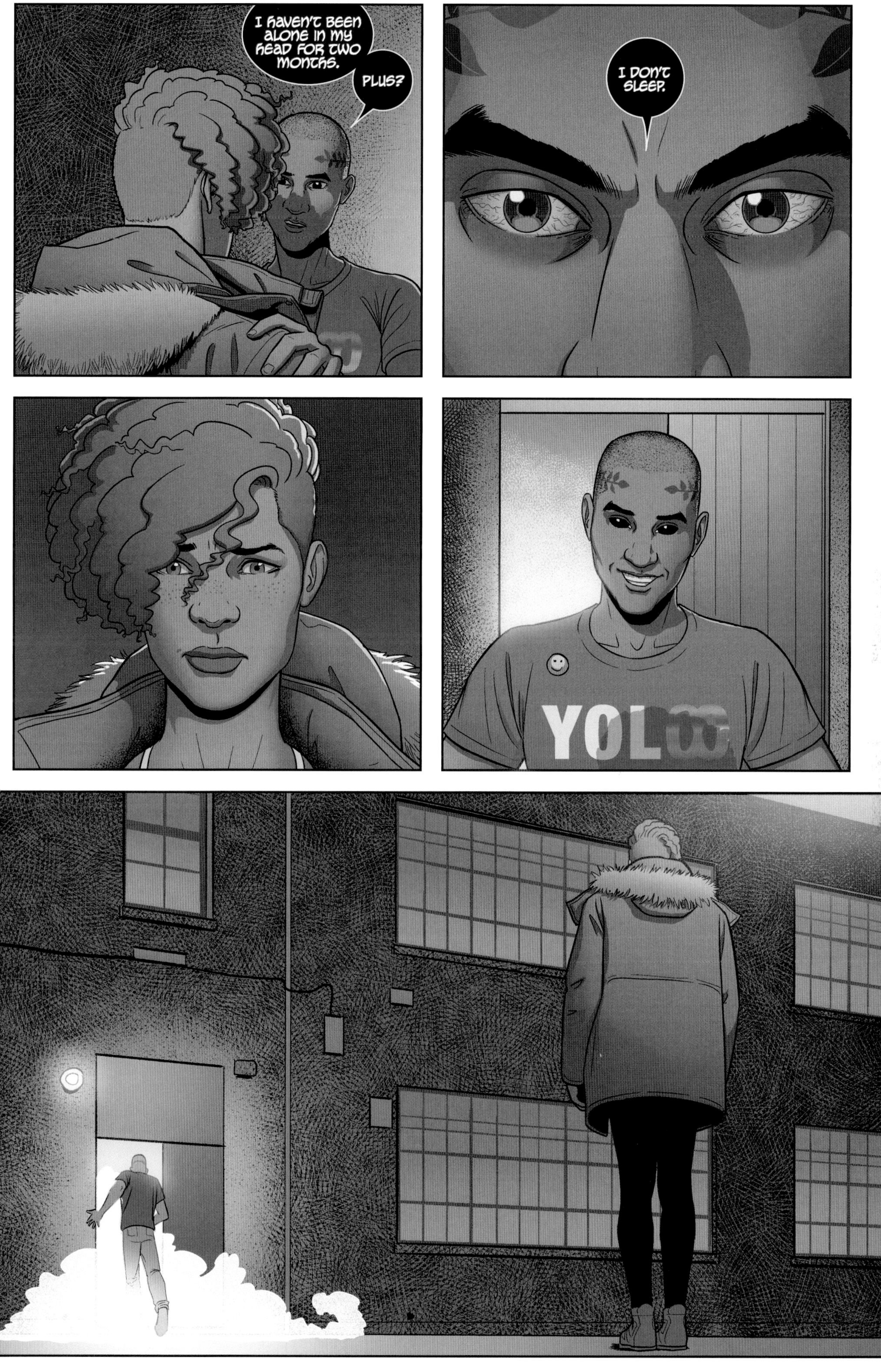
I HAVEN'T BEEN ALONE IN MY HEAD FOR TWO MONTHS.
PLUS?
I DON'T SLEEP.

NEVER GOING TO
BE ALONE AGAIN

19 MAY 2014

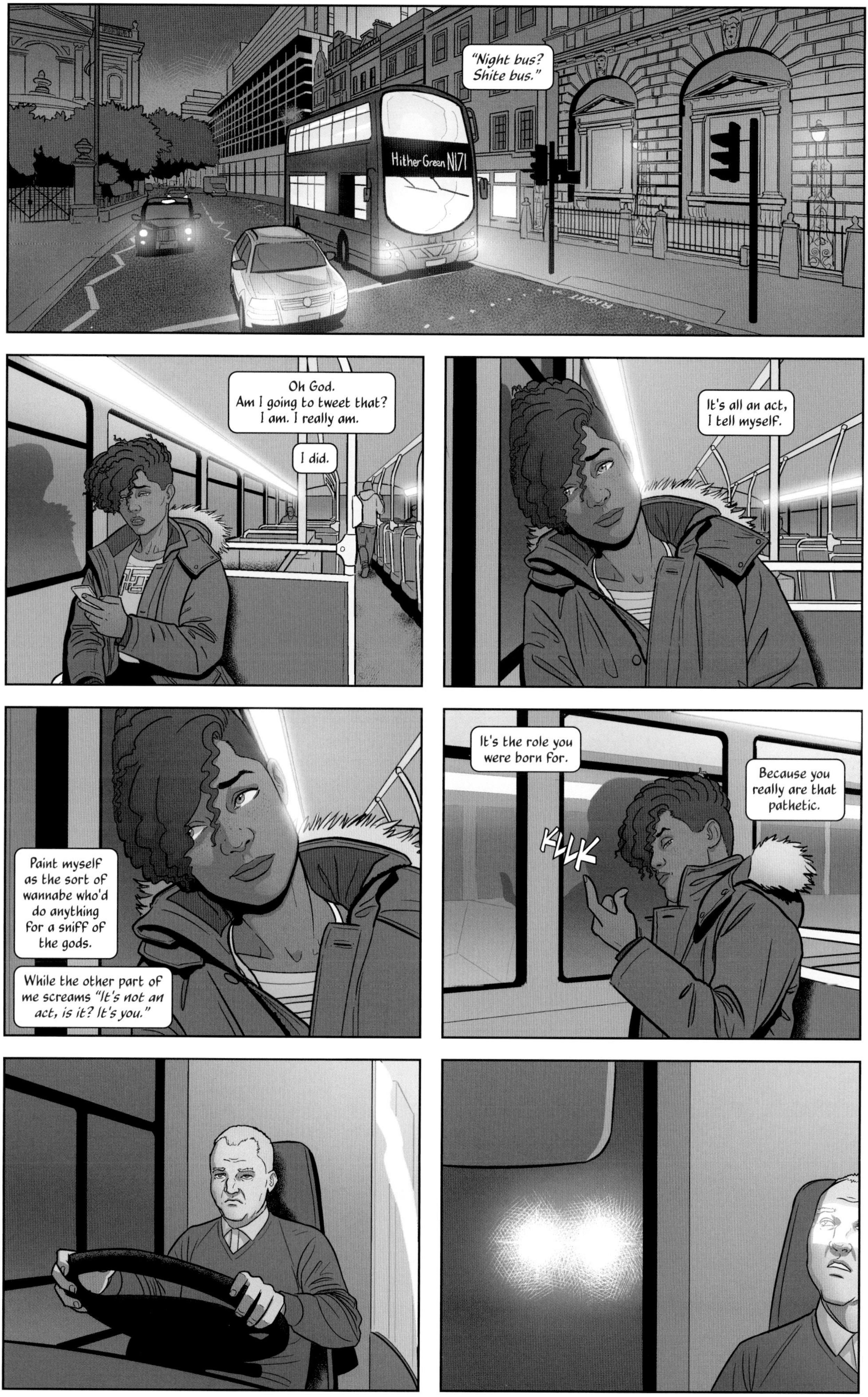
"Night bus? Shite bus."
Hither Green N171
Oh God. Am I going to tweet that? I am. I really am.
I did.
It's all an act, I tell myself.
Paint myself as the sort of wannabe who'd do anything for a sniff of the gods.
While the other part of me screams "It's not an act, is it? It's you."
It's the role you were born for.
KLLK
Because you really are that pathetic.

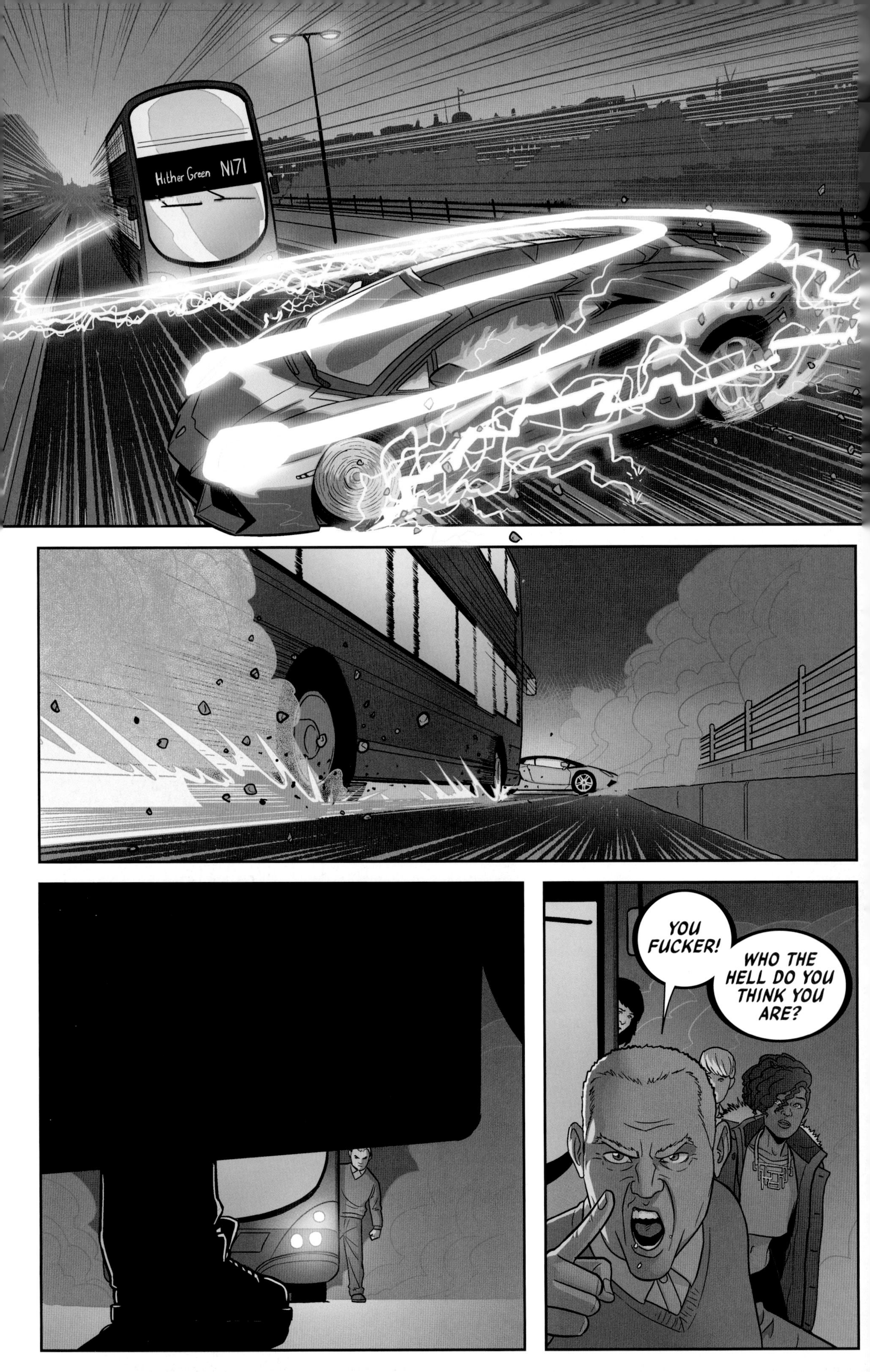
Hither Green N171
YOU FUCKER!
WHO THE HELL DO YOU THINK YOU ARE?

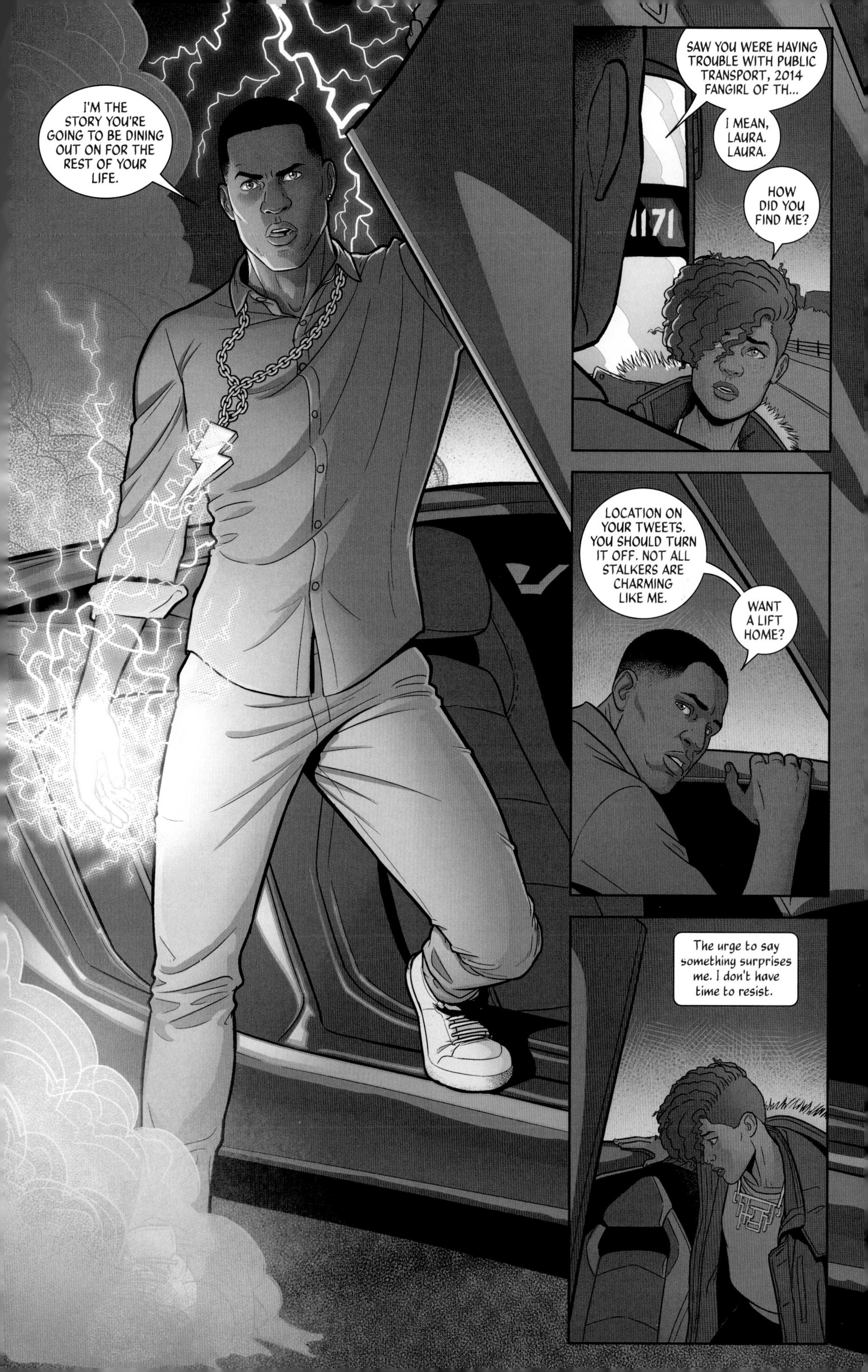
I'M THE STORY YOU'RE GOING TO BE DINING OUT ON FOR THE REST OF YOUR LIFE.
SAW YOU WERE HAVING TROUBLE WITH PUBLIC TRANSPORT, 2014 FANGIRL OF TH...
I MEAN, LAURA. LAURA.
1171
HOW DID YOU FIND ME?
LOCATION ON YOUR TWEETS. YOU SHOULD TURN IT OFF. NOT ALL STALKERS ARE CHARMING LIKE ME.
WANT A LIFT HOME?
The urge to say something surprises me. I don't have time to resist.

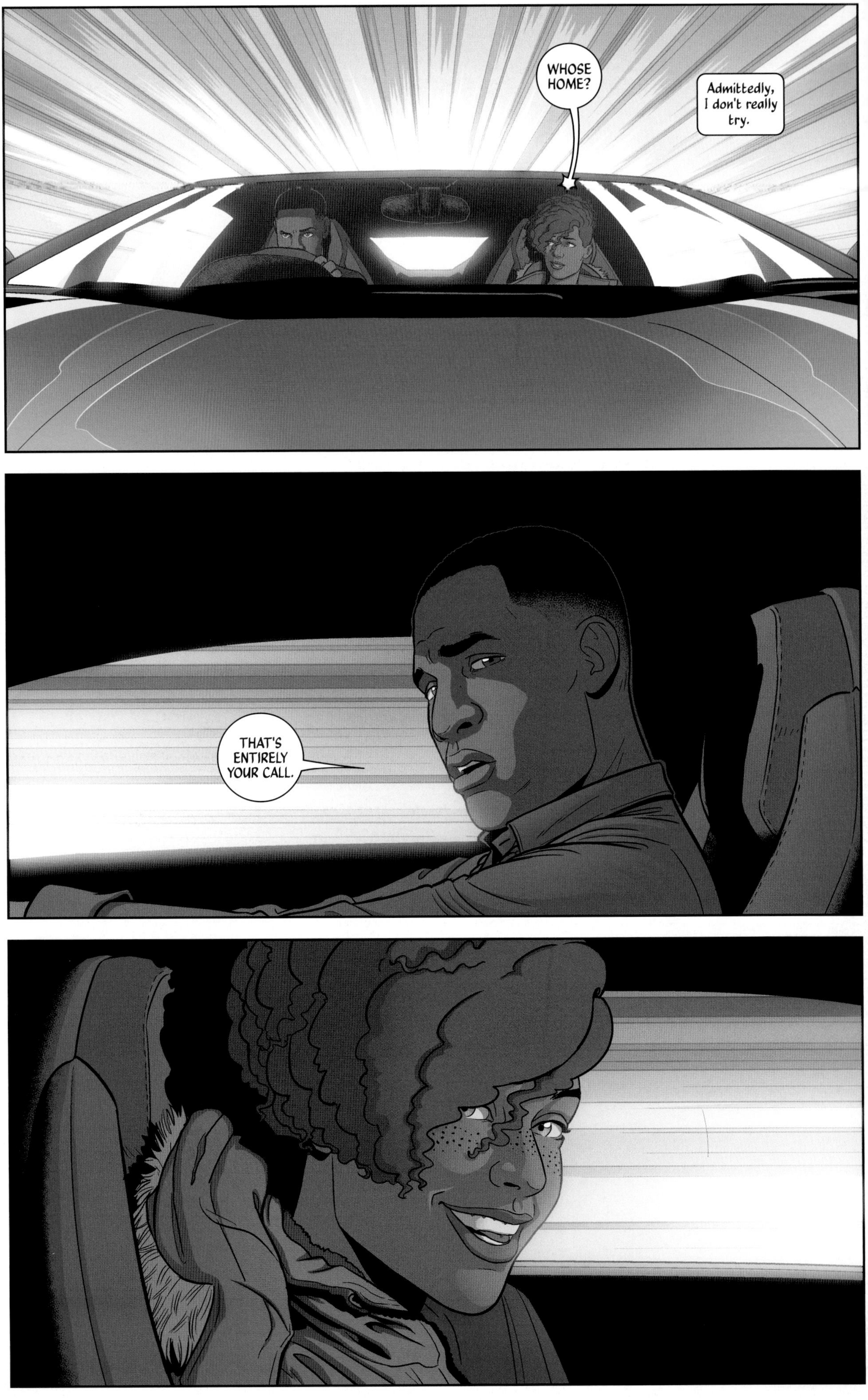
WHOSE HOME?
Admittedly, I don't really try.
THAT'S ENTIRELY YOUR CALL.

UH-HUH

19 MAY 2014

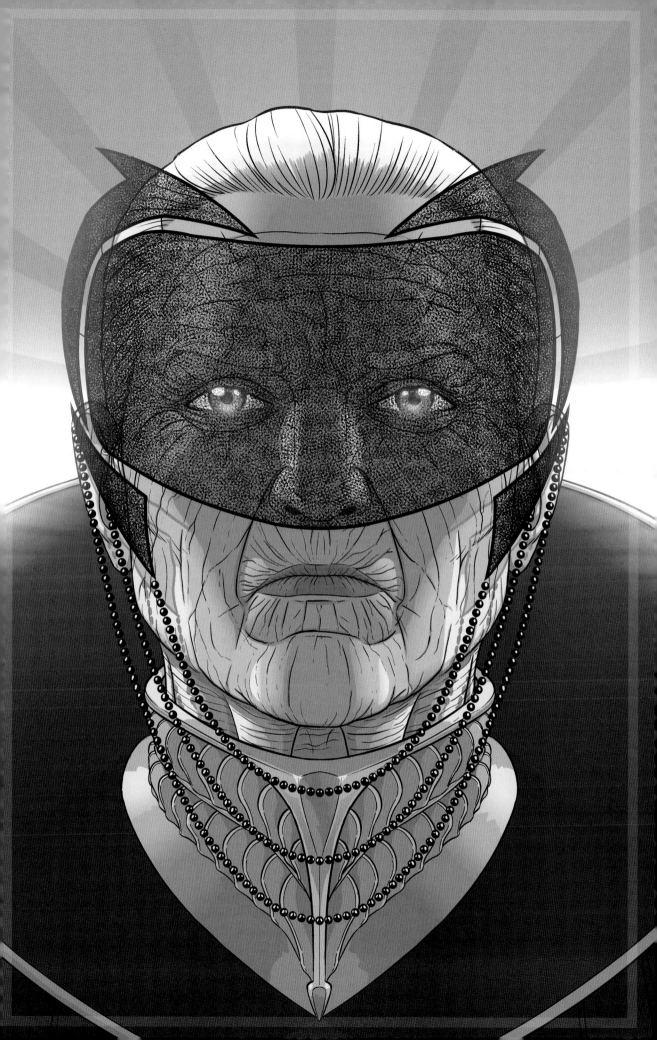

THE
WICKED
+
ƎNIΛIᗡ
ƎHT

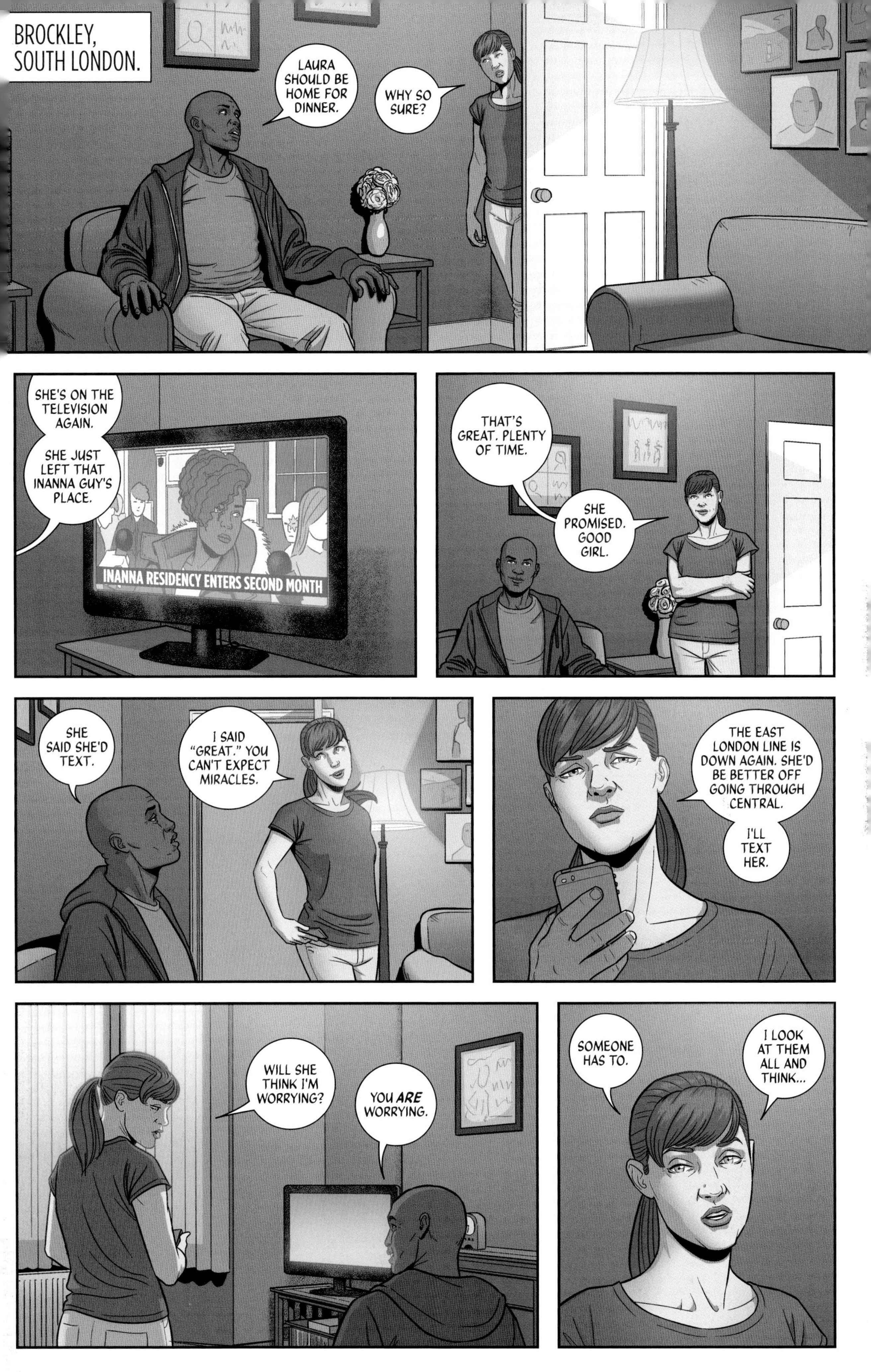
BROCKLEY, SOUTH LONDON.
LAURA SHOULD BE HOME FOR DINNER.
WHY SO SURE?
SHE'S ON THE TELEVISION AGAIN.
SHE JUST LEFT THAT INANNA GUY'S PLACE.
INANNA RESIDENCY ENTERS SECOND MONTH
THAT'S GREAT. PLENTY OF TIME.
SHE PROMISED. GOOD GIRL.
SHE SAID SHE'D TEXT.
I SAID "GREAT." YOU CAN'T EXPECT MIRACLES.
THE EAST LONDON LINE IS DOWN AGAIN. SHE'D BE BETTER OFF GOING THROUGH CENTRAL.
I'LL TEXT HER.
WILL SHE THINK I'M WORRYING?
YOU *ARE* WORRYING.
SOMEONE HAS TO.
I LOOK AT THEM ALL AND THINK...

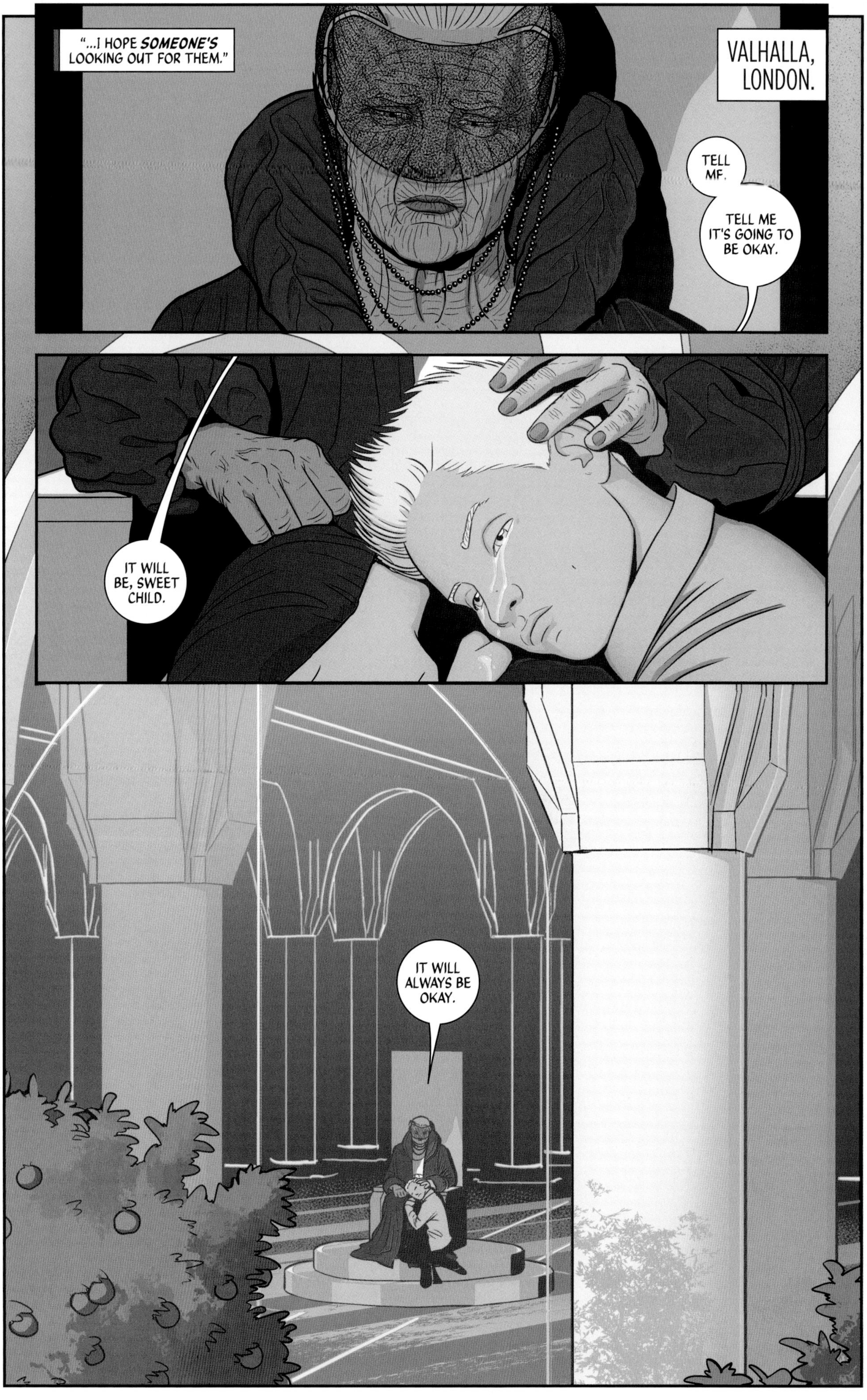
"...I HOPE **SOMEONE'S** LOOKING OUT FOR THEM."
VALHALLA, LONDON.
TELL ME.
TELL ME IT'S GOING TO BE OKAY.
IT WILL BE, SWEET CHILD.
IT WILL ALWAYS BE OKAY.

THIS IS A GIFT

28 JUNE 2014

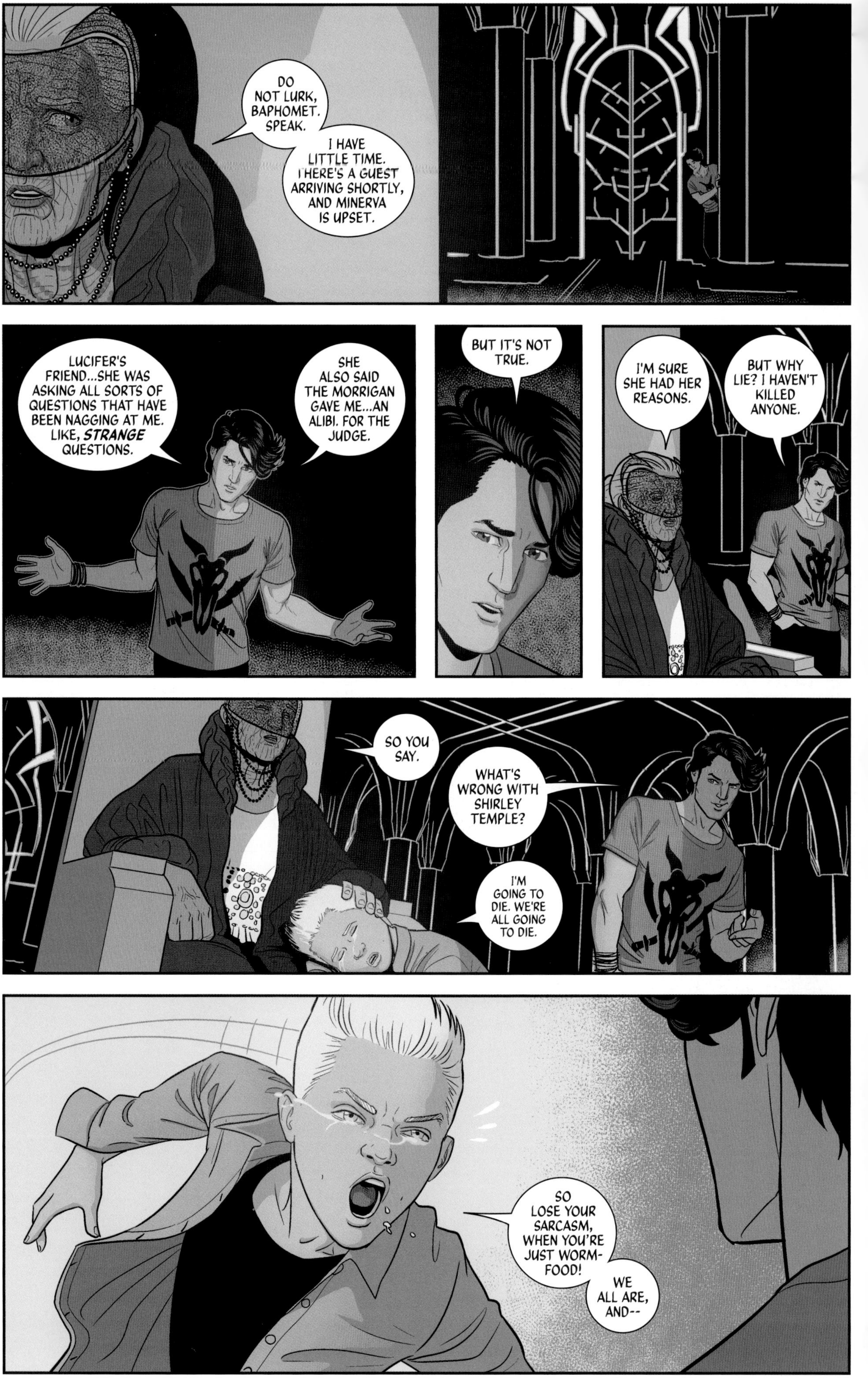
DO NOT LURK, BAPHOMET. SPEAK.
I HAVE LITTLE TIME. THERE'S A GUEST ARRIVING SHORTLY, AND MINERVA IS UPSET.
LUCIFER'S FRIEND...SHE WAS ASKING ALL SORTS OF QUESTIONS THAT HAVE BEEN NAGGING AT ME. LIKE, ***STRANGE*** QUESTIONS.
SHE ALSO SAID THE MORRIGAN GAVE ME...AN ALIBI. FOR THE JUDGE.
BUT IT'S NOT TRUE.
I'M SURE SHE HAD HER REASONS.
BUT WHY LIE? I HAVEN'T KILLED ANYONE.
SO YOU SAY.
WHAT'S WRONG WITH SHIRLEY TEMPLE?
I'M GOING TO DIE. WE'RE ALL GOING TO DIE.
SO LOSE YOUR SARCASM, WHEN YOU'RE JUST WORM-FOOD!
WE ALL ARE, AND--

FUC--

LANGUAGE.

LEAVE US, MINERVA.

YOU DIDN'T COME TO TALK ABOUT LUCIFER.

YOU CAME TO HAVE YOUR HEAD STROKED TOO.

I HAVEN'T FELT RIGHT SINCE THAT COP SHOT ME. DON'T EVEN SEE HOW HE WAS ABLE TO HURT ME.

YOUR DEFENCES ARE AT YOUR WEAKEST WHEN YOU PERFORM.

YOU REVEAL YOURSELF. YOU MAKE YOURSELF VULNERABLE.

ALL GIFTS HAVE THEIR PRICE.

I'M NOT SURE I CAN STAND ANOTHER STIRRING RENDITION OF *ALWAYS LOOK ON THE BRIGHT SIDE OF DEATH*, ANANKE...

I WILL SPARE YOU. THERE IS SOMETHING ELSE.

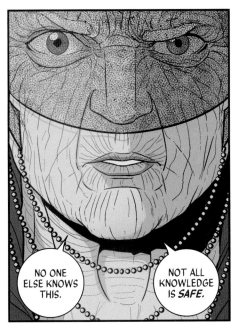

NO ONE ELSE KNOWS THIS.

NOT ALL KNOWLEDGE IS *SAFE*.

THAT'S WHY I DISMISSED MINERVA. HER MORAL COMPASS IS NOT DEVELOPED. THE YOUNGEST ARE MOST LIKELY TO ACT OUT, IN MY EXPERIENCE.

I WOULD RATHER NONE OF YOU KNOW...BUT YOU ARE *YOU,* AND NO FOOL.

YOU ARE EXPLORING YOUR DIVINITY. YOU COULD EASILY CHANCE UPON IT YOURSELF. AND AS THE FEAR IS HEAVY UPON YOU, YOU COULD BE TEMPTED...

WHAT ARE YOU TALKING ABOUT?

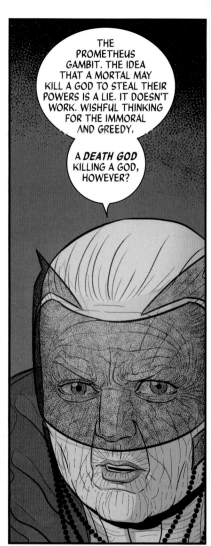

THE PROMETHEUS GAMBIT. THE IDEA THAT A MORTAL MAY KILL A GOD TO STEAL THEIR POWERS IS A LIE. IT DOESN'T WORK. WISHFUL THINKING FOR THE IMMORAL AND GREEDY.

A *DEATH GOD* KILLING A GOD, HOWEVER?

YOU COULD TEAR A FEW MORE YEARS FOR YOURSELF.

THEIR LIFE FOR YOUR LIFE.

NOW HEED MY WORDS, BAPHOMET.

ONLY YOU KNOW THIS. IF A GOD IS MURDERED, *I WILL HUNT YOU DOWN.*

I CAN AID YOU IN COMING TO TERMS WITH THIS LIFE YOU HAVE, IN CONNECTING WITH YOUR IMMORTAL PAST AND FUTURE.

DO NOT SUBMIT TO THE FEAR. I CAN HELP YOU.

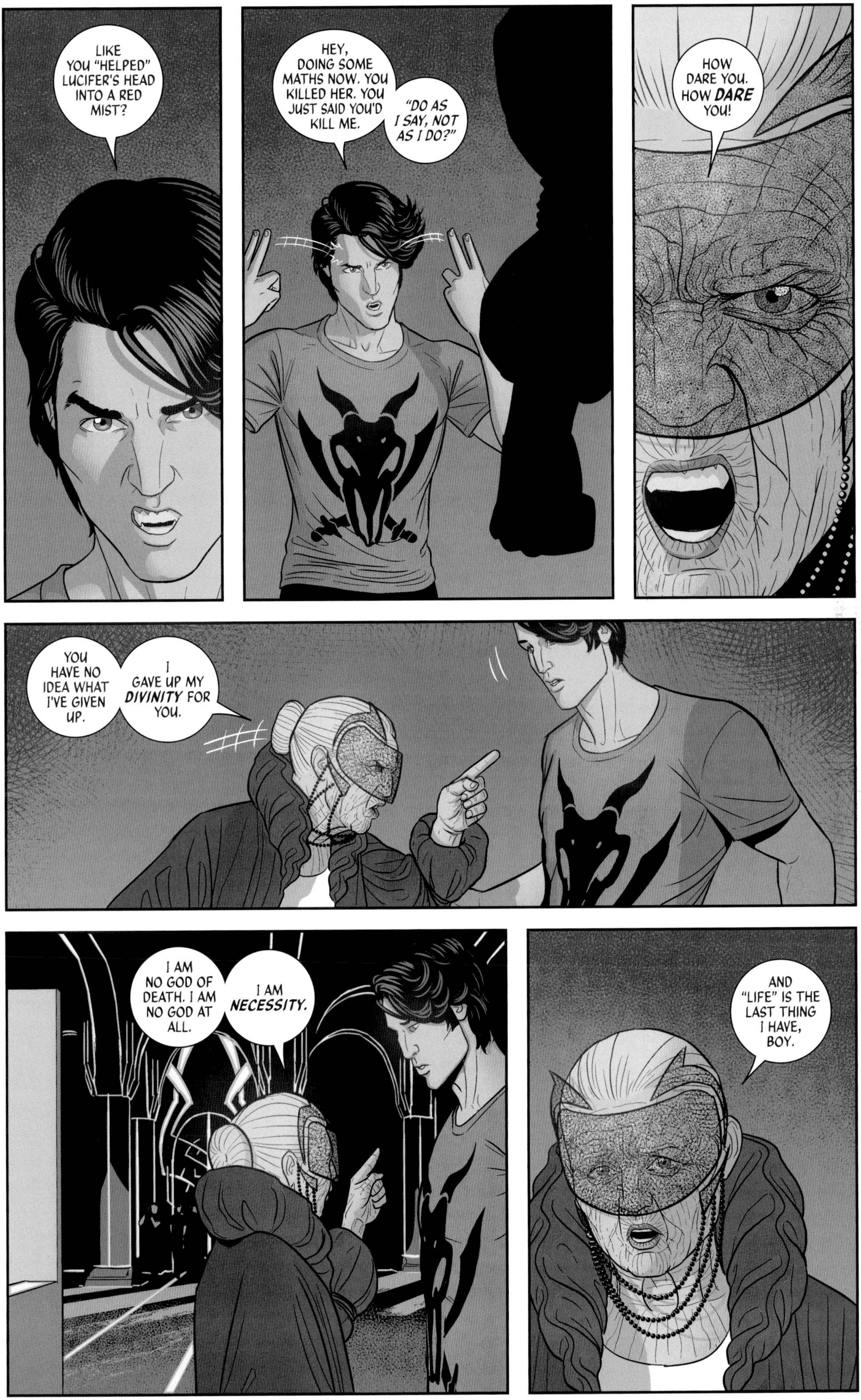
LIKE YOU "HELPED" LUCIFER'S HEAD INTO A RED MIST?
HEY, DOING SOME MATHS NOW. YOU KILLED HER. YOU JUST SAID YOU'D KILL ME.
"DO AS I SAY, NOT AS I DO?"
HOW DARE YOU. HOW DARE YOU!
YOU HAVE NO IDEA WHAT I'VE GIVEN UP.
I GAVE UP MY DIVINITY FOR YOU.
I AM NO GOD OF DEATH. I AM NO GOD AT ALL.
I AM NECESSITY.
AND "LIFE" IS THE LAST THING I HAVE, BOY.

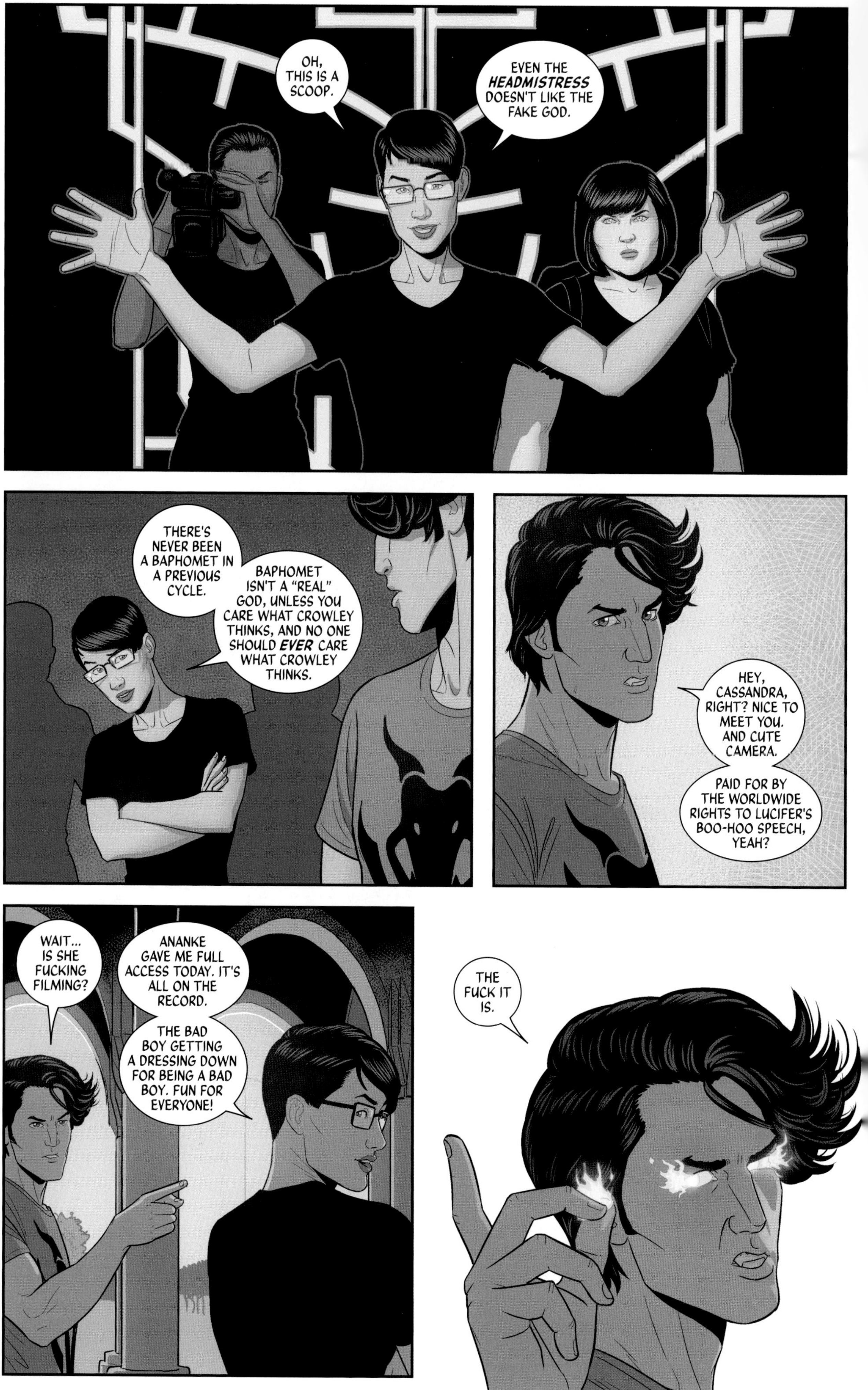
OH, THIS IS A SCOOP.
EVEN THE HEADMISTRESS DOESN'T LIKE THE FAKE GOD.
THERE'S NEVER BEEN A BAPHOMET IN A PREVIOUS CYCLE.
BAPHOMET ISN'T A "REAL" GOD, UNLESS YOU CARE WHAT CROWLEY THINKS, AND NO ONE SHOULD EVER CARE WHAT CROWLEY THINKS.
HEY, CASSANDRA, RIGHT? NICE TO MEET YOU. AND CUTE CAMERA.
PAID FOR BY THE WORLDWIDE RIGHTS TO LUCIFER'S BOO-HOO SPEECH, YEAH?
WAIT... IS SHE FUCKING FILMING?
ANANKE GAVE ME FULL ACCESS TODAY. IT'S ALL ON THE RECORD.
THE BAD BOY GETTING A DRESSING DOWN FOR BEING A BAD BOY. FUN FOR EVERYONE!
THE FUCK IT IS.

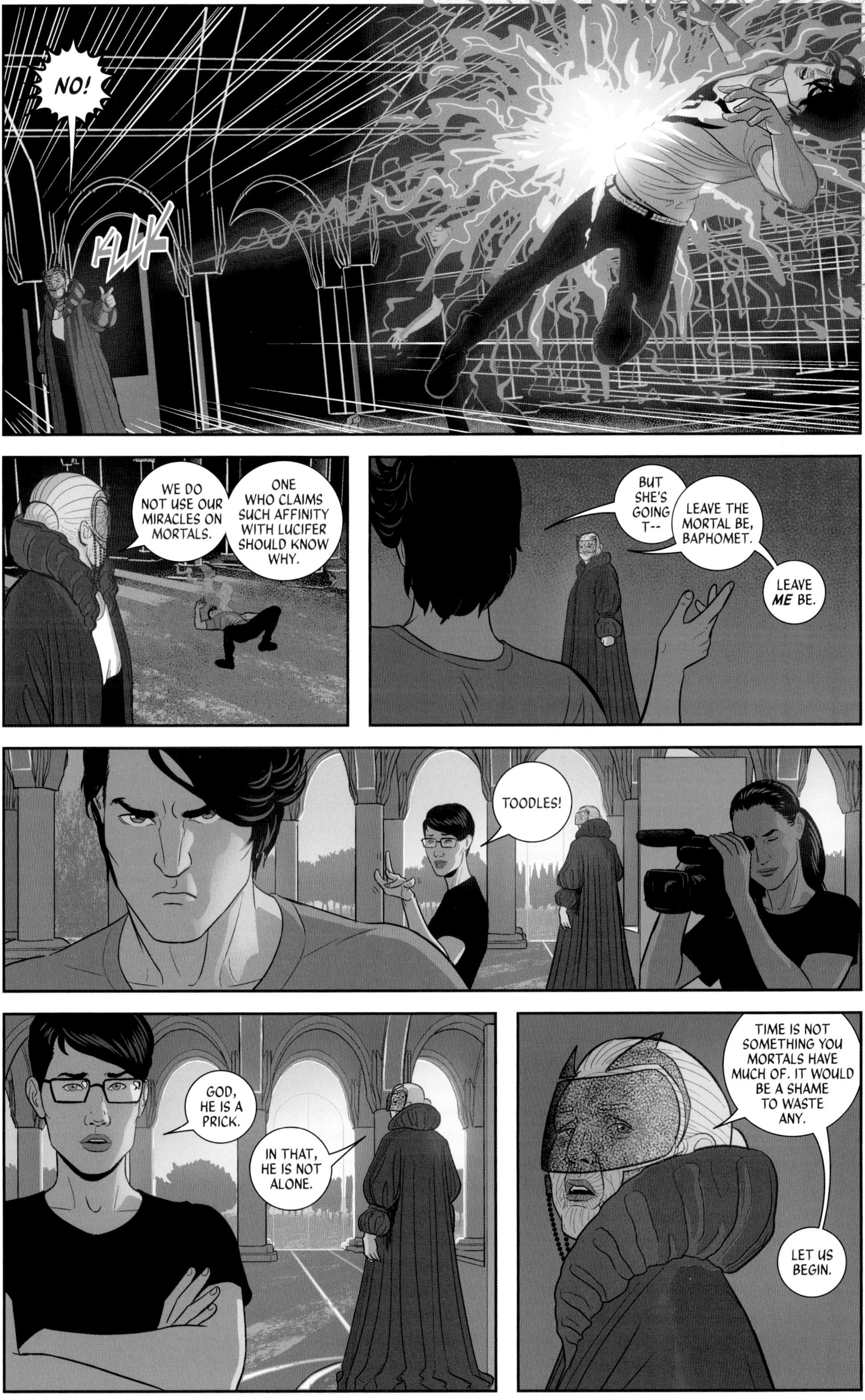
NO!
KLIK
WE DO NOT USE OUR MIRACLES ON MORTALS.
ONE WHO CLAIMS SUCH AFFINITY WITH LUCIFER SHOULD KNOW WHY.
BUT SHE'S GOING T--
LEAVE THE MORTAL BE, BAPHOMET.
LEAVE *ME* BE.
TOODLES!
GOD, HE IS A PRICK.
IN THAT, HE IS NOT ALONE.
TIME IS NOT SOMETHING YOU MORTALS HAVE MUCH OF. IT WOULD BE A SHAME TO WASTE ANY.
LET US BEGIN.

FEAR
AND LOATHING
IN ETERNITY

28 JUNE 2014

FIRST QUESTION. WHY AN INTERVIEW?

WODEN TOLD ME YOU WANTED TO TALK. YOU *NEVER* TALK. YOU'RE BARELY A GHOST IN THE LITERATURE. YOU'RE THIS BIG EXCITING MYSTERY AND YOU SPEAK TO ME NOW... WHY?

YOU ARE RESEARCHING THE CIRCUMSTANCES OF LUCIFER'S DEATH.

I WANT TO HELP YOU.

WAIT. HOW DID YOU--

I DIDN'T. I DO NOW.

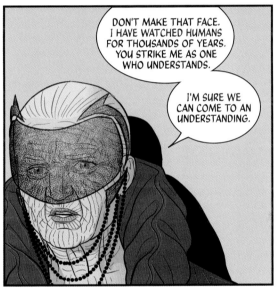

DON'T MAKE THAT FACE. I HAVE WATCHED HUMANS FOR THOUSANDS OF YEARS. YOU STRIKE ME AS ONE WHO UNDERSTANDS.

I'M SURE WE CAN COME TO AN UNDERSTANDING.

OKAY. SERIOUSLY, YOU'RE "IMMORTAL"? PROVE IT.

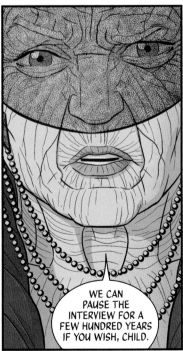

WE CAN PAUSE THE INTERVIEW FOR A FEW HUNDRED YEARS IF YOU WISH, CHILD.

DON'T PATRONISE ME. YOU CAN'T EXPECT ANYONE TO ACCEPT THAT. GIVE US SOME PROOF OF...

WHAT? TELL YOU HOW NAPOLEON LIKED TO EAT HIS EGGS OR WHAT THE SUN LOOKED LIKE RISING OVER THE COLOSSUS OF RHODES? THAT GRAPES PLUCKED FROM THE HANGING GARDENS WERE INFERIOR TO THOSE IN YOUR LOCAL GROCER'S?

THIS IS NOT THAT KIND OF STORY.

MINE IS A LONELIER STORY THAN THAT.

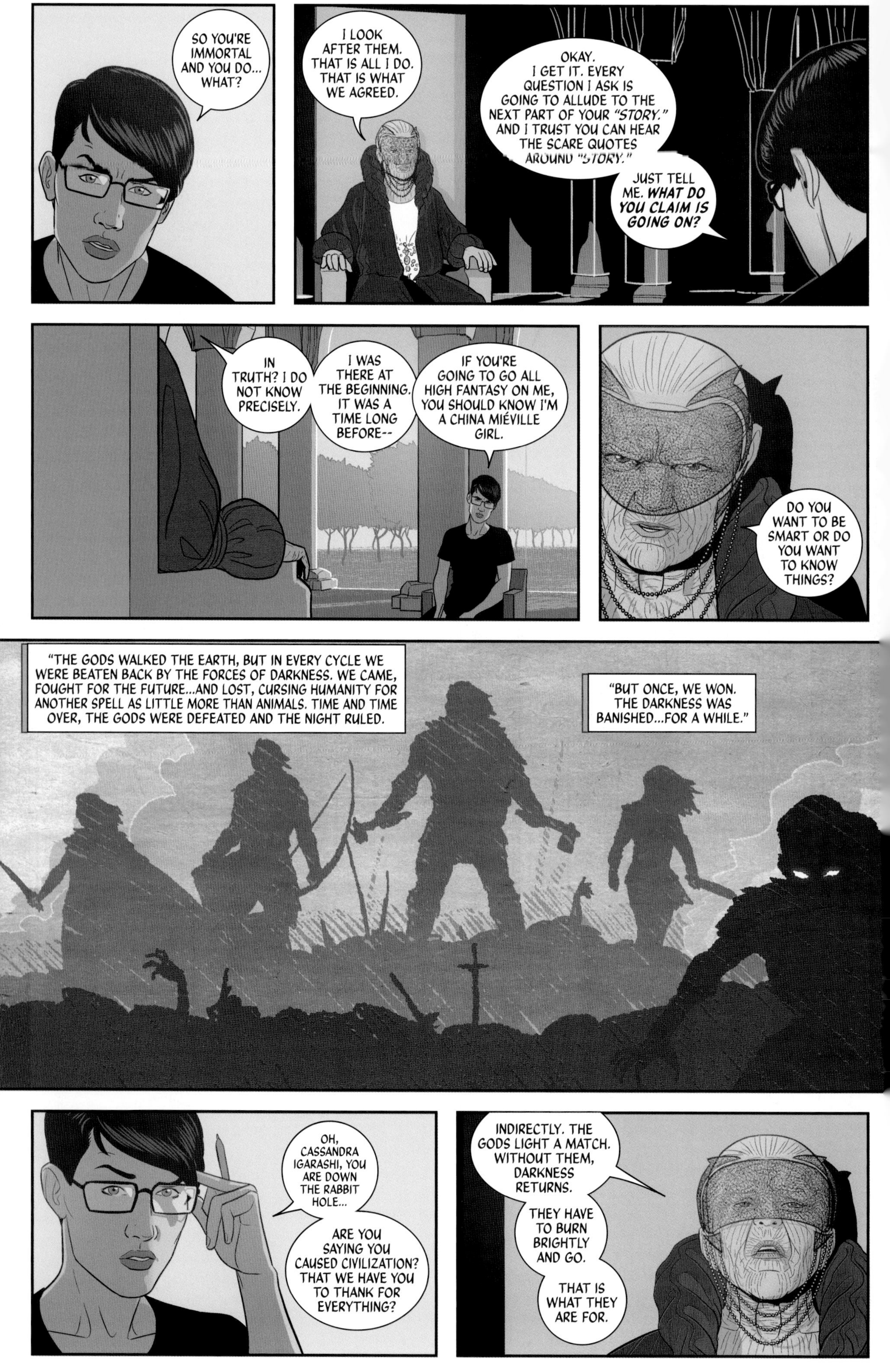
SO YOU'RE IMMORTAL AND YOU DO... WHAT?
I LOOK AFTER THEM. THAT IS ALL I DO. THAT IS WHAT WE AGREED.
OKAY. I GET IT. EVERY QUESTION I ASK IS GOING TO ALLUDE TO THE NEXT PART OF YOUR "STORY." AND I TRUST YOU CAN HEAR THE SCARE QUOTES AROUND "STORY."
JUST TELL ME. WHAT DO YOU CLAIM IS GOING ON?
IN TRUTH? I DO NOT KNOW PRECISELY.
I WAS THERE AT THE BEGINNING. IT WAS A TIME LONG BEFORE--
IF YOU'RE GOING TO GO ALL HIGH FANTASY ON ME, YOU SHOULD KNOW I'M A CHINA MIÉVILLE GIRL.
DO YOU WANT TO BE SMART OR DO YOU WANT TO KNOW THINGS?
"THE GODS WALKED THE EARTH, BUT IN EVERY CYCLE WE WERE BEATEN BACK BY THE FORCES OF DARKNESS. WE CAME, FOUGHT FOR THE FUTURE...AND LOST, CURSING HUMANITY FOR ANOTHER SPELL AS LITTLE MORE THAN ANIMALS. TIME AND TIME OVER, THE GODS WERE DEFEATED AND THE NIGHT RULED.
"BUT ONCE, WE WON. THE DARKNESS WAS BANISHED...FOR A WHILE."
OH, CASSANDRA IGARASHI, YOU ARE DOWN THE RABBIT HOLE...
ARE YOU SAYING YOU CAUSED CIVILIZATION? THAT WE HAVE YOU TO THANK FOR EVERYTHING?
INDIRECTLY. THE GODS LIGHT A MATCH. WITHOUT THEM, DARKNESS RETURNS.
THEY HAVE TO BURN BRIGHTLY AND GO.
THAT IS WHAT THEY ARE FOR.

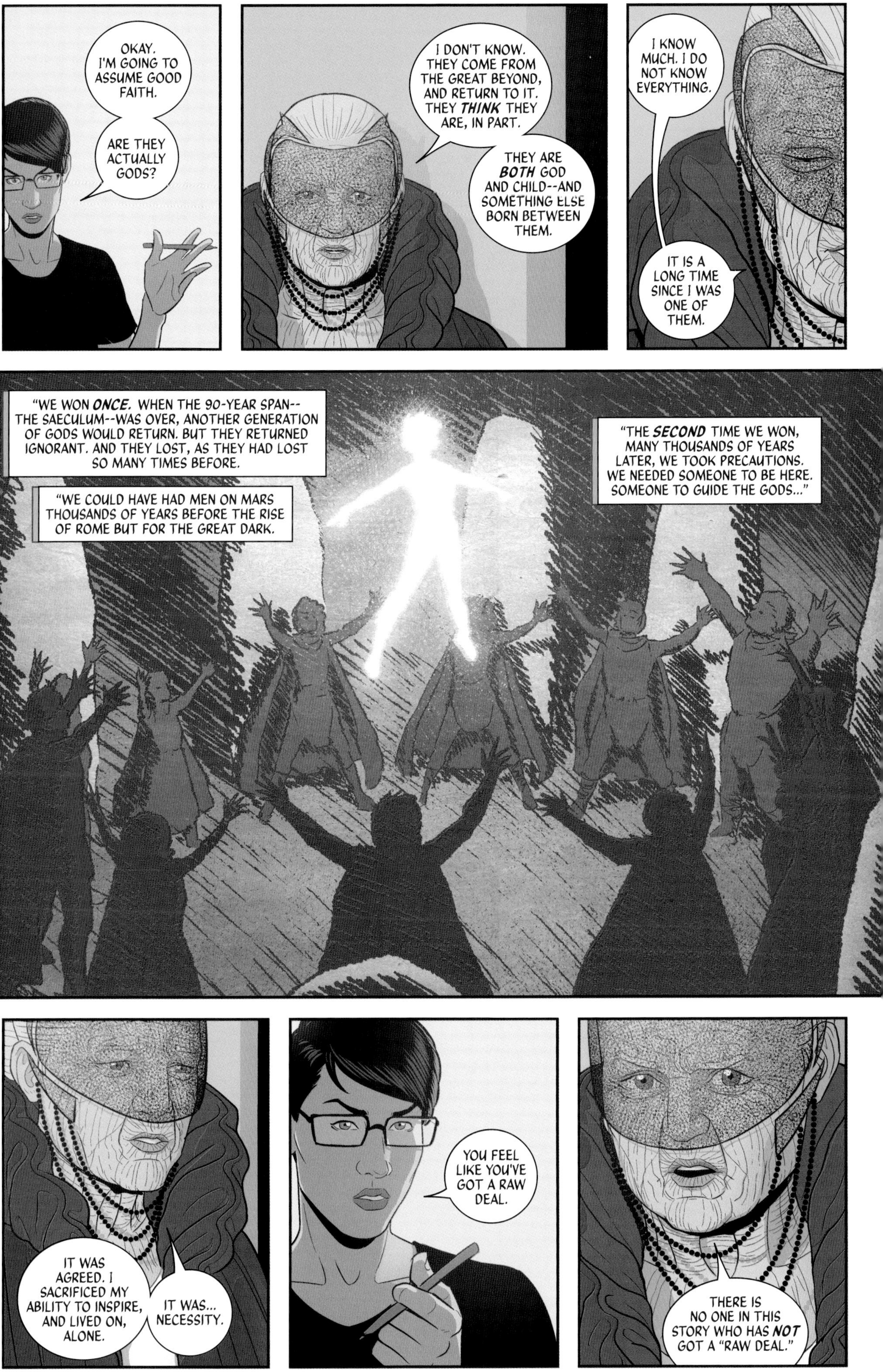
OKAY. I'M GOING TO ASSUME GOOD FAITH.
ARE THEY ACTUALLY GODS?
I DON'T KNOW. THEY COME FROM THE GREAT BEYOND, AND RETURN TO IT. THEY *THINK* THEY ARE, IN PART.
THEY ARE **BOTH** GOD AND CHILD--AND SOMETHING ELSE BORN BETWEEN THEM.
I KNOW MUCH. I DO NOT KNOW EVERYTHING.
IT IS A LONG TIME SINCE I WAS ONE OF THEM.
"WE WON ***ONCE.*** WHEN THE 90-YEAR SPAN--THE SAECULUM--WAS OVER, ANOTHER GENERATION OF GODS WOULD RETURN. BUT THEY RETURNED IGNORANT. AND THEY LOST, AS THEY HAD LOST SO MANY TIMES BEFORE.
"WE COULD HAVE HAD MEN ON MARS THOUSANDS OF YEARS BEFORE THE RISE OF ROME BUT FOR THE GREAT DARK.
"THE ***SECOND*** TIME WE WON, MANY THOUSANDS OF YEARS LATER, WE TOOK PRECAUTIONS. WE NEEDED SOMEONE TO BE HERE. SOMEONE TO GUIDE THE GODS..."
IT WAS AGREED. I SACRIFICED MY ABILITY TO INSPIRE, AND LIVED ON, ALONE.
IT WAS... NECESSITY.
YOU FEEL LIKE YOU'VE GOT A RAW DEAL.
THERE IS NO ONE IN THIS STORY WHO HAS ***NOT*** GOT A "RAW DEAL."

BUT IT CAN BE--LET US SAY IT HAS BEEN A BAD CENTURY FOR ME. SO MUCH CHANGE. I'VE FELT OLDER THAN I EVER HAVE.

I WAS WEAK. I TALKED TO ANOTHER MORTAL...

...GAVE A DRUNKEN DIATRIBE, IF TRUTH BE TOLD...

...IN THE 1910s, TO A MAN CALLED GRAVES.

ROBERT... GRAVES. *"THE WHITE GODDESS"*?

YOU'RE SAYING THAT *YOU* INSPIRED *THE WHITE GODDESS*?

I SHARED SOME THOUGHTS. HE LISTENED. HE GOT THE GENERAL GIST.

YOU'VE READ THE BOOK, I TAKE IT. DID YOU UNDERSTAND?

YES, OF COURSE.

I DOUBT IT. YOU'RE GOOD AT BEING CRITICAL... BUT YOU'RE NOT EXACTLY A GOOD CRITIC.

FUCK YOU--

IS WHAT YOU SAY TO OTHERS. YOU DISMISS WHAT OTHERS FEEL IN THE PRESENCE OF THE GODS.

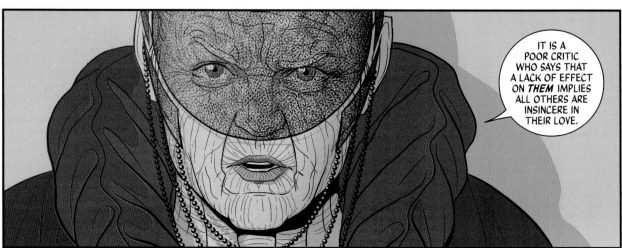

IT IS A POOR CRITIC WHO SAYS THAT A LACK OF EFFECT ON *THEM* IMPLIES ALL OTHERS ARE INSINCERE IN THEIR LOVE.

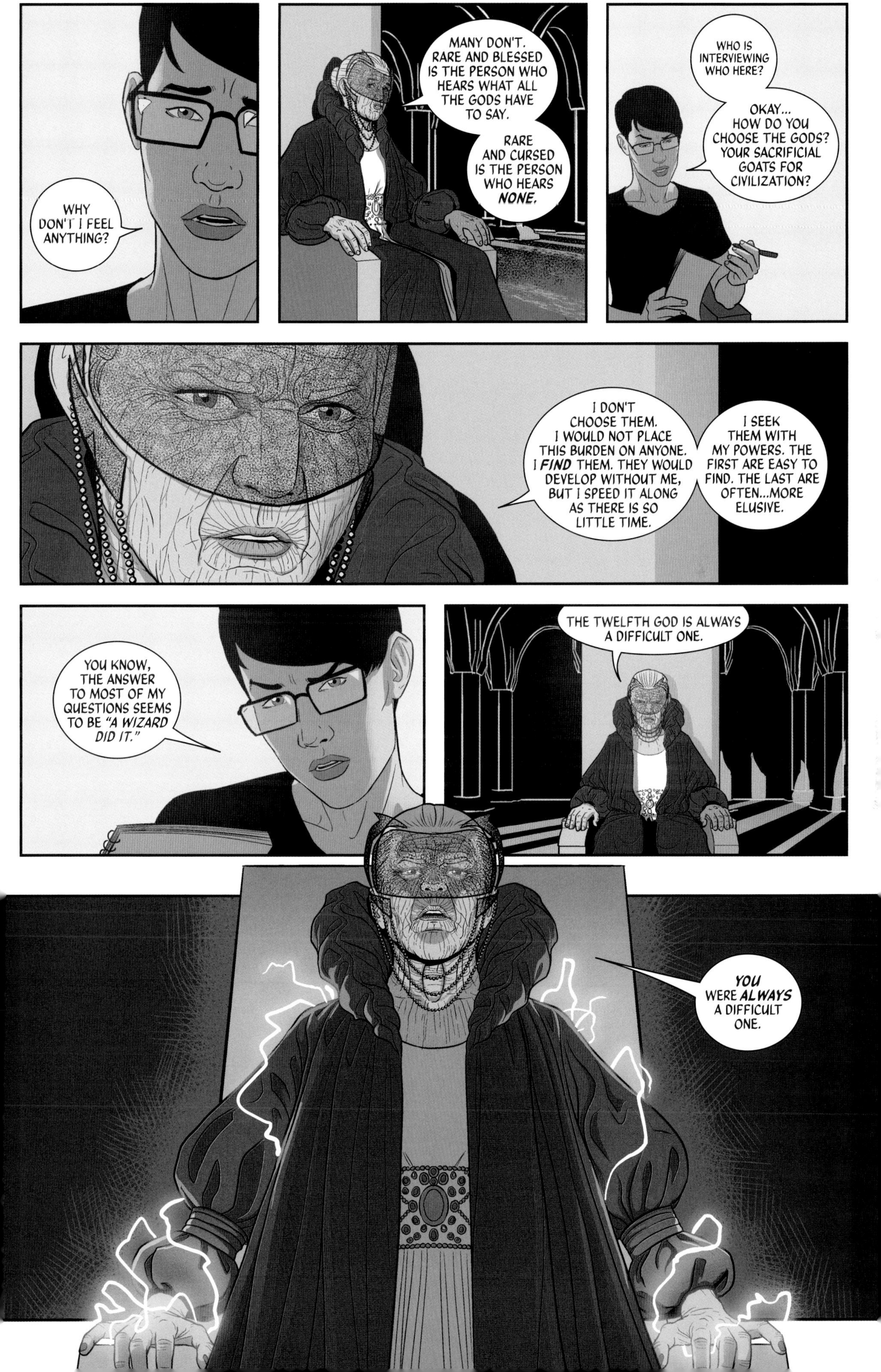
WHY DON'T I FEEL ANYTHING?
MANY DON'T. RARE AND BLESSED IS THE PERSON WHO HEARS WHAT ALL THE GODS HAVE TO SAY.
RARE AND CURSED IS THE PERSON WHO HEARS ***NONE.***
WHO IS INTERVIEWING WHO HERE?
OKAY... HOW DO YOU CHOOSE THE GODS? YOUR SACRIFICIAL GOATS FOR CIVILIZATION?
I DON'T CHOOSE THEM. I WOULD NOT PLACE THIS BURDEN ON ANYONE. I ***FIND*** THEM. THEY WOULD DEVELOP WITHOUT ME, BUT I SPEED IT ALONG AS THERE IS SO LITTLE TIME.
I SEEK THEM WITH MY POWERS. THE FIRST ARE EASY TO FIND. THE LAST ARE OFTEN...MORE ELUSIVE.
YOU KNOW, THE ANSWER TO MOST OF MY QUESTIONS SEEMS TO BE *"A WIZARD DID IT."*
THE TWELFTH GOD IS ALWAYS A DIFFICULT ONE.
YOU WERE ***ALWAYS*** A DIFFICULT ONE.

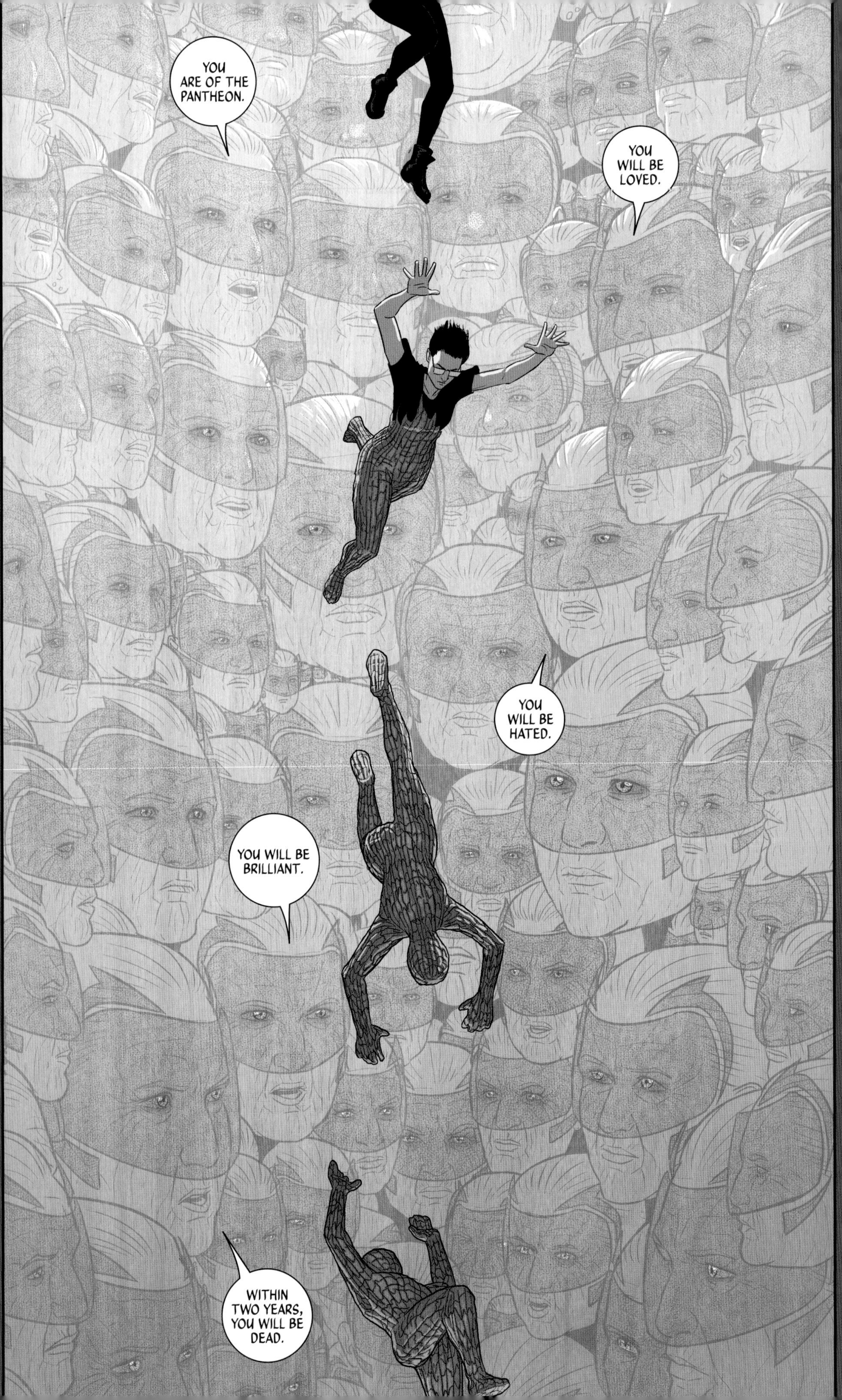
YOU ARE OF THE PANTHEON.
YOU WILL BE LOVED.
YOU WILL BE HATED.
YOU WILL BE BRILLIANT.
WITHIN TWO YEARS, YOU WILL BE DEAD.

YOU SIT WITH YOUR SISTERS, BENEATH ALL CREATION.
SHE WHO SPINS THE THREAD OF LIFE.
YOU ARE THE QUEEN OF SEERS, ALL-SEEING.
OF WHAT IS.
OF WHAT MUST BE.
OF WHAT MUST NOT BE CONCEALED.

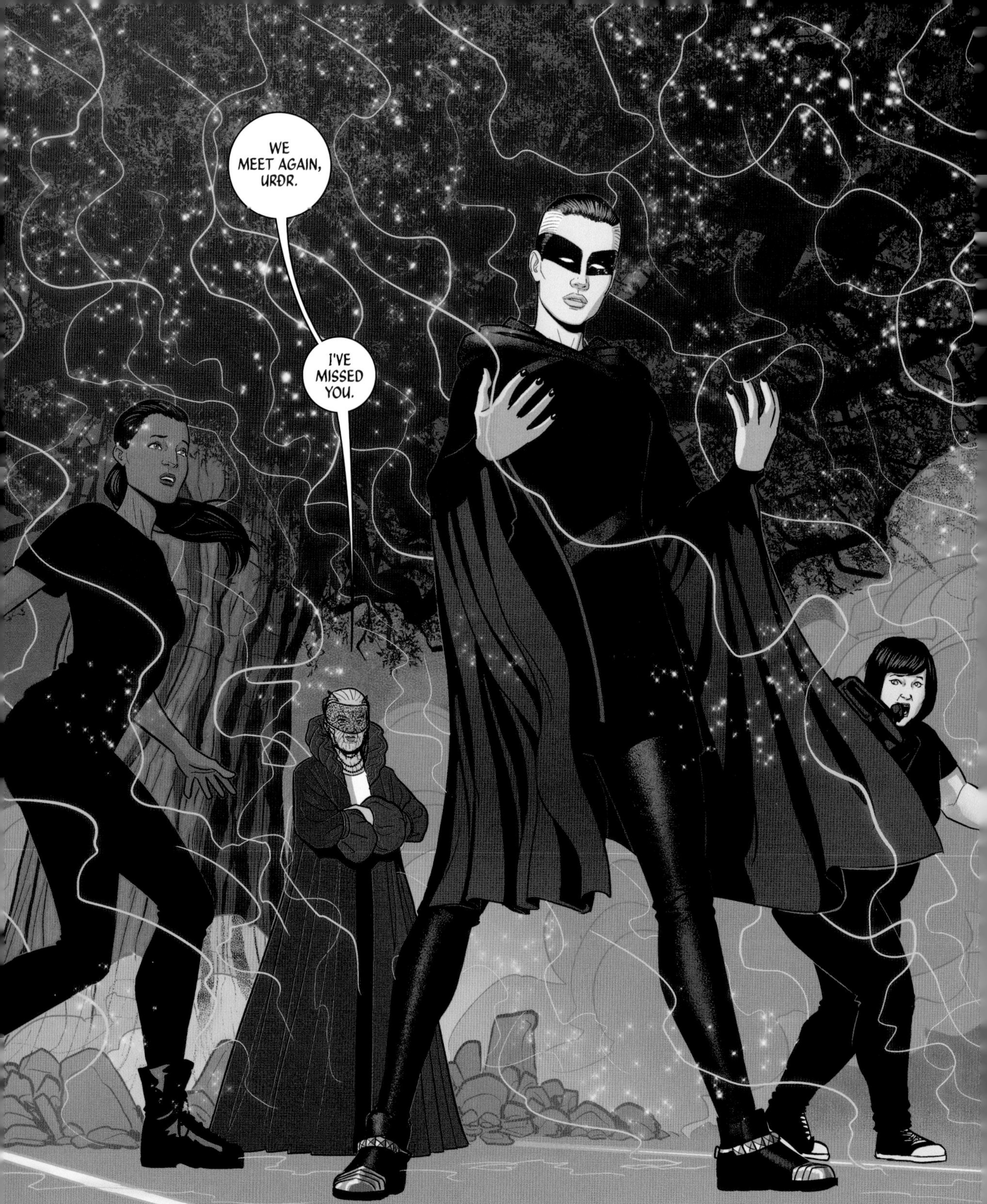
WE MEET AGAIN, URÐR.
I'VE MISSED YOU.

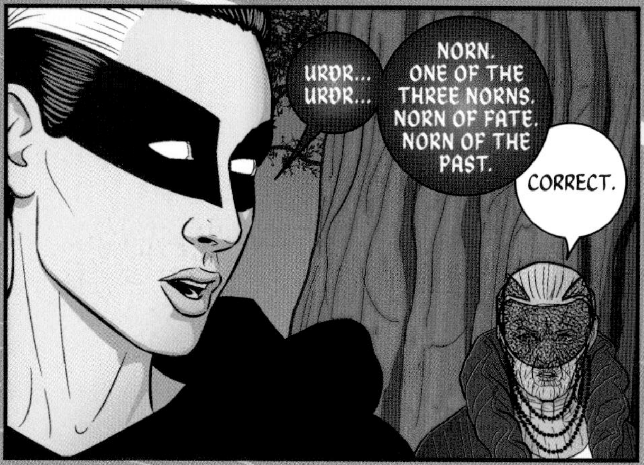
URÐR... URÐR...
NORN. ONE OF THE THREE NORNS. NORN OF FATE. NORN OF THE PAST.
CORRECT.

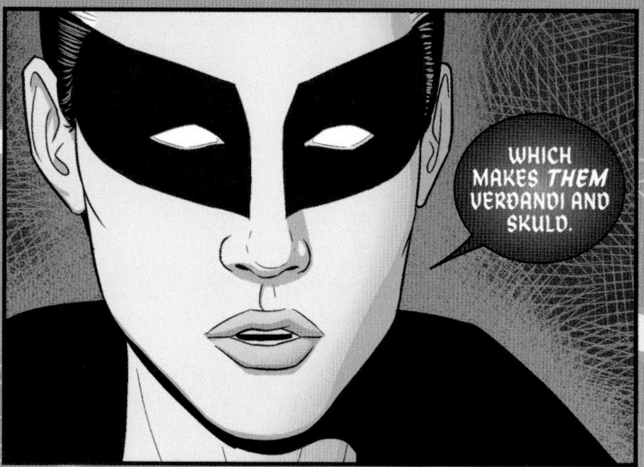
WHICH MAKES *THEM* VERÐANDI AND SKULD.

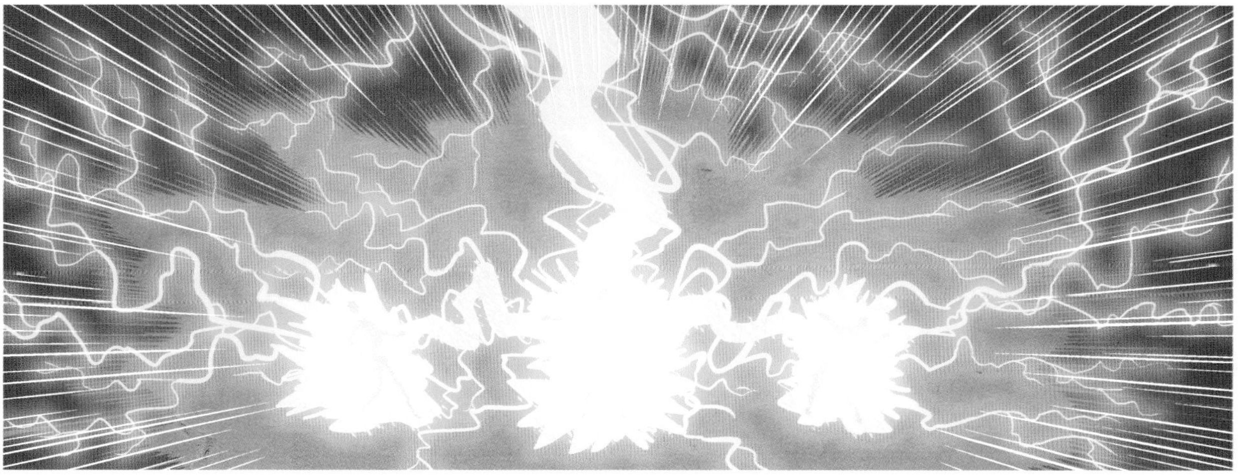

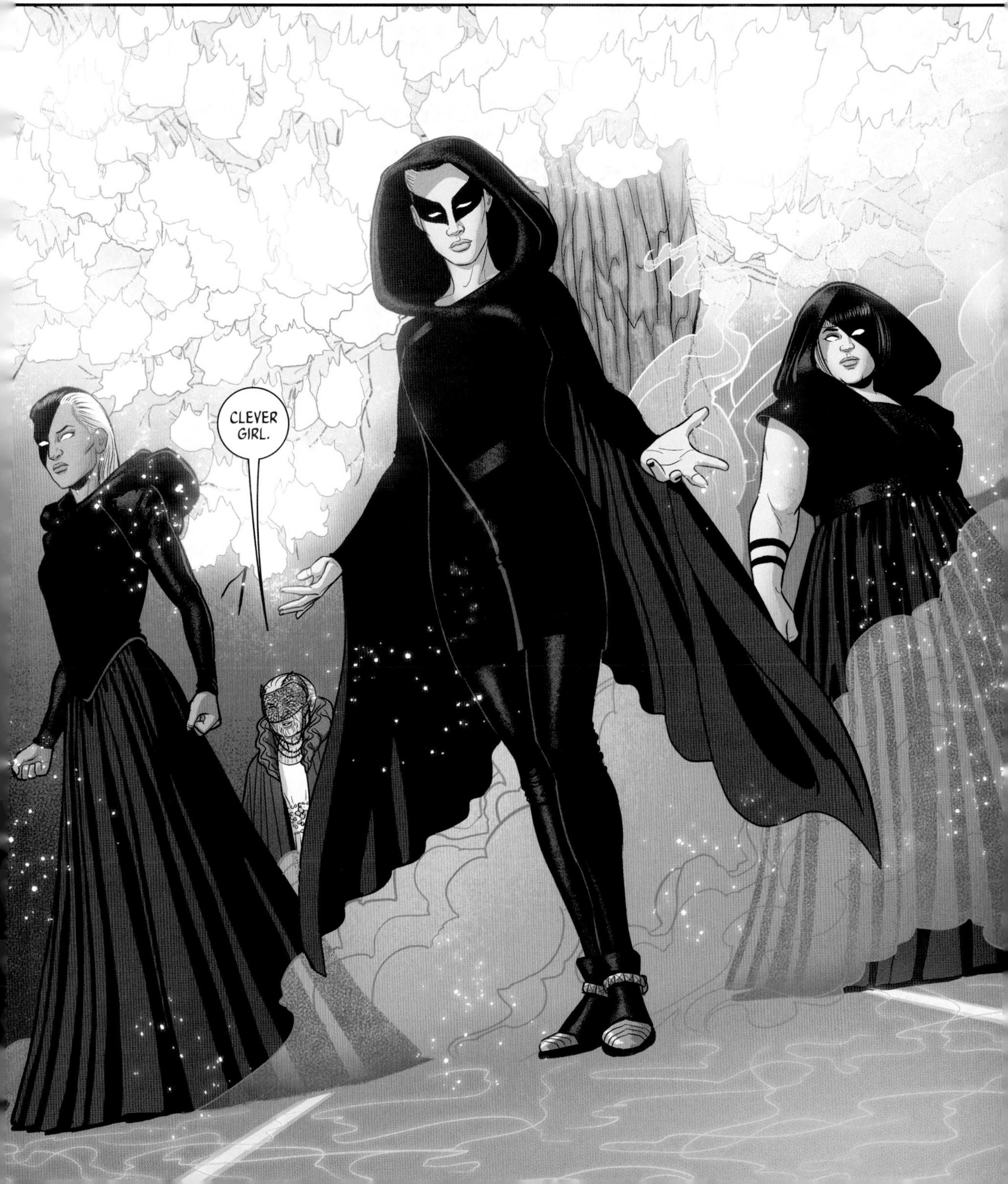
CLEVER GIRL.

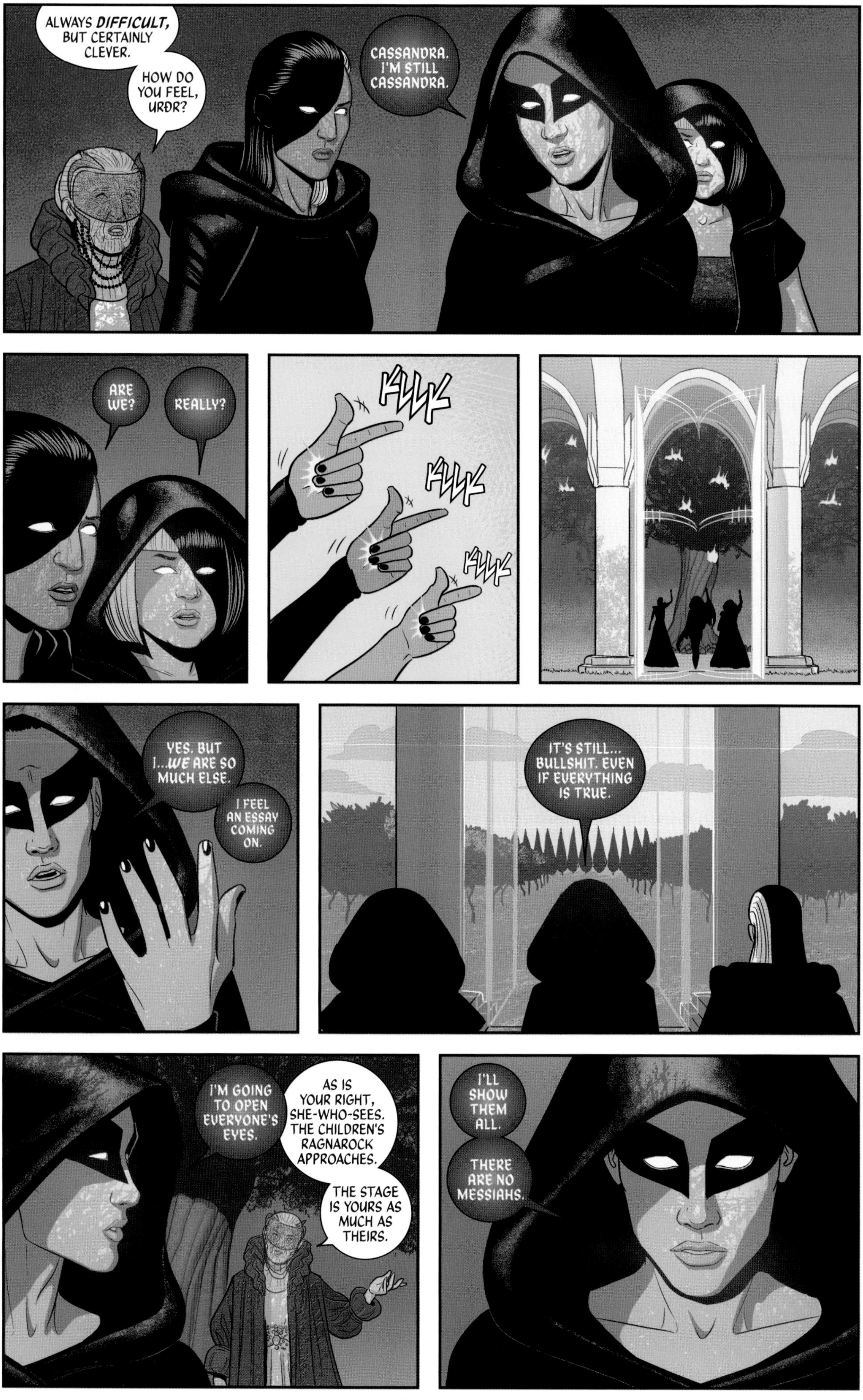
ALWAYS *DIFFICULT*, BUT CERTAINLY CLEVER.
HOW DO YOU FEEL, URÐR?
CASSANDRA. I'M STILL CASSANDRA.
ARE WE?
REALLY?
KLLK
KLLK
KLLK
YES. BUT I...*WE* ARE SO MUCH ELSE.
I FEEL AN ESSAY COMING ON.
IT'S STILL... BULLSHIT. EVEN IF EVERYTHING IS TRUE.
I'M GOING TO OPEN EVERYONE'S EYES.
AS IS YOUR RIGHT, SHE-WHO-SEES. THE CHILDREN'S RAGNAROCK APPROACHES.
THE STAGE IS YOURS AS MUCH AS THEIRS.
I'LL SHOW THEM ALL.
THERE ARE NO MESSIAHS.

I COULDN'T KILL BAAL. I WOULDN'T KILL MINERVA. I WANT TO KILL MORRIGAN HALF THE TIME.
BUT YOU, CASSY?
WOULDN'T IT BE A TRAGEDY IF YOU WENT AND JUST DIED.
WHAT'S WRONG? ARE YOU OKAY?
TIRED. RELIEVED. THIS IS ALWAYS A STRAIN, TO SAY THE LEAST.
FINDING YOU. FEAR THAT IT'LL GO WRONG...
IT'S GOOD THAT YOU'RE ALL HERE. I'VE MISSED YOU. I MISSED YOU ALL.
THE PANTHEON IS COMPLETE.
ONCE AGAIN, WE RETURN.

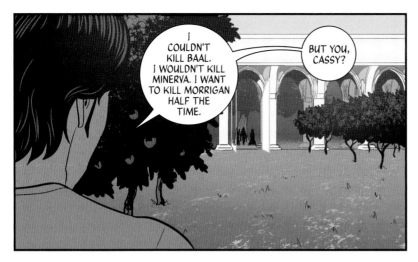

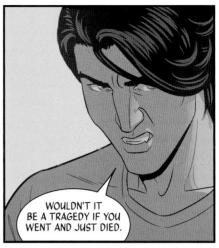

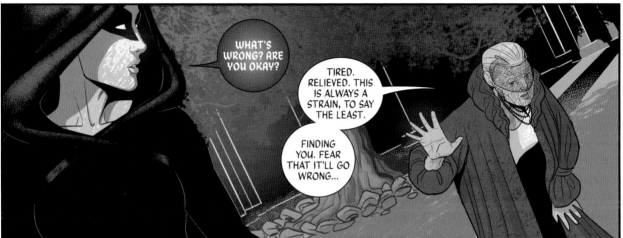

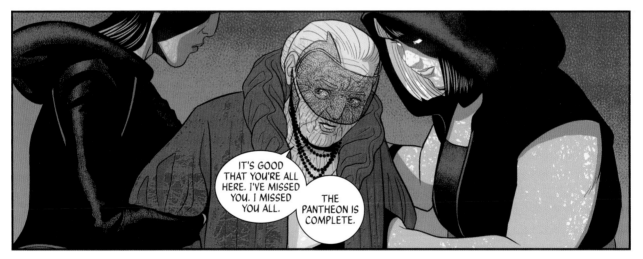

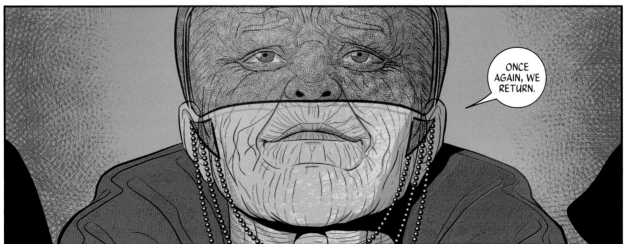

THE NORNS

28 JUNE 2014

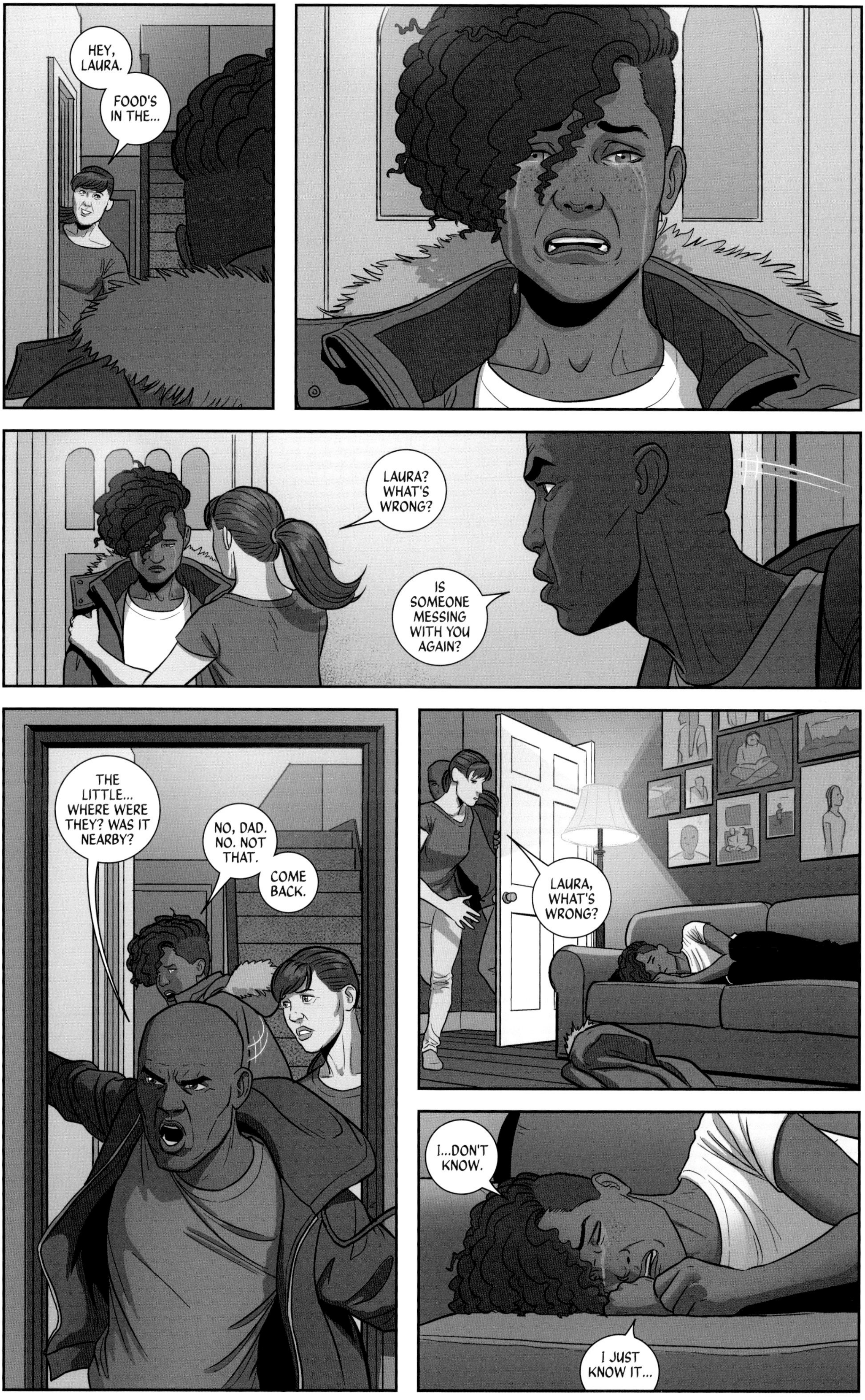

HEY, LAURA.
FOOD'S IN THE...
LAURA? WHAT'S WRONG?
IS SOMEONE MESSING WITH YOU AGAIN?
THE LITTLE... WHERE WERE THEY? WAS IT NEARBY?
NO, DAD. NO. NOT THAT.
COME BACK.
LAURA, WHAT'S WRONG?
I...DON'T KNOW.
I JUST KNOW IT...

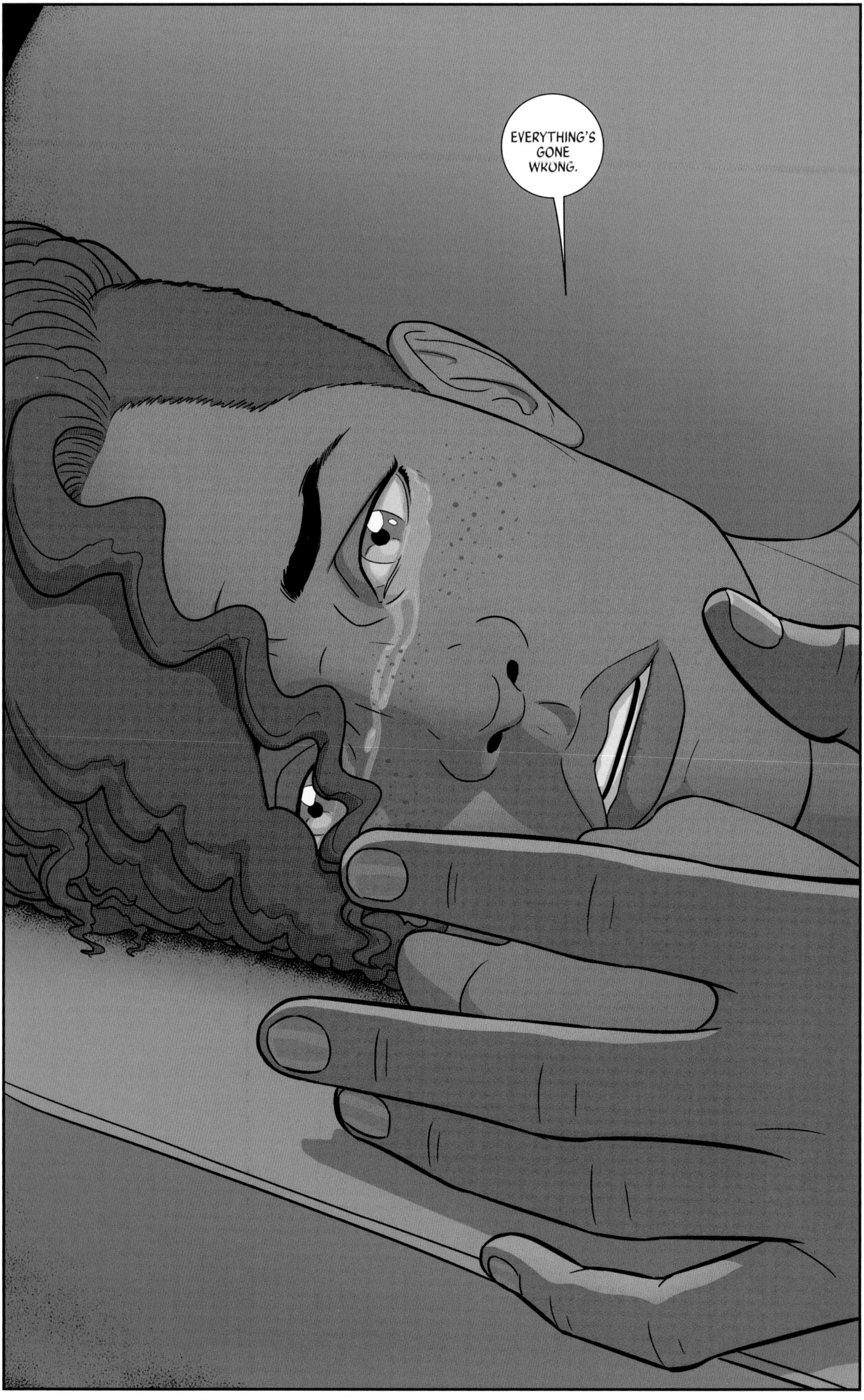
EVERYTHING'S GONE WRONG.

YOU ARE
CORDIALLY INVITED
TO THE DEATH OF
YOUR DREAMS

28 JUNE 2014

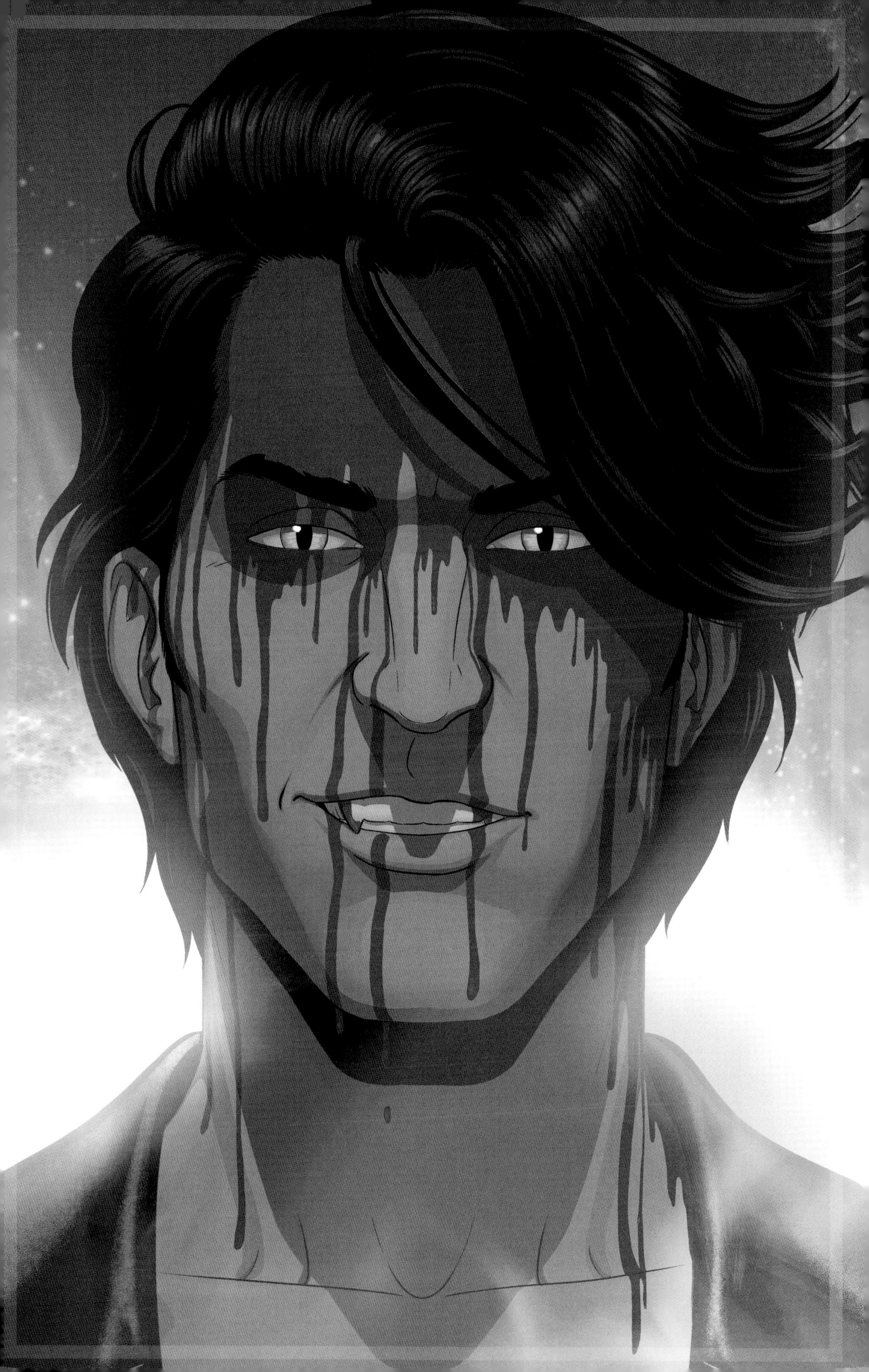

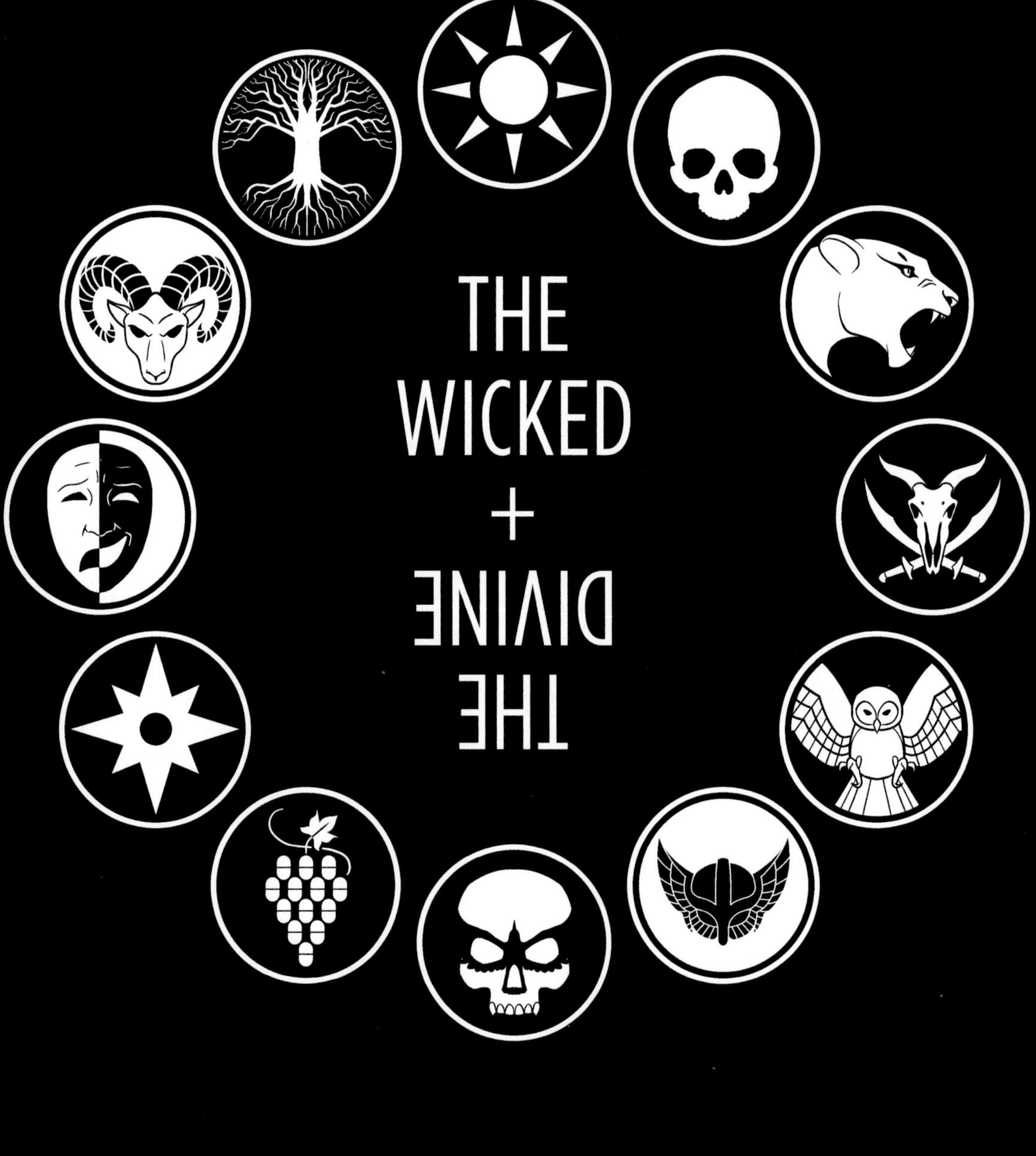
THE WICKED + THE DIVINE

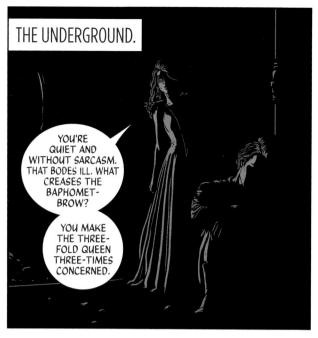

THE UNDERGROUND.

YOU'RE QUIET AND WITHOUT SARCASM. THAT BODES ILL. WHAT CREASES THE BAPHOMET-BROW?

YOU MAKE THE THREE-FOLD QUEEN THREE-TIMES CONCERNED.

NOT NOW, MARIAN. I'M NOT FEELING PLAYFUL.

DON'T PRETEND TO CARE. YOU DOOMED ME.

I DOOMED YOU *BECAUSE* I CARED.

THIS IS ALL YOU EVER WANTED.

IT'S ALL I EVER WANTED...

...BUT I WANT MORE.

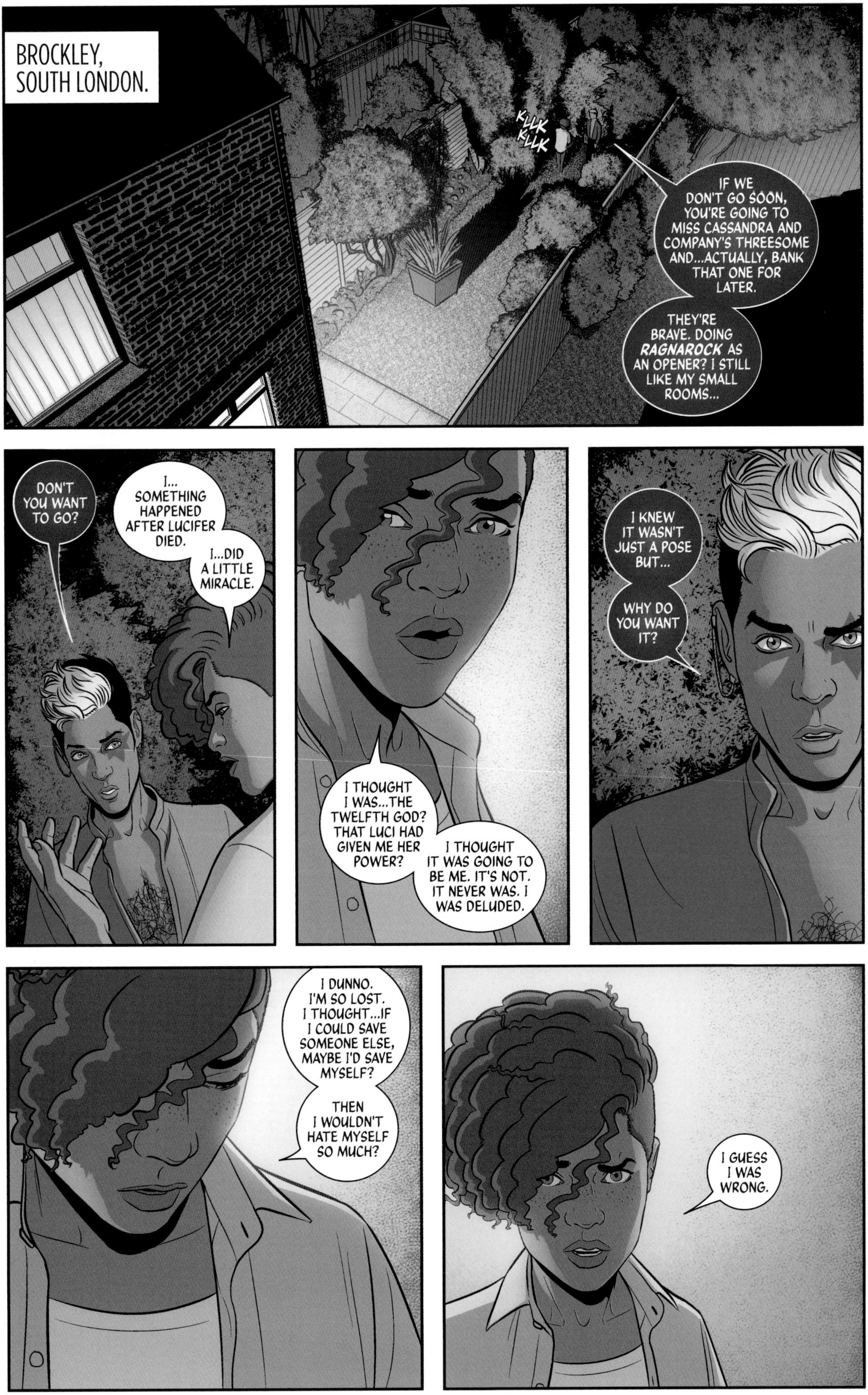

BROCKLEY, SOUTH LONDON.
KLLK KLLK
IF WE DON'T GO SOON, YOU'RE GOING TO MISS CASSANDRA AND COMPANY'S THREESOME AND...ACTUALLY, BANK THAT ONE FOR LATER.
THEY'RE BRAVE. DOING **RAGNAROCK** AS AN OPENER? I STILL LIKE MY SMALL ROOMS...
DON'T YOU WANT TO GO?
I... SOMETHING HAPPENED AFTER LUCIFER DIED.
I...DID A LITTLE MIRACLE.
I THOUGHT I WAS...THE TWELFTH GOD? THAT LUCI HAD GIVEN ME HER POWER?
I THOUGHT IT WAS GOING TO BE ME. IT'S NOT. IT NEVER WAS. I WAS DELUDED.
I KNEW IT WASN'T JUST A POSE BUT...
WHY DO YOU WANT IT?
I DUNNO. I'M SO LOST. I THOUGHT...IF I COULD SAVE SOMEONE ELSE, MAYBE I'D SAVE MYSELF?
THEN I WOULDN'T HATE MYSELF SO MUCH?
I GUESS I WAS WRONG.

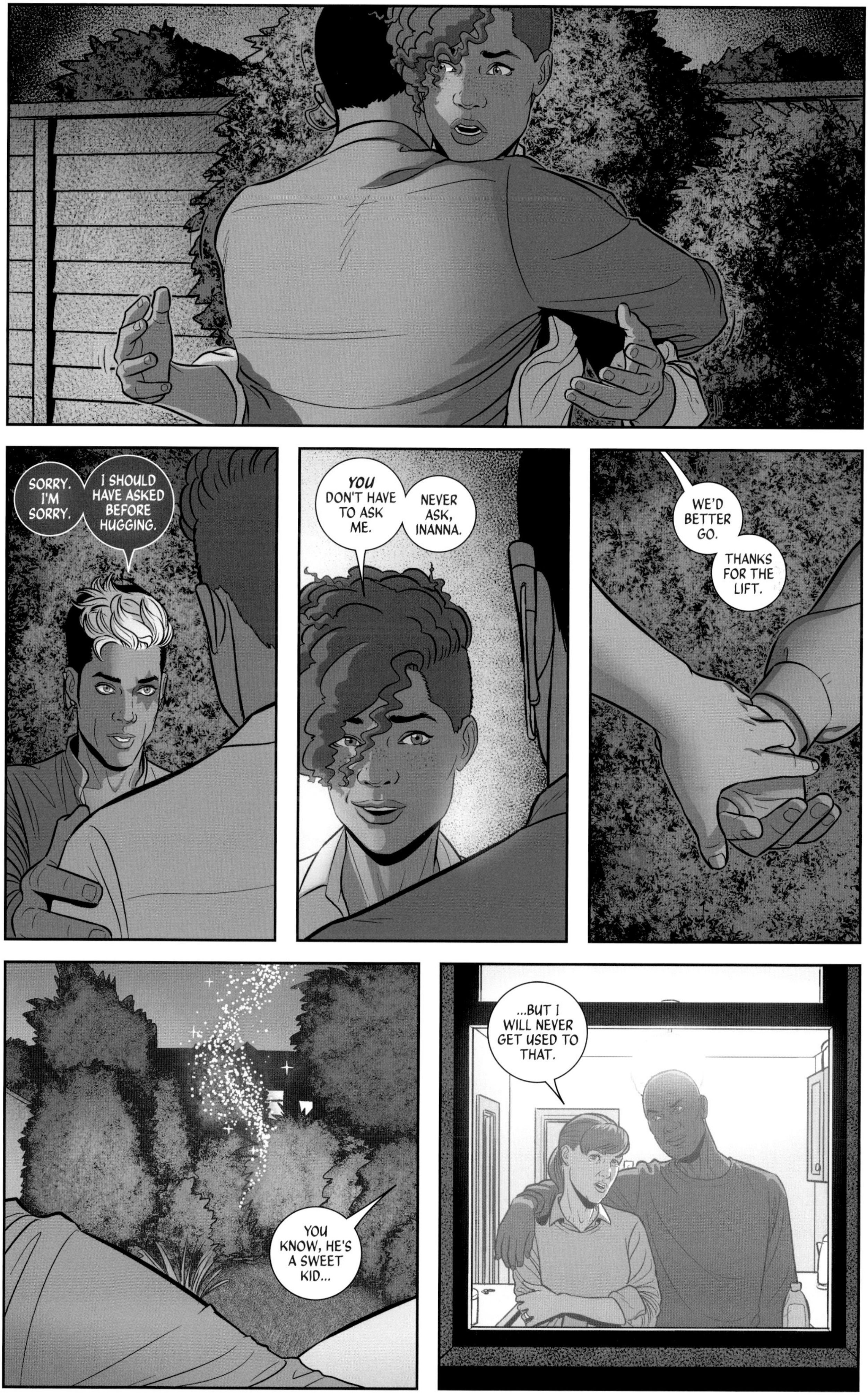
SORRY. I'M SORRY.
I SHOULD HAVE ASKED BEFORE HUGGING.
YOU DON'T HAVE TO ASK ME.
NEVER ASK, INANNA.
WE'D BETTER GO.
THANKS FOR THE LIFT.
YOU KNOW, HE'S A SWEET KID...
...BUT I WILL NEVER GET USED TO THAT.

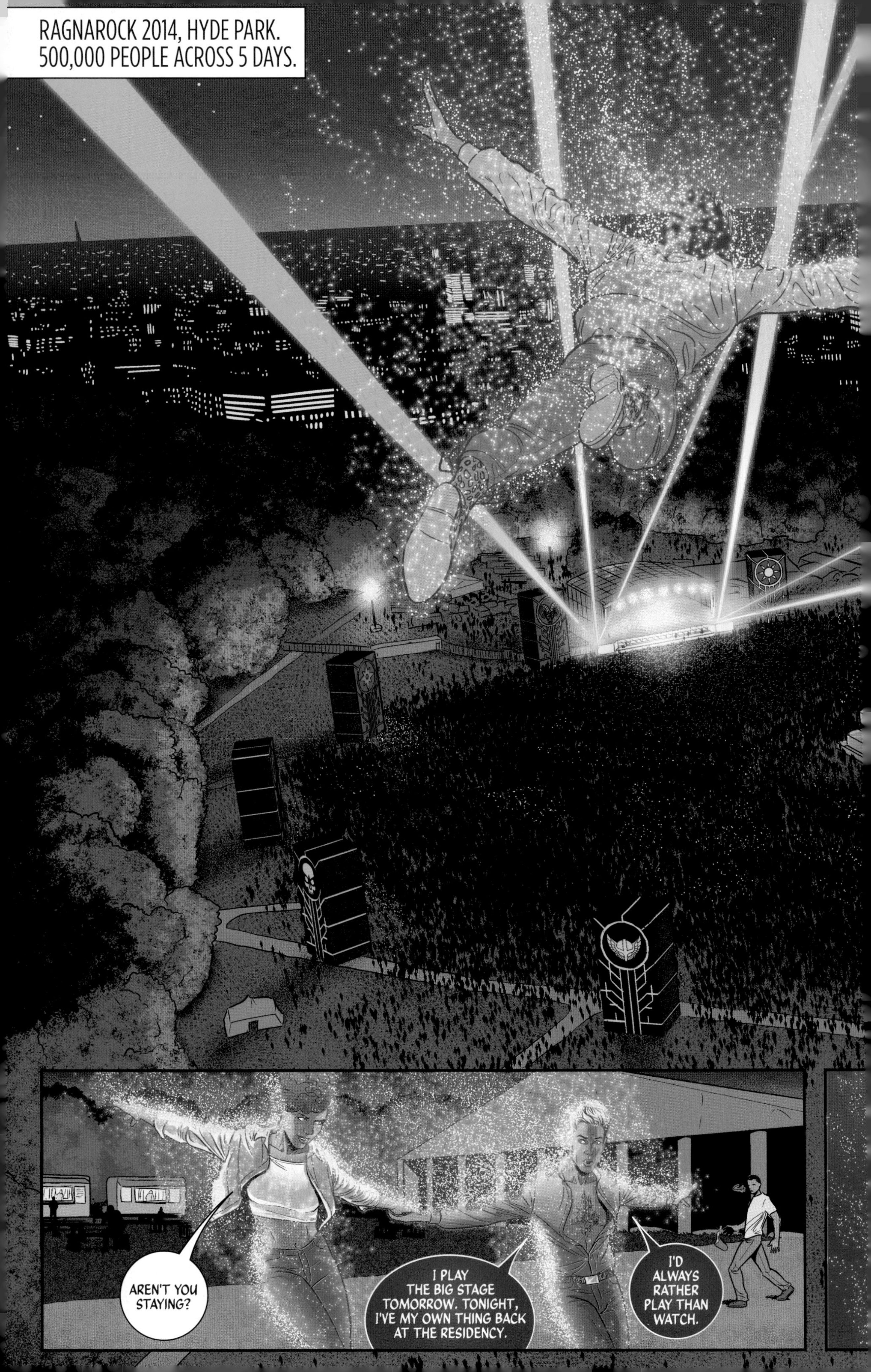
RAGNAROCK 2014, HYDE PARK.
500,000 PEOPLE ACROSS 5 DAYS.
AREN'T YOU STAYING?
I PLAY THE BIG STAGE TOMORROW. TONIGHT, I'VE MY OWN THING BACK AT THE RESIDENCY.
I'D ALWAYS RATHER PLAY THAN WATCH.

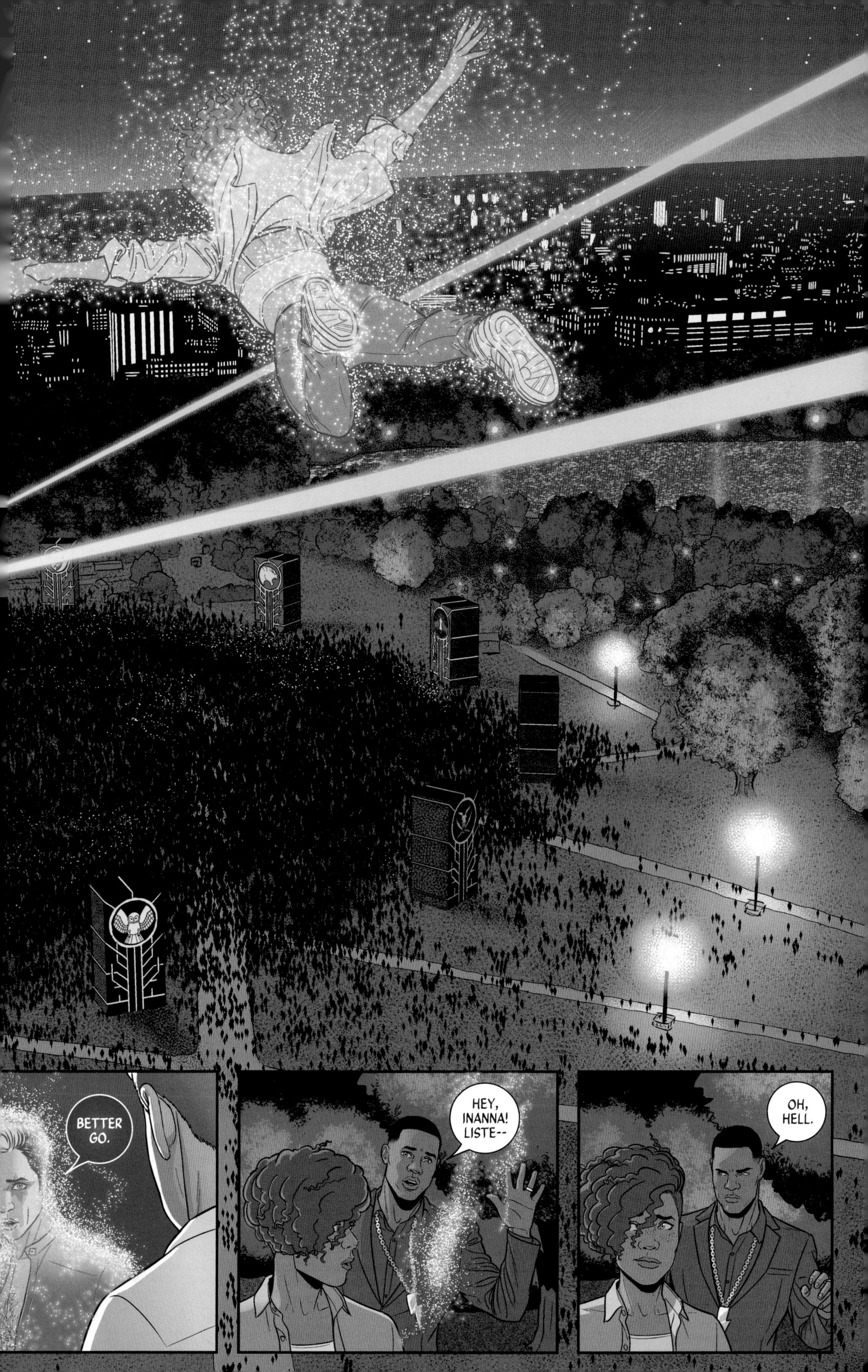
BETTER GO.
HEY, INANNA! LISTE--
OH, HELL.

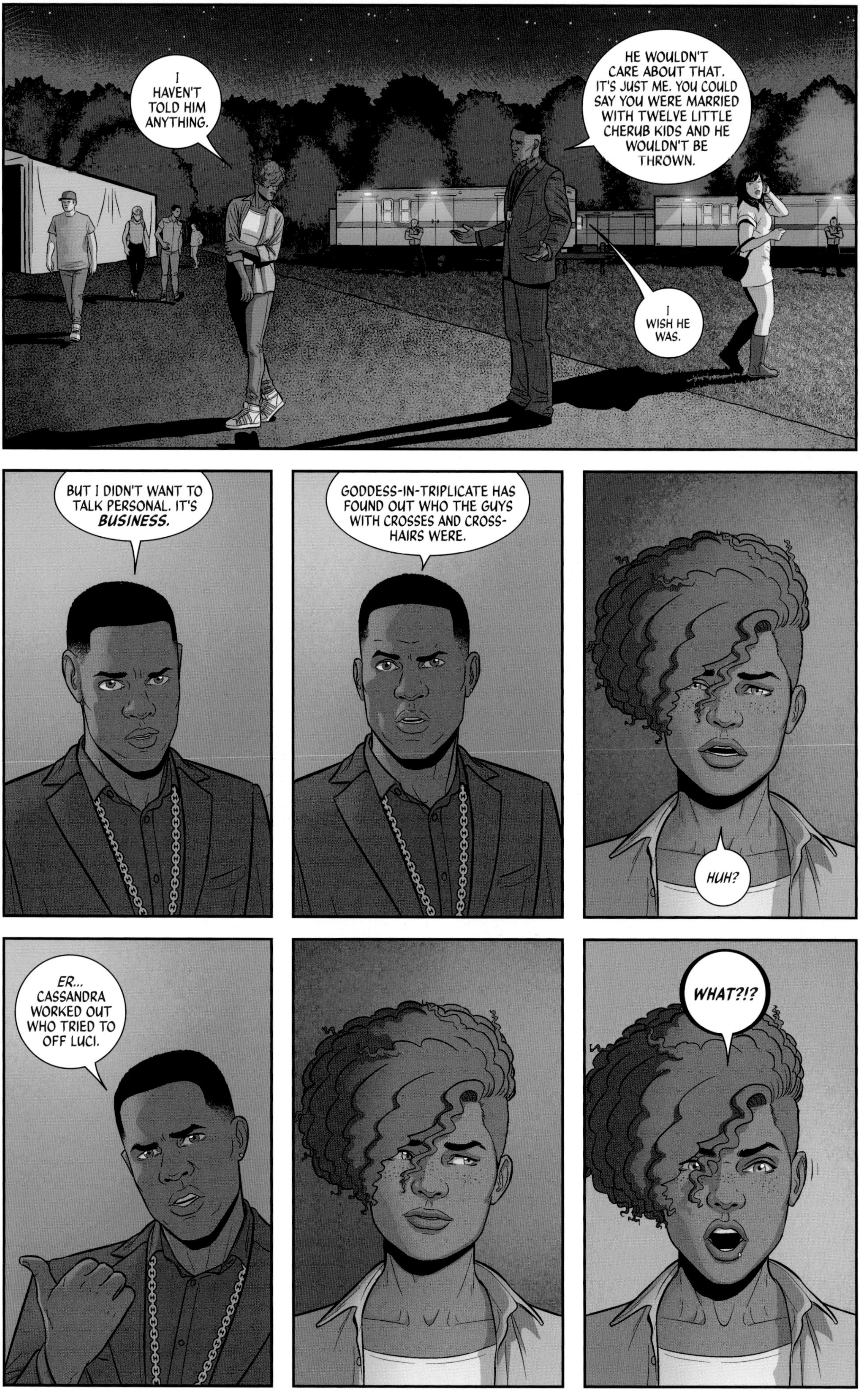
I HAVEN'T TOLD HIM ANYTHING.
HE WOULDN'T CARE ABOUT THAT. IT'S JUST ME. YOU COULD SAY YOU WERE MARRIED WITH TWELVE LITTLE CHERUB KIDS AND HE WOULDN'T BE THROWN.
I WISH HE WAS.
BUT I DIDN'T WANT TO TALK PERSONAL. IT'S *BUSINESS.*
GODDESS-IN-TRIPLICATE HAS FOUND OUT WHO THE GUYS WITH CROSSES AND CROSS-HAIRS WERE.
HUH?
ER... CASSANDRA WORKED OUT WHO TRIED TO OFF LUCI.
WHAT?!?

NOT HER STORY

2 AUGUST 2014

THEY'RE NOT SEEING ANYONE.

BIG NIGHT FOR HER.

I'M SORRY, I'M DAVID BLAKE.

WE'VE MET BEFORE. I'M--

I KNOW WHO YOU ARE.

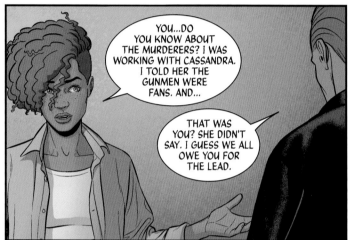

YOU...DO YOU KNOW ABOUT THE MURDERERS? I WAS WORKING WITH CASSANDRA. I TOLD HER THE GUNMEN WERE FANS. AND...

THAT WAS YOU? SHE DIDN'T SAY. I GUESS WE ALL OWE YOU FOR THE LEAD.

YES. *URÐR* WAS WORKING WITH ME TOO. I COLLATED A LIST OF PEOPLE WHO'VE DISAPPEARED FROM THE FANDOM.

THERE ARE A LOT OF... LONELY PEOPLE. THERE'S ALWAYS A CHURN. PEOPLE DISAPPEARING.

SO WHO WERE THEY?

DUNCAN ACKFORD AND ONE OF HIS GRAD STUDENTS, TOM WILKES.

DUNCAN... WHO?

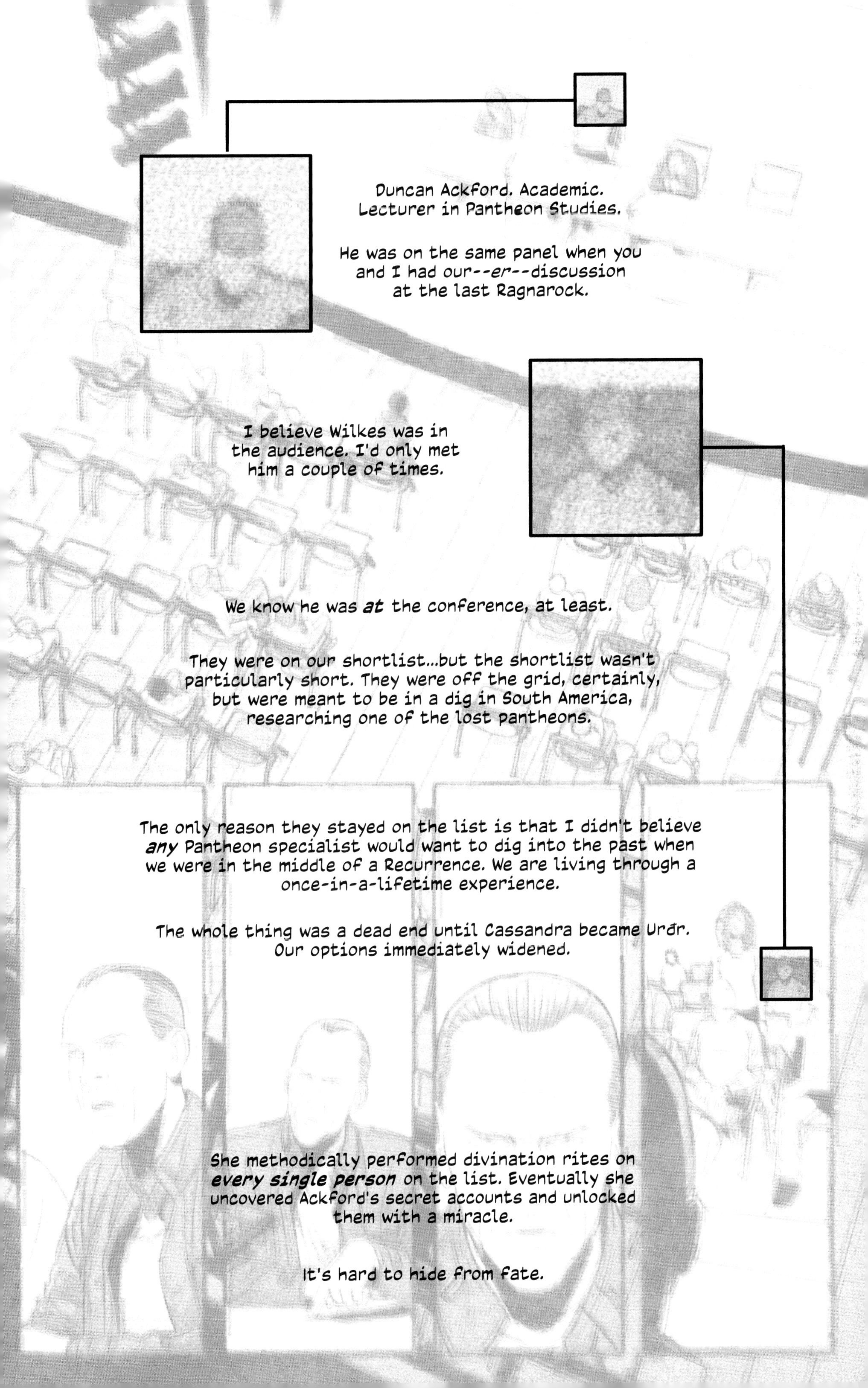
Duncan Ackford. Academic. Lecturer in Pantheon Studies.
He was on the same panel when you and I had our--*er*--discussion at the last Ragnarock.
I believe Wilkes was in the audience. I'd only met him a couple of times.
We know he was ***at*** the conference, at least.
They were on our shortlist...but the shortlist wasn't particularly short. They were off the grid, certainly, but were meant to be in a dig in South America, researching one of the lost pantheons.
The only reason they stayed on the list is that I didn't believe ***any*** Pantheon specialist would want to dig into the past when we were in the middle of a Recurrence. We are living through a once-in-a-lifetime experience.
The whole thing was a dead end until Cassandra became Urðr. Our options immediately widened.
She methodically performed divination rites on ***every single person*** on the list. Eventually she uncovered Ackford's secret accounts and unlocked them with a miracle.
It's hard to hide from fate.

She found almost a million words of everything obsessive and twisted about Fandom. Escape routes, cover stories, the whole deal.

The dig didn't exist. They suspected the Pantheon would be after them once they'd killed Lucifer, so had arranged to hide and then re-emerge as the new gods if they could, or remain in hiding if they couldn't.

Very much the Prometheus Myth cult. Kill a god, get their powers. A ludicrous fantasy.

 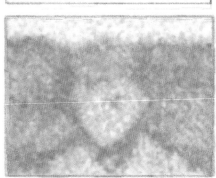

Ackford was lying to Wilkes too, telling him the powers could be shared. He didn't believe that for a second. Ackford had plans to get rid of him if Wilkes caused any problems...

 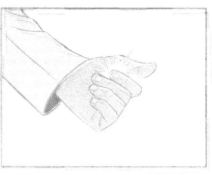

The documents are just disturbing. The researcher part of me knows that intensive study will lead to a lot of interesting work, but when you find your own papers mixed in with theirs, it becomes a little too personal.

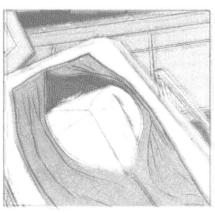 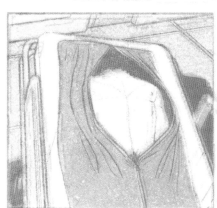

At least we know now. The families can get some peace.

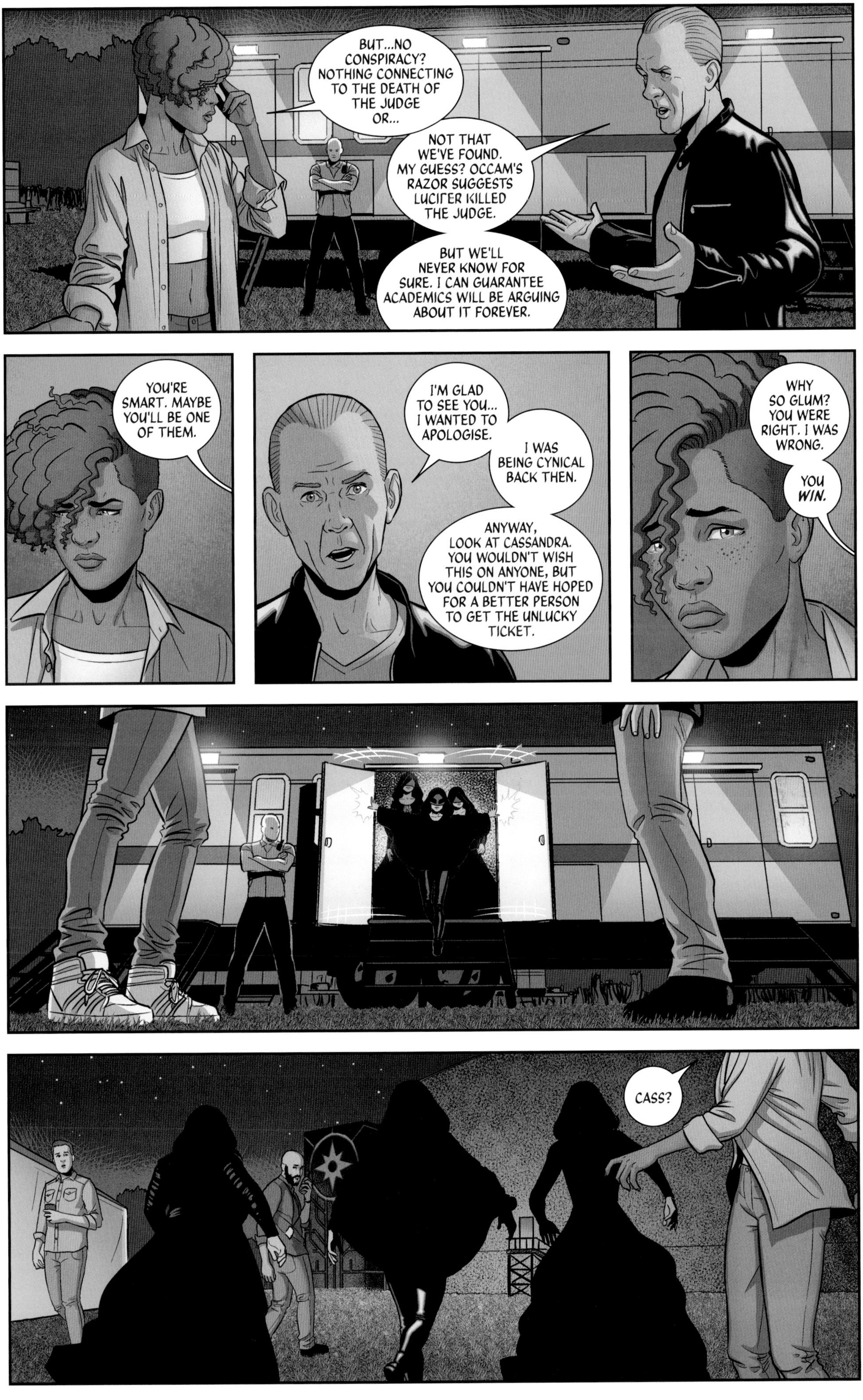
BUT...NO CONSPIRACY? NOTHING CONNECTING TO THE DEATH OF THE JUDGE OR...
NOT THAT WE'VE FOUND. MY GUESS? OCCAM'S RAZOR SUGGESTS LUCIFER KILLED THE JUDGE.
BUT WE'LL NEVER KNOW FOR SURE. I CAN GUARANTEE ACADEMICS WILL BE ARGUING ABOUT IT FOREVER.
YOU'RE SMART. MAYBE YOU'LL BE ONE OF THEM.
I'M GLAD TO SEE YOU... I WANTED TO APOLOGISE.
I WAS BEING CYNICAL BACK THEN.
ANYWAY, LOOK AT CASSANDRA. YOU WOULDN'T WISH THIS ON ANYONE, BUT YOU COULDN'T HAVE HOPED FOR A BETTER PERSON TO GET THE UNLUCKY TICKET.
WHY SO GLUM? YOU WERE RIGHT. I WAS WRONG.
YOU *WIN.*
CASS?

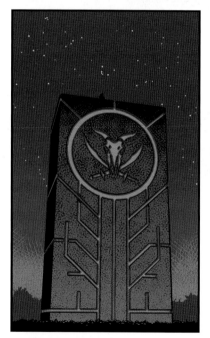

LISTEN. AND. UNDERSTAND.

"KILL THEM? REALLY?"

I CAN'T DO IT.

HELP ME.

KLIK

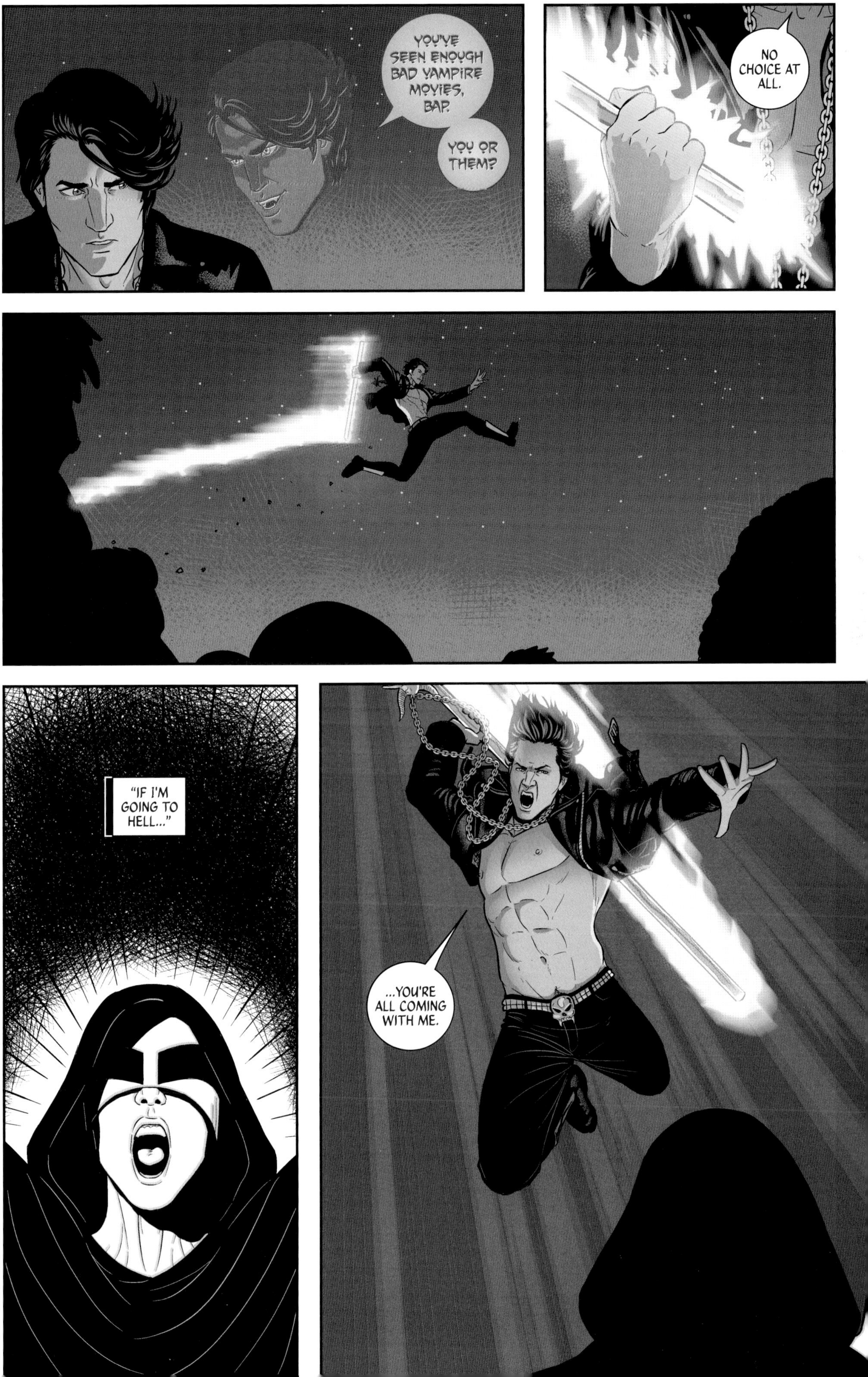
YOU'VE SEEN ENOUGH BAD VAMPIRE MOVIES, BAP.
YOU OR THEM?
NO CHOICE AT ALL.
"IF I'M GOING TO HELL..."
...YOU'RE ALL COMING WITH ME.

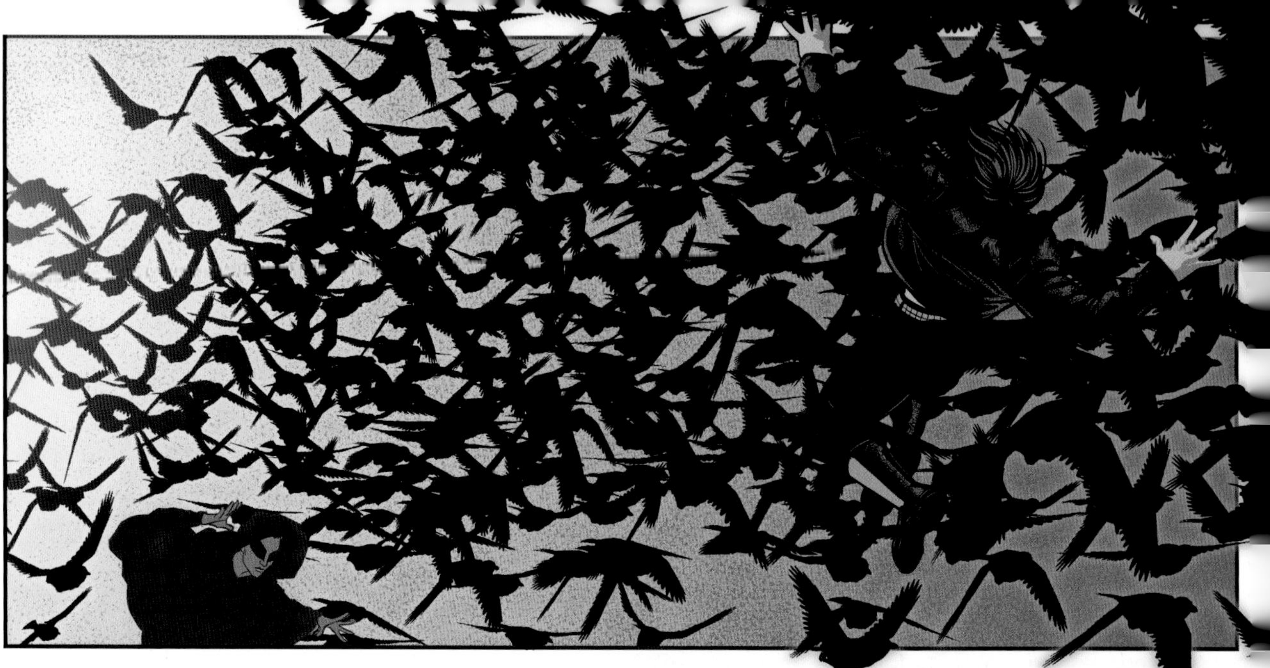

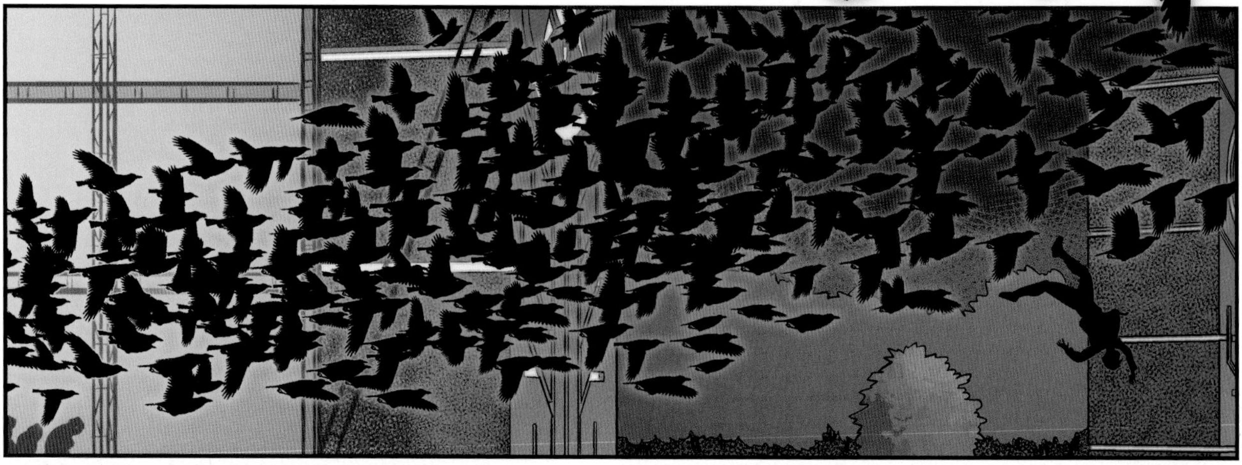

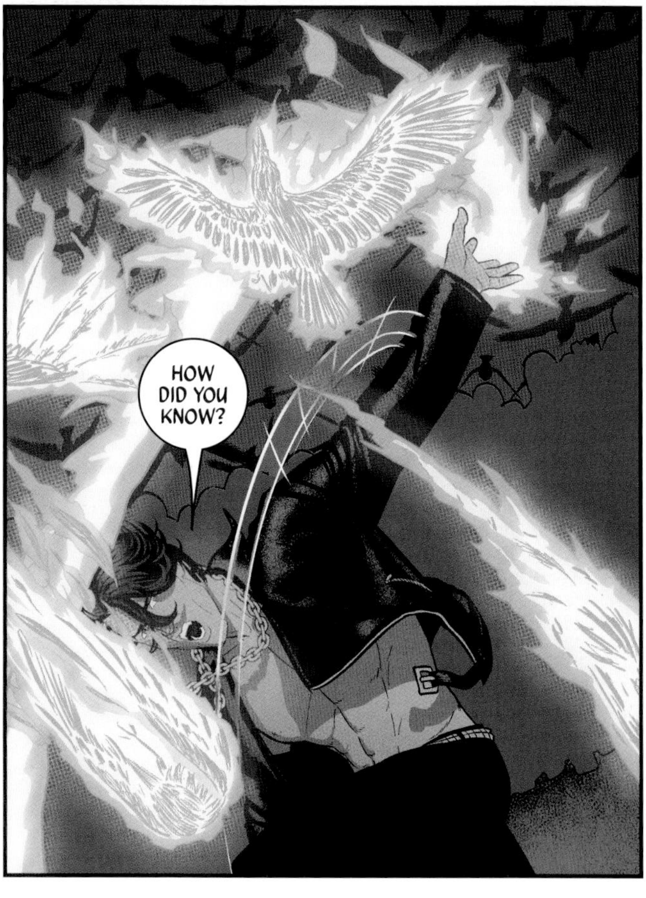
HOW DID YOU KNOW?

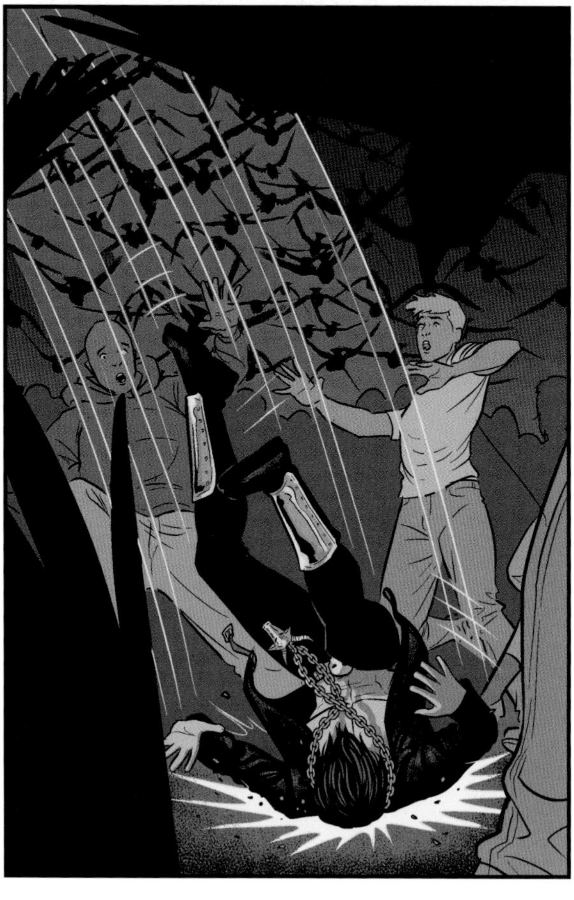

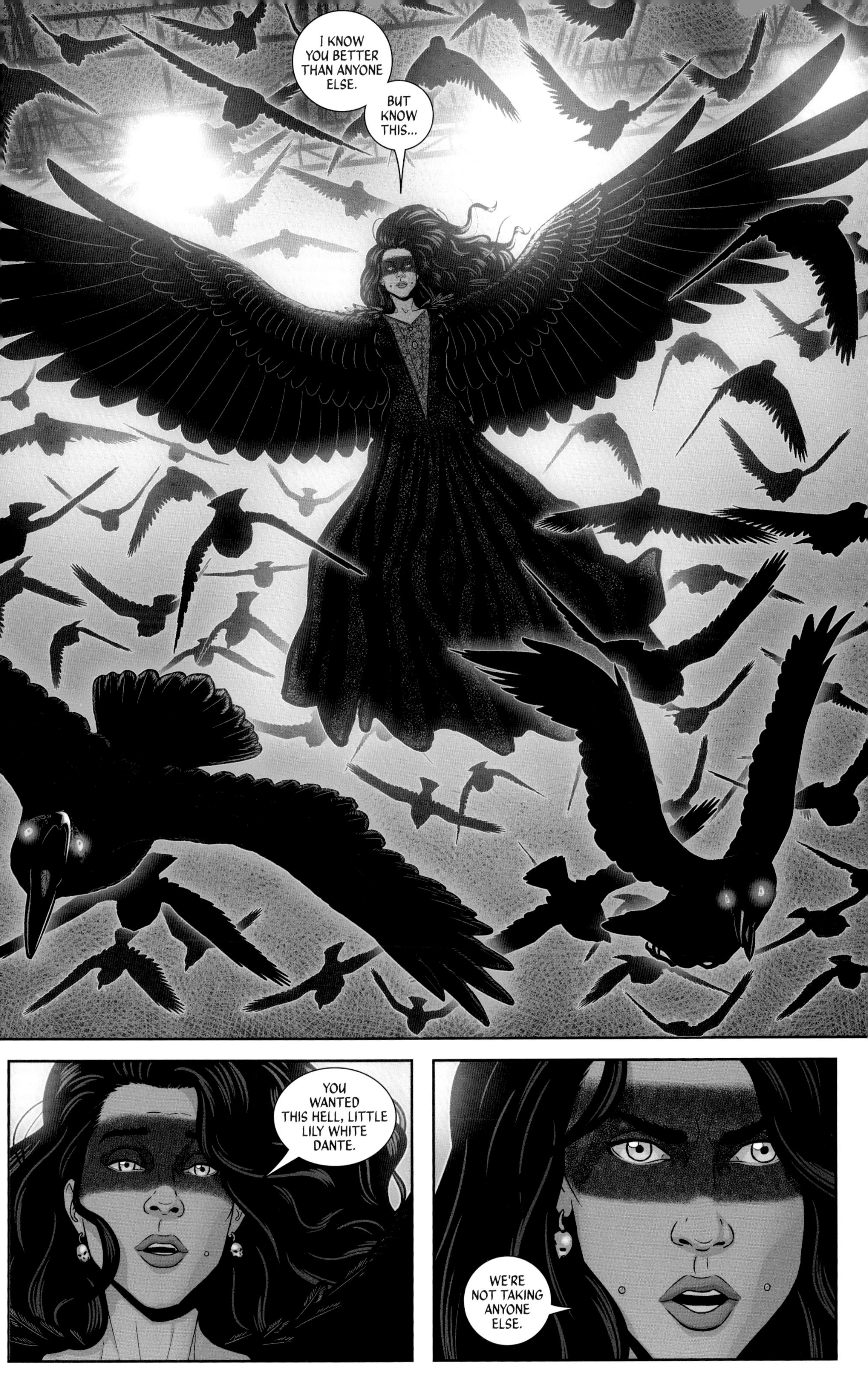
I KNOW YOU BETTER THAN ANYONE ELSE.
BUT KNOW THIS...
YOU WANTED THIS HELL, LITTLE LILY WHITE DANTE.
WE'RE NOT TAKING ANYONE ELSE.

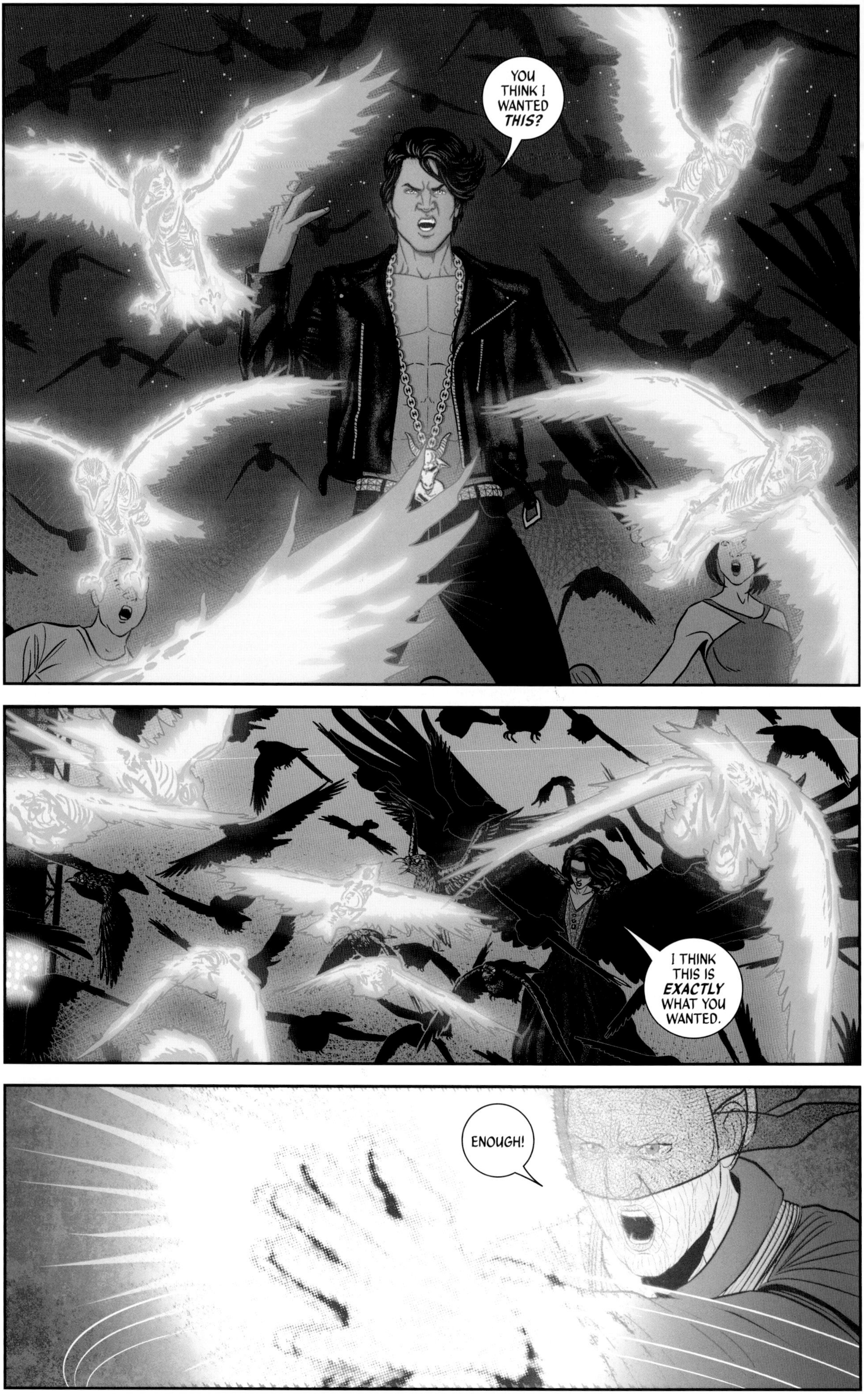
YOU THINK I WANTED *THIS?*
I THINK THIS IS *EXACTLY* WHAT YOU WANTED.
ENOUGH!

YOU HAVE MOVED WITH MURDEROUS INTENT.

YOU KNOW THE COST OF YOUR CRIME. THIS CANNOT BE ALLOWED TO CONTINUE.

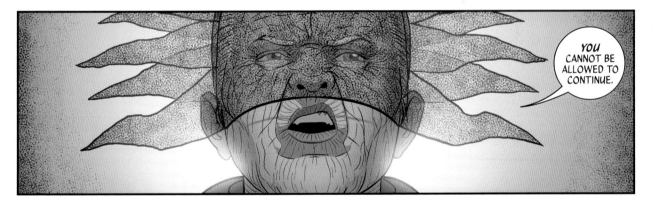

YOU CANNOT BE ALLOWED TO CONTINUE.

I STOPPED HIM. NO BLOOD IS SPILLED. I *GUARD* HIM, ANANKE.

FUCK YOU AND YOUR JUDGMENTAL FUCKING FUCKING FU--

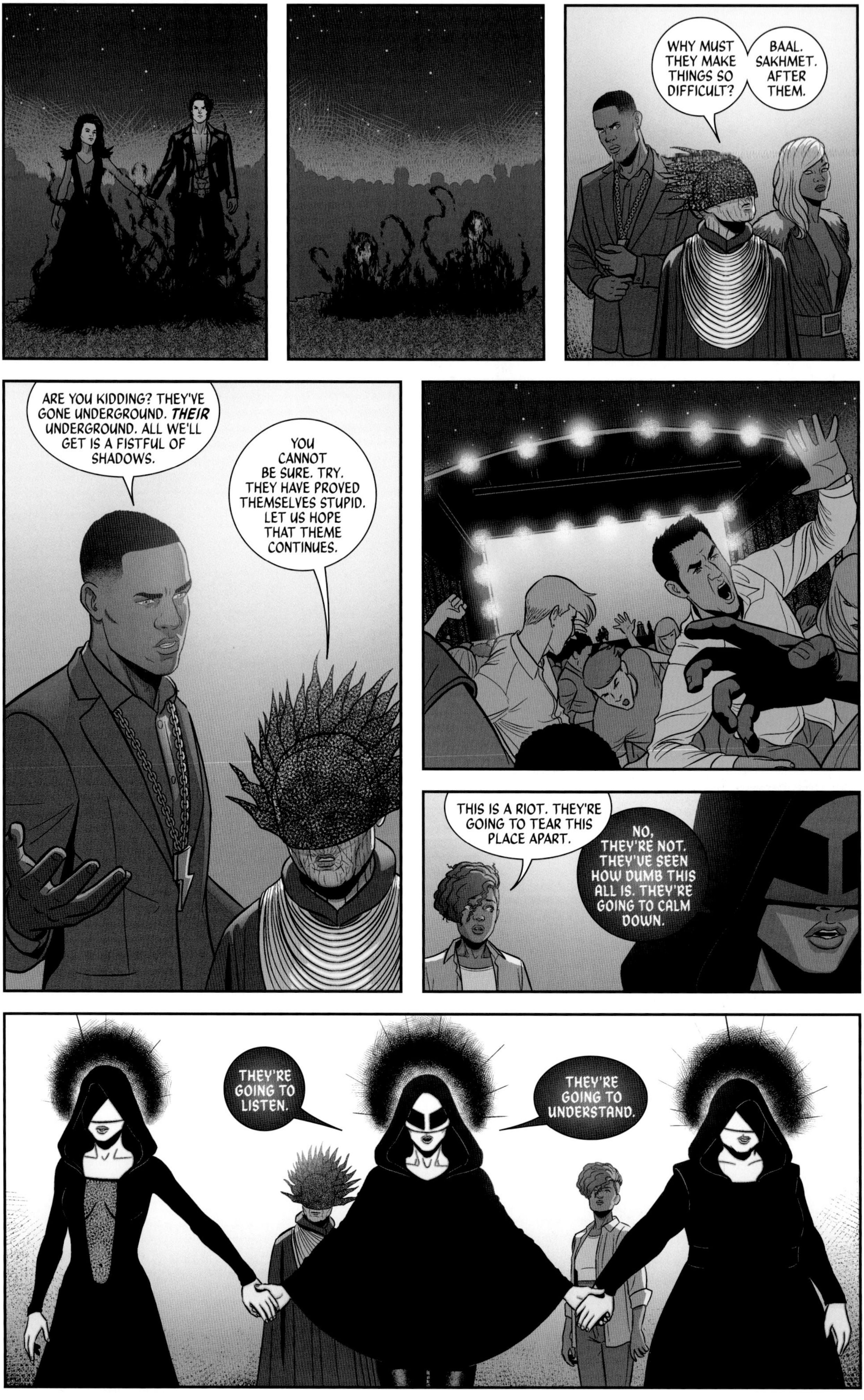
WHY MUST THEY MAKE THINGS SO DIFFICULT?
BAAL. SAKHMET. AFTER THEM.
ARE YOU KIDDING? THEY'VE GONE UNDERGROUND. *THEIR* UNDERGROUND. ALL WE'LL GET IS A FISTFUL OF SHADOWS.
YOU CANNOT BE SURE. TRY. THEY HAVE PROVED THEMSELVES STUPID. LET US HOPE THAT THEME CONTINUES.
THIS IS A RIOT. THEY'RE GOING TO TEAR THIS PLACE APART.
NO, THEY'RE NOT. THEY'VE SEEN HOW DUMB THIS ALL IS. THEY'RE GOING TO CALM DOWN.
THEY'RE GOING TO LISTEN.
THEY'RE GOING TO UNDERSTAND.

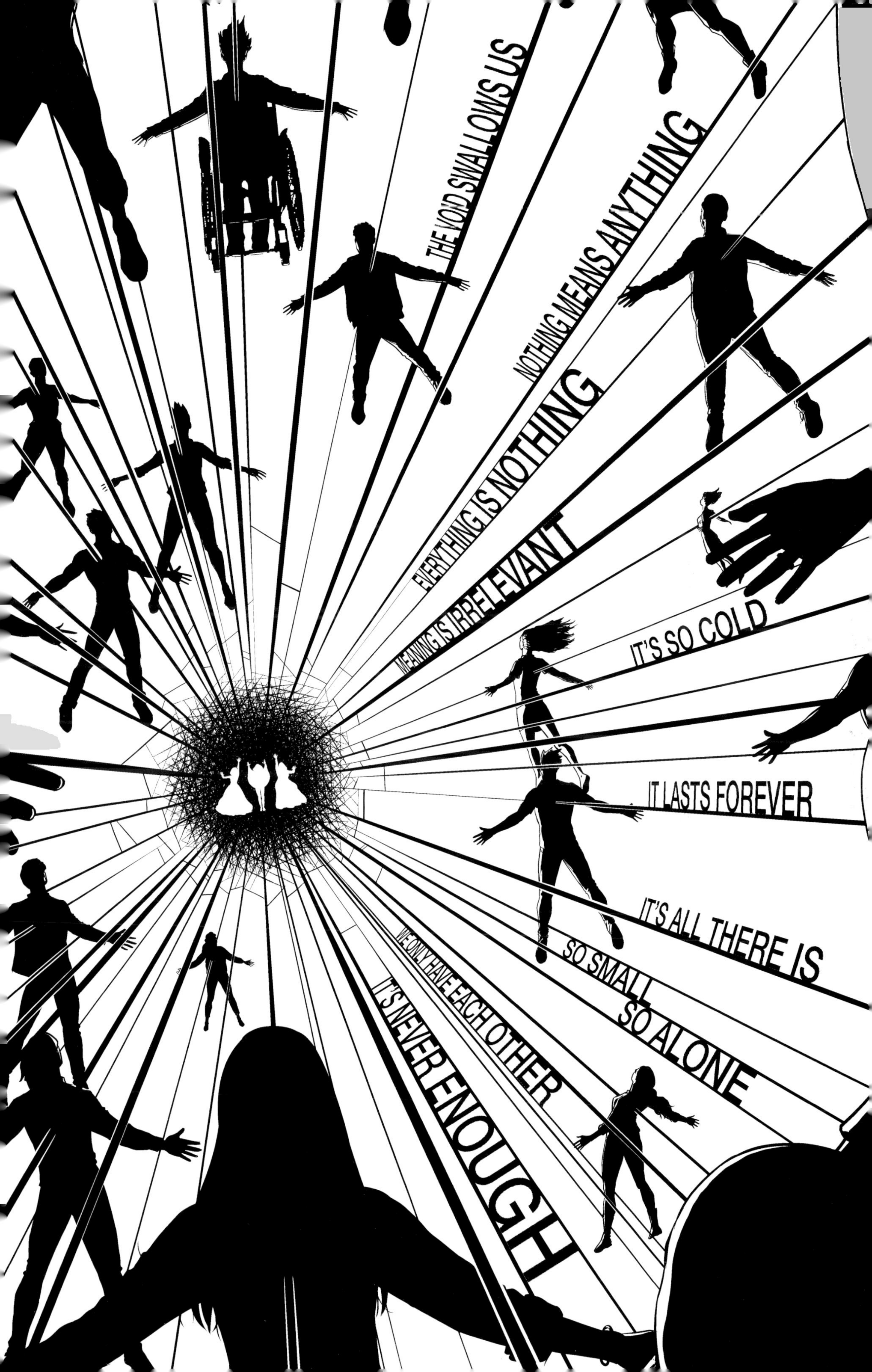
THE VOID SWALLOWS US
NOTHING MEANS ANYTHING
EVERYTHING IS NOTHING
MEANING IS IRRELEVANT
IT'S SO COLD
IT LASTS FOREVER
IT'S ALL THERE IS
SO SMALL
SO ALONE
WE ONLY HAVE EACH OTHER
IT'S NEVER ENOUGH

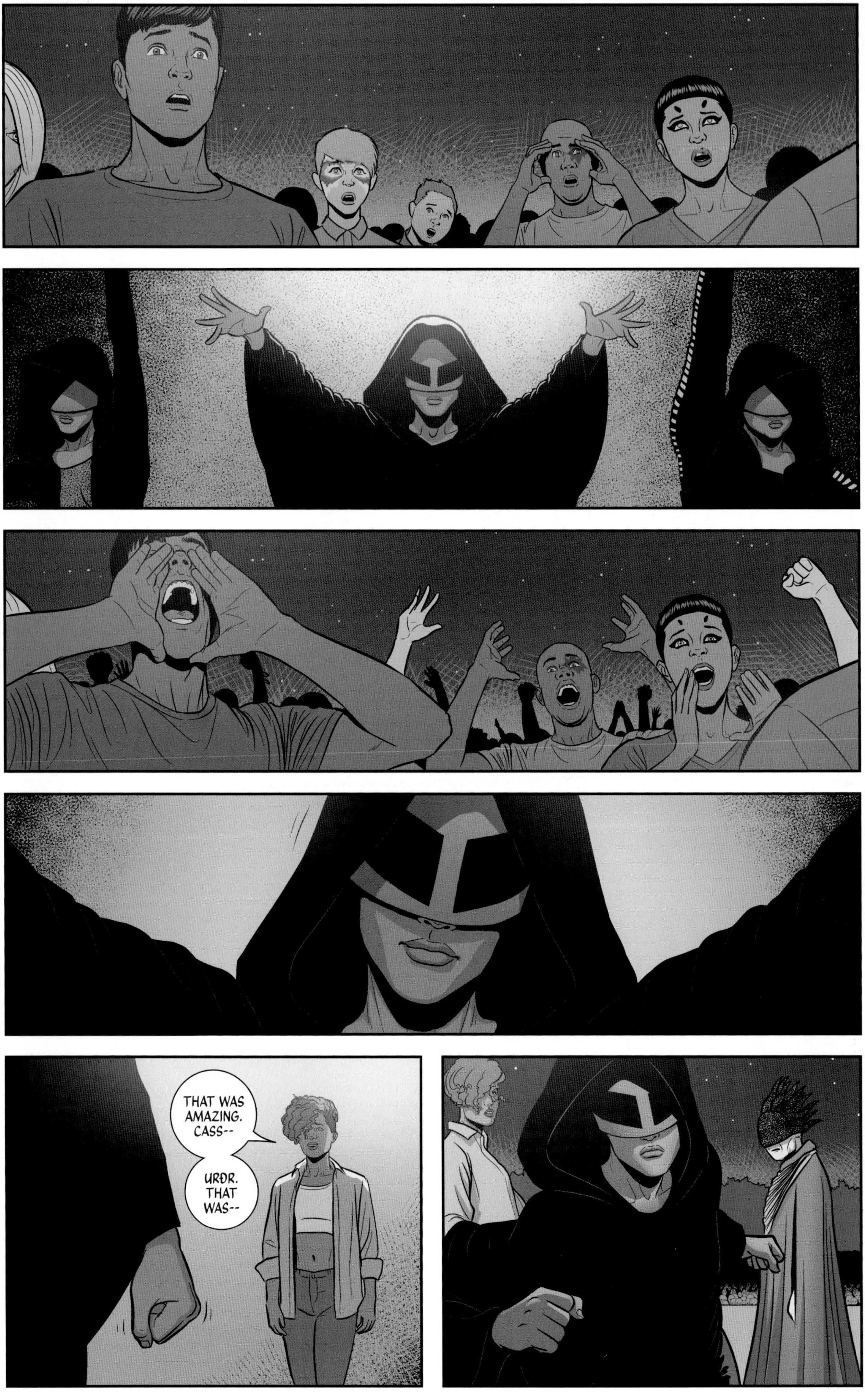
THAT WAS AMAZING. CASS--
URÐR. THAT WAS--

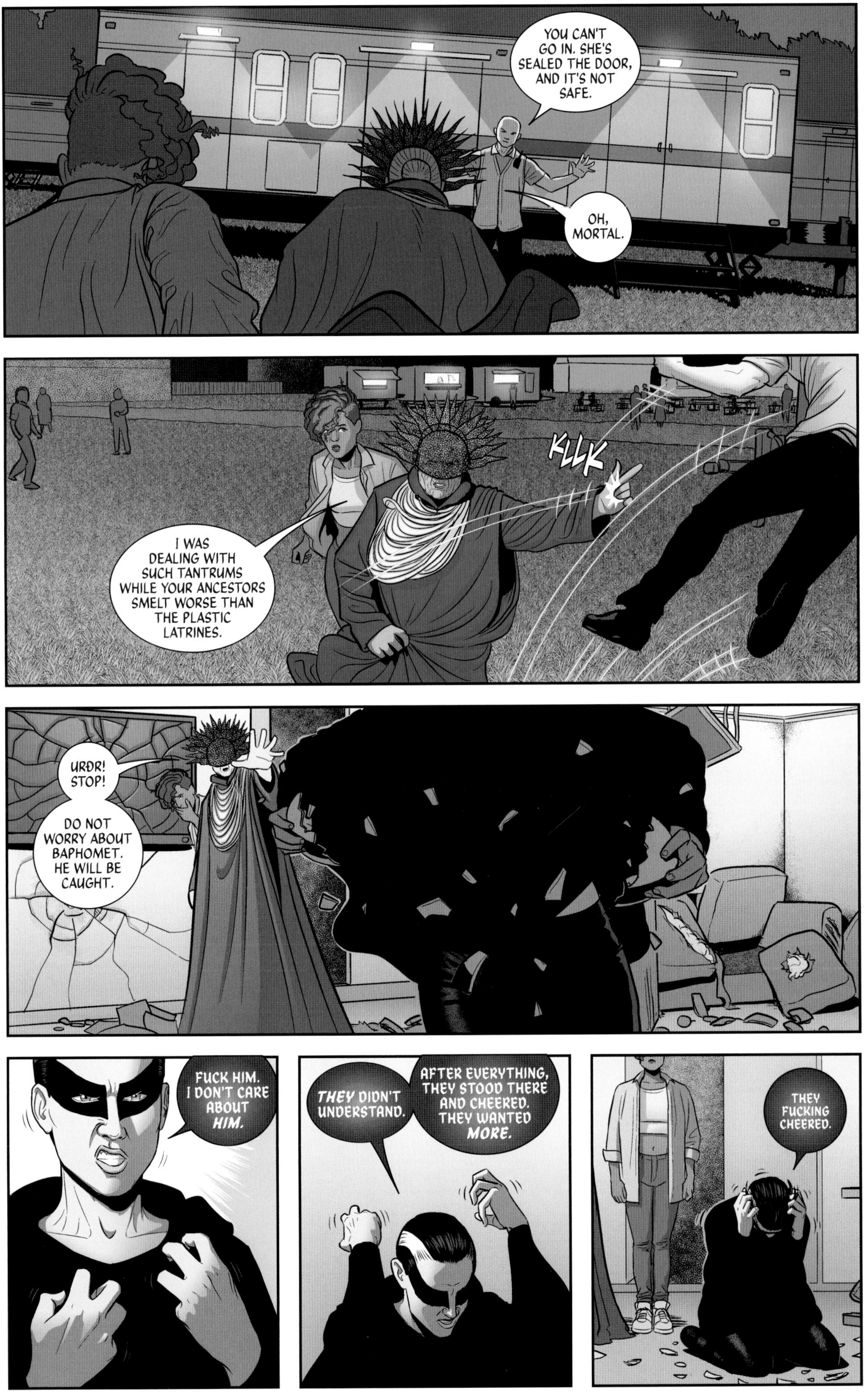
YOU CAN'T GO IN. SHE'S SEALED THE DOOR, AND IT'S NOT SAFE.
OH, MORTAL.
KLLK
I WAS DEALING WITH SUCH TANTRUMS WHILE YOUR ANCESTORS SMELT WORSE THAN THE PLASTIC LATRINES.
URÐR! STOP!
DO NOT WORRY ABOUT BAPHOMET. HE WILL BE CAUGHT.
FUCK HIM. I DON'T CARE ABOUT *HIM.*
THEY DIDN'T UNDERSTAND.
AFTER EVERYTHING, THEY STOOD THERE AND CHEERED. THEY WANTED *MORE.*
THEY FUCKING CHEERED.

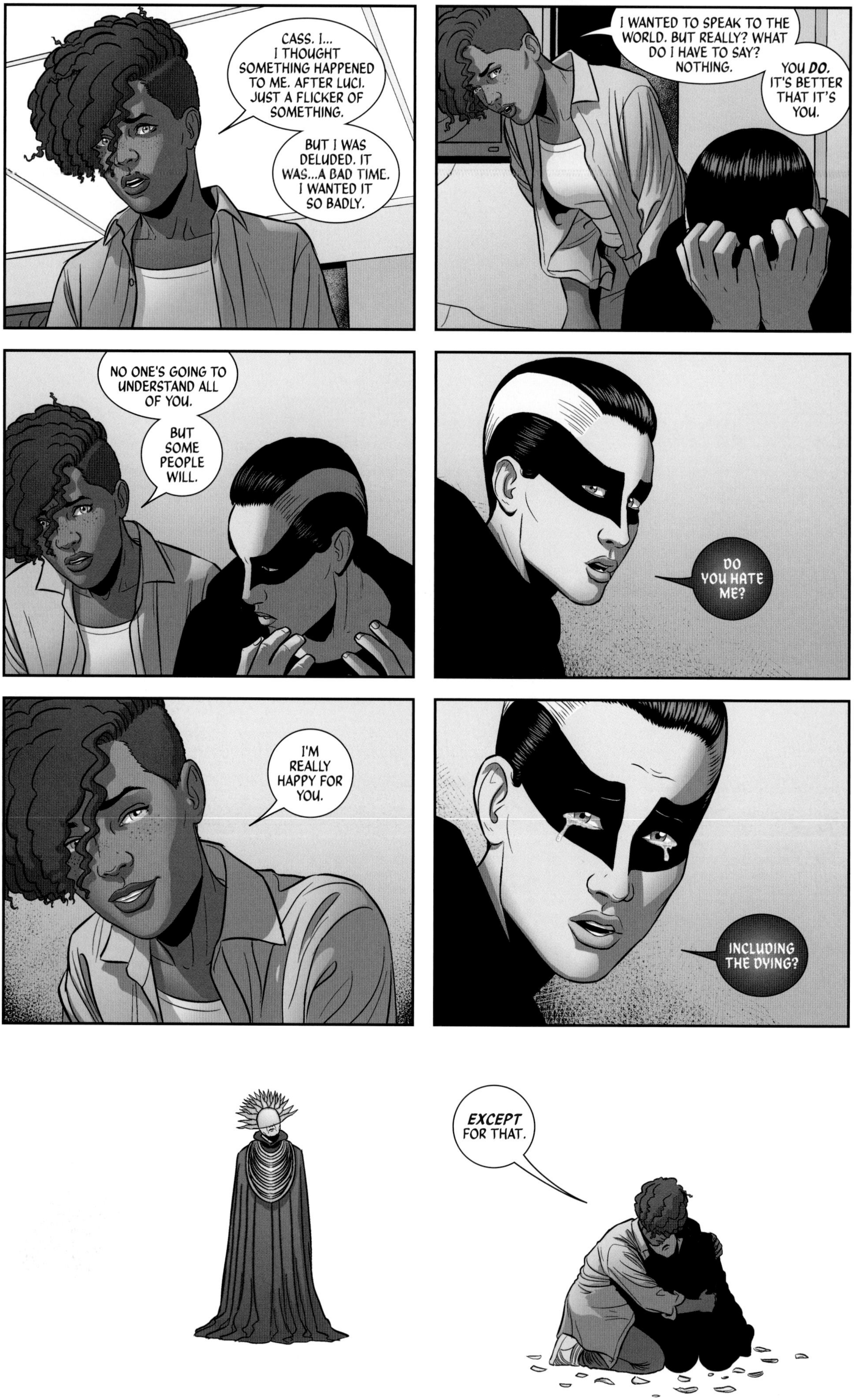
CASS. I... I THOUGHT SOMETHING HAPPENED TO ME. AFTER LUCI. JUST A FLICKER OF SOMETHING.
BUT I WAS DELUDED. IT WAS...A BAD TIME. I WANTED IT SO BADLY.
I WANTED TO SPEAK TO THE WORLD. BUT REALLY? WHAT DO I HAVE TO SAY? NOTHING.
YOU *DO.* IT'S BETTER THAT IT'S YOU.
NO ONE'S GOING TO UNDERSTAND ALL OF YOU.
BUT SOME PEOPLE WILL.
DO YOU HATE ME?
I'M REALLY HAPPY FOR YOU.
INCLUDING THE DYING?
EXCEPT FOR THAT.

WE ONLY HAVE
EACH OTHER

2 AUGUST 2014

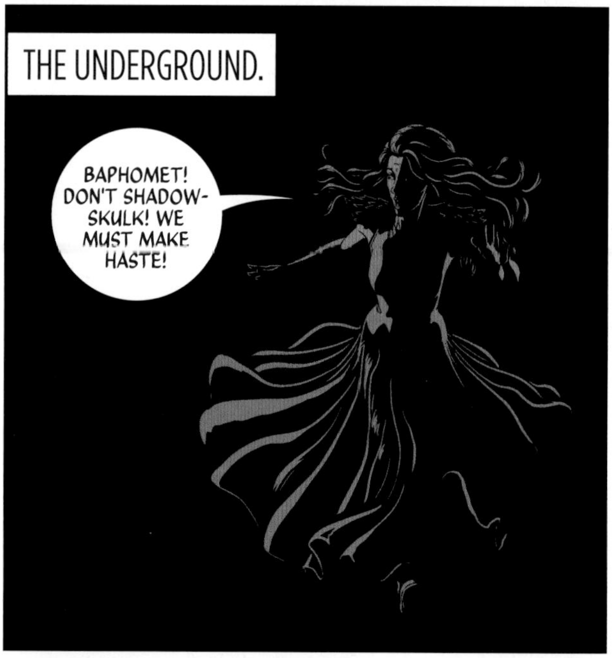
THE UNDERGROUND.
BAPHOMET! DON'T SHADOW-SKULK! WE MUST MAKE HASTE!
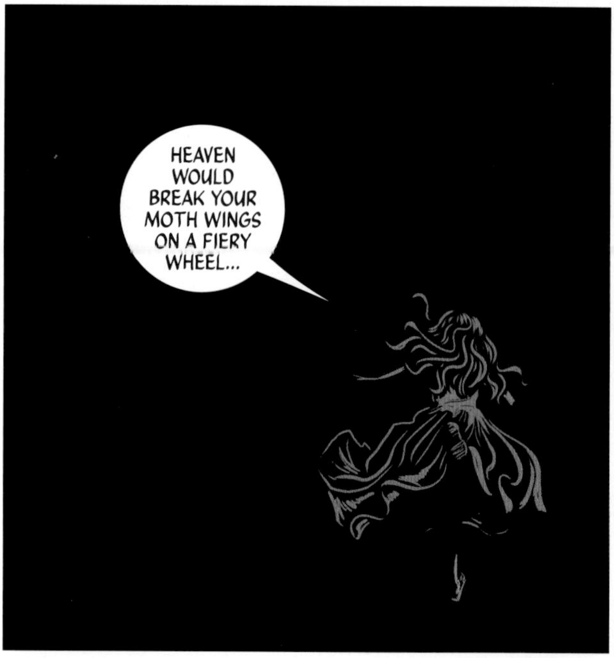
HEAVEN WOULD BREAK YOUR MOTH WINGS ON A FIERY WHEEL...
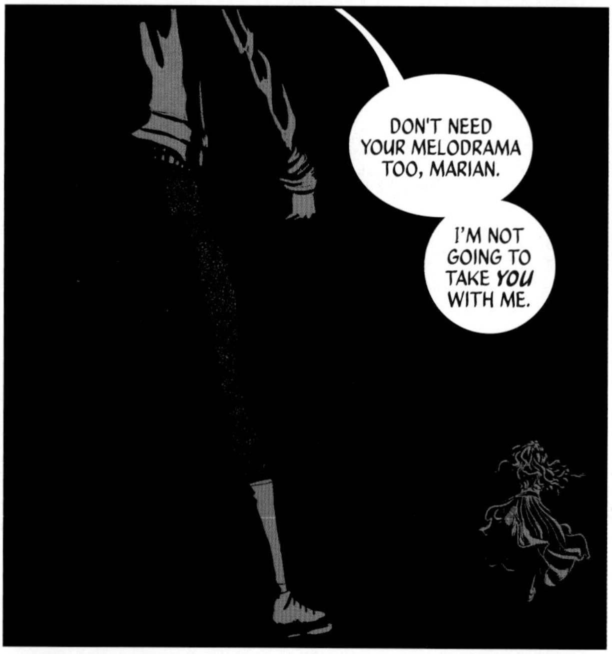
DON'T NEED YOUR MELODRAMA TOO, MARIAN.
I'M NOT GOING TO TAKE *YOU* WITH ME.
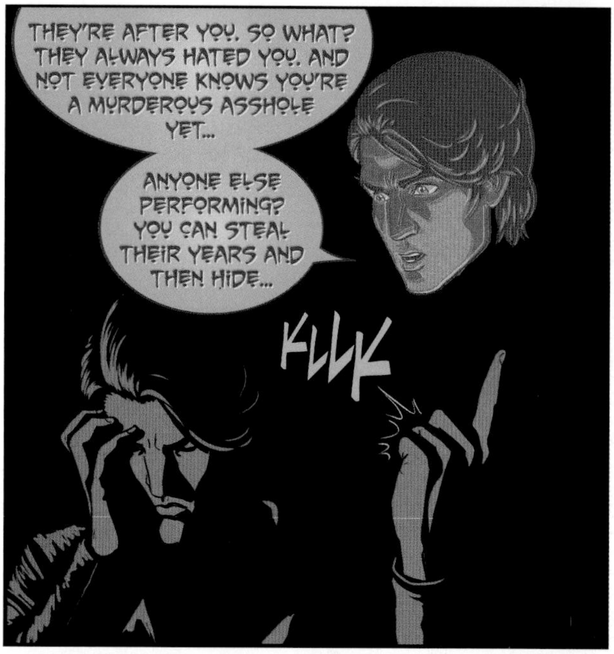
THEY'RE AFTER YOU. SO WHAT? THEY ALWAYS HATED YOU. AND NOT EVERYONE KNOWS YOU'RE A MURDEROUS ASSHOLE YET...
ANYONE ELSE PERFORMING? YOU CAN STEAL THEIR YEARS AND THEN HIDE...
KLLK
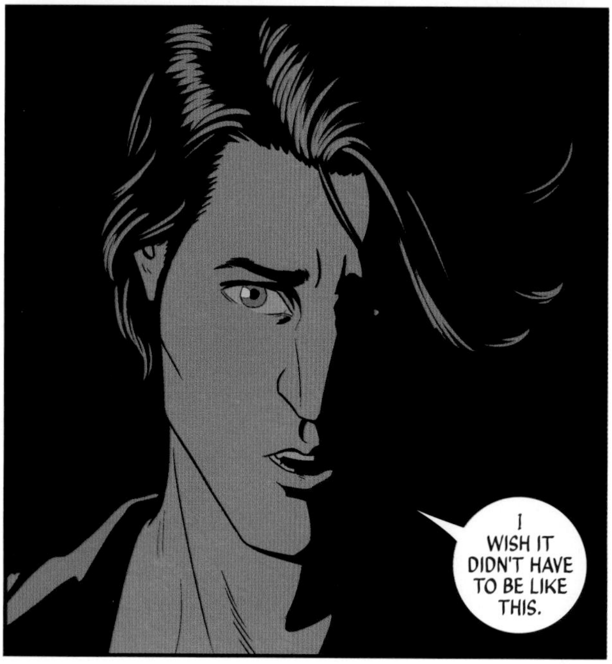
I WISH IT DIDN'T HAVE TO BE LIKE THIS.
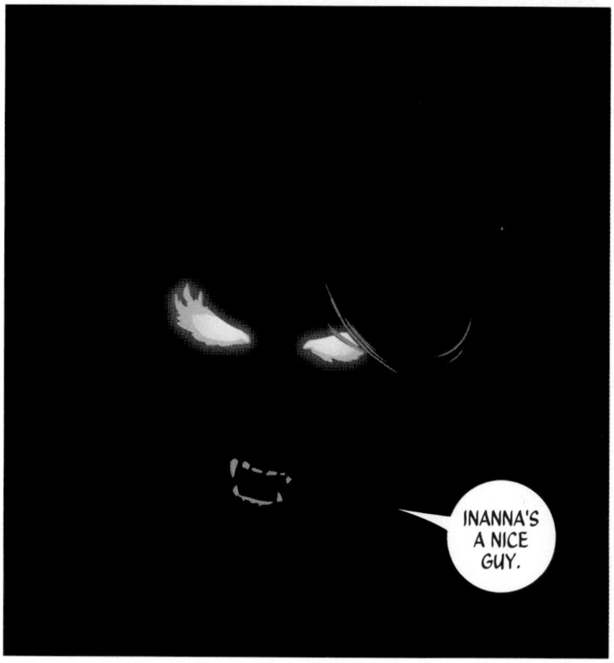
INANNA'S A NICE GUY.

NEVERMORE

2 AUGUST 2014

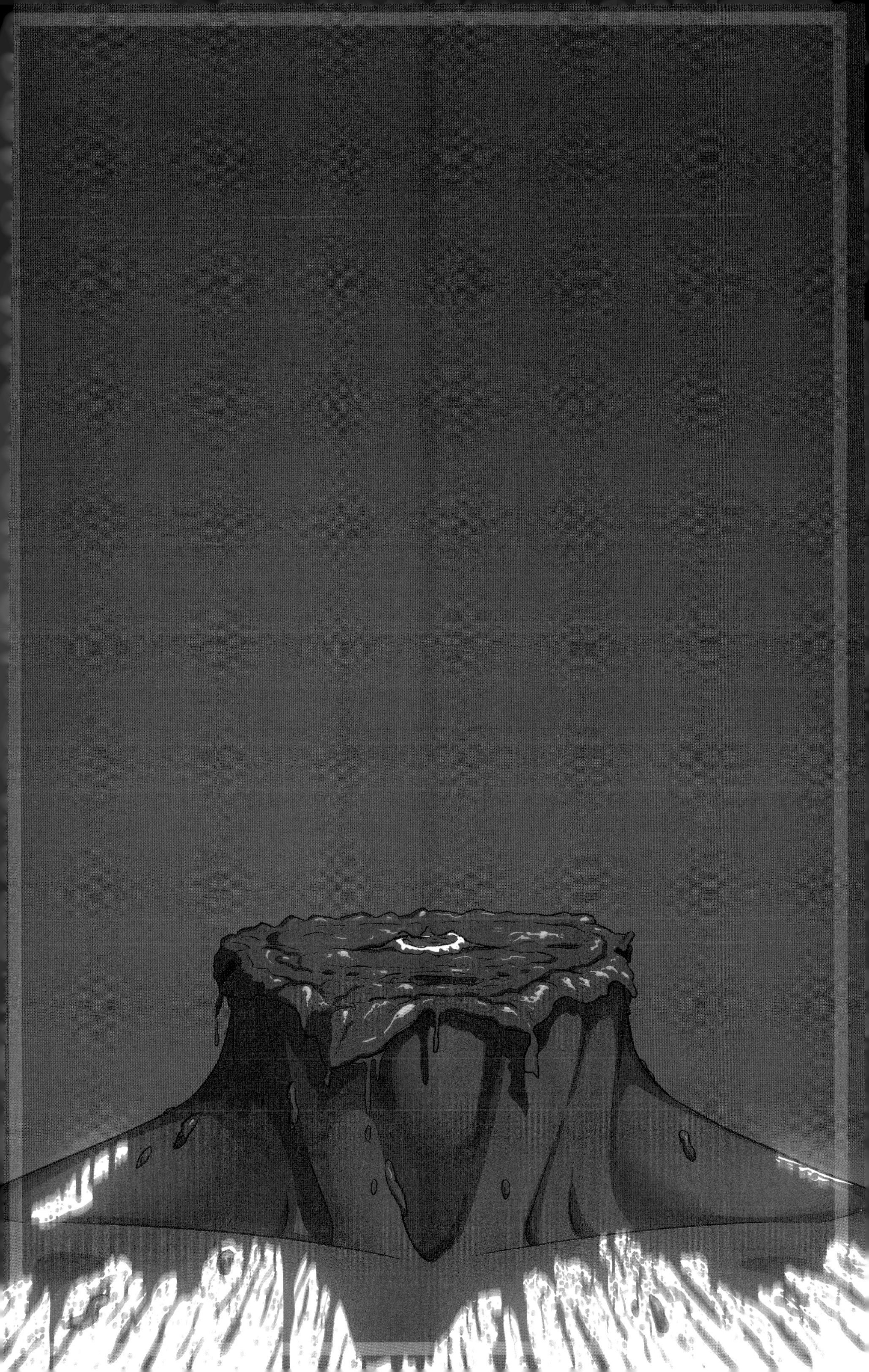

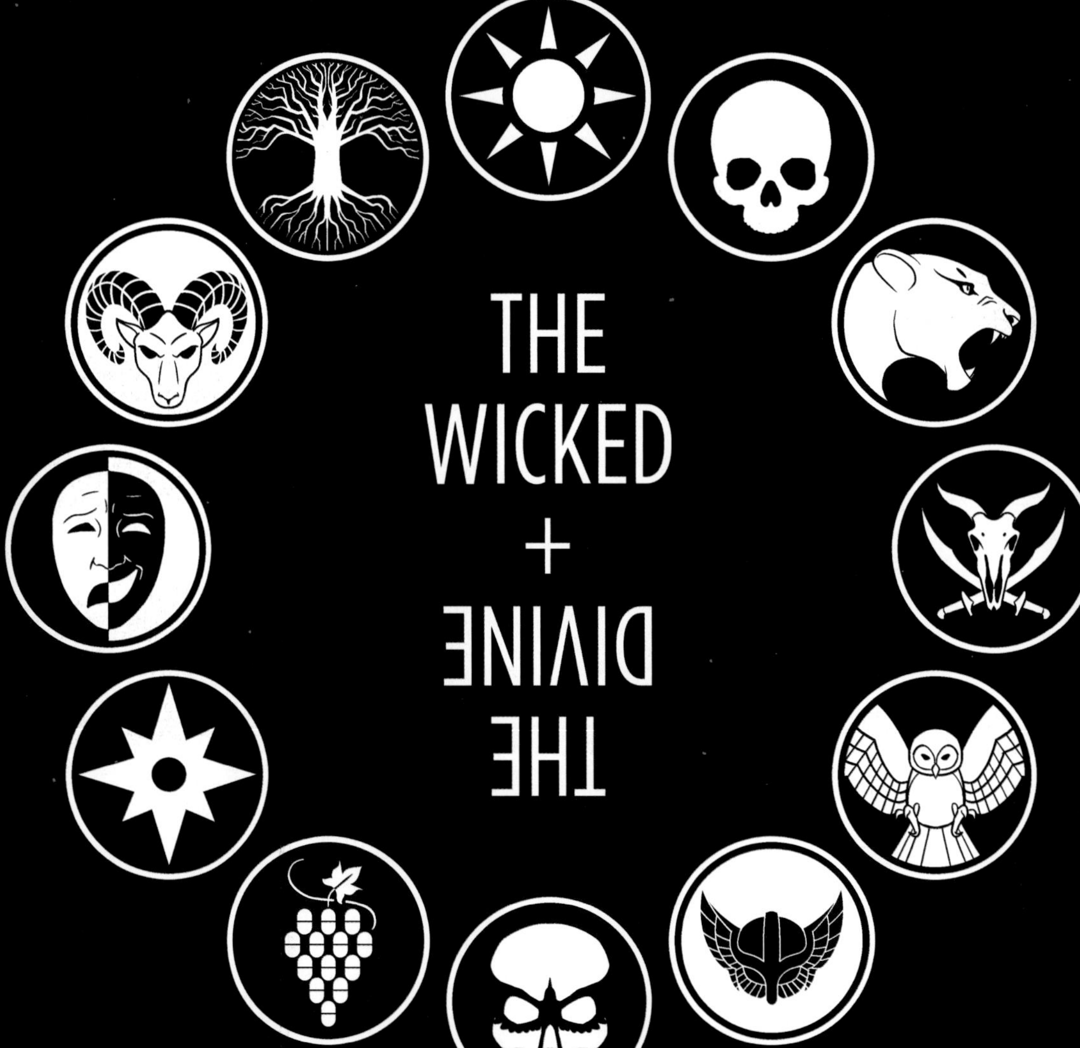
THE
WICKED
+
DIVINE
THE

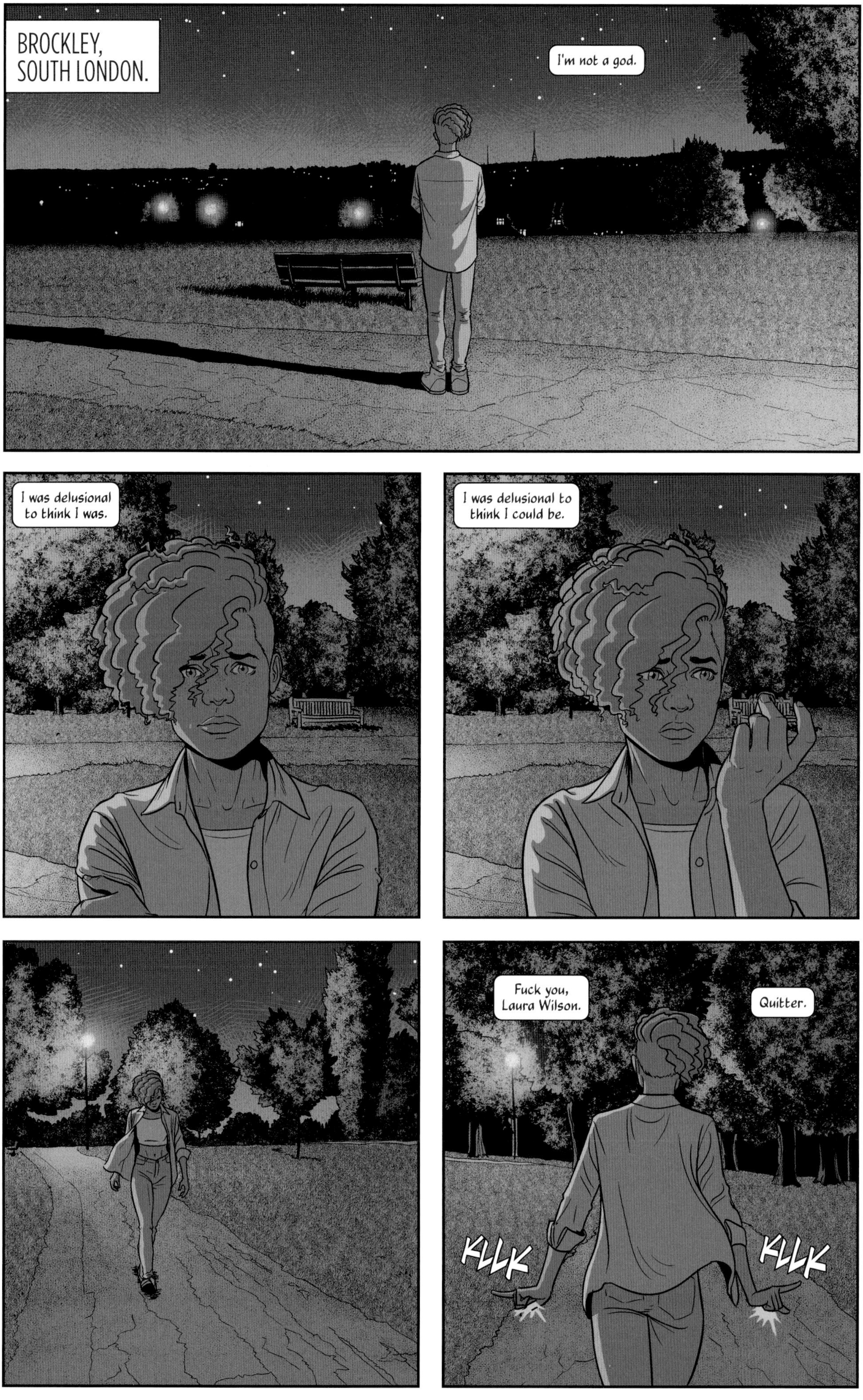
BROCKLEY, SOUTH LONDON.
I'm not a god.
I was delusional to think I was.
I was delusional to think I could be.
Fuck you, Laura Wilson.
Quitter.
KLLK
KLLK

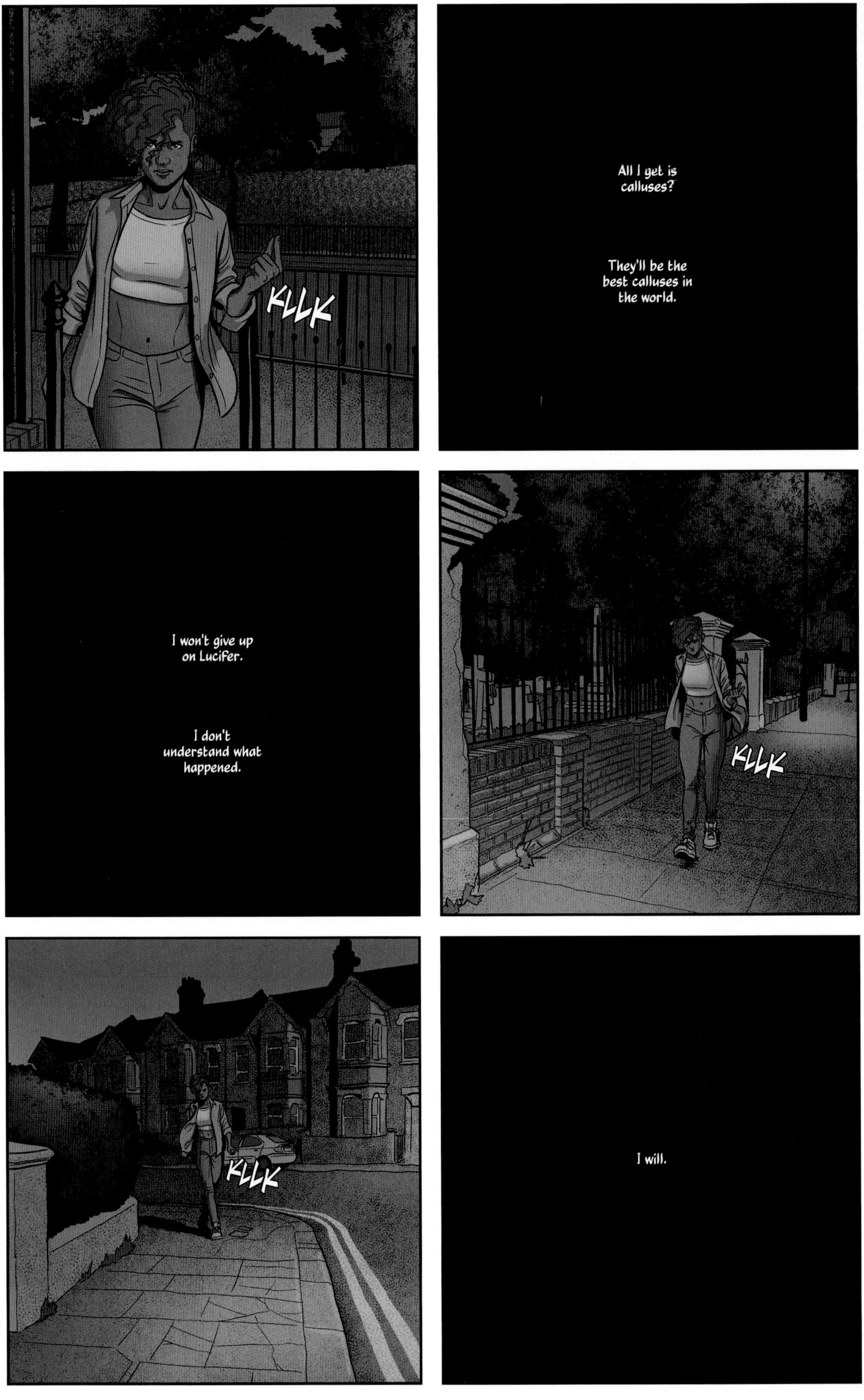
KLLK
All I get is calluses?
They'll be the best calluses in the world.
I won't give up on Lucifer.
I don't understand what happened.
KLLK
KLLK
I will.

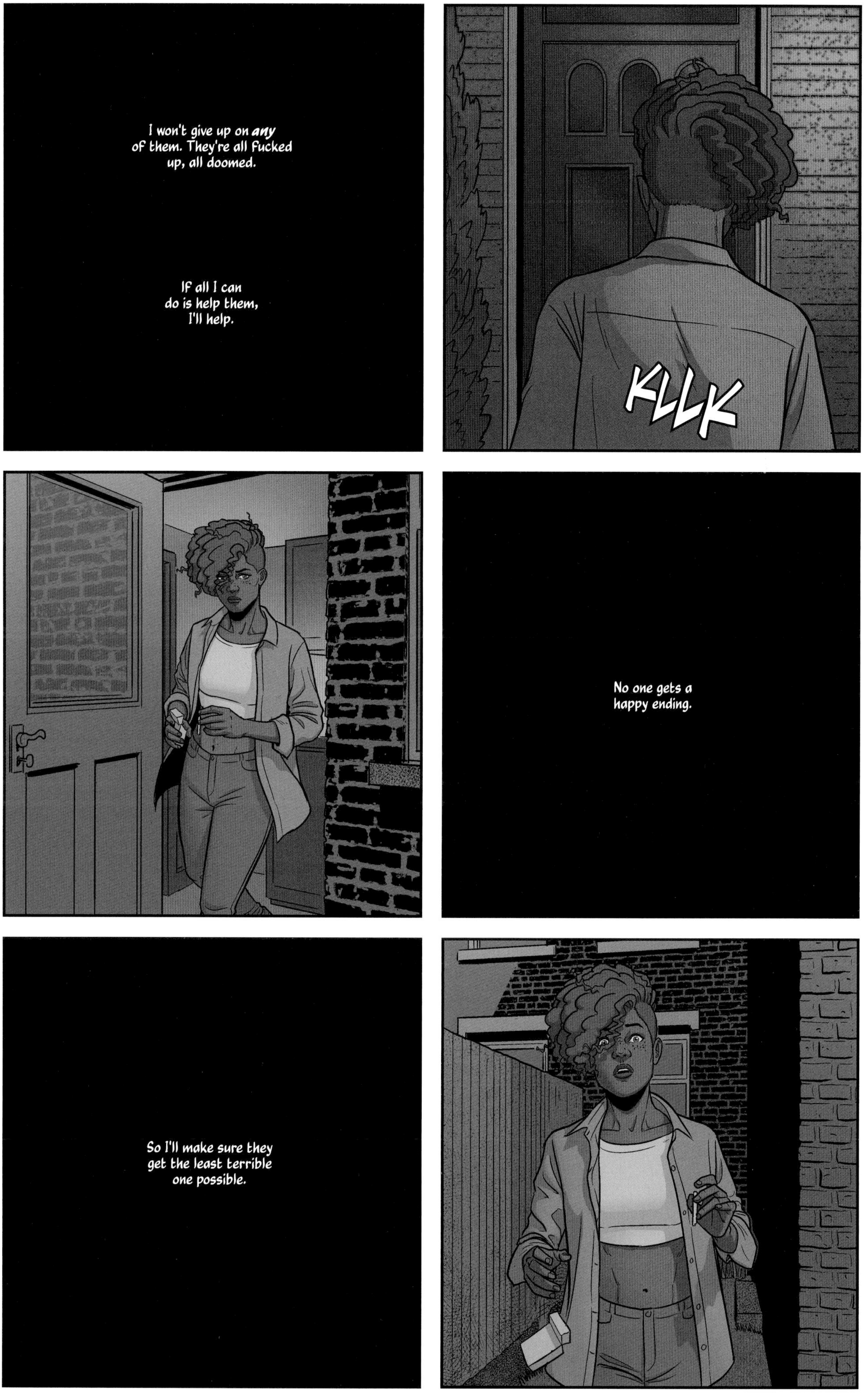
I won't give up on *any* of them. They're all fucked up, all doomed.
If all I can do is help them, I'll help.
KLLK
No one gets a happy ending.
So I'll make sure they get the least terrible one possible.

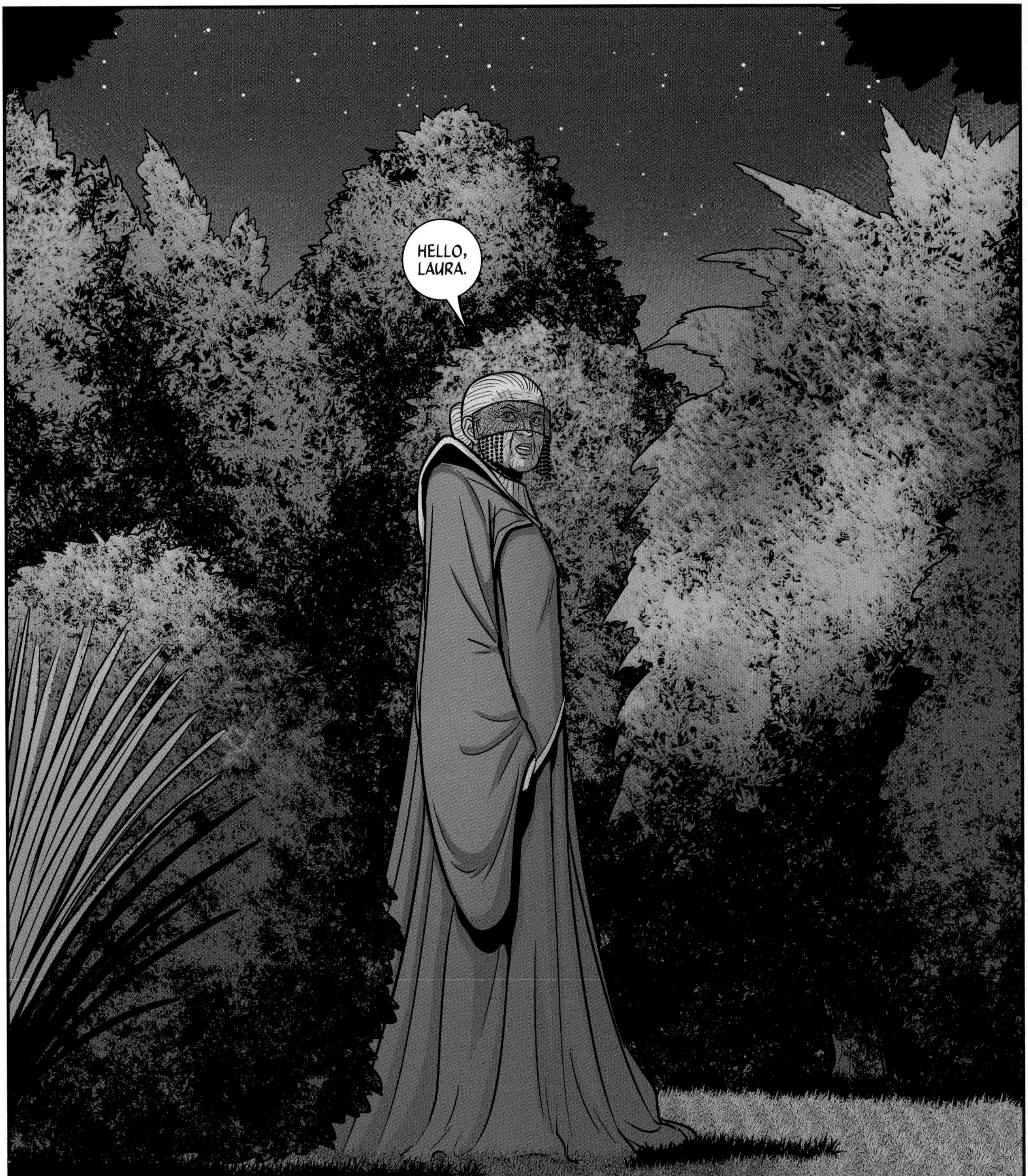
HELLO, LAURA.
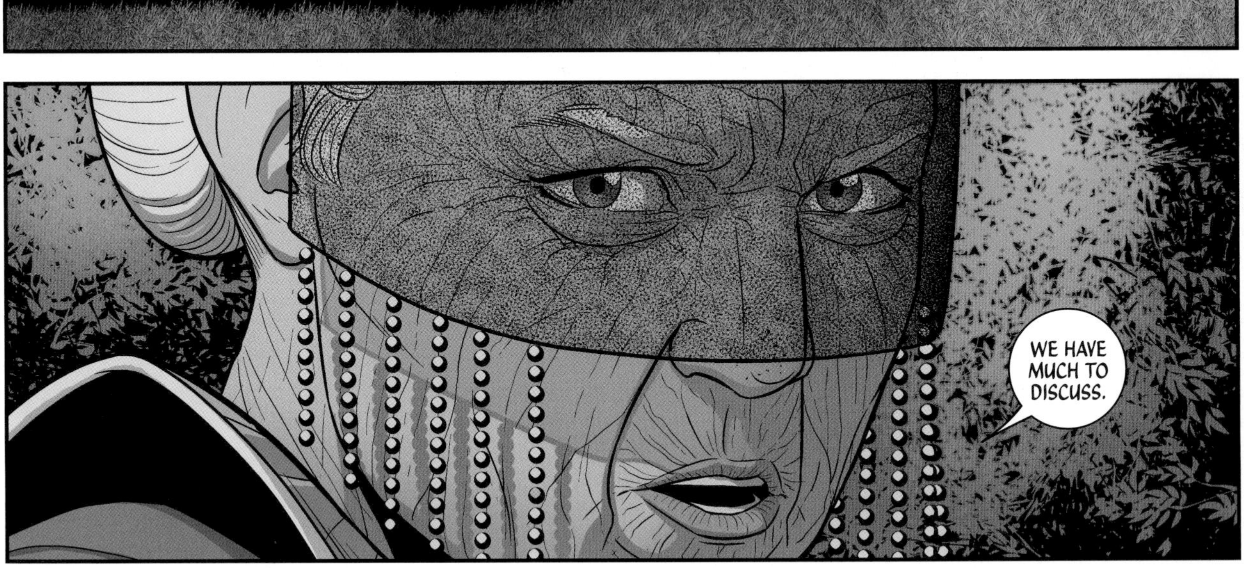
WE HAVE MUCH TO DISCUSS.

IT'S GOING
TO BE OKAY
(SLIGHT RETURN)

3 AUGUST 2014

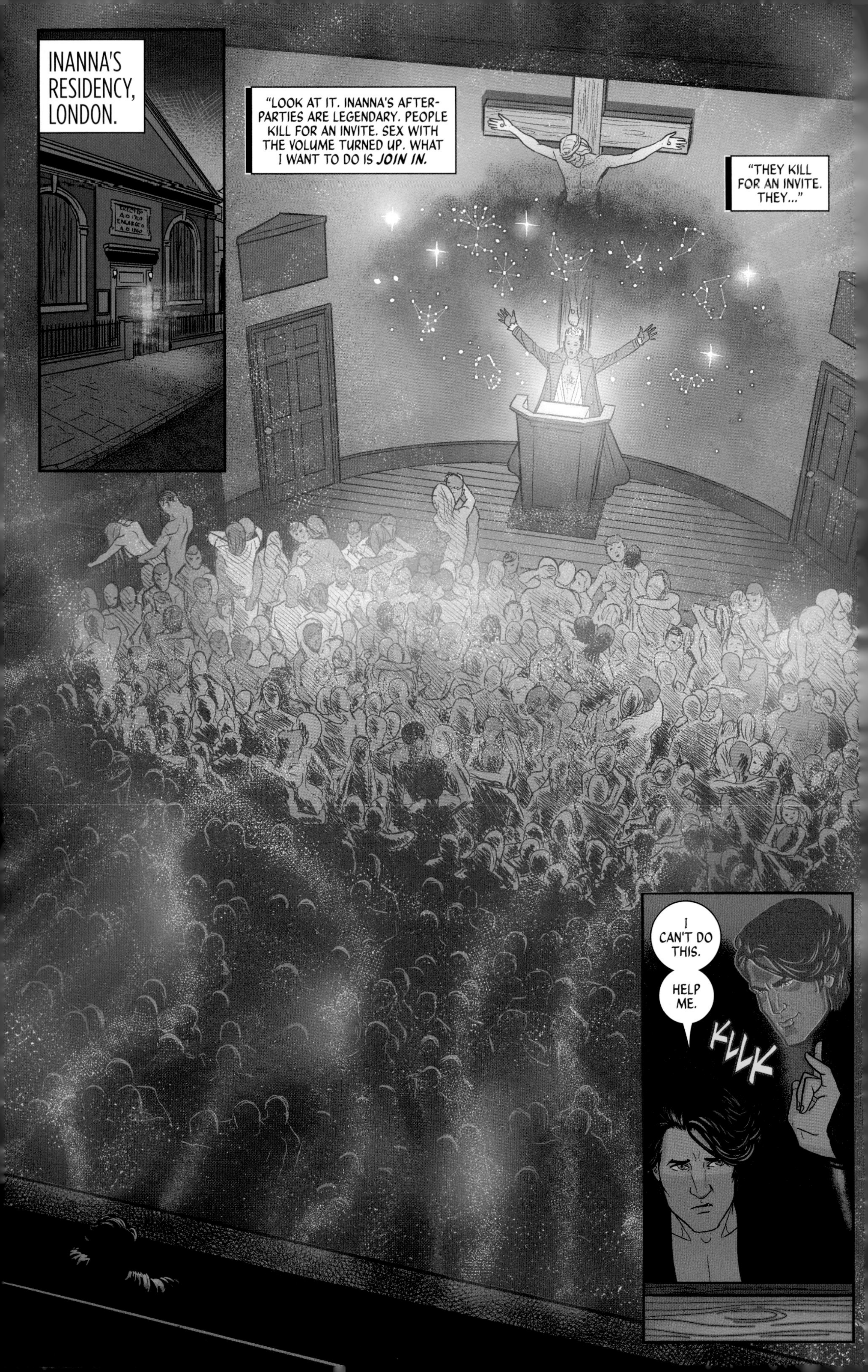
INANNA'S RESIDENCY, LONDON.
"LOOK AT IT. INANNA'S AFTER-PARTIES ARE LEGENDARY. PEOPLE KILL FOR AN INVITE. SEX WITH THE VOLUME TURNED UP. WHAT I WANT TO DO IS *JOIN IN.*
"THEY KILL FOR AN INVITE. THEY..."
I CAN'T DO THIS.
HELP ME.
KLLK

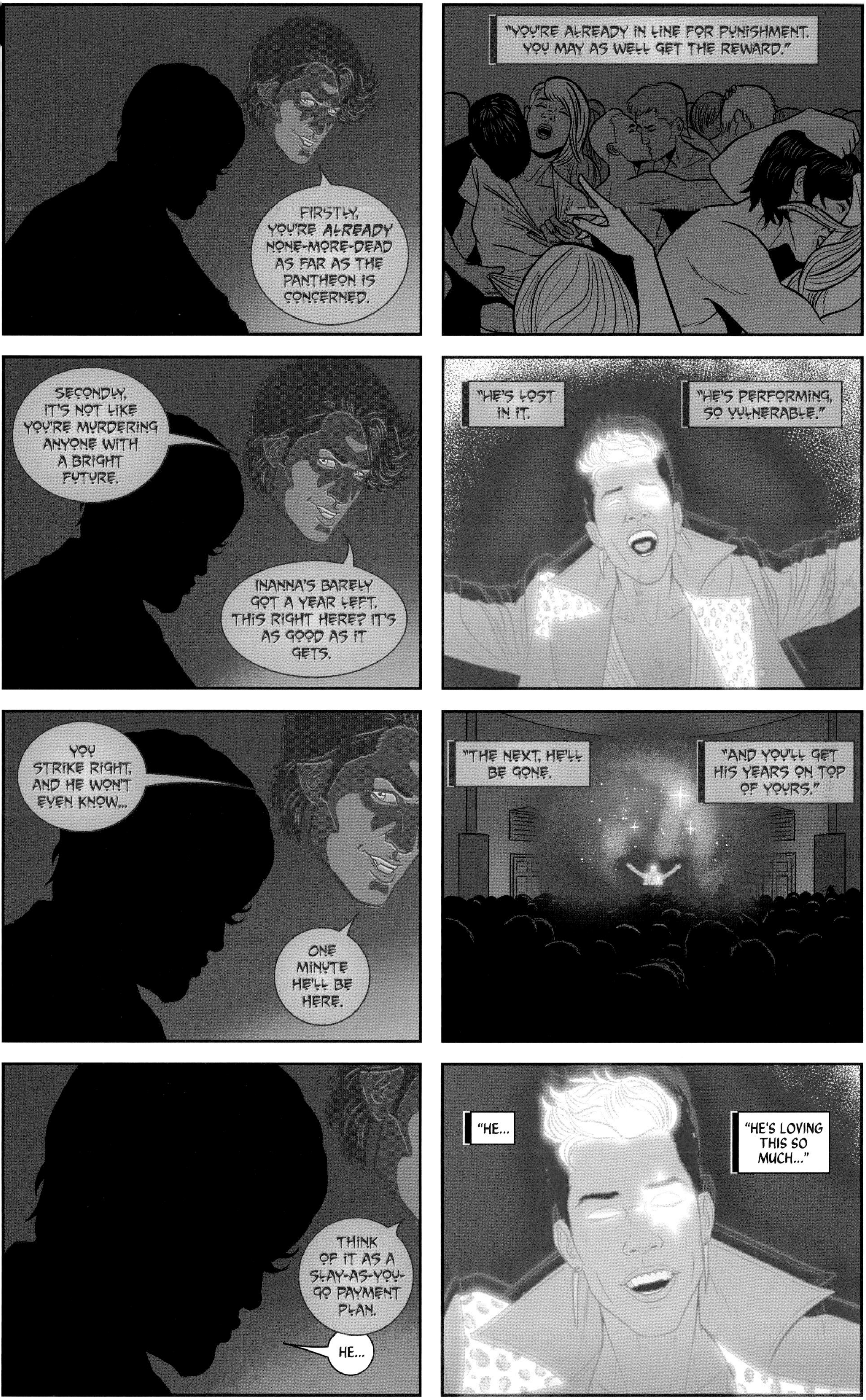
FIRSTLY, YOU'RE ALREADY NONE-MORE-DEAD AS FAR AS THE PANTHEON IS CONCERNED.
"YOU'RE ALREADY IN LINE FOR PUNISHMENT. YOU MAY AS WELL GET THE REWARD."
SECONDLY, IT'S NOT LIKE YOU'RE MURDERING ANYONE WITH A BRIGHT FUTURE.
INANNA'S BARELY GOT A YEAR LEFT. THIS RIGHT HERE? IT'S AS GOOD AS IT GETS.
"HE'S LOST IN IT.
"HE'S PERFORMING, SO VULNERABLE."
YOU STRIKE RIGHT, AND HE WON'T EVEN KNOW...
ONE MINUTE HE'LL BE HERE.
"THE NEXT, HE'LL BE GONE.
"AND YOU'LL GET HIS YEARS ON TOP OF YOURS."
THINK OF IT AS A SLAY-AS-YOU-GO PAYMENT PLAN.
HE...
"HE...
"HE'S LOVING THIS SO MUCH..."

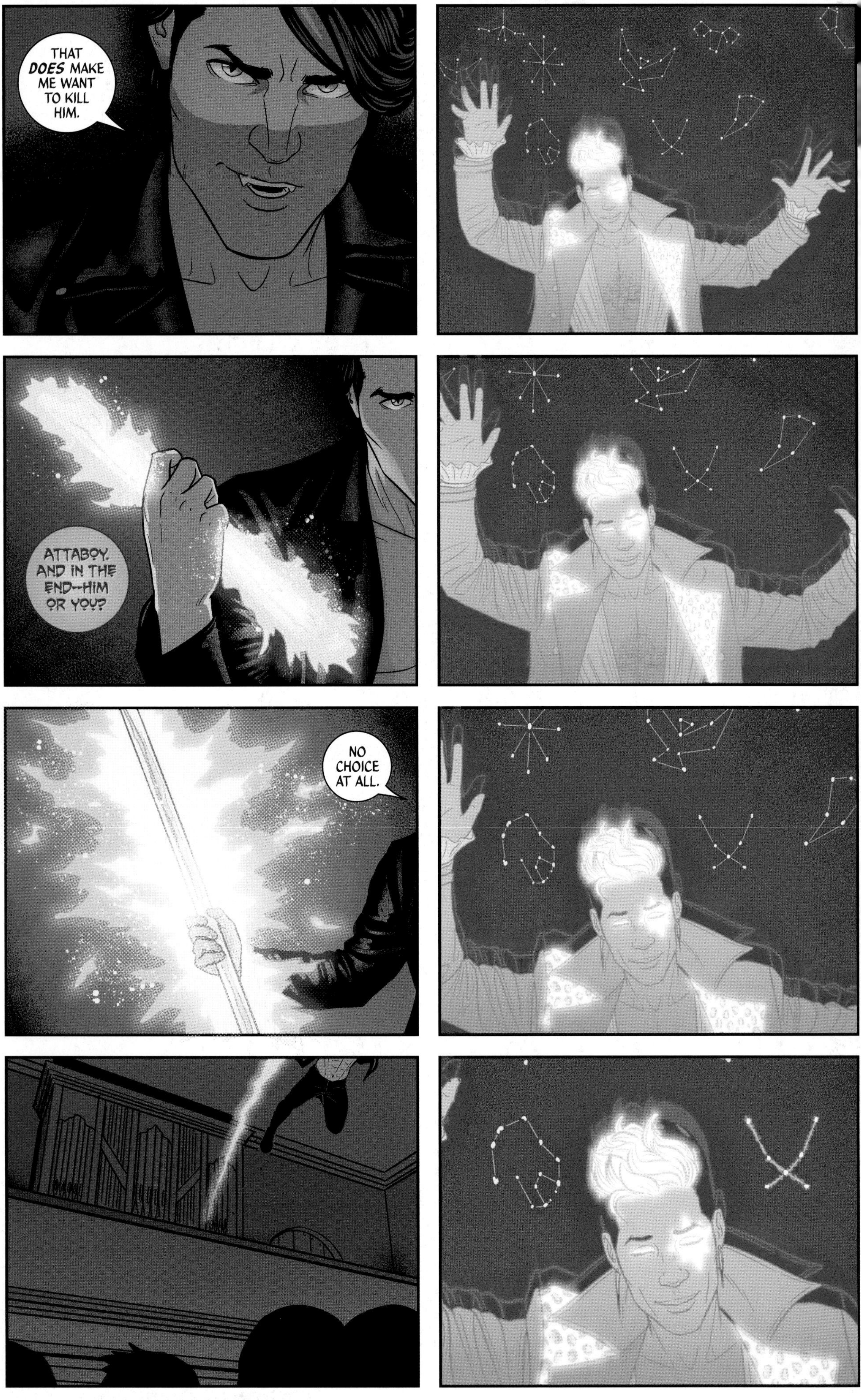
THAT DOES MAKE ME WANT TO KILL HIM.
ATTABOY. AND IN THE END--HIM OR YOU?
NO CHOICE AT ALL.

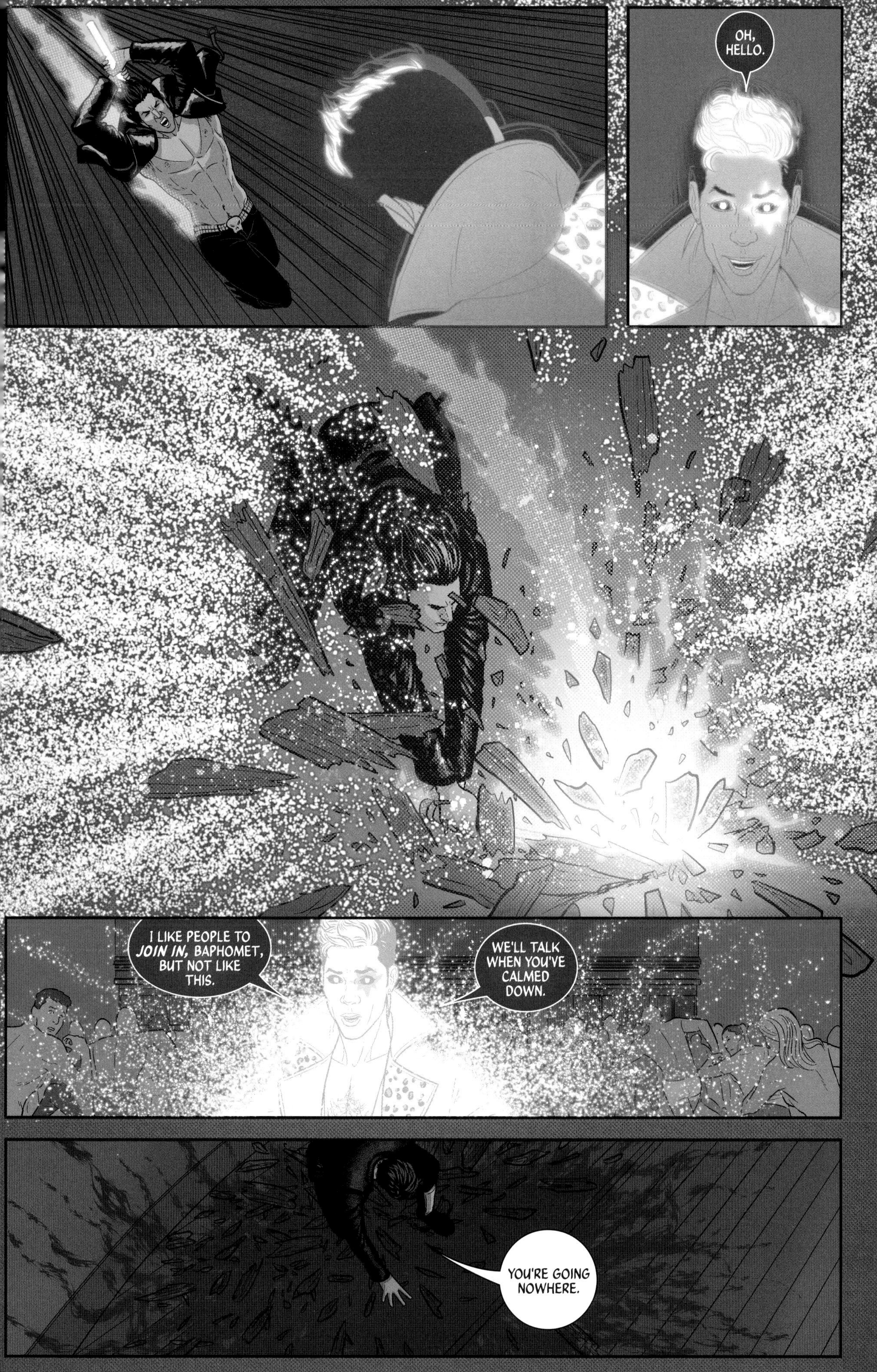
OH, HELLO.
I LIKE PEOPLE TO *JOIN IN,* BAPHOMET, BUT NOT LIKE THIS.
WE'LL TALK WHEN YOU'VE CALMED DOWN.
YOU'RE GOING NOWHERE.

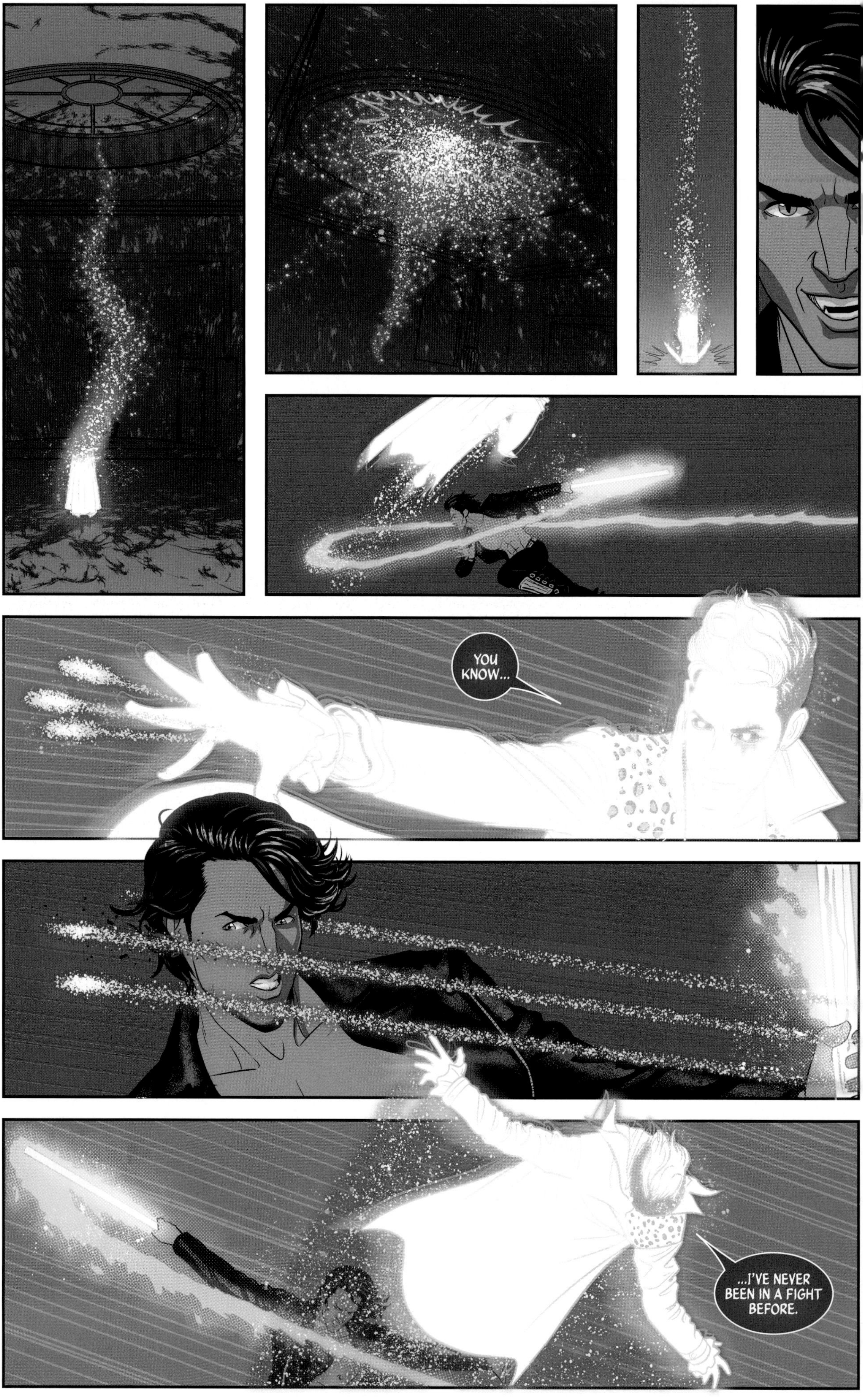
YOU KNOW...
...I'VE NEVER BEEN IN A FIGHT BEFORE.

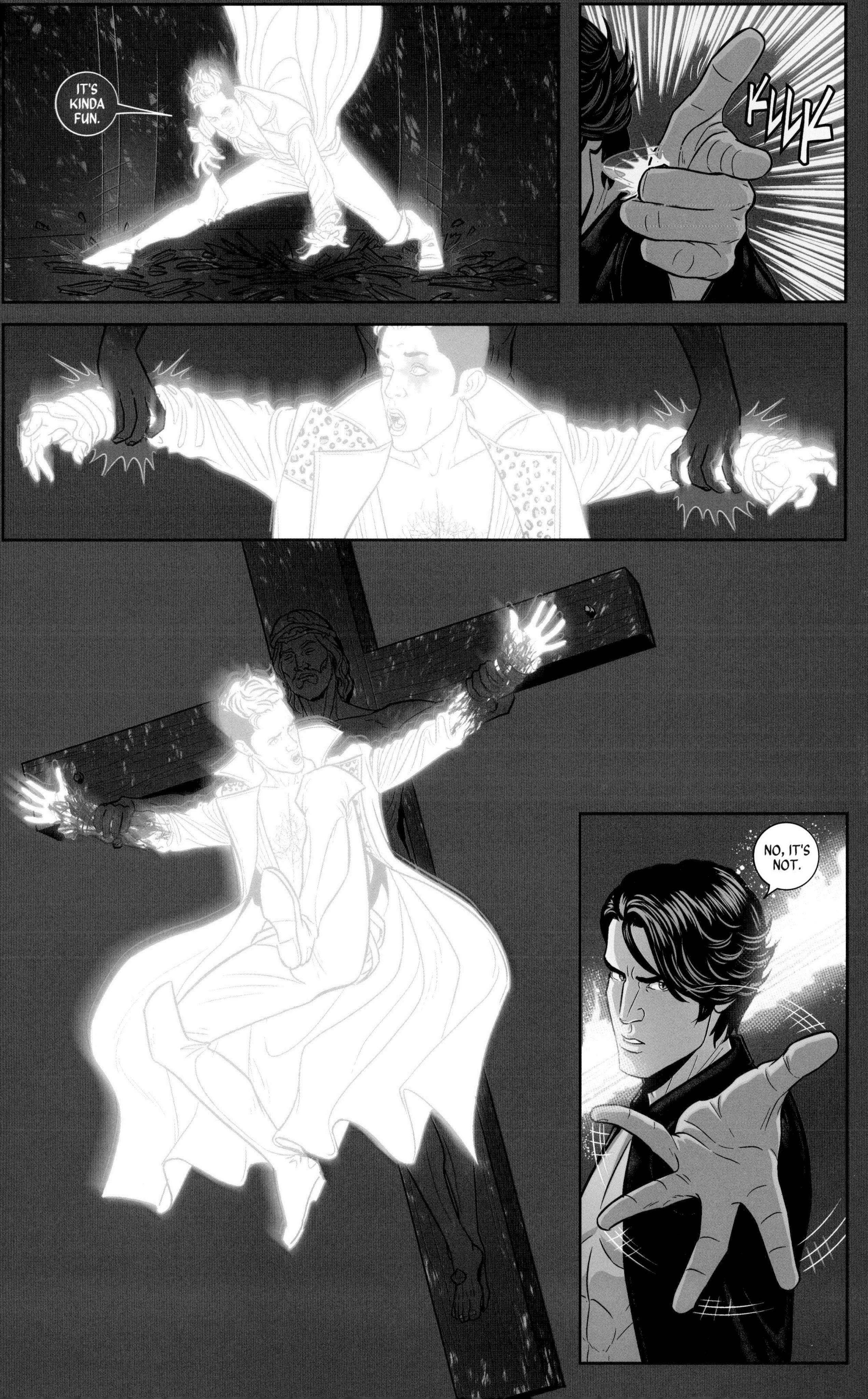
IT'S KINDA FUN.
KLLK
NO, IT'S NOT.

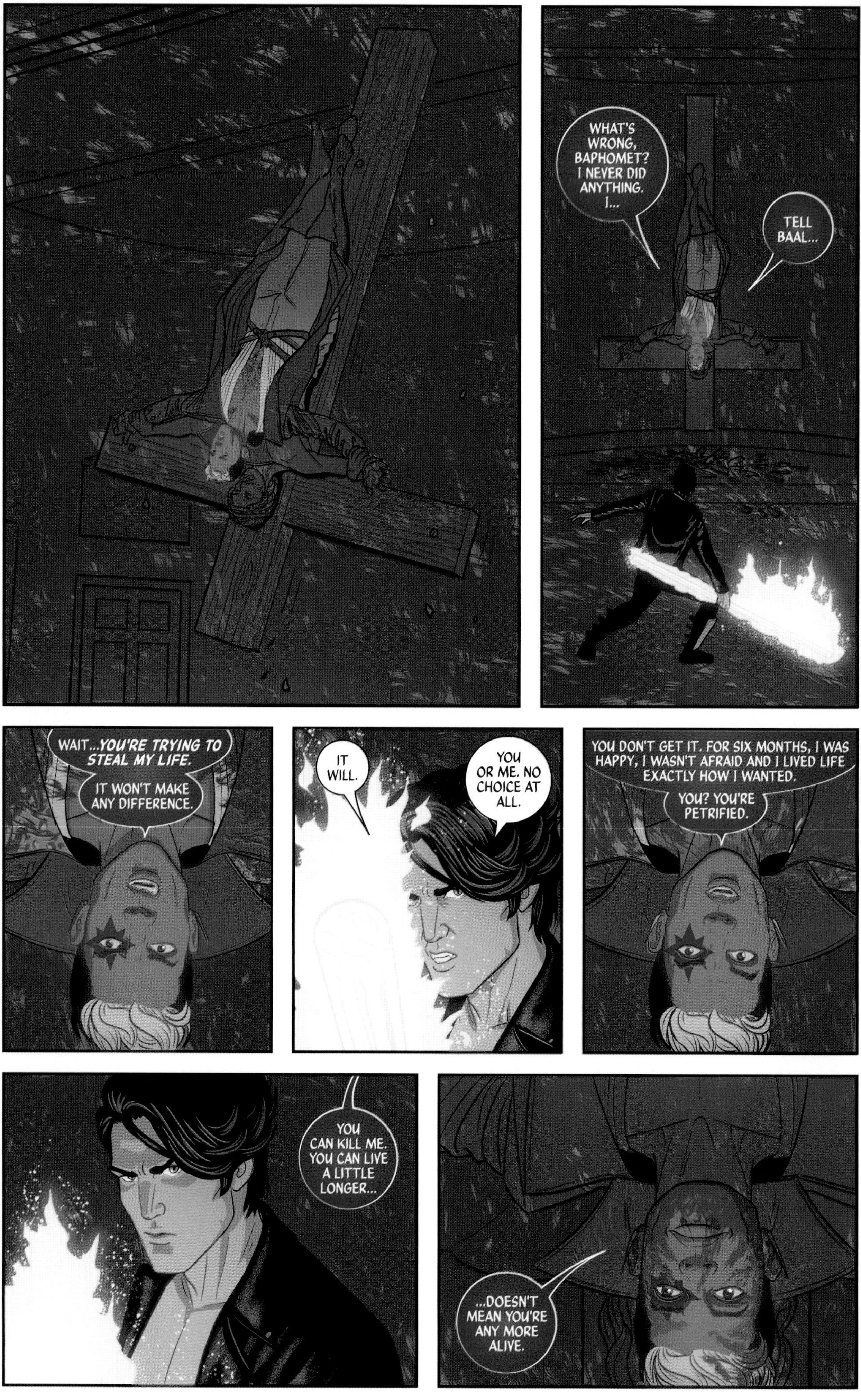

WHAT'S WRONG, BAPHOMET? I NEVER DID ANYTHING. I...
TELL BAAL...
WAIT...*YOU'RE TRYING TO STEAL MY LIFE.*
IT WON'T MAKE ANY DIFFERENCE.
IT WILL.
YOU OR ME. NO CHOICE AT ALL.
YOU DON'T GET IT. FOR SIX MONTHS, I WAS HAPPY, I WASN'T AFRAID AND I LIVED LIFE EXACTLY HOW I WANTED.
YOU? YOU'RE PETRIFIED.
YOU CAN KILL ME. YOU CAN LIVE A LITTLE LONGER...
...DOESN'T MEAN YOU'RE ANY MORE ALIVE.

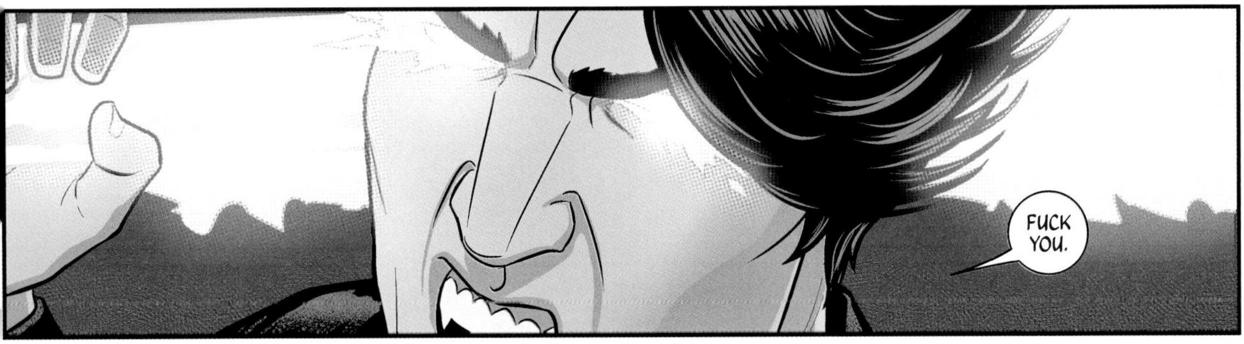
FUCK YOU.
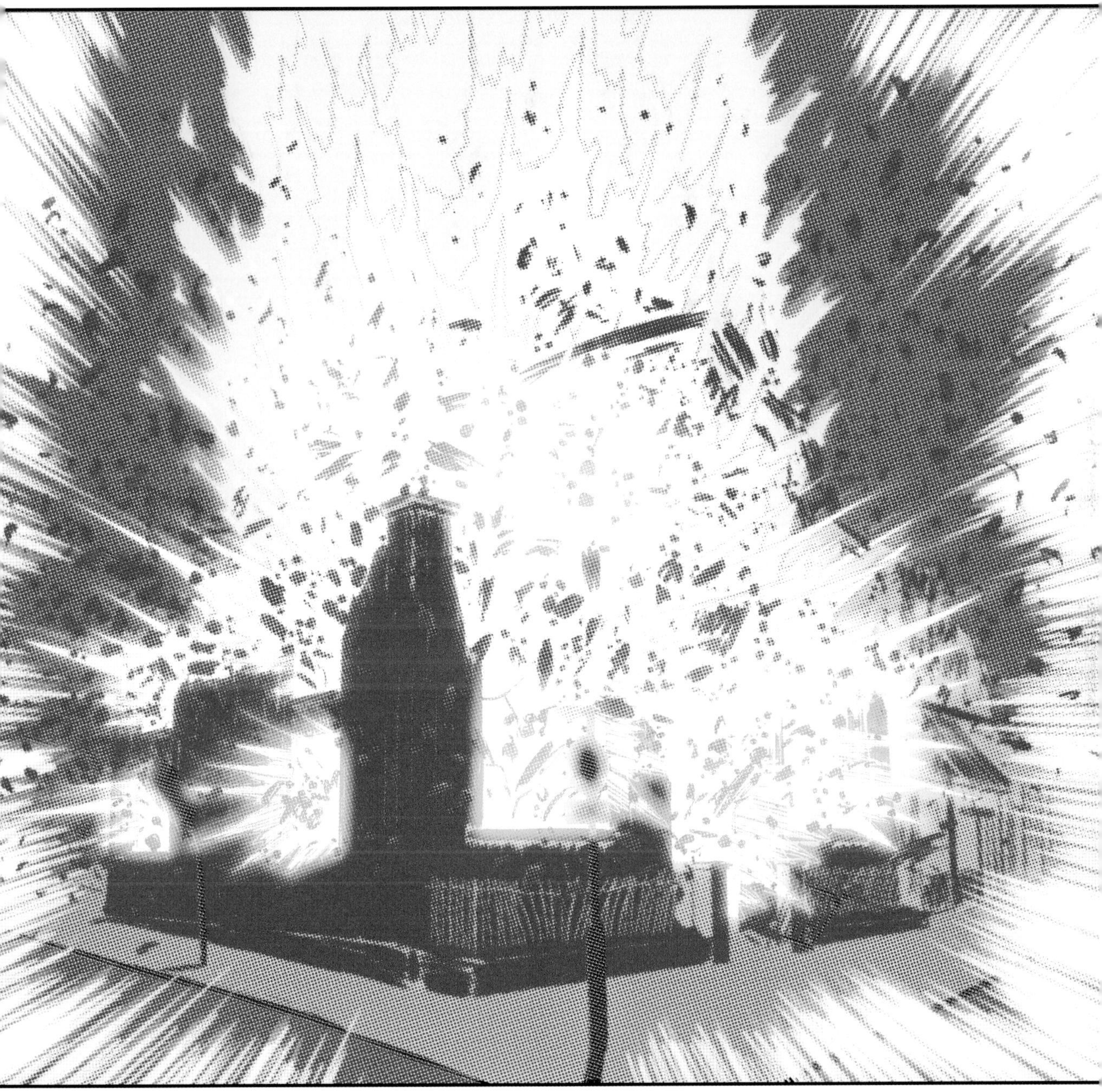
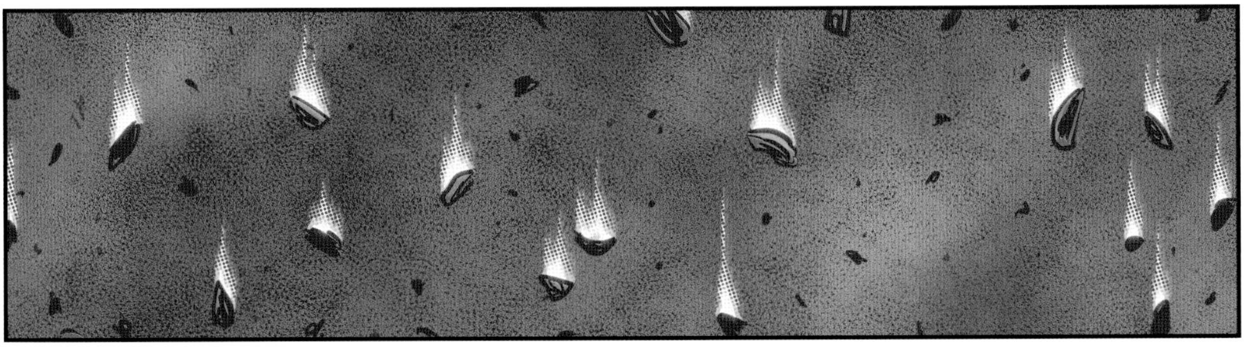

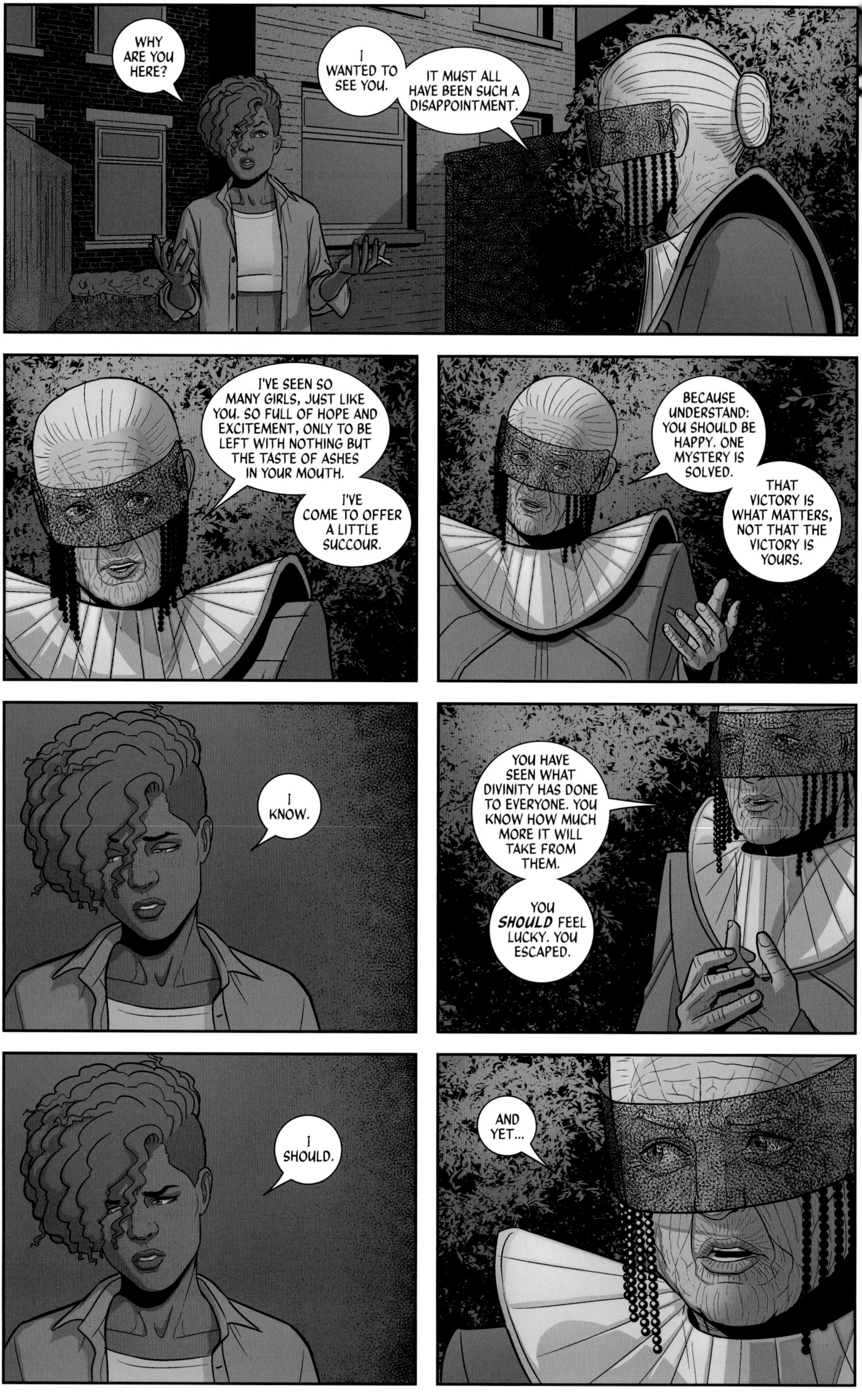
WHY ARE YOU HERE?
I WANTED TO SEE YOU.
IT MUST ALL HAVE BEEN SUCH A DISAPPOINTMENT.
I'VE SEEN SO MANY GIRLS, JUST LIKE YOU. SO FULL OF HOPE AND EXCITEMENT, ONLY TO BE LEFT WITH NOTHING BUT THE TASTE OF ASHES IN YOUR MOUTH.
I'VE COME TO OFFER A LITTLE SUCCOUR.
BECAUSE UNDERSTAND: YOU SHOULD BE HAPPY. ONE MYSTERY IS SOLVED.
THAT VICTORY IS WHAT MATTERS, NOT THAT THE VICTORY IS YOURS.
I KNOW.
YOU HAVE SEEN WHAT DIVINITY HAS DONE TO EVERYONE. YOU KNOW HOW MUCH MORE IT WILL TAKE FROM THEM.
YOU ***SHOULD*** FEEL LUCKY. YOU ESCAPED.
I SHOULD.
AND YET...

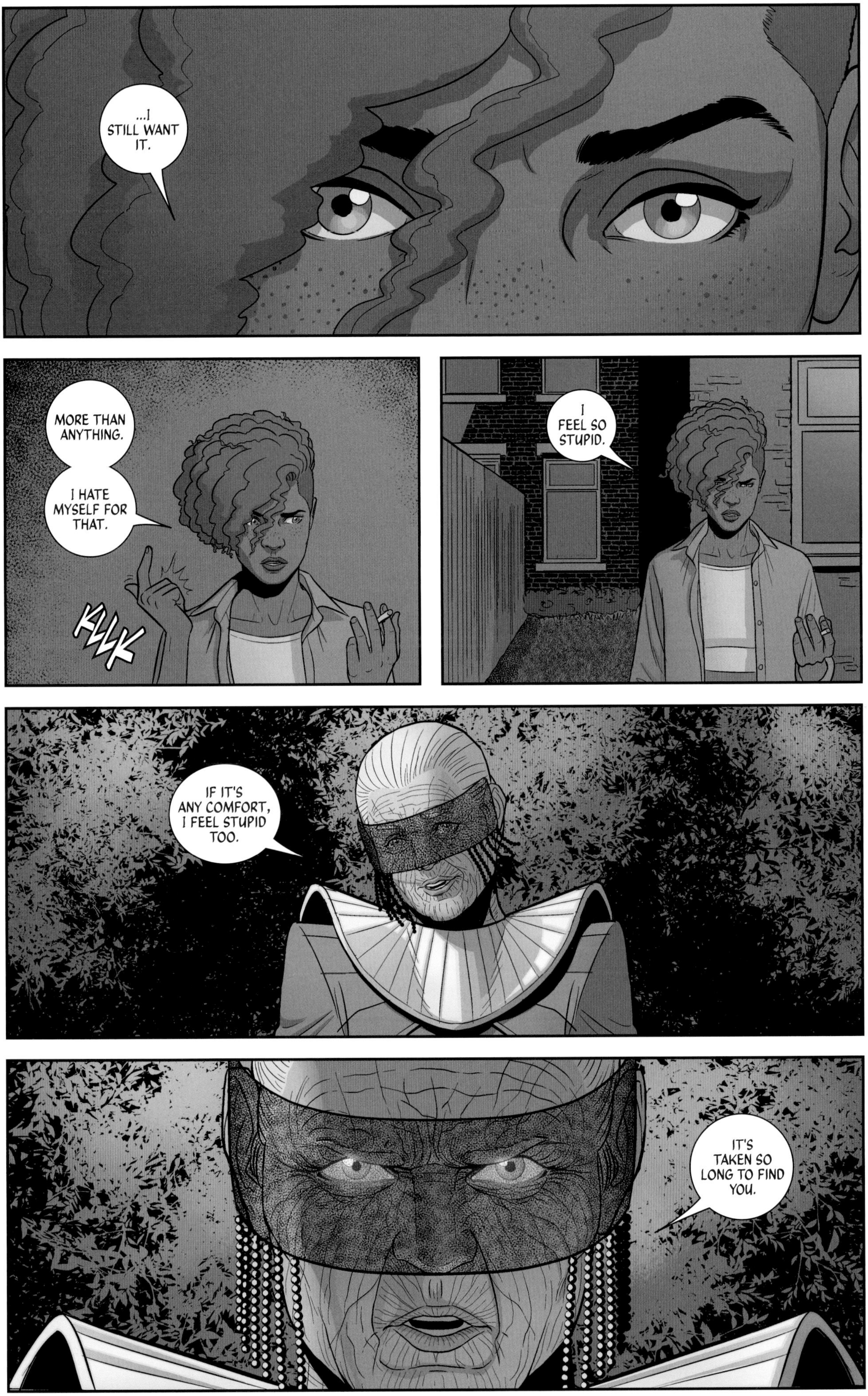
...I STILL WANT IT.
MORE THAN ANYTHING.
I HATE MYSELF FOR THAT.
KLLK
I FEEL SO STUPID.
IF IT'S ANY COMFORT, I FEEL STUPID TOO.
IT'S TAKEN SO LONG TO FIND YOU.

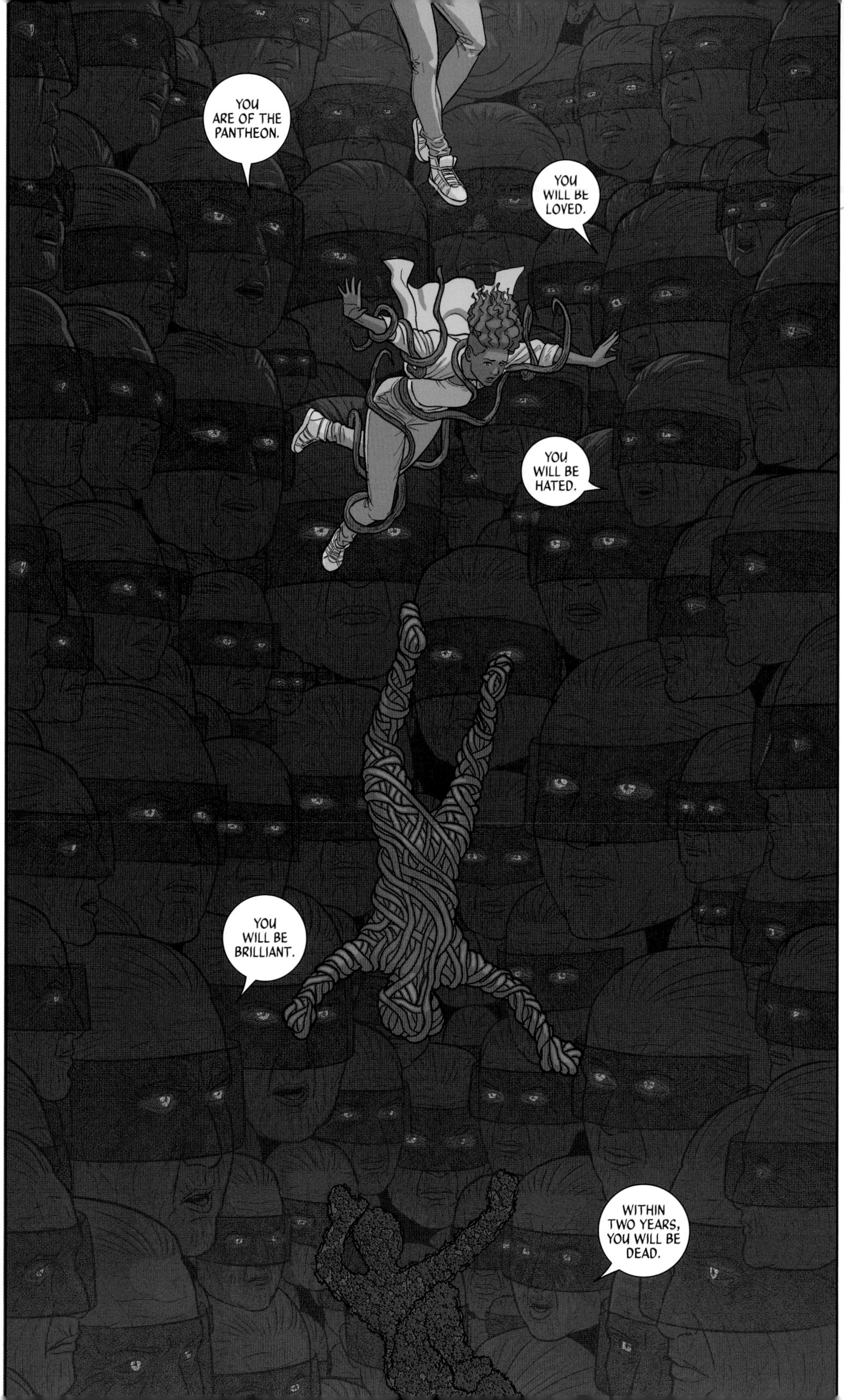
YOU ARE OF THE PANTHEON.
YOU WILL BE LOVED.
YOU WILL BE HATED.
YOU WILL BE BRILLIANT.
WITHIN TWO YEARS, YOU WILL BE DEAD.

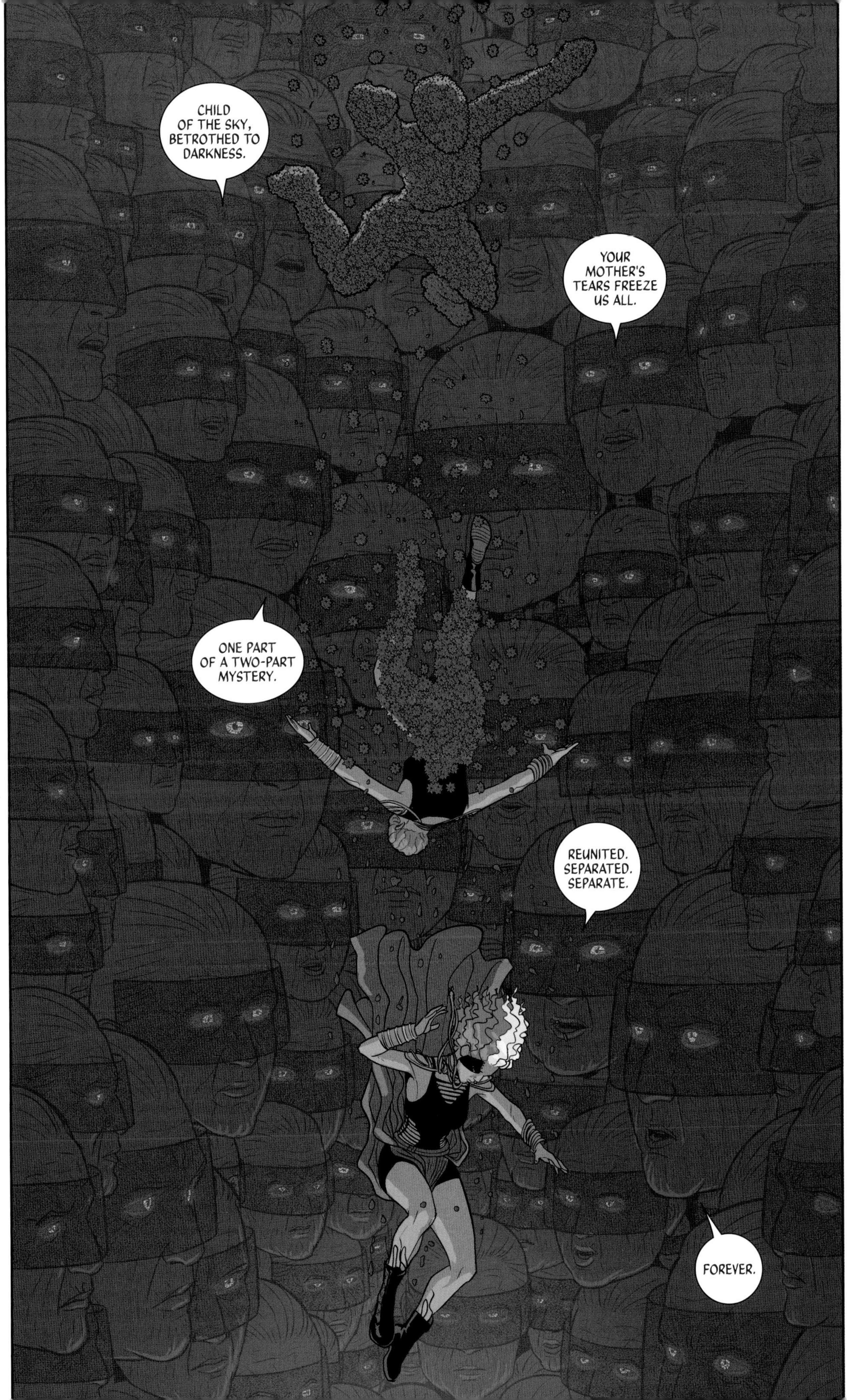
CHILD OF THE SKY, BETROTHED TO DARKNESS.
YOUR MOTHER'S TEARS FREEZE US ALL.
ONE PART OF A TWO-PART MYSTERY.
REUNITED. SEPARATED. SEPARATE.
FOREVER.

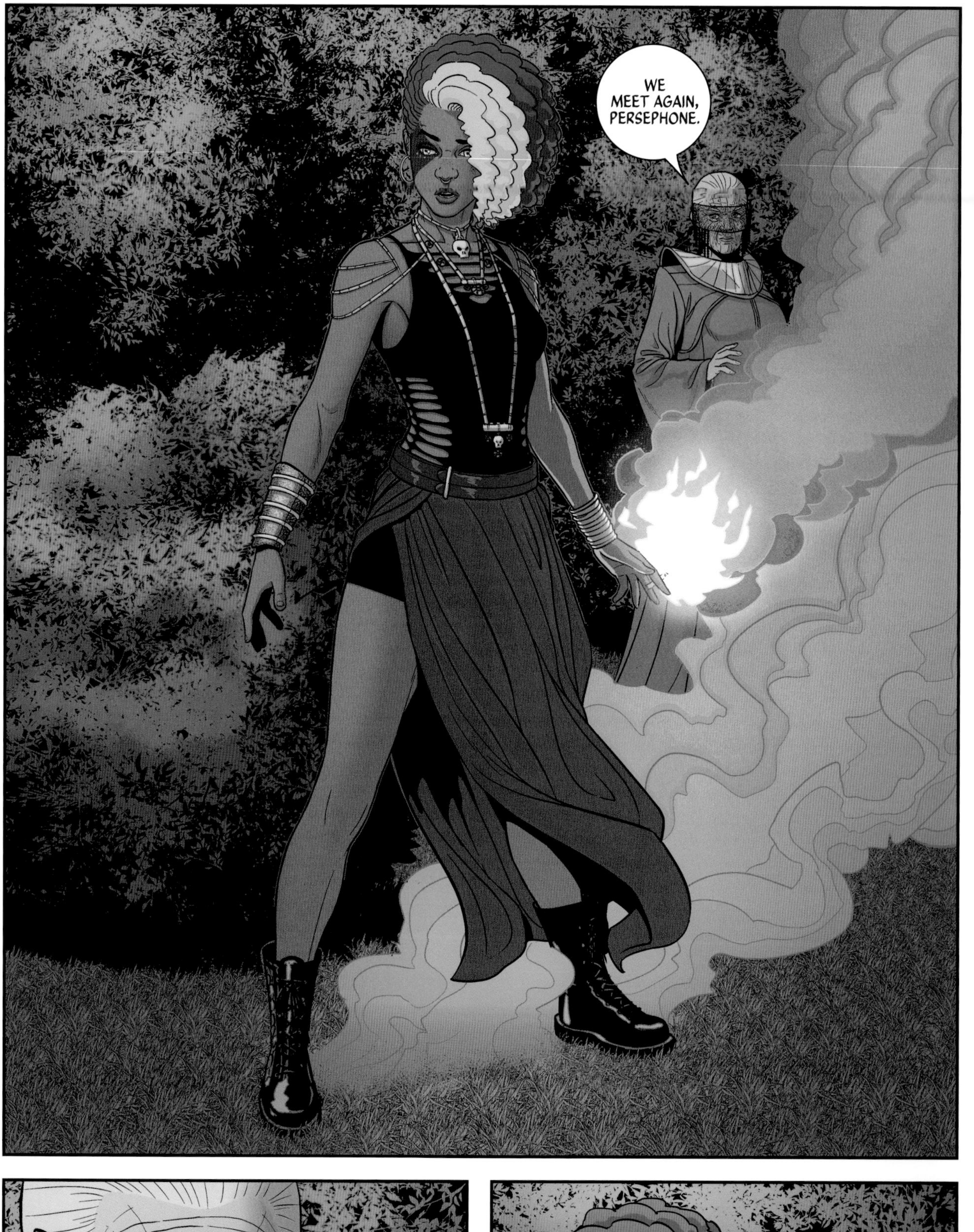
WE MEET AGAIN, PERSEPHONE.
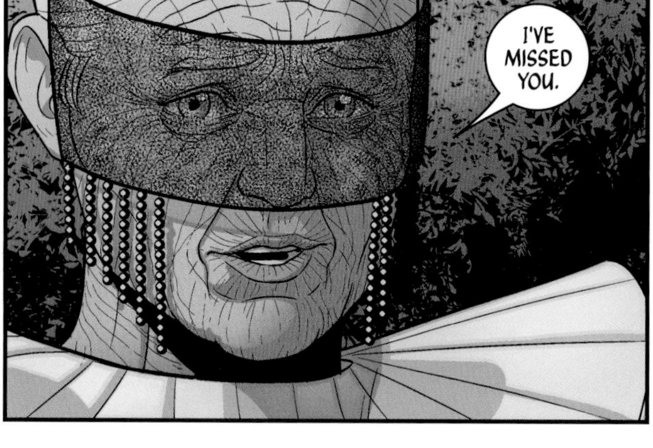
I'VE MISSED YOU.
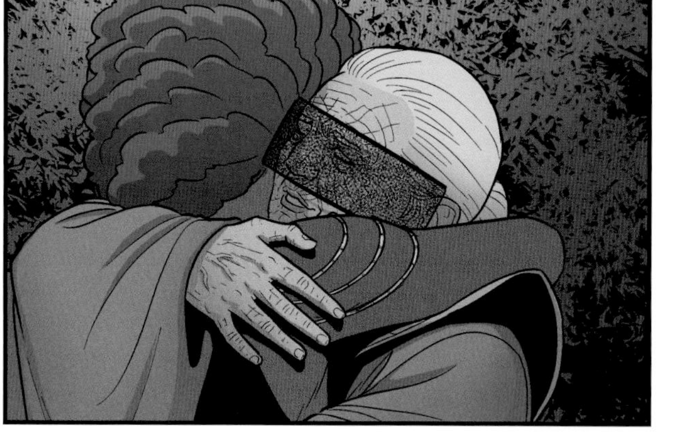

PERSEPHONE

3 AUGUST 2014

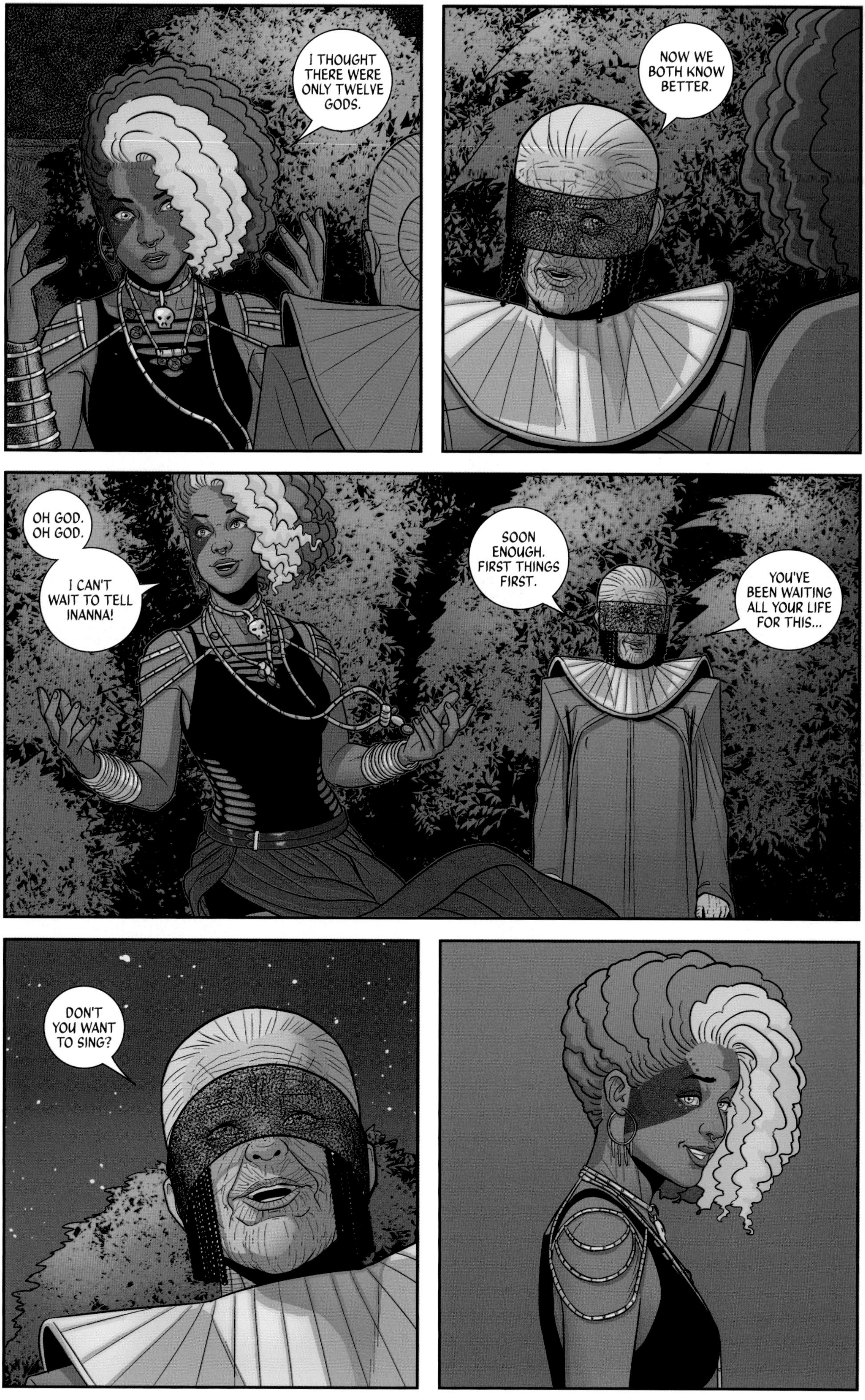
I THOUGHT THERE WERE ONLY TWELVE GODS.
NOW WE BOTH KNOW BETTER.
OH GOD. OH GOD.
I CAN'T WAIT TO TELL INANNA!
SOON ENOUGH. FIRST THINGS FIRST.
YOU'VE BEEN WAITING ALL YOUR LIFE FOR THIS...
DON'T YOU WANT TO SING?

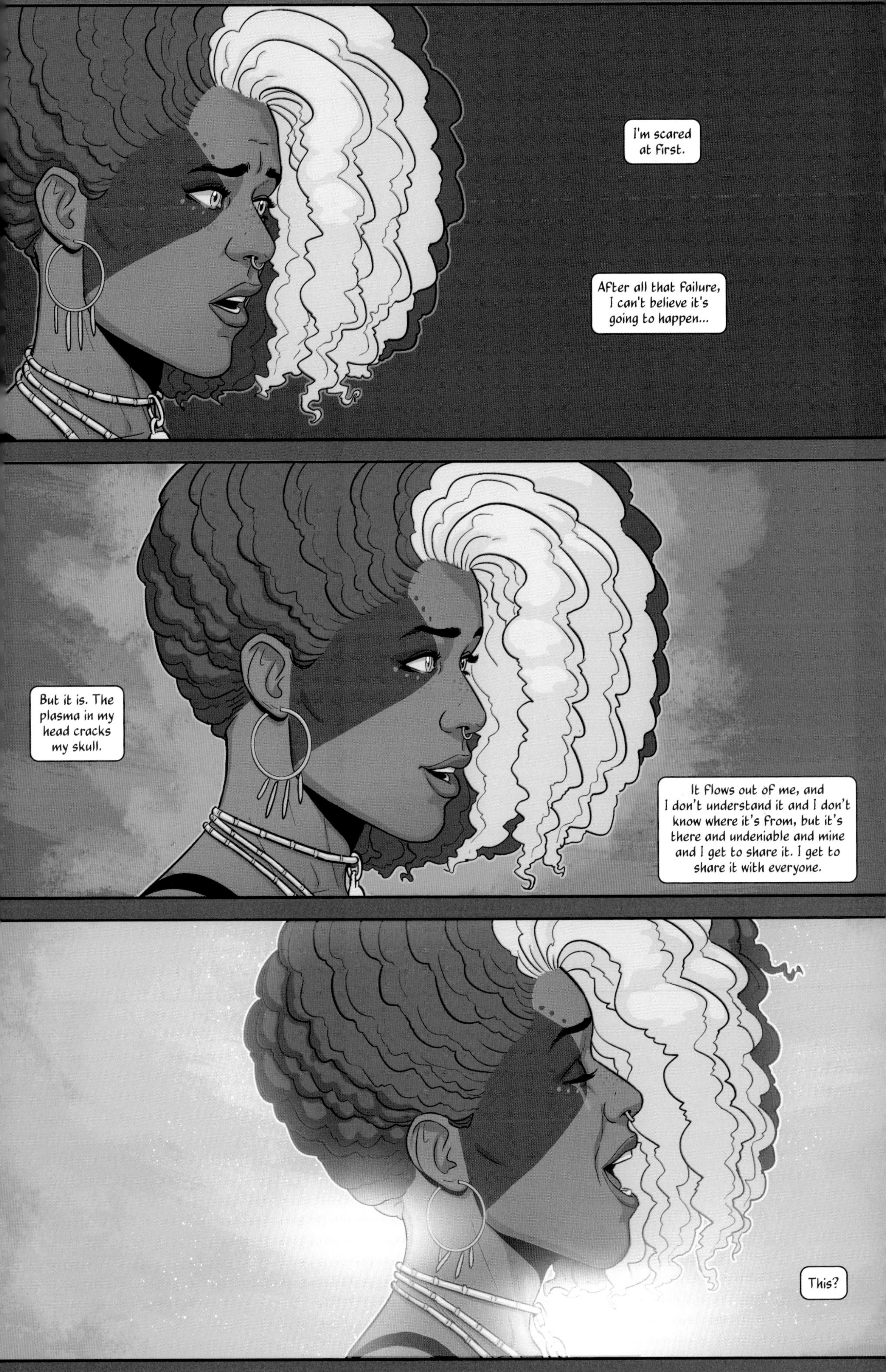
I'm scared at first.
After all that failure, I can't believe it's going to happen...
But it is. The plasma in my head cracks my skull.
It flows out of me, and I don't understand it and I don't know where it's from, but it's there and undeniable and mine and I get to share it. I get to share it with everyone.
This?

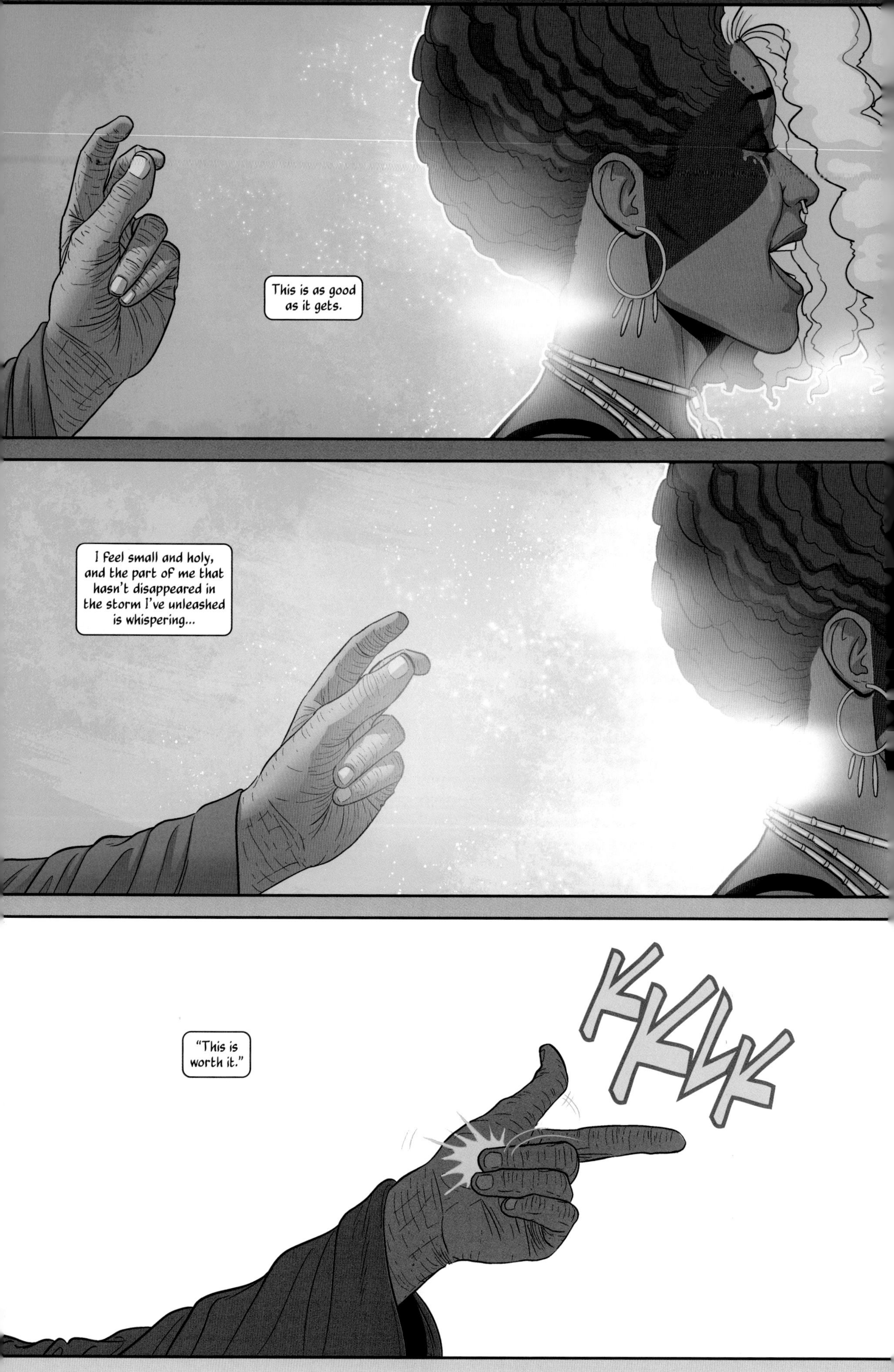
This is as good as it gets.
I feel small and holy, and the part of me that hasn't disappeared in the storm I've unleashed is whispering...
"This is worth it."
KKLK

I don't remember
anything after
that.

I guess I'm
grateful.

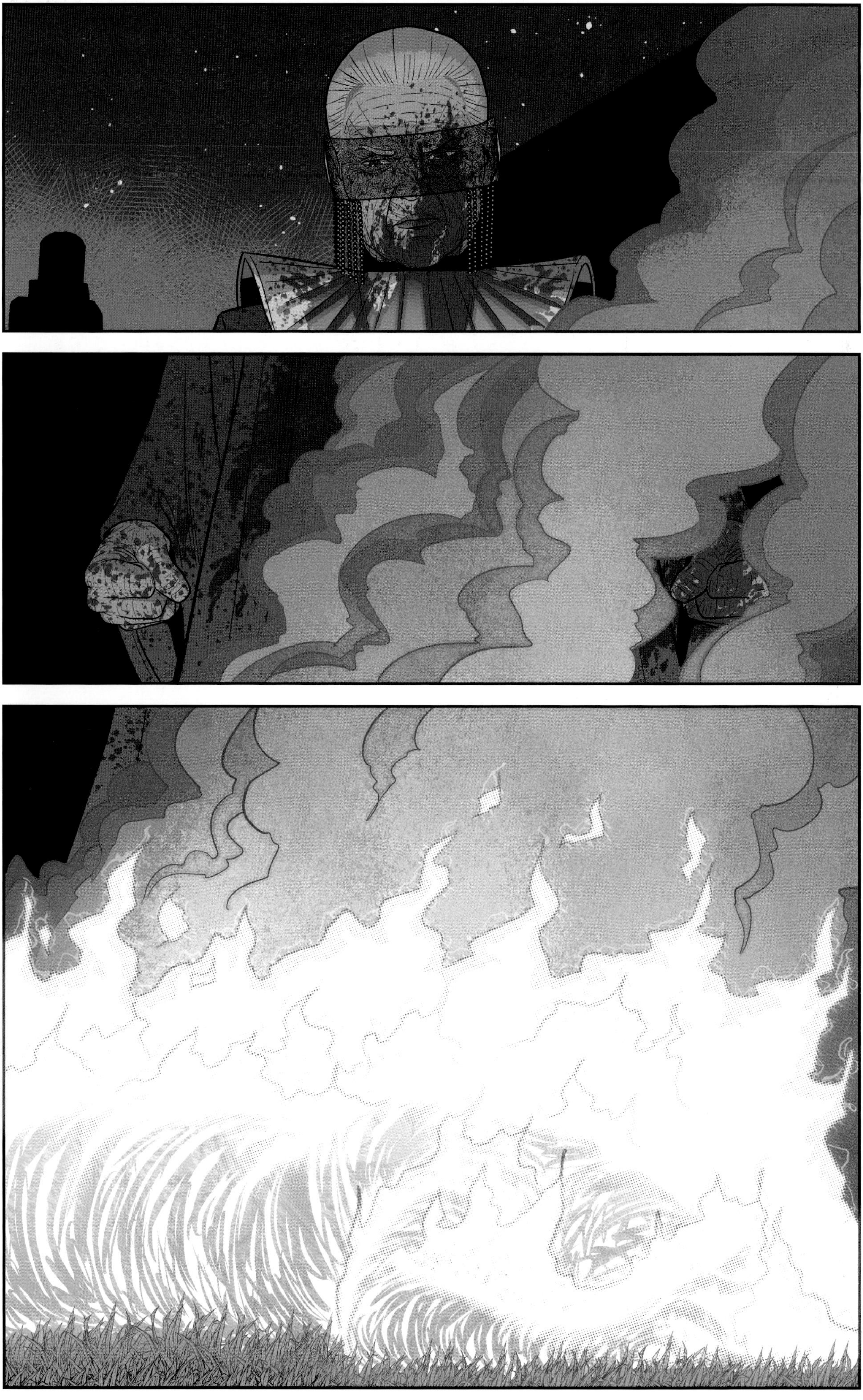

WHAT THE HELL DO YOU THINK YOU'RE DOING?
YOU'RE...
THAT FIRE. THERE'S...
NO.
FORGIVE ME.
I SHOULD HAVE LEFT MORE SWIFTLY.
SOME MURDERS ARE NECESSARY.
OTHERS ARE NOT.
KLLK

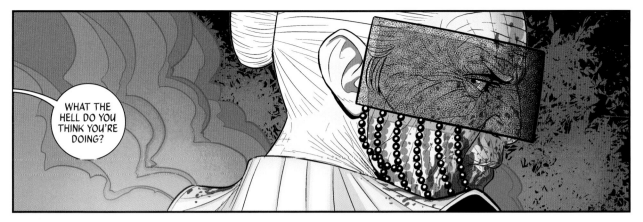

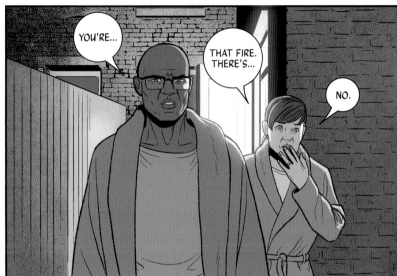

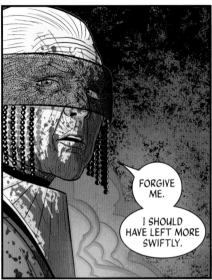

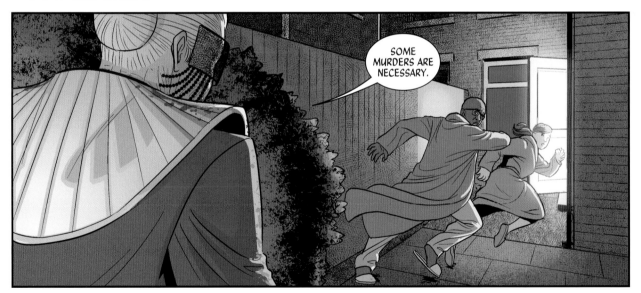

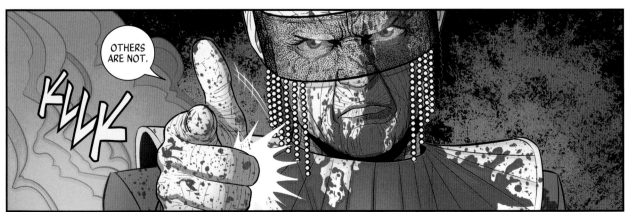

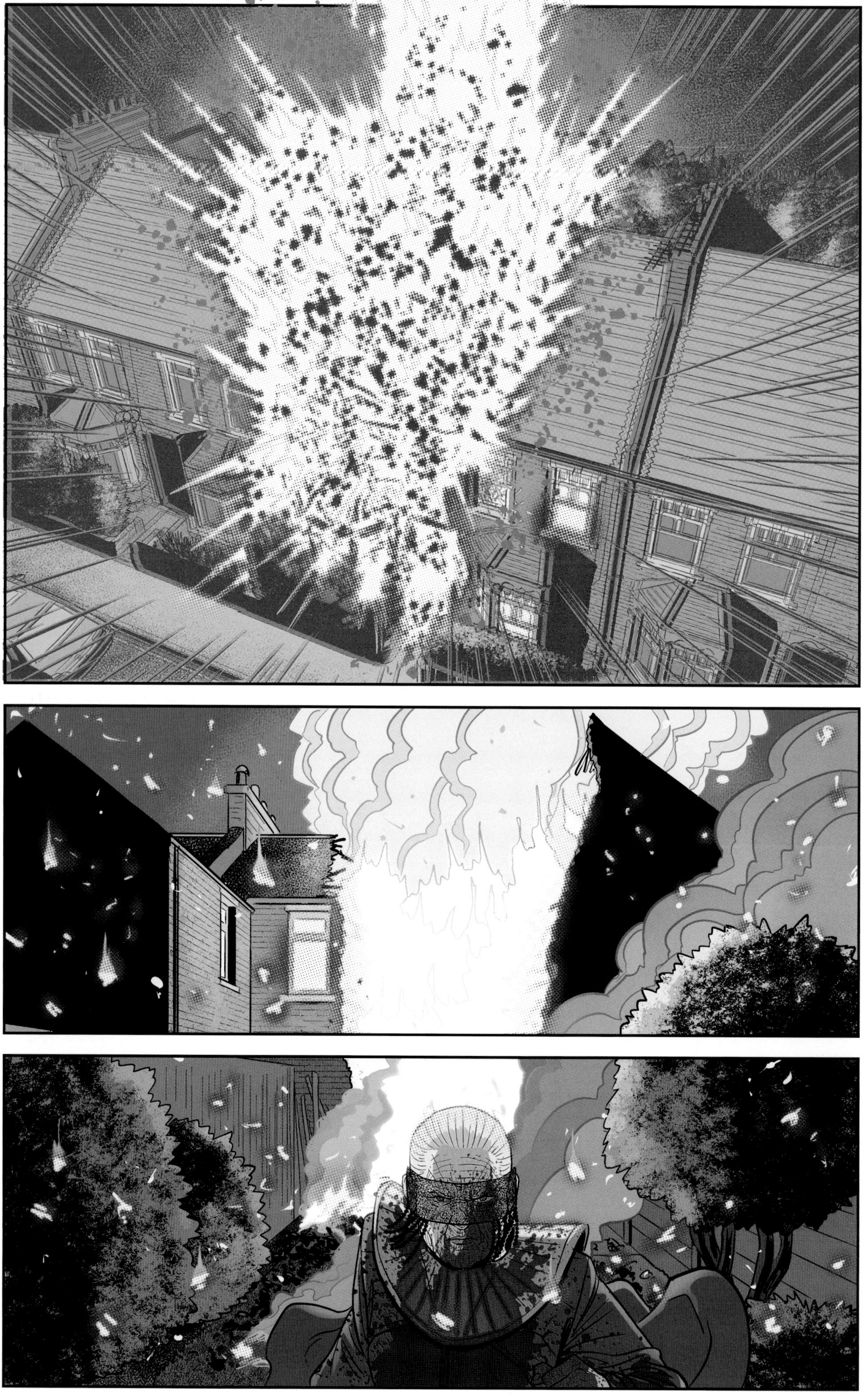

IT WAS NEVER
GOING TO BE OKAY

3 AUGUST 2014

ALTERNATE
COVERS

For most books, alternate covers act primarily as a device to drive sales. In *WicDiv*, they ended up as something else, and unless something changes dramatically across our run, we'll have an alternate for every issue. In a book that's so much about the characters as icons, treating them as such, and inviting our talented friends to interpret them in their own style, seemed to be an excellent thing to do. We strongly suspect that the following gallery proves our point, and if you disagree, we'll fight you. Yeah, you heard.

Jamie McKelvie
Issue one cover
(Coloured by Matthew Wilson)

Bryan Lee O'Malley
Issue one cover

Matthew Wilson,
Jordie Bellaire
Issue one colour variants
(Bellaire bottom right)

Matthew Wilson,
Jamie McKelvie
Issue one and two colour variants
(McKelvie bottom right)

Jamie McKelvie
Issue two cover

Chip Zdarsky
Issue two cover

Jamie McKelvie
Issue three cover

Stephanie Hans
Issue three cover

Kevin Wada
Issue four cover

Jamie McKelvie
Issue five cover

Becky Cloonan
Issue five cover

David Lafuente
Issue six cover

Christian Ward
Issue seven cover

Brandon Graham
Issue eight cover

Matthew Wilson,
Jamie McKelvie
Issue nine ECCC cover

Marguerite Sauvage
Issue nine cover

Frazer Irving
Issue ten cover

Fiona Staples
Issue eleven cover

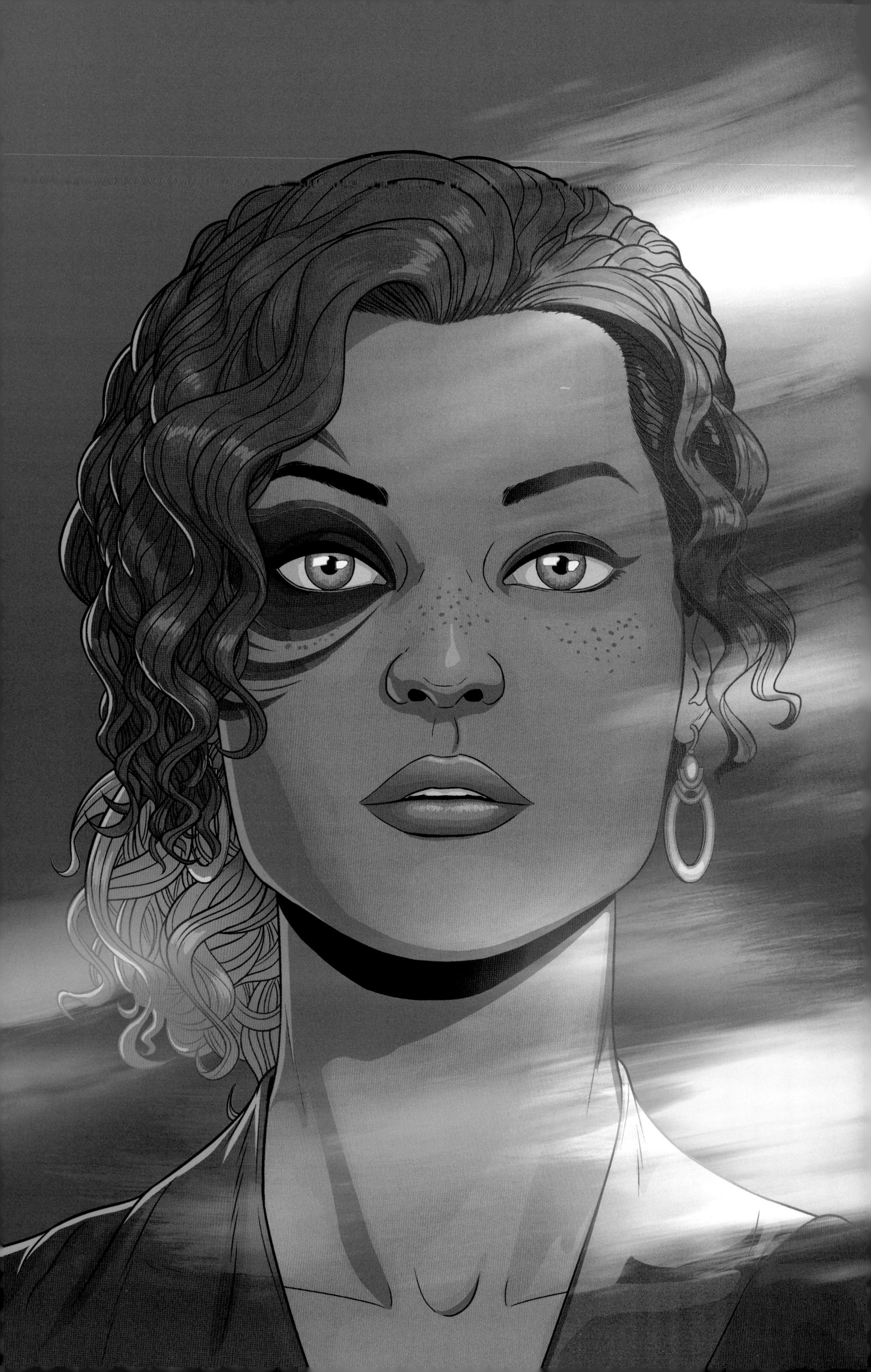

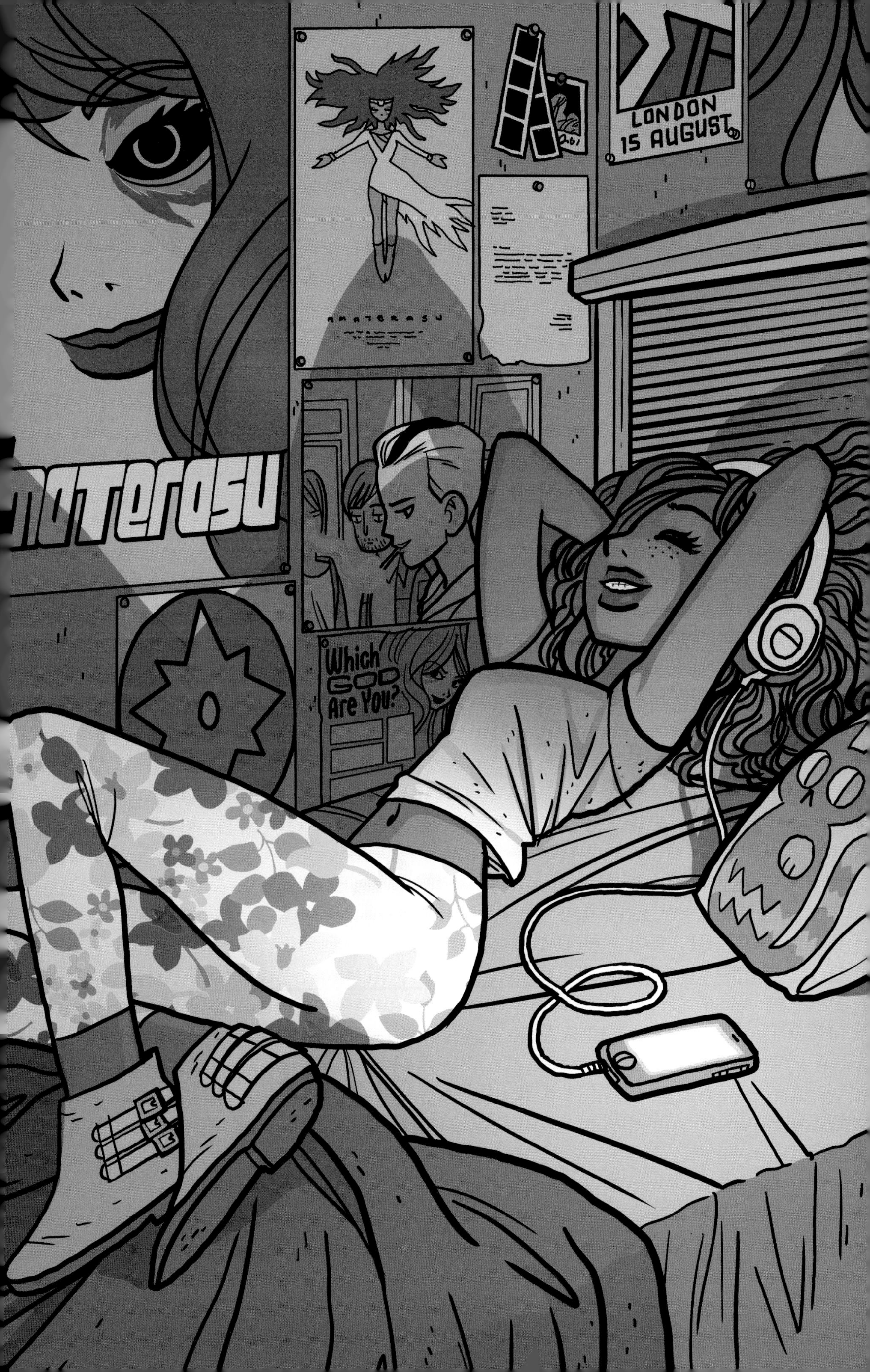
LONDON
15 AUGUST
Which GOD Are You?

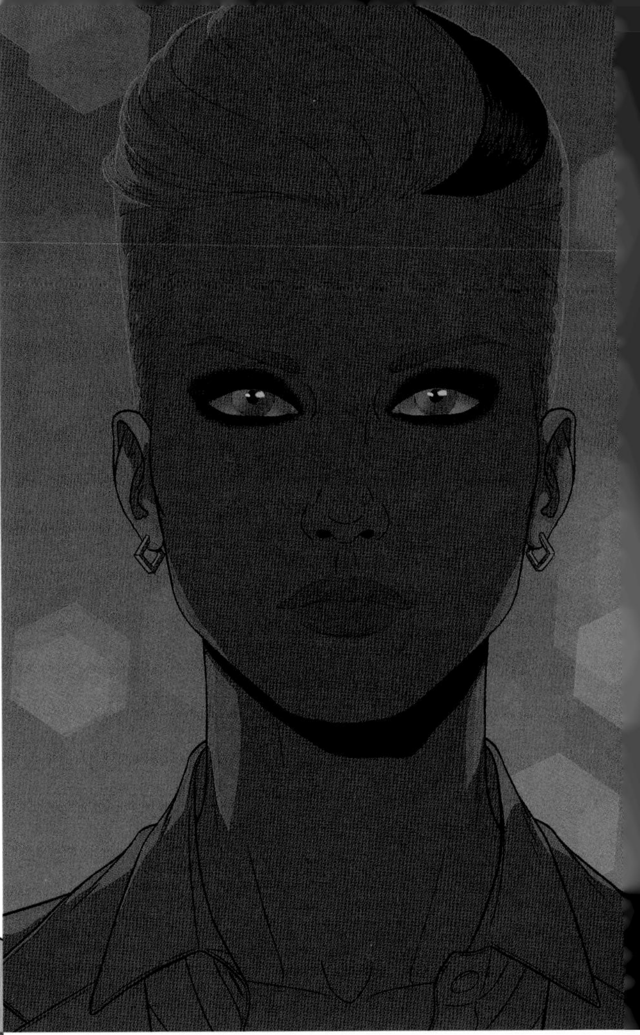
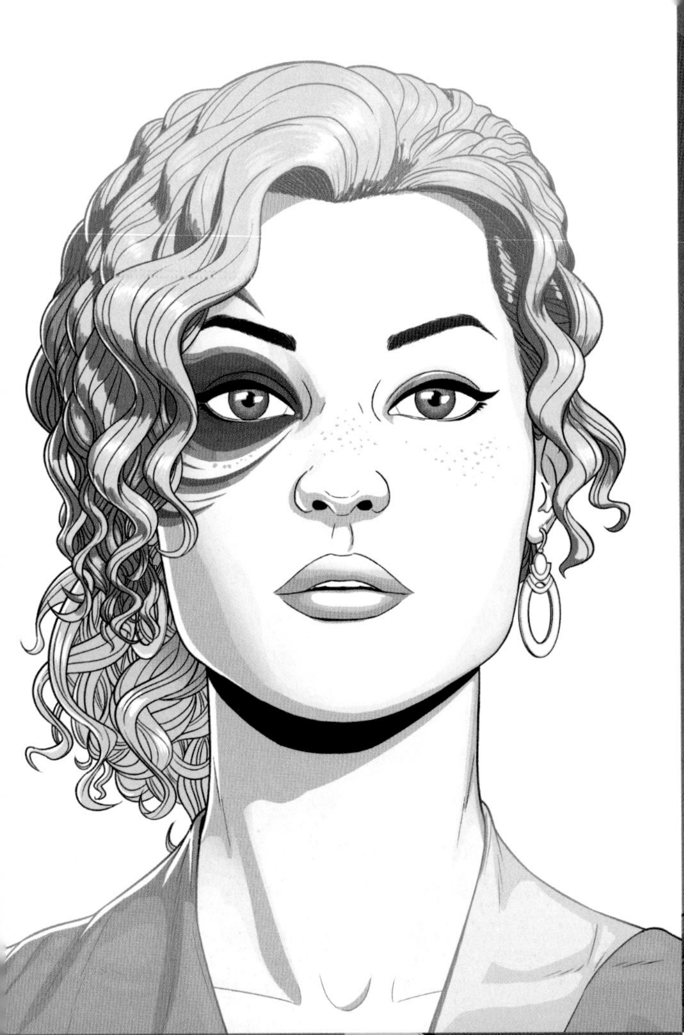
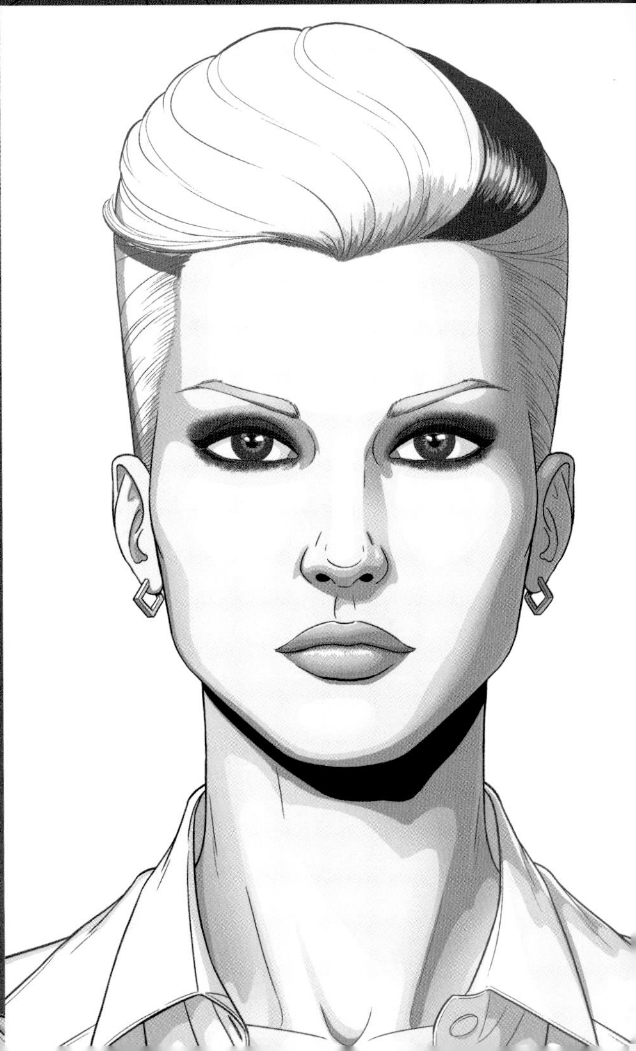
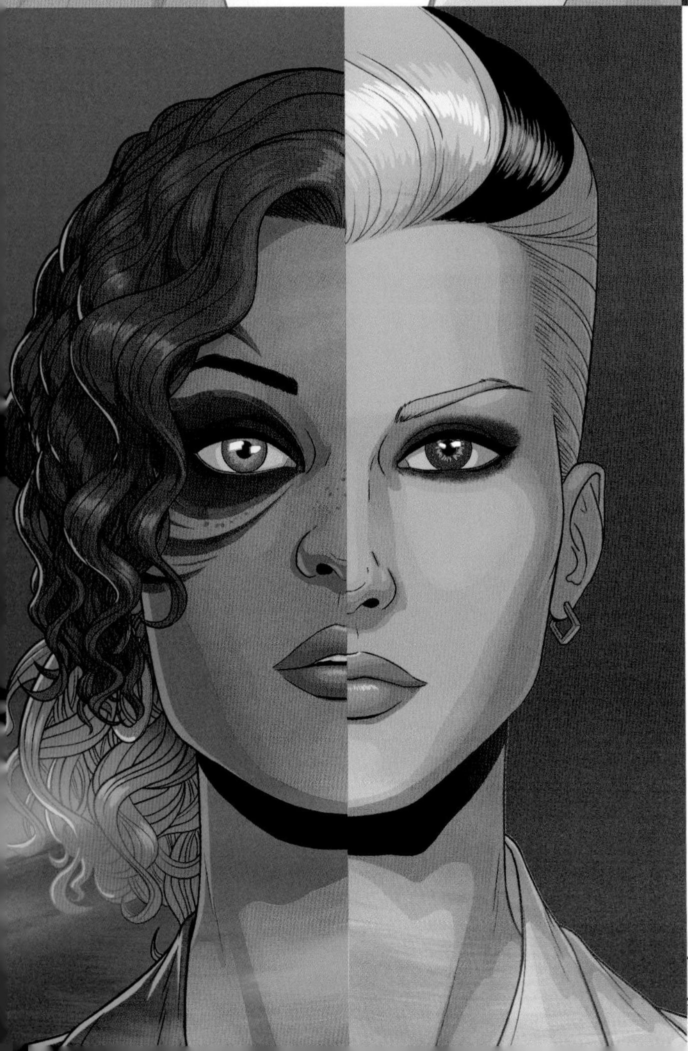

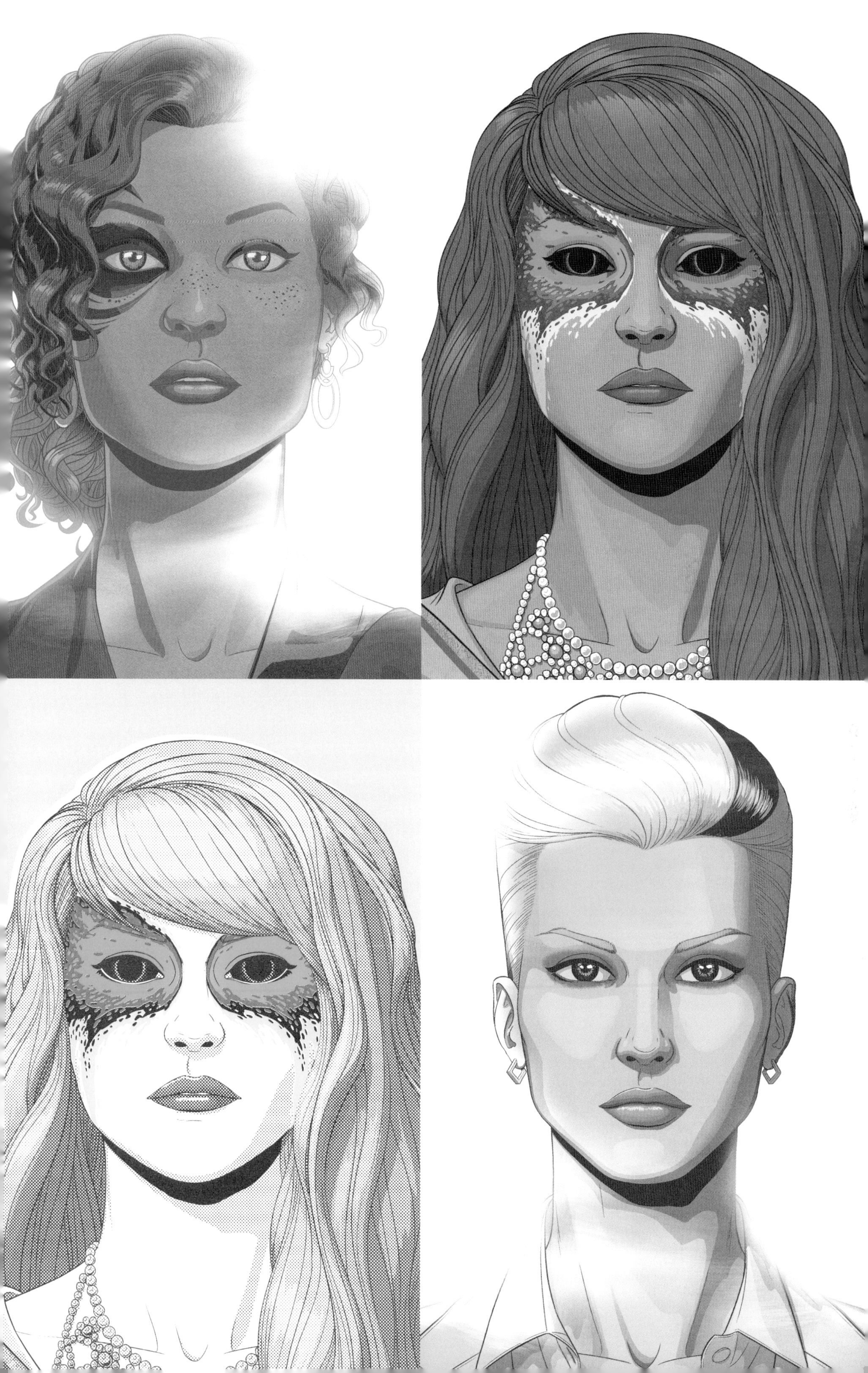

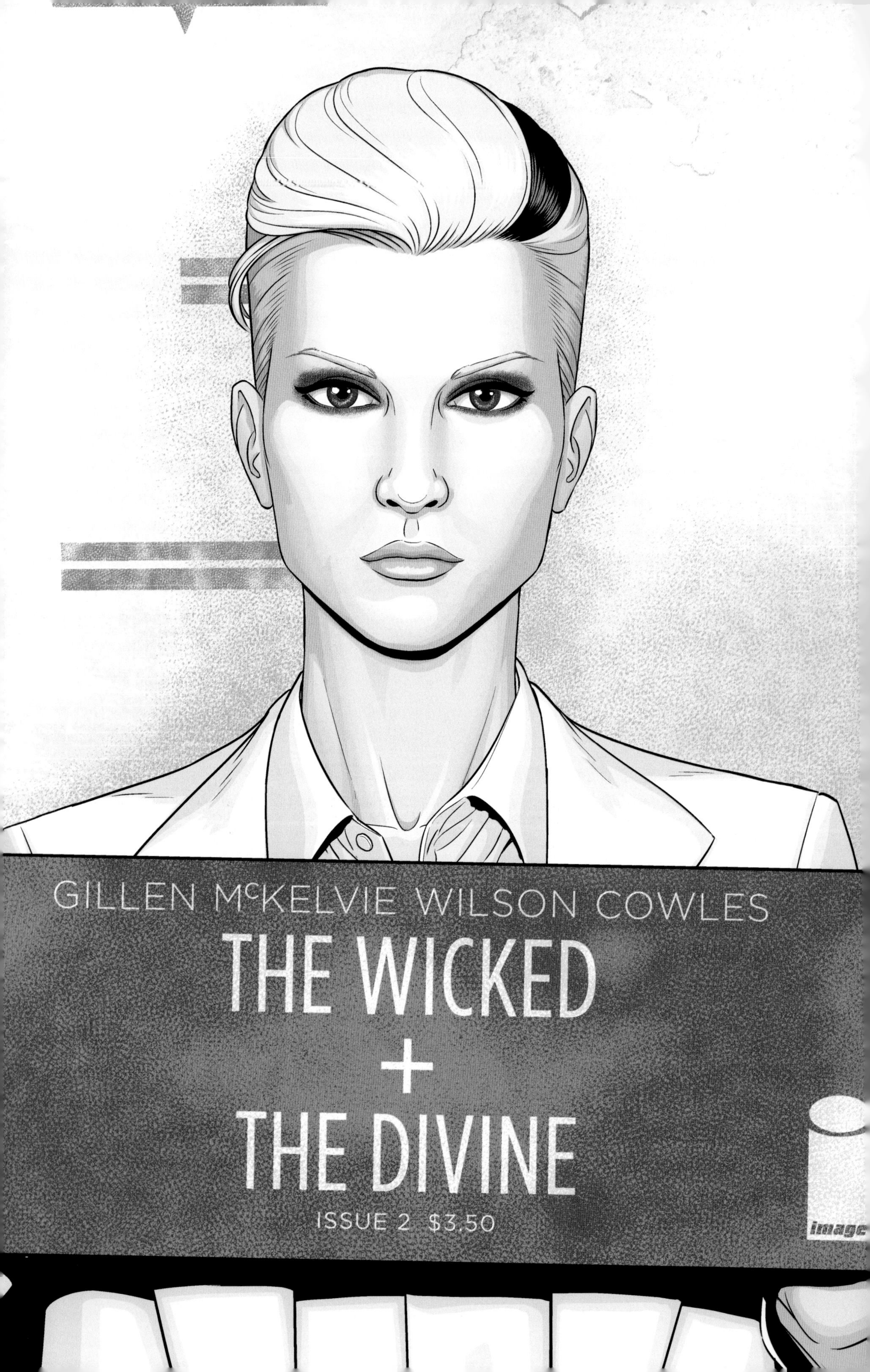
GILLEN McKELVIE WILSON COWLES
THE WICKED
+
THE DIVINE
ISSUE 2 $3.50
image

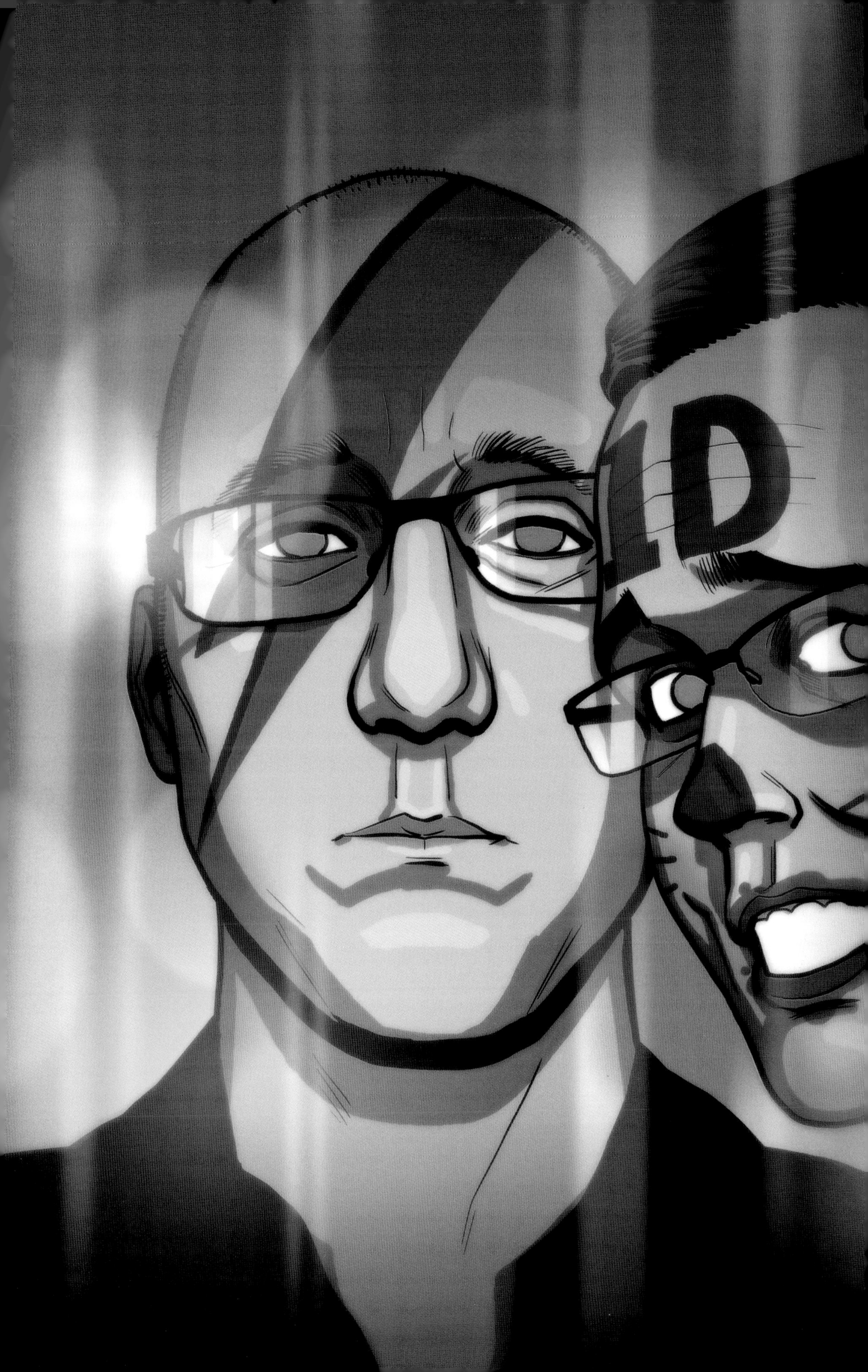
1D

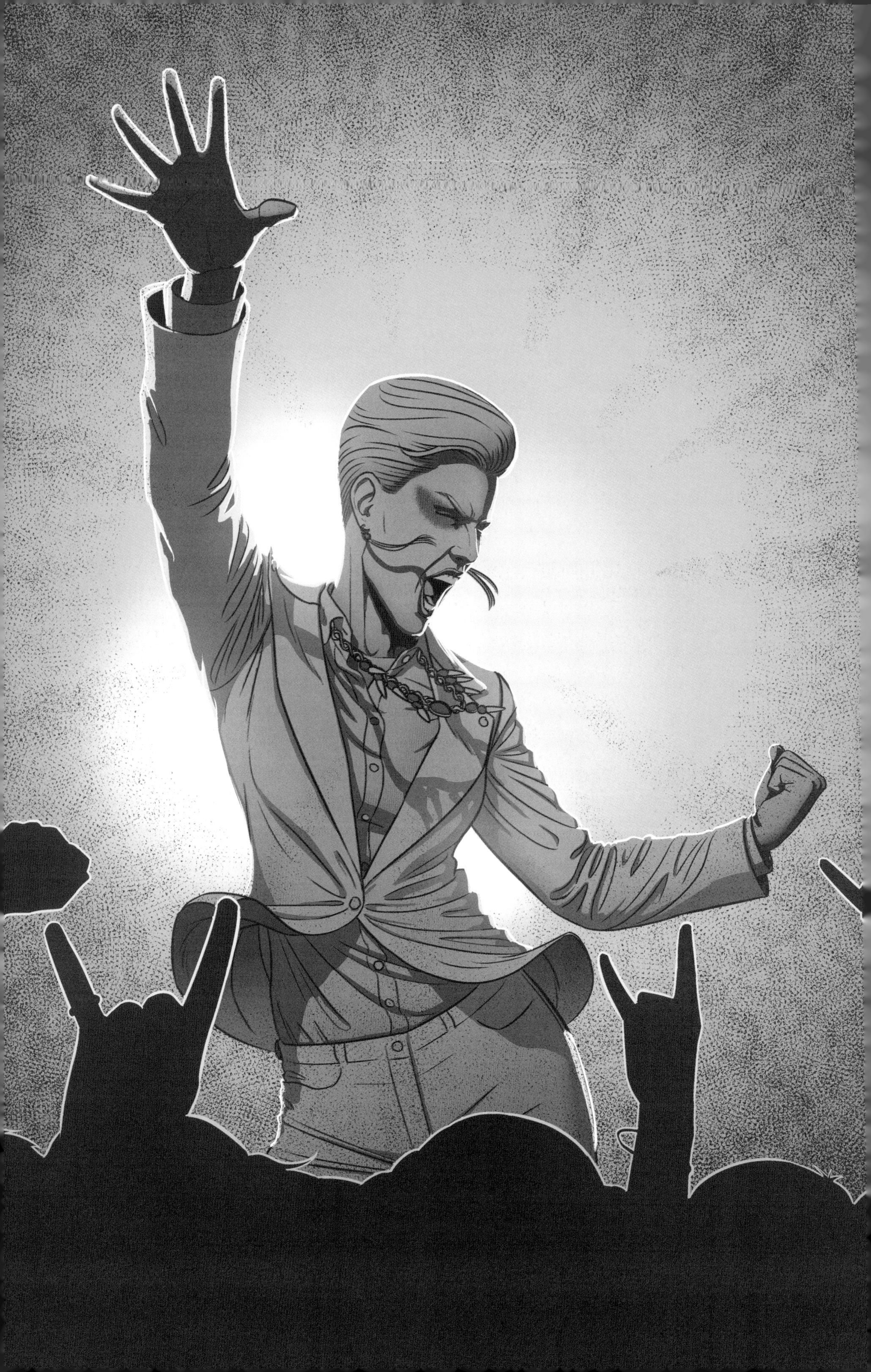

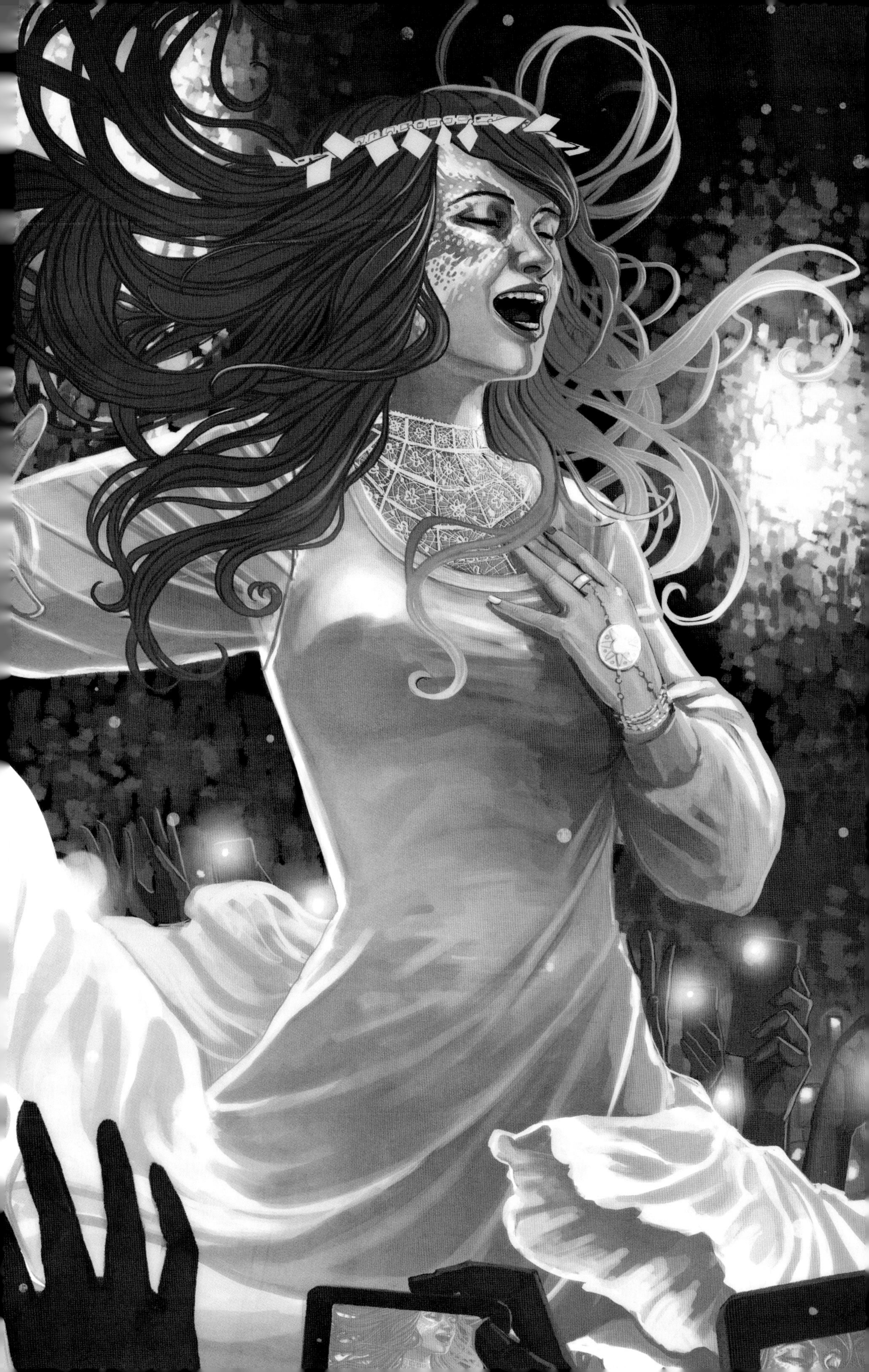

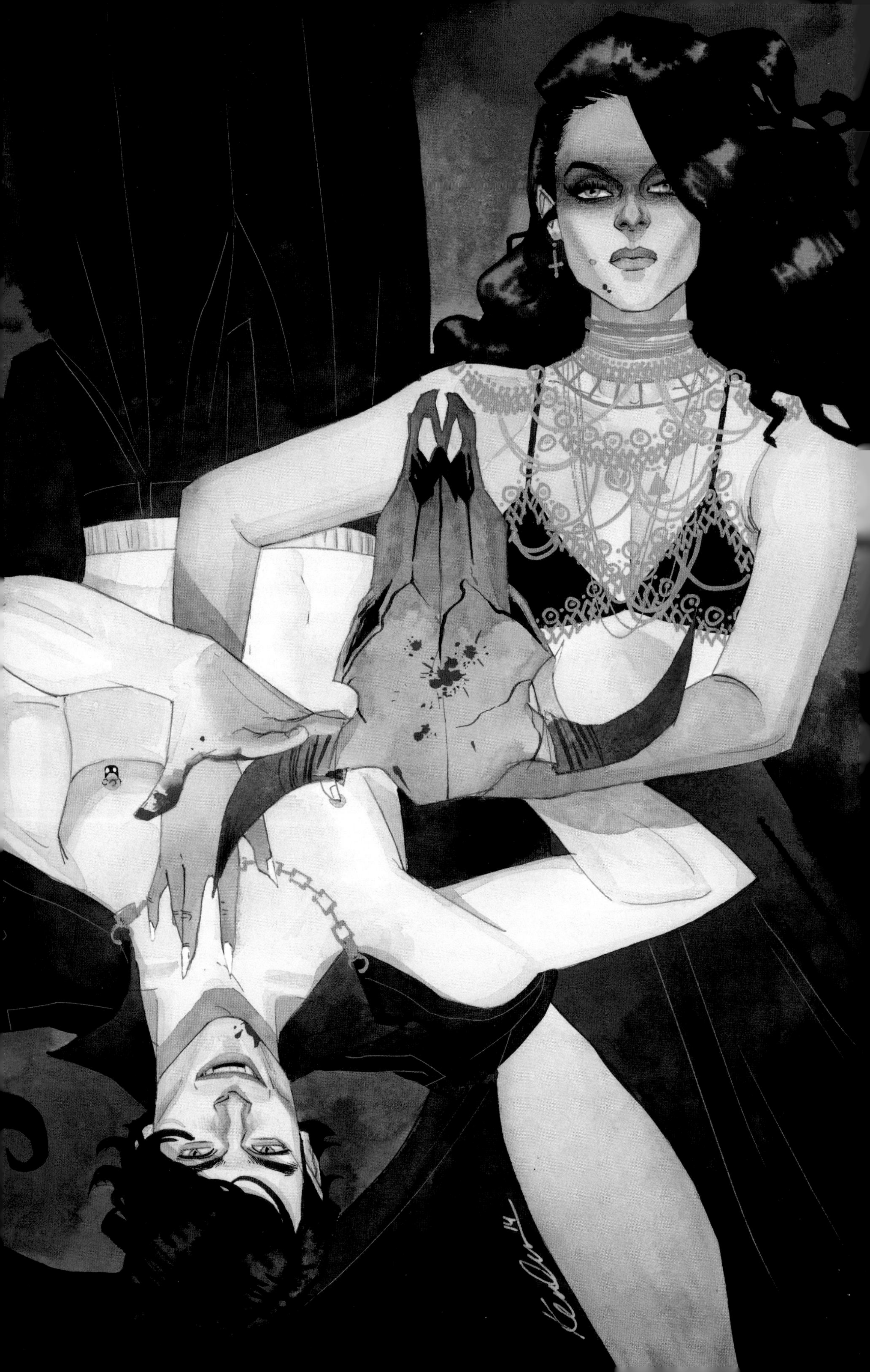

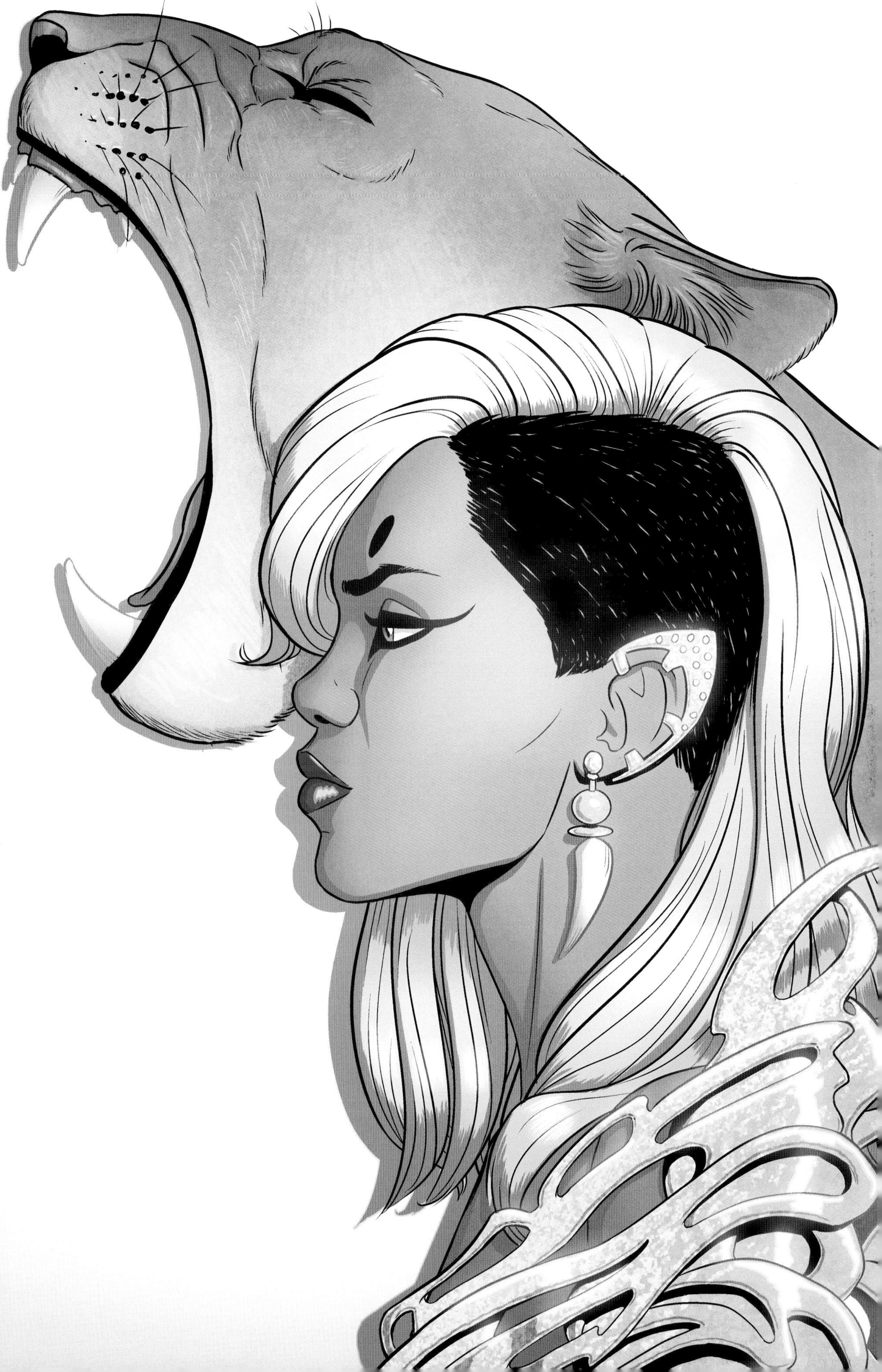

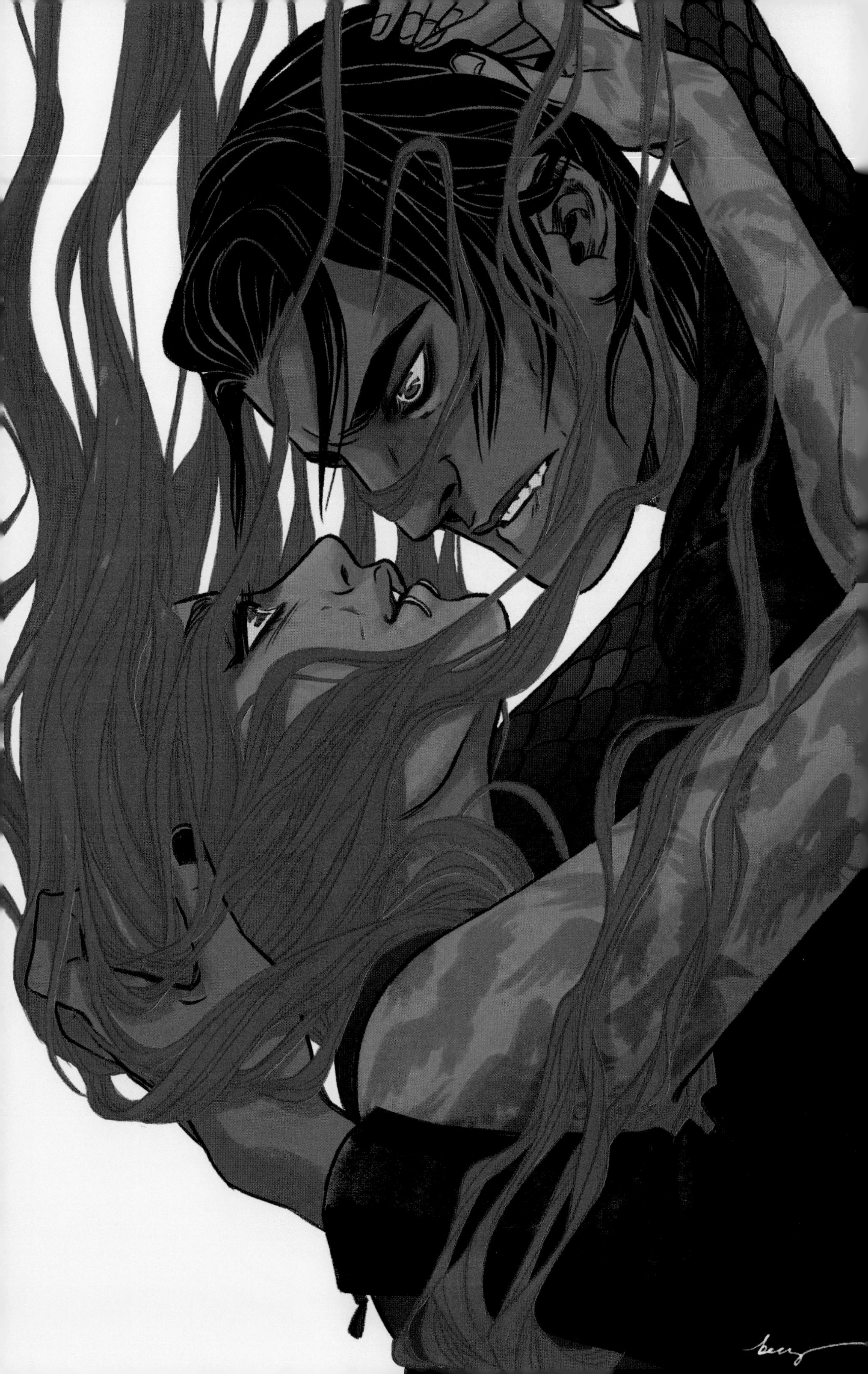

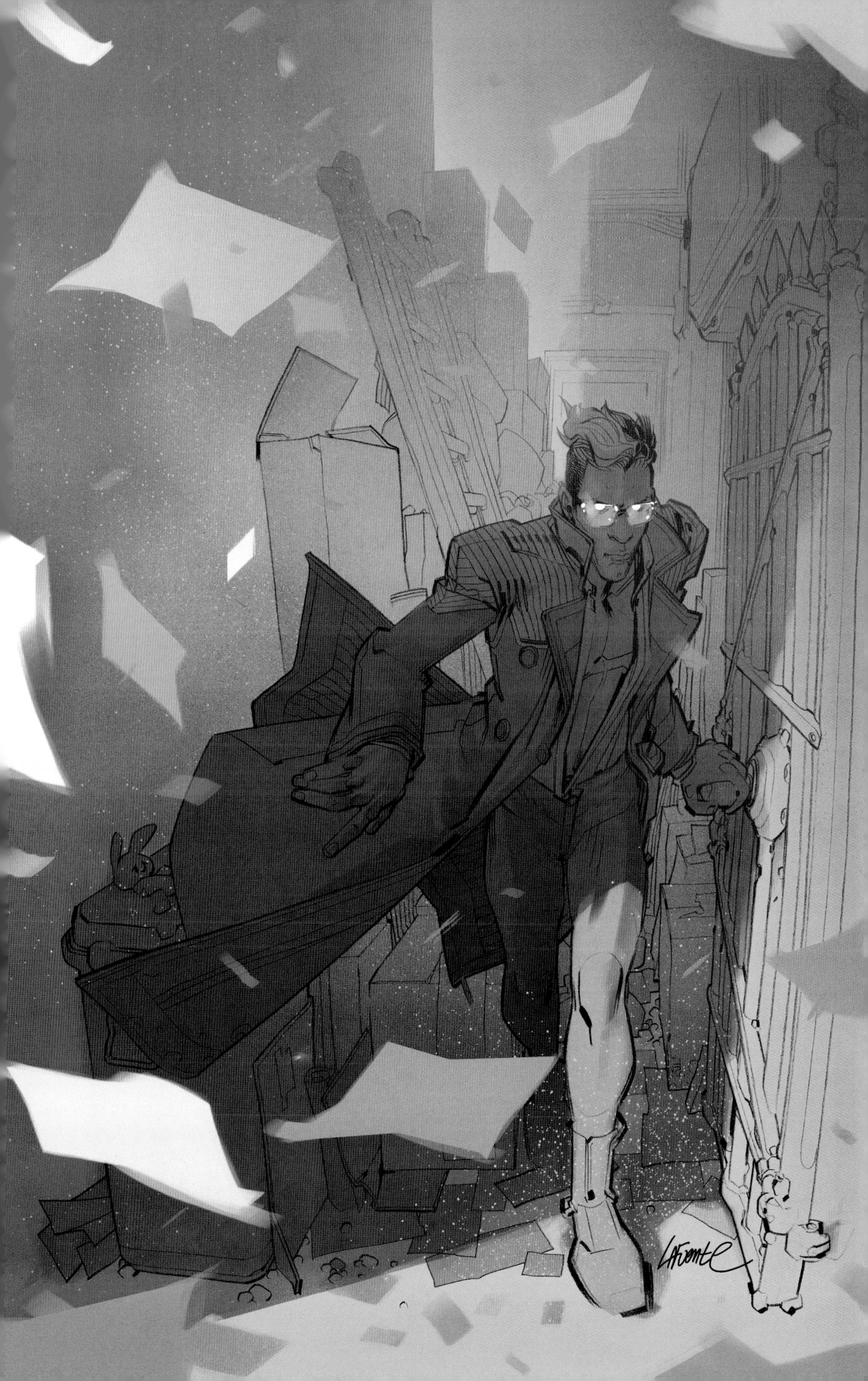

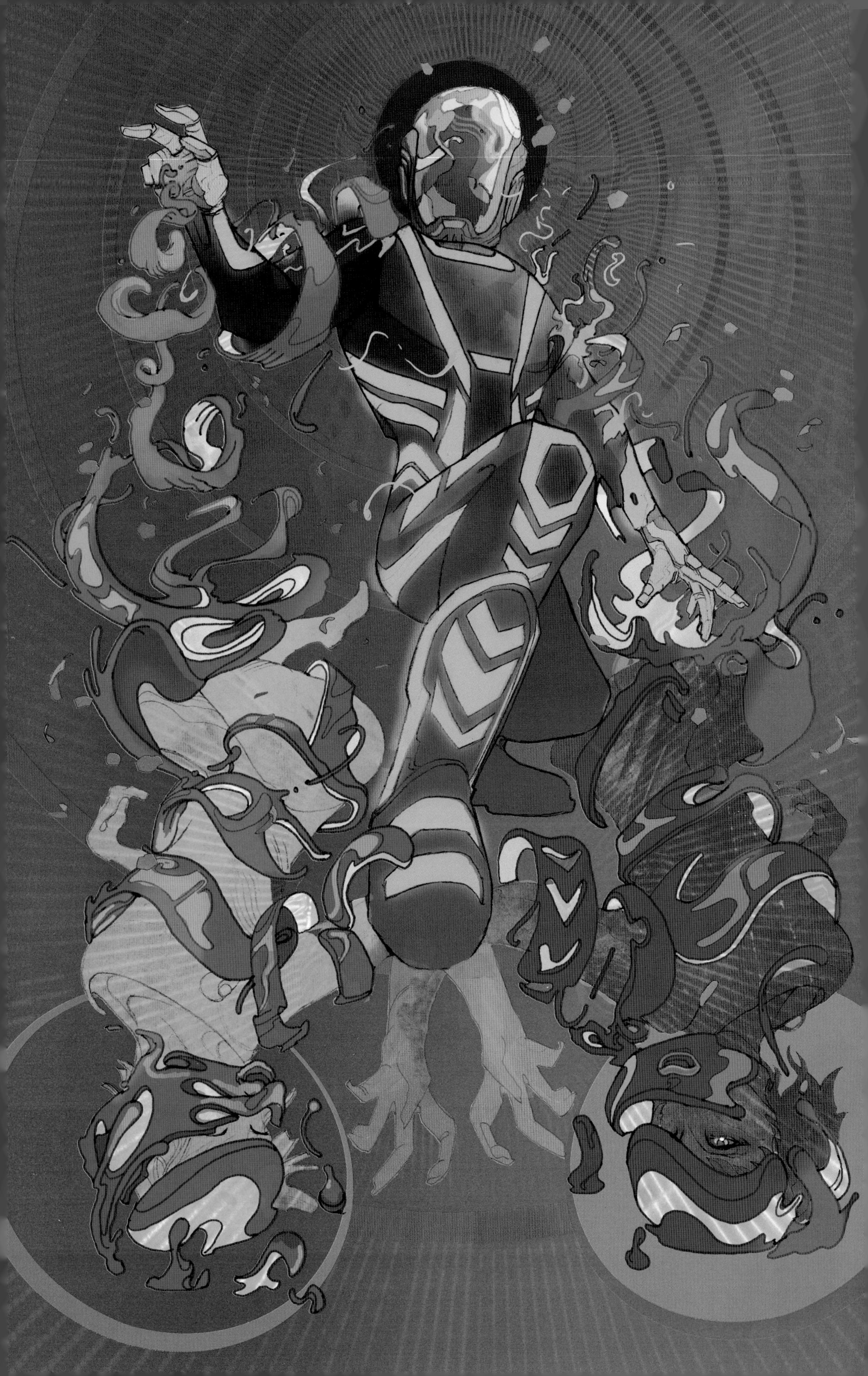

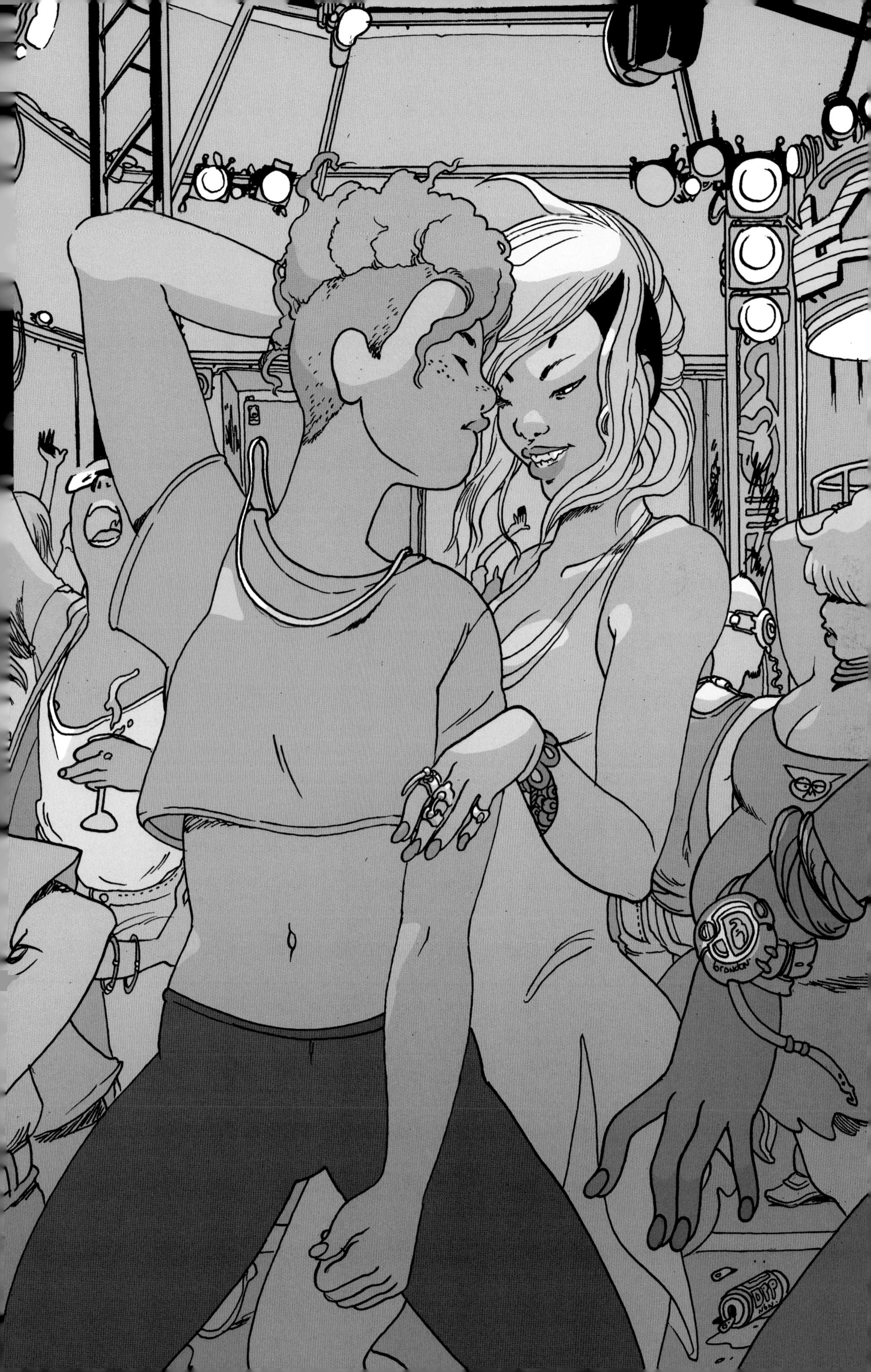

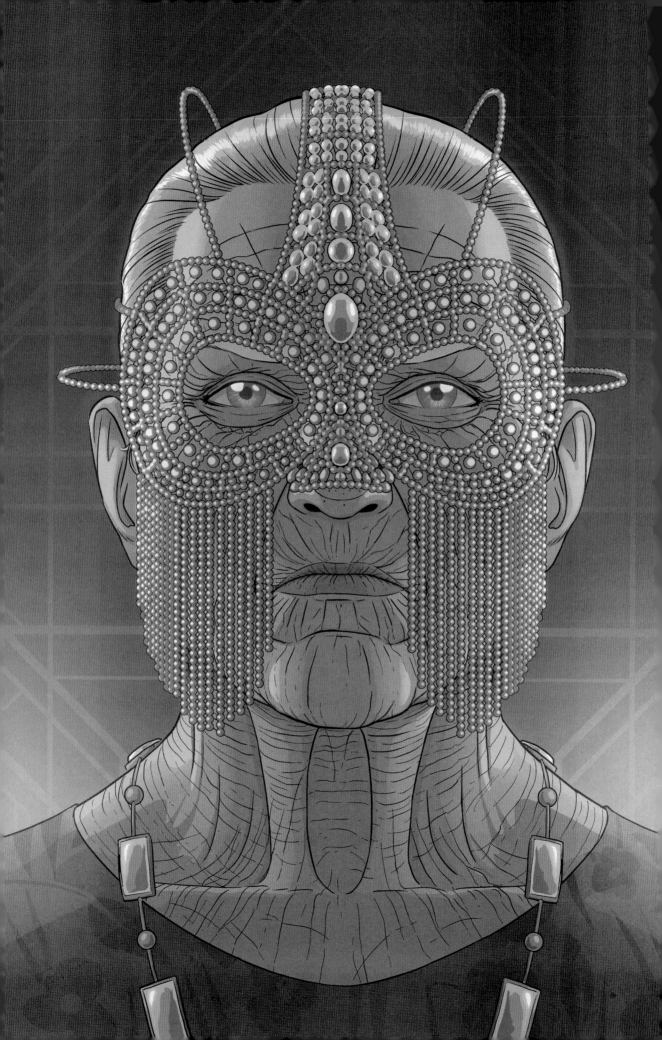

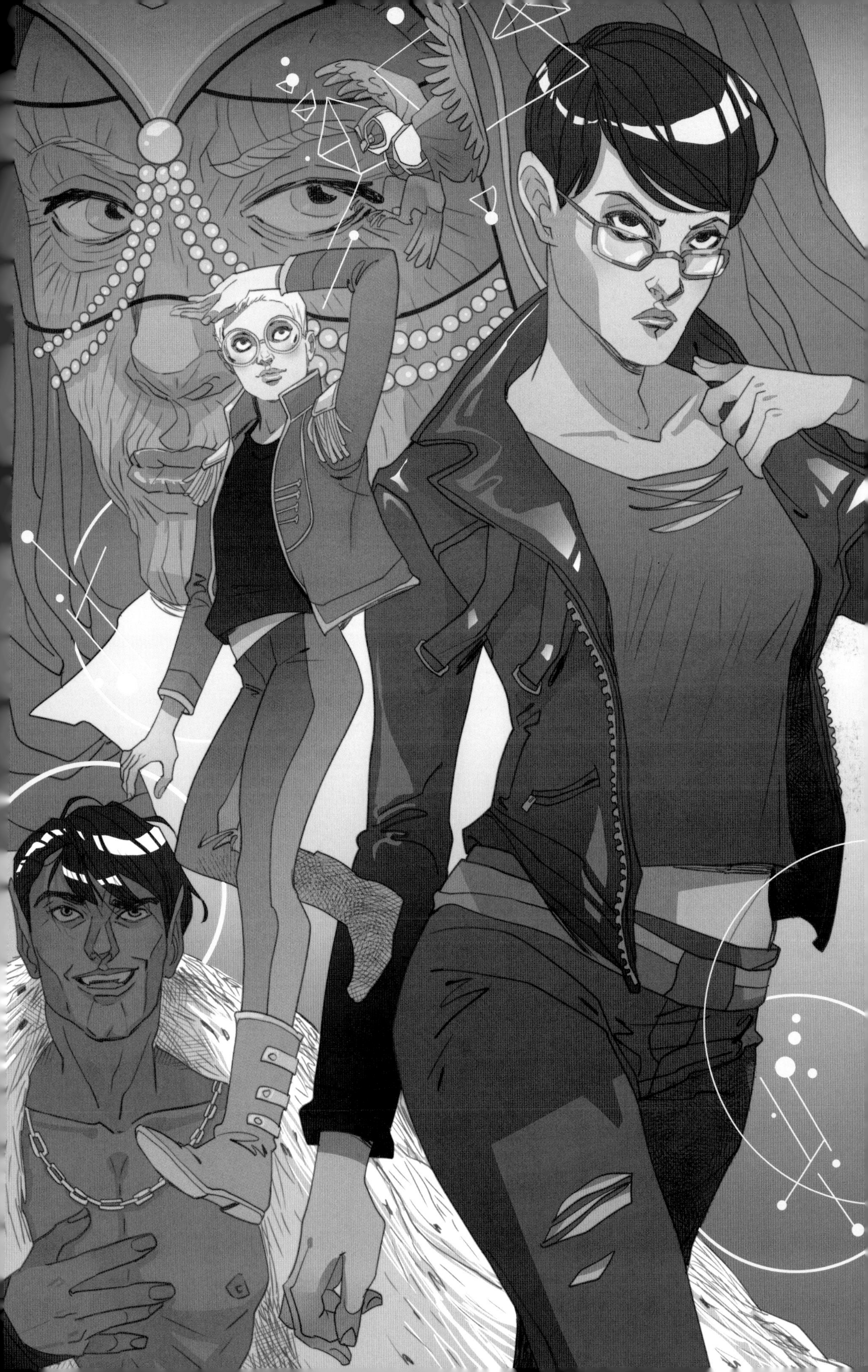

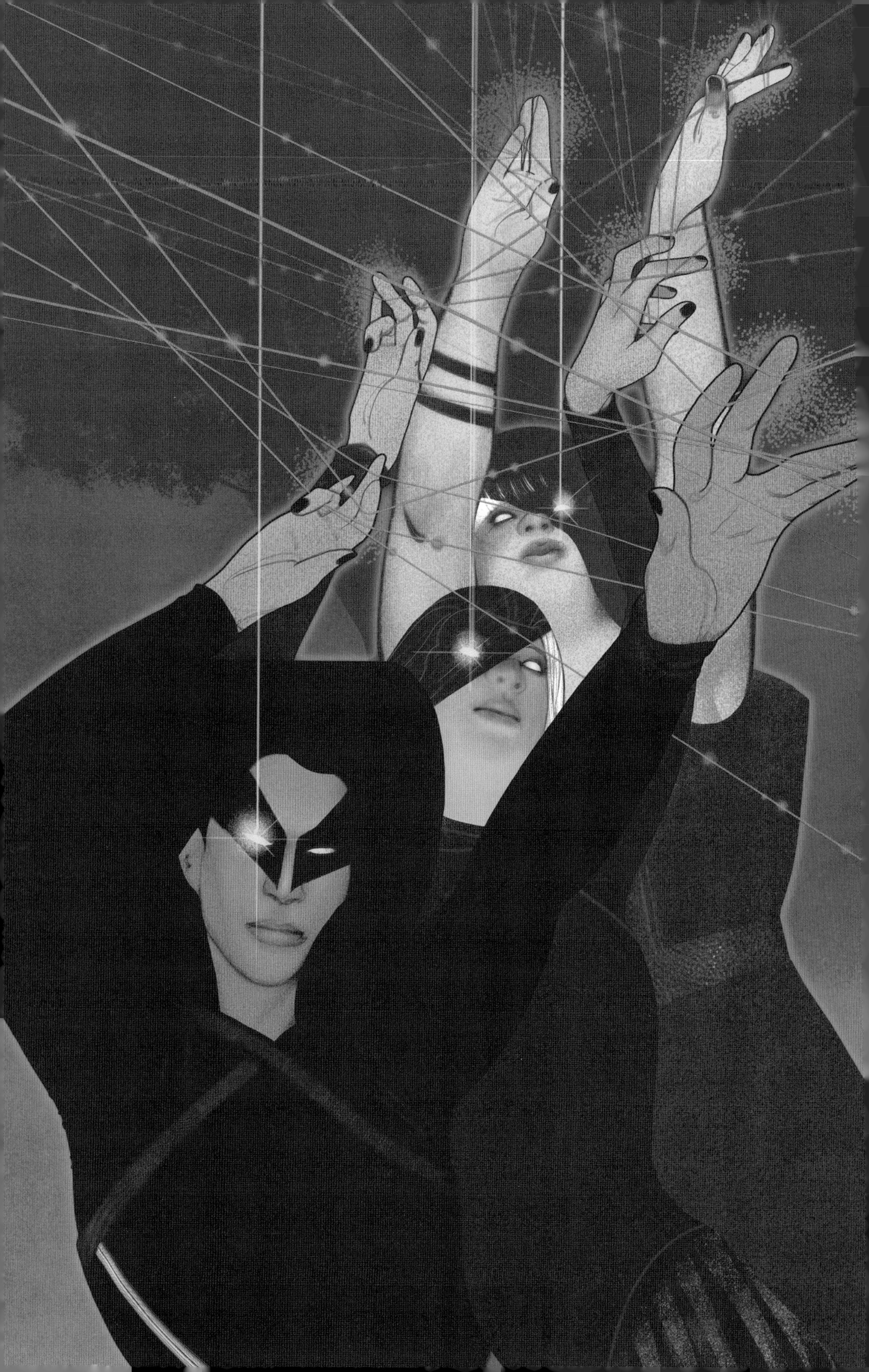

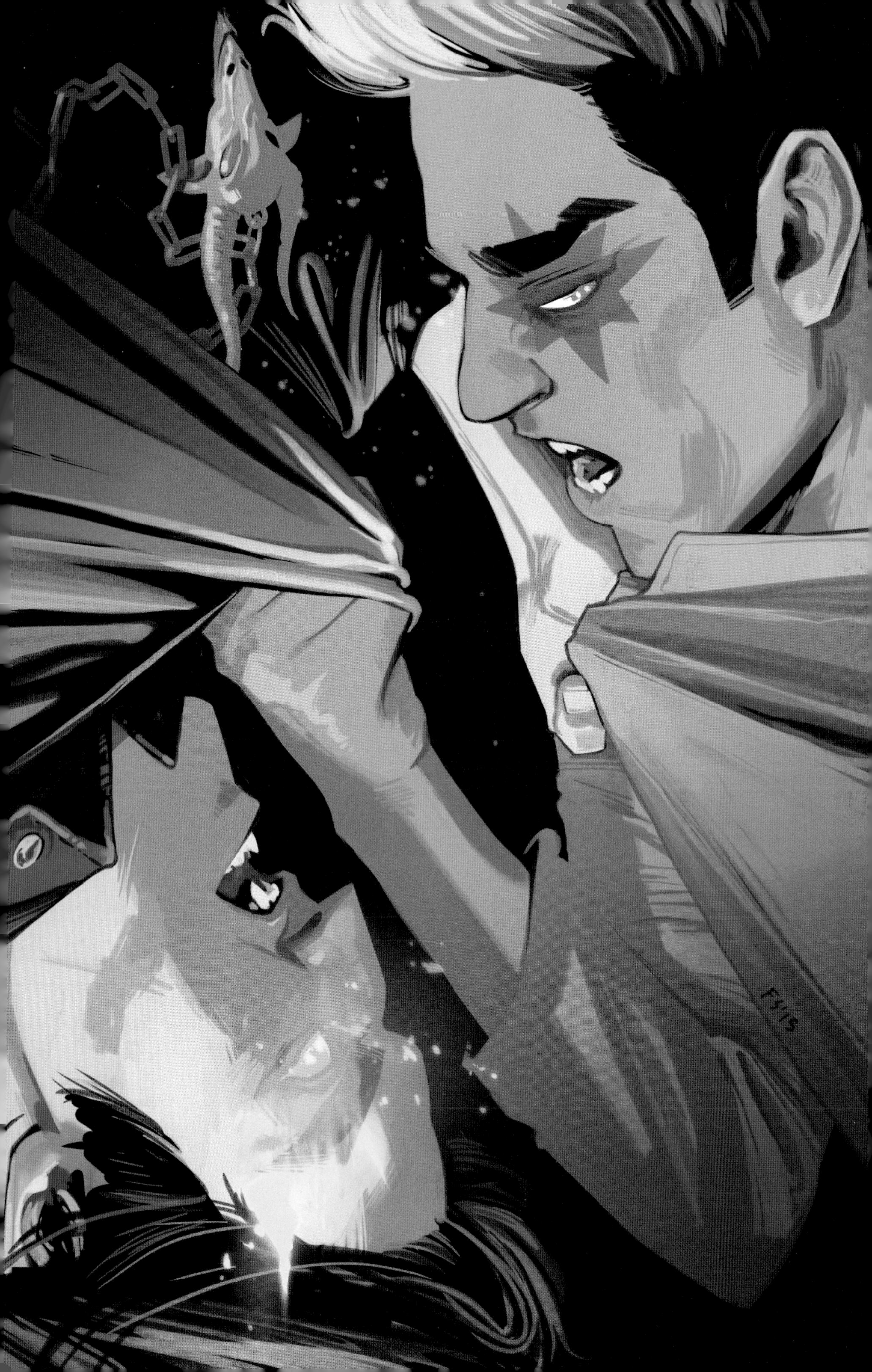

MAKING OF

There's always a question of how much people want to know about how the sausage gets made, especially when the sausage is made of humans, and the humans are us lot. Still — along the journey to the finished issues, a bunch of material was generated. We gathered some selected highlights, which you'll find in the following pages. This is true. We wouldn't lie to you at a time like this, not after you've spent all that money on this fancy hardback.

WicDiv Bible

Kieron Gillen 30th December 2013 ★ ↩

to Jamie McKelvie ➕

Hi Jamie

Attached is basically the first take on the bible. It'll be expanded from now on, and I'll edit it depending on any conversations we have following this. There's certain bits where we can definitely go different ways, and as these are often character visual issues as much as anything else, clearly would like your input.

This is the basic backstory for the series, plus various bits and pieces, plus character profiles for the primary cast. It's about 7000 words, and I wrote 4000 this morning, so expect a few typos, but you've worked with me before, so you know what I'm like.

Anyway — grab a coffee, print out, go read this fucking mess. See what you think about these guys.

I'll do my take on the first script tomorrow, and my plan is to mail it to you at 12:01 Jan 1st, because I'm exactly that kind of prick.

Excited by this. There's really a story here now.

Speak soon.

KG

....

1 Attachment ⬇

📄 WicDiv_Bible.pdf

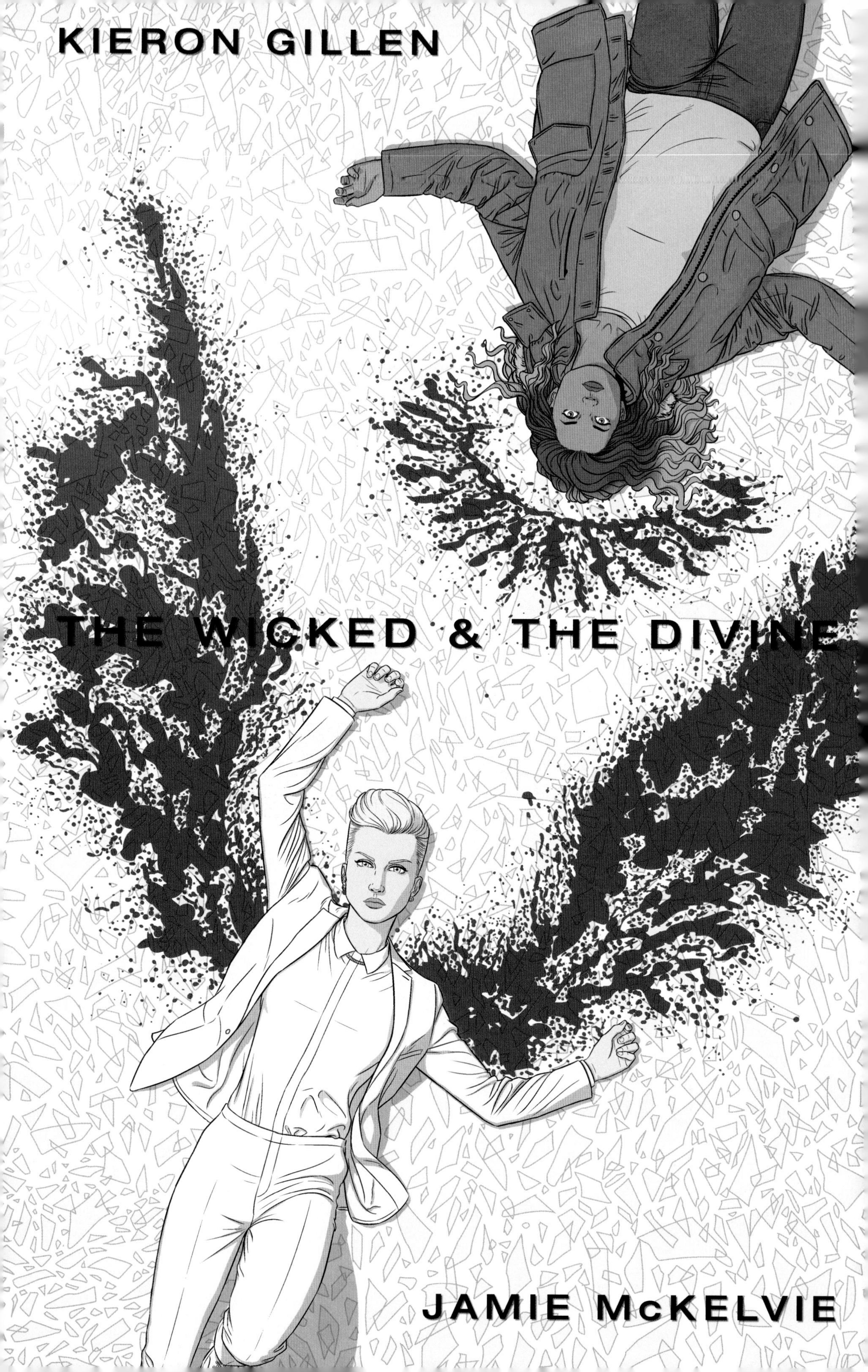
KIERON GILLEN
THE WICKED & THE DIVINE
JAMIE McKELVIE

ANNOUNCEMENT (left)

We announced *The Wicked + The Divine* at the Image Expo in San Francisco on 9th January 2014. This was the first piece of art produced for the comic. As the relationship between Laura and Luci was so core to the book, we wanted to focus on them. Jamie instantly regretted having all that broken glass, as he had to ink it all.

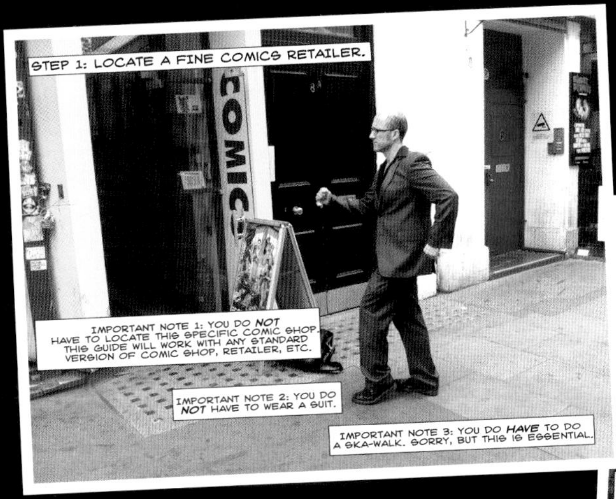
STEP 1: LOCATE A FINE COMICS RETAILER.
COMIC
IMPORTANT NOTE 1: YOU DO NOT HAVE TO LOCATE THIS SPECIFIC COMIC SHOP. THIS GUIDE WILL WORK WITH ANY STANDARD VERSION OF COMIC SHOP, RETAILER, ETC.
IMPORTANT NOTE 2: YOU DO NOT HAVE TO WEAR A SUIT.
IMPORTANT NOTE 3: YOU DO HAVE TO DO A SKA-WALK. SORRY, BUT THIS IS ESSENTIAL.

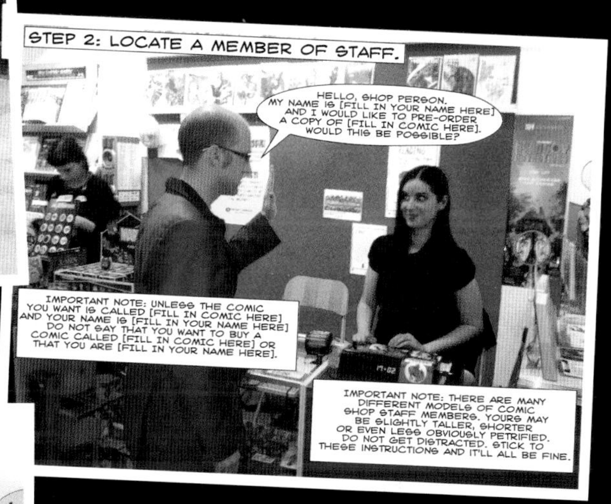
STEP 2: LOCATE A MEMBER OF STAFF.
HELLO, SHOP PERSON. MY NAME IS [FILL IN YOUR NAME HERE] AND I WOULD LIKE TO PRE-ORDER A COPY OF [FILL IN COMIC HERE]. WOULD THIS BE POSSIBLE?
IMPORTANT NOTE: UNLESS THE COMIC YOU WANT IS CALLED [FILL IN COMIC HERE] AND YOUR NAME IS [FILL IN YOUR NAME HERE] DO NOT SAY THAT YOU WANT TO BUY A COMIC CALLED [FILL IN COMIC HERE] OR THAT YOU ARE [FILL IN YOUR NAME HERE].
IMPORTANT NOTE: THERE ARE MANY DIFFERENT MODELS OF COMIC SHOP STAFF MEMBERS. YOURS MAY BE SLIGHTLY TALLER, SHORTER OR EVEN LESS OBVIOUSLY PETRIFIED. DO NOT GET DISTRACTED. STICK TO THESE INSTRUCTIONS AND IT'LL ALL BE FINE.

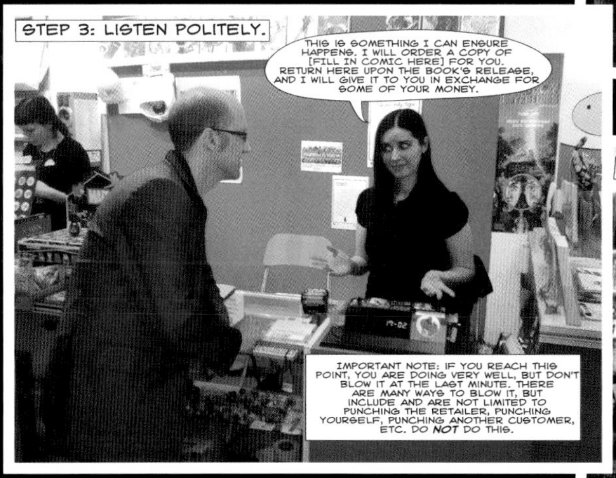
STEP 3: LISTEN POLITELY.
THIS IS SOMETHING I CAN ENSURE HAPPENS. I WILL ORDER A COPY OF [FILL IN COMIC HERE] FOR YOU. RETURN HERE UPON THE BOOK'S RELEASE, AND I WILL GIVE IT TO YOU IN EXCHANGE FOR SOME OF YOUR MONEY.
IMPORTANT NOTE: IF YOU REACH THIS POINT, YOU ARE DOING VERY WELL, BUT DON'T BLOW IT AT THE LAST MINUTE. THERE ARE MANY WAYS TO BLOW IT, BUT INCLUDE AND ARE NOT LIMITED TO PUNCHING THE RETAILER, PUNCHING YOURSELF, PUNCHING ANOTHER CUSTOMER, ETC. DO NOT DO THIS.

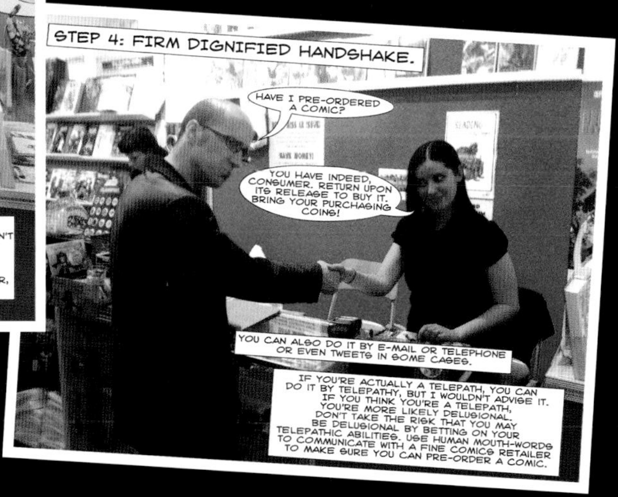
STEP 4: FIRM DIGNIFIED HANDSHAKE.
HAVE I PRE-ORDERED A COMIC?
YOU HAVE INDEED, CONSUMER. RETURN UPON ITS RELEASE TO BUY IT. BRING YOUR PURCHASING COINS!
YOU CAN ALSO DO IT BY E-MAIL OR TELEPHONE OR EVEN TWEETS IN SOME CASES.
IF YOU'RE ACTUALLY A TELEPATH, YOU CAN DO IT BY TELEPATHY, BUT I WOULDN'T ADVISE IT. IF YOU THINK YOU'RE A TELEPATH, YOU'RE MORE LIKELY DELUSIONAL. DON'T TAKE THE RISK THAT YOU MAY BE DELUSIONAL BY BETTING ON YOUR TELEPATHIC ABILITIES. USE HUMAN MOUTH-WORDS TO COMMUNICATE WITH A FINE COMICS RETAILER TO MAKE SURE YOU CAN PRE-ORDER A COMIC.

HOW TO PRE-ORDER COMICS

As this book was such a big deal for us, we completely went into hype-monster mode. In the final week, feeling disgusted with himself and somewhat demented, Kieron decided to try and turn his exhortations on how to pre-order a comic into art. Outsider art, admittedly, but that's neither here nor there. He did this, released it with all the typos, and the Internet seemed to find it amusing. Hurrah, etc.

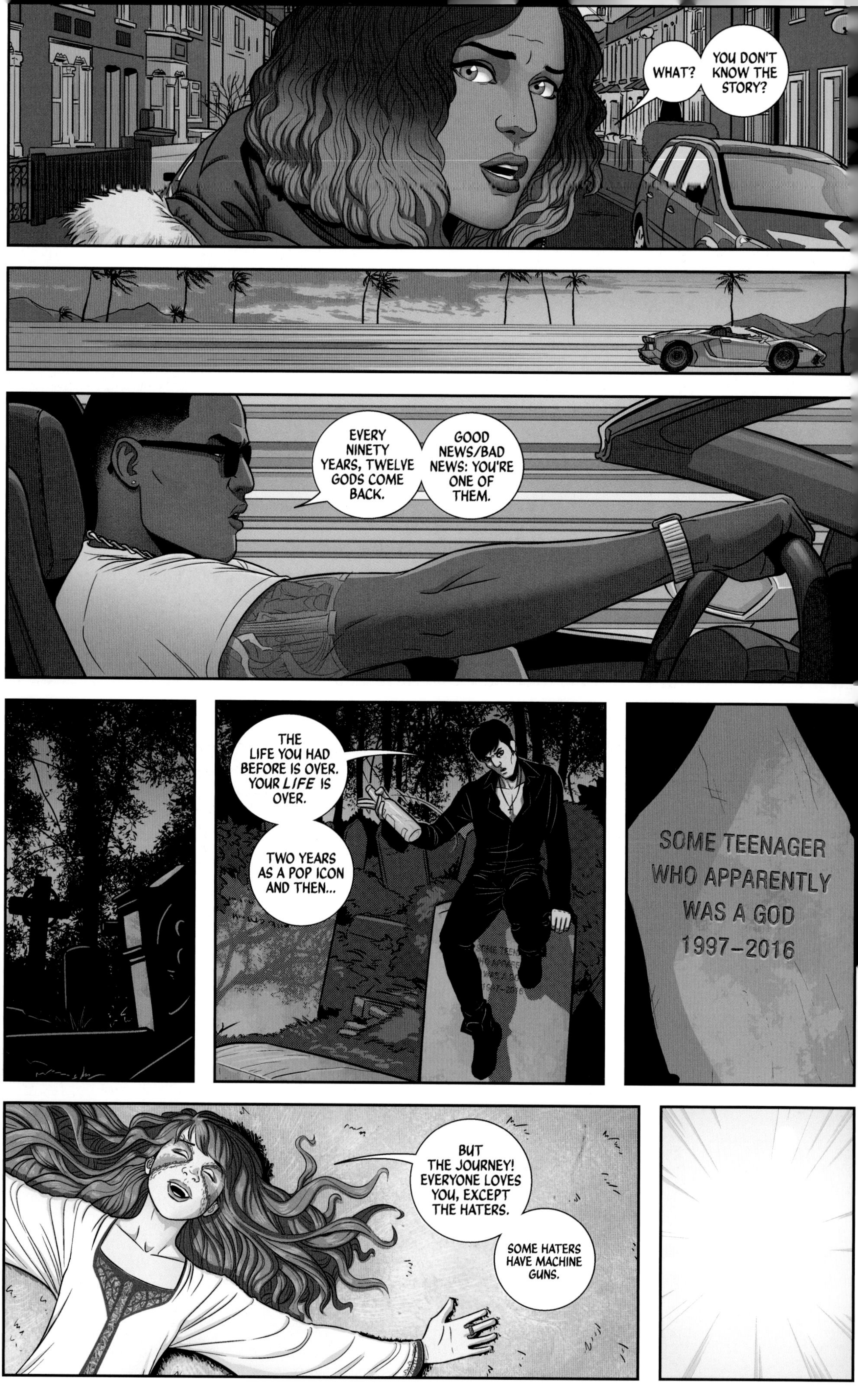
WHAT?
YOU DON'T KNOW THE STORY?
EVERY NINETY YEARS, TWELVE GODS COME BACK.
GOOD NEWS/BAD NEWS: YOU'RE ONE OF THEM.
THE LIFE YOU HAD BEFORE IS OVER. YOUR *LIFE* IS OVER.
TWO YEARS AS A POP ICON AND THEN...
SOME TEENAGER WHO APPARENTLY WAS A GOD 1997–2016
BUT THE JOURNEY! EVERYONE LOVES YOU, EXCEPT THE HATERS.
SOME HATERS HAVE MACHINE GUNS.

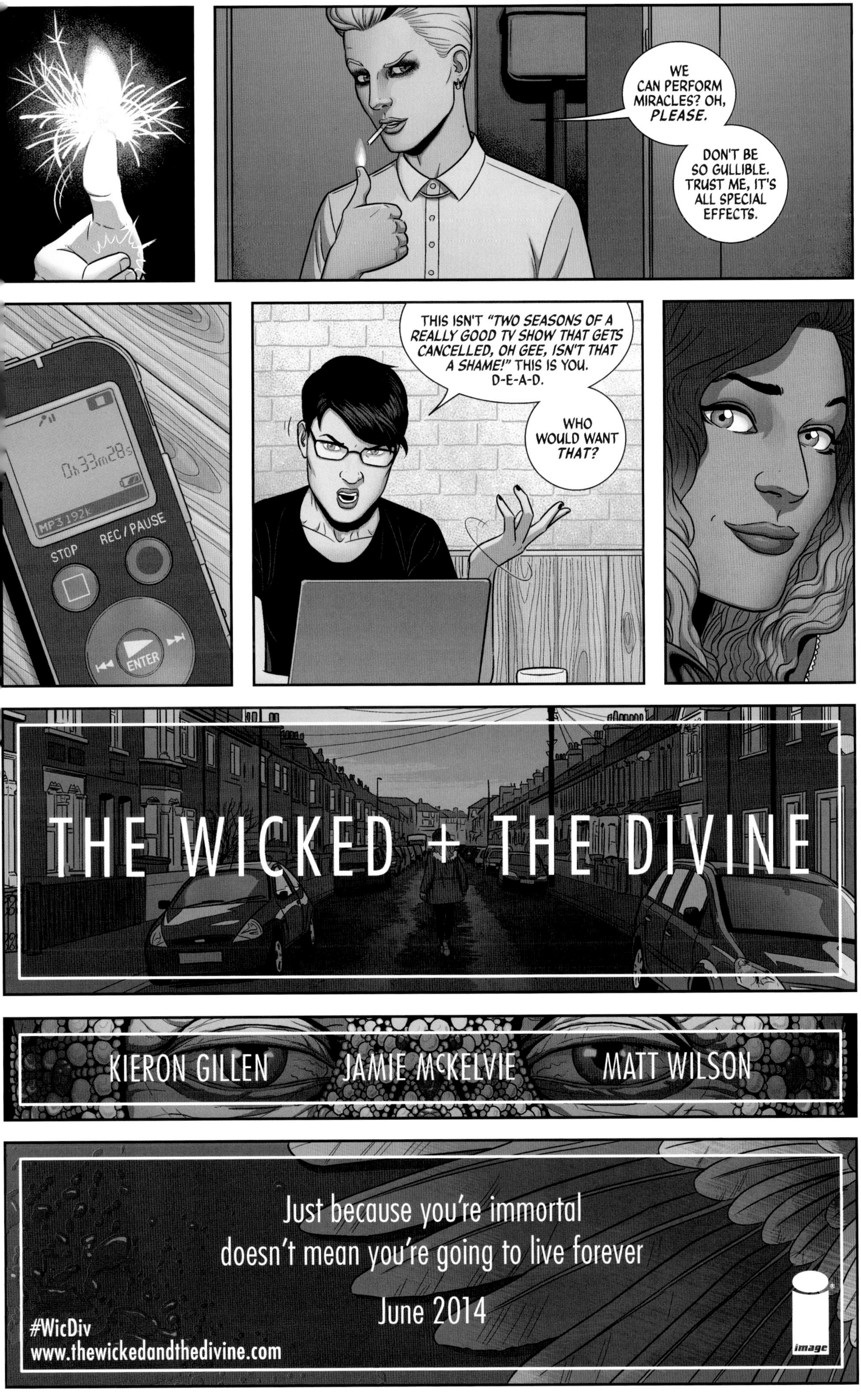
WE CAN PERFORM MIRACLES? OH, *PLEASE.*
DON'T BE SO GULLIBLE. TRUST ME, IT'S ALL SPECIAL EFFECTS.
0h33m28s
MP3 192k
STOP
REC / PAUSE
ENTER
THIS ISN'T *"TWO SEASONS OF A REALLY GOOD TV SHOW THAT GETS CANCELLED, OH GEE, ISN'T THAT A SHAME!"* THIS IS YOU. D-E-A-D.
WHO WOULD WANT *THAT?*
THE WICKED + THE DIVINE
KIERON GILLEN
JAMIE McKELVIE
MATT WILSON
Just because you're immortal
doesn't mean you're going to live forever
June 2014
#WicDiv
www.thewickedandthedivine.com
image

TEASER (previous pages)

One part of *Phonogram* we always were kind of happy with was the short advert teaser. Rather than repurposing panels from the book or dropping a preview, we created a bespoke one-page story that introduced the concept. We decided to do it again for *The Wicked + The Divine*, except when seeing the script, Jamie decided it'd be better on two pages. This is the first sign that Team *Phonogram* were entering their opulent phase.

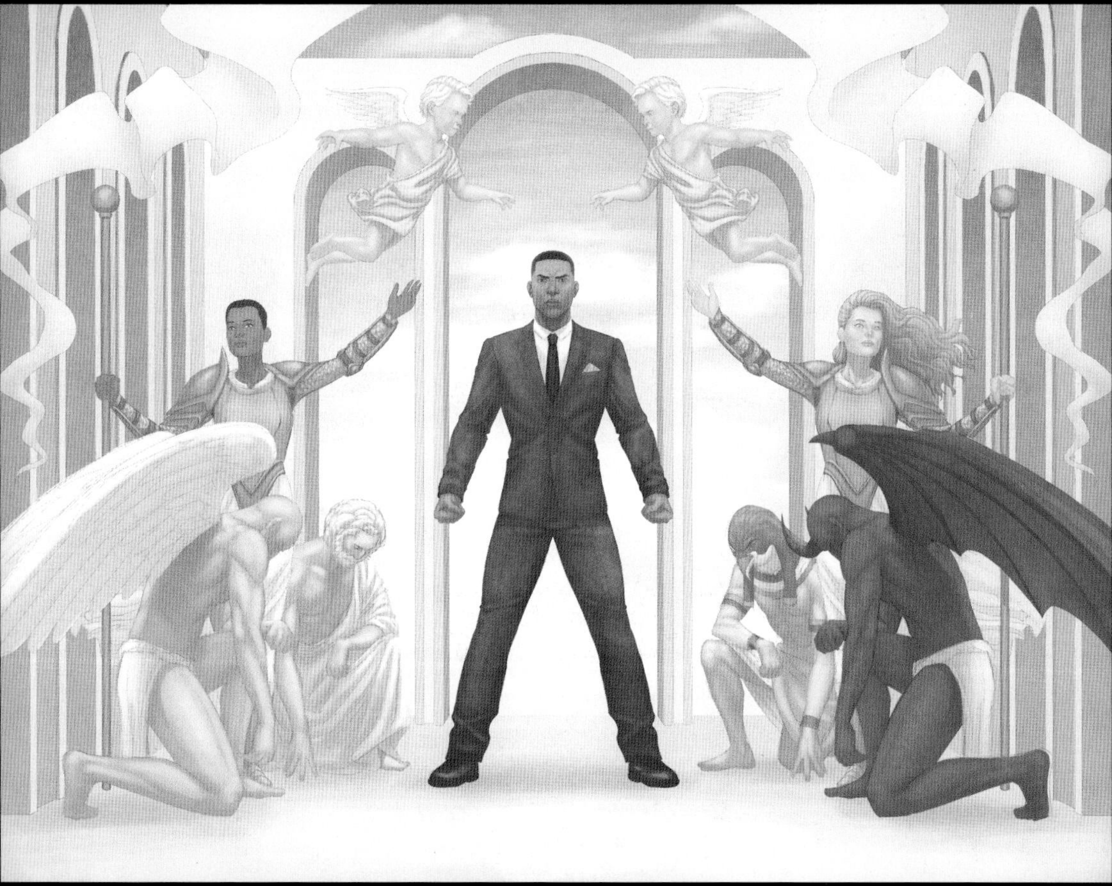

NATHAN FAIRBAIRN FRESCO

When seeing the script for issue four, Jamie had the bright idea that rather than Matt colouring the fresco, we reach out to another colourist with a very different style. Nathan Fairbairn was up for it, rendering over Jamie's art in a fully painted style, leading to this wonderful image. We're very happy. That said, us paying a completely different colourist to do a small piece of an issue's art is another example of us going into the aforementioned decadent phase. We look forward to the Barbarians arriving and killing us all. It's more than we deserve.

SKETCHES

Here are some head sketches Jamie did of three of the characters when trying to get the hang of their respective looks. Originally, he had Morrigan with shorter, scruffier hair, but Kieron wanted it to be longer. He had both Urðr and Persephone's designs down straight away, though he played with a couple of colour choices for Persephone.

The designs came from their descriptions in the *WicDiv* bible, and indirectly via both Kieron and Jamie posting images to the *WicDiv* Style blog (which you can find here: http://wicdivstyleblog.tumblr.com). The *WicDiv* bible features a whole bunch on all the characters, pretty much none of which is able to be shared. But here are a few fragments we can give you, edited and also faked for our purposes...

PERSEPHONE
Our lead. Black dad, white mum, south London. Aspirational working class girl, who has one eye on going to art school. 17. Slightly pretentious, desperately ambitious, wanting to escape everything. She's the fangirl who views her heroes as inspirations rather than objects of pure devotion. There's this odd mix of wonder on the surface and steel beneath.

   Oddly, writing this, it strikes me that she reminds me of you a little, Jamie. I say that to possibly give you a way into her...

   Archetypes: MIA, Siouxsie Sioux, Sky Ferreira And FKA Twigs. A whole lot of FKA Twigs.

THE NORNS
Are tricksy, and the last god of the main twelve to emerge. However, they appear in the first issue.

   The Norns are the journalists who are covering the gods. A sound person, a camera person and the lead interviewer. The lead is the key of the three, with the other two as supporting. She is the hyper-smart voice of knowledge and logic early on. She picks apart the faults of the characters, and even the concept of the book. She's one of the older of the gods — 22 or so — and has just left university on a cultural studies degree about myth. She knows everything, and thinks this is bullshit.

THE MORRIGAN
The Morrigan is basically a living Pixies record. Imagine taking all the classic Celtic mythological figures, and then changing them into the sort of people Frank Black used to sing about. Incest, violence, death, general wide-eyed lunacy. She could literally be wearing a Pixies T-shirt at one point.

   There's more in the mix, of course, and it does alter depending on which of the aspects she's in. Either way, as she changes between aspects, we change her powers, her personality and details of her appearance. She's one of the most obviously otherworldly and scary to be around of all the gods.

   Badb is a god of battle and crows, is related to the Banshee — working in the panic of Nemain would be a good idea. There's lots of imagery here. This would be the freak out mode, I suspect.... Gentle Annie as another would be interesting — where she would be very calm, and about comforting the dead. Or just finishing them off... Morrigan herself sits between the two. There's crow imagery in there too, but you could limit to a pet or a single example, while Badb would turn into a cloud of them. It would be the basal state, basically, swinging to either side.

   Archetypes: KatieJane Garside, Karen O, Patti Smith, PJ Harvey. All my favourite alt-girl stars.

FROM SCRIPT TO PAGE

PAGE 18

This is the one real sequence of magic in the issue. It's possible you may want to spread it to more pages if you feel like it... but maybe not. It's a quiet magical thing, as is this issue.

We're in a morgue, at night. It's all still. There is a roof in the ceiling or small high windows. Through it, we can see the night sky. Stars twinkling out there, all distant. Perhaps beams of lights fall across this clinical empty space, from the moonlight...

And then, in the beams of light, we start to get twinkles of purple, like tinkerbell-gone-Purple-Rain.

And then, out of the light itself, Inanna steps out. Not all there yet — just swirling stardust in part.

And then he's there, looking around. He's not entirely at ease. This place is creepy.

CAP: Miracle options.

FROM ISSUE 6 SCRIPT

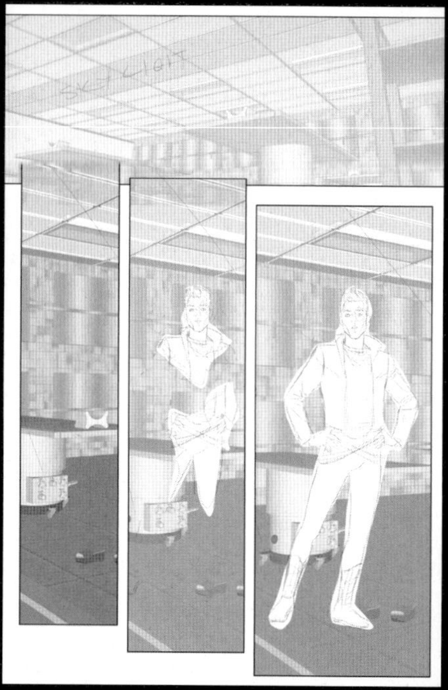

PENCILS

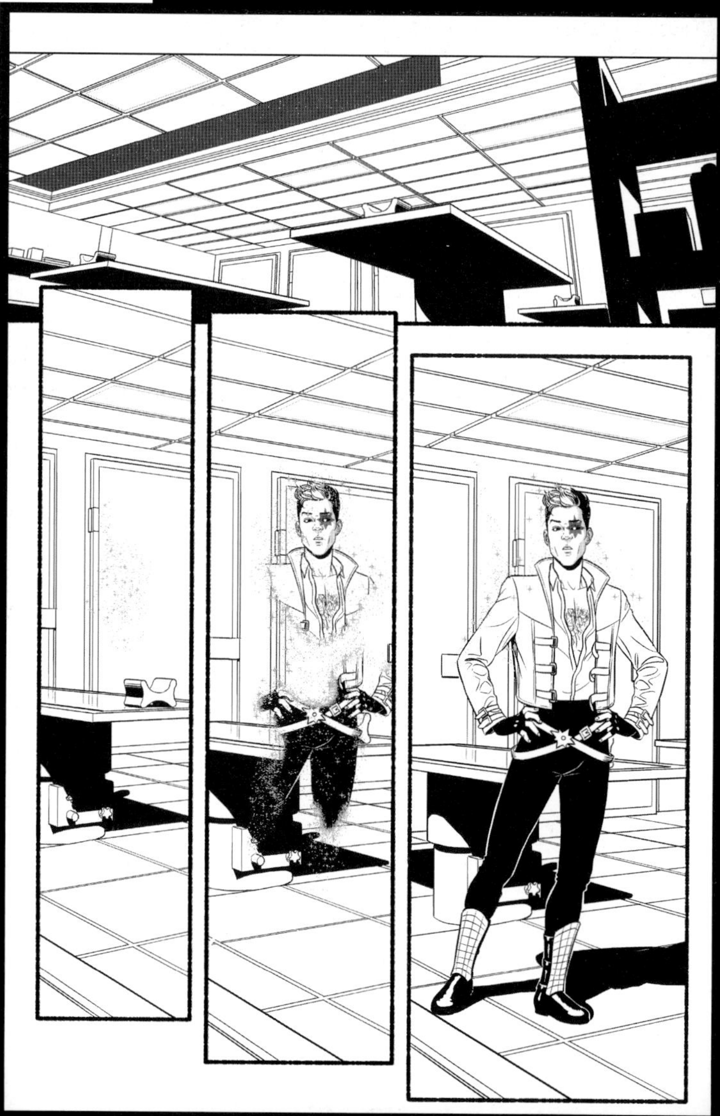

COLOURS

FLATS

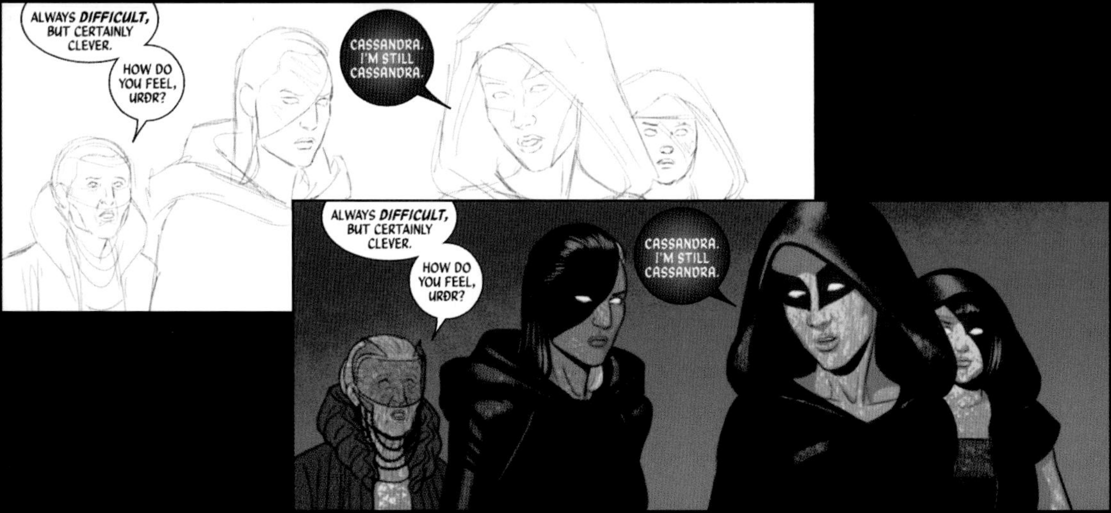
ALWAYS DIFFICULT, BUT CERTAINLY CLEVER.
HOW DO YOU FEEL, URÐR?
CASSANDRA. I'M STILL CASSANDRA.
ALWAYS DIFFICULT, BUT CERTAINLY CLEVER.
HOW DO YOU FEEL, URÐR?
CASSANDRA. I'M STILL CASSANDRA.

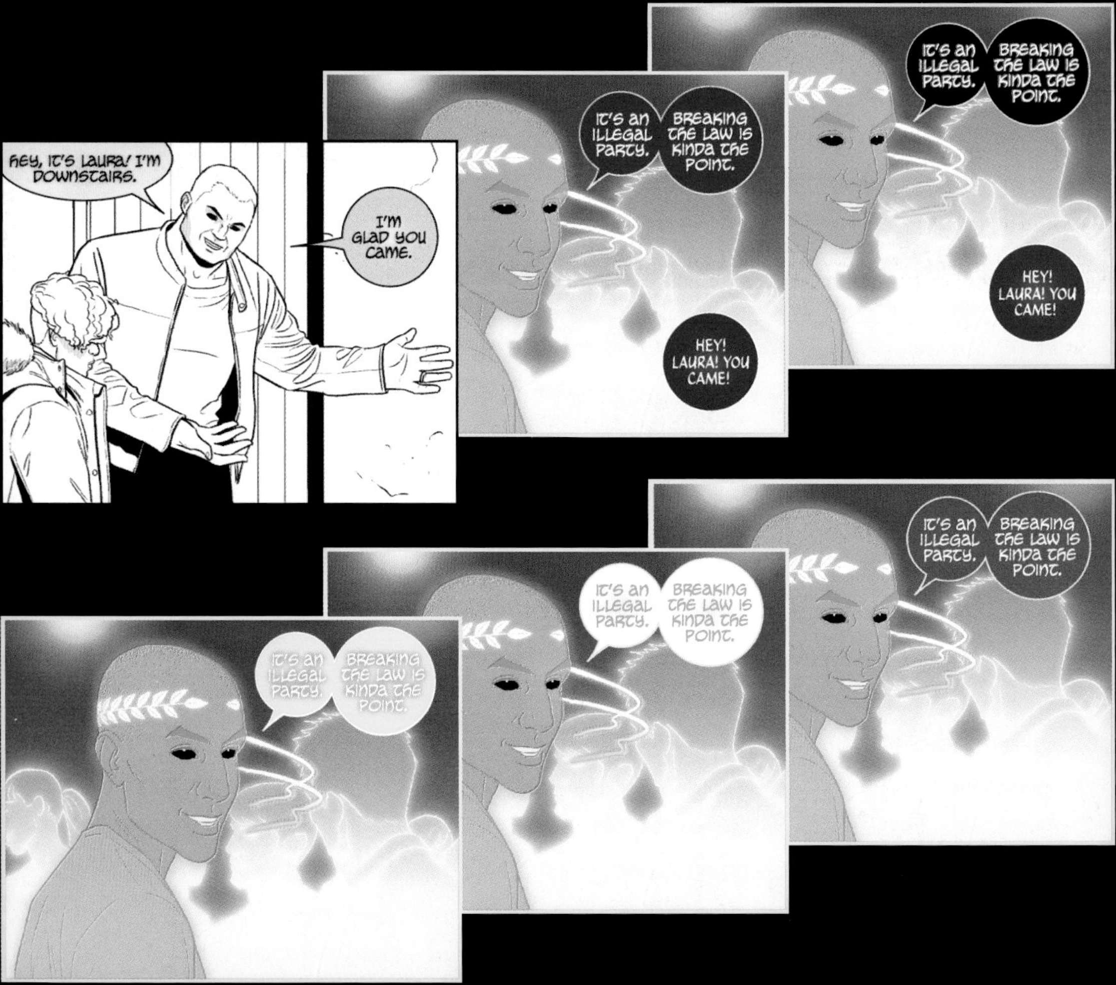
HEY, IT'S LAURA! I'M DOWNSTAIRS.
I'M GLAD YOU CAME.
IT'S AN ILLEGAL PARTY.
BREAKING THE LAW IS KINDA THE POINT.
HEY! LAURA! YOU CAME!
IT'S AN ILLEGAL PARTY.
BREAKING THE LAW IS KINDA THE POINT.
HEY! LAURA! YOU CAME!
IT'S AN ILLEGAL PARTY.
BREAKING THE LAW IS KINDA THE POINT.
IT'S AN ILLEGAL PARTY.
BREAKING THE LAW IS KINDA THE POINT.
IT'S AN ILLEGAL PARTY.
BREAKING THE LAW IS KINDA THE POINT.

You'll see particular differences here between how the script started out and what was subsequently drawn. Things we haven't shown you, for example, include an extensive email chain between Jamie, Kieron and Chrissy debating festival venues, sites and capacities.

PAGE 4-5

4-5.1
Double Page spread with inserts in bottom right of the spread.
(It could have other insert panels if you wanted to take it that way, but I'm not doing many images in the comic which get the sense of what Ragnarock is... so we may want to lean into the spectacle here. Ideally, it would be a full DPS, but I needed some panels here to lead into the next page.)
We are with Laura and Inanna, high in the air. Like, Superman high. They hold hands, falling in stardust, but with incredible grace – Inanna as Peter Pan to Laura's Wendy. Remember that Miss America panel that opened Young Avengers? That had grace and power. This is very much leaning to grace. We follow them, and before them is...
Well, it's a cross between Glastonbury and a religious festival. Which makes it Glastonbury x Glastonbury.
It's night. Across the countryside below a 100,000 campfires dot the landscape. A moon hangs over the land. The northern star especially glints – Inanna's Star.
The main stage is epochal. Part of me actually wanted to set this at actual Stonehenge, but I don't think that's going to be possible, as Laura needs to make her own way back. Let's set it at whatever Heath is biggest – I'm using Hampstead Heath for now.
While the Stage is at one end, in front of it are several-hundred-feet quasi-stone blocks, arranged in a circle. It's as if Spinal Tap got their Stage Stonehenge, but with the scale flipped the wrong way. They glint in techno-magnificence – presumably made by Woden. There's twelve of them. Each one has a symbol of the gods on it. This would include Lucifer. Perhaps each one could have unearthly fire sparking into the sky. Perhaps except Lucifer's. This looks awesomely ritualistic.
The crowd mills inside the circle, visible through their lighters. The actual people at the gig would be 300,000.
LOC CAP: Ragnarock 2014.
LOC CAP: Hampstead Heath.

4-5.2
And we're at the back stage area. Have you ever been backstage at a festival? Backstage at Glastonbury, except a fantasy of that – one part Glastonbury and one part Garden of Eden.
We don't have much here, so we can have people milling around. We have Laura and Inanna stepping out of the stardust, beautiful.
I see this as a long, almost page width panel...
LAURA: Aren't you staying?
INANNA: I play the big stage tomorrow. Tonight, I've my own thing back at the residency.
INANNA: I'd always rather play than watch.

4-5.3
Small panel. On Inanna, turning to light. He's glancing over Laura's shoulder. He's a little trepidatious. He's basically escaping!
INANNA: Better go.

4-5.4
Baal stepping up... and Inanna takes to the air, in stardust. Baal is reaching and caught half greeting.
BAAL: Hey, Inanna you--
BAAL: Oh, hell.

FROM ISSUE 10 SCRIPT

TOP VIEW
STAGE
Pillars (and one more)
CROWD!
CAMPING!
CAMPING
CAMPING
CAMPING
ENORMOUS
GLOW

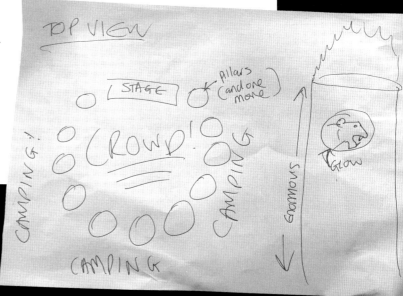

KIERON'S SKETCH

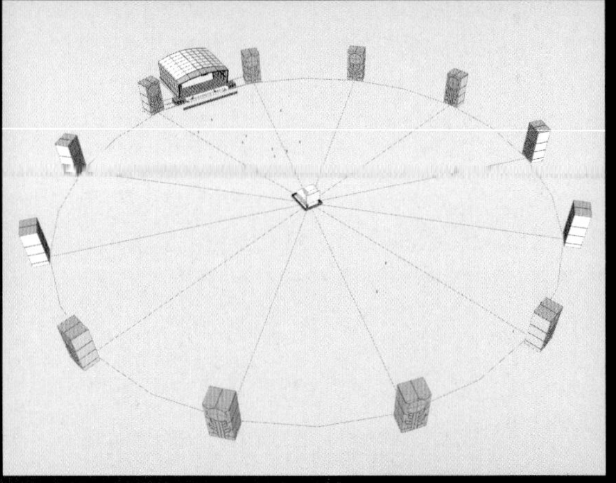

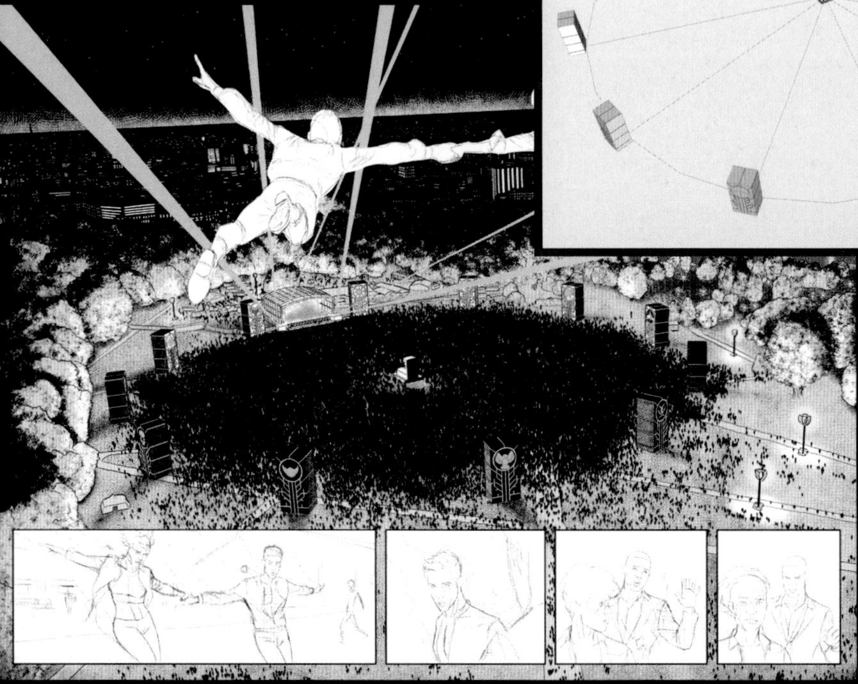

PENCILS

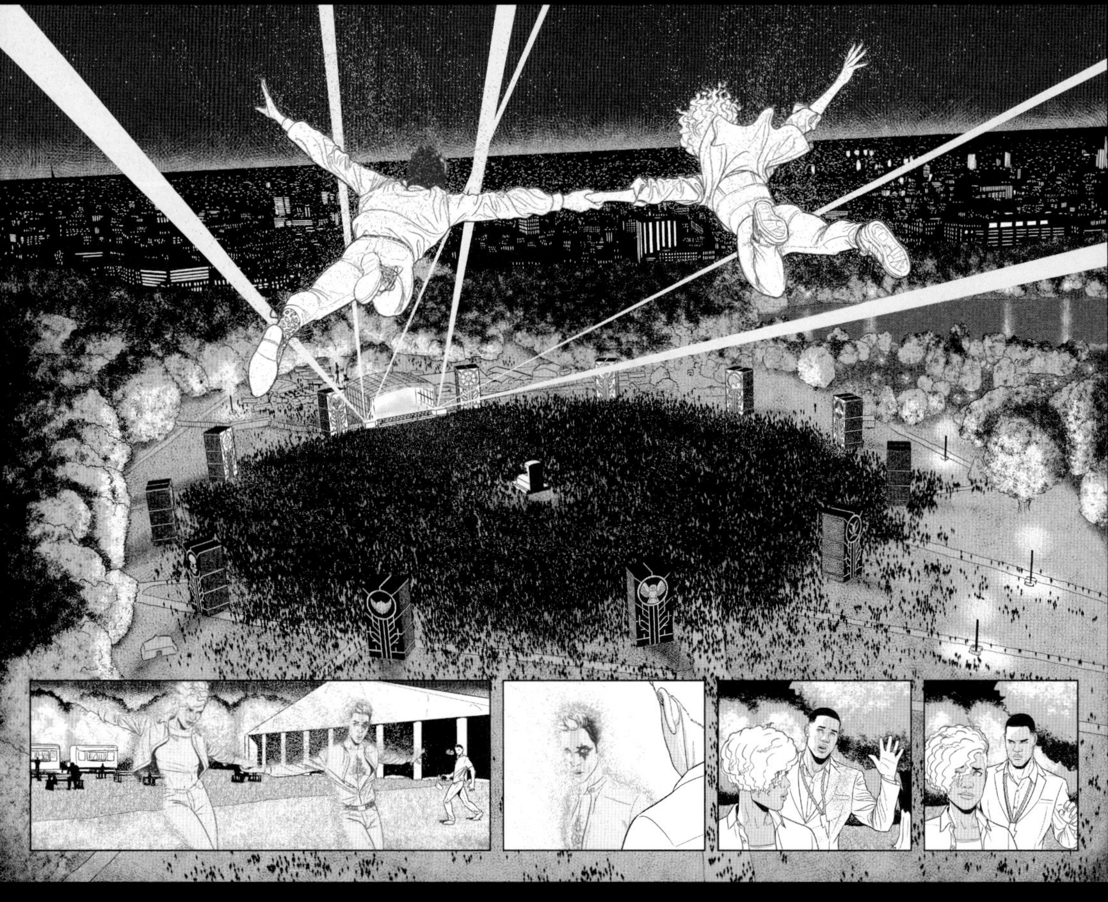

INKS

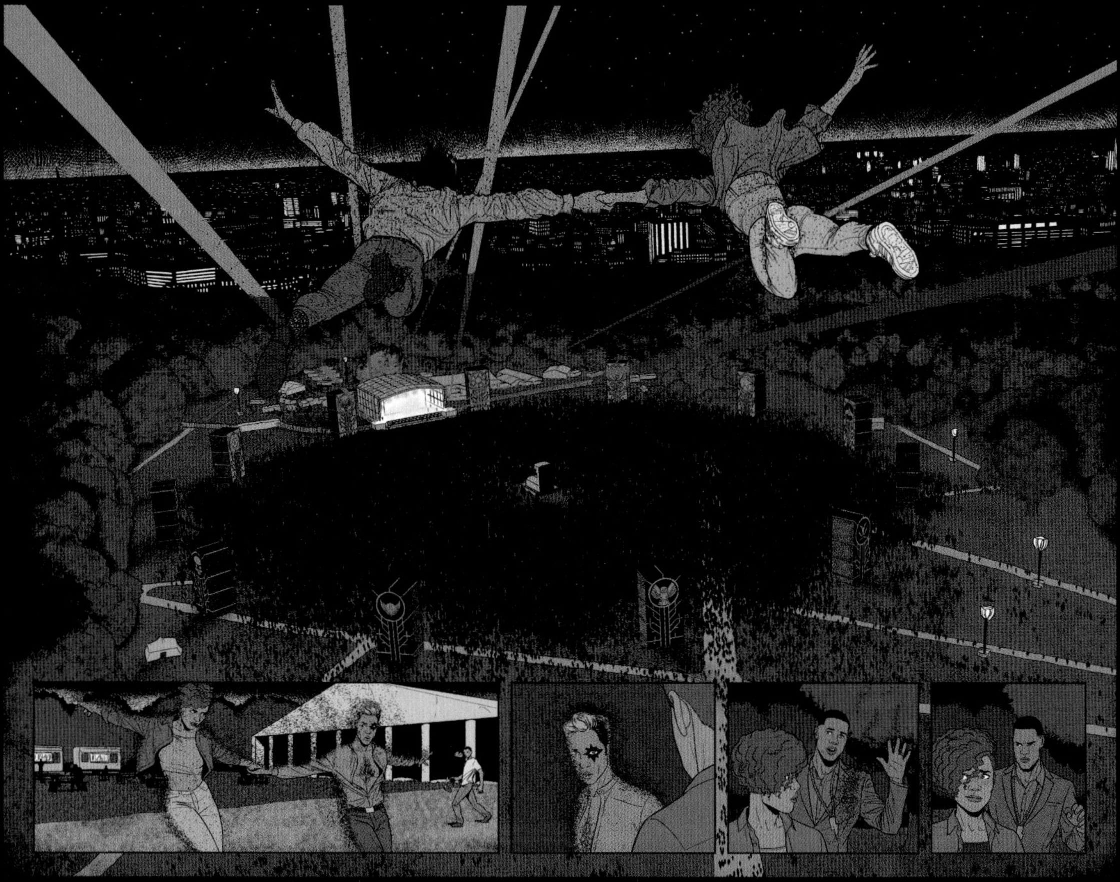

FLATS

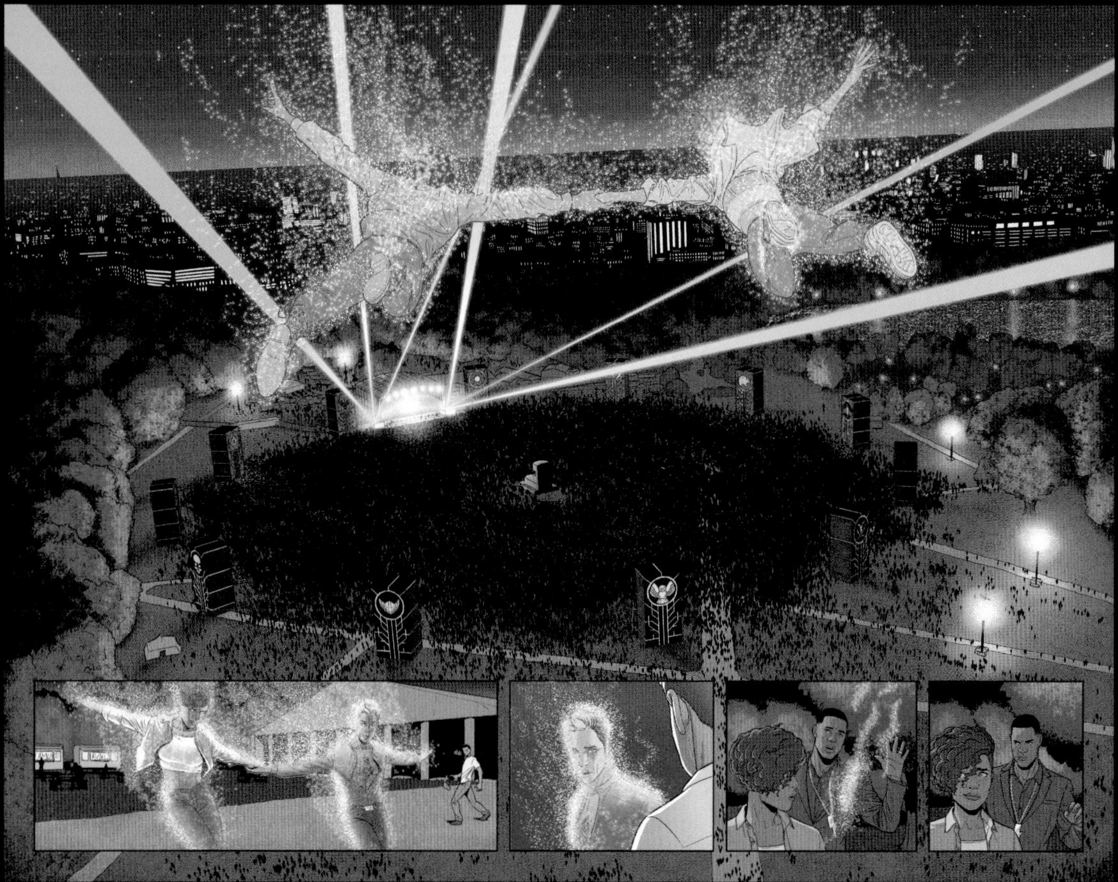

COLOURS

issue 8 came close to killing everyone. Kieron's final resort was to push pieces of paper around and scribble grid structures down to try and work out how it could possibly hold together.

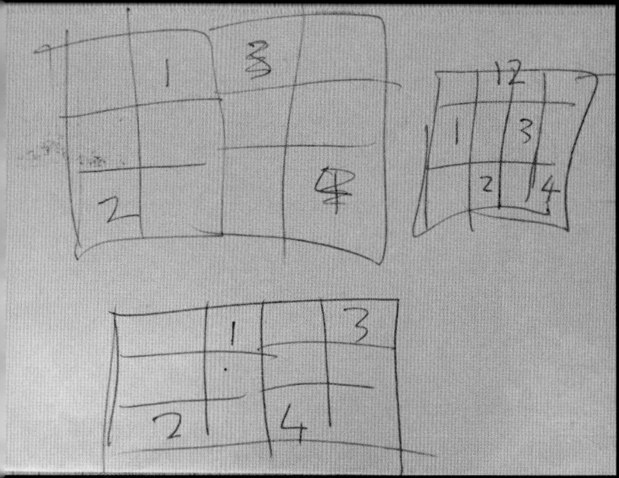

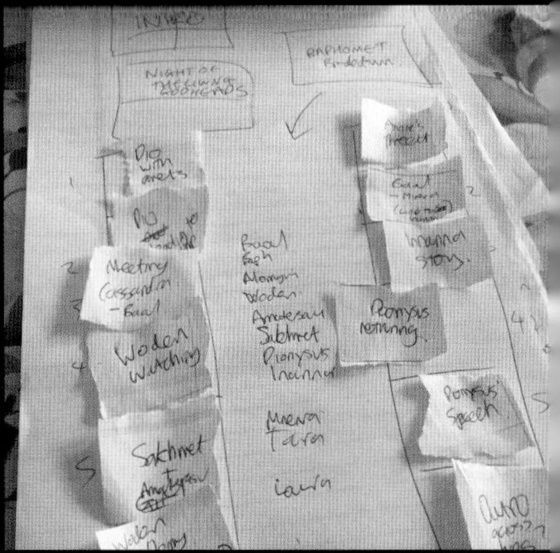
BAPHOMET
Meeting Cassandra - Baal
Woden watching
Sakhmet
Baal
Morrigan
Woden
Amaterasu
Sakhmet
Dionysus
Inanna
Minerva
Tara
Laura
Dionysus returning
Dionysus' Speech

These sketches Kieron did for issue 10 show why we don't let him draw.

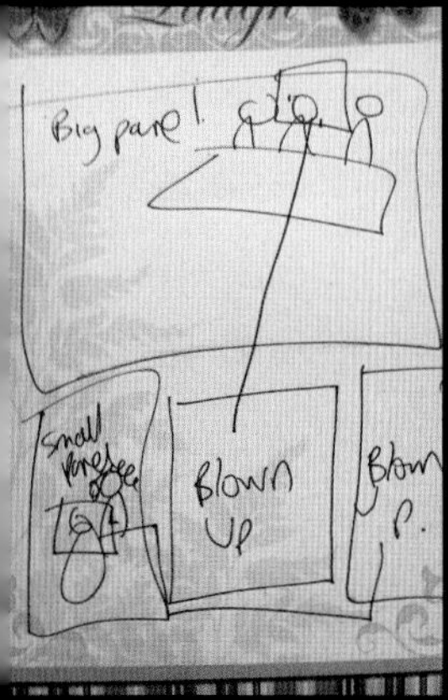
Big panel!
Blown Up

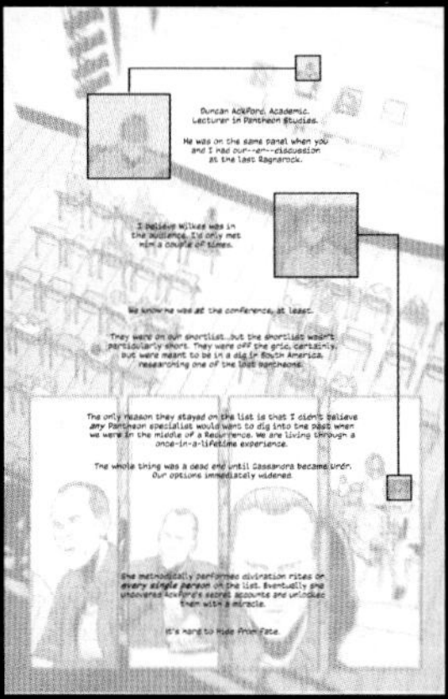

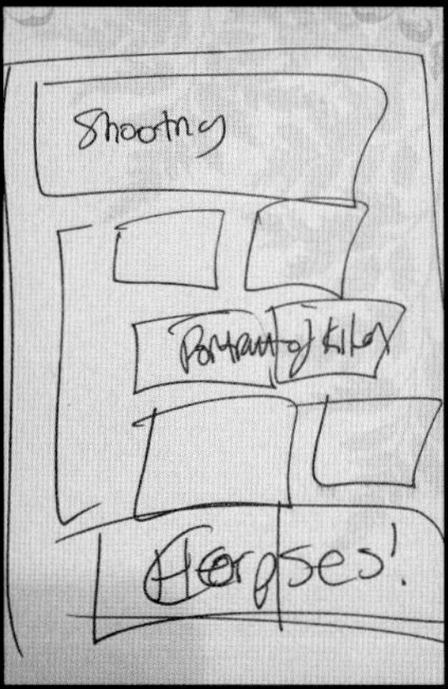
Shooting
Corpses!

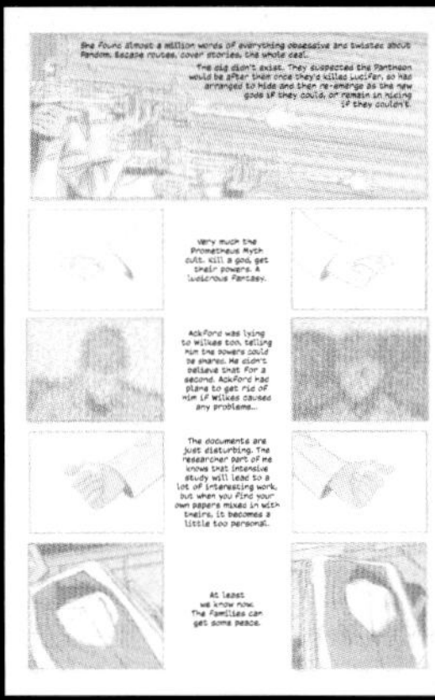

Classic owl correction was required for this panel in issue 7.

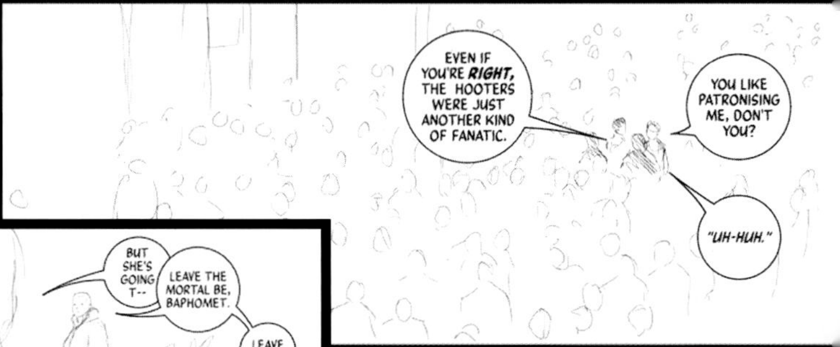
EVEN IF YOU'RE ***RIGHT,*** THE HOOTERS WERE JUST ANOTHER KIND OF FANATIC.
YOU LIKE PATRONISING ME, DON'T YOU?
"UH-HUH."

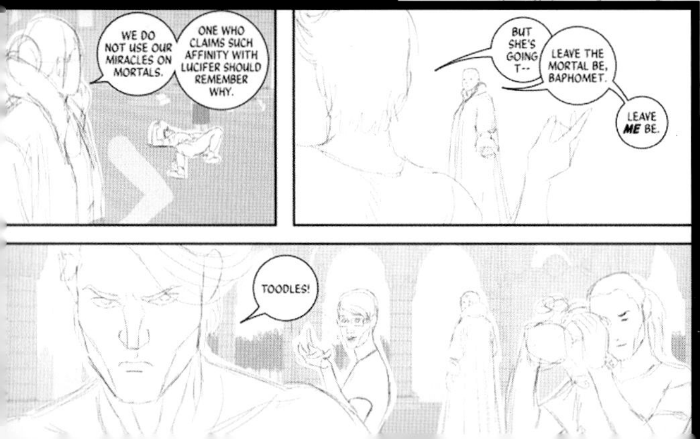
WE DO NOT USE OUR MIRACLES ON MORTALS.
ONE WHO CLAIMS SUCH AFFINITY WITH LUCIFER SHOULD REMEMBER WHY.
BUT SHE'S GOING T--
LEAVE THE MORTAL BE, BAPHOMET.
LEAVE ***ME*** BE.
TOODLES!

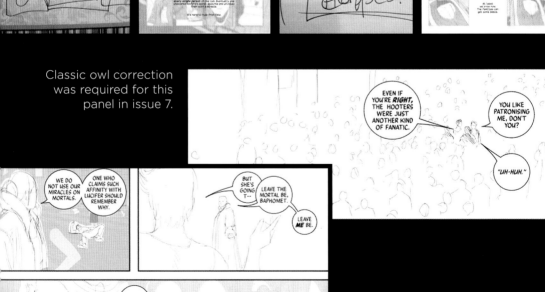

The bottom panel here in issue 10 needed correcting after Cassandra's line was accidentally misattributed to Baphomet. Aww, grumpy Baphomet was *grumpy*.

When putting together the hardback, David Bowie died. Bowie was an enormous influence on everyone on the team. Kieron wrote the following.

IMMORTALITY, OF A KIND

The girl in the white suit hid her nerves behind the cigarette.

The curtains opened. A pale man in pressed flannel frowned.

"Who are you," he said, rubbing sleep from his eyes, "and what the hell are you doing on my window-ledge?"

The girl balanced on her bare heels, rocking back and forth.

"I... am a fan," she said, "Don't worry. I'm perfectly safe."

"I wasn't worried," he said, "Lose the cigarette."

"Sorry," she said. Her face twisted, as if her muscles used to make apologetic expressions had atrophied through neglect.

"I wanted to ask some advice," she said as she flicked the cigarette into the void behind her.

The man thought of his breakfast cooling.

"Make it quick," he sighed.

There was silence, or as close to silence as the rumble of the city far below would ever allow.

"I have so much I want to do, and so little time," she said, "I want everything. Is that so much to ask? Everyone says so. Everyone says 'be reasonable'. But then I look at you, and everything you've achieved, and know that 'reasonable' is defeatist. Any one sliver of what you've done would be an enviable career. That it takes it all in, is an impossibility. There's so little time, and so much work I want to do. I'm going to die but I want to be immortal. I'm trying so many things, but I'm afraid of losing myself in a–"

"Enough," said the man, "I've two things for you. Listen carefully."

"Always finish the album," said the man, "and get the hell off my window ledge."

The girl nodded.

"You were my inspiration," she said, as she stepped backwards, turning to a shower of ash and sulphur, leaving tiny sooty footprints on the ledge.

The man sighed as he turned from the window. A girl dressed in a white suit, smoking, with that hair? And I was apparently inspiration? No shit.

Still — she was far from the first, and she'd be far from the last.

Immortality, of a kind.

WRITER'S NOTES

After each issue comes out, Kieron throws a few thoughts out onto tumblr, which he somehow expands out into several thousand words. There's definitely times when you can tell that Kieron used to work in a job where he was paid by the word. Basically, think of it as a director's commentary sort of thing, with Kieron saying some of the things that were going through the team's heads when pulling the issue together. If you want to follow them as they come out, check the writer-notes tag on http://kierongillen.tumblr.com

ISSUE 1

It's probably best I restate what these notes are. They are, as you'll soon discover, a ramble. They will contain craft stuff and random "where ideas emerged" stuff. I will do some tech stuff, but I'm going to try hard to avoid actually just explaining the whole card trick. It's hard, as it's the way my brain is wired, but I'll try.

Also, they're not normally this long. First issue, y'know?

Probably the main thing to stress: this isn't everything there is to say about the book. It barely counts as the tip. Do not take anything said below as the sole reason we did anything.

I've been running a podcast called *Decompressed* for the last year. It's sporadic, especially recently, but I did a lot of talking to people in public. A lot of it was about first issues. In a real way, if you listen to them now, be aware I was thinking about *The Wicked + The Divine* for the whole of that time, and what on Earth I was going to do with the first issue. The questions of "What should a first issue do" may as well be me talking to the mirror.

Right? Onwards.

Cover(s). Jamie's high concept, Hannah's design. The designer Hannah Donovan is a long term friend of ours, and she did a little comic work with me on *Three*. She wanted to be involved early, and we were glad to have her. She's very much the high level aesthetic conductor of the book.

Jamie's concept was portraits, done in the style of a fashion magazine, specifically with those colouring effects. The full-page logo is the sort of thing which retailers a decade ago would have been outraged about, I suspect, but which didn't get a mention now. Not sure what that says, but I think it's a good thing.

We considered losing our names entirely from the cover, but had a moment of sense.

I'm still amazed we went with the name. We went through a mass of them — *Young Gods* was the original title, but that would have been *shameless* for a half dozen reasons, as well as copyright infringing — and it took a while to reach the final one. I thought we'd get something else, and it was only when I was backstage at the Image expo, about to go on stage, that I realised "Oh man! It's totally too late to change it now." I never said I was smart.

We played with some radical ideas, especially when we had the dual-cover concept. The duality of the title is key. We were considering releasing two covers every issue, one entitled *The Wicked* and the other *The Divine*. We'd never actually say what the title of the book was, so the book just existed as this Schrödinger's title. Half the print run would have one cover on the front, the other half would have the other (And the other one on the reverse — we didn't want to gouge). It's a fun idea, but we realised it was probably a good idea for people to be able to walk into a shop and actually say the name of the comic they wanted to buy. To quote the email I sent to Jamie that started this whole thing: "For once in our life, let's not be stupid."

My fave minor thing? The idea of the "+" instead of "And/&" (Hannah's, I believe), which both gives a nod towards christianity while also resembling a cross-hair right in the middle of the character's face, in a Public Enemy fashion. This may just be me.

Icons. Black, black, black. GOTH AS FUCK.

This is our "standard" title page we'll use throughout the book. As people learn to read the icons, it'll act as a soft recap of the state of play. Time is important because, as the high concept comes in, each of those days is incredibly important to the cast.

In passing, design pages like this in books are (for WFH books) pretty much free (i.e. don't come from the budget). In books like ours, they take much less effort in terms of time than a drawn page (i.e. they don't come from our "budget"). If you see a design page like this, it was never going to be a page of art. If it wasn't a designed page, it'd almost certainly be a house-ad. I've never asked Hickman if it bugs him when reviewers complain about it, but if I were him, I'd be walking around the house with an axe any time someone said anything about wasting pages which solely existed due to the creator's desire to give the reader more content.

But I'm a famously axe-stompy kinda guy. Jonathan is much more chill.

Actually, it was Hickman's ownership of icons over the last five years that gave us second thoughts about doing this. We've been doing design based stuff since *Rue Britannia*, and I was specifically thinking about an update of the opening image of *The Singles Club* trade — i.e. social group as circular diagram — but I was aware it'd be filed as Hickman-derived stuff, just because of how much he's made it his signature.

Basically, we decided fuck it.

Each icon is a god. No, we won't be confirming — at least for a while — what god means what. In my script I said the icons would be the same no matter what generation of gods we were in. I did that as a "this could end up a lot of work" thing. Jamie said he wanted to do individual styled icons for each period, hence the art-deco vibe of these four. Jamie is a good one.

Note: No indicia. I didn't want commerce to be the first thing anyone sees in a book. Equally, no creative team. Art first, commerce last. Art first, creators last. Yes, I know. We contain multitudes.

1. GOTH AS FUCK.

If you've read any of the interviews about this, you'll know I've said it's a book about death. I work this in with subtle, almost invisible subtext by having a big fucking skull on the front page staring at you.

We spent quite a bit of time deciding where the balloon should come from. Top right, so you read the sentence before you actually reach the skull was the decision. Top right, as that's where the masked lady is.

I called for the hyper-shadow hyper-real art-mode Jamie did for his Horror-Oubliette in *Young Avengers*, and he's leaned into it.

This borders on the "not pointing out cleverness" stuff, but this is very much me lifting from *Watchmen*. In *Watchmen*, the cover is the first panel of the story. Here, the transition from the alive face to a skull is the point. The "cover as part of the comic" is something Jamie and I do a lot in our indie work, though never as an actual panel transition before now.

Originally had a Location Caption on this page, but decided to lose it.

Several people have picked up on the line of dialogue's similarity to the first line of 90s pop-comics counter-cultural classic *The Invisibles*. They would be correct. As a general rule, if a line's ringing bells, it's ringing bells for a reason. However: the devil is in the details. It's not the same line, and the stressing is always key. Also a good time to re-stress the "everything is done for more than one reason?" point I did in the intro? It's not just an *Invisibles* riff.

The Invisibles is great, btw. If you want a picture of the 90s, it's one of the best, flaws and all. And no work of art worth a damn is without its flaws. *Invisibles* changed peoples lives.

Look at Matt's colouring choices throughout this sequence. Sepia choices, which always reminds me of bone. The whole scene looks like bleached bone. Matt's one hell of a colourist, as I'll talk about anon. He wasn't even pleased with the work on the first issue. As good as the first issue is, now that I've seen the second, I kinda see why. It's an astounding rollercoaster structure based around hue — but I'll talk about that next month.

2. You know, thinking about this after talking about Hickman earlier, this opening scene really is a Hickman move, at least for his Indie work. As in, dropping you into a situation with no explanation and trusting the audience to keep up with it.

I'll admit, I was primarily thinking of the opening of *Gangs Of New York*, a film I have very little time for, but I do love that whole opening sequence. Fundamentally, we see the end of the previous movie. This is a little like that.

To return to a key thing in current-aesthetic action comics — space is importance. Could you have done this scene in less pages? Sure, but it'd bleed it of all meaning and impact. Space also lets us stress lots of the details. Yes, you won't understand this all on first reading... but you probably will on the second, as there's a lot of single images to let you dwell on it.

Christ, look at all the black going on here. Man! Jamie is owning the black.

Love the Gods of the Jazz Age designs. Jamie outdid himself here. If I wasn't planning to do more with them before, I would have when I saw them.

Obviously — circles and skulls are the shapes we're playing with.

3. The masked lady is totes mysterious. She hasn't been named yet in the story, but will soon enough. When designing her, I noted that she wouldn't be wearing this outfit particularly often (as it's a period one) so Jamie could go to town and do something that he wouldn't want to draw every issue, but can just about handle for a scene. This is what results.

People talk about comics' infinite budget on the page. It's true, but only as far as it goes. The budget is what the artist is willing to actually draw without wanting to set themselves (and the writer) on fire.

Susanoo teases a line...

4. ...And goes a different way on the page turn. Lighter. He's the only character named in the scene, which you have to presume is for a reason.

For those who never did French at high school, Au Revoir = Until we meet again.

Italics for foreign language. Use of italics, quotation marks and bold is a little off standard comic-forms in *WicDiv*.

I wrote a lot in the script about the implicit relationship between these gods, and their personal relationships, and Jamie did some wonderful things here. How do you think the guy in the second panel feels about Susanoo, y'know?

Like all the gods, I weighed what spelling to use for Susanoo before ending up with this one.

5. Various iconic, memetically sticky bits of the book are introduced: skulls, the finger-clicks (or snaps, if you're that way inclined), 1-2-3-4.

Debating how we'd write KLLK was one of the better editorial debates herein. Me being me, I'd written it in various ways, and we standardised to this.

The page turn is really well done by Jamie here. Silence...

6. ...Noise.

Colour, light, and a return to "Once again, We return."

7. Title page, more icons, more figuring out. 1-2-3-4 is probably already sinister by this point, I suspect.

We're not confirming to people which icon symbolises which god, so they'll have to do a little deduction. It'll be clear sooner rather than later.

January 1st 2014 is when we officially started work on *WicDiv*. I sent Jamie the first script a few seconds after the new year.

Hmm... this is probably a good place to talk about some of the more fucking oddball stuff I do. The — for want of any word to say this which isn't even more fucking pretentious — shamanistic parts of it. The magical thinking parts.

The task of *WicDiv* is trying to keep the odd oblique power of the Too-Much-Information Too-Much-Us that you get when you try and funnel existence into art without a barrier, while not just collapsing into utter incoherence. As a writer, the part of me which works on instinct and the part of me that runs on numbers are always at war. You'll see different books doing it to different levels. *Über* is probably the one where the math brain is most in effect, as I tend to be just as coldly mechanistic as the characters and the world it portrays. There is no magic in *Über*. The only pure magical thinking stuff is the short apocalypse romance stuff — even *Phonogram* has a hard structural maths edge to it, especially in *The Singles Club*.

WicDiv's driving force is to make the two work together. It's another iteration of the duality that's clear from the title downwards, y'know?

Okay — what I'm saying is that's what I'm thinking about when trying to make all the choices in the book. There are a lot of darlings and deciding whether they should live or die is the work. If I remove too few, the book doesn't work as genre fiction. If I remove too many, the reason I'm doing the book disappears and I may as well have never bothered.

8-9. Brockley is near where I live. I could have set it anywhere, but as Laura is primarily inspired by the Girls On The Bus, I wanted to be precise about it. Also this is me buying in emotionally. As I walk about the area, I'm thinking "What would Laura make of that?" when I see something.

It also obviously makes it easy to get photo ref.

Why London at all? I was considering making it worldwide, but knew that it would reduce Laura's normality (and so the contrast between her life and the gods) if she had to travel internationally. If she has to go to (say) Glasgow, I can have her hiding in a toilet, dodging fare. Doing something like that with a plane turns her either into a very rich girl or someone who's basically the Black Widow.

I was also aware that, culturally speaking, I can write London better than I can write (say) New York. The book requires a certain literacy with how a city and its people work, and having the experience matters.

Also — why *not* London? I'm a Brit. I'm interested in Jason writing the South. I'm interested in anyone writing about where they're from. I always think when writing that my own tastes can't be that unusual.

Basically, shamanistic reasons and easy photo ref. You know us.

(I joke: once again, there's a shitload of other reasons, some I've just deleted.)

The 1-2-3-4 panels was an early idea. I often considered whether it would be a good idea to kill them to do other things with the space. In the end, I'm glad we didn't. My main worry was whether Laura's intro would be too bitty. I played with other choices of what to show her doing — tube stuff, approaching the venue – but ended up focusing in on those two key scenes. The leaving the house and the transformation.

Laura's our abstract lead, and PoV character. As such, my worry is always having her too passive and not clear as a person rather than an observer. However, there's the secondary urge — the story requires us, as readers, to be interested in Lucifer's fate at the end of the issue. As such, we need to sell Lucifer as hard — or even harder.

Anyway — what I mean by all that is that when the pages came back and panels 4 and 6 of page 9 were there, I felt a lot better. Jamie saves the universe with another perfect pair of expressions.

Laura's name comes from Bat for Lashes' 'Laura', one (if not the) key *WicDiv* songs.

Hannah's choice of font is epic. We considered different colours for the 1-2-3-4 background, but settled on the boldness of the white.

10-11. We said we weren't doing many double-page spreads from now on. They were a *Young Avengers* thing. But — y'know — occasionally they're called for.

"1-2-3-4... She was just seventeen" is the first of the classic rock references in the issue. From 'I Saw Her Standing There'. First track on the first Beatles album. 1-2-3-4 and... pop music.

Not on the *WicDiv* playlist because the Beatles aren't on Spotify.

This image — obviously a key one — was one of the shamanistic pieces of it all. On a transatlantic flight. Listening to the plane's music system, and 'Shake It Out' by

Florence drops and it's just one of those moments when a record which I'd felt conflicted over suddenly transmutes into something else, and I'm paralysed by it. The fact the lyrics are carved from purest doggerel ceases to matter, and the words take on a power above and beyond everything else that's happening. I'm crying and get the key image — the girl on the stage and the girl in the crowd, the space between them.

(Clearly, for all their lack of subtlety, the lyrics of 'Shake It Out' are extremely *WicDiv*, and when they're at their best and sung with all the force she can muster, it feels like something we're aspiring to)

So, yes, there's a lot of Florence in here, but not just her. We try and keep the archetypes we're touching on relatively wide — there's a lot of Kate Bush and Stevie Nicks in the mix too.

Jamie just kills here. Matt does too. The composition of the one face in the crowd and Amaterasu on stage. Fuck yeah.

12-13. Oh, the pose is great, but it's Matt's colouring that takes centre-stage here. The original idea was a little more conservative and realistic, but we urged Matt to press more towards the emotional effect. And then in come all the whites.

First rush of names here. World buildy-build-build.

Hmm. I do like using brackets in captions. Hmm.

First appearance of "orgasm" in *WicDiv*. I suspect it won't be the last.

I think Jamie's got something really powerful with the expression in the last panel of twelve. Amaterasu is divine, but here she looks terrifying and a little terrified. And Matt nails those eyes-as-solar-eclipse effects. Eye effects are kind of a motif for all our indie work. They're all over *Phonogram*.

Page 13, panel 1: See the face on the left? You know Jamie often takes photo ref of himself for expressions? Now imagine Jamie, at home, trying to pull an O-face. I'd like to think he committed and method-wanked the expression, but that's much more Zdarsky's style.

Page 13, panel 3: Originally had extra captions on, but we realised that it was much more powerful with the single one. One of the things about captions in a panel is that they render it timeless. You have literally no idea how long that moment is. The second you add dialogue, or even thought balloons, it implies a certain length of time. Anyway — that, here.

Page 13, panel 5: I love Laura's freckles here.

Last panels were originally a fade to black, but when the colours started coming in, we realised a white out is a far better idea.

14. And hello to Luci.

You know, my *Uncanny X-Men* character Unit was originally based on a character I'd had lying around since I was 21 or so, and I decided to just drop him into the MU as he'd never work outside any large shared universe and I had no desire to make one. A gender-switched Lucifer who preferred 'Luci' dates from the same period. Good to get her out in front of a crowd.

The big influence on Luci is obvious, as we've said it in interviews — namely Thin White Duke era Bowie. To be honest, there's stuff I've taken from different periods as well. But there's certainly a lot more in the mix as well, not least... oh, we'll get to that in a minute.

Anyway — introduction is important. Trying to get the cross between the divine and the normal, which switches mid-page. What kind of book are we doing? This kind of book.

Laura's legs in panel 2 were redrawn after Matt Fraction said Jamie would regret it if he didn't. Turned out much better second time.

15. We're meeting a god for the first time, as a human. Clearly the relationship is going to be key going forward. The push and pull is fundamental — Luci being outrageous and Luci showing a little bit of humanity before letting the mask take over again.

Editor Chrissy added a lot to this page — it was one we argued about in terms of aim versus effect and all that. Let Luci be a deliberate attempt to be an outrageous troll early on, but in the original draft Laura didn't call her on it nearly as hard as she does here. I'll be saying this for the whole run, but this is a book *about* problematic people who will do problematic things. The book is *about* problematic things. Making sure that "about" is present is always on my mind.

Originally didn't have quotation marks around the Beatles or Larkin quotes, but we decided we really had to make the scene clear. Even if you don't know the quote, you need to know it's a quote. The quote marks with italics is our style guide for direct quotation of something famous, versus the straight speech marks without italics we use for more normal ironic distance.

Eight-panel grid. Our first one, and not the last. I love eight-panel grids. I fucking adore them. Jamie wants to kill me, but they're the very best.

16. I really like how Jamie handles Laura trying to stumble to apologise.

Panel 3 — you know, we really do a lot of hand-reaching-out gestures in our comics.

Panel 3 — Hmm. The guy on the left looks like Kid With Knife has been juicing.

17. How did they get to the afterparty? Who cares, sez I. Cut to the chase.

What I quite like about Jamie is how we've simultaneously got what's clearly a fancy room, but he's presented it objectively. This is an establishing shot without glamour. All the subjective angles of the gigs to sell the glamour, and now we go behind the curtain and... it's this.

It obviously works as an establishing shot as well – the layout of the room is key for the action sequence. Both Jamie and I are very much in the school who likes our fight scenes to be follow-able.

And we meet Sakhmet.

I initially considered Bast/Bastet for her, but I felt using her would have been basically like using Thor or Loki. Thor and Loki are always going to be in part about the Marvel Universe, and Bast would always be taken in part as *Sandman* critique. I dug a little further into the Egyptian mythology, and Sakhmet — there's various spellings, obv — stood out for a number of reasons.

The pop star archetype is spottable, with a major influence (Rihanna) perhaps a little too visible here. There's another influence worth noting, which is my own cat Lemon. Having Lemon in my life has made me think about cats a bunch.

18-19-20. Doing a comic about gods as pop stars does mean that we can do interviews and use them in a similar way. This is, in terms of cold, hard details of the world, the most exposition-including scene.

In the original sort of rough draft when I was still doing the larger scale world building, the interviewer was a one-off character. This would obviously would have been a mistake. This scene is an interview, and clearly about the gods generally — but it's just as much about Cassandra. Cassandra is just as key to the book as Laura is. They're opposites, the fan and the hater, the unquestioning devotee and the critic. Here, she's the book's autocritical voice.

It's the scene which (as I suspected) has proved to be the Rorschach test in the readership, normally based on how they feel about Cassandra. I could write more about that, but it'd be wiser to not.

Obviously this whole section was worked to death. What is too oblique? What is too obvious? What is too many fucking words? I managed to get page 18 down enough so we could have that silent panel at the end.

Page 18, panel 5: quoting my own series' tagline in the story is a very me move, innit? I'm despicable.

Page 19 has some of my favourite panels in the book. Panel 3 kills me — there's little of the girl there, and a lot of the god. The casual arrogance. I believe her there.

Page 20 is the poster child for "This book is about problematic people doing problematic things" lampshading. There's nothing that Cassandra says that isn't correct. By putting it in the text, it's our way of giving the nod to the readership that this is what the book's *about* rather than blundering around with no awareness. In short: if you want to do a story *about* something, it has to be included as an element in the story. This is us saying: "We know, you know, go with us." It's also a sign to say "if you're *not* willing to go with us, you probably should get off the train. The book is only going to frustrate you."

Last panel of 20 — I've only just noticed that Luci's shoes have fallen off, which is an amazing detail.

21. Yes, the idea for this whole scene came from playing with Lemon.

Sakhmet's expression in panel 4 is just great. Nice work, Jamie.

22. And a sudden change of mood, innit? We've front-loaded the possibility of violence with the opening (one of the structural reasons for having it as the opening before going into the real world) and now we're diving in.

Lots of lovely art details you can pick up on — the curving of the bullets around Amaterasu is one of my faves.

That's totally a Jack Kirby sort of pose in the last panel, innit? Also — look at the panel break. Jamie doesn't do it often.

1-2-3...

23. ...and 4! We talked about including one, perhaps in a caption, perhaps coming out the window, but decided it would be ugly as hell and had faith that after all the 1-2-3-4s so far, you'd fill the four in yourself in your head – and the 4 would be the explosion.

When the gods are doing their powers, it was Matt's idea to up all the lights. Everything is brighter. Showtime, etc.

Nice view of London in the background. We're looking towards the South Bank, which is just one of my favourite places.

24-25. Panel 1 is the first time "Lucifer" is explicitly mentioned in the book, which gives us the chance for Luci to do the Rolling Stones reference.

Nice use of background in the second panel. Was that Jamie or Matt? I can't remember.

When I was doing *Phonogram*, I had the urge to do a comic that basically took the structure of a musical, but applying it to superhero comics. You know — in musicals, when people are feeling something, they just burst into songs. We'd do that, but instead of songs, we'd have fight scenes. A fight scene would always be about that. While we're not doing that in *WicDiv* (it's more like what we did in *Young Avengers*, to be honest) there is a lot of the idea that the combats are also treated like performances. The timing, the pop art colouring, etc.

In terms of first issue saying what the book is about, I considered this whole sequence necessary. This isn't *Phonogram*, which primarily used genre as a structure to drape philosophy over. This is genre. In its own warped way, this is a superhero story, at least as much as *Buffy* or the *Matrix* are.

When I saw Jamie drawing panels of Teddy punching apart the goo-people in *Young Avengers*, I suspected Jamie would handle the violence fine. This is horrible stuff, but with the eye on the emotional effect of it — that distant shot after the two pop-art head-explosions is what sells it, for me. The headless body on fire, falling to the ground...

Last panel on 25 may be my favourite Luci expression in the issue. I wish I could have lost the caption and had it just as a one-liner panel, but without it, the transition loses people. It's a really hard cut, and needed to be softened.

26. The captions being a late add meant that the word EXACTLY was used both here and in Luci's dialogue. The last change I made to the issue was getting Clayton to change the dialogue one to PRECISELY, at about half-eleven. The captions serve another purpose. Laura has been very quiet for a while in the book. It restates that she's our viewpoint, and we're following her. Her captions on the last page serve the same purpose. I think the rough take for Luci's speech was the first thing I actually wrote for *WicDiv*. Just playing with the voice, playing with the concept of a miracle, etc. Luci is a glorious troll here, bless her.

27-28-29. In terms of panelling, you'll probably see that *WicDiv* is a lot more restrained than a lot of our work. There's lots of mad stuff down the line, but while we're inching people in, we don't want to distract them. Just very clean storytelling...

Actually, changed my mind. Luci's expression in the last panel of 28 is my fave of her expressions.

Or maybe it's the first of 29.

(Those motion lines make me laugh in that panel — just the implication of the back and forth tease,)

Three panels on 29. Why do this? Well, there's the practical thing. I want the page turn before people discover what actually happens. But it's also about extending the moment as much as we can.

It's also one of those sickening things where you realise that if you give an artist who can do what Jamie does a simple three-tier page, they will create something that works, every single fucking time. It's a bit depressing, in many ways.

30. More Jamie violence. More Matt leaning into the pop-art for the non-realist colours. Non-realist colours as parts of our performances is a very *WicDiv* thing.

When looking at Jamie's art doing violence, I find myself thinking about Brian Talbot circa *Heart of Empire*, if you see what I mean.

31-32. Sitting and looking at this page, and the only thing I don't like about it is that I should have asked Jamie to have a few small bits of fire as well as the smoke. Man! I suck.

Lots of key expressions. This is always Jamie's secret weapon, and you fucking use it. Luci has been in control throughout the book (with the exceptions of those rare flashes of vulnerability). This is not something we've seen before. A trickster god being played.

In a strict storytelling fashion, we don't actually need Laura's captions here, but they reconnect us to her, and hint towards what's next in the story by implication.

And on 32, full page cliff-hanger. I don't always end (or start) WicDiv with a splash, but it's rarely a bad idea. It does create closure.

And a cliffhanger — as much as the combat, another signifier that this book is going to be working in a certain way. "Lucifer is apparently framed for murder" is a plot hook that you could comprehend even without any of our world building. I could talk about murder mysteries as a plot-driver, but perhaps I'll save that for next time. This has already gone on a long time and my eyes are very tired.

33. And credits! Including Indicia, but I've already mentioned that. Designed by Hannah.

Back Cover. Quotes from the character on the cover are totally our thing. My only worry is that I write such long sentences, will they fit?

Right, that's enough for now.

Thank you for reading. The response to the book has been overwhelming. I want to hug you all, but if I did that, I'd just infect everyone with everyone else's germs, and that'd be rubbish.

See you next month.

ISSUE 2

Main Cover. Amaterasu, as seen in the previous issue. Doesn't feature much in this issue, which may make you wonder why we went with her. Primarily, she's one we've introduced already. We could have used Baphomet, for example, but that'd have spoiled the end — which is similarly why we didn't use Baphomet for *next* issue. We're being relatively careful in terms of when and where we introduce the gods, and the aesthetic effect inherent in that. That we're in a medium where you could get to see a cover 3 months before release changes a few things.

Not that it's not possible to play games with that. But we'll get there eventually....

Chip Zdarsky Cover. Chip asked to do it as a joke on twitter. Jamie said yes. And then it happened.

The great joy of creator-owned books like this is that you can totally just go ahead and do this kind of fun stuff. Worth annotating? I dunno if Chip is doing me as Ziggy or Gaga, and don't care. Jamie's in One Direction make-up, and cat-make-up because his old nickname was "Kitten." It's been retired.

My photo was taken in my mum's back garden by Chrissy, and took about 40 attempts to get right. It's quite funny that Jamie is doing the more active part and I'm doing the stoic role, as in real life we play completely opposite roles. Chip has never actually met us in the flesh, which seems strange now I've actually written it down. Oh, Chip. When will I know your kind embrace?

In passing — buy *Sex Criminals*.

Beach Ball Cover. A riff on the Rochester Police Bowie Mugshot.

McKelvie's idea. Strong call, and obviously appropriate for the story.

Icons. Note the change on an icon. Bars in front of it. We use these as status updates. Which god is in prison? That's Lucifer's icon.

I try to do synopses for my books. Partially it's to allow newcomers to dive in if they want to, but it's as much about reminding people what happened previously. A month is a long time. They've got more things to think about than your comickybook. Give a few prompts to remind people, y'know?

As some have noted, it's "young people" not "teen-agers".

1. Pick up from last panel. Three-panel grid. Nice use of the colour close-up, as called for by Jamie in the choice.

Tweaked the dialogue a bunch here, in terms of what information went in each balloon.

I like how the blood is visible as a halo around Lucifer's head on the right side of the panel, as if it's coming from Lucifer's head.

2. And hello, Baal. I'll save writing about him properly when he arrives in the story properly. First man of the gods to appear. In interviews I've described him as inspired by the archetype that runs from Bo Diddley doing 'Who Do You Love' to Kanye doing 'Power', which was primarily a device to help explain some of the core concepts of the series — in this case, that we're not talking about specifics but archetypes. Trying to make any of the present gods a 1:1 comparison to any real world figure isn't the point, etc. There's obviously more

in there. I like Baal a lot. He's not the first male character I made up for the book, but he was the second.

Laura's front room and her family is something we've discussed a lot, and the details will come out as we press on, though there's some details in the picture if people wanted to unpack it. We always do the environment-as-storytelling approach to comics.

I feel sorry for Laura's sister.

3. Interview storm out, and done in style.

I originally had Laura's panel silent, but added a caption in this rare case. Laura hasn't "said" anything in the book, and I wanted her a little more active — and there was a strength in being a little more specific about her feelings towards Baal and her feelings towards her feelings toward Baal.

Towards the end of the page, Laura's dad is basically what mine was like. Professional wind-up merchant.

4. Lots of details to ground it in the real world, while giving it a twist. Using a phone to look up shit. As natural as it gets. A girl with a broken phone. Says key things too.

The twist of subjectivity in panel 5 was something I chewed over. I like to think the joke stands alone (and it's not just a joke — it's more a way of seeing the world) but there was a nagging doubt that it may require a different kind of reading. With Fraction/Aja on *Hawkeye*, when they did the EVERYTHING AWFUL headline in a paper, I saw *reviewers* asking why a newspaper would ever print that headline. Perhaps it would be best to add a hand-holding caption in 6 to make sure everyone got it.

Problem being, that steps on the joke and ruins it for anyone who actually **did** get the gag.

There's no right answer in terms of art vs directness. You go all in on directness, and your book appears crass to any sophisticated reader. You go all in on art, and four people understand what the fuck is going on.

Generally speaking, I try and respect the audience's ability to keep up. I went with this. Fuck fear. Fuck making your book worse to make it appeal to a larger group of people at a less intense level.

5. One Week Later rather than a date, as the reader won't recall when it was actually set, and a relative time movement requires no context other than an understanding when the "now" is.

6. Holloway is a women's prison in North London.

When the page arrived from Jamie, I'd forgotten I'd asked for some explicitly Lucifer Fans outside the place, so I was wondering why he wasn't actually doing more individual outfits for the people outside the prison. I am an idiot.

You know, if the narration earlier hadn't started making some things clear about Laura, this monologue probably does.

'No Future' will always carry a little of the Sex Pistols with it.

I love what Jamie did with Laura's clothes here.

'Religious Studies' was originally R.E. In my first draft. You may have seen us ask whether people got what it meant on Twitter.

To quote Matt Fraction's notes on *Rex Mantooth*, we probably owe Jack Kirby money for the hand pose in panel 2.

7. The finger-protectors were Jamie's idea. A wonderfully materialistic response to someone who appears to be able to do miracles.

Sticking someone like Lucifer in a clear room like this immediately presses all kinds of genre-related buttons. Jamie uses space here well, to both establish the environment while also — by composition — underlying Luci's isolation.

Another book could have spent half an episode on Laura trying to hunt down the lawyer, but SKIP TO THE END, etc.

A couple of great "expressions" with Lucifer here.

8. This is probably the most fiddled with page in the entire issue, in terms of amounts of dialogue tweaked. Most of it went on trying to make sure what we wrote couldn't be taken to court.

Laura does say "Nuh-uh" a lot. We debated considerably how "Nuh-uh" should be spelled. Comics!

Luci's reintroduction, so she really does push it a bit. Lots of people's favourite lines from the issue seem to be from this page.

9. Flashback. There's a slight change in colouring here... and, generally speaking, read the issue with an eye on the colour palettes. There's a sort of rollercoaster of it, with a strong division between palettes which I really like. I write a bit about this later.

This was actually written Marvel Method style, which is odd, as it's one of the more traditional pages in the thing.

Introduction of Luci's parents on the quiet.

Is it stating the obvious to say there's shitloads of semiotic markers on the page, in terms of trying to nail down Luci's parents?

After miniguns and club toilets, swings may be the main recurring visual element in my comics. I mean, I was once biffed on the head by a swing by my Aunt, but I don't think it scarred me mentally *that* badly.

Luci struck me as the sort of girl who'd go for a knife.

(In passing: Scott McCloud "captions telling a different story to the images" beat here in panel 5. Which is entirely what we did in the previous panel, which was to bring them together to try and get the greater sense of the moments in her narrative.)

And hello Ananke! In a more easily drawable mask!

10-11. You know when we were talking about trying to do things similar to our DPS stuff in *YA*, but on single pages? This kind of thing.

Yes, you may send regards to Jamie's poor aching hand for drawing these two pages.

This issue is, in part, about selling key parts of our mythology — this is, in a partial way, Luci's origin sequence. It's the moment you realise you aren't a muggle.

(I hate that word.)

12. Jamie and Matt do lovely things here in terms of mood — the heat of the pinks, versus the white. Jamie throwing off another Lucifer outfit, to underline the idea that our characters don't have costumes — they have *styles*.

13. Discussing Fingercuffs was also a worryingly lengthy component of this issue.

" " at the start of a sentence is a very me thing to do. Implied pause before the start of speech. I over-use it in scripting, and lose a lot at the lettering stage. Marvel are particularly anti it. I'm not entirely sure who or where I picked it up from.

14. "Damnation is delightful. Everyone should try it". Originally a different line, but tweaked it to this, which resonates fairly obviously with our last project. Compare/Contrast.

Next to Tara, Woden is definitely the character who gets the most bashing in conversation.

Last panels were originally in a different order, but editor Chrissy noted that we could simplify the dialogue, rearrange, and get the silent final panel that we wanted. Comics are an agreeably remixable medium. It's less often in the visual — the ability to "dub" a scene after it's drawn is more where most of the flexibility is — but there's still a little of it there.

15. Change of scene to the National Portrait Gallery. A real place, which you can visit. Also, free to go into. It's a great way to spend an afternoon.

This scene is in the Romantics Room. I actually wrote it sitting in there, facing those portraits — or rather, the portraits which we riffed on.

The caption in the third panel was originally something much more elaborate, which nailed down some of the specifics of Cassandra and Laura's prior relationship — Laura was defining them as "people who she talked shit about who for some reason hadn't blocked her."

In the end, we went through half a dozen versions before I had a moment of clarity and realised that less was much, much more.

The three portraits you can see are riffing on Mary Wollstonecraft/Shelley, Lord Byron and Shelley. You can work out what gods they were on your own, except for the one I give away in two pages' times.

Better look at Cassandra's team. They're very much our book's equivalent to Silent Girl.

16. You discover characters whilst writing, in many ways. Their voice grows. My main surprise with Cassandra is how fucking sweary she is. There's someone else who comes close, but even he's not quite as full on.

(I've just finished doing some tweaks for *WicDiv* 3's lettering, and one of the things I'm removing is Luci saying "Fucking" and changing it to something a little more circular. Not that Luci wouldn't say fucking, but it depends much more about the context.)

This did involve some serious debate about whether Wikipedia could sue us.

17. "Mad, bad and dangerous to know" is the famous description of Lord Byron. Obvious implication.

Do I need to write more about the back and forth between Cassandra and Laura, and their dynamic? I think the point's pretty obvious.

In terms of writing, they're good sounding boards for once another.

18. Cassandra is the main device for giving nods to people who actually know the mythology. The little half-aside twists and ughs hopefully work as a wink.

The "Tara from fucking Buffy" was actually a late addition when I was trying to work out how to precisely load the first solid information about Tara other than Laura's dislike of her. One of the more popular lines from the issue. Sometimes it's stuff which you've had from the start. Sometimes it's the moment of inspiration.

The inserted thought-caption in panel 7 worked really well.

Last panel is already building up the mood for the next bit, which is utterly key.

19-20-21-22. One of the most loved sequences in the book. Probably best to not read this if you're highly adverse to sausage making.

Now, Marvel comics are basically 20 pages each. I've written a lot of them, and was there when the 22 page story got cut to a 20. That was an interesting writing challenge, which I believe I touched on a few times on *Decompressed* — maybe the Fraction episodes?

Anyway — one of the quiet things I did on my Marvel book was trying to get more pages which were basically free. Just little tricks and stylistic approaches that meant we could get more pages in the book without going over budget. Because, as I said last time, there's things (text pages, etc) that don't count towards the budget, which is spent on getting an artist to draw a page of art. The text and title pages are a pretty obvious example, but I did a lot more. The double-page spread that was just coloured red in the fourth issue of *Origin II* would be a pretty nifty example, but there was stuff like in *Journey into Mystery* where I used the same piece of art repeatedly and changed the lettering/colouring on it, etc.

I had a few ideas circa *Young Avengers* how to push it even further. If you took a page with six panels on, then put them on two pages, you can use the space for interesting effects. You can do text shout outs, do stuff with pacing, do stuff with design. Abstractly, you get two pages for the price of one.

The problem with doing that in WFH is that it basically is just opening a door for all sorts of exploitation. It doesn't matter how much work a page is, you get paid a page rate. It's the same for writers. If you start cheating that, or allowing editors to say "Well, that doesn't really count as a page" it could be doom.

Now, *WicDiv* is our book. We can do whatever the hell we want.

You may think "Well, just draw as many pages as you like." Problem is, we've still got a budget — which is basically "we need to get the book done and out and hit our deadlines and — y'know — Jamie needs to eat, and his time isn't free, etc". So abstractly each normal issue of *WicDiv* is 20 pages.

(Plus the interstitials and backmatter, which — as I mentioned — are free)

There will be exceptions, normally based around us looking at an issue objectively and trying to work out

whether it's feasible in terms of the deadline. Jamie added a page to Issue 3, just to ensure we got that full first image of the Morrigan's head, for example.

Anyway — in this case, I'm breaking down the issue and seeing how much space everything needs. And I ended up realising, basically, I needed to do the descent into the underground in one page.

This is a problem. The ending would just about work, but would work a damn sight better with a slower build.

So I come back to the ideas Jamie was playing with, and suggest basically using the work of one page, and splitting it into either two or four pages. (To keep the page turn on the final image.)

Basically a four-panel page, arranged on the blackness, arranged to give the the idea of a descent.

Jamie says yes, and (well) it looks more like nearly two pages' work rather than one, so he's being very kind... but artists are oft perfectionists, and I salute that instinct.

Extending to the full four meant I had to expand the monologue as well — all of which slows the process, and with the huge chunks of black, kind of adds to the atmosphere. I especially love what Jamie did with the escalator panel, leading us down. Plus when you get to the bottom, you get the claustrophobic towering amount of black above you...

In short: an idea we wanted to try which worked well. We wouldn't do it like this again, but we could do it in a different way.

My fave fan comment about this issue was the person who wondered exactly how long Baphomet hung in the dark until someone gave him an intro line. This is true.

Yes, Tara posters on the escalator.

21. And Fire! Have a look at how Matt works colour over the issue — the tonal rise and fall throughout it is one of my favourite things in the book. Each scene really has its own sense of place and colour scheme, and the movement of one to another is key. The black to the fire is the most obvious — but the calming turquoise of the National Portrait Gallery to the black is also startling.

I think we wrote this page Marvel Method.

I described the crowd as my dream The Specials audience gig.

22. And meet Baphomet, who may not be a very nice man. There are subtle tells.

Baphomet's archetype is pretty clear — leathers, attitude, fuck you, with me specifically digging into the early Nick Cave/Andrew Eldritch mode — though being a modern book has added a lot of sit ups.

23. And icons back! A new one added, with added flames to guide your eye there.

Thanks for reading. See you next month.

ISSUE 3

As always, these are just some random thoughts from flicking through the issue, and shouldn't be taken as any kind of holy writ that this is everything there is to think about the issue.

This issue was nightmarish to do, due to a variety of

compounded deadlines. As an example, I was signing off files at 2:30am, the night before my brother's wedding, sitting in the corridor of the hotel. There were a lot of tears and head banging against my desk that week, basically, and I suspect it was just as intense in different ways for everyone else.

But still: None More Goth, etc.

Generally speaking the idea of this issue is to have Laura go and have herself a nice adventure in the underground (framed in the structure of something akin to a gig) before returning to the surface. Obviously this also gives us an introduction to two of the gods. When one of them is the Morrigan — one of the more complicated figures in the book — she did need the space.

I think it's my least favourite of the first five. It works better than I thought it would, but it's serving a lot of masters.

Main Cover. The Morrigan in full effect, continuing the head shots. Colour choices telling. I have enjoyed that people have had a shot of cosplaying the characters before anything other than their heads are visible.

Stephanie Hans Cover. Due to the aforementioned chaos — this part entirely on us — Stephanie basically came in at the last minute and turned this around over the weekend. Stephanie is a force of nature here. Now that four of our guest variants are out there, I do smile at them, as a sort of cross-section of powerful and individual takes by artists of completely different styles, yet still speaking to the project. That's wanky for "I think our covers are pretty neat."

Beach Ball Cover. As we haven't seen Lucifer perform yet, Jamie thought it'd be a good idea to do one. I agree. There's a lot of *WicDiv* which is about distance-to-the-gods. The first time we see or hear them doing their thing may not even be in the narrative, but in the larger diaspora of STUFF around us.

Er... I *am* wanky today. I'll get a cup of tea and see if it normalises me.

1. Just like Issue 1, this is a cover-to-page-1 transition. Issue 2 had a note of it, but only thematically. This is even more (no pun intended) in your face.

In the first draft of the script, it didn't exist. I wanted it to be in there, but if I was writing for 20 pages, there just wasn't space. This was one of those negotiated conversations Jamie and I have, and in the end, Jamie just wanted to do it that much. There's 23 pages of comic art in the issue, though obviously we're doing our OPTIMISE WORK stuff in certain points. Black is our friend.

Anyway — from head to decapitated head, Laura captions recontextualise everything.

2. I really like what Jamie has done with the crowd shot — that curling fiery ceiling makes me recall music video format too. People taking pictures reflexively is a very us beat.

Took me a while to work out what I was going to do with Baphomet's voice. His internal life is one thing, but how that is expressed (or rather, how he chooses to express it) was a little elusive. In the first draft, he was a little more straight vamp melodramatic rather than the

pop-cultural, pun-obsessed fucking irritant show-off that I ended on. In a real way, Baphomet is a bit of a troll. He wants to annoy people who care, while simultaneously show how little he cares at all. The act is, as we see, somewhat brittle.

Anyway, he turns up with a magically created head and uses it in an act of Grand Guignol-esque theatre. This is reminiscent of... well, god knows how many bands there are who like playing with this stuff. It's more of a metal beat than a goth one, I suspect.

"Your new favourite god" was very close to being "who's your favourite new god, now and forever" but that would make me nearly as bad as Baphomet.

3. The only problem with adding a page at the start was that it moved the "head has started talking" beat to a right hand page (i.e. it isn't a surprise). In the end, we decided it was worth it.

In the drawing script, there was a lot more dialogue in panel 3. This was all moved to panel 4, because having multiple lines of dialogue in a panel that's clearly set in a very short period of time (like panel 3) is something that always looks terrible.

"TS Eliot is an anagram of Toilets" is something Editor Williams likes noting.

4-5. Jamie wanted a DPS. Jamie gets a DPS, and we do the frenzy of the crows.

Jamie actually drew the lettering on the boy, which involved some back and forth between the team.

6. And enter the Badb aspect of the Morrigan. As I said, she's complicated, and I wanted to treat her as complicated. She's an explicit mystery, so that's how we treat her. The reader is asked to puzzle her out.

The Morrigan is a triple goddess, as anyone who's been to Wikipedia will know. The opinion of what the aspects are varied, and obviously I had reasons for choosing the three I did.

The Morrigan is a warrior goddess, but clearly the way I'm writing Badb, she's taking point on the most obviously direct fuck-you attitude of that.

Originally the first panel was silent, but I figured that it was worth being a little explicit earlier on rather than just leaving the reader to puzzle it out from what Baphomet does later.

I smiled when I saw this page, as part of me was thinking "Now we're totally a 90s Image book" and grinning.

Badb's hair was originally a more natural red, but we ended up moving it to this. While Amaterasu's hair actually is dyed red in internals, the most famous images of her appear to be more of a bright natural (or semi-natural) redhead, and that's very much the iconic resonance most people use for her in fanart, cosplay, etc. As such, it seemed that Amaterasu owned natural-redhead now... which means that Badb gets to be the Pillarbox Red Queen.

I'll admit, I wanted her to have that look more than anyone else on the team. Moving from the unnaturally-haired Badb, to the Morrigan's relatively restrained natural look, to Annie's complete removal of hair was a sort of interesting contrast.

And there's autobio reasons for it as well. As always.

Last panel makes it kinda clear how Badb rolls. Writing her dialogue had me sort of blinking at my keyboard a lot.

7. All of this changes in tone when we talk about the Morrigan and Baphomet having been lovers, of course. This is a big melodramatic and childish shouting match, which is fine, except when they're gods.

Badb's voice was… not easy, but certainly came out in a great black flood. The problem was more editing. She makes her own compound words from other words (i.e. performing acts of violence against language and refusing to obey anyone else's rules, whatevvvvvva).

Interrogation of male fear and demonisation of female sexuality is a pretty obvious theme in my work (The Disir being the most obvious example over in *JIM*). You can probably file Badb in there, though she's coming at a different angle. As such, I was thinking of Sheela Na Gig statues, from the statue's perspective (And, yes, obviously there's more than a little PJ Harvey in the mix with the Morrigan). "Chasm-Cunted" is apex of the "Er… not sure if I get to write that, no matter what my intent" but after arguing it with Williams, decided it was okay. This is a statement of absolute power, etc. People seemed to have liked it. The Misandry is fierce.

(I like the bit on the previous panel where Badb says she implies she's going to use his shin-bone as a dildo. Oh, Badb.)

That said, we could probably lose all the dialogue and just have kept Jamie's immaculate little finger gesture and it'd have worked.

Let's talk colour for a second — this is a particularly lovely section from Matt — look at panel 2, and how he's turning the colours of Morrigan to make her almost burn up all red, etc.

Anyway — by the end of the page, Baphomet's actually had his ego pricked and he abandons his mask and goes a little more 4 Real.

8. Matt's colouring really makes the page here. The ghosts weren't quite working raw in terms of the effect, and the distortion makes it unearthly. It keeps Baphomet's mockery, but does something else. This is not normal.

And Laura returns with her caption voice seemingly caught in their melodrama. I keep on wanting to say "ravens" for the Morrigan, but they're actually crows. Heaven help the *JIM* fans — I could have changed it to magpies.

9. And Laura tries to solve a problem. This page took a lot of rewriting. It just about holds together, but it's still far from my favourite thing in the issue. Do love Laura here though, in her "WILL THIS DO???!??!" and framing it in the concept of an interview. Laura is, as Baphomet notes later, almost certainly someone who did drama at school.

(I almost started rambling about Laura's family background, but realised that's probably for the comic, eh?)

Using doggerel to fight doggerel strikes me as a very me beat.

End of page panel transition, trying to use framing to guide the eyes. We never see the Morrigan change, which is kind of the point. She's not changing forms in any way that we'd understand. She's the three-in-one.

Lovely expression on Badb counting to four. Badb really would rather kill someone, but not the time or the place.

(Also Laura in panel 3. That glance to the side.)

And enter the Morrigan, this time with a body (though tellingly out of panel). As those who know the myths will realise, she's (probably) Macha. For our purposes, as she's the "core" personality that Badb and Gentle Annie are the alt-modes, so goes by the Morrigan.

Er… some people have been confused by the Morrigan, but I'm saying it certainly could be worse.

I actually caught an interesting review. It's someone who didn't like the first two issues that much, but dug the third (and, in fact, in retrospect decided he liked the first two). He'd realised that the problem was he was trying to read it like most other books (i.e. fast). He'd forcibly slowed himself down, even to the point of actually reading it aloud. Now he likes them all. That struck me as interesting, and got me thinking. Especially in Issue 3, the language is written to be decoded, this mass of wordplay, word destruction and general mass of allusions. It's not the most naturalistic of books anyway, and Morri vs Baphomet is the apex (or nadir) of that particular trend in there. As the Shakespearean riffs may suggest here, this is a performance. He may have something. It's not a book that works well at a speed-read, at least in the issues so far.

Obviously not saying anyone who hates it "just isn't reading it right". If you have a low tolerance for people spouting this kind of stuff, it's obviously going to trip you right up. Just generally intrigued at responses. It's an odd book at times.

10. I have no idea why, but I still find NOCOCK HOLMES funny.

Morrigan's voice keeps a little of the artificiality of Badb, but loses some of her extremities (both in terms of twisting sentences and words, and content) for directness. She shares some wordplay with Baphomet — there's moments here when I can see why the pair of them hooked up. Badb is a force of Id-y nature. Annie works on her own logic. Morrigan is the queen, and more deliberate.

The Morrigan's inspiration actually came from the Pixies' 'Tame', but drifted considerably. I thought about transferring the incest-and-torture delirium of Frank Black's American South into the lands of the sidhe. There's some of it in there, but there's more elements to it. I probably could still use the concept in another project.

Second panel has the quote-on-back-of-issue drop. I haven't talked about these properly yet, have I?

I don't think I will.

Adding None More Goth to the actual issue was a relative late addition.

Really like Morrigan's shout on the left of the last panel.

The caption going off the page at the end was a choice, trying to get the idea of reality breaking down. Had a bunch of people presume it was a printing error. Probably should have pushed it even further, to make it clear it was deliberate.

11. This whole page is lovely work by Matt and Jamie. The slightly sickly orange warmth just being swallowed alive by the darkness.

12-13. Negative space ftw.

The performances are such an odd part of what we do. Hmm.

14. The swallowing and release by the dark works pretty well atmospherically, I think. The caption was chewed over considerably, with its positioning trying to at least give a little hand holding on what's going on.

Laura really does over-worry about the Gods.

Good finger point by Baphomet at the end.

15. Matt's sickly colouring really makes this whole sequence strange and (for me) scarier. In the inks, this looks like a natural fire. With the colours, it's something entirely else, and really oddly horrible. Also a return to the pop art violence of Issue 1.

Captions were an addition to give more of an impression of time passing. After pencils, Baphomet's escape was moved from four to three, which also extends the moment.

The "foot in end of page to intro a newcomer" panel is something I probably do a bit too much.

16. And here's Gentle Annie, one of the euphemisms for "Anann". Call her that in fear of pissing her off, basically. Primarily, she's a death goddess.

Gentle Annie's voice is the simplest of the three aspects, in terms of choices of language. She has her own obsessional concerns and interests, and that obviously comes through.

I've seen readings of Morrigan as a id/ego/super-ego model, and… well, it's undeniably there a bit.

I keep on wanting to call her Lazy Susan, which would be a very different sort of character.

Matt is selling the coming-back-to-life transformation here, in terms of really leaning into the flushing of the skin.

17. Sharing framing and stance in panels 2 and 3 to underline the transformation.

I probably owe Fraction money for the transforming into crows things. At least we can do a Casanova vs Morrigan crossover when we decide to really sell out.

Last two panels turn oddly physical comedy. Also a chance to look at Laura's skirt. Is it PVC? THAT'S MY FAVOURITE PLASTIC.

I'm sorry, Kenickie moment.

18. We really did use a lot of black ink this issue.

The last panel is really strong, I think — the ominousness of that policeman really works. Nice work, guys.

19. Bouncing between the normal life and the glamour of these adventures is, at least, part of the point.

I didn't want to do dialogue here, and just do internal narrative, as the specifics here matter far less than what the page says.

Last panel is a semi-reprise of a panelling choice from *The Singles Club*. The straight six-panel grid and story-telling choices are another step back towards something more traditionally indie, underlying the normality of it.

20. "Cthonic" as the underworld and "Homesick Blues" as in a Dylan riff and… oh, don't mind me.

21. And we begin again. One of the odd things about this issue is that it's more two issues — a sort of liminal place between the two. The first half is actually the conclusion of the previous issue, and the last few pages are more a prologue to the other part. We do things with the interstitial pages to try and make the THIS IS A UNIT OF ENTERTAINMENT clear. There's meant to be a pause for breath.

22-23-24. Now, as we wanted to give Morrigan the space, it turns this section dense. I suspect it works depending on how much you enjoy hearing Lucifer bitch about her "friends." Luci does strike you as the sort of person who has a prepared insulting description of everyone she's ever met.

Actually, as a murder mystery, having Lucifer's take on everyone struck me as a required scene. Lucifer has an opinion who did it. Let's see what she thinks. There's also the small issue that Lucifer isn't in this issue at all, and giving her a little face time is paramount. This arc is primarily her and Laura, and as such, we need to keep her around.

The "we don't hear Laura actually speak" anti-naturalism of this bit is something… I like? I think I like it. It obviously wouldn't have worked at all without Jamie and Matt. I mean, the comic wouldn't be there if it wasn't for Jamie and Matt, but I mean specifically in this particular section. Nice use of distortion by Jamie. Consistent.

Cassandra going "ugh" is totally us lampshading, I fear.

You ever heard a bunch of stories about someone before you've actually met them? That. This is meant to feel like that. Plus the social group-ness of the gods. They are more than a little cliquey.

Heh. Re-reading this, there is a lot of Luci being Luci here. HIGH CONCENTRATE LUCI. The Luci/Cassandra double-act strikes me as key. I wish they were friends.

I'm pleased that all the Carthaginian scholars in the audience haven't raked me over the coals for "Carthaginian God Of Fuck You".

25. Oh, hello, Baal. We were just talking about you.

I would kill to own this suit, btw.

Thanks for reading.

See you next month.

ISSUE 4

This is the sort of issue that inevitably turns up in far too many of my stories. It's often a narrative weakness, at least for a certain preference of readers. It's the "let's stop and have a nice walk around a place and explain what's been going on". If it's a three issue arc, you'll find it in issue two. If it's a four issue arc, you'll find it in issue three. If it's a five issue arc, you'll find it in issue four. If it's a six issue arc, I rarely use it, because that's too much delay before answer — or alternatively, enough space to leak out the secrets more gradually so it's a little less obvious.

I say this in part so that it ruins any story I've ever written, because now I've told you this, you won't be able to look at my work in the same way ever again, and so it'll force me to try other things. Or, at least, mix it up a little.

To be honest, it's something a lot of writers do. My problem is that I both like mystery (i.e. withholding information as long as possible) and complexity (i.e. amount of moving parts. This should not be confused with depth or intelligence or any other positive synonym. Complexity is an entirely neutral description in terms of quality — in fact, if anything, it leans negative, because for the same level of aesthetic kick something that does it more quickly is almost certainly better than something which requires more work. There is nothing intrinsically better about more work. The only justification for complexity is that it gives more than a simple solution) which means that a very natural structure leads to backloading of a lot of information, which causes this tumorous bulge in the narrative. I have a lot of things to say and hold it off as long as possible. Hence, this before-climax mass of *stuff*.

(Yes, the enormous parenthetical break in the middle of that paragraph was an illustration of my point. You stop and have to explain something too complicated, and you risk forward momentum just falling apart.)

To be honest, I actually kinda like it in many of the works I love: the essay-as-comics structure. Ideas, detail, character. I dig that, so it's no big surprise that I do things like (say) doing an entire issue where an analogue of Tony Wilson explains to Loki exactly why any conception of Britain-as-Arthurian-bullshit is bullshit. I don't read comics for plot. I read comics for *content*. I don't care what the content actually is — but just that it justifies my time. However, if you *don't* like that stuff, it's dead air.

That said, there's a certain school of comic fan who views anything not involving one person punching another as dead air, so you sort of have to shrug. You write what you find interesting. If you lose contact with that, you're fucked.

Anyway, *WicDiv* 4

Main Cover. I don't think Matt knows Tinie Tempah, but there's a lot of him in the mood here. First bloke on the cover too.

Kevin Wada Cover. Kevin Wada in full effect. You know, with Becky's cover just coming out, it has me thinking on actually what our alt covers are doing narratively speaking. Just because it's not in the story doesn't mean it doesn't feed into our iconography. Michaelangelo didn't do anything in the Bible, but is of fundamental importance to the Catholic faith, y'know?

Point being, it got me thinking that the Baphomet/Morrigan covers sell something about the two of them which absolutely is not there in the issues. We've only got to see them as a couple arguing in a nightclub, in an awful terminal state. The covers do something else, and all these things interact.

Er… am I stating the obvious in bringing up the playing-card structure, yeah? Thought so.

Kevin does sex incredibly well, in the "this is something people actually do" way, rather than the standard cheesebeefcakeisms. I want to see him draw FKA Twigs art, basically.

Talking to him also inspired…

1. …the page transition. When I wrote the Fresco, Jamie had the idea of rather than getting Matt to colour it, we'd get someone else. Nathan Fairbairn did the honours. Honestly, seeing Jamie's stuff with Nathan's full painting on it is a complete revelation, and immediately made me imagine somehow getting the budget to do a whole comic with it for a suitable aesthetic purpose.

It's also telling that *WicDiv* has been a hit. If we were doing it on *Phonogram* money, we would have never thought "Hey — let's pay a completely different colourist to do a whole fresco just as a detail on couple of pages for a comic" because we'd rather be thinking "how can Jamie eat this month with this money? Or rather, how can Jamie eat something which actually is nutritious rather than — for example — moss and twigs?"

Yeah, another cover —> first page transition. It may be a theme or something.

Cassandra's expression is hilarious for me here.

2. And the rest of the Fresco. Done as a single Jamie McKelvie spread, then coloured.

First two pages are a character intro. Either you find this amusing and like Baal for it, or you don't. As in all things, it says as much about you as Baal.

I've already talked about Baal being inspired by the whole line of archetypes between Bo Diddley doing 'Who Do You Love?' and Kanye West doing 'Power'. Most people have picked up on the (incredibly foreshadowed) Kanye-isms, which is fine, as they are very much to the fore.

3. Oh, my. Me and my puns.

4. At this point of writing, 'Monster' has just turned up on shuffle. Oddly, one of my friends has recently been personality-smeared on a site by people who didn't recognise a quote of Minaj's rap during 'Monster'. Sigh. Sigh. Sigh.

Relevantly, in the script for panel 4, amongst a lot of other of my usual nonsense I said…

"Anyway — him giving a glance back over his shoulder. And… this is very much the LOOK THAT NICKI MINAJ HAILS IN 'SUPER BASS'."

Jamie nailed that look.

First appearance of Laura's internal monologue, which is absolutely key this issue. Laura does very little in the first few pages, but Jamie (via framing and responses) and me (via my usual captiony nonsense) are making sure she's present, even when Baal and Cassandra are going at it.

Baal was one of the first gods I knew I wanted in the book. I love the whole school of Caananite/Phoenician gods. The confusion over "what-Baal-anyway?" is very me.

5. Valhalla as digital future thing is a lot of fun. We'll get to Woden in a minute, of course. Jamie and Matt were trying to get a slow build towards the centre, adding more of the electronic brightness.

(In passing, fuck me — this issue was hard as hell. Jamie basically catching some awful Norovirus half way through, and we lost a week. This involved of a lot of pain towards the end for everyone. That the issue is as strong and coherent as it is says a lot about what Matt, Clayton and Jamie can do together. Round of applause.)

Baal's doing a bunch of things here. We're getting larger scale ideas based around the gods generally and specific things about how he sees it — Baal is a fatalist and a realist.

We also introduce another key idea of the series here, which Ananke nods towards later on — what the gods actually *do*. I occasionally talk about *WicDiv* being a summation of everything I've ever loved and anything I've ever done — it's only here I realised that there was more than a little of my *Busted Wonder* in the mix as well.

There's one verbal tick with Baal, which is basically a *The Thick of It*-esque avoidance of calling anyone by their actual name. He doesn't do it all the time, but this is me trying to get a little of the verbal playfulness of some of my favourite rappers in the mix. It's clearly an ongoing balance.

The amount of debate between Chrissy and me over whether it should be "Play it cool!" or "PLAY IT COOL!" in the final panel was not exactly a small thing. I talk about this a bit later.

6. The joy of working with Jamie is that you write a scene like this and you know he'll nail it. It's like a director working with one of the foremost character actors in the world.

As you'll know the first three panels, I'll direct you to the fourth — I love how Baal absolutely doesn't buy into anything. Also panel 1 — how Jamie draws the expression so that there is no question mark in the sentence. Baal isn't asking *anything*. Baal already knows.

More Baal fatalism, and the first appearance of some of Woden's foreshadowed Valkyries.

I love Halberds, but can never spell one. Ever. When I was in Venice earlier this year, going around the Doge's armouries and naming all the weapons shows me to be a man who is on first name terms with the AD&D manual. I just call it "A".

Honestly, I love that Laura is going to meet the gods in a pair of fucking dungarees. Jamie is a wonder.

7. I would too.

8-9. This was originally written as a single page, for space reasons. Jamie insisted on a DPS, because he (rightly) argued that it'd be more effective with the circular design. Not that doing a circular design in a medium like comics is exactly easy.

We've met Amaterasu and Sakhmet before, but in the *WicDiv*-ian mode of style > costumes, Jamie's gone for a new look. I really like Amaterasu's Cosplaying-A-Healer look. I could never wear it, as I'd be covered in stains in the first four seconds.

Minerva and Woden are the new ones — plus one of Woden's Valkyries. Frankly, if there hadn't already been two warnings in the story so far about Woden, the fact he's possessively holding a towering valkyrie in pink glowing armour should probably send alarm bells ringing. *Dude.*

Minerva… oh, she's an interesting mess of semiotics. The retro uniform was used by more than a few people — from the Beatles to the Libertines to MCR to Queen to the Manics to fuck knows else. Plus a mechanical owl. Who can resist a mechanical owl, eh?

(Yes, *Jason & The Argonauts* is certainly in the mix there. *WicDiv* is everything I've ever loved and all that.)

Fave Jamie addition: each seat has the god's icon above it. They actually replace if anyone swaps seat. Cute.

Clayton obviously had his work cut out trying to work out how to do Woden's vocoder-impression vocal style. I suspect it'll only get more extreme as we go on.

10. The problem with Jamie asking for a DPS in the previous page means that it knocks all the page turns out of whack. As there are important page turns later in the issue that we want to keep where they are (not least Luci's escape) we wanted to add a page earlier. In fact, we added it here – expanding the silence before Ananke speaks. Originally 10-11 happened on the same page.

Of course, originally there was no re-intro of the gods mid-panel either. This was written quiet to build tension, but at lettering we realised that now would be a very good time to have a formal reintroduction to them.

There's a few bits in this section that nag a little, but I suspect that's at least in part as I know how I wrote the original monologue.

11. We totally missed the icon in panel 3. Fixed for the trade. Sorry. Jamie's Norovirus, remember. REMEMBER.

The last panel had the "A" missing from it until literally minutes before it was sent. Chrissy thought I was just doing ancient-god-esque speech, when in fact, I'd typoed like a big ol' idiot. Comics!

12. Perhaps obviously, this is where we blow apart the murder mystery. The plot as stated dissolves, at least assuming everyone here is telling the truth. Murder mysteries imply that one can solve the crime in a normal way. Here we go "Nah". This is not that kind of story.

4 and 5 are odd issues. I actually wrote them both simultaneously, bouncing between the two. This sequence was the last thing I wrote the first draft of. It changed intensely between that draft and the second one — it was far more static, with both Laura and the gods being almost spectators to Ananke. Now, there's certainly artistic reasons for doing that — and that's probably what I was thinking — but I'm much happier with where its ended up. Yes, Ananke takes the lead, but we get all the gods to chip in appropriately a lot more — plus Laura is much more of an active character.

Obviously, there's a lot of world building going on, but I most love Amaterasu here.

13. And in panel 5 we return to the idea of gods as conduits for inspirations that Baal brought up earlier. This was a core thing in *Busted Wonder*, which I really must get around to trying to talk someone into printing.

I'm really do like Sakhmet. She's coming from a very different place to the rest of the gods.

14. In terms of my favourite very late addition to the script, Minerva's beat is probably my favourite.

In terms of my favourite quite late twists of the scene, Laura's "This is such bullshit" outburst would be one. I actually had her being a lot more timid in the first draft, and being basically a messenger between the pantheon and Luci. However, for doing this, I love Laura.

15. Great selection of expressions here. I think Sakhmet takes it.

(Woden doesn't even really compete.)

Also, Laura has more confidence than I would have. I'd never face down anyone while wearing dungarees, let alone a bunch of gods.

16. I believe this is the second time the title is lifted from dialogue spoken actually inside the section. The first was the ONCE AGAIN which opened Issue 1.

Important. May come back to it.

17. Jamie is very good at this comics human emotion thing.

As a basic writer craft note, a hard cut from a scene which is loaded with information to a scene later, after one character has explained everything they've just heard to the other one is a classic move. Obviously wasting time repeating everything is awful, but there's a real power in making the reader's understanding of information entirely line up with a character's. In this case, Luci and the reader both learn what's going on with the pantheon simultaneously.

18. Eight-panel grid, Jamie doing acting thing, this is what we dooo-ooo-oooo.

Er... very important page. Maybe I'll talk about it down the line.

19. I've been mildly obsessed with Matt's choice for the pink to purple in the first panel. That's a very unusual choice. I didn't want to ask Matt why he did it, as I almost didn't want the magic spoiled. If he said "I just felt like it" I would have been very disappointed.

Laura's phone re-enters. I quite like how many people haven't realised Luci has totally stolen the phone in a few pages.

Part of me feels terrible that *WicDiv* has call-back jokes based around cocaine and cigarettes. It's not a very big part.

20-21. Page turn is key here, of course.

Jamie does lovely stuff here. We talked about a variety of things in the script, but this relatively clean but quietly dynamic approach is probably best. For an issue that's been as static as it has been in terms of panel layout, even slight change of panel-shapes and grid is deeply impactful.

The "sprinkler not hitting Luci" is splendid, but I think my favourite panel is the melting of the plastic screen. There's something really visually interesting about the perfect circles forming in front of Luci that really captures the supernatural element of it.

Wonderful stuff by Matt as well — all the reds here are great. The Luci-blowing-apart-cuffs shot is especially strong.

22. Jamie added the silent panel, which is a really strong choice, and has led to some interesting readings of this scene. It's certainly a charged one, and a key one for understanding Lucifer.

I had to attack this in a few ways when writing it. I suspect this is where we at least feel that Laura is 4 Real. In the first draft, Laura was the person who brought up the deal, which changes that entirely.

Those bottom three panels. Jamie, you are quite the guy. Laura's hair being totally soaked is strong.

23. One misreading of the book I've seen quite a lot of is thinking Luci is playing 'The Last Time'. She's not. As the text says, she's playing the B-side, the sepulchral threat of 'Play With Fire'. I did expect that, and thought about suggesting Jamie change the iPhone image to some Stones Compilation with it on... but I kinda like the doubling down of it.

It being Laura's phone is also loaded, of course.

I think this is the first time we ALL CAPPED a Laura Caption. Originally the PLAY IT COOL! PLAY IT COOL! from earlier in the issue was also all caps. Decided it was overkill, though it was a much longer argument than that.

24. And one of those key images in the series I knew was coming all along, and got terribly excited about when it turned up.

That said, for a formative image, the final line got rewritten a *lot*. I had a number of different approaches, and a *lot* of specific implementations of each of them. I ended up on a carefully worked version of one of the earliest concepts — specifically, the caffeine intake joke, married to some specific choices of language, and (the last part which came, and probably the key thing which makes it feel like closure) a call back to Ananke's warning.

Anyway — hopefully that leaves everyone ready for the big first arc climax.

Thanks for reading. This one was fun.

ISSUE 5

We may be taking "Kill Your Darlings" a little too literally.

It's a tricky one to write about, this, as obviously it's simultaneously the climax of these five issues and the start of the larger 30-60 issue thing. As such, talking about design in terms of the small scale may be revealing about the larger scale, and vice versa. In other words, the standard advice of "do not assume this is even the smallest fraction of the thinking behind the comic" stands more than ever. I'm telling you stuff, but I'm also not telling you stuff.

In a real way, as always, a lot of this is actually trivia.

When the first issue dropped, McK dropped me a line asking "So, are you worried that we're going to be killing the most popular character off?" to which I — being a fairly rational human — answered "YES, OF COURSE."

It's core to the design, of the arc and *WicDiv* generally. In a real way, it's a tragedy, and *Hamartia* — yes, I had to google that, as I have no education — is at the core of it. For our purpose, the necessary momentum of there being no way out was part of the conception.

Luci is the most darlingest of all my darlings, the distillation of what could be roughly phrased as a Kieron Gillen Character. One part *Dangerous Liaisons*, one part a cursory skim of The Bluffer's Guide To Popular Culture Of

The Last 4000 Years. My Emily Aster, my Loki, my Emma Frost and all the rest — a core character I return to to explore a bunch of things I find fundamental about me.

So, yes, she dies first. She has to die first. It's simultaneously the expected move, but also a distancing one from all our previous work. *WicDiv* is about everything we (and I) have done, but it's also an attempt to break with our (and my) own tradition. As such, self-immolation is entirely necessary. This is what you know about us, and also a break from it.

If you want a minor bit of trivia, for a few seconds before settling on Lucifer, I played with the idea of having the Lucifer role be Loki. I rejected it for a bunch of reasons — too on the nose, for one. Too parasitic, for two. But it sits in there as subtext.

Main Cover. Fucking Tara!

Becky Cloonan Cover. This is just great. I've talked in previous sets of notes about how the Alt Covers do a lot to establish the characters as icons, with their own internal history, but Becky completely nails that. All the doomed needy romance of everything is here, and it's not really in the story, etc.

In passing, if anyone could art direct all my kisses in my life, it would be Becky.

Jamie's Sakhmet Cover. Very regal, nice composition and Matt Wilson can really colour a fucking lion. Sakhmet has been kept at a distance, despite being one of the first gods we've met, and this doesn't really break that.

Intro. "Fuck That" makes me smirk. Sigh. I am 12.

1. This page caused hilarious problems. Obviously another transition from the first page — IF IT'S GOOD ENOUGH FOR *WATCHMEN*, etc...

The problem was that I'd written it as something that worked as a page but when I had a moment of looking at things from a higher level, I noticed something was off. In fact, so did Jamie. And our consultant. Everyone agreed there was a problem.

The thing was that the doodles were basically Lucifer drawing a beard on Tara. Other stuff as well, but a beard was in the mix. Written solely as a traditional thing people graffiti on pictures. Fine, out of context. In context, with the Cassandra beat later, this creates a whole different set of resonances. It's made worse by Lucifer's original line in the third panel being something else that could code as transphobic — and that would interact with the later scene in a way which undermines everything that's happening there.

The line was an easy fix, but the image was a problem. With an impossible deadline, it'd require a complete redraw to move the finger, and it'd break the composition no matter what. So the question became what could we have on the image which could end her finger in that position. I'm pretty pleased with what we ended up with — the devil horns weren't in the first draft, and are a definite improvement — and I suspect you would have never have known we had to tweak anything if I hadn't told you. Oops.

I really like Luci's coffee sipping.

2. The corner of Highbury & Islington. Oddly, a pretty important locale for *Phonogram* 3 too, which is accidental, except not really. I was originally planning to have the final fight in central London, near the National Portrait Gallery from the second issue, but I just didn't buy the distance travelled by Lucifer before everything kicking off. I was idly thinking of it happening by the HUMANITY statue outside there.

Of course, being near Trafalgar would have made this a crossover with *Über* instead of *Phonogram*. It's all linked. You may think of *Über* for another reason in this issue, of course.

There's nothing I don't love about Jamie's work here.

3. SHIT BEING FLUNG FANWARDS was a line I was resisting throughout the whole process, before going "Fuck it" at the last minute. I think it was the right call. Cassandra is a little bit that person.

Craft fans should note us trying to reintroduce the idea of the original offence with Lucifer here – the quotation marks on "Cassandra". It's been five issues since then, and *everyone* would have missed it at the point. It's on the Chekovian shelf, but we have to at least remind people it exists.

I kinda love how utterly clueless Amaterasu can be. Bless her. Jamie did this after going to see Kate Bush live, and you can see the influence all over this issue. Kate was wearing a similar tassle-y outfit in her opening set.

4. Nice colouring nimbus on panel 3 by Matt. I believe "remove the headphones on panel 1" was an editorial note, and one Jamie does wonderfully. I especially like the blankness of Lucifer. "Ammy" in quotation marks was me reacting to how Jamie had drawn the page. Important to do such things.

The lightning bolt in the last panel is glorious, of course.

5. Probably the best Punch Jamie's thrown in his career. And, yes, it's around this point I suspect the superhero DNA of the book comes a lot more to the fore. We're never going to be a throw-down-every-issue book, but when we choose to do it, we'll really go for it.

(There's an issue down the line which will be my take for the best fight comic of all time. I suspect it'll say more about my definition of best fight comic than anything else, but I'm looking forward to it enormously)

Matt played a lot with the colouring effect. Earlier drafts had a more superheroic mainstream hyper-bright-ism to it, which was wonderful state of the art superhero stuff, but we wanted something a little more a step to the left. The digital distortion, like reality being sampled and remixed, speaks to a bunch of stuff. Strong work, Matt.

6. DISCO INFERNO, etc.

Okay — on a craft level, the trick this issue was keeping the back and forth. More genre-aware readers would be suspecting doom for Lucifer. Those who don't double-think the books would be going for the story as is. Trying to get a rollercoaster of back and forth is absolutely key. Luci doing this kind of stuff is to the core of it.

This is probably the most Warren Ellis beat I've ever written, I fear.

7. This whole section was written Marvel Method, so the dialogue was often responding to the page. I really wanted to say as little as possible. This is a good page to examine what Matt is doing to Jamie's work — the third panel is completely Daft Punk.

8. Yes, Sakhmet turns up to a fight to the death in thigh-high boots and leather hotpants. It's just how she rolls.

Sakhmet's fire from mouth is probably something that has the more mythic-aware folks going OH, I SEE WHAT YOU'RE DOING, etc.

When writing this issue, I wrote a few sections in Marvel Method. One was this, the other one was the latter rescue by The Morrigan. I wrote both for two pages, but had a note that if we had time, expanding either sequence (or both) to four pages was something that could serve the material. Jamie expanded his sequence — from Baal's arrival to Laura running — but kept the latter sequence as written. This was the wiser take — the opening being that the first god/god action is our first impression. The "bigger" it gets, the better. We don't do a lot of it, so it needs to be memorable.

9. We moved the location of this around a little, and debated on whether trains would even be running. The fight being a little away and having the police line gave us the plausible deniability, I suspect.

There were originally more Laura captions here — terse, but more of them. They disappeared across the various drafts. When one went, the rest fell quickly, as they were primarily about the momentum between them. You lose one, the rest become increasingly extraneous.

Lovely lip bite in panel 4.

10. I rarely do multiple punctuation marks in my comics, but I suspect panel 1 is as good an excuse for it as any.

I believe my script had a note that this is the most irresponsible scene I've written in my life.

11. One of my favourite pages in the entire issue. Jamie added a panel into the mix here, which allowed him to basically construct the page into two units — the top, which is a moment to moment transition (which uses the stillness of the image's framing to create the impact of all the other movement) and the other *another* moment-to-moment which uses the stillness of the composition to create atmosphere. It looks even better — as those who do edits have discovered — if you just lose all the dialogue and have the Morrigan merging with the black to her right. Wonderful stuff.

SHE ASKED/I TOLD HER was a late addition to bridge the transition, which was feeling a little awkward. Generally speaking, this is the sort of thing you look out for in the transition between script to pages to final letters.

The Morrigan has a little Kate Bush influence too, I suspect. Jamie was really taken by the gig.

12. Sakhmet really doesn't give a fuck.

The four panels on the right read a little quick — the first line in the second panel was added which changes the pacing significantly. Originally it was just the second line, which changes the beat of the sequence.

Jamie uses a lot of digital stuff for the ravens, perhaps unsurprisingly, which lead to this panel in the rough pencils.

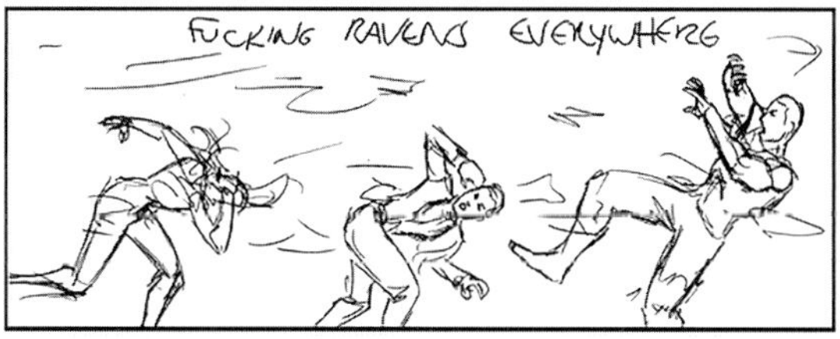
FUCKING RAVENS EVERYWHERE

Which is absolutely my favourite.,

The 12-13 was the other sequence that I suggested maybe could do with expanding to four pages. Jamie didn't, and it's interesting to examine how he did it, if you've got your craft head on. It's sub-page unit stuff.

The layout did cause one problem, however - notice that Baal is pretty undressed here? Remember that.

13. Luci in the first panel makes me laugh.

Panels 2 and 3: we're not subtle, us. Also a call back to Issue 1. Not alone in that.

I get the image of whoever's house this is coming in from the right, and giving all these kids a good talking to.

Panel 6 is GPOY.

14. Obviously one of the more reworked pages in this issue. Lots of eyes on it. Also a scene I chewed over a bunch, not least that it could have pissed off literally everyone. The part of the audience who views diversity as pandering will hate it just because Cassandra is a trans character. The part of the audience who is social justice may not be able to deal with Luci having deliberately having used a transphobic insult as a weapon.

In the end, we seem to have got away with it. From conversations I've seen on both sides of what I'd call the cultural divide, when someone brought up the responses I expected, someone else nodded towards the nuance I was trying to work in.

But in a real way, I don't write to comfort. I write to both explore and provoke uncertainty.

The LUCI! From off-panel was a late addition that seemed to smooth the transfer.

I smile at the passing of the cigarette — that line was another one that was reworked to death — because... well, I was writing Issues 4 and 5 simultaneously. I was bouncing between both issues, and filling in the gaps, as it all basically existed in my head at the same time. It was also — er — probably my most agitated state of mind of the year.

Anyway, when I came back to polish the final draft a few months later, I read through it all, and it was only in the final scene where I realised that Luci hadn't actually given Laura the cigarette for her to light at any point whatsoever. Plotting FTW!

I kinda like the CREDIBLE UNDERGROUND ARTIST gag. I did have another gag from Lucifer in here — Luci calling Laura something other than her name — but that's Baal's schtick. I'll probably use it in his mouth at some point.

15. Page structure identical to Issue 1. Nice big panels to give it as much build up as possible.

Now, one thing I don't like about having it like this is that it has this reveal on the RIGHT hand page. That means that you can see it when you're reading the pages in print copies. As in, for most readers, they'll be aware that some bad shit is just about to happen, which colours the reading of the Cass/Luci scene.

Which is interesting. Obviously in digital, this wouldn't be true — I suspect I'll be interested in quizzing people who read it digitally or in print and seeing whether it altered their reading experience.

I mean, I **could** have expanded a page, and had the clicks and the death shot on the same double-page spread... but that removes the page turn, which has a power of its own. The element of complicity and tension/release in comics is something I love. My own comics origin includes buying THE NEW SCUM for *Transmetropolitan* and being a little saddened and surprised that they'd have (er) the end of a certain character on a right side page, which means that the equivalent build up was wasted. Of course, trades are tricky fuckers.

Anyway.

Also — what a great look by Ananke? You're rocking it, girl.

Also — the central expression there. "Don't" indeed. Nice work, Guys.

16. Well, yeah.

Obviously lots of work here on the head-shot. There were a variety of different takes on the colours, and we ended up on hot pink.

There was dialogue in the script in this panel, but when Jamie has this frozen moment of horror, I decided to lose it and lean into the timelessness of the panel. Especially...

17. ...when we go for this next.

Necessity is a mother of invention. As you may have guessed, this issue was enormously packed, in terms of fitting everything in — and, even more importantly, fitting everything in and making it emotionally meaningful. This led to me growling that there wasn't really space for anything just after the moment and...

Well, we don't need to. In fact, it's better if we don't.

18. Great anguish here. Various people have picked up on the classical pose here, but what I really like is that Jamie's made it feel much more down to earth. Up to this point in the issue, it's very much classic action comic storytelling. The characters are generally speaking larger than life. This isn't. Before, Luci was a god. Here, she's a lump of meat.

(Special marks for the Ananke pose too.)

First panel did have one element that required a tweak. Namely, Baal was basically topless in the original inks, and it was (er) somewhat distracting. As it was the first time we became aware he'd lost his clothes, it was something that drew attention beyond what was appropriate for the moment. So we added some more clothes.

Gentle Annie is the world's greatest diagnostician.

(I suspect people who were a bit bewildered by Issue 3 may see its purpose in this issue.)

19. And Ananke's bid at YouTube superstardom was actually one of the first speeches I wrote on the proj-

ect. I can't remember if it was in the first rough notes I hammered out, or whether Luci's speech in Issue 1 came first. They were close together though, and possibly in the same session.

20. At this point I realised that the characters have run a long way in their cloud of ravens. NICE TRY.

21-22. I kinda love Laura's parents here.

This sequence is leaning into the "maximum amount of artistic effect for the same work" axis that we've been exploring in *WicDiv*. I could have merged all six panels into a single page... but why the hell should I? This works much better.

23. I originally wrote this scene in Laura's bedroom, reprising the O'Malley cover of Issue 1... but I realised I wanted to save that for something else, and the familial space we set up in Issue 2 is probably more resonant.

24-25. I originally wrote this as a traditional ending single image, but it just didn't seem to be us. Seeing it light is one thing... but I'd rather say more. In which case, we came up with this, which (for me) is the apex of our trying to rethink the concept of pages-vs-work. Doing what is basically half a page of art, but recoloured to create a completely different effect. Took quite a while to get it right, but when I got Matt's colours when he mailed it through in the pub, I shouted fuck yeah *that's* what we were looking for.

Nice work, guys.

26-27. Obviously "Sympathy" has a lot of connotations. *Sympathy for You Know Who* was the working title for the arc before *The Faust Act*.

Yes, that's Luci's symbol replaced with a skull, which probably is the last clue you needed to get the circle that opened Issue 1.

The responses to this issue have been amazing. For those of you who are worrying, it was written in what was the peak level of (er) a heightened emotional state this year. I'm in a better place now. The next arc, which I'm currently writing, is an interesting one — while I'm more together than I was, I'm also specifically writing *about* that period. We'll see how it goes.

Thanks for reading. Hope you join us next time.

ISSUE 6

Seems an odd time to be writing this. Issue 7 is just being uploaded to the printer. Passed Jamie the Issue 8 script. And now chewing over Issue 6. And Christmas Eve. And the ISS has just flown past our house.

Okay, I'm just overloading everything here. Let's go.

(As always, this is primarily trivia and shouldn't be taken to be everything.)

Odd issue, in many ways. There's really two ways you can go, and either one would have defined the book. After five, we could accelerate into the quasi-superhero warfare mode. But no, that's not our style. We slow down, and take the events seriously. Of course, there's precursors here — I suspect this issue reminds genre anglophone fans of those after-arc issues in Claremont's *X-Men* where characters actually get to have a little downtime to have emotions and act like humans.

And most importantly, we refocus on Laura.

Main Cover. Yes, clearly to show the Claremont influence, we have Shatterstar on the cover.

David Lafuente Cover. I love David's stuff, and I've wanted to do a project with him for years. We did a *Phonogram* B-side, and he's done a couple of covers for our books, but that's been it. Must do something about that, eh? Fact: this is the alleyway near where he used to live in North London.

Icons. We're going to have increasing problems with our recap pages, I think.

1. We start really quietly. It's a mood thing, using the number of pages to show the implied vignette of what life has been like.

The T-shirts are interesting — when I saw them, I immediately asked Jamie how he was doing it, and how difficult it was to do. It's done with a single image, which he uses the warp tool on to distort it appropriately. It's a really strong effect.

We plan to do this as merch down the line, after the other T-shirt.

2. The T-shirt is a very Jamie and me collaboration. The one-liner was me, the design was his.

We'll be soliciting this for April, btw. We'll be doing it in black as well as white, because we are total goth.

Yes, Laura is in a bad place. No, not Brockley. Brockley is a lovely place.

3-4. As reintroduction, we have to work in a bunch of world building here, and this is where we start it. It's an arc about fans. We start with human horror and smalltalk.

Inanna's residency in Camden has been mentioned a few times, of course.

We debated whether the second heave was clear enough. It probably isn't, but the only way to make it clear would be to add an SFX, and I thought that turned it into far too much of a comedy beat. Sound effects are, by their nature, humorous. This isn't funny at all, except in the blackest way possible.

Matt's idea for the recolouring of the panel, and a typically unusual choice. Strong.

5. So, about a month later. A lot of time passes in the second arc.

6. Lots of teamwork here. The bits of scrolling text which aren't completed were a giggle. The "Rolling Stones' 1969 Classic" ends with a note that it's gone to #1 in the charts, for example.

Baal in rare form here.

We side-step the obvious plot. Frankly, the "Oh no, the government are scared of these people" plot has been done to death for the last 80 years of superhero comics. I have absolutely no desire to do it, at least in its

standard state. But, yes, this statement raises as many questions as it answers.

I suspected as this is obviously such a shitty job to have to admit impotence, Clegg would get it.

Hmm. I'm not quite sure if I'm taking the piss out of my favourite scene in *St. Swithin's Day* with the Baphomet scene or not. Hmm.

7. Space=meaning. This is clearly the biggest thing, and we treat it as such.

Probably best not to say much else.

Laura's parents are the long suffering heroes of this book.

8. Jamie's idea to drop to the white, which I think works really well — it stresses the complete alienation from the environment and a bunch of other stuff, while also giving him a chance to do some full-length acting.

This sort of stream of consciousness ramble isn't necessarily what comics are best at, except with burning a lot more panels, but it works well enough.

I suspect the PLASMA! line is me being influenced a little by *Doctor Who* writing. It's also me trying to write about that wonderful bit in *England's Dreaming* where Jon Savage is talking about putting together his zines in the work toilets, trying to let the A-bombs in his head out. That was one of my own OH I GET IT THIS IS HOW YOU FEEL sort of moments.

Uh-huh is an oddly flexible catchphrase.

9. This issue is so low key that even the formally wanky things are sort of crushing. I suspect it really is meant as a downbeat cousin of Issue 4 of *Young Avengers*.

Tricky to talk about this page. Hmm. Hmm. A mixture of jokes and plot-relevant Chekovian guns and jokey plot-relevant Chekovian guns. And red herrings. And everything.

The L is missing. Because it's hidden.

The bedroom is based on Bryan's cover for Issue 1, and expanded. I like trying to tie as much of *everything* connected to *WicDiv* into the book.

10. The landline joke still makes me smile.

We had a big debate internally about what Inanna does in this page. I did it a different way, wrote the script, then Jamie accidentally drew the original, which also works fine. TEAM *WICDIV* IN FULL EFFECT.

The Inanna lettering is pretty nifty. Strong work by Clayton.

11. Yes, Luci's parents were Mr and Mrs Rigby, and being Britpop heads who had kids young, completely submitted to their evil Britpop urges. Laura's not wrong with the Larkin callback.

We tweaked the colours a little from the initials, as it made her DOB appear to be 1993. It's actually 1995. Yes, you can work out when she was conceived if you like.

Trying to work out how to get the Inanna balloon looking good in terms of positioning was tricky. It seems to basically work.

12. And helllllllloooo Inanna.

Important character, kept off stage for the first arc, for lots of reasons. The most obvious one being that with Luci gone, we need someone else with a little charisma and likeability. As we see, he's a very different sort of god to Luci. I'm pleased people seem to like him.

I want his coat.

For those who were looking at the early unlettered preview pages, you'll note we added the glow to the rain. It was an effect we wanted to get right before showing anyone, y'know? Matt was inspired. It adds a lot to this scene's mood.

(The fantasy element heightening a very grounded experience is something that's especially key about this issue, and *WicDiv* generally.)

13. As evidenced here, Inanna has clearly processed a bunch of stuff which other gods (and people, for that matter) have trouble with. He came from various places — the obvious archetype is Prince, but a lot of other things are worked in the side.

Panels 4 and 5 — what Matt is doing with the lights? Fuck me, he's good.

Oh, wait, we've mentioned Ragnarock a few times before, etc.

14. The caption with "Purgatorial" in was originally much longer. It's one of the ones which is so overwritten in first draft, we tried to rework it in order to keep the clever stuff, and then just set fire to. I was resisting "Purgatorial" for a long time, as I always connect it to a scene in *Dangerous Liaisons*.

(A scene I love.)

No, according to the maths I've provided, there wasn't a pantheon in 1640.

15. Yes, digging into Laura is a key thing in this arc, and especially this episode. We've known she's a fangirl, but that's a broad church.

Jamie does some really strong things with the mapping of this room. There's another panel next issue, which would make an interesting compare and contrast.

Also – that last panel? Jamie is strong.

On a technical element, we're doing a lot of quite complicated story-in-story and single-panel flashbacks and other things. They're techniques I use a lot elsewhere, but which I avoided in the first arc. I suspect the fact this issue is as complicated as it is, and never actually feels like that, is the thing I'm most happy about. It's got a sort of conversational ramble to it.

16. In terms of my personal connection to the material, it comes from an off-the-cuff comment my friend Clara said to me earlier in the year, which was pretty much "you need to get more in contact with your inner Prince". Someone having their inner Prince let out was very much my Inanna origin story.

Yes, of all the gods' statements of intent, Inanna's is definitely the one which is most openly optimistic.

Man, making these notes is making me want to wear more leopardskin.

There's something oddly funny and sinister about Ananke, just sitting on his bed.

17. We did discuss whether the characters would know Deep Throat as a political reference. We decided yes, though it's more borderline for Laura.

Clearly, both can make deep throat jokes, though Inanna is more likely to.

Working out where the bodies would be kept was a lot of fun.

18. Jamie contacted Morgue Specialist Carla Valentine to discover what the set up would be here.

This is such a quiet issue, with relatively little magic in it, I wanted to give as much space as possible to introduce Inanna's signature effect. Matt especially excels here. Just wonderful.

(Honestly, I'm not someone who thinks about anyone adapting any of our work much, but seeing Inanna's star-walking animated could be pretty amazing.)

19. Signature Team *Phonogram* eye-changing.

Jamie also sources what wounds would have been inflicted in the post-mortem. A serious, gothy young man, our Jamie.

Yes, star systems based on our gods.

20. AND NEW INFORMATION.

Love the expression here. I gave it as much space as I could, though "space" in *Fandemonium* means a different thing than in *The Faust Act*. We're leaning on the eight-panel much more, which means the double-panel counts as "Space."

Panel 4: Honestly, Matt? Are you trying to get a raise? This is fucking great.

21-22. I worked out which off-licence in Brockley would be open this late at night. Then Jamie couldn't get reference for that one, and went for one down the road instead. For people who are trying to shop very late at night be aware that, in the real world, this place isn't actually open then.

Yes, Laura got her phone back. And yes, it's even more cracked than before. Sad emoticon.

I asked Jamie if it was okay to expand this to two pages, and he said yes. Clearly, I could have done it in one, but I really wanted to stretch it out and show that the decision isn't a light thing.

When I re-read this page, I totally want to go and eat fried chicken.

Hmm. Is it worth noting that Laura doesn't actually really smoke until now? Info set up with the missing L's phrasing. Smoking is something that's loaded with Laura's own personal history, of course.

"Fuck it" is kind of a Laura catchphrase now.

23. Upping the Dante, etc.

Thanks for reading. See you next month. And Merry Christmas things.

ISSUE 7

An odd issue this. Actually mildly surprised how well it went down. The sort of detail-heavy character-heavy things rarely get people smiling, and the mass of formally playful bits are normally overlooked (Or rather, no one really cares about them). But no, people seem very excited by it. This makes me happy.

You'll have probably noticed that the second arc is a little more like *The Singles Club* in terms of its storytelling and intent. We fracture.

Obvious thing — the issue actually is two stories. The main story is up to Woden leaving, and takes about the length of a normal issue (or rather, a normal *Singles Club* issue). The second story operates more like the B-sides did in *The Singles Club*. Here's a fragment which is almost solely driven by character (thats said, most of the A-sides on *The Singles Club* were also character pieces).

Right — diving in.

Main Cover. Jamie likes Woden, as Woden is the easiest of the gods' heads to draw. Phew.

Christian Ward Cover. Christian is lovely, and another Lewisham-based creator (i.e. we spend some time in his pub). I wanted him for the Woden issue, just to see what his hyper-brightness would do to with the techno-pop stylings of Woden. Strong.

1. The Excel is home to both the MCM Expo and the London Super Comic Con, which are some of London's biggest general pop cultural things. A lot of the aspects of this story were inspired by last year's London Super Comic Con (which was, shall we say, a momentous weekend) but I've been going there forever so have lots of fondness for the events.

Look at me reprise the story so far in narrative, like a real grown up writer.

Laura's glance in the last panel is excellent.

2. London Fantheon. This issue is probably the densest selection of puns yet seen in *WicDiv*. I suspect we'll back off sharpish.

I called for the crowds to be outlines, to get that sense of alienation and distance. Jamie suggested the specific grey, which is a really good call for lots of reasons. Laura lost in the fog of the con is very much the vibe.

3. Oh god. Another pun.

4-5. When writing this issue I found myself wanting to explore some aspects more. Also, as we're selling pretty well, I thought we could use some of our money to pay for designers to do something which would work in the book without breaking Jamie's aesthetic.

Alison Sampson is a brilliant artist, designer and friend, and struck me as an excellent choice. I forwarded her a brief of what we were doing, and them met her for a meal in Chinatown, where she presented me with this mass of rough maps, and talked me through the set up of the building, its people flow and everything else. This

ended up feeding back into the story, with me moving certain key scenes around. Here's a photo from the pub...

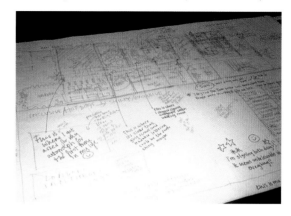

Alison then went to town, and there was a bunch of back and forth. Alison had lots of wild ideas for visual puns, but we ended up having to step away from some them — as an in-world object, it had to be primarily a functional object. The more literal puns in the key are a mix of mine and Alison's. God, I Want A Coffee is Alison's, which makes me laugh a lot.

The handwriting is Alison's, who is now official LAURA HANDWRITING.

My favourite note to Alison about this involved removing stars from a bit of writing as it was too cheerful.

Pleased with how this came out. Does a lot in a little space.

6. You can spot the start of a running joke here easily enough.

I once spent an entire con standing at the doors, trying to hand people flyers hyping *Phonogram* before it came out. The whole weekend. I still remember certain pros who turned down a flyer. Not that I hold grudges.

Cassandra's "Fuck Off, Superstar" makes me smile. Also, nice visual transition to sort of underline the point of the grey people "thing."

7. You'll note that this issue is very grid-y and intense. We're working at something much closer to the *Phonogram* trad eight-panel modified grid throughout, and obviously here. The seven panels on an eight-panel grid is one of the rhythms I really like.

Originally I had Cassandra not say anything in panel 4, and just use the gesture, but in a motionless medium, the pointed finger isn't quite enough to carry the meaning.

Matt originally gave Blake a red T-shirt. We changed it, as Blake totally is less interesting than that.

8. First panel. Space=Meaning, as always. Of course, when you're working on an eight-panel grid, that takes on a different sort of meaning. Good expression here too. Cassandra has all the fun.

Panel 6: perhaps unsurprisingly, Cassandra's main sense of humour is based around extreme sarcasm. I like Laura's little smirk here.

Man, that off-panel-line scene introduction is getting a lot of work this issue.

9. And we meet Beth, finally getting a speaking line after hanging around in the background all the way since Issue 1. Beth's replacement is hanging around in all the Cassandra scenes, though we won't get a good look at her until Issue 9, I suspect.

Panel 5 is clearly a little bit cramped, but needs must.

The fan/fanatics thing is something I was a little surprised I haven't seen anyone mention since the whole Prometheus Gambit was revealed in Issue 6. I had a prepared "CASSANDRA IS IN YOUR CORNER!" answer for anyone who sent an ask to me about it. No one did. Sad face.

My favourite crowd shot in the issue in the last panel.

10. Er... I first read this issue at the Image headquarters after the Expo, and spotted something startling in this sequence which made me swear loudly. No one's talked about it online that I've seen, so I'm not going to say it, as I suspect pointing out will make it worse.

I'm writing quite close to Jamie's deadlines with *WicDiv*, for various reasons, which means that I'm giving him the issue in chunks, and with fewer dialogue passes than usual — which means I edit a lot when we get to lettering. We lost a lot of Brunhilde's dialogue here. Walking the line in her accusations at Woden was the hardest part, as there's various bullshit narratives we had no desire to buy into.

11. "Brunhilde's animated suit" is clearly our master-level cosplay challenge for the issue. For those who think the demiurge costume is too easy.

12. Jamie is doing some interesting things here in terms of moderating the panel size to create momentum and force across what could have been a standard eight-panel.

13. Spoiler: Woden is a bit of a shit.

I've been interested in the response to Woden, as a lot more people have at least some sympathy for him than I thought would. He's being a monster, but he's got his reasons, as bad as they are. I guess as the writer of *Darth Vader* I shouldn't be surprised by that.

The transition here was rewritten a lot. I wanted to very much link it back to why this conversation would be interesting to Laura, in terms of the real reason why she's here. I didn't have a caption originally, thinking the subtext was clear enough, but repeated re-reads made me realise it wasn't. That I see a few reviewers didn't get the link even with the handholding makes me suspect I could have gone further.

14. Her phone being the one that Lucifer stole, of course.

I really do want all of Baal's suits.

SATAN'S LITTLE HELPER was a line I came up with for Issue 5, which would have been Lucifer saying it to Laura. I deleted it, as that sort of name-play isn't Lucifer's thing. It *is* Baal's, however.

It's quite sweet at the end of the page, in terms of Laura trying to dissemble her feelings on an issue. She is trying very hard here.

The "aesthetic" line seems to be a lot of people's "favourite" from the issue.

15. Hmm. I wonder if people being able to bear Woden is based around the fact he's as unrepentant as he is. Even his hypocrisy is very self-aware. Hmm.

"Nice Guy" is as loaded as the gun on the next page.

This issue was against some nightmarish deadlines, and we only caught that the sign on the wall didn't have any writing on just before it was going to press. Phew.

16. I don't always know what line is going to go on the back of the cover when I'm writing an issue. When I hit "I'm a God, Not a Saint" I immediately knew it was the right one.

The Laura captions were strimmed enormously here. Having a bulky caption in the third panel obviously breaks this scene. I had some stuff about the various entrances (all seen on the map) but frankly, no one really cares about that. I have a weakness of wanting to over-explain why something isn't a plot hole, which actually ends up breaking the story in a different way.

(Of course, if you don't explain at all, you end up with people who just go with their immediate "oh — that's a problem" and don't think about why it isn't. There is no right answer, just the least wrong one.)

17. There's a bunch of fan-suggested headcanons which make me laugh, especially when one indirectly hits upon somewhere I'm planning to go in the book. Baal and Minerva's relationship would be one of these.

This scene was originally written to be in the area between the VIP area and the main stage. It was moved after Alison's map went to town, adding the entire secondary circulatory system to the venue. The odd mix of the supernatural and the very low key behind-the-curtain is very us.

18. I think that's probably the hardest swearing we've had in *WicDiv*, and obviously chewed it over.

I spent some time trying to work out how we could have paced this so Woden gets the Valkyrie to call the Bifröst, but it simply doesn't work. It's fine like this.

19. "Bad Company" is a very common phrase in pop culture, and people have traced it around. The fact that it's also Jamie's big brother's drum & bass group is an added bonus.

20. And we start the second story. Obviously, this gives the issue its somewhat odd pacing.

This is a real area. There aren't really many places to eat near the expo. You can eat bar food in the Fox, but generally speaking, the China Palace would be where I'd suggest eating.

Multiple references to Stephen King's *It* in this sequence, a book which I saved from being burned by a teenage friend of mine.

21. As you'll have noticed, *WicDiv*'s fancy comics sequences tend to be a little more low key than *Young Avengers*'. This is a good example. The approach reminds me of platformers like *N*.

The lettering is obviously unconventional, in that it's getting you read right to left via placing, but I haven't seen anyone not get it, so JOB'S A GOOD 'UN. That was Jamie's suggestion. This whole sequence was written in the extended Marvel Method style, with lots of suggested dialogue, etc.

This sequence obviously is a call back to Issue 3.

22. Badb is singing 'It's Not Okay (I Promise)' by My Chemical Romance.

Er... this sequence is directly inspired by a few Karaoke and con experiences I had in a social group last year. Specifically, this is the Karaoke Dungeon, which lurks beneath the restaurant. To get to the room, we found ourselves descending a mass of seemingly endless tunnels, which ended up making us think of Moria. After several hours down there, I found myself thinking that we could emerge to find the Earth taken over by Zombies or Triffids. Clearly, that will be my cold open if I ever do a *Walking Dead* rip-off.

The MCR just struck me as appropriate. I also did that at another Karaoke Session in the excellent Lucky Voice. It was this of 'This Corrosion', which is another of my faves to bawl.

Yes, there's another reference/quotation here.

23. Panels 1 and 2 are what I'm happiest with this issue. Not a particularly happy happy, of course, but it just about holds together. Maybe this whole page, in fact. Hmm.

Also — nine-panel grid, which changes things entirely. I'm twitchy around the nine-panel, but it worked really well here. I probably should dig into it more. As well as the Moore, it brings me to mind of *St. Swithin's Day*, which has a certain part of the mood. The two-panel sub-page transition stuff is also key, and that's a *St. Swithin's Day* beat.

Morrigan got the shading to her character in the first arc. Baphomet gets his here.

Hmm. Those middle three panels. Probably an essay here, but one I could only really write years down the line.

24. And running joke concludes. Three, it's the magic number, etc.

The patented fade-into-the-shadows by Morrigan and Baphomet.

Making the flyer slightly transparent to ease the transition to the flyer was a late addition from Matt and Jamie, but a really useful one. Without it, we don't really make the leap that intuitively.

25. The flyer was done by Tom Muller, given guidelines to make it feel a little inspired by an old-skool rave flyer. I did a little text to start with, and then did a little more when Tom came up with the design.

Tom's design work is great. Have a look at his covers for *Zero*.

26. And... another icon. Whoop!

Right. Issue 8 goes to press shortly, and I still need to write Issue 9, so better get back to it.

Thanks for reading.

ISSUE 8

Actually, before I start, I want to give a formal notice of a sort. You may see this is the latest I've ever done *WicDiv* issue notes. Previous ones have been coming later too, and you may wonder if this is a trend. In all honesty, it may be. As I've written before, this schedule is utterly frenzied this year. It's do-able, but it also requires a lot of discipline — and at least part of that discipline is not working too hard. I'm leaving space to recharge batteries, as otherwise I know I risk burn-out.

(This all sounds quite bleak but it's all just part of working as a creative.)

Anyway — that means that a lot of things I've done which basically tap the same emotional reserves as "work" are lower on my priorities than last year. This would include the Writer Notes. As fun as they are, they are very much a case in point in me just not turning off. I had vague plans of perhaps reducing them to a one-set-of-notes-per-arc sort of thing for other books, but as I haven't done anything yet, it's probably telling.

In short: if there's not many of these for the rest of the year, I'm sorry, but it's a casualty to the work. And on a personal level, I'd appreciate if you don't ask after them specifically. It stresses me out, and I could do without that.

That level of self-centered woe-is-me bullshit out of the way, let's get on with it.

A divisive issue, it seems, which isn't really that surprising when it's the closest thing we've done to a *Phonogram* issue yet. The structure obviously is about trying to do our best to mirror a certain form of musical experience, a semi-sequel to the *Wolf Like Me* issue of *The Singles Club*, as well as trying to do the whole of *The Singles Club* floating-perspective thing in a single issue.

The idea originated in a paragraph pitch I lobbed at Vertigo when I was doing a dance with them early in my career. Let's dig it out...

HIGHER STATE

In the long summer of 1967 some believed they were at the cusp of the next stage of human evolution; that a new age was dawning on the streets of Haight-Ashbury with humanity rising up on lysergic wings. They were disappointed. Problem being, they'd been born into the wrong summer of love. Twenty one years later, all across England, thousands gather to dance in fields, in warehouses — anywhere they can, to hear new sounds on new drugs. The transcendent moment comes as a rave just outside the M25 literally detonates, leaving a sole survivor amongst the charred remains: Seb Michaels. At first he's treated as a monster, before it becomes clear he contains the consciousness of everyone present at the rave. Immediately he's the focus of the country's attention, treated as everything from Public Enemy Number One to spiritual prophet of the Ecstasy Age. But whether England will be one nation under a groove

is only really decided after other hive-minds start to emerge. *Higher State* remixes the social history of the UK rave scene and general emergence of dance culture into an alternately bleak and funny piece of grounded psychic horror.
In short: *Akira* meets *24-Hour Party People*.

The idea of the communality of the dancefloor as a psychic communion is something that struck me as fun. I had the big formalist structure beneath it, trying to get a whole issue done with that beat. The trick was trying to make it work, which pretty much broke the whole team. This was by far the hardest issue of the series.

Main Cover. Dionysus isn't a pop star. He's a dance floor. *The Crowd is the Star* to use the old line. As such, one of the major influences was a gentleman called Umar, who I pretty much only met on the Thought Bubble dancefloor for a few years. His determined leading of the dancefloor stuck in my head, and when I pictured this unstoppable party animal, he quickly came to mind.

In the same way as *Wolf Like Me* was about Kid-with-Knife, Dionysus is a little like the Kwk of the cast. Obviously with a lot of differences, but a few shared core instincts.

Brandon Graham Cover. Love all of the fleshy litheness of Brandon's work here, and the seething of the crowd. Strong!

1. We're still in the period where I was writing only just ahead of Jamie. The last sequence and the first sequence were done, then I worked into the middle. I was trying to wrestle it from the ether.

This meant writing with less time to pick things over. While there's some things I worry about on the page, the fact that I get interrogated by Jamie and Chrissy means most of it gets caught.

The worry here was the cigarette. I originally had Laura pass her cigarette to Inanna to go in, as I wanted a reason for Inanna not to go in with Laura. Of course, this is me over-thinking it — Inanna can just hang back for any one of dozens of reasons, and Inanna as a smoker definitely seems to be crossing the Glamourising Smoking line we've already skirted close to.

And a second's thought reveals that Inanna isn't a smoker anyway.

Thankfully, I'm now actually ahead of Jamie by a considerable margin. I've written to Issue 12 now.

ANYWAY!

The "her" is a "I haven't communed with a god since *Lucifer died*." In a real way, this issue is about Laura having actual pleasure for the first times in months. It's about Laura remembering why she cared not about the gods as people — but the gods as experiences, etc.

As always Clayton played around with a lot of ideas — the psychic changing of the person's voice is a fairly standard special effect, so we had to have one which was very much ours. I am, generally speaking, pro hot pink.

2. I like what Matt's doing with mood here.

Heh. This page is dense with allusions, both internal and external. YOL∞ was one of my terrible T-shirt ideas, and does make me smile. The acid badge, as we call out later, is the symbol of acid house and very much the pure myth I'm hailing in this issue. I was slightly too young to do Acid House, which is something of a regret. It's also the symbol of *Watchmen*, but I'll talk about that later. Obviously, this is the most formalist *WicDiv* issue so far. We are wearing our influences on our sleeve. Or rather, lapel.

If you're wondering which of the fans in Issue 3 was Dio btw, here you go:

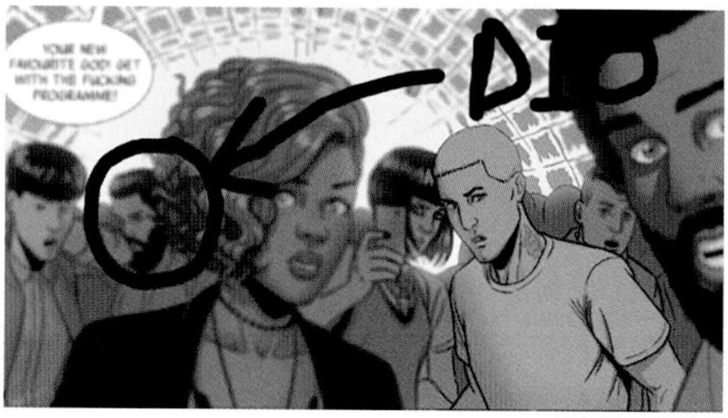
DIO

3. The debating of the portal in space colouring was good. Clearly, the club-god has a magical cloak room.

I suppose that's the other influence worth mentioning — I was explicitly thinking about the clubbing episode in seminal British comedy *Spaced*. Jamie and I are enormous fans, and it's one of the most magical ones. It was clearly an E episode, and caught all that's good about clubbing without ever mentioning the E. It was just naturalistic, and full of life lived and warm hearted and the rest. We're clearly a lot more pretentious than *Spaced*, but the urge to do something that sure of itself was part of it. An episode that's as clearly about drugs as this one is can be just plain embarrassing. While people have said lots of bad things about the issue, I haven't seen anyone say it doesn't feel convincing. That's a major victory, and I have to be happy with it.

In short: everyone go watch *Spaced*.

Anyway — I mentioned it's a hive mind earlier. We set up how different it is.

We didn't have a glow on the finger tips originally, but C argued that we really needed a soft magical tell. She's right. I think this works quite well.

4-5. And yes.

A bunch of people have picked apart these two pages, which is gratifying. The original urge was to do a pulling in and out of focus and losing the flow of linear space. That sort of SNAP refocusing and all that. Frankly, there's a bunch of craft in here, from the whole team, and I suspect it's best to let you obsess over it if you're of that bent.

There were a couple of other purposes though — as I mentioned earlier, I was writing this piecemeal. When I was doing this sequence I had no idea which 1-2-3-4 grid I was going to settle on (more on THAT soon). One of the grids I was playing with would have involved moving the reading line from the standard page-based system, to one which reads across the double-page spread. I was thinking it may work as a useful metaphor for how Laura was feeling different, and that the club was a different place for her. To that end, this page was also meant to introduce people to reading from left to right across the spread rather than normally. While there's no real single path, that the whole thing has an increasing pressure to make you read across the spread would have ideally have set people up for that.

It serves its own purpose now, but it makes me smile anyway.

6. The whole sequence is very page-as-stanza — or bar, if we're using *Phonogram* musical terminology. Matt's using the page as a single aesthetic entity — however, the colour choices also do rise and fall as we progress. I was hopeful that this may actually be less work for Matt (as there's less rendering, etc) but in the end, the amount of experimentation meant that it really wasn't.

Matt tried several treatments for the lines — the white out approach in the last panel of the page was tried throughout, and we decided it just got overwhelming. Instead, it captures momentary sharpness.

Okay — the grid. This was actually the thing which kept me puzzling longest, and delayed me starting for quite a while. I knew I wanted to do the 1-2-3-4 as a repeat. But what grid to use? What spacing? I've got notepads and doc files full of...

1X	4X		1X	3X
2X	1X	Or...	X2	X4
3X	2X		XX	XX

Or anything fucking else, from eight-panel to four-panel grids and everything. If you look through my files for this issue, it's some real *The Shining* shit. I was puzzling over questions like what kind of scenes can you do with two panels? What do you do with one? What patterns do the numbers take? Is a sequence which breaks the pages better or worse? One that repeats every four pages?

I was resistant on the eight-panel for a long time, simply because it's one of our standard tools, and that we'd done the opening 1-2-3-4 scene in Issue 1 in the six-panel grid. There was something powerful about doing them with square panels, with each one with their regular four sides, etc.

But when I hit on this basic layout, I realised it was just rock solid. Four to a page, diagonal shape to cascade down the page. It was going to be a confusing issue, but it'd lend it a little momentum.

Anyway — we break you in softly. Things get stranger, but this is almost normal.

This is also the apex of our "using space in lieu of work" thing. Each one of these pages is actually half a page of Jamie's art, which meant we could have twice as many of them. It's why we expanded the issue to 40 pages. Same amount of work, over a larger space.

(Yes, I was a little pissed off with the couple of reviewers who thought Jamie drew less than normal.)

Heh. I can see why I put off writing this fucker for all this time. This is *tiring*.

7. This conversation came from Jamie's conversation with me, and through it realising a few things about Dionysus.

In terms of keeping the beat, one thing I tried to do, then abandoned in the detail, was make the dialogue in each panel be of a similar length, to add to the sense of the rhythm. If it was a *Singles Club* story, I'd have done this more, but *WicDiv* has other fish to fry, and a lot of story elements to forward. There's a lot going on at the party, so pure formalism was let go. Kill your darlings and all that

8-9. I think I budgeted this for a page of comics — as the whole top half of the spread is actually black with an integrated logo, but frankly Jamie didn't listen to me and did a full spread.

Especially have love for Gentle Annie doing a certain mode of early nineties rave girl pose here.

One of my fondest memories of this issue was us debating what the trace-lines are called.

The title is a riff on the Public Enemy track.

10. Of the first bunch of pages which Clayton lobbed over, this is the one which initially blew me away. I just love the vector traces.

Ah, the Badge. The "here is a comics reference which we're not going to reference in text as comics culture and it's terribly incestuous" is a very me beat, to the level where I used it in the first page of *Phonogram* with Kohl's T-shirt.

I'm still not sure what I make of *Pax Americana*. I mean that in a literal way. I've owned two copies and lost both of them on the way home. One was left on a train, heading far to the south. One fell out my pocket when running for a bus in New Cross. Alcohol may have been involved in both stories. I read it several times in the space, and I'm not sure which side of the reading I'm on — the two takes are either that it's a we-can-do-this-too-if-we-want piece of formalist arguable defensiveness or it's a celebration of what that form of oddly hermetically sealed comics can do. Or both. But I did find myself thinking about the nature of that kind of six year in the making concept-rock prog *thing* and thinking of the issue as a bit of a riposte to all that, in terms of being ramshackle and thrown together in a month and formally challenging in its own way but very much designed as a pop object with edges. It was an interesting way into the issue, in terms of me realising the areas I completely didn't want to go.

11. Laura's blues here are just wonderful.

12. Matt getting a little bit of a pulse, the hugs juxtaposed with all those warm oranges. Cassandra with another sledgehammer classical culture reference in case anyone missed it.

This is really a page about all that sort of touchy-feely stuff. The "You're full of stars too" panel may be one of my favourite in the whole series, just in terms of how it shows the gap between the two characters.

Also: last of the recapitulation of what's happened so far, a last step of familiarity before...

13. Hulllllloooo Baal.

We've done Laura disassociative in and of herself.

Here, by moving between Baal/Cassandra/Laura and Woden, we start to move the focus across the crowd. The narrative perceptive whirls around the rest of the issue, while obviously having Laura as an anchor. We've kept the whole series very focused on Laura — I believe there's two scenes so far that she hasn't been present for. The opening scene of the book, and the brief section when Laura runs away from the fight between Lucifer and Baal/Sakhmet. The rest of the club sequence becomes Laura as one part of the crowd, in the same way as she's one part of the hive-mind.

Also, we have to have a bunch of talking between other folks.

Also: Woden in hyper creepy mode.

(Nice Cassandra panel here — I suspect it may be the definitive Cassandra panel, in many ways. The character in a beat.)

14. The colours were talked about a lot here, which catches a different moment of intensity. If perspective is loosening on the previous page, here time is as well. This is very much how I remember nights out — those sorts of fragmented vignettes. (**Ed's Note** — there's more on KG's planning for this in the "Making Of" section.)

Basically, whenever I resort to papercraft, you normally know I'm operating in a difficult place. I was originally not really thinking of a page as stanza approach here, but when the eight-panel 1-2-3-4 solidified it made me realised I'd better lean into it. Perhaps I'll go another way another time.

15. What could Woden be offering her?

(Note here the moving back to Laura and her perpetual KLLK machine from the sequence. Jamie is really working some tricky shit here.)

16-17. I originally tried to write the top bit as a single panel, as a big shot of a crowd is a beautiful thing, but I instantly realised it had to be a progression. We lose some of the subjective joy from the choice — the opening panel isn't as FUCCCK YEAH as the last crowd scene, obviously — but it's necessary 100% for storytelling.

Yes, Baphomet is very cute on this page. For once.

The choice of how to do Baphomet in the last panel was chewed over a fair bit. We went for the subjective distancing in the narrative (and for Laura's perspective of him) rather than Baphomet's returning to how he was at the start of the page, where he's visually coded as part of the crowd.

18-19. The pink! It is hot pink!

After the break, things are getting more melancholic, step by step, the conversations more grounded. Follow how the colours work in this sequence, up to Dionysus' return, as Matt is powerful.

Minerva shows our flashback colouring, which turns up in a few pages with Lucifer again.

Baal's line with the FUCKING YOU UP was rewritten as many times as anything else in this issue, I think.

20. Oh man. Look how dreary the colours are getting! ASTOUNDING MATT WILSON.

This is some Inanna stuff I wanted to get into Issue 6, but it just didn't fit.

21. And hello, Lucifer. I sort of wanted to do a lot more of these, in terms of pillow-talk-in-Inanna's-beds, but it's not really 100% necessary.

Oh, Inanna.

AND DIONYSUS BRINGS THE BEAT BACK.

22. The hot red was chosen as this is the most intense burst of Dionysus in the book. You'll have noticed that we do these occasional god-intro issues, which are constructed in a way to really let you get to know one of the gods. As a latecomer, Dionysus informs the issue's structure, and this is the key thing.

Laura with her face held is just wonderful. Jamie, you are lovely.

23. I think I first saw this running dialogue across panels trick in the last episode of *Codeflesh* by Joe Casey and Charlie Adlard. We're miles away from the specific execution here — Casey doesn't break sentences and the narrative perspective is something else — but I was very aware I was processing that. It's a wonderful issue, btw.

This is one of my favourite pages in the issue, in terms of everyone on the team basically working together to try and get an acceleration of pace towards the end of the page — Matt with the colours, Jamie with the tightening angle, me with the reduction in sentence length so you read quicker until...

24-25. We collapse into the night. The collapse from the intensity of a club into the cold and utterly still streets is one of my favourite things about clubbing, and what I was trying to get here.

Of course, after this positive energy thrill, we have to mix in a little darkness. More than a little darkness. When I was writing the *WicDiv* bible originally, I saw Dionysus as perhaps the character who would be least likely be anyone's crush in the cast. The second I hit on this second string to him, I realised he had tragic doomed crushworthyness with the best of them.

26. Justice vs Simian nod, which was on the soundtrack for ages until I realised it was capturing something I was feeling about Dionysus. I was wandering across Charing Cross station going for the last train with it blaring loud in my ears, and it sort of clicked.

27. No, there's no autobiography here. Definitely not.

We originally had this page on a bus which didn't run this route at the weekend. Chrissy caught it, and we changed the numbering. We may worry about this kind of stuff too much.

28-29. This is one of the scenes I've wanted to write since I conceived of the book. It is VERY BAAL.

The driver is based on a guy I had an argument with in Bath, for the record.

Baal definitely is good at his mobile phone. And... well, you unpick Baal. His line through the last few issues has been fun to do, in a quiet way.

30. It's good to see Laura smile again, but it screams trouble. Good work, Jamie.

31. I spent some time working out what to call that chapter break, before I realised Laura's own catchphrase was a shoe-in.

Anyway — that's it. Hope you come back for next month's issue and... wait, it's out tomorrow. I'm due to write another one of these. Oh noes!

ISSUE 9

Where we learn that you can make readers swallow any amount of exposition if you don't tell them anything for eight issues.

Main Cover. On my second ever comic, the lead character at the end of the story was really old. When I saw the page, I remember writing to the artist that old people just look amazing in comic art. It's all in the detail. I suspect artists hate it, because wrinkles = more work. Perhaps that's the secret reason why superhero characters never get any older. Laziness. That's normally the solution.

Marguerite Sauvage Cover. This was a lot of fun. This is our first cover which feels like a classic movie poster, with a montage of the cast — tellingly not including Laura. Subconsciously we set up the idea that this story isn't Laura's.

ECCC Cover. We originally planned a flyer for the party, but with deadlines crushing and not having a party anyway, Jamie suggested doing a period Ananke. I know I talk a lot about how we try and work out shortcuts to artistic effects, but adding a completely different mask to the same figure, and then recolouring is a very strong one.

1. On my original *WicDiv* document, my plan was that this issue would bounce between Laura's parents and Ananke. So we got the parents' perspective on Laura's life juxtaposed with Cassandra's interview. In the end, as it was primarily pure character work to give a different look at Laura's life, I went the other way and gave more space to Baphomet.

"You can't expect miracles." I am a shit.

2. Obviously the original plan of the issue was about drawing a line between parental perspectives on the younger cast, so we get the core of that in the transition.

I normally hate off-panel dialogue, but in this case, this let us focus on the actual key response.

A few words on Matt's colouring for all of this, which is just lovely. Jamie saw it like this, but for some reason I was thinking about Valhalla being much colder and more austere. With the sci-fi Olympian vibe of Jamie's inks, that's what I get. The soft pinks and sunlight were something else entirely. MATT WILSON FOR EISNER, etc.

3. A month gap since the last issue again. I occasionally wonder whether I should do something a little more stressing the time gaps — I saw some people not realise this is a month after Laura gets in Baal's car, and therefore thinking her response this issue was to do something like that. Hmm.

The title is a Florence & The Machine reference. Florence being a star right at the heart of *WicDiv*, with her inspiring the initial image in the series — as in, Amaterasu and Laura.

4. Jamie really wants to do this T-shirt as merch. A lot of people have asked. It would be cool.

Looking at Ananke really makes me want to go to the McQueen exhibit in London. Very excited. Very!

I chewed over whether the Shirley Temple nod was right or wrong. It is a very old reference — I'm always careful about making sure the cultural references are the ones the character would use — but it was also a very old reference even for me. I think it's just classic now.

5. Chrissy wondered in script form whether it would be clear enough that Baphomet was cut to the core. I said I'd tweak it if it's not, but it's Jamie, and I had every faith it would be. My faith was not misplaced.

There was originally another Monty Python nod in this issue, but it was distracting in mood, so I cut it. We're thinking about doing some equivalent of outtakes and blooper reels for the trade, so I may include it in there.

6. The Prometheus Gambit has haunted this arc. Here's the twist.

I suspect in retrospect Baphomet's character arc across the series is a little more obvious.

Panel 2 with Baphomet basically getting his Keanu Reeves 'looking confused' on.

I like what Jamie's done with the lecturing from Ananke — this is conspiratorial, direct at us. She's sharing this information with Baphomet, sure, but also with the reader. It's a small circle.

Also, death gods can apparently extend their life by choking out one of their own. Ananke immediately hits Baphomet with the "I can help you for the time you already have" as if she didn't give him the ultimate loophole. I'm sure Baphomet will be sensible about this. I mean the cover for the next issue is him smirking and covered in blood but who knows. Could be cherryade.

Good work, Jamie.

7. I love panel 2. Hilarious, Baphomet.

I would suggest it's normally a good idea to at least hint at a later reveal before the reveal happens. As in, hint in a way which is noticeable. If it's not a question people may be wondering, a reveal risks being empty. This is setting up Ananke's origin later.

Quote for the back page of the single issue at the end. Picking these is always tricky. It's trying to find the core statement of the issue.

8. And hullllllo Cassandra. She's at her best and worst this issue, to say the least.

I think this is the first good look at her new assistants. This was set up in Issue 7, of course, in the scene with Beth. I'll write a bit about this later in the transformation sequence.

I saw some people surprised that Cassandra was as dismissive to Crowley as she is here.

She's paraphrasing some key real-world facts about Baphomet, and adding some of our in-universe ones.

Yes, Woden was inviting Cassandra to do an interview with Ananke at the club. That was me using my own origin story — a writer from a magazine came up to me in a club and asked if I wanted to write for a magazine. I similarly punched the air. Yes. Yes. Yes.

9. There was one awesome blooper on this page. I hope we have space in the page.

I wrote this issue basically in a linear fashion, hammering out all the conversations. I *think* this was the first Ananke/Cassandra interaction I wrote. I immediately knew this would be an interesting pairing, bringing out the worst in both of them.

Actually, I'm lying — I know the first interaction I wrote, but it was one of those big set-pieces which I tend to have lying around in the *WicDiv* bible. This was the first bit I wrote in the process of doing the issue.

10. I played with a bunch of titles for this. *Actually It's About Metaphysics In Journalism* was the one that made me laugh, but was deleted for a bunch of reasons. Far too in jokey, far too tied to a certain time and space, not actually fun enough, and adding a taint to the comic. Frankly, *WicDiv* is important to me, and letting any of that in diminishes it.

Obviously a Hunter nod. Riffing on *Fear and Loathing* for titles is very much Journo cliché, and deeply unimaginative. The awareness of both is key, obv.

11. "First question. Why an interview?"

The structure of *Fandemonium* so far has actually been a series of interviews. There was more than a little of that in *The Faust Act* too. Each issue, we have a sequence where a god gets to lay down their practised lines to our ingénue. This issue we make it explicit, just to end it. And Cass is far from an ingénue, so it takes a different route.

Panel 3: oooh, oldest trick in the book, Cass. Raise your game.

I wrote a lot more examples of things which Ananke didn't see in her long life.

12. Chrissy and I talked over Cass and Ananke a lot. Cass has basically been the voice of reason for a lot of *WicDiv*. Repeatedly here, her voice-of-reason actually ends up crossing over being into plain abusive and defensive.

(She's got a chance of a lifetime, and she's doing all manner of posturing stuff. This is very much what the Internet thinks a confrontational interview is like, y'know? She's dropping her insults too early, too worried about her own ego rather than the story. I've said all the characters are me, but Cass is doing something I did for a long time, and know her well.)

It's always been there, but actually meeting someone like with Ananke turns the volume up to 11. Ananke drops a lot of one liners in this issue, but "Do you want to be smart or do you want to know things?" is probably the closest to nailing Cass.

Fantastic expression by Jamie on that line too.

China is well worth reading, btw. I mean, you almost certainly knew that, but if you haven't dive in. One of my odder memories of my honeymoon is my wife and I both reading *Perdido Street Station* simultaneously.

Jamie suggested we drop Cassandra's full name in this issue. Her ethnicity was being overlooked far too often for our liking, so we wanted to make it explicit in the text.

An idea akin to the one Ananke is forwarding has actually turned up in my work before. *Busted Wonder.* Go read.

13. Oh man. In my ranting I didn't mention this for the last page — didn't Matt do wonderful stuff with the colouring on Ananke's prehistory storytelling? When he lobbed this as us, I said that when this is all wrapped up, we should do an Indie RPG together. Matt mentioned he was a fan of *Banner Saga*, which I admit, was entirely what I was thinking about.

"There is no one in this story who has not got a 'raw deal'" is one of the earliest lines in my *WicDiv* document, I think.

"Necessity" is basically what Ananke is a god of in the real world. Though "god" is stretching it.

14. Heh.

I've got a pile of books where I work, and I've been hiding *The White Goddess* from every shot I take of it for the last year or so. Very much a rabbit hole for anyone who wishes to go there. To state the obvious, anything you need to know about the book will be mentioned explicitly in the text. That said, if you read it, you'll be able to spot the stuff Ananke is talking about. But, I suspect, only in retrospect. *The White Goddess* includes a lot of stuff, and has a basal setting of abstruse.

Wow, Ananke really has Cassandra on the ropes on this page.

I've seen the last panel taken and reblogged and RTed a lot. It is very much the sort of panel you can lift. I said earlier about the line which most skewers Cassandra was the "Smart" thing. With second thought, it's probably this. That said, it's also one which hits a lot of bad critics. Occasionally *entertaining* critics, but intellectually dishonest cowards.

The best of them get over it.

Generally speaking, that full-row ¼ page panel is reserved for key lines in *WicDiv*. We use it a bunch.

15. Favourite thing here — Cass actually not getting offended. She's gone past offence and become vulnerable... before she closes up again ("Who is interviewing who here?").

I said the whole thing about delayed exposition earlier, but the issue is actually about the push and pull between the two personalities. That's how we get away with it. The facts are one thing, but the drama is about the characters' responses to the facts.

(I think Cass's question in the third panel is one place where she actually nails an aggressive question. It's obviously trying to rile Ananke, but it's got a lot less posture to it.)

Heh. Notes for this one are strange. I'm analysing my characters, and I wrote the fucker. Critics writing critics writing critics.

(In passing — if you ever find yourself interviewing an Ananke, the "A Wizard Did It Line" is the sort of thing you build towards. Cass would have come out of it a lot better (and not got Ananke's beat down) if she actually reeled Ananke in, gained evidence, and then delivered her coup de grâce.

16-17. Re-used background, with added masks. Still a lot of work, but saving space. After Issue 8, I knew this one should be as easy as possible, ideally to make up more time. Sadly, Jamie was sick, so we didn't gain back anything. Comics!

An odd thing about Cass and her crew as the twelfth god: no one anywhere I'd seen had actually publicly guessed at it. We sent it on a Friday night, and the first person I saw who dropped the theory said it on Saturday morning. That struck me as interesting. As in, when it's finalised and printing, people in the world... just knew.

I'd suspected more people would have got it in advance, but that's fine. Someone will always get a twist. If no one gets it, that's a problem. Execution is the key thing. And, a hard twist on the execution to make it fresh to those who figured it out — in this case, that it isn't just Cass. It's also her assistants.

Anyway, Cass turns into Batman!

18-19. Actually, no, it's Urðr.

I mentioned earlier the set-piece line? The "Clever Girl" exchange was the first one I wrote.

Clayton chewed over the style a lot. The aim was to try and get something sepulchrally goth.

The influences on The Norns are a little more subtle than many of the gods. The primary influences are basically intense girl groups who wear too much black, leaning alt. The original one is Savages, whose 'She Will' you'll see really near the start of the *WicDiv* playlist. If you read a Savages interview, you can easily imagine Cassandra saying a lot of it. Other stuff — Elastica, Ladytron, Electrelane, even some Sleater-Kinney. There's a bunch of McQueen in there too.

When we were completing the pantheon just as we were finishing Issue 1, we did realise that we had really bad variation body types. Looking across the cast, the ones which we could move to a heavier build created different problems (Morrigan was the best candidate... but the one heavier character being obviously mentally unstable is problematic in a completely different way.) I realised that we had a *very* good excuse to kick out one of Cassandra's assistants and replace her. Clearly, we'll also see more of just-missed-godhood Beth. I wouldn't have wasted a page on her if we didn't have plans for her, y'know?

20-21. Being a trans girl, the question of names and identity is something that is very close to her. I wanted to at least make it clear that it's on her mind.

Jamie does a lot on this page. Kinda wincing for asking him to do it.

Key Cassandra beats on this page, of course.

You know, I wonder if I'd actually written Urðr in caps and realised all the bad 'Urðr on the Dancefloor' caps, whether I'd have chosen her.

There were a lot more jokes on this page, but I cut them. Mood is much more serious than that.

22. Ugh. I messed up here. I should have had an interstitial here, with THE NORNS as a title, so that the final two story pages were split over a page turn. I'll include it in the trade. (**Ed's Note** — Hey presto! We included an interstitial here! We've moved KG's page refs for the following notes on a page so they now make sense. Well, as much sense as these notes were ever going to.)

23. The second panel on 23 is heartbreaking. Oh, Laura. Laura.

I think we get away with the transition from four to five, just about. If it went wrong, it'd have been a classic rookie error.

24. One reason for wanting the page turn here was to keep the same structure as all the other god introductions.

25. It was originally YOU ARE CORDIALLY INVITED TO THE DEATH OF ALL YOUR DREAMS but the "ALL" was just a little too much and made it cramped. So we lost it. Man!

Nice complete design, eh? Whoop!

Anyway — *WicDiv* 10 is at the printer, where the plot kicks into over-drive.

Thanks for reading.

ISSUE 10

Issue 10. Crikey. *10*. We normally say that the book will be between 30 and 60 issues, with my gut feeling of about 40. That means we're a quarter of the way through, which is intimidating in all sorts of ways.

But I'm happy. It's basically going well, and where we go in the next few issues is probably the strongest period of the book yet. The first two guest stories are perhaps my favourite issues I've written, in very different ways.

Abstractly, this would have been the end of the second arc. The plan was five issues, each one with a gap of about a month between them. When I sat down and did the serious planning, I realised that there was absolutely no way the last part was going to fit in a single issue. Hence six, with the last two parts basically being the end-of-season double-sized finale.

Main Cover. Our Flame-Grilled Whopper cover, with Ketchup.

We do a lot of thinking about the covers, the functions they serve and the various places they're going to be seen. In many ways, like everything, we over-analyse. Well, not true — we work from our instincts and gut, and then really analyse exactly what's going on. Covers are seen in multiple places — they're in previews, they're online and people following the book closely will have three months to chew over them, they're on shelves of the week of release, and they're then retrospectively part of the book's iconography — and, of course, how we use them as chapter headings.

This is hardest on people who follow the book closely. In the same way the blood trickling at the chapter headings of *Watchmen* makes you know something awful is coming, seeing that an issue three ahead of the one you're reading has something like this on adds a sense of awful brooding anticipation. Obviously next issue's cover is more so.

On a more basic note, I love how Matt treats fire. This is just astounding stuff.

Frazer Irving Cover. If I recall the conversation correctly, when planning who we wanted to do each of the alt covers, basically we went "Norns!" and then went "Frazer." He's an old friend, his work is ever more strong, and in terms of who we wanted to present the first iconic image of the Norns, he was the top of this list. Very weird with a y.

1. We've touched on the Underground before, with that triple-pun, but here we kind of lean into it further. The removal of backgrounds is something we've done before, with Mother's dimension in *Young Avengers*. This is obviously the opposite. Jamie's merging of the characters inks with the shadows back in Issue 5 very much worked, so we rolled with it. Also, I believe Jamie did these in white inks on a black canvas, like this:

I suspect I should have put the Morrigan's revelation here a little earlier in the story — I suspect people would have swallowed Issue 3 a little easier if I'd given people more emotional hooks that they could grasp (i.e. a reason why they were fighting with one another rather than a mystery of a reason why they were fighting with one another). C'est la vie. You live, you learn. I've been writing a little of Morrigan's issue this week, actually, which I'm liking a lot.

The last two panels' dialogue were originally in panel 5, with the line on the back of the issue on panel 6. They're both good lines, but you don't need both, and having both hurts it. Only problem was Hannah had already laid out the back cover, so she would have killed me if I'd made her change it. I found another home for it, as you see.

There are a lot of lyrically allusive elements in this issue, from both on the playlist and not. More, the Sisters of Mercy here.

2-3. Originally a lot more was written for these pages, but I cut it right back. A little sad melancholic mood here with Matt's colours — that odd sad halo from the light in the house.

Inanna is a total sweetie — love what Jamie did on the hug.

I never stop loving what Matt does with Inanna's teleportation. Trying to get a signature look for the gods' powers is obviously a big thing, and very much in the superheroic tradition.

I saw someone say that Laura's parents are the real heroes of *WicDiv*, and I don't think they're wrong.

4-5. Yeah, boom. MATT WILSON FOR COLOURIST EISNER. JAMIE CAN COME TOO.

We're including this page in the "Making Of" in the back of the trade, with a step-by-step account of how we did it, including my script. My main note was I was calling for a modernised Peter Pan shot — Inanna as Peter, taking Laura's Wendy off across London to Neverland. Jamie nailed it, and I haven't seen a flying shot I've liked as much since the first panel of the .1 story in *Young Avengers*. Comparing and contrasting the two of them is interesting, Inanna and America are fundamentally doing it differently.

There was a lot of internal debate on where to have Ragnarock. We could have made it even bigger if we moved it further outside London, but we decided that'd cause a different set of comic problems. We played with a weekend, a week and all manner of other things. There's not really any places in London that can fit much more than a crowd of 100,000 — and Hyde Park seemed the best of them. I kinda wanted the cool million, but the maths didn't work. Jamie generally speaking pushes me to be more conservative on things like numbers, and I push things further in the red, in a Print The Myth way. I think it's a good compromise.

Jamie did one of his 3D models for this one. The inspiration was basically a cross between Stonehenge and speaker stacks. Circles are one of the key *WicDiv* visual elements, of course.

Having the row of panels at the bottom of the page worked much better than I hoped it would. It allowed me to reclaim space to make the next page work properly with its pauses, but I worried it'd lose the impact of the top image. In short: no it didn't.

Good expression by Laura in the last panel. Also, love the guy in panel 2 dropping his drink.

6. Modified nine-panel grid structure to make sure we had enough space for the pauses and reactions to sell the joke. The long top panel lets us show how much space there is between Baal and Laura, which is something I find pretty effective — I called for a similar effect with Kate and Marvel Boy in the penultimate issue of *Young Avengers*.

7. Originally the second space was deleted, but we decided that people would extrapolate in the wrong way from that.

8. That Blake comes back at this point perhaps shows some of the DNA of the original plan — if this *was* the last issue, Blake and Laura's conversations bookending the arc is very much the sort of circular narrative structure I lean into.

We had a debate about where Blake's balloon from the first panel should be from. I wanted bottom, Jamie wanted right, we settled on middle-right with that semi-long train.

Er... you may be seeing that anti-climax and crushing disappointment is one of the big themes across this issue.

9-10. Yes, it's a Kieron-Works-Out-How-To-Get-Two-Pages-Of-Art-For-Free special.

I mentioned that we'd be doing this to Jamie back in the script for Issue 6, so it was on our minds back then. (**Ed's Note** — See the backmatter for sketches...)

We kind of lost it, but the fuzzy-zoom was meant to be a little tribute to Brett Ewins who recently passed. The distorted-photo-copied zoom was one of his signature effects.

Matt originally had different colouring on the two panels, but we ended up making them identical. You know when the press only get one really bad shot of a murderer and have to re-use it constantly? I was trying to get something a little like that.

The colours were also bleached a little as we progressed, to aid legibility.

11. Yeah, I'm less twisting the knife, more attaching the device to a boring device and leaving it to gouge away.

We're packing a lot into this issue — I mean, we're trying to also claim space for a properly impressive fight scene, and doing a lot of heavy plot-based lifting. The mid-page transitions are a sign of that. Other than that, I actually tried to keep the storytelling pretty simple. Yes, there's set-pieces, but there is a lot of moving pieces in this issue, and I don't want to lose people.

I love Cassandra and company doing the badass walk here.

12. Odd page this — we're doing something that's almost like an aspect to aspect transition, as we change our focus. Sits oddly.

I do like Baphomet sitting on top of his own monolith. Subtle, dude.

BLACK/WHITE was very much the Norns' thing already, but Jamie suggested completely dropping all colour when the Norns do their thing. It does speak to their nature.

13. Devil on your shoulder, obv. The font may ring a few bells. It's very similar to the one we used for Mephisto on *Journey Into Mystery*.

Baphomet having a big shiny metal pole does amuse me enormously.

This is where that line for the back cover found its home. Works better here for a few reasons, not least that by putting it closer to Morrigan's interjection it reminds us of part of his original reasons to be doing this.

The penultimate panel probably would be an off-panel balloon in most books, but I try to avoid that.

Good pose in the final panel, in terms of sense of power.

14-15. Fucking ravens everywhere, etc.

The page turns here are interesting, and telling in terms of how I'm actually choosing to pace it. In a real way, a lot of the right hand pages would work better as a left hand page — but by doing that you lose a lot of other stuff. In the original script, the fight sequence was a page shorter — and that was just too cramped. We turned The Norns' performance into a single page to reclaim that, which also altered the page turns.

I think we're fine. Of the two choices, this one is better.

This whole sequence was directly inspired by the Under The Sea Kate Bush performances last year. You had to be there. We felt like Kate Bush was trolling us with that final image, so we sent it back at her.

I quite like "Lily White Dante".

When I showed this issue to the always-excellent Ray Fawkes, he noted he was surprised we were seguing into tragedy so early. I suspect with the melodramatic tendencies of Morrigan and Baphomet, that was inevitable. They really are the full Shakespeare.

16-17. Yet more fucking amazing flame effects from Matt.

This has gone completely Warhammer Fantasy Battle. We don't do a lot of fight scenes in *WicDiv*, but I'm really pleased with them when we do.

The distortion of image when powers are used was Matt's idea from the Issue 5 fight scene, and we're sticking with it. Most visible in the two panels where Ananke does her thing. I love how he's worked its intensity across the panel — look how fucked up it is near her hands, and how it moves away.

Despite the high stakes here, part of me laughs hard at Baphomet's sudden swearing.

18. Friend of *WicDiv* Hannah noted that this immediately made her think of 'No Children' by the Mountain Goats. Yes, that's what I was thinking of. It's not on the playlist, but it's always on my mind. I haven't put it on it, as it was the last song on the *Young Avengers* playlist, and it felt too close.

Fuck it. It's on the playlist now.

I considered adding some dialogue to the first two panels, but Chrissy talked me out of it. She was right. Good editor.

Lots going on in this page — Jamie is increasingly good at this sort of compressin. Post-*Hawkeye* and Aja, it feels like something readers roll with a lot more than (say) a decade ago.

Lots of debate over exactly how much Baal had to say. There's a lot of necessary exposition in here — making clearer the actual nature of The Underground is 100% key to what happens by the end of the issue.

The half panel in inks and half in colour is just wonderful. Inverted *Wizard Of Oz*. If we ever colour the first trade of *Phonogram*, I suspect that'll be what we do for the Memory Kingdom sequence as well. That whole issue in black and white, like old newsprint.

19. A performance page. First one for a while, actually, unless you count Issue 8 (Which I hope you do.)

I settled the text early, so Jamie could design the whole page around it. Strong perspective, Jamie.

I'm pleased people liked the page. This sort of thing I always worry about, because it's very easily mocked if people don't buy into the book's conceit. I think people are aboard now though.

20. Extremely strong silent page here. I love the guy who's holding his head in the first panel, who I imagine is basically doing the Bill and Ted "whooooooooooa" noise.

Also — tiny fist shake in penultimate panel.

We were a bit worried people wouldn't realise Laura followed the Norns to the stage, but I think we got away with it. We perhaps over-worry about some stuff like that.

21. As someone who has been backstage at quite a few festivals, I can confirm their toilets aren't necessarily much better than the ones out in the wild. Bands aren't entirely full of shit. I've seen the evidence. Worst toilet I ever used in my life was backstage at Reading in 2000. As on a much-worse-than-that-bog-in-*Trainspotting* level.

Er... I digress.

Another page where we're cramming a lot in. I regularly say, Space = Meaning but I'm really pleased by how powerful those last the panels are. Look at Cass' position across the three panels too — the use of space is really interesting. In the third panel, look how small she is.

I suspect how this one played out was inspired by the crying snotty mess I ended up in after my first performance by the relatively acceptable band I was in once. We were terrible, but actually had a few ideas. Anyway, crying snotty mess. Giving a toss is an odd burden sometimes.

22-23. Chrissy and I debate a lot of stuff involving *WicDiv*. One day she'll have stories to tell about my various responses to stuff, which basically start as "REALLY? I WILL HAVE TO REWRITE THE WHOLE COMIC NOW!" petulance and end up after two minutes' stomping turning into "Actually, I can tweak this one line and it's okay." Anyway — one thing she does is hold up a useful more critical eye to Laura, which leads to lots of interesting thinking.

Anyway — this is her favourite moment of Laura's, and I think it may be mine too. I'm proud of you, Laura. You've come a long way. Obviously this is the in-issue resolution of the anti-climax/disappointment element, in terms of how Laura is responding to all that.

That last panel is lovely. Strong choice of colours, framing, etc.

I also find Ananke's head tilt very funny.

24. Morrigan's lines were a last minute rewrite. The original lines were just as ornate, but not nearly as good. Also, they oddly reminded me of 'Bohemian Rhapsody', so had to go.

I think "Murderous Asshole" was a late addition I quite like.

Originally the reveal he's going after Inanna was the penultimate panel, but we realised that was a much weaker ending. Basic writing trick to maintain interest is keep the most important element of a sentence until the end. As such, people pay attention to the sentence as information is withheld. Same thing here, really.

24. Obvious Poe reference, calling back to both the various ravens and Baphomet's stated desire at the start, etc. We really are unbearable.

Anyway — we're finishing off Issue 11 this week, and it'll hopefully be with you soon. Thanks for reading.

ISSUE 11

"Second verse, same as the first."

I've talked about the origins of *WicDiv* a few times. As in, where I got the original idea from. However, in terms of constructing its initial vision, it grew while I was doing *Young Avengers*, and solidified in early 2014. It came from a period which I euphemistically describe as a heightened emotional intensity. As in, I was a hot fucking mess. I had far too much stuff to fit inside this year, and it's bulged occasionally, hot metal about to rupture its veins. There's stuff I wanted that was strimmed away, but it's mostly in there. I think I'm actually happier with the second year — it's just as intense, but it's a little more at ease and I don't have the intellectual corsetry of THIS VISION FOR THE FIRST YEAR OF THE BOOK.

The short version of it is that dual structure, where we spend the first year in these two cycles. We do this to Luci. Then we do this to Laura. And we dovetail back and forth, and create this whirl, by which point we've created what I tend to describe as the Drama Engine. All the characters now have stakes we understand, and they'll go tearing into each other. Yes, we have someone who seems to be the villain, but that's only half the problem.

But yeah. *Faust Act* is *Faust Act*. *Fandemonium* is the rest of *Charlie & The Chocolate Factory*, with the remaining tickets being found. Deal with disappointment. Oh, there was a final golden ticket. Oh, oh, shit.

We were pleased with this one. Everyone did well. There's a lot of craft by everyone here, as I think people can tell by the response.

Anyway – let's do this.

Main Cover. I think we were originally thinking of doing this subversion of our own status quo well down the line, but we realised it sat much better at the punchline to the first year before we move off and do something else. Works worryingly well, shall we say.

Fiona Staples Cover. Fiona's success across the last few years has been incredibly heartwarming. She's got great style, use of colour, mood, romance. She asked if she'd made Inanna too angry here. I thought it fine. I mean, there's a time to be angry, and this would be it.

1. Specifically this is Hilly Fields in Brockley, looking East. Laura would have walked from Brockley Station, and for some reason decided to head across the park. It's dark here. I suspect she would have probably not gone this way in a normal state of mind. Except, evidently, she's not exactly in a normal place. She is totally heightened Emotional Intensity.

Jamie and I went and walked the route and took reference photos for this. The cemetery on the next page is the one I walked around before starting the first page of *WicDiv*. I was listening to 'Laura'. Yes, None More Goth.

Only colour notes were adding the lights to the towers — which, of course, Matt didn't know about. London is interesting.

Played with the lettering and pacing a lot here. Moving captions either side of Laura in the last panel, to match with the KLLKs, was a late tweak, but a useful one

I think. Gained us the silent panel previously, which helps pacing, and an interesting delay.

2-3. Another of the page expansion tactics. This is one page of content expanded into two. We do a lot of it this issue — we actually fill the whole comic with content via it — but it's in a far less intrusive way than Issue 8. You can pretty much see everything we've learned from the last year of comics in this one. Working out how to get space and page turns (and what page turns needed to be protected) was absolutely key.

Why not do this in one page? Because Ananke on page 4 *is* a page turn worth keeping. We need to create a meaningful cliffhanger to make people want to come back to Laura after we cut away to Inanna/Baphomet.

Have I ever mentioned that I do what Laura does? Clicking my fingers when walking is one of my nervous gestures. Well, now I have. My reasons are very different from Laura's.

To state the obvious — the black panels in a six-panel grid are the first of the issue's many call backs to Issue 5.

4. Space = Meaning, etc.

Okay — I've talked about the dual cycle of the first eleven issues. This issue also has its own internal back and forth. We need to both intro Laura and her state of mind, and leave her in an interesting place. You could do it quicker than in the space I gave it, but I suspect it'd lack meaning.

5. Title last seen in Laura and Luci's exchange in Issue 4. With its given response there, you may suspect it to be one of the key refrains of the book. You know when we did what we did to Leah in *JIM*, and I started noting that words like "Forever" and "Change" will probably be underlined in everyone's copies by now? Well, this is fairly obviously one of the core things the book is about.

Have I actually said where I got the phrase from? I don't think I said it last time. If I did, I won't repeat it. In time, I think.

'Slight Return' is a Hendrix nod.

6. The Baphomet/Inanna sequence was tricky in terms of space management. It needs to be as big and as showy as the Luci/Baal/Sakhmet fight in Issue 5, but we have much more to do. As such, we're really trying to work out how to cram stuff in.

This is actually sort of inspired by Stoke Newington Unitarian Church. In the *WicDiv* universe, it isn't actually a church, and has a very different history, which we'll get to in time. If you look who actually went to the Church back in the day, I suspect you'll probably get a clue.

So, no, don't go to there in real life and expect to see an orgy. Or, in fact, this layout.

Kate Leth has been asking for actual kissing for eleven issues. I guess this one is for her.

I think it's interesting how Jamie has shot stuff. We're an M rated book. We totally could show a lot more actual nudity than we do here. I do like the couple doing it doggy-style on the far left.

Matt is doing wondrous things with the colouring here. That pink!

7-8. First way of stretching the pages — only half the page are "real" panels. The other half are repeats with a zoom. In effect, it's five panels a page, with three repurposing material. Clearly, this is still more than just two pages (and probably more in terms of work from Jamie) but I give some pages which are deliberately less demanding later. Jamie was fine with it. I had other ideas if it was too much — but I'm glad we was cool with it, not least as I'd have had to rework the whole pacing of the page turns again. Point being: it's a dialogue between the team.

It was on this page when the floating Baphomet head realised that it may be some late-90s residual *Red Meat* influence showing.

The sudden glow of a symbol in the last panel on page 8 is basically us doing a spider-sense. There's more than a little of Spider-Man to Inanna's fighting style too.

9. The dance between Baphomet and Inanna's colours is full on.

Worth noting, that the rest of the fans have got out. Phew. Baphomet isn't a *mass* murderer.

10. This is some of my favourite action storytelling from Jamie (and Matt, for that matter). I saw I had a page for the main "battle" part and winced, as I wasn't sure how much of the balletic nature of the fight this could capture. I saw them flipping around the place, the fight-as-dance-routine brought to the fore. So I packed a lot in, and basically through my hands up in a "Hey — David Aja makes it work. We should give it a shot…" way.

Jamie nails it, for me. Look at use of storytelling and space. Those first four panels take something that's really quite odd and esoteric, and show the emotions. I mean, we hadn't seen *Mad Max* at this point, but basically that's what *Mad Max* does for two hours.

This was written Marvel Method. Bits of dialogue were in that, but a lot of the arrangement was done when Jamie did a page.

11. This sequence was at least in part inspired by dancing in a church. It was to 'Like A Prayer'. I didn't actually realise the crucifix part of it when I thought it up. That came to me as I was writing it, in a weirdly gothic melodrama…

12. And then I realised I had to invert it too. NONE MORE GOTH.

I sort of blinked at myself after I had the idea. This really couldn't be more the product of a catholic boy who read the *Realm Of Chaos* Warhammer manual at an impressionable age.

In passing, 'Crucified' by Army Of Lovers is very much an Inanna track, and every time I listened to it, I was thinking about writing this scene.

I saw one reader actually say that this sign reminded them a little of Kid Loki's final speech in *JIM* — pyrrhic victory. That's explicitly the kind of the expression I called for in the script.

13. You may note that this isn't a page turn. Ideally it would be, but that'd have caused more problems later. I tried to work out how to do page 14 and 15 in one page (so 16-17 could be on the page turn), and had to sacrifice so much stuff that was required. You moved too quickly from the chaos of Baphomet and Inanna, etc. Pacing. Pacing.

Call back to Issue 1, obv.

14-15. And silence. We really do need these two pages.

Yes, with how the story goes, Ananke really is being a monster here.

First panel of page 15 is a device we do quite a bit in *WicDiv* — that full-tier single image, at the top of a page. We come back to it time and time again, and it's normally to stress a key line. Space is meaning, and if you're working on an eight-panel grid, that (relatively speaking) is much more powerful.

Honestly, I think *Sex Criminals* was in my head quite a bit in *Fandemonium*. We stuck to our traditional eight-panel, but trying to find more smaller moments was an underlying urge.

16-17. And we get the falling sequence again, with a different colour take. Matt and Jamie went back and forth over the colour choices here — the poppies are an especially great touch, I think. Jamie was mailing me ideas when I was out and about, which is always a strange thing to get. "Hey, how about vines?"

Hmm. Memory is foggy on this for some reason.

18. And hello, Persephone.

Her design was pulled from a few places. I was thinking about Sky Ferreira, whose album was one of the bigger influences on Laura (All Sky songs on the playlist are Laura songs). MIA was in there, in terms of art school girls in London. Siouxsie Sioux I nodded to too.

And then when we were under way, FKA Twigs emerged. South London mixed-race girl with a background that wasn't 100 miles away from Laura's. An alien sex and death aesthetic. As I occasionally note in my tracks of the year list, Pop Music Provides.

Yes, Laura's look was foreshadowed in her cosplay. Yes, Laura's cigarette is finally burning. Yes, she does scrub up well.

We tried various colour schemes, with Jamie making the call on the reds.

Really pleased with this. Having to reblog all the fan art as links is killing me.

19. White out page, as first seen in the first issue of *The Singles Club*.

20. Oh god. The turn of the knife in the "I can't wait to tell Inanna! I hope he isn't dead or anything! That'd be terrible!" :(

21. This and the next page are abstractly the "easier" pages I planned to make up for those extra panels earlier in the comic. Of course, easier is relative. It's a simple couple of pages in terms of layout, number of panels, its perspective, and a single slow pan, but Jamie has so much acting to do here, it's not as if there's many artists working in comics who could have pulled it off. I'm very proud of the fucker.

Equally, there's a shitload of work put on Matt in terms of telling the story through the intensity in the colour (we started a little more reserved and amped this up, as this really is the most rhapsodic we've ever gone. Laura's been on a long road to be here.)

Regarding the earlier page turn conversation, you can see this is one that I had to do everything to keep. It's more important than anything else.

22. Yeah.

Sorry.

23. Once again, maintaining the page turn. Once again, with the call back. Once again, we return. What was more important? Which came first? Ideally, it's impossible for the reader to tell. I'm not sure if I even remember.

24. You know, I'm beginning to suspect that Ananke's motives may not be entirely benevolent.

This page arrived when I was in bed. We were watching Netflix on C's laptop, and a Dropbox Update appeared in the top right. I grabbed my tablet, and dug it out, and this was the last thing I saw before going to bed. Brr.

Chatting to Dan Hart of *Need To Consume* before the issue dropped, he said that he thought there would actually be no body count this issue, because doing a stump on the cover would be a spoiler, and that's not really our style. He would be right. If there was *one* corpse at the end.

At least one reason why the structure of the issue has been a shocker isn't just that we did this to our lead. It's that when we see the church explode, there's a narrative assumption that Oh, It's Inanna. From then on, it's that rollercoaster of positive and negative beats, going from the height of the series to the backstab.

25-27. This is strictly speaking a double-negative beat, which is something I suspect you have to be careful about. Go google that kind of thing. Here, I think it's necessary. This is the ashes in the mouth moment. Knowing that this was going to happen to Laura's parents at the end of the arc probably in retrospect makes the reason for some of the work we did with them in this arc clearer.

Strong dressing gown looks from the Wilsons too.

28. And the second half of that key phrase.

Due to a last-minute design miscommunication the Inanna skull was removed from this, and his symbol placed back there. Jamie caught it just before it went to print. This issue is brutal, but that would be just cruel.

So, yes. What's next? The first of the guest issues, with the main story from Kate Brown (who you may remember from Issue 6 of *Young Avengers*).

As well as the main story, Jamie and Matt will be doing a back up story in all the guest issues, featuring the cover star. So, yes, more Inanna. That knife twists so much it's basically attached to someone spinning in their own grave.

The response to this one was overwhelming. I think you'll be interested in where we take you in the second year.

Thanks for reading.

ISSUE 1

PAGE 1

1.1

Full page image.

A skull, lying on an expensive oaken table, filling the panel entirely. Looming.

Detailed as you can make it. More than anything else we show in the comic, this object feels real.

Hyper-real, in fact. Maybe use the heavy-shadow effects from the Oubliette sequence in Young Avengers.

A skull is always ominous. This is the most ominous skull you've ever drawn, but not because it's fantastical. Just because this is the bone which has the lump of meat that's everything you are crammed inside it, and one day, it'll be gone, and we'll be left with this cold, dry lump of bone.

Low-lights. It's possible we may see some of the background from the next page. It's possible that it may be out of focus, so we're just on the skull. It's possible that a figure walking behind the skull may be out of focus. If so, the voice comes from her. If not, the voice comes from off panel.

LOC CAP: LONG ISLAND, U.S.A.

ANANKE: And once again, we return to this.

(PROBABLY OFF)

ALSO BY THE CREATORS

THE WICKED + THE DIVINE

VOL. 1: THE FAUST ACT
#1—5 COLLECTED

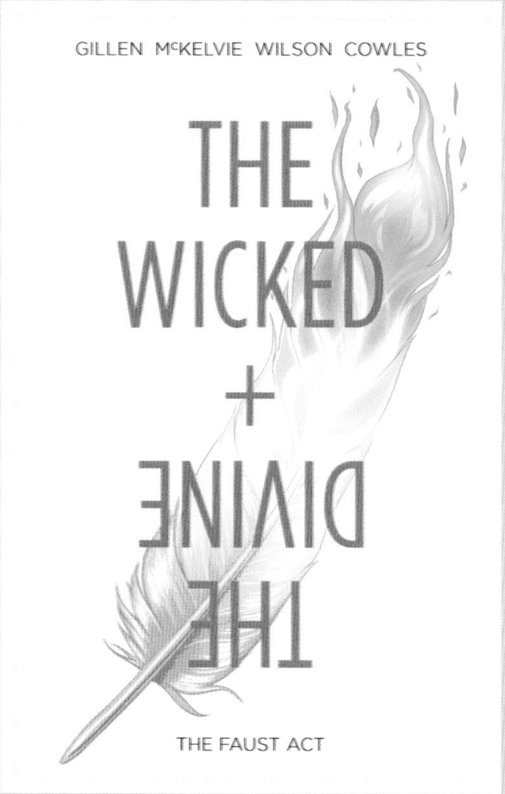
GILLEN McKELVIE WILSON COWLES
THE WICKED + THE DIVINE
THE FAUST ACT

VOL. 2: FANDEMONIUM
#6—11 COLLECTED

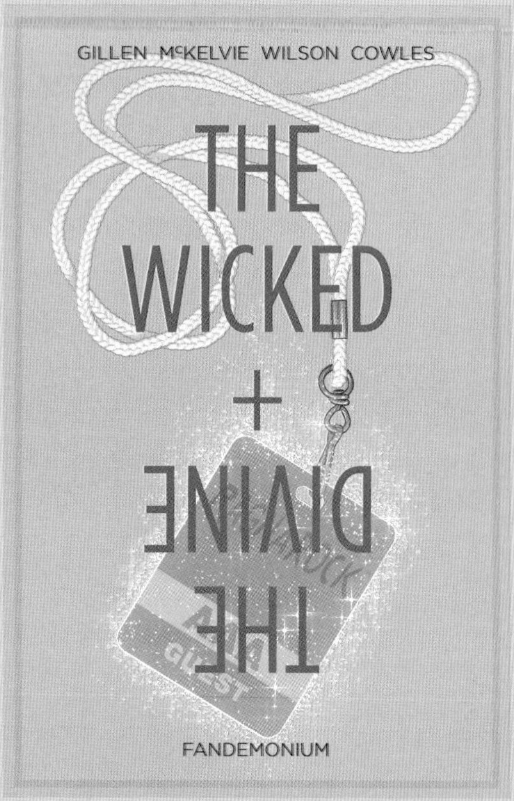
GILLEN McKELVIE WILSON COWLES
THE WICKED + THE DIVINE
FANDEMONIUM

VOL. 3: COMMERCIAL SUICIDE
#12—17 COLLECTED

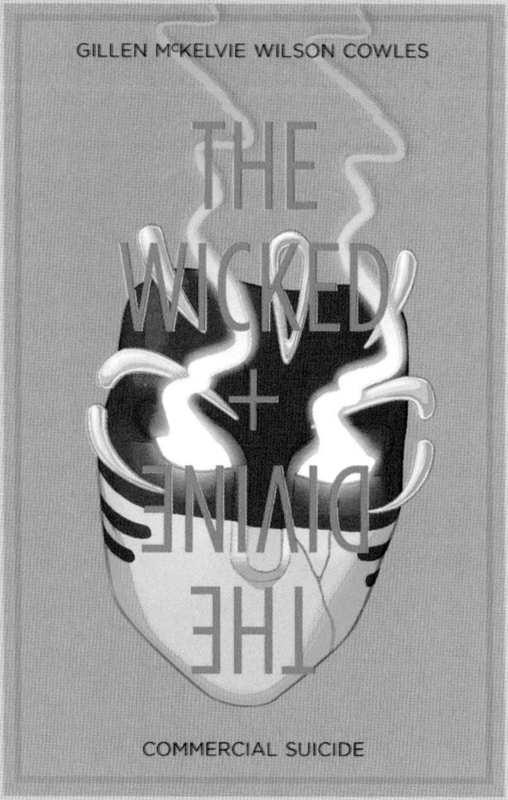
GILLEN McKELVIE WILSON COWLES
THE WICKED + THE DIVINE
COMMERCIAL SUICIDE

SUBURBAN GLAMOUR

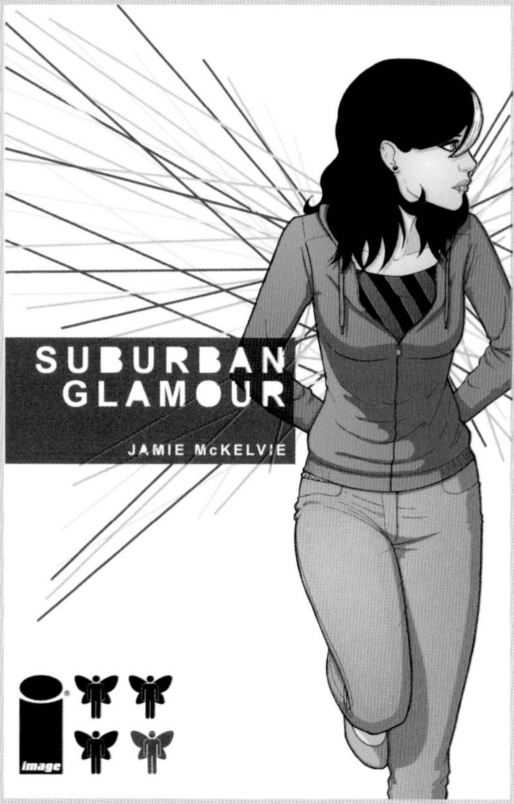
SUBURBAN GLAMOUR
JAMIE McKELVIE
image

PHONOGRAM

VOL. 1:
RUE BRITANNIA

PHONOGRAM
RUE BRITANNIA
Kieron
GILLEN
Jamie
McKELVIE

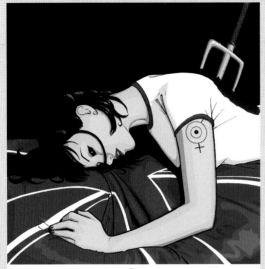

VOL. 2:
THE SINGLES CLUB

PHONOGRAM
THE SINGLES CLUB
KIERON GILLEN & JAMIE McKELVIE

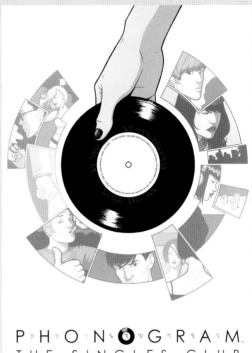

VOL. 3:
THE IMMATERIAL GIRL

PHONOGRAM
THE IMMATERIAL GIRL

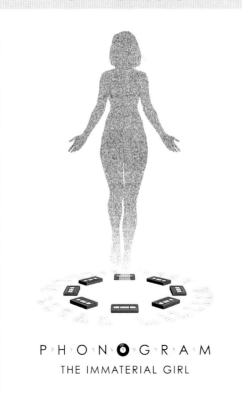

FOR FURTHER INFORMATION ON
THE WICKED + THE DIVINE:

www.wicdiv.com

major news, new issues,
merchandise.

#WicDiv

the hashtag on twitter
for WicDiv Discussion

WicDiv

the general tag on tumblr
for the community.

bit.ly/WicDivPlaylist

the ever-updated Spotify
Playlist for the series.

Kieron Gillen is out of focus. He writes.
Jamie McKelvie is in focus. He draws.
Matthew Wilson isn't pictured. He colours.

Photo by Dan Griliopoulos